DEVIANCE AND SOCIAL CONTROL

DEVIANCE AND SOCIAL CONTROL

A Reader

Edited by

Ronald Weitzer

Boston   Burr Ridge, IL   Dubuque, IA   Madison, WI   New York   San Francisco   St. Louis
Bangkok   Bogotá   Caracas   Kuala Lumpur   Lisbon   London   Madrid   Mexico City
Milan   Montreal   New Delhi   Santiago   Seoul   Singapore   Sydney   Taipei   Toronto

McGraw-Hill Higher Education

A Division of The *McGraw-Hill* Companies

DEVIANCE AND SOCIAL CONTROL: A READER
Published by McGraw-Hill, an imprint of The McGraw-Hill Companies, Inc. 1221 Avenue of the Americas, New York, NY, 10020. Copyright © 2002 by The McGraw-Hill Companies, Inc. All rights reserved. No part of this publication may be reproduced or distributed in any form or by any means, or stored in a data base or retrieval system, without the prior written consent of The McGraw-Hill Companies, Inc., including, but not limited to, in any network or other electronic storage or transmission, or broadcast for distance learning.

Some ancillaries, including electronic and print components, may not be available to customers outside the United States.

This book is printed on acid-free paper.

1 2 3 4 5 6 7 8 9 0 FGR/FGR 0 9 8 7 6 5 4 3 2 1

ISBN 0-07-245900-X

Editorial director: *Phillip A. Butcher*
Sponsoring editor: *Sally Constable*
Developmental editor: *Maggie Barbieri*
Editorial coordinator: *Alyson DeMonte*
Senior marketing manager: *Daniel M. Loch*
Project manager: *Jill Howell*
Production associate: *Gina Hangos*
Producer, Media technology: *Jessica Bodie*
Coordinator freelance design: *Mary L. Christianson*
Supplement producer: *Nate Perry*
Freelance cover designer: *Design Solutions*
Cover image: © *PhotoDisc*
Typeface: *10.5/12 Times Roman*
Compositor: **TECH**BOOKS
Printer: *Quebecor World Fairfield Inc.*

Library of Congress Cataloging-in-Publication Data

Deviance and social control : a reader / edited by Ronald Weitzer.
    p. cm.
   ISBN 0-07-245900-X (alk. paper)
    1. Deviant behavior. 2. Social control. 3. Criminal behavior. I. Weitzer, Ronald

HM811 .D52 2002
302.5'42–dc21   2001031683

www.mhhe.com

ABOUT THE AUTHOR

Ronald Weitzer received his Ph.D. in sociology from the University of California, Berkeley, in 1985. He is currently a professor of sociology at George Washington University in Washington, DC. His research includes extensive work on police relations with minority groups in the United States, South Africa, and Northern Ireland. He is also an expert on the sex industry, and has written several articles on prostitution in the United States. He has published four books: *Current Controversies in Criminology* (Prentice Hall, forthcoming 2002), *Sex for Sale: Prostitution, Pornography, and the Sex Industry* (Routledge 2000), *Policing under Fire: Ethnic Conflict and Police–Community Relations in Northern Ireland* (State University of New York Press 1995), and *Transforming Settler States: Communal Conflict and Internal Security in Northern Ireland and Zimbabwe* (University of California Press 1990).

PREFACE

Deviance and Social Control provides readers with a selection of articles that examine core issues in the field of deviant behavior and social control. Major areas covered in the book include how individuals "become deviant"; effects of deviance on the identities of people; efforts by deviants to justify their unconventional conduct; the role of the mass media in framing popular impressions of deviants; how deviants are treated by control agencies and how this treatment changes over time; social and political conflicts over deviance and over appropriate methods of suppressing or managing deviant populations; and ways in which deviant actors attempt to "fight back" to reject stigmatization, enhance their self-esteem, and struggle for their rights. Types of deviance examined in the book include drug use and drug dealing, corporate crime, pornography, governmental deviance, rape and other violence against women, prostitution, homosexuality, cyberdeviance, AIDS, cheating among college students, transgenders, and many others.

Key features of the book include:

- A mix of both classic essays and recent, cutting-edge studies;
- Selections on theories of deviance and control and empirical studies based on each theory;
- Articles describing the research methods commonly used in studying deviant behavior;
- Selections covering major substantive areas in the field, including some previously neglected perspectives and issues;
- Study questions for each article.

The book addresses the following key questions in the field:

How are the core concepts of *deviant behavior* and *social control* defined? What causes people to engage in deviant behavior? How do the reactions of others (friends, strangers, the authorities) affect deviants' self-images and their behaviors? What variables shape the creation of laws to control deviant populations and the operations of agencies that control deviance? Part I (Introductory Issues) and Part II (Theories of Deviance) cover these central issues. Six major theories are presented in the book, both micro-level and macro-level theories. Each theoretical essay is coupled with articles that are research applications of the theory.

How do social scientists study deviant behavior and social control? What are the special challenges facing researchers who investigate marginal groups and individuals who are engaged in stigmatized or illegal behavior and who have an interest in avoiding detection? What are the advantages and disadvantages of studying deviants in their "natural settings," including field observations of individuals actually engaged in deviant activities? What are the pros and cons of studying persons currently incarcerated in prisons or mental institutions? How do social scientists make use of data collected by government agencies, like the FBI's crime statistics? What are the limitations of these kinds of statistics? These and other issues are addressed in Part III on "Researching Deviance."

What role do the mass media and the Internet play in shaping public perceptions of deviance and popular ideas about appropriate methods of controlling deviant behavior? To what extent do the media exaggerate problems associated with deviant behavior, or distort public impressions of both the amount and seriousness of deviance, resulting in public demands for more punishment or preemptive control (for instance, the recent spate of school shootings)? How has the advent of the Internet shaped deviance? The section on "Deviance in the Media and on the Internet" addresses these questions.

If there is a great deal of *consensus* in public attitudes toward some kinds of deviant behavior (child molestation, for instance), there is much more *discord* regarding other kinds of deviance (whether the behavior is deviant at all, how deviants should be treated by the authorities). Indeed, some kinds of deviance are routinely fought over in both private and public settings. The ongoing debate about illegal drugs in the United States is just one example of politically contested deviance and control, with interest groups pitted against one another in their campaigns to influence government policy. Should "medical marijuana" be legally available to persons suffering from cancer? Should persons who are convicted of simple possession of marijuana be sent to prison? Similar conflicts are currently raging in many other areas: Should greater restrictions be placed on the tobacco industry and on cigarette smoking in public places? Should sex offenders be subjected to public shaming and greater social control (via community notification, under Megan's Law statutes) once they are released from prison? Should they be committed to mental institutions after they have served their prison terms? Should the law against polygamy be more vigorously enforced in Utah than it has been in the past? What should be done about violence on television? Should the federal government and local governments do more to control pornography? Should prostitution be legalized? These and many other behaviors have become increasingly politicized and struggled over in America. Such conflicts are examined in the section "Politics and the Control of Deviance," as well as in some other articles in the book.

Part V examines issues of deviant identity, the interactional dynamics between deviants and conventional persons, and efforts by deviant actors to "normalize" their behavior, challenge those who condemn them, and fight for their rights. What effect does deviance have on the identities of people engaged in deviant activities? How do deviant individuals and groups deal with the stigma, rejection, and discriminatory treatment by "normal" others? In what ways do deviants attempt to manage others' impressions of them, by "passing" for normal, selective disclosure, or neutralization of others' negative attributions and justification of their deviant conduct? What leads some deviants to actively resist, either individually or collectively, stereotyping and negative treatment by others? Some have formed lobbying groups to advance their interests. The final section of the book, "Fighting Back: Organized Resistance by Deviants," examines ways in which deviants have struggled for public acceptance and to win their rights. Unfortunately, this very important dimension of deviance and control has been missing from most scholarly writing in the field; indeed, there is a pervasive bias in the theoretical literature, empirical research studies, and most deviance textbooks that portrays deviants as altogether powerless and incapable of fighting back. *Deviance and Social Control* shows that deviants are not necessarily so passive and impotent.

Ronald Weitzer

CONTENTS

PART ONE

Introductory Issues

DEFINING DEVIANCE   2

   Introduction   2

1-1 **Images of Deviance and Social Control** 5
   Stephen Pfohl

CONSTRUCTING AND CONTROLLING
DEVIANCE   9

   Introduction   9

1-2 **Moral Entrepreneurs**   10
   Howard S. Becker

1-3 **Ironies of Social Control**   13
   Gary T. Marx

PART TWO

Theories of Deviance

THEORIES OF DEVIANCE   24

   Introduction   24

FUNCTIONALIST THEORY   31

2-1 **The Sociology of Deviance**   31
   Kai T. Erikson

2-2 **Television News Magazines and Functionalism** 36
   Maria Elizabeth Grabe

SOCIAL DISORGANIZATION THEORY   45

2-3 **Deviant Places**   45
   Rodney Stark

2-4 **Broken Windows**   54
   James Q. Wilson and George L. Kelling

ANOMIE THEORY   64

2-5 **Social Structure and Anomie**   64
   Robert K. Merton

2-6 **Anomie and Corporate Deviance**   69
   Nikos Passas

LEARNING THEORY   74

2-7 **Differential Association Theory**   74
   Edwin H. Sutherland

2-8 **Becoming a Marihuana User** 76
Howard S. Becker

2-9 **The Training of House Prostitutes** 83
Barbara Sherman Heyl

LABELING THEORY 92

2-10 **Outsiders** 92
Howard S. Becker

2-11 **Societal Reaction to
Deviant Behavior** 95
John I. Kitsuse

2-12 **Labeling the CIA Deviant** 103
William B. Waegel, M. David Ermann,
and Alan M. Horowitz

CONFLICT THEORY 111

2-13 **Capitalism, Class, and
Crime in America** 111
David M. Gordon

2-14 **The Police and the Black Male** ✓ 119
Elijah Anderson

2-15 **Fraternities and Rape on Campus** ✓ 126
Patricia Yancey Martin and
Robert A. Hummer

→ 2-16 **The Manufacture of Deviance in
the Soviet Purge** 134
Walter D. Connor

PART THREE

Researching Deviance

Introduction to Researching Deviance 144

3-1 **Measuring Crime** 149
Joseph J. Senna and Larry J. Siegel

3-2 **Number Jumble Clouds Judgment
of Drug War** 153
Jeff Leen

3-3 **Improving Surveys on Violence
Against Women** 157
Michael D. Smith

PART FOUR

Institutional Contexts

DEVIANCE IN THE MEDIA AND
ON THE INTERNET 168
Introduction 168

4-1 **Media Constructions of Crime** 170
Vincent F. Sacco

4-2 **Deviants on Talk Shows** 177
Joshua Gamson

4-3 **Log on to Sex: Erotic Cyberspace
as a New Frontier** 185
Keith F. Durkin and Clifton D. Bryant

MEDICINE AND PSYCHIATRIC
INSTITUTIONS 195
→ *Introduction* 195

→ 4-4 **Medicine as an Institution of** ✓
Social Control 196
Peter Conrad and Joseph W. Schneider

→ 4-5 **On Being Sane in Insane Places** ✓ 205
D. L. Rosenhan

POLITICS AND THE CONTROL
OF DEVIANCE 214
Introduction 214

4-6 **Politics of Marihuana
Decriminalization** 215
Albert DiChiara and John F. Galliher

4-7 **The Meese Commission on the Road** 235
Carole S. Vance

4-8 **Prostitution Control in America** 243
Ronald Weitzer

PART FIVE

Identity, Interaction, and Resistance

BECOMING DEVIANT: IDENTITY AND
BEHAVIORAL CHANGE   258
    Introduction   258

5-1 Drifting into Drug Dealing   260
Sheigla Murphy, Dan Waldorf, and
Craig Reinarman

5-2 Becoming Homosexual   272
Richard R. Troiden

**5-3 Coming Out as a
Transgendered Person**   282
Patricia Gagné, Richard Tewksbury,
and Deanna McGaughey

MANAGING DEVIANCE: PASSING,
DISCLOSURE, AND
NEUTRALIZATION   301
    Introduction   301

5-4 Living with the Stigma of AIDS   304
Rose Weitz

**5-5 Situational Ethics and Cheating
Among College Students**   313
Donald L. McCabe

5-6 Denying the Guilty Mind   318
Michael L. Benson

5-7 Rapists' Vocabulary of Motive   327
Diana Scully and Joseph Marolla

5-8 How Women Experience Battering   339
Kathleen J. Ferraro and
John M. Johnson)

FIGHTING BACK: ORGANIZED
RESISTANCE BY DEVIANTS   352
    Introduction   352

5-9 The Prostitutes' Rights Campaign   353
Ronald Weitzer

5-10 Pedophile Organizations   367
Mary deYoung

**5-11 Political Activism Among the
Disabled and Mental Patients**   371
Renee R. Anspach

5-12 Gay and Lesbian Movements   381
Steven Epstein

PART ONE

INTRODUCTORY ISSUES

DEFINING DEVIANCE

Introduction

Deviant behavior is behavior that is viewed negatively and condemned: it is considered abnormal, offensive, immoral, harmful, or reprehensible. This definition covers a broad range of behaviors and conditions, including drug dealing, robbery, child molestation, corporate crime, prostitution, mental illness, and many others.

The field of deviance and social control covers both deviant individuals (social "actors") and the people who view them as deviant and seek to control them (social "audiences"). In condemning acts that they consider deviant, an audience may invoke social norms to support their case. *Norms* are rules or prescriptions that govern social behavior, and they include standards of etiquette and custom, moral codes, and the law. An appeal to a norm is not always straightforward, however, since some norms are ambiguous (e.g., cross-dressing), honored in the breach (e.g., drinking in public, traffic violations), politically contested (e.g., drug use), or applicable to only some people (e.g., children may not buy alcohol and cigarettes). And some norm violators do so with impunity; for whatever reason, including selective enforcement by the authorities, they are not treated as deviant by any audience. In short, while norms certainly influence the behavior of both actors and audiences, deviance is not simply a matter of norm violation. Whether a person is considered deviant also depends on the *reactions* of others, reactions that *may or may not* be influenced by some norm.

Social control refers to efforts to induce people to conform to general societal norms or to the standards of a particular group, as well as efforts to punish people for violating norms. Social control may be *informal* (exercised in encounters between ordinary members of society) or *formal* (exercised by agents of institutions like the church, medical profession, criminal justice system, and the legislature). Agents of formal control operate with the support of some established code of conduct, such as the criminal law, and have formal sanctions at their disposal.

The field examines social control not only at the micro level (in face-to-face interactions) but also at the macro level (the creation of rules and sanctions by the government or some leading social institution). In other words, we are interested in both the labeling and treatment of *individuals* as deviants and the creation of general *categories* of deviance at the societal level—how certain types of behavior come to be designated as deviant. Since categories of deviance and norms of behavior change over time, it is important to study the dynamics of rule creation and the development of new types of control. Previously tolerated acts like cigarette smoking, alcoholism, drunk driving, child abuse, and television violence have in recent years become more stigmatized, restricted, or punished than in the past.

In sum, the field of deviance is concerned with understanding and explaining two different things: (1) deviant behavior and (2) norm creation and social control. Central issues in the field covered in this book include the following:

- why people engage in deviant behavior;
- how deviants explain or justify their behavior;
- changes in their identities as they become increasingly involved in deviance;
- how deviance is socially organized at the group or subcultural level;
- why norms and sanctions change over time, in either a more rigid or more tolerant direction;
- effects of social control on deviant actors and on society;
- the role of others (family, friends, strangers, police, psychiatrists, etc.) in identifying individuals who are engaged in unacceptable behavior, attaching labels to them, and discriminating against them in some fashion.

Scholars who study deviant behavior make several important distinctions. First, there are *different degrees of deviance,* from the minor aberration (e.g., urinating in public) to the most serious crimes (e.g., mass murder). Second, audience reactions to deviance and efforts to control deviant actors *vary in their intensity and in their consequences* for the deviant actor. Negative treatment ranges along a continuum that includes avoiding deviants, gossiping about them, shaming them in public, firing them from their job, incarcerating them in a prison or asylum, and, at its most extreme, murdering or legally executing them. As a general rule, the more serious the rule breaking, the greater the intensity of condemnation by the audience. Third, the *amount of participation* in deviant activity varies. Some types of deviance are fairly widespread in American society, whereas other types of deviance are engaged in by small numbers of people. Even if most people conform to most of society's rules most of the time, the overwhelming majority of the American public has, at some time, engaged in deviant acts, and many people believe that at least some of these acts should not be punishable.

The implications are twofold: First, deviant behavior is not limited to the bizarre acts of a few but is a more common aspect of everyday life. Second, there may be considerable *disagreement* in society regarding some norms, and substantial slippage between certain laws and public support for those laws. At the same time, other behaviors are *widely abhorred.* Indeed, some conduct is nearly unanimously defined as deviant by the American public. While there is a high degree of societal conflict over certain behaviors, as to whether or not they are deviant and should be punished (e.g., abortion, pornography, homosexuality), other types of behavior register a high degree of consensus that they are reprehensible and should be severely sanctioned (murder, child molestation, robbery). Even some nonviolent acts are widely disapproved. A recent opinion poll, for instance, found that 77 percent of Americans believe that extramarital sex is "always wrong" (Michael et al. 1994).

The first chapter in this book, Stephen Pfohl's "Images of Deviance and Social Control," raises a number of important questions about how individuals and groups categorize some acts as "deviant" and others as "normal." He suggests that the central distinction between deviance and normality is not what is harmful to individuals or to society, but depends instead on *power relations.* Deviant categories, according to Pfohl, are types of behavior that are condemned by powerful interests, not necessarily by the wider population. At the same time, the agents of dominant social and political institutions are left free, for the most part, to engage in practices that injure large numbers of people. Readers should keep Pfohl's thought-provoking essay in mind when reading other selections in this book. Power dynamics are important not only in shaping what kinds of conduct are deemed deviant at the macro–societal level (Pfohl's focus) but also at the micro level, in face-to-face interactions between individuals. The balance of power between individual actors and audiences determines who will be treated as deviant and whose behavior will be tolerated. You will see that *power* is a central concept in labeling theory and conflict theory, and it also receives special attention in the section on Politics and the Control of Deviance.

REFERENCE

Michael, Robert T., John H. Gagnon, Edward O. Laumann, and Gina Kolata. 1994. *Sex in America: A Definitive Survey.* New York: Little, Brown.

Images of Deviance and Social Control

Stephen Pfohl

The story of deviance and social control is a battle story. It is a story of the battle to control the ways people think, feel, and behave. It is a story of winners and losers and of the strategies people use in struggles with one another. Winners in the battle to control "deviant acts" are crowned with a halo of goodness, acceptability, normality. Losers are viewed as living outside the boundaries of social life as it ought to be, outside the "common sense" of society itself. They may be seen by others as evil, sleazy, dirty, dangerous, sick, immoral, crazy, or just plain deviant. They may even come to see themselves in such negative imagery, to see themselves as *deviants*.

Deviants are only one part of the story of deviance and social control. Deviants never exist except in relation to those who attempt to control them. Deviants exist only in opposition to those whom they threaten and those who have enough power to control against such threats. The outcome of the battle of deviance and social control is this. Winners obtain the privilege of organizing social life as they see fit. Losers are trapped within the vision of others. They are labeled deviant and subjected to an array of current social control practices. Depending upon the controlling wisdom at a particular moment in history, deviants may be executed, brutally beaten, fined, shamed, incarcerated, drugged, hospitalized, or even treated to heavy doses of tender loving care. But first and foremost they are prohibited from passing as normal women or men. They are branded with the image of being deviant.

From Stephen Pfohl, *Images of Deviance and Social Control: A Sociological History,* 2nd ed., New York: McGraw-Hill, 1994. Reprinted by permission of the McGraw-Hill Companies.

When we think of losers in the battle to control acceptable images of social life, it may seem natural to think of juvenile gang members, serial killers, illegal drug users, homosexuals, and burglars. Indeed, common sense may tell us that such people are simply deviant. But where does this common sense come from? How do we come to know that certain actions or certain people are deviant, while others are "normal"? Do people categorized as deviants really behave in a more dangerous fashion than others? Some people think so. Is this true?

Think of the so-called deviants mentioned above. Are their actions truly more harmful than the actions of people not labeled as deviants? In many cases the answer is no. Consider the juvenile gang. In recent years the organized drug dealing and violent activities of gangs have terrorized people living in poverty-stricken and racially segregated urban neighborhoods. Gang-related deviance has also been the focal point for sensational media stories and for social control policies ranging from selective "stop-and-search" police tactics to the building of new prisons and (in Los Angeles) even the criminalization of alleged gang members' parents.

But what about the people most responsible for the oppressive inner-city conditions that lie at the root of many gang-related activities? What about the "gangs" of bankers whose illegal redlining of mortgage loans blocks the investment of money in inner-city neighborhoods? What about the "gangs" of corporate executives whose greed for short-term profits has led to the "offshoring" of industrial jobs to "underdeveloped" countries where labor is cheap and more easily exploitable? Aren't the actions of such respectable people as costly as, if less visible than, the activities of most inner-city gangs? Yet, there is an important difference: unlike gangs of elite deviants, inner-city youths have little or no real access to dominant institutions in which contemporary power is concentrated.

A related question may be posed concerning serial killers. The violence of serial killers haunts our nightly news broadcasts. Indeed, the seemingly random character of serial killings—although they are most commonly directed against women and children—instills a deep and alarming sense of dread within society as a whole. Nevertheless, the sporadic violence of serial murderers, no matter how fearful, is incomparable in terms of both scope and number to the much less publicized "serial killings" perpetrated by United States-supported *death squads* in countries such as El Salvador and Guatemala. The targets of such death squads are typically people who dare to speak out in the name of social justice. From 1980 to 1991, for instance, approximately 75,000 Salvadoran civilians were secretly killed or made to "disappear" by paramilitary executioners. Why is it that such systematic murders are rarely acknowledged as true serial killings? Why, moreover, do such cold-blooded killings provoke so little U.S. public outrage in comparison to the attention given to the isolated violence of individual murderers, such as Ted Bundy or Jeffrey Dahmer? Is it because the people who authorize them are respectable persons, sometimes even publicly elected officials? Is it because, though we feel vulnerable to other serial killers, we ourselves—at least those of us who are white, male, North American, and economically privileged to live at a distance from the violence that historically envelops the daily lives of others—feel protected from death squads?

Similar questions might be raised about drug users. When we speak of the abuse of drugs, why do we often think only of the "controlled substances" that some people use as a means of achieving psychic escape, altered consciousness, and/or bodily pleasure? True, we as individuals and as a society may pay a heavy price for the abuse of such drugs as cocaine and heroin. But what about

other—legal—substances that many of us are "on" much of the time? Some of these drugs are even more dangerous than their illicit counterparts. In addition to alcohol, tobacco, chemical food additives, and meat from animals that have been fed antibiotics and hormones, our society openly promotes the use of prescription and over-the-counter drugs for everything from losing weight, curing acne, and overcoming anxiety to building strong bodies, fighting depression, and alleviating allergies caused by industrial pollution. Certainly many of these substances have their salutary effects and may help us adjust to the world in which we live. However, even legal substances can be abused; they too can be dangerous. The effects can be direct, jeopardizing an individual's health or fostering addiction, or they can be indirect and more insidious. For example, consider the role drugs play in creating and sustaining our excessively image-conscious, age-conscious environment and in promoting our tendency to avoid dealing with personal conflicts and everyday problems in a thoughtful and responsible manner. Also—not to belabor the issue—just think of what we are doing to our planet, to our future, with our use of pesticides, fertilizers, and other industrial products and by-products. To raise such concerns is not to claim that legal drugs are more dangerous than illegal drugs, but simply to suggest that what is officially labeled illegal or deviant often has more to do with what society economically values than with whether the thing is physically harmful per se.

Further consider the actions of sexist heterosexuals. Such persons may routinely mix various forms of sexual harassment with manipulative patriarchal power and an intolerance of alternative forms of sexual intimacy. Despite the harm these heterosexist individuals cause, they are far less likely to be labeled deviant than are gay, lesbian, or bisexual lovers who caress one another with affection. The same goes for corporate criminals, such as the executives recently implicated in the savings and loan scandal. The stealthy acts of such white-collar criminals have cost the U.S. public as much as $500 billion. Yet the elite deviance of the upper echelon of rule breakers is commonly less feared than are the street crimes of ordinary burglars and robbers.

From the preceding examples it should be evident that many forms of labeled deviance are not more costly to society than the behaviors of people who are less likely to be labeled deviant. Why? The answer is that labeled deviants are viewed as such because they threaten the control of people who have enough power to shape the way society imagines the boundary between good and bad, normal and pathological, acceptable and deviant. This is the crux of the effort to understand the battle between deviance and social control. Deviance is always the flip side of the coin used to maintain social control.

Whether we are dealing with a strange-acting roommate, an unfaithful lover, a frightening mugger, or a politician promising to support the death sentence, we are confronted daily with questions of deviance and the often harsh realities of social control. Nor are such questions easy. In fact, they are quite uneasy. They are uneasy in two senses. They are uneasy because questions about what causes deviance and its control are difficult to answer. Some place the burden of deviance on the free choice of nonconformists. Others view deviance as biologically or psychologically determined. Another views it as something which is learned. Still another sees deviance as primarily a problem of overly repressive social control. Which, if any, of these views are correct? By what standards is correctness measured? The task before us is an uneasy one. It requires that we dig deeply into the social, political, and economic landscapes out of which images of deviance are born and upon which they implant their vision of social control.

What are the major perspectives that humans have used to make sense of deviance and to make sensible certain programs of social control? Where do these perspectives come from? Like acts of deviance and strategies of social control, theoretical images are produced at certain moments of history. Put into practice, they create history as well. What are their consequences? How well have they stood the tests of time, experience, and systematic re-

search? How exactly have they been translated into social control policy and practice? What are their social, political, or economic implications? What should we think of them? Are they sound or unproven, helpful or useless, good or bad? They are not easy questions to answer. They require that we combine questions of theory with questions of research and practice.

Questions about deviance and social control are uneasy at a second level as well—the level of our own personal choices, feelings, and political commitments. At this level, questions about deviance and social control challenge us to go beneath our surface thoughts and feelings, to become reflective and critical about things we have come to take for granted as acceptable and things we oppose or are even repulsed by. How is it that we have come to accept or reject certain ways of thinking, feeling, and acting? How have we been influenced or shaped by the processes which promote social control and/or deviance? What are the consequences for others and for ourselves of living within the confines of our present social, economic, and political realities?

How do we benefit or lose by accepting or deviating from the dominant realities of our time? How are the lives of others directly or indirectly influenced by the way we presently endorse normality and oppose deviance? Could we do better? Should we seek to alter the images of deviance produced in the context of present social, political, and economic arrangements? Would we be deviants if we did? This is the second set of uneasy questions that confront us. These questions will not and should not make us feel comfortable. They ask us not only about who we are but about whom we could become as well.

The uneasy nature of our questions about deviance and social control is quite real. It is not an uncommon experience for the serious student of such matters to experience an initial sense of dizziness, a sense of lost innocence about the "natural" character of things that were previously taken for granted as being simply deviant. If you are unwilling to risk having this discomforting experience, stop reading now. If, on the other hand, you are willing to examine critically the simultaneous formation of deviant and normal realities, including the ways that your own personal realities have been shaped by the ever-present processes of social control, the end experience can be quite exhilarating.

Our worlds can become wider and deeper. This expansion will lead behind and below the ordinary surface of everyday social life by taking a hard look both at deviants—who they are and what they do—and at control processes—who or what gets controlled, how, and why. This expansion can provide us with the freedom of greater personal and social movement. Some of the old, "seemingly natural" binds, bonds, taboos, and rules may loosen up. This new awareness may permit us greater space within which to celebrate the dance that is human life. It may also present us with new senses of human responsibility for our actions and the actions of our fellow deviants and controllers alike.

CONSTRUCTING AND CONTROLLING DEVIANCE

Introduction

How do norms and new types of deviance emerge? In his chapter, Howard Becker argues that "moral entrepreneurs"—persons who find a form of deviance evil and take action to stamp it out—are key players in the construction of new deviant categories. Examples of moral entrepreneurs are activists who work for Mothers Against Drunk Driving, anti-abortion groups, the Moral Majority, and the Partnership for a Drug-Free America. If successful, the efforts of these "rule creators" may lead to the passage of a new law or to greater enforcement of existing laws. Moral entrepreneurs are not always successful or satisfied with the results of their crusade against deviance. They do not always get the kind of cooperation they want from "rule enforcers" like the police, who have to consider the practicalities of vigorous enforcement and may decide to enforce the law selectively or rarely. Sodomy laws are a perfect example: Twenty states have sodomy laws (prohibiting oral and anal sex) yet the laws are seldom enforced.

It goes without saying that agents of social control often fail to discover deviant acts and to apprehend or otherwise control offenders. What is less often recognized is that the authorities may *encourage* deviant behavior among people who otherwise would not have engaged in rule breaking, or they may *increase* the amount of deviant behavior among those who are already involved in some rule breaking—whether the authorities intend to do this or not. Gary Marx ("Ironies of Social Control") identifies three practices by the authorities that may increase, rather than suppress, deviant behavior: escalation, nonenforcement, and covert facilitation. Marx's article is a major contribution to the field because it shows that the relationship between deviance and control is more complex than the conventional view that deviance begets control. The causal direction may be reversed: Control may lead to deviance. Agencies like the police act in ways that can produce or amplify deviant behavior. And it is well known that "correctional" institutions tend to have the effect of reinforcing deviant behavior among the inmates. After all, prisons have long been called "schools of crime" and mental hospitals are notorious for perpetuating patients' abnormal behavior.

Moral Entrepreneurs

Howard S. Becker

Rules are the products of someone's initiative and we can think of the people who exhibit such enterprise as *moral entrepreneurs*. Two related species—rule creators and rule enforcers—will occupy our attention.

RULE CREATORS

The prototype of the rule creator, but not the only variety as we shall see, is the crusading reformer. He is interested in the content of rules. The existing rules do not satisfy him because there is some evil which profoundly disturbs him. He feels that nothing can be right in the world until rules are made to correct it. He operates with an absolute ethic; what he sees is truly and totally evil with no qualification. Any means is justified to do away with it. The crusader is fervent and righteous, often self-righteous.

It is appropriate to think of reformers as crusaders because they typically believe that their mission is a holy one. The prohibitionist serves as an excellent example, as does the person who wants to suppress vice and sexual delinquency or the person who wants to do away with gambling.

These examples suggest that the moral crusader is a meddling busybody, interested in forcing his own morals on others. But this is a one-sided view. Many moral crusades have strong humanitarian overtones. The crusader is not only interested in seeing to it that other people do what he thinks right. He believes that if they do what is right it will be good for them. Or he may feel that his reform will prevent certain kinds of exploitation of one person by another. Prohibitionists felt that they were not simply forcing their morals on others, but attempting to provide the conditions for a better way of life for people prevented by drink from realizing a truly good life. Abolitionists were not simply trying to prevent slave owners from doing the wrong thing; they were trying to help slaves to achieve a better life. Because of the importance of the humanitarian motive, moral crusaders (despite their relatively single-minded devotion to their particular cause) often lend their support to other humanitarian crusades. Joseph Gusfield (1955:223) has pointed out that:

> The American temperance movement during the 19th century was a part of a general effort toward the improvement of the worth of the human being through improved morality as well as economic conditions. The mixture of the religious, the equalitarian, and the humanitarian was an outstanding facet of the moral reformism of many movements. Temperance supporters formed a large segment of movements such as sabbatarianism, abolition, woman's rights, agrarianism, and humanitarian attempts to improve the lot of the poor. . . .
>
> In its auxiliary interests the WCTU revealed a great concern for the improvement of the welfare of the lower classes. It was active in campaigns to secure penal reform, to shorten working hours and raise wages for workers, and to abolish child labor and in a number of other humanitarian and equalitarian activities. In the 1880's the WCTU worked to bring about legislation for the protection of working girls against the exploitation by men.

As Gusfield (1955:223) says, "Moral reformism of this type suggests the approach of a dominant class toward those less favorably situated in the economic and social structure." Moral crusaders typically want to help those beneath them to achieve a better status. That those beneath them do not always like the means proposed for their salvation is another matter. But this fact—that moral crusades are typically dominated by those in the upper levels of the social structure—means that they add to the power they derive from the legitimacy of their moral position, the power they derive from their superior position in society.

Naturally, many moral crusades draw support from people whose motives are less pure than those of the crusader. Thus, some industrialists supported Prohibition because they felt it would provide them with a more manageable labor force (McCarthy 1959:395–396). Similarly, it is sometimes rumored that Nevada gambling interests support the opposition to attempts to legalize gambling in California because it would cut so heavily into their business, which depends in substantial measure on the population of Southern California.

The moral crusader, however, is more concerned with ends than with means. When it comes to drawing up specific rules (typically in the form of legislation to be proposed to a state legislature or the Federal Congress), he frequently relies on the advice of experts. Lawyers, expert in the drawing of acceptable legislation, often play this role. Government bureaus in whose jurisdiction the problem falls may also have the necessary expertise, as did the Federal Bureau of Narcotics in the case of the marihuana problem.

By leaving the drafting of the specific rule in the hands of others, the crusader opens the door for many unforeseen influences. For those who draft legislation for crusaders have their own interests, which may affect the legislation they prepare. It is likely that the sexual psychopath laws drawn by psychiatrists contain many features never intended by the citizens who spearheaded the drives to "do something about sex crimes," features which do however reflect the professional interests of organized psychiatry.

THE FATE OF MORAL CRUSADES

A crusade may achieve striking success, as did the Prohibition movement with the passage of the Eighteenth Amendment. It may fail completely, as has the drive to do away with the use of tobacco or the anti-vivisection movement. It may achieve great success, only to find its gains whittled away by shifts in public morality and increasing restrictions imposed on it by judicial interpretations; such has been the case with the crusade against obscene literature.

One major consequence of a successful crusade, of course, is the establishment of a new rule or set of rules, usually with the appropriate enforcement machinery being provided at the same time. I want to consider this consequence at some length later. There is another consequence, however, of the success of a crusade which deserves mention.

When a man has been successful in the enterprise of getting a new rule established—when he has found, so to speak, the Grail—he is out of a job. The crusade which has occupied so much of his time, energy, and passion is over. Such a man, at loose ends, may generalize his interest and discover something new to view with alarm, a new evil about which something ought to be done. He becomes a professional discoverer of wrongs to be righted, of situations requiring new rules.

When the crusade has produced a large organization devoted to its cause, officials of the organization are even more likely than the individual crusader to look for new causes to espouse. This process occurred dramatically in the field of health problems when the National Foundation for Infantile Paralysis put itself out of business by discovering a vaccine that eliminated epidemic poliomyelitis. Taking the less constraining name of The National Foundation, officials quickly discovered other health problems to which the organization could devote its energies and resources.

Only some crusaders, then, are successful in their mission and create, by creating a new rule, a new group of outsiders. Of the successful, some find they have a taste for crusades and seek new problems to attack. Other crusaders fail in their attempt and either support the organization they have created by dropping their distinctive mission and focusing on the problem of organizational maintenance itself or become outsiders themselves, continuing to espouse and preach a doctrine which sounds increasingly queer as time goes on.

RULE ENFORCERS

The most obvious consequence of a successful crusade is the creation of a new set of rules. With the creation of a new set of rules we often find that a new set of enforcement agencies and officials is established. Sometimes, of course, existing agencies take over the administration of the new rule, but more frequently a new set of rule enforcers is created. The passage of the Harrison Act presaged the creation of the Federal Narcotics Bureau, just as the passage of the Eighteenth Amendment led to the creation of police agencies charged with enforcing the Prohibition Laws.

With the establishment of organizations of rule enforcers, the crusade becomes institutionalized. What started out as a drive to convince the world of the moral necessity of a new rule finally becomes an organization devoted to the enforcement of the rule. Just as radical political movements turn into organized political parties and lusty evangelical sects become staid religious denominations, the final outcome of the moral crusade is a police force. To understand, therefore, how the rules creating a new class of outsiders are applied to particular people we must understand the motives and interests of police, the rule enforcers.

Although some policemen undoubtedly have a kind of crusading interest in stamping out evil, it is probably much more typical for the policeman to have a certain detached and objective view of his job. He is not so much concerned with the content of any particular rule as he is with the fact that it is his job to enforce the rule. When the rules are changed, he punishes what was once acceptable behavior just as he ceases to punish behavior that has been made legitimate by a change in the rules. The

enforcer, then, may not be interested in the content of the rule as such, but only in the fact that the existence of the rule provides him with a job, a profession, and a *raison d'être*.

Enforcers of rules, since they have no stake in the content of particular rules themselves, often develop their own private evaluation of the importance of various kinds of rules and infractions of them. This set of priorities may differ considerably from those held by the general public. For instance, drug users typically believe (and a few policemen have personally confirmed it to me) that police do not consider the use of marihuana to be as important a problem or as dangerous a practice as the use of opiate drugs. Police base this conclusion on the fact that, in their experience, opiate users commit other crimes (such as theft or prostitution) in order to get drugs, while marihuana users do not.

Enforcers, then, responding to the pressures of their own work situation, enforce rules and create outsiders in a selective way. Whether a person who commits a deviant act is in fact labeled a deviant depends on many things extraneous to his actual behavior: whether the enforcement official feels that at this time he must make some show of doing his job in order to justify his position, whether the misbehaver shows proper deference to the enforcer, whether the "fix" has been put in, and where the kind of act he has committed stands on the enforcer's list of priorities.

The professional enforcer's lack of fervor and routine approach to dealing with evil may get him into trouble with the rule creator. The rule creator, as we have said, is concerned with the content of the rules that interest him. He sees them as the means by which evil can be stamped out. He does not understand the enforcer's long-range approach to the same problems and cannot see why all the evil that is apparent cannot be stamped out at once.

When the person interested in the content of a rule realizes or has called to his attention the fact that enforcers are dealing selectively with the evil that concerns him, his righteous wrath may be aroused. The professional is denounced for viewing the evil too lightly, for failing to do his duty. The moral entrepreneur, at whose instance the rule was made, arises again to say that the outcome of the last crusade has not been satisfactory or that the gains once made have been whittled away and lost.

REFERENCES

Gusfield Joseph R. 1955. "Social Structure and Moral Reform: A Study of the Woman's Christian Temperance Union." *American Journal of Sociology* 61.

McCarthy Raymond G. (ed.). 1959. *Drinking and Intoxication.* New Haven and New York: Yale Center of Alcohol Studies and The Free Press of Glencoe.

READING 1-3

Ironies of Social Control

Gary T. Marx

Situations where social control contributes to, or even generates, rule-breaking behavior include these three ideal types:

A. Escalation (by taking enforcement action, authorities unintentionally encourage rule breaking).
B. Nonenforcement (by strategically taking *no enforcement action,* authorities intentionally permit rule breaking).
C. Covert facilitation (by taking *hidden or deceptive enforcement action,* authorities intentionally encourage rule breaking).

These are analytic distinctions. In a given empirical instance all may be present.

Documents and published accounts are [my] major sources. However, I have also drawn on interviews and observations made over a seven-year period in 18 U.S. police departments while studying community police patrols, community service officers, civilian police planners, and performance measures, plus those made during a year spent studying English and French police.

Reprinted from *Social Problems* 28:3 (Feb. 1981), 221–233, by permission of the author and the publisher. © 1981 by the Society for the Study of Social Problems.

ESCALATION

The clearest cases of authorities contributing to rule breaking involve escalation. As with facilitation, authorities' intervention is conductive to deviance. However, secrecy need not be involved (the facilitation can be overt), and the final consequence is generally not consciously, or at best publicly, sought by controllers when they initially enter the situation.[1] It is not simply that social control has no effect, rather that it can amplify. In escalation the very process of social control directly triggers violations. In urging that attention be focused on the deviant act as such, Cohen has written:

> The history of a deviant act is a history of an interaction process. The antecedents of the act are an unfolding sequence of acts contributed by a set of actors (1965:9).

---

[1] Because of their intentionality, nonenforcement and covert facilitation are social control strategies; this cannot be said of escalation which is defined by its unintended consequences, though these may be present with the former as well. Sometimes, of course, police may follow a policy of deliberate provocation in the hope of encouraging escalation so that they can legally use force, bring heavier charges, or dispense "alley justice."

Nowhere is this logic clearer than in the case of escalation. Five major analytic elements of escalation are:

1. An increase in the *frequency* of the original violations.
2. An increase in the *seriousness* of violations, including the greater use of violence.
3. The appearance of *new* categories of violators and/or victims (without a net diminution of those previously present).
4. An increase in the commitment and/or skill and effectiveness of those engaged in the violation.
5. The appearance of violations whose very definition is tied to social control intervention.

Escalation may stem from initial or postapprehension enforcement efforts.

Police involvement in family conflict, crowd, and automobile chase situations can contribute to violations when none were imminent, or it can increase the seriousness of these situations. In responding to challenges to their authority or to interpersonal conflict situations, preemptive police actions (euphemistically called by some with a sardonic smile, "constructive coercion" and "preventive violence") may lead to further violence.

A three-year study of police-citizen incidents in New York City notes "the extent to which the handling of relatively minor incidents such as traffic violations or disorderly disputes between husbands and wives seemed to create a more serious situation than existed prior to the police attempt to control the situation" (McNamara 1967). Family disturbance calls are an important source of police injuries to citizens and vice versa. Bard has similarly observed that "there is more than ample evidence that insensitive, untrained, and inept police management of human problems is a significant breeding ground for violence" (1971:3). Certain styles of intervention are likely to provoke aggressive responses.

An English policeman characterized the 1960s' riot control behavior of American police in some cities as "oilin' the fire." Police responses to crowd situations offer many examples of escalation (Marx 1970; Stark 1972). Provocative overreaction (referred to by another English policeman as "cracking a nut with a sledgehammer") can turn a peaceful crowd into a disorderly one. In the 1967 riot in New Haven, for example, a small group of angry but as yet law-abiding blacks marched in the street—to be met by police tear gas; this then provoked a small riot. Or in Detroit a small riot emerged during the Poor People's March when, during a meeting in a large hall, police inside the building tried to push people outside, at the same time that mounted police outside were trying to push people back inside. Such police reactions and subsequent arrests may occur in the most benign of circumstances, such as at sporting events or concerts.

High-speed chases offer another all too tragic example. They result in injuries, in death, and often in manslaughter charges against persons who, in the absence of the chase, might have faced minimal or no charges. For example, in a Boston suburb, a car being chased by two police cruisers at speeds of 95 miles an hour killed a foot-patrolman. The young driver of the car was subsequently charged not only with speeding but with manslaughter. The same day a 15-year-old youth facing manslaughter charges hung himself in a jail in a nearby town. He was arrested the week before, following a high-speed chase in which his car killed two people (*Boston Globe,* November 21, 1975). The high-speed chase, perhaps because of the risks and emotions involved and the denial of police authority, also figures disproportionately in situations where prisoners are abused. The escalation here has second-order effects, coming to involve new offenders (police themselves) as well as new offenses (e.g., assault and denial of civil rights).

One consequence of strong enforcement actions can be to change the personnel and social organization of those involved in illegal activities. For example, stepped-up enforcement efforts with respect to heroin and cocaine appear to have moved the drug traffic away from less sophisticated and skilled local, often amateur, groups to more highly skilled, centralized, better organized criminal groups (Young 1971; Sabbag 1976; Adler et al. forthcoming). The greater skill and sophistication of those now drawn into the activity may mean the development of new markets. Increased risks may mean greater profits, as well as incentives to develop new consumers and markets. The more professional criminals are more likely to be able to avoid prosecution and are in a better position to induce police corruption.

Increased corruption, a frequent escalatory consequence of stepped-up enforcement efforts, is one of a number of second-order forms of illegality which may indirectly appear. Even attacking corruption may generate other problems. Thus, following reform efforts in one city (Sherman 1978:257), police morale declined and citizen complaints went up sharply, as did police use of firearms. In Boston a recent increase in high-speed chases and attendant offenses and injuries is directly traceable to an order to enforce traffic laws more stringently. Another second-order effect can be seen in the monopoly profits which may accrue to those who provide vice in a context of strong enforcement pressures. These profits can be invested in still other illegal activities. Thus, some of the tremendous profits earned by organized crime groups that emerged during prohibition, and the skills developed then, went into gambling, labor racketeering, and narcotics. Violence may increase among criminal groups contending for new monopoly profits. Their monopoly may also have been aided by informing on competitors. The increased cost of the product they provide may mean increased illegality on the part of customers facing higher prices (Schur 1965). A link between drug addiction and street crime, for example, has often been argued.

Authorities may directly provide new resources which have unintended effects. Part of the increased homicide rates in the 1970s, for example, particularly among minority youths, has been attributed to vastly augmented amounts of federal "buy" money for drugs. This increased the opportunity for youths

to become informers, and some of them were subsequently killed. The drugs, stolen goods, money, weapons, and tips sometimes given to informers and others who aid police may be used in subsequent crimes. A more benign resource may be the youth workers sent to work with gangs in their environment. Some of the detached street-worker programs, aimed at reducing gang delinquency, may have actually increased it: By strengthening identification with the gang, they made it more cohesive and encouraged new recruits (Klein 1969). Klein observes that the assumed advantages of group work with gangs are "mythical," and he advocates abandoning standard detached worker programs. In Chicago, antipoverty funds for self-help programs among gangs offered resources, opportunities and incentives which created a context for fraud, extortion and violence (Short 1974).

Contemporary American law has evolved an increasing number of crimes which emerge solely as an artifact of social control intervention. These emerge incidentally to efforts to enforce other laws. If authorities had not taken action, the offense would not have been committed. Resisting arrest or assaulting an officer are familiar examples. The prosecution of white-collar crimes offers a different example.

Prosecutors who initially set out to make cases of corruption, fraud, or food and drug violations may be unable to prove the targeted crime, yet still be able to prosecute for perjury or obstruction of justice. The latter violations become possible only after an investigation begins and can exist regardless of the quality of evidence for the case the prosecutor originally hoped to make.

More routine are white-collar offenses involving the violation of requirements imposed on citizens to aid in the investigation of still other crimes. In and of themselves the violations need not produce social harm. In the effort to detect and sanction infractions the criminal justice system can promote crimes because of its own need for information. Failing to file reports or filing a false statement to the U.S. government are examples. Failure to file an income tax form is a crime even if one owes no taxes.[2]

Most of the escalation examples considered here have involved the initial enforcement effort and one point in time. The work of Wilkins (1965) and that of Lemert (1951, 1972) call attention to postapprehension escalation and a person's "career" as a deviant. Wilkins sees a spiraling interactive process whereby rule breaking leads to sanctioning, which then leads to more serious rule breaking, which in turn leads to more serious sanctioning and so on. Lemert focuses on how people may change their lives and self-conceptions in response to being formally processed, punished, stigmatized, segregated, or isolated. To the extent that their lives and identities come to be organized around the facts of their publicly labelled deviance, they are secondary deviants.

However, postapprehension escalation can occur without an accelerating spiral or changes in self-image. Having been apprehended for one offense, or identified as a rule violator, can set in motion actions by authorities that make additional violations more likely. For one thing, contact with the criminal justice system may alter one's status (e.g., to probationer, inmate, or parolee) so that one is guilty of a misdemeanor or felony for acts that would be legally inoffensive if committed by others. In addition, being placed in such statuses may provide actors with inducements to the commission of a crime, either by way of opportunity or pressure, to which others are not exposed.

Among the most poignant and tragic examples of escalation are those that emerge from the application of the initial sanction. Prisoners, such as George Jackson, who are sent up at a young age for a short term, then who find their sentences continually lengthened because of their behavior in prison, are clear examples. According to one study, only 6 of 40 offenses punishable in one state prison would be misdemeanors or felonies if done outside (Barnes and Teeters 1959, as cited in Lemert

1972:81). Similarly, violation of some of the regulations faced by those on parole or probation can send them to prison, but the same acts are not illegal when done by others.

For those not yet in prison, the need to meet bail and expensive legal fees can exert pressure to obtain such funds illegally. Clarence Darrow reported the case of a young thief who wanted the famous lawyer to defend him. Darrow asked if he had any money. The young man said, "No," and then with a smile said he thought he could raise some by that evening. An undercover narcotics detective (more taken by the seeming stupidity of those he arrests than of the system that generates their behavior) reports, "I even make buys again from guys who I've arrested and come right back out to make some fast bread for their expenses in court" (Schiano and Burton 1974:93). There seems to be the possibility of infinite regress here.

NONENFORCEMENT

In nonenforcement, the contribution of authorities to deviance is more indirect than with escalation or covert facilitation. Rule breaking does not expand unintentionally and authorities do not set people up and covertly facilitate it. Instead, those involved in nonenforcement relationships (e.g., with police) may break rules partly because they believe they will not be appropriately sanctioned. Here we have an exchange relationship between police and offenders. Offenders perform services for police; in return they are allowed to break rules and may receive other benefits.

When it is organized and specialized, nonenforcement is the most difficult of the three forms of interdependence to identify empirically. As a strategy it is often illegal and is more likely to be hidden. One does not find conditions for its use spelled out in policy manuals. Indeed the opposite is more apt to be true. In prohibiting nonenforcement, training and policy guidelines often go to great lengths to point out its dangers. Police are sworn to uphold the law: Not to do so may involve them in malfeasance, aiding and abetting a felon,

---

[2] As Jack Katz has pointed out in a private communication, "Such laws reflect the fact that in a way large sections of our society are always under investigation for a crime."

compounding a felony, perjury, and a host of other violations. Some anticorruption policies are from one perspective antinonenforcement policies. They seek to create conditions that will work against collusive nonenforcement relations; at the same time the realities of the police job are such that it emerges as a major fact of police life.

Nonenforcement may literally involve taking no enforcement action, passing on information regarding police and criminal activities (including tips on raids), using improper procedures that will not stand up in court, offering ineffective testimony, helping a person facing charges to obtain leniency, giving gifts of contraband, and taking enforcement action against competitors. While there is sometimes overlap, we can differentiate "self-interested nonenforcement" involving traditional police corruption from "principled nonenforcement"—of most interest here—where police actions are thought to serve broader organizational goals.[3] Nonenforcement or leniency can be an important resource that authorities offer to those engaged in rule breaking whose cooperation they need. It is protected by the legitimate discretion in the police role and the United States' comparatively high standards of proof and rules of evidence required for conviction.

Police may adopt a policy of nonenforcement with respect to (1) informants who give them information about the law breaking of others and/or help in facilitating the controlled commission of a crime; (2) vice entrepreneurs who agree to keep their own illegal behavior within agreed upon bounds; (3) individuals who either directly regulate the behavior of others using resources police lack or means they are denied, or who take actions desired by authorities but considered too politically risky for them to undertake.

A former director of the FBI states, "Without informants we're nothing" (*New York Times,* April 16,

1974). The informant system, central to many types of law enforcement, is a major source of nonenforcement. Informants can offer police a means of getting information and making arrests that cannot come from other sources, given strictures against electronic surveillance, search and seizure, coercion, and the difficulty of infiltration. In return the system can work to the advantage of rule breakers. In the words of an FBI agent known for his ability to cultivate informants among those in organized crime:

> They [informants] worked with agents because it was profitable for them: They avoided prison, got reduced sentences or parole for friends and relatives, maybe enjoyed some revenge against guys who had betrayed them, and picked up informer fees and some very substantial sums in the way of rewards paid by insurance companies delighted to refund five percent in return for saving the ninety-five percent liability (Villano 1977:103).

The system can be used by both police and informants as a form of institutionalized blackmail. Potentially damaging action such as arrest or denouncement of someone as an informant or offender is withheld as long as the cooperation sought is forthcoming.

The tables can also get turned, as the informant manipulates the control agent into corrupt activities (or merely acquiesces in the agent's desire for these). For example, in the case of drugs, the exchange of immunity or drugs for information can, in a series of incremental changes, lead to joint marketing and other criminal ventures (Commission 1972). The nonenforcement may become mutual and the balance of power shift. The informant not only controls the flow of information but could even threaten exposure, which may entail greater risk for the police officer than for the drug dealer (Moore 1977; Karchmer 1979).

Where the informant is involved in the controlled commission of a crime, social control actions may generate rule breaking in two ways. Criminogenic effects may be present because police ignore illegal activities of the informant. But they may also be present because informants covertly facilitate the rule breaking of others. Informants facing charges

---

[3] Here we ignore the many other sources of nonenforcement such as lack of resources, intimidation, bureaucratic timidity, lack of belief in the rule, or compassion, as well as the suspension of law enforcement in order to have something to hold over a person should the need arise later.

or desiring drugs, for example, may have strong incentives to facilitate others' deviance.

Louis Tackwood, an informant for the Los Angeles Police Department for ten years, worked first in traditional crime and later in radical politics. He appears to have committed numerous crimes, yet never to have been sentenced. He recalls:

> I never worried about getting caught. It was the idea of the money, the free crime. Here's a cat, a person, who like me has been successful in forming several organizations for crime. Here are the police officers telling me, hey, we want you to work for us. Two things went through my mind then—money and I got a free hand to do anything I want to do (Citizens Committee and Tackwood 1973:24).

In more muted terms, a former commander of detectives in Chicago hints at how the informant system in a context of secrecy and specialization may work at cross-purposes:

> The burglary detectives may be inclined to "pass" a junkie with a small amount of drugs if he can turn up stolen property, while the narco squad will forget a few nickel and dime burglaries in return for cooperation in apprehending a major peddler. Homicide investigators looking for information on a murder will view a busy prostitute only as a source of information (Reppetto 1976).

People often become informants while in jail, or facing arrest. Sentencing may be deferred for a period of time while the informant "works off" the charges (for example, see Cloyd 1979). In some police circles this is known as "flipping" or "turning" a man. With respect to drug enforcement, in some cities a point system is used whereby the informant receives one point for each marijuana purchase and two points for the purchase of harder drugs. If the informant earns a fixed number of points, such as ten, charges will be dropped. There is no doubt considerable variation among departments and within. Accounts such as that offered by Tackwood are perhaps best treated as ideal-typical illustrations.

In return for noninterference from police (often further bought by the payment of bribes), vice entrepreneurs may agree to engage in self-policing and operate with relative honesty (i.e., run orderly disorderly houses), restrict their activities to one type of vice, stay in a given geographical area, and run low-visibility operations. By favoring certain vice operators and cooperating with them to keep others out, police may introduce a degree of control and stability into what would otherwise be a chaotic cutthroat situation.

Vigilante-type groups offer another example. Police may look the other way and essentially delegate certain enforcement rights to a group that wishes to take action that police might like to take but are unwilling to. The summary justice of the southern lynch mob, and group violence against blacks, were often conspicuous because of the lack of a restraining police presence. Until recently in many areas of the South, police (when not themselves members) ignored or gave encouragement to the Klan. The weak, if not openly supportive, attitude of many southern leaders in the face of discrimination and white violence significantly encouraged the Klan. This greatly hampered the federal effort to enforce civil rights laws and protect civil rights workers. With respect to traditional offenses, it has been claimed that in some urban minority areas police have been less than diligent in investigating the murders of drug pushers supposedly carried out by vigilantes seeking to rid their communities of pushers.

Still another type of nonenforcement can originate in some criminals' possession of unique skills, or even in their having the same enemies as authorities do. The fact that organized crime and the United States government have had some common enemies (Mussolini in Italy and Castro in Cuba) has sometimes led to cooperation between them.

Recent reports of connections between the CIA and the underworld may simply be the continuation of an old American tradition. The CIA with its "executive action program" designed to "eliminate the effectiveness of foreign leaders" also delegated some of its dirty work (such as assassination efforts directed against Castro and Lumumba) to underworld figures. In Castro's case organized crime figures were thought to have "expertise and contacts not available to law-abiding citizens." They also had a motive which it was thought would take attention away from sponsorship of the U.S. government. According to one estimate (Schlesinger 1978), Castro's coming to power cost organized crime $100 million a year. Outsiders were used by the CIA to avoid having "an Agency person or government person get caught" (Select Committee 1975:74).

A former bank robber and forger involved in the unsuccessful plot to assassinate Lumumba was given plastic surgery and a toupee by the CIA before being sent to the Congo. This man was recommended by the Chief of the CIA's Africa Division as a "field operative" because "if he is given an assignment which may be morally wrong in the eyes of the world, but necessary because his case officer ordered him to carry it out, then it is right, and he will dutifully undertake appropriate action for its execution without pangs of conscience. In a word, he can rationalize all actions" (Select Committee 1975:46). It appears that in extreme cases one crucial element which agents of social control may obtain in such exchange relationships is a psychopathic personality not inhibited by conventional moral restraints.

Still another type of strategic nonenforcement, one not involving exchanges, happens when authorities fail to take action about a violation they know is planned, or in progress, until the violation is carried out. This permits arrest quotas to be met and can lead to heavier charges, greater leverage in negotiations, better evidence, and a higher level of offender arrest. For example, an experienced cocaine smuggler, who could easily identify "amateurs" in the business, argues that federal agents always waited for such persons to be arrested before talking to them. He notes:

> Rather than walk up to someone obviously headed for trouble—where they might flash a badge and say, "Get smart, kid, it's not going to work"—they will, as a matter of policy, allow him to risk his life with the local heavies, get a few snorts of pure, and walk into jail at the airport back home. Why prevent smuggling when you can punish it—isn't that what jails are for? (Sabbag 1976:120)

COVERT FACILITATION

In the case of covert facilitation, authorities consciously seek to encourage rule breaking: Getting someone to break the rule is the major goal. Both law and internal policy are often favorable to police facilitation of crime. A not atypical policy manual of one police department contains a section on "permissible tactics for arranging the controlled commission of an offense." Police are told that they or their agents under appropriate conditions may:

A. affirmatively suggest the commission of the offense to the subject;
B. attempt to form a relationship with the subject of sufficient closeness to overcome the subject's possible apprehension over his trustworthiness;
C. offer the subject more than one opportunity to commit the offense;
D. create a continuing opportunity for the subject to commit the offense;
E. minimize the possibility of being apprehended for committing the offense.

For the purpose of this paper we identify at least three types of covert facilitation:

1. disguised police or their agents cooperating with others in illegal actions;
2. police secretly generating opportunities for rule breaking without being coconspirators;
3. police secretly generating motives for rule breaking without being coconspirators.

With respect to the "controlled commission of an offense," police or their agents may enter into relationships with those who don't know that they are police, to buy or sell illegal goods and services or to victimize others. The former is the most common. Agents of social control may purchase or sell drugs, pose as tourists seeking prostitutes, as prostitutes seeking customers, or as homosexuals seeking partners. They may pose as fences buying or selling stolen goods, as hit men taking a contract, as criminals trying to bribe prosecutors, and as entrepreneurs running pornographic bookstores. They may join groups that are (or become) involved in car theft, burglary, or robbery. They may infiltrate political groups thought to be dangerous. The last decade reveals many examples of covert facilitation as authorities responded to widespread protest (Marx 1974).

Both of the two other types of covert facilitation (deceptively creating opportunity structures or motives but without collusion) have a "give-them-enough-rope" quality. Police activity here is more passive and the deception is of a greater order from that involved in the "controlled commission of an offense." Police do not directly enter into criminal conspiracies with their targets, and charges of entrapment would not be supported—but they do attempt to structure the world in such a way that violations are made more likely.

The use of decoys to draw street crime is a major form of police creation of opportunity structures. Police anticrime squads, increasingly in vogue, may disguise their members as old women, clerics, derelicts, tennis players, and bike riders; they may use attractive police women in civilian clothes to induce robbery and assault, with other police watching from close by (Halper and Ku 1976). Private guards posing as inattentive customers paying for small purchases with large bills routinely test cashier honesty. Plain-clothed "security inspectors" may test employee vigilance by seeing if they can get away with shoplifting. There is almost no limit to the variety of attractive opportunities for property theft that can be generated. Other examples include leaving packages in a watched unmarked decoy car with its windows open, leaving expensive skis (which, when moved, emit an electronic signal audible only to guards) in a conspicuous place at ski resorts, and opening crates of expensive merchandise at airport storage terminals and dusting it with an invisible powder that can be seen only by an ultraviolet light machine that employees pass as they leave work (Marx 1980).

Covert facilitation involving the creation of motives can be seen in many counterintelligence activities. Here the goal may be disruption and subversion (rather than strictly law enforcement). In "dirty tricks" campaigns, police may take clandestine actions in the hope of provoking factionalism and violence. In one extreme example, an FBI agent in Tucson, Arizona, instigated a series of bombings of a Mafia home and a business to encourage fighting among rival organized crime groups (Talese 1972). In one of the more bizarre cases of the last decade, the FBI, in "Operation Hoodwink," sought to encourage conflict between the Communist Party and elements in organized crime (Donner 1976). The FBI was also responsible for burning cars of leftist activists so that it appeared to be done by rival political groups (*New York Times,* July 11, 1976). Undercover agents operating on opposing sides apparently played an important role in the violent split that occurred between the Huey Newton and Eldridge Cleaver factions of the Black Panthers. Perhaps more common are efforts to make it appear that an individual involved in criminal or radical politics is an informant, by planting information or contriving leaks. The "informant" may then be subject to possible retaliatory violence. This may be done by a genuine informant as part of a strategy of subversion or to cast blame elsewhere if arrests are to be made where it will be obvious that an informant was present (Schiano and Burton 1974; Villano 1977).

In a version of turnabout as fair play (at least to reform police executives), covert facilitation may also be turned inward in efforts to deal with corrupt police and assess police honesty. Tactics recently used by the New York City police include: planting illegally parked cars with money in them to see if police tow truck operators would steal it; planting "lost" wallets near randomly selected police to see if they would be turned in intact; offering bribes to arresting officers; putting through a contrived "open door" call to an apartment where marked money was prominently displayed to see if two officers under suspicion would steal it (they did); establishing phony gambling operations to see if police sought protection money; and having an undercover officer pose as a pusher to see if other undercover narcotics agents paid out the full amount of "buy" money they claimed (*New York*

Times, November 29, 1972, and December 28, 1973; Sherman 1978).

Government lawyers, judges, and congressmen may also be targets of such tactics. Thus Sante A. Bario, a federal drug agent, posed as Salvatore Barone, a Las Vegas underworld figure, and was "arrested" in a Queens bar for carrying two loaded pistols. He then offered an assistant district attorney under suspicion $15,000 and the "charges" were dismissed (as was the assistant D.A.; Lardner 1977); Operation Abscam, part of a federal bribery investigation, involved undercover agents posing as Arab sheiks who offered money to congressmen in return for favors (*New York Times,* February 4, 1980).

For convenience we have thus far treated three types of interdependence as if they were distinct empirically as well as analytically. However, there are deviance and social control situations in which each or several are present—or where they merge or may be temporally linked. One of the things rule breakers may offer to police in return for nonenforcement is aid in covertly facilitating someone else's rule breaking. The arrest that emerges out of this can involve escalation. For example, a drug informant's petty theft may be ignored (nonenforcement) in return for his making controlled buys (covert facilitation). The arrest growing out of this may lead to additional charges if the suspect is involved in a high-speed chase and fights with the arresting officers after they call him a name. Escalation may lead to a later policy of nonenforcement in those situations where authorities perceive that their intervention would in fact only make matters worse.[4] Stepped-up enforcement may also lead to nonenforcement by increasing opportunities for police corruption.

---

[4] In the case of civil disorders, however, underreaction as part of a policy of nonenforcement can have the unintended consequence of encouraging the spread of disorder. The three largest civil disorders of the 1960s (Watts, Newark, and Detroit) were all characterized by the initial period of police underreaction. Given the infraction-generating potential of both over- and underreaction, police often find themselves criticized no matter how they respond, and policies are cyclical.

REFERENCES

Adler, P. A., P. Adler and J. Douglas. Forthcoming. "Organized crime: Drug dealing for pleasure and profit." In J. Douglas, *Observations of Deviance,* second edition. New York: Random House.

Bard, M. 1971. "Iatrogenic violence." *The Police Chief* (January):16–17.

Barnes, H. and N. Teeters. 1959. *New Horizons in Criminology.* Englewood Cliffs, N.J.: Prentice Hall.

Citizens Research and Investigation Committee and Louis F. Tackwood. 1973. *The Glass House Tapes.* New York: Avon Books.

Cloyd, J. 1979. "Prosecution's power, procedural rights, and pleading guilty: The problem of coercion in plea bargaining cases." *Social Problems* 26(4):452–466.

Cohen, A. 1965. "The sociology of the deviant act." *American Sociological Review* 30:5–14.

Commission to Investigate Allegations of Police Corruption and the City's Anti-Corruption Procedures (1972). *The Knapp Commission Report on Police Corruption.* New York: Braziller.

Donner, F. 1976. "Let him wear a wolf's head: What the FBI did to William Albertson." *Civil Liberties Review* 3 (April–May):12–22.

Halper, A. and R. Ku. 1976. *New York City Police Department Street Crime Unit.* Washington, D.C.: U.S. Government Printing Office.

Karchmer, C. 1979. "Corruption towards performance: Goals and operations in proactive law enforcement." Paper presented to Western Political Science Association, Portland, Oregon.

Klein, M. 1969. "Gang cohesiveness, delinquency and a street work program." *Journal of Research in Crime and Delinquency* 6(1):135–166.

Lardner, J. 1977. "How prosecutors get nabbed." *New Republic,* January 29:22–25.

Lemert, E. 1951. *Social Pathology.* New York: McGraw-Hill.

———. 1972. *Human Deviance, Social Problems and Social Control.* Englewood Cliffs, N.J.: Prentice Hall.

Marx, G. 1974. "Thoughts on a neglected category of social movement participant: Agents, provocateurs and informants." *American Journal of Sociology* 80 (2):402–442.

———. 1980. "The new police undercover work." *Journal of Urban Life* 8(4):400–446.

McNamara, J. H. 1967. "Uncertainty in police work: The relevance of police recruits' background and training."

Pp. 163–252 in D. Bordua (ed.), *The Police,* New York: Wiley.

Moore, M. 1977. *Buy and Bust.* Lexington, Mass.: Lexington Press.

Reppetto, T. A. 1976. "The uneasy milieu of the detective." Pp. 130–136 in A. Niederhoffer and A. Blumberg (eds.), *The Ambivalent Force,* 2nd edition. Hinsdale, Ill.: Dryden.

Sabbag, R. 1976. *Snow Blind.* New York: Avon.

Schiano, A. and A. Burton. 1974. *Solo.* New York: Warner.

Schlesinger, A. 1978. *Robert Kennedy and His Times.* Boston: Houghton Mifflin.

Schur, E. 1965. *Crimes Without Victims.* Englewood Cliffs, N.J.: Prentice Hall.

Select Committee to Study Governmental Operations With Respect to Intelligence Activities. 1975. *Alleged Assassination Plots Involving Foreign Leaders.* Washington, D.C.: U.S. Government Printing Office.

Sherman, L. 1978. *Scandal and Reform.* Berkeley: University of California Press.

Short, J. F. 1974. "Youth, gangs, and society: Micro- and macrosociological processes." *Sociological Quarterly* 15 (Winter):3–19.

Stark, R. 1972. *Police Riots, Collective Violence and Law Enforcement.* Belmont, Calif.: Wadsworth.

Talese, G. 1972. *Honor Thy Father.* Greenwich, Conn.; Fawcett Crest.

Villano, A. with G. Astor. 1977. *Brick Agent.* New York: Quadrangle.

Wilkins, L. 1965. *Social Deviance.* Englewood Cliffs, N.J.: Prentice Hall.

Young, J. 1971. "The roles of the police as amplifiers of deviancy." Pp. 27–61 in S. Cohen (ed.), *Images of Deviance.* London: Penguin Books.

STUDY QUESTIONS

1. According to Howard Becker, why are "rule enforcers," such as the police, sometimes at odds with "rule creators"?

2. Becker discusses "moral entrepreneurs." Think of an example of a recent crusade in America led by moral entrepreneurs; what are its goals?

3. Based on the essay by Gary Marx, why do the authorities engage in practices that result in the escalation, nonenforcement, and covert facilitation of deviance?

4. In what ways does Marx's essay broaden and enrich our understanding of the relationship between deviant behavior and social control?

PART TWO

THEORIES OF DEVIANCE

THEORIES OF DEVIANCE

Introduction

Theories are an essential part of any scientific enterprise. A *theory* may be defined as a set of testable propositions designed to explain a general class of phenomena, such as deviant behavior or the conditions under which social control is likely to be exercised. Theories can advance our *understanding* of the social world and can also be used to *predict* both deviant behavior and social control practices. Each theory covered in this book identifies unique variables that distinguish it from other theories. And each theory has attracted empirical research that appears to support at least some of the theory's propositions.

Theories of deviance and control can be critically evaluated. Some theories are more cogent and illuminating than others. Readers are encouraged to interrogate each theory in this section of the book by asking the following questions:

1. How is deviance *defined* (explicitly or implicitly) by the theory: Is it simply a matter of norm-violation, or is deviance defined differently?
2. Does the theory focus mostly on deviant *behavior,* mostly on social *control,* or does it provide a more *balanced* model incorporating both deviance and control?
3. Are the *cause → effect relationships* clearly spelled out in the theory? What are the main causes and effects?
4. Is the theory a *general* theory, applicable to all forms of deviance? Or is it best suited to explaining some kinds of deviance but weak in explaining other kinds of deviance?

For each of the six theories of deviance covered in this section, the first essay outlines core elements of the theory, and the selections that follow are research applications of the theory. Each research-based study is designed to illustrate or test at least some of the theory's main propositions.

Functionalist theory is, in some respects, the most radical perspective because it takes an *appreciative* stance toward deviance. Unlike perspectives that begin with the assumption that deviance is pathological and should be stamped out, functionalism asserts that deviance is a *natural* feature of all societies and that deviant behavior and its control serve *positive functions* for groups and societies. As Emile Durkheim (1966/1895) wrote more than a century ago, "Crime is, then, necessary; it is bound up with fundamental conditions of all social life, and by that very fact it is useful, because these conditions . . . are themselves indispensable to the normal evolution of morality and law." For

Durkheim, crime and punishment are functional because they help to clarify and ratify normative boundaries in society—that is, the boundaries between acceptable and unacceptable behavior. Public punishment of offenders helps to strengthen norms and highlights the line between good and evil, and has the added benefit of increasing cohesion and solidarity among the conforming members of society. Kai Erikson expands on Durkheim's argument in his essay, "The Sociology of Deviance," and Maria Grabe ("Television News Magazines and Functionalism") applies the theory to television reports on crime. Her analysis of 272 hours of television news stories found that the reports demonized offenders, drew stark contrasts between good and evil, promoted public outrage toward criminals, and, by dramatizing the arrests of suspects, communicated the message that crime doesn't pay—thus ratifying societal norms.

Social disorganization theory emphasizes "location, location, location." Unlike theories that focus on "kinds of people" explanations for deviant behavior (for instance, young males who commit violent crimes), the social disorganization approach examines the effects of "kinds of places" (specifically, different types of neighborhood) in fostering conditions favorable or unfavorable to deviant behavior. Neighborhoods differ in their capacity to control the behavior of people in public places, which is related to variables such as the lack of community friendship networks, family disruption (one-parent families), residential turnover, poverty, and unsupervised teenage peer groups that might be prone to get into trouble. The more socially disorganized a neighborhood is along these dimensions, the greater likelihood of local deviance. The theory was first advanced in the 1920s and 1930s and applied in Chicago by Clifford Shaw and Henry McKay (1942), and the perspective has experienced a revival in recent years.

Rodney Stark's article, "Deviant Places," is a perfect example of this perspective. He presents 30 propositions that seem to explain why deviance is more prevalent in some neighborhoods than in others. James Wilson and George Kelling ("Broken Windows") examine two aspects of social disorganization: the tendency for isolated signs of neighborhood decay (e.g., graffiti, abandoned cars) and disorder (e.g., panhandling, street prostitution, drug dealing) to become more widespread if left unchecked and the need for residents and police to confront miscreants before they get out of hand and ruin the neighborhood. In other words, consistent with social disorganization theory, residents must be vigilant in maintaining social control in the neighborhood—both through their own informal actions and with the help of formal agents of control like the police. Since its publication in 1982, Wilson and Kelling's article has had a major influence on the policies of many police departments, who have begun to crack down on signs of neighborhood disorder and street deviance.

Anomie theory holds that deviance results from a disjunction between two basic features of social structure: cultural goals and institutionalized norms or means for pursuing those goals. The theory was originally designed by Robert Merton ("Social Structure and Anomie") to explain four types of deviant adaptation to the goals-means disjunction, but Merton was most interested in the "innovative" deviance of lower-class persons who sought to pursue the American Dream of material success but faced blocked opportunities in achieving success. The use of illegitimate means to pursue the success goal is more prevalent, Merton argues, in the lower class than in the middle and upper classes because the latter have more opportunities to pursue success through legitimate channels. But how then do we explain crime among affluent people, who appear to have access to legitimate means for achieving success? The chapter by Nicos Passas ("Anomie and Corporate Deviance") attempts to show that anomie theory can also be applied to affluent, corporate criminals. Corporations put a very high premium on maximizing profit and undercutting competing firms, and these elevated success goals may be hard to achieve through normal, legal means—thus setting the stage for innovative deviance.

Anomie theory can be expanded to include goals other than material success. In fact, it can be applied to any situation in which highly esteemed values and goals are out of reach for some people. Examples include athletes who will do anything it takes to win a match (such as taking steroids) and police officers who violate the law in order to fight crime, including improper searches, use of illegal tactics to induce suspects to confess to a crime, and the "street justice" or summary punishment of suspects when officers have insufficient evidence to warrant an arrest.

Learning theory holds that deviant behavior is learned in the same way that conventional behavior is learned. As Edwin Sutherland ("Differential Association Theory") argues, learning is a necessary precursor to all criminal activity, and individuals learn crime through association with others involved in crime. Learning includes both behavioral techniques and the values and beliefs that support nonconformity, including justifications for the behavior. Sutherland's claim that learning is confined to persons who directly associate with others has been criticized by other scholars, and prompted Daniel Glaser (1956) to modify Sutherland's theory with the idea of "differential identification." Glaser points out that people may learn deviance not only by direct association with other deviants but also by *identifying* with persons who are quite remote from the actor, including people portrayed in the mass media, like serial murderer Jeffrey Dahmer or the "Unabomber" Ted Kaczynski. As Glaser (1956) writes, "a person pursues criminal behavior to the extent that he identifies himself with real or imaginary persons from whose perspective his criminal behavior seems acceptable." Sutherland's and Glaser's propositions may be easily combined: individuals learn deviance by either direct association or indirect identification with other deviants.

Sutherland's "differential association" version of learning theory is applied in the chapters by Howard Becker ("Becoming a Marihuana User") and Barbara Heyl ("The Training of House Prostitutes"). Becker's classic article, published in 1953, centers on how novice marijuana users learn techniques for properly smoking marijuana as well as how to perceive the drug's effects and how to interpret those effects as pleasurable. Becker also challenges the conventional view that aberrant motives lead to deviant behavior. Motivations do not precede marijuana smoking but instead are *learned* in the course of smokers' experiences with the drug. Becker writes that "the motivation or disposition to engage in the activity is built up in the course of learning to engage in it and does not antedate this learning process." The same dynamic may characterize at least some other types of deviance as well.

Heyl's study of brothel prostitutes describes how they are resocialized to perform this kind of work. They are taught by the madam of the house distinctive values, norms, and skills, and consequently experience a change in their identities as well.

Labeling theory differs from the other perspectives in its emphasis on *audience reactions* to deviant actors and the effects of these reactions on the actors. What is most important, according to labeling theorists, is not norm violation but rather how individuals are *perceived and treated* by audiences. No behavior is deviant in the abstract; it only becomes deviant when some audience observes it, labels it deviant, and treats the actor differently because of the imputed deviance. Howard Becker ("Outsiders") uses the concepts of "pure deviance" and "falsely-accused deviance" to demonstrate that the most important variable is how an actor is regarded by others, not whether he or she actually broke some norm. Pure deviants are individuals who have broken a norm and are viewed as deviant by others, whereas falsely-accused deviants are those who have violated no norm but are nevertheless perceived and treated as deviant by an audience. Another of Becker's concepts, "secret deviance," appears more problematic. Secret deviance is the opposite of falsely-accused deviance: the secret deviant violates norms but is not perceived by others as deviant. "No one notices it or reacts to it," Becker writes. The notion of secret deviance has been criticized by other scholars as being inconsistent with the labeling perspective. If, as Becker writes, "The deviant is one to whom a label has successfully been applied," then deviance cannot be secret since no labeling has occurred. One way to resolve the discrepancy between secret deviance and the idea that labeling must precede deviance would be to argue that a secret deviant's behavior would likely be condemned and branded deviant *if* it became known to some audience. As Erving Goffman (1963) points out, we can distinguish between "discredited" persons (pure or falsely-accused deviants) and "discreditable" persons (secret deviants) who stand a high chance of being discredited if their rule-breaking behavior is discovered.

John Kitsuse elaborates on the central argument of labeling theory in his article, "Societal Reaction to Deviant Behavior." He writes, "Forms of behavior per se do not differentiate deviants from nondeviants; it is the responses of the conventional and conforming members of the society who identify and interpret behavior as deviant which sociologically transform persons into deviants." In other words, behavior is not deviant or normal in the abstract; it depends entirely on how an *audience* views and treats an actor. Kitsuse identifies three stages in the interactional production of deviance: (1) a reactor *interprets* an actor as a deviant, (2) a reactor then *categorizes* the actor as a certain kind of deviant (insane, alcoholic, anorexic), and (3) a reactor then *treats* the actor differently because of the imputed deviance. Kitsuse applies this model to the labeling of homosexuality. In interviews with college students, subjects relied on two types of "evidence" in reaching a conclusion that another person was homosexual: direct observation and indirect evidence. Both types of evidence can be dubious grounds for drawing conclusions about another's sexual orientation, but this did not prevent audience members from doing so.

Labeling is not always successful. William Waegel and his colleagues ("Labeling the CIA Deviant") discuss attempts to attach a deviant label to the Central Intelligence Agency for its improper or illegal activities, and the agency's successful repudiation of such imputations. This chapter shows quite clearly that labeling efforts may be frustrated, and it demonstrates the importance of *power* in the labeling process. Like other powerful organizations, the CIA has considerable capacity to prevent deviant labels from "sticking."

Conflict theory centers on patterns of class, racial, and gender domination in society and the ways in which inequality gives rise to conflict, crime, and repressive social control. Challenging the functionalist assumption that consensus exists over the norms and that the norms serve the interests of the entire population, conflict theory holds that there is more conflict than agreement over the norms and that norms reflect the interests of powerful groups. The government and social institutions generally protect the interests of economic and political elites by imposing controls on powerless segments of society—such as the poor and the working class, racial minorities, and women. The chapters reprinted here examine each of these populations. David Gordon's article ("Capitalism, Class, and Crime in America") is a general analysis of class inequality and crime. He argues that most crime is a rational response to class inequality in capitalist societies.

Elijah Anderson ("The Police and the Black Male") examines how police officers stereotype and discriminate against African Americans. Officers stop, harass, and abuse black men on the streets, even when they have done nothing wrong—an illustration of the way race is used by agents of control to keep blacks in a subordinate position. Not all police officers do this, however; Anderson found that "downtown" police from outside the neighborhood treated blacks more harshly than "local" police who knew residents better and were thus less likely to engage in racial profiling. Social class may also influence police behavior, insofar as officers treat African Americans in poor neighborhoods worse than blacks living in middle-class neighborhoods (Weitzer 1999).

Patricia Yancey Martin and Robert Hummer ("Fraternities and Rape on Campus") investigate gender relations and male deviance at universities. The authors focus on the male culture of university fraternities, which reinforces the notion that females are sex objects to be exploited, even if this results in rape. Of course, this indictment does not apply to all fraternities; some fraternities actively reject the "rape culture" that others accept (Boswell and Spade 1996). This variation also applies to entire societies. Consistent with conflict theory, societies where inequality between men and women is low and where the value system does not objectify women appear to discourage rape, compared to other societies (Sanday 1981).

Conflict theory was originally formulated as a critique of capitalist societies, but some key tenets of the theory can also be applied to socialist societies, such as the former Soviet Union. According to Walter Connor ("The Manufacture of Deviance in the Soviet Purge") Josef Stalin's purge of alleged political deviants during the 1930s reflected a "radical disparity of power" between the rulers and the ruled. In addition, the purge netted a large number of persons who were falsely accused of deviant acts—people who had violated no norm. Connor challenges the functionalist idea that the purge was necessary to strengthen the moral boundaries of Soviet society; instead, it had negative, or dysfunctional, consequences for society.

REFERENCES

Boswell, A. Ayres, and Joan Z. Spade. 1996. "Fraternities and Collegiate Rape Culture: Why are Some Fraternities More Dangerous Places for Women?" *Gender and Society* 10:133–147.

Durkheim, Emile. 1966 [1895]. *The Rules of Sociological Method.* New York: Free Press.

Glaser, Daniel. 1955. "Criminality Theories and Behavioral Images." *American Journal of Sociology* 61:433–444.

Goffman, Erving. 1963. *Stigma.* Englewood Cliffs, NJ: Prentice Hall.

Sanday, Peggy Reeves. 1981. "The Socio-Cultural Context of Rape: A Cross-Cultural Study." *Journal of Social Issues* 37:5–27.

Shaw, Clifford R., and Henry D. McKay. 1942. *Juvenile Delinquency and Urban Areas.* Chicago: University of Chicago Press.

Weitzer, Ronald. 1999. "Citizens' Perceptions of Police Misconduct: Race and Neighborhood Context." *Justice Quarterly* 16:819–846.

FUNCTIONALIST THEORY

READING 2-1

The Sociology of Deviance

Kai T. Erikson

In 1895 Emile Durkheim wrote a book called *The Rules of Sociological Method* which was intended as a working manual for persons interested in the systematic study of society. One of the most important themes of Durkheim's work was that sociologists should formulate a new set of criteria for distinguishing between "normal" and "pathological" elements in the life of a society. Behavior which looks abnormal to the psychiatrist or the judge, he suggested, does not always look abnormal when viewed through the special lens of the sociologist; and thus students of the new science should be careful to understand that even the most aberrant forms of individual behavior may still be considered normal from this broader point of view. To illustrate his argument, Durkheim made the surprising observation that crime was really a natural kind of social activity, "an integral part of all healthy societies" (Durkheim 1958).

Durkheim's interest in this subject had been expressed several years before when *The Division of Labor in Society* was first published (Durkheim 1960). In that important book, he had suggested that crime (and by extension other forms of deviation) may actually perform a needed service to society by drawing people together in a common posture of anger and indignation. The deviant individual violates rules of conduct which the rest of the community holds in high respect; and when these people come together to express their outrage over the offense and to bear witness against the offender, they develop a tighter bond of solidarity

From Kai T. Erikson, *Wayward Puritans: A Study in the Sociology of Deviance*. New York: John Wiley and Sons, 1966. Reprinted by permission of Allyn & Bacon.

than existed earlier. The excitement generated by the crime, in other words, quickens the tempo of interaction in the group and creates a climate in which the private sentiments of many separate persons are fused together into a common sense of morality.

> Crime brings together upright consciences and concentrates them. We have only to notice what happens, particularly in a small town, when some moral scandal has just been committed. They stop each other on the street, they visit each other, they seek to come together to talk of the event and to wax indignant in common. From all the similar impressions which are exchanged, for all the temper that gets itself expressed, there emerges a unique temper . . . which is everybody's without being anybody's in particular. That is the public temper. (Durkheim 1960:102)

The deviant act, then, creates a sense of mutuality among the people of a community by supplying a focus for group feeling. Like a war, a flood, or some other emergency, deviance makes people more alert to the interests they share in common and draws attention to those values which constitute the "collective conscience" of the community. Unless the rhythm of group life is punctuated by occasional moments of deviant behavior, presumably, social organization would be impossible.

When one describes any system as boundary maintaining, one is saying that it controls the fluctuation of its constituent parts so that the whole retains a limited range of activity, a given pattern of constancy and stability, within the larger environment. A human community can be said to maintain boundaries, then, in the sense that its members tend to confine themselves to a particular radius of activity and to regard any conduct which drifts outside that radius as somehow inappropriate or immoral. Thus the group retains a kind of cultural integrity, a voluntary restriction on its own potential for expansion, beyond that which is strictly required for accommodation to the environment. Human behavior can vary over an enormous range, but each community draws a symbolic set of parentheses around a certain segment of that range and limits its own activities within that narrower zone. These parentheses, so to speak, are the community's boundaries.

Now people who live together in communities cannot relate to one another in any coherent way or even acquire a sense of their own stature as group members unless they learn something about the boundaries of the territory they occupy in social space, if only because they need to sense what lies beyond the margins of the group before they can appreciate the special quality of the experience which takes place within it. Yet how do people learn about the boundaries of their community? And how do they convey this information to the generations which replace them?

To begin with, the only material found in a society for marking boundaries is the behavior of its members—or rather, the networks of interaction which link these members together in regular social relations. And the interactions which do the most effective job of locating and publicizing the group's outer edges would seem to be those which take place between deviant persons on the one side and official agents of the community on the other. The deviant is a person whose activities have moved outside the margins of the group, and when the community calls him to account for that vagrancy it is making a statement about the nature and placement of its boundaries. It is declaring how much variability and diversity can be tolerated within the group before it begins to lose its distinctive shape, its unique identity. Now there may be other moments in the life of the group which perform a similar service: wars, for instance, can publicize a group's boundaries by drawing attention to the line separating the group from an adversary, and certain kinds of religious ritual, dance ceremony, and other traditional pageantry can dramatize the difference between "we" and "they" by portraying a symbolic encounter between the two. But on the whole, members of a community inform one another about the placement of their boundaries by participating in the confrontations which occur when persons who venture out to the edges of the group are met by policing agents whose special business it is to guard the cultural integrity of the community. Whether these confrontations take the form of criminal trials, excommunication hearings, courts-martial, or even psychiatric case conferences, they act as boundary-maintaining devices in the sense that they demonstrate to whatever audience is concerned where the line is drawn between behavior that belongs in the special universe of the group and behavior that does not. In general, this kind of information is not easily relayed by the straightforward use of language. Most readers of this paragraph, for instance, have a fairly clear idea of the line separating theft from more legitimate forms of commerce, but few of them have ever seen a published statute describing these differences. More likely than not, our information on the subject has been drawn from publicized instances in which the relevant laws were applied—and for that matter, the law itself is largely a collection of past cases and decisions, a synthesis of the various confrontations which have occurred in the life of the legal order.

It may be important to note in this connection that confrontations between deviant offenders and the agents of control have always attracted a good deal of public attention. In our own past, the trial and punishment of offenders were staged in the market place and afforded the crowd a chance to participate in a direct, active way. Today, of course, we no longer parade deviants in the town square or expose them to the carnival atmosphere of a Tyburn, but it is interesting that the "reform" which brought about this change in penal practice coincided almost exactly with the development of newspapers as a medium of mass information. Perhaps this is no more than an accident of history, but it is nonetheless true that newspapers (and now radio and television) offer much the same kind of entertainment as public hangings or a Sunday visit to the local gaol. A considerable portion of what we call "news" is devoted to reports about deviant behavior and its consequences, and it is no simple matter to explain why these items should be considered newsworthy or why they should command the extraordinary attention they do. Perhaps they appeal to a number of psychological perversities among the mass audience, as commentators have suggested, but at the same time they constitute one of our main sources of information about the normative outlines of society. In a figurative sense, at least, morality and immorality meet at the public scaffold, and it is during this meeting that the line between them is drawn.

Boundaries are never a fixed property of any community. They are always shifting as the people of the group find new ways to define the outer limits of their universe, new ways to position themselves on the larger cultural map. Sometimes changes occur within the structure of the group which require its members to make a new survey of their territory—a change of leadership, a shift of mood. Sometimes changes occur in the surrounding environment, altering the background against which the people of the group have measured their own uniqueness. And always, new generations are moving in to take their turn guarding old institutions and need to be informed about the contours of the world they are inheriting. Thus single encounters between the deviant and his community are only fragments of an ongoing social process. Like an article of common law, boundaries remain a meaningful point of reference only so long as they are repeatedly tested by persons on the fringes of the group and repeatedly defended by persons chosen to represent the group's inner morality. Each time the community moves to censure some act of deviation, then, and convenes a formal ceremony to deal with the responsible offender, it sharpens the authority of the violated norm and restates where the boundaries of the group are located.

For these reasons, deviant behavior is not a simple kind of leakage which occurs when the machinery of society is in poor working order, but may be, in controlled quantities, an important condition for preserving the stability of social life. Deviant forms of behavior, by marking the outer edges of group life, give the inner structure its special character and thus supply the framework within which the people of the group develop an orderly sense of their own cultural identity. Perhaps this is what Aldous Huxley had in mind when he wrote:

> Now tidiness is undeniably good—but a good of which it is easily possible to have too much and at too high a price. . . . The good life can only be lived in a society in which tidiness is preached and practiced, but not too fanatically, and where efficiency is always haloed, as it were, by a tolerated margin of mess. (Huxley 1949:13)

This raises a delicate theoretical issue. If we grant that human groups often derive benefit from deviant behavior, can we then assume that they are organized in such a way as to promote this resource? Can we assume, in other words, that forces operate in the social structure to recruit offenders and to commit them to long periods of service in the deviant ranks? This is not a question which can be answered with our present store of empirical data, but one observation can be made which gives the question an interesting perspective—namely, that deviant forms of conduct often seem to derive nourishment from the very agencies devised to inhibit them. Indeed, the agencies built by society for preventing deviance are often so poorly equipped for the task that we might well ask why this is regarded as their "real" function in the first place.

It is by now a thoroughly familiar argument that many of the institutions designed to discourage deviant behavior actually operate in such a way as to perpetuate it. For one thing, prisons, hospitals, and other similar agencies provide aid and shelter to large numbers of deviant persons, sometimes giving them a certain advantage in the competition for social resources. But beyond this, such institutions gather marginal people into tightly segregated groups, give them an opportunity to teach one another the skills and attitudes of a deviant career, and even provoke them into using these skills by reinforcing their sense of alienation from the rest of society (Erikson 1957; Goffman 1962; Sykes 1958). Nor is this observation a modern one:

> The misery suffered in gaols is not half their evil; they are filled with every sort of corruption that poverty and wickedness can generate; with all the shameless and profligate enormities that can be produced by the impudence of ignomiy, the rage of want, and the malignity of dispair. In a prison the check of the public eye is removed; and the power of the law is spent. There are few fears, there are no blushes. The lewd inflame the more modest; the audacious harden the timid. Everyone fortifies himself as he can against his own remaining sensibility; endeavoring to practise on others the arts that are practised on himself; and to gain the applause of his worst associates by imitating their manners. (Anonymous author quoted in Howard 1929:10)

These lines, written almost two centuries ago, are a harsh indictment of prisons, but many of the conditions they describe continue to be reported in even the most modern studies of prison life. Looking at the matter from a long-range historical perspective, it is fair to conclude that prisons have done a conspicuously poor job of reforming the convicts placed in their custody; but the very consistency of this failure may have a peculiar logic of its own. Perhaps we find it difficult to change the worst of our penal practices because we *expect* the prison to harden the inmate's commitment to deviant forms of behavior and draw him more deeply into the deviant ranks. On the whole, we are a people who do not really expect deviants to change very much as they are processed through the control agencies we provide for them, and we are often reluctant to devote much of the community's resources to the job of rehabilitation. In this sense, the prison which graduates long rows of accomplished criminals (or, for that matter, the state asylum which stores its most severe cases away in some back ward) may do serious violence to the aims of its founders, but it does very little violence to the expectations of the population it serves.

These expectations, moreover, are found in every corner of society and constitute an important part of the climate in which we deal with deviant forms of behavior.

To begin with, the community's decision to bring deviant sanctions against one of its members is not a simple act of censure. It is an intricate rite of transition, at once moving the individual out of his ordinary place in society and transferring him into a special deviant position (Parsons 1951). The ceremonies which mark this change of status, generally, have a number of related phases. They supply a formal stage on which the deviant and his community can confront one another (as in the criminal trial); they make an announcement about the nature of his deviancy (a verdict or diagnosis, for example); and they place him in a particular role which is thought to neutralize the harmful effects of his misconduct (like the role of prisoner or patient). These commitment ceremonies tend to be occasions of wide public interest and ordinarily take place in a highly dramatic setting (Garfinkel 1956). Perhaps the most obvious example of a commitment ceremony is the criminal trial, with its elaborate formality and exaggerated ritual, but more modest equivalents can be found wherever procedures are set up to judge whether or not someone is legitimately deviant.

Now an important feature of these ceremonies in our own culture is that they are almost irreversible. Most provisional roles conferred by society—those of the student or conscripted soldier, for example—include some kind of terminal ceremony to mark the individual's movement back out of the role once its temporary advantages have been exhausted. But the roles allotted the deviant seldom make allowance for this type of passage. He is ushered into the deviant position by a decisive and often dramatic ceremony, yet is retired from it with scarcely a word of public notice. And as a result, the deviant often returns home with no proper license to resume a normal life in the community. Nothing has happened to cancel out the stigmas imposed upon him by earlier commitment ceremonies; nothing has happened to revoke the verdict or diagnosis pronounced upon him at that time. It should not be surprising, then, that the people of the community are apt to greet the returning deviant with a considerable degree of apprehension and distrust, for in a very real sense they are not at all sure who he is.

A circularity is thus set into motion which has all the earmarks of a "self-fulfilling prophesy," to use Merton's fine phrase. On the one hand, it seems quite obvious that the community's apprehensions help reduce whatever chances the deviant might otherwise have had for a successful return home. Yet at the same time, everyday experience seems to show that these suspicions are wholly reasonable, for it is a well-known and highly publicized fact that many if not most ex-convicts return to crime after leaving prison and that large numbers of mental patients require further treatment after an initial hospitalization. The common feeling that deviant persons never really change, then, may derive from a faulty premise; but the feeling is expressed so frequently and with such conviction that it eventually creates the facts which later "prove" it to be correct. If the returning deviant encounters this circularity often enough, it is quite understandable that he, too, may begin to wonder whether he has fully graduated from the deviant role, and he may respond to the uncertainty by resuming some kind of deviant activity. In many respects, this may be the only way for the individual and his community to agree what kind of person he is.

Moreover this prophesy is found in the official policies of even the most responsible agencies of control. Police departments could not operate with any real effectiveness if they did not regard ex-convicts as a ready pool of suspects to be tapped in the event of trouble, and psychiatric clinics could not do a successful job in the community if they were not always alert to the possibility of former patients suffering relapses. Thus the prophesy gains currency at many levels within the social order, not only in the poorly informed attitudes of the community at large, but in the best informed theories of most control agencies as well.

In one form or another this problem has been recognized in the West for many hundreds of years, and this simple fact has a curious implication. For if our culture has supported a steady flow of deviation throughout long periods of historical change, the rules which apply to any kind of evolutionary thinking would suggest that strong forces must be at work to keep the flow intact—and this because it contributes in some important way to the survival of the culture as a whole. This does not furnish us with sufficient warrant to declare that deviance is "functional" (in any of the many senses of that term), but it should certainly make us wary of the assumption so often made in sociological circles that any well-structured society is somehow designed to prevent deviant behavior from occurring.

Perhaps we can conclude, then, that two separate yet often competing currents are found in any society: those forces which promote a high degree of conformity among the people of the community so that they know what to expect from one another, and those forces which encourage a certain degree of diversity so that people can be deployed across the range of group space to survey its potential, measure its capacity, and, in the case of those we call deviants, patrol its boundaries. In such a scheme, the deviant would appear as a natural product of group differentiation. He is not a bit of debris spun out by faulty social machinery, but a relevant figure in the community's overall division of labor.

REFERENCES

Durkheim, Emile. 1958. *The Rules of Sociological Method.* Trans. S. A. Solovay and J. H. Mueller. Glencoe, Ill.: The Free Press.

———. 1960. *The Division of Labor in Society.* Trans. George Simpson. Glencoe, Ill.: The Free Press.

Erikson, Kai T. 1952. "Patient Role and Social Uncertainty: A Dilemma of the Mentally Ill." *Psychiatry* 20:263–274.

Garfinkel, Harold. 1956. "Successful Degradation Ceremonies," *American Journal of Sociology* 61:420–424.

Goffman, Erving. 1962. *Asylums.* New York: Bobbs-Merrill.

Howard, John. 1929. *The State of the Prisons.* London: J. M. Dent and Sons.

Huxley, Aldous. 1949. *Prisons: The "Carceri" Etchings by Piranesi.* London: The Trianon Press.

Parsons, Talcott. 1951. *The Social System.* Glencoe, Ill.: Free Press.

Sykes, Gresham. 1958. *The Society of Captives.* Princeton, N.J.: Princeton University Press.

READING 2·2

Television News Magazines and Functionalism

Maria Elizabeth Grabe

The injustice and human suffering which result from crime have been well-documented and lamented. Yet, the widespread occurrence of crime persists. Emile Durkheim (1933, 1938, 1951), Kai Erikson (1966), Michel Foucault (1979), and George Herbert Mead (1918) provide a controversial explanation of the persistence and prevalence of crime over the centuries. Unlike the popular belief that crime is a menace that must be obliterated, these scholars argue that crime is an inherent part of a healthy society. Rituals whereby crime is processed and punished function on a number of levels to sustain social structure. Whether there is consensus as to the desirability of the system that is maintained, of course, does not affect the functionality of these rituals in aiding that system's stability.

The existence of crime provides society's members with the opportunity to publicly draw and recognize the line between good and evil. Furthermore, crime rituals promote social cohesion. When the criminal is presented as violating the collective sentiments of a society, its members unify in their condemnation of the criminal. Crime, and the punishment thereof, can also be viewed as a form of social control, where potential criminals are scared into submission to society's rules and regulations.

Beyond the mass media's ritualization of the three Durkheimian functions of crime—to construct morality, promote cohesion, and impose social control—this study is concerned with the mass media's functional presentations of demographic relationships between criminals and victims. According to Gerbner et al. (1979), demographic

profiles of violent criminals and the portrayed repercussions of their actions often demonstrate power relations to society's members by communicating "who gets away with what against whom" (p. 181). Although Gerbner takes a functionalist view on this construction of a social order, he fundamentally opposes the notion that crime, and the mass mediation thereof, is a "healthy" part of social systems. Instead he views the narratives of crime stories (fictional or non-fictional) as cultivating an oppressing "scary view" of the world which musters support for police power and ultimately aids in maintaining the status quo.

THE STUDY OF NARRATIVE CONTENT

The above functional views of crime assume the mass dissemination of rituals and myths surrounding the occurrence of criminal acts by which the immorality of deviant behavior is made known. In other words, crime becomes functional when it is constructed into a narrative and made public. Before the existence of mass media, societies relied on public rituals like torture and executions to demonstrate the notion of justice (Cromer 1978; Erikson 1966; Foucault 1979; Garfinkel 1956; Rusche and Kirchheimer 1939; Schattenburg 1981). In fact, Erikson (1966) links the disappearance of public execution with the development of the newspaper. It is therefore not unreasonable to suspect that contemporary mass media provide the platform for public rituals and communication of myths about crime.

CRIME NEWS AS MYTH AND RITUAL

Ericson (1991) observes that the mass media and the justice system constitute two institutions jointly responsible for much of what we learn about the

From *Critical Studies in Mass Communication* 16(2) (July 1999) 155–171. Reprinted by permission of the National Communication Association. © 1999 by the NCA.

social order. Together they turn events in the physical world into narratives ". . . of what ought to be, fusing facts with normative commitments, values, and myths" (Ericson 1991:223). Many scholars have described journalism as a process of mythmaking. Following Carey's (1975) ritual view of communication, news is not information but drama—it does not describe the world, but portrays an arena of dramatic forces and action. Along the same lines Condit (1987), Glasser and Ettema (1989), Ettema and Glasser (1988), Gans (1979), and Knight and Dean (1982) argue that through ritualistic mythmaking, journalism reinscribes and updates society's consensual views on morality by publicly defining what is right and wrong, innocence and guilt. Gans (1979:293) goes so far as to claim that the news media helps to "punish those who deviate from these values."

In order to investigate the pragmatic potential of news to perpetuate the moral order, promote social cohesion, impose social control, and define power relations, it is necessary to uncover the specific functional myths that underlie crime stories. Durkheim (1933:65–110; 1951:335–392) argues that the ritualization of crime is a powerful means to draw publicly the line between good and evil, thereby constructing morality. Thus if crime news stories play a part in constructing morality, we could expect them to clearly assign the roles of good and evil to police and criminals and prominently frame crime in terms of the struggle between good and evil. This leads to the first hypothesis:

H1: News stories will frame crime in terms of a struggle between good and evil and primarily assign police and criminals to these roles.

Durkheim (1933:73–74) and Ericson and Haggerty (1997:448) theorize that criminal violations of public sentiments provoke a shared outrage aimed at the criminal (and not the societal causes of crime) among society's members which indirectly promotes social cohesion and integration. Fictional television crimes are commonly portrayed as resulting from individual causes such as material greed and psychological instability (Barrile 1980, 1986; Haney & Manzolati 1981). By ignor-

ing possible structural causes for crime, such as poverty or racism, the criminal is portrayed as society's enemy who deserves shared hate and banishment. If crime news stories play a part in promoting social cohesion we could expect them to promote outrage against criminals by presenting them as irrational villains who are responsible for violating society's moral values. This leads to the second hypothesis:

H2: News stories will present criminals as villains who are personally responsible for violating society's moral values.

Durkheim (1933:65–110; 1951:335–392) and Ericson and Haggerty (1997:53, 54 and 360, 361) argue that the processing and punishment of crime provides an opportunity to discourage those who contemplate criminal behavior and intimidate them into submission to society's rules and laws. Dominick (1973) and Estep and Macdonald (1985) reveal that in television fiction, almost without exception, crime doesn't pay. If crime news stories play a part in promoting social control, they will prominently present the idea that crime is not profitable. This leads to the third hypothesis:

H3: News stories will prominently feature the crime does not pay myth.

According to Gerbner et al. (1979) demographic profiles of criminals and their victims have the narrative potential of communicating society's power structure to its members. Research on fictional narratives reveals the marginalization of women and African Americans. Emphasis on African Americans as society's criminals promotes suspicion and distrust of this race group and when women are routinely featured in fictional crime stories as victims of crime this gender group's vulnerable social position is reaffirmed. If crime news stories contribute to the perpetuation of hierarchical power relationships we can expect these stories to present women as the victims of crime and African Americans as the criminal villains. This leads to the fourth hypothesis:

H4: News stories will present women as the victims of crime and African Americans as criminals.

METHOD

This study focuses on news magazine programs because they feature self-contained narrative segments and allow for relatively lengthy and elaborate storytelling compared to the short and fragmented format of stories on local and national newscasts. In recent times scholars have argued that the distinction between the so-called tabloid and traditional approaches to news reporting is disappearing (Bird 1992; Knight 1989; Knight & Dean 1982). For the purpose of this study both tabloid and traditional news magazine programs were included in the investigation. The specific tabloid programs are: "Inside Edition," "A Current Affair," "American Journal," and "Hard Copy." The specific traditional programs are: "Dateline NBC," "Prime Time Live," "Turning Point," "48 Hours," "Eye to Eye with Connie Chung," "60 Minutes," "Day One," and "20/20."

Instead of a composite month of television programming, the news magazine programs examined in this study were exhaustively sampled over a six month period (October 1, 1994 to March 31, 1995). An additional week of these television broadcasts (April 1–7, 1995) was used in coder training sessions. Half a year of television news magazine programs provided 713 programs and 2,783 individual story segments which amounted to 272 hours of material for the analysis. It is important to use an uninterrupted time period for this study because major crime stories tend to evolve over several weeks and a randomly sampled composite month of television content would only provide fragments of this evolving storytelling process. Although this study is not directly concerned with how crime stories evolve over time, there was concern about creating a sample which could only provide fragmented episodes in a complex, interrelated, and evolving social process. The six month period was long enough for prominent crime stories to develop (e.g., the O. J. Simpson case, Susan Smith's murder of her two infant sons, the Ferguson train massacre trial in New York City, and two skinhead brothers killing their parents and brother). Such highly publicized crime cases, together with lower profile stories, represent the typical course of crime reporting.

CODING INSTRUMENT

Coding was based on what was portrayed, reported, suggested, or implied in the content of the news programs. Two different sampling units were used.

Sampling Unit One: The News Magazine Program

The prevalence of crime was assessed through items pertaining to the number of program segments and crime segments in each news magazine program, as well as the duration of crime segments. Items concerning the positioning of the crime segment within the story line-up provided insight into the prominence of crime in news magazine programs.

Sampling Unit Two: The Crime Segment

The second sampling unit concerned individual crime segments within news magazine programs. A crime story is defined as a program segment which features one or more acts of breaking the law as central to the narrative. Only a subset of all segments, based on this criterion, was coded. Segments identified as "crime stories" by virtue of their focus on crime were analyzed using the portrayed, mentioned, or inferred criminal, victim, and criminal act as three separate recording units. A crime story may have multiple crimes, criminals, and victims, and in such instances, coders coded each criminal, victim, and crime separately. The criminal was identified as the person, group, or organization suggested, suspected, accused, charged, or found guilty of a crime. Three important aspects were considered when coding a criminal. First, the criminal had to be central to the crime narrative. In other words, the criminal had to make a considerable and critical contribution to the construction of the crime narrative. Second, "suspect," "accused," "perpetrator," or "sentenced criminal" were all coded. Once someone was identified as a criminal suspect (lawfully guilty or not) and presented as such in the story, he/she was included in this investigation. Third, this study also included group and corporate criminality. In such instances each of the identified members of the corporation or group responsible for the crime were [sic] separately coded as criminals.

The victim was identified as the person or group which suffered due to criminal actions. Four important aspects were considered when coding a victim. First, as with the criminal, the victim had to be central to the crime narrative. Stories may provide criminals without victims. In such instances only the presented criminal was coded. Second, in cases of group victimization each central victim appearing, inferred, or described was coded separately. Third, when animals were presented as the victims of a crime, the "other" option was coded on all items except those related to the severity of the victimization. Finally, in order for someone to be coded as a victim, he/she had to be a direct or primary victim of the criminal act. When acquaintances or family members of the primary victim were portrayed as secondary victims (e.g., they lost the murdered family member) they were not coded as victims.

The crime is the act committed by the criminal, which establishes a relationship with a victim (except of course in the case of a victimless crime). As with the criminal and victim, each criminal act central to the crime narrative was coded. Presentation of the criminal act was scrutinized for its nature, motivation, and the aftermath. The outcome of the crime was examined on a number of different levels. The prevalence of the "crime doesn't pay" myth, the struggle between good and evil, and the portrayed roles of the criminal, victim, and law enforcement system in the struggle between good and evil were recorded. The coding instrument also assessed the physical and psychological harm done to the victim as a result of the crime.

Criminals and victims were coded for demographic information including gender, race, age, class, occupational status, criminal history of the suspect, and the alleged criminal's guilt or innocence. Two separate items pertained to the presentation of

the criminal's guilt and innocence. Both categories had "yes" and "no" options. In other words, the coding instrument allowed for the possibility that in one story both innocence and guilt could have been implied.

The operational definitions of crime, criminal, and victim used in this study are not attempts to describe the "essence" of these constructs. These definitions were merely useful within the parameters of this study, which involves more inclusive treatment of crime portrayals than what is stipulated in criminal justice definitions of crime.

ESTABLISHING A MORAL ORDER

The majority of society's members believe in the efficiency, accuracy, and fairness of the criminal justice system. With few exceptions, law enforcement officers are viewed as the protectors of society's members, and the mass media generally reaffirm this notion by portraying the officers of the system as effective and fair in their efforts to guard common morality. In the programs under investigation, law enforcement officers were cast as the good force (78% of cases) fighting against evil criminals in the classic battle between these two forces, confirming Hypothesis 1. The victim was in most cases (91.3%) the helpless good person whom the criminal preyed upon. The criminal took the prominent role as the evil force in 93.5% of cases. By unambiguously assigning police officers to the role of the good force fighting evil, criminals to the role of the evil force, and victims to the role of the helpless prey of evil, clear lines between acceptable and unacceptable behavior are drawn—thereby contributing to constructing society's moral values.

PROMOTING SOCIAL COHESION

Support for Hypothesis 2 was found on two levels. First, the patterned presentation of criminals as guilty before the criminal justice system has taken its course prematurely vilifies suspects. Most crime reports preceded the criminal's day in court. Most often (in 86.5% of cases) the suspect was arrested, yet in most cases (69.7%) the outcome of the criminal justice process after the arrest remained unknown. In only 17.9% of cases the arrested criminal was shown to have been found guilty and in only 14.4% of cases was the criminal sentenced. This did not discourage presentations of the criminal as guilty. More than 95% of the portrayed criminals were presented as guilty (see Table 2-1). Similar character assassinations of alleged criminals are common in television fiction (Cromer 1978). Garfinkel (1956) refers to these portrayals as mass mediated degradation ceremonies which publicly deliver a curse upon the criminal and call for all of society to witness the ritual destruction of the deviant character. Ultimately these degradation ceremonies serve to promote social solidarity because the members of a society unify in their outrage against the criminal's violation of their common values. The criminal fulfills the important function of representing the evil force in society's never-ending battle against evil. Therefore, it is noteworthy that news magazine programs were quick to turn suspects into guilty and evil criminals.

Second, the criminal was presented as having sole responsibility for violating society's moral values. From Table 2-1 it is clear that of all the motivations for crime, psychological instability was featured most often. Most important though is that portrayals of individual causes for crime (such as psychological instability—91%, revenge—55.2%, protection of social status—26%, greed—17%, drug abuse—13%, and avenging justice—3%) overshadowed structural causes of crime such as poverty (1%). Barrile (1986) reports similar emphases on individual causes for crime in television fiction and labels it the "personalized" crime perspective. By virtually ignoring possible structural causes for crime (such as poverty or racism) criminals are portrayed as society's irrational enemies who deserve little sympathy because they presumably act as a result of their own will. In the Durkheimian (1933:73–74) view, these supposedly self-interested acts that violate the common morality of society's members provoke a shared outrage against the criminal (and not societal

TABLE 2-1

PROMOTING SOCIAL COHESION

Variable	Frequency	%
Criminal Arrested		
Yes	1119	86.5
No	166	12.8
Unknown/Other	8	0.7
Criminal Found Guilty?		
Yes	231	17.9
No	162	12.5
Unknown/Other	900	69.7
Criminal Sentenced?		
Yes	186	14.4
No	97	7.5
Unknown/Other	1010	78.1
Implied That the Criminal Is Guilty?		
Yes	1238	95.7
No	37	2.9
Unknown/Other	18	1.4
Implied That the Criminal Is Innocent?		
Yes	92	7.1
No	1196	92.5
Unknown/Other	5	0.4
Motivation		
Greed	223	17.2
Material Desperation	13	1.0
Protection of Social Status	336	26.0
Psychological Instability	1177	91.0
Romantic/Domestic Revenge	714	55.2
Alcohol/Drug Abuse	168	13.0
Avenging Justice	17	1.3
Other Motivation	30	2.3

Note: The "unknown" option includes cases in which no suggestion or information related to the categorical issue at hand was provided. The "other" item is an attempt to exhaust options within categories. It comprises cases which could not be fitted into either of the options within categories. The motivations of crime were not coded as mutually exclusive categories. This allowed coders to indicate if more than one of the above motivations were presented as the reason for a criminal act.

institutions), promote social cohesion and integration, and ultimately camouflage the need to change the status quo.

It is noteworthy that 97.7% of all crimes were fully explained in terms of the above motivations (i.e., as a result of greed, material desperation, protection of social status, psychological instability, revenge, alcohol or drug abuse, and avenging justice). The FBI's uniform crime reports provide limited insights into the causes of crime. Yet, there are indications that individual causes of crime play a remarkably small role in motivating criminal behavior. Only 6.91% of murders are motivated by greed and 4.93% of murders are committed because of revenge (Federal Bureau of Investigation 1994). Nevertheless, the television news magazine world functionally emphasizes individual causes for crime, thereby promoting a view of criminals as self-interested violators of social values.

IMPOSING SOCIAL CONTROL

As Table 2-2 shows, the vast majority of news magazine crimes (88.6%) were violent. Yet, the FBI's uniform crime reports (Federal Bureau of Investigation 1994) indicate a vastly different ratio between violent and non-violent crime: Only 13.4% of crimes are violent. Yet murder was the most prevalent (71.1%) outcome of the criminal act in the news magazine programs. By contrast, FBI (1994) crime statistics indicate that murder constitutes just 0.16% of all crimes and 1.23% of all violent crimes committed in the United States. Only 10.7% of victims in news magazine programs escaped without any physical injuries (see Table 2-2). Psychological injury as a result of the crime appeared prominently (93%) in the news stories under investigation.

This disproportionate emphasis on violence and injury reflects what Gerbner (1988) describes as the process of cultivating fear in television viewers. As we become socialized and observe patterned portrayals of violence in the symbolic world of primetime, we make our own calculations about the risk of becoming a victim of crime (Gerbner 1988). If the members of a society are repeatedly instructed that violence and psychological injury are common outcomes of crime, their understanding of the seriousness of this act is greatly inflated.

TABLE 2-2

IMPOSING SOCIAL CONTROL

Variable	Frequency	%
Crime Type		
Violent	1145	88.6
Weapon Used	871	67.4
Sex	142	11.0
Property	129	10.0
Financial	53	4.1
Physical Harm		
Killed	1102	71.1
Serious Injury	119	7.7
Light Injury	96	6.2
Unharmed	167	10.7
Unknown/Other	66	4.3
Psychological Injury		
Yes	386	93.0
No	29	7.0
Unknown/Other	0	0.0
Suggested That Crime Doesn't Pay		
Yes	952	73.6
No	86	6.7
Unknown	255	19.7
Suggested That Crime Pays		
Yes	224	17.3
No	678	52.4
Unknown	391	30.3
Punishment Other Than the Criminal Justice System		
Yes	419	32.4
No	828	64.0
Unknown	46	3.6

The drama and narrative potential of crime stories as powerful lessons about social control, morality, social cohesion and power relations are therefore enhanced.

Social control was further promoted in the content of the programs under investigation by making it clear that crime doesn't pay. This study assessed the prevalence of this crime lesson in two ways. First, the inevitability of a criminal's arrest (86.5%

of cases, see Table 2-1) implies that virtually all criminals are brought into the cold light of justice. The tendency to portray law enforcement efforts as swift, effective, and fair is common in television fiction. Knutson (1974:29) argues that in television detective series, police officers are presented as dedicated protectors of morality. Haney and Manzolati (1981) did not find a single instance where the "wrong man" was in custody at the end of television fiction shows. This tendency to portray the police as infallible creates an illusion of certainty and trust in law enforcement (Haney & Manzolati 1981).

Second, the outcome of 73.6% of all crime stories was coded as presenting the "crime doesn't pay" myth. Even when criminals escaped the long arm of the criminal justice system (32.4% of cases), they faced alternative forms of punishment (i.e., personal tragedy or victimization by another criminal), thereby reaffirming that crime doesn't pay (see Table 2-2).

Narratives about police efficiency and the unprofitability of crime were prominently featured in news magazine crime stories, supporting Hypothesis 3. Public displays of arrests can be interpreted as fear-provoking warnings against criminal pursuits of self-interest. As Durkheim (1933:86), Mead (1918:587), and Foucault (1979:32–69) argued, they are a way of instilling the paralyzing fear of retribution in the minds of those who contemplate evil.

REAFFIRMING POWER RELATIONS

Hypothesis 4 was also supported. Criminals in news magazine programs are mostly male (85%), African American (53.3%), adult (68.1%), upper-class (50%), and legitimately employed (66.7%). Considering the race and age of criminals, the FBI's demographic profile for criminals differs noticeably from what was found in the content of the programs under investigation. In fact, according to uniform crime reports (Federal Bureau of Investigation 1994) state prison inmates are most often Caucasian (49.1%) and young adults (45.7%). However, similar to the content of news magazine

TABLE 2-3

CROSSTABULATION OF CRIMINAL'S AND VICTIM'S RACE AND GENDER

Victim	Criminal		
Race	Caucasian	African American	Latino
Caucasian	39.2	58.0	2.8
African American	29.7	67.6	2.7
Latino	40.0	10.0	50.0
Gender	Male	Female	
Male	75.2	24.8	
Female	94.9	5.1	

Note: Data presented in percentage.

programs, FBI reports indicate that most criminals are employed (67.3%) and male (94.5%).

The focus on African Americans as the group most likely to commit criminal behavior may contribute to the marginalization of this race group. It is important to note that African American criminals were also portrayed as the most prominent victimizers of both Caucasians (58%) and people from their own race (67.7%, see Table 2-3). These portrayals have the potential to reaffirm Caucasian distrust of African Americans. Indeed, it hardly promotes the social integration of this race.

The demographic profile of the victim differs from that of the criminal in all variables but social class (i.e., Caucasian, 87.9%; female, 53%; young adult, 39.5%; upper-class, 40.6%; and legitimately employed, 36.8%). Unlike what is reported in the news magazine programs under investigation, the FBI crime reports indicate that young black males are most likely to become crime victims (Federal Bureau of Investigation 1994).

Caucasian, young adult, upper-class, females who are legitimately employed could be viewed as the group most frequently competing with males in the workplace. It is therefore noteworthy that women were presented as most likely to be victims of crime. One can certainly argue that this portrayal serves the existing social order by communicating to aspiring females that they are the group in society most likely to become victims of crime.

Crosstabulations of gender and labor status reveal that working women (58.7%) were more likely than working men (29.40%) to be victimized in the work-place. Furthermore, the group of working women that was portrayed as victims was also more likely to be victimized in the workplace (58.7%) than at home (31.4%). There is reason to argue that these portrayals send the discouraging message to women that the workplace is a dangerous environment.

As Table 2-3 shows, male criminals were more likely to victimize females (94.9% of female vic-timizations) than people of their own sex (75.2% of male victimizations). Weapons like knives and guns, as well as the male body itself, were used in the process of victimization. Male criminals (72%) were more likely than female criminals (32.7%) to use weapons during the crime and men (11.9%) were responsible for more sex crimes than women (3.9%). These prominent portrayals of men using weapons and sex against their female victims is an intimidating reaffirmation of male dominance.

The race variable also produced noteworthy re-sults pertaining to sex crimes, the use of weapons other than the body, and ultimately the communi-cation of power relations. Caucasians (20.6%) and males (11.9%) were most likely to commit sex crimes while African Americans were most likely to be the victims (25.4%) of these crimes. Thus when white males were presented as violent crim-inals they most often used the physical force of sex to establish their superiority over other races. The body and its sexual imposition on women and African Americans was portrayed as the Caucasian male's means of dominance. On the other hand, human-made weapons provided African American criminals with the means to achieve dominance over their victims. As a group, African American criminals were most likely to use guns, knives, and other weapons (83.1%) against their victims. These portrayals of the African American as armed and dangerous deepen this group's marginalization and perhaps even perpetuate justification for police bru-tality against African American offenders.

The relationship between the criminal's gender and the portrayed motivations for the crime offer insight into how society publicly distinguishes between demographic groups. Crosstabulations of the criminal's gender and motivation for crime reveal that female criminals were presented as more irrational than male criminals. In fact, female crim-inals were more likely than male criminals to be portrayed as committing crimes because of greed (29.4% vs. 15.6%) and drug or alcohol abuse (86.7% vs. 13.3%). By contrast, the male criminal was motivated by more "rational" needs (i.e., protection of his social status—27.9% vs. 1.8% of females). These portrayals emphasize the view of women as unstable, substance abusing, and patho-logically greedy beings. This image of women as greedy is further encouraged by the fact that more female (19%) than male (8.8%) criminals were portrayed as committing property crimes. When a society succeeds in constructing demographic distinctions like these, the inclusion and exclusion of distinct groups in different aspects of social life become inevitable.

CONCLUSION

Although many efforts have been made to study crime in television fiction and newspapers, crime portrayals in television news have, thus far, been neglected. This study's findings contribute to com-prehensive knowledge about the mass media's por-trayals of crime. The theoretical significance of this study lies in the functionalist perspective of the role that crime occupies within society. Popular con-demnations of humankind's long-standing fascina-tion with crime overlook the instructional value of mass mediated crime stories. Indeed, this study found support for the notion that the rituals whereby crime is made public serve social func-tions. In the Durkheimian tradition, the results of this study suggest that crime stories provide a po-tential means for negotiating society's morality by drawing clear lines between good and evil. Moreover, by frequently and prominently offering the criminal for public scrutiny and by promoting outrage against the criminal's violation of the public's common morality, social solidarity and integration may be promoted.

Through the unambiguous communication of the idea that crime doesn't pay, there is tremendous potential for mass mediated social control. In line with cultivation analysts' reasoning, this study also suggests that the construction of crime narratives involves the casting of demographic groups at different levels of the social order, thereby reinscribing hierarchical power relations and re-establishing stereotypes. African Americans were presented as criminals who cannot be trusted while women were marginalized as helpless victims, particularly those who dare to leave their homes to pursue careers. These messages are strikingly conservative in times when institutionalized support of women and minorities is supposedly correcting inequalities between race and gender groups. In fact, this study's results support the notion that television mass disseminate messages to nurture the survival of the existing social order.

REFERENCES

Barrile, L. G. (1986). "Television's 'bogeyclass'?: Status, motives, and violence in crime drama characters." *Sociological Viewpoints* 2:39–56.

Bird, S. E. (1992). *For inquiring minds: A cultural study of supermarket tabloids*. Knoxville, TN: The University of Tennessee Press.

Carey, J. W. (1975). "A cultural approach to communication." *Communication* 2:1–22.

Condit, C. M. (1987). "Crafting virtue: The rhetorical construction of public morality." *Quarterly Journal of Speech* 73:23–38.

Cromer, G. (1978). "Character assassination in the press." In C. Winick (ed.), *Deviance and mass media* (pp. 225–241). Beverly Hills, CA: Sage.

Dominick, J. R. (1973). "Crime and law enforcement on prime time television." *Public Opinion Quarterly* 37:241–250.

Durkheim, E. (1933). *The division of labor in society*. New York: The Free Press.

———. (1938). *The rules of sociological method*. New York: The Free Press.

———. (1951). *Suicide*. New York: The Free Press.

Ericson, R. V. (1991). "Mass media, crime, law and justice." *The British Journal of Criminology* 31:219–249.

Ericson, R. V., and Haggerty, K. D. (1997). *Policing the risk society*. Toronto: University of Toronto Press.

Erikson, K. T. (1966). *Wayward puritans*. New York: Macmillan.

Estep, R., and Macdonald, P. T. (1985). "Crime in the afternoon; murder and robbery on soap operas." *Journal of Broadcasting and Electronic Media* 29:323–331.

Ettema, J. S., and Glasser, T. L. (1988). "Narrative form and moral force: The realization of innocence and guilt through investigative journalism." *Journal of Communication* 38:8–26.

Federal Bureau of Investigation. (1994). *Uniform Crime Reports*. U.S. Government Printing Office.

Foucault, M. (1979). *Discipline and punish*. New York: Vintage Books.

Gans, H. J. (1979). *Deciding what's news*. New York: Pantheon.

Garfinkel, H. (1956). "Conditions of successful degradation ceremonies." *American Journal of Sociology* 61:420–424.

Gerbner, G. (1988). *Violence and terror in the mass media*. Paris, France: Unesco.

Gerbner, G., Gross, L., Signorielli, N., Morgan, M., and Jackson-Beeck, M. (1979). "The demonstration of power: Violence profile no. 10." *Journal of Communication* 29:177–196.

Glasser, T. L., and Ettema, J. S. (1989). "Investigative Journalism and the Moral Order." *Critical Studies in Mass Communication* 6:1–20.

Haney, C., and Manzolati, J. (1981). "Television criminology: Network illusions of criminal justice realities." *Human Behavior* 12:278–298.

Knight, G. (1989). "Reality effects: Tabloid television news." *Queen's Quarterly* 96:94–108.

Knight, G., and Dean, T. (1982). "Myth and the structure of news." *Journal of Communication* 32:144–161.

Knutson, P. (1974). "Dragnet—The perfect crime?" *Liberation* 18:28–30.

Mead, G. H. (1918). "The psychology of punitive justice." *The American Journal of Sociology* 23:577–602.

Rusche, G., and Kirchheimer, O. (1939). *Punishment and social structure*. New York: Russell & Russell.

Schattenberg, G. (1981). "Social control functions of mass media depictions of crime." *Sociological Inquiry* 51: 71–77.

SOCIAL DISORGANIZATION THEORY

Deviant Places

Rodney Stark

Norman Hayner, a stalwart of the old Chicago school of human ecology, noted that in the area of Seattle having by far the highest delinquency rate in 1934, "half the children are Italian." In vivid language, Hayner described the social and cultural shortcomings of these residents: "largely illiterate, unskilled workers of Sicilian origin. Fiestas, wine-drinking, raising of goats and gardens . . . are characteristic traits." He also noted that the businesses in this neighborhood were run down and on the wane and that "a number of dilapidated vacant business buildings and frame apartment houses dot the main street," while the area has "the smallest percentage of home-owners and the greatest aggregation of dilapidated dwellings and run-down tenements in the city" (Hayner 1942:361–363). Today this district, which makes up the neighborhood surrounding Garfield High School, remains the prime delinquency area. But there are virtually no Italians living there. Instead, this neighborhood is the heart of the Seattle black community.

Thus we come to the point. How is it that neighborhoods can remain the site of high crime and deviance rates *despite a complete turnover in their populations?* If the Garfield district was tough *because* Italians lived there, why did it stay tough after they left? Indeed, why didn't the neighborhoods the Italians departed to become tough? Questions such as these force the perception that the composition of neighborhoods, in terms of characteristics of their populations, cannot provide an adequate explanation of variations in deviance rates. Instead,

From *Criminology* 25, No. 4 (1987), 893–909. Reprinted by permission of the American Society of Criminology and the author.

there must be something about places as such that sustains crime.

This paper attempts to fashion an integrated set of propositions to summarize and extend our understanding of ecological sources of deviant behavior. In so doing, the aim is to revive a *sociology* of deviance as an alternative to the social psychological approaches that have dominated for 30 years. That is, the focus is on traits of places and groups rather than on traits of individuals. Indeed, I shall attempt to show that by adopting survey research as the *preferred* method of research, social scientists lost touch with significant aspects of crime and delinquency. Poor neighborhoods disappeared to be replaced by individual kids with various levels of family income, but no detectable environment at all. Moreover, the phenomena themselves became bloodless, sterile, and almost harmless, for questionnaire studies cannot tap homicide, rape, assault, armed robbery, or even significant burglary and fraud—too few people are involved in these activities to turn up in significant numbers in feasible samples, assuming that such people turn up in samples at all. So delinquency, for example, which once had meant offenses serious enough for court referrals, soon meant taking $2 out of mom's purse, having "banged up something that did not belong to you," and having a fist fight. This transformation soon led repeatedly to the "discovery" that poverty is unrelated to delinquency (Tittle, Villemez, and Smith 1978).

Yet, through it all, social scientists somehow still knew better than to stroll the streets at night in certain parts of town or even to park there. And despite the fact that countless surveys showed that kids from upper and lower income families scored the same on delinquency batteries, even social scientists knew that the parts of town that scared them were not upper-income neighborhoods. In fact, when the literature was examined with sufficient finesse, it was clear that class *does* matter—that serious offenses are very disproportionately committed by a virtual under class (Hindelang, Hirschi, and Weis 1981).

So, against this backdrop, let us reconsider the human ecology approach to deviance. To begin, there are five aspects of urban neighborhoods which characterize high deviance areas of cities. To my knowledge, no member of the Chicago school ever listed this particular set, but these concepts permeate their whole literature starting with Park, Burgess, and McKenzie's classic, *The City* (1925). And they are especially prominent in the empirical work of the Chicago school (Faris and Dunham 1939; Shaw and McKay 1942). Indeed, most of these factors were prominent in the work of 19th-century moral statisticians such as the Englishmen Mayhew and Buchanan, who were doing ecological sociology decades before any member of the Chicago school was born. These essential factors are (1) density; (2) poverty; (3) mixed use; (4) transience; and (5) dilapidation.

Each of the five will be used in specific propositions. However, in addition to these characteristics of places, the theory also will incorporate some specific *impacts* of the five on the moral order as *people respond to them*. Four responses will be assessed: (1) moral cynicism among residents; (2) increased opportunities for crime and deviance; (3) increased motivation to deviate; and (4) diminished social control.

Finally, the theory will sketch how these responses further *amplify* the volume of deviance through the following consequences: (1) by attracting deviant and crime-prone people and deviant and criminal activities to a neighborhood; (2) by driving out the least deviant; and (3) by further reductions in social control.

Proposition 1: *The greater the density of a neighborhood, the more association between those most and least predisposed to deviance.*

At issue here is not simply that there will be a higher proportion of deviance-prone persons in dense neighborhoods (although, as will be shown, that is true, too), rather it is proposed that there is a higher average level of interpersonal interactions in such neighborhoods and that individual traits will have less influence on patterns of contact. Consider kids. In low-density neighborhoods—wealthy suburbs, for example—some active effort is required for one 12-year-old to see another (a ride from a parent often is required). In these settings, kids and their parents can easily limit contact with bullies and those in disrepute. Not so in dense urban neighborhoods—the "bad" kids often live in the same building as the "good" ones, hang out close by, dominate the nearby playground, and are nearly unavoidable. Hence, peer groups in dense neighborhoods will tend to be inclusive, and all young people living there will face maximum peer pressure to deviate—as differential association theorists have stressed for so long.

Proposition 2: *The greater the density of a neighborhood, the higher the level of moral cynicism.*

Moral cynicism is the belief that people are much worse than they pretend to be. Indeed, Goffman's use of the dramaturgical model in his social psychology was rooted in the fact that we require ourselves and others to keep up appearances in public. We all, to varying degrees, have secrets, the public airing of which we would find undesirable. So long as our front-stage performances are credible and creditable, and we shield our back-stage actions, we serve as good role models (Goffman 1959, 1963). The trouble is that in dense neighborhoods it is much harder to keep up appearances—whatever morally discreditable information exists about us is likely to leak.

Survey data suggest that upper-income couples may be about as likely as lower-income couples to have physical fights (Stark and McEvoy 1970). Whether that is true, it surely is the case that upper-income couples are much less likely to be *overheard* by the neighbors when they have such a fight. In dense neighborhoods, where people live in crowded, thin-walled apartments, the neighbors do hear. In these areas teenage peers, for example, will be much more likely to know embarrassing things about one another's parents. This will color their perceptions about what is normal, and their respect for the conventional moral standards will be reduced. Put another way, people in dense neighborhoods will serve as inferior role models for one another—the same people would *appear* to be more respectable in less dense neighborhoods.

Proposition 3: *To the extent that neighborhoods are dense and poor, homes will be crowded.*

The proposition is obvious, but serves as a necessary step to the next propositions on the effects of crowding, which draw heavily on the fine paper by Gove, Hughes, and Galle (1979).

Proposition 4: *Where homes are more crowded, there will be a greater tendency to congregate outside the home in places and circumstances that raise levels of temptation and opportunity to deviate.*

Gove and his associates reported that crowded homes caused family members, especially teenagers, to stay away. Since crowded homes will also tend to be located in mixed-use neighborhoods (see Proposition 9), when people stay away from home they will tend to congregate in places conducive to deviance (stores, pool halls, street corners, cafes, taverns, and the like).

Proposition 5: *Where homes are more crowded, there will be lower levels of supervision of children.*

This follows from the fact that children from crowded homes tend to stay out of the home and that their parents are glad to let them. Moreover, Gove and his associates found strong empirical support for the link between crowding and less supervision of children.

Proposition 6: *Reduced levels of child supervision will result in poor school achievement, with a consequent reduction in stakes in conformity and an increase in deviant behavior.*

This is one of the most cited and strongly verified causal chains in the literature on delinquency (Thrasher 1927; Toby and Toby 1961; Hirschi 1969; Gold 1970; Hindelang 1973). Indeed, Hirschi and Hindelang (1977:583) claim that the "school variables" are among the most powerful predictors of delinquency to be found in survey studies: "Their significance for delinquency is nowhere in dispute and is, in fact, one of the oldest and most consistent findings of delinquency research."

Here Toby's (1957) vital concept of "stakes in conformity" enters the propositions. Stakes in conformity are those things that people risk losing by being detected in deviant actions. These may be things we already possess as well as things we can reasonably count on gaining in the future. An important aspect of the school variables is their potential for future rewards, rewards that may be sacrificed by deviance, but only for those whose school performance is promising.

Proposition 7: *Where homes are more crowded, there will be higher levels of conflict within families weakening attachments and thereby stakes in conformity.*

Gove and his associates found a strong link between crowding and family conflict, confirming Frazier's (1932:636) observations:

> So far as children are concerned, the house becomes a veritable prison for them. There is no way of knowing how many conflicts in Negro families are set off by the irritations caused by overcrowding people, who come home after a day of frustration and fatigue, to dingy and unhealthy living quarters.

Here we also recognize that stakes in conformity are not merely material. Indeed, given the effort humans will expend to protect them, our attachments to others are among the most potent stakes in conformity. We risk our closest and most intimate relationships by behavior that violates what others expect of us. People lacking such relationships, of course, do not risk their loss.

Proposition 8: *Where homes are crowded, members will be much less able to shield discreditable acts and information from one another, further increasing moral cynicism.*

As neighborhood density causes people to be less satisfactory role models for the neighbors, density in the home causes moral cynicism. Crowding makes privacy more difficult. Kids will observe or overhear parental fights, sexual relations, and the like. This is precisely what Buchanan noted about the dense and crowded London slums in 1846 (in Levin and Lindesmith 1937:15):

> In the densely crowded lanes and alleys of these areas, wretched tenements are found containing in every cellar and on every floor, men and women, children both male and female, all huddled together, sometimes with strangers, and too frequently standing in very doubtful consanguinity to each other. In these abodes decency and shame have fled; depravity reigns in all its horrors.

Granted that conditions have changed since then and that dense, poor, crowded areas in the center cities of North America are not nearly so wretched. But the essential point linking "decency" and "shame" to lack of privacy retains its force.

Proposition 9: *Poor, dense neighborhoods tend to be mixed-use neighborhoods.*

Mixed use refers to urban areas where residential and commercial land use coexist, where homes, apartments, retail shops, and even light industry are mixed together. Since much of the residential property in such areas is rental, typically there is much less resistance to commercial use (landlords often welcome it because of the prospects of increased land values). Moreover, the poorest, most dense urban neighborhoods often are adjacent to the commercial sections of cities, forming what the Chicago school called the "zone of transition" to note the progressive encroachments of commercial uses into a previously residential area. Shaw and McKay (1942:20) describe the process as follows:

> As the city grows, the areas of commerce and light industry near the center encroach upon areas used for residential purposes. The dwellings in such areas, often already undesirable because of age, are allowed to deteriorate when such invasion threatens or actually occurs, as further investment in them is unprofitable. These residences are permitted to yield whatever return can be secured in their dilapidated condition, often in total disregard for the housing laws. . . .

Shaw and McKay were proponents of the outmoded concentric zonal model of cities, hence their

assumption that encroachment radiates from the city center. No matter, the important point is that the process of encroachment occurs whatever the underlying shape of cities.

Proposition 10: *Mixed use increases familiarity with and easy access to places offering the opportunity for deviance.*

A colleague told me he first shoplifted at age eight, but that he had been "casing the joint for four years." This particular "joint" was the small grocery store at the corner of the block where he lived, so he didn't even have to cross a street to get there. In contrast, consider kids in many suburbs. If they wanted to take up shoplifting they would have to ask mom or dad for a ride. In purely residential neighborhoods there simply are far fewer conventional opportunities (such as shops) for deviant behavior.

Proposition 11: *Mixed-use neighborhoods offer increased opportunity for congregating outside the home in places conducive to deviance.*

It isn't just stores to steal from that the suburbs lack, they also don't abound in places of potential moral marginality where people can congregate. But in dense, poor, mixed-use neighborhoods, when people leave the house they have all sorts of places to go, including the street corner. A frequent activity in such neighborhoods is leaning. A bunch a guys will lean against the front of the corner store, the side of the pool hall, or up against the barber shop. In contrast, out in the suburbs young guys don't gather to lean against one another's houses, and since there is nowhere else for them to lean, whatever deviant leanings they might have go unexpressed. By the same token, in the suburbs, come winter, there is no close, *public* place to congregate indoors.

Thus, we can more easily appreciate some fixtures of the crime and delinquency research literature. When people, especially young males, congregate and have nothing special to do, the incidence of their deviance is increased greatly (Hirschi 1969). Most delinquency, and a lot of crime, is a social rather than a solitary act (Erickson 1971).

Proposition 12: *Poor, dense, mixed-use neighborhoods have high transience rates.*

This aspect of the urban scene has long attracted sociological attention. Thus, McKenzie wrote in 1926 (p. 145): "Slums are the most mobile . . . sections of a city. Their inhabitants come and go in continuous succession."

Proposition 13: *Transience weakens extra-familial attachments.*

This is self-evident. The greater the amount of local population turnover, the more difficult it will be for individuals or families to form and retain attachments.

Proposition 14: *Transience weakens voluntary organizations, thereby directly reducing both informal and formal sources of social control* (see Proposition 25).

Recent studies of population turnover and church membership rates strongly sustain the conclusion that such membership is dependent upon attachments, and hence suffers where transience rates reduce attachments (Wuthnow and Christiano 1979; Stark, Doyle, and Rushing 1983; Welch 1983; Stark and Bainbridge 1985). In similar fashion, organizations such as PTA or even fraternal organizations must suffer where transience is high. Where these organizations are weak, there will be reduced community resources to launch local, self-help efforts to confront problems such as truancy or burglary. Moreover, neighborhoods deficient in voluntary organizations also will be less able to influence how external forces such as police, zoning boards, and the like act vis-à-vis the community, a point often made by Park (1952) in his discussions of natural areas and by more recent urban sociologists (Suttles 1972; Lee, Oropesa, Metch, and Guest 1984; Guest 1984).

In their important recent study, Simcha-Fagan and Schwartz (1986) found that the association between transience and delinquency disappeared under controls for organizational participation. This is not an example of spuriousness, but of what Lazarsfeld called "interpretation" (Lazarsfeld, Pasanella, and Rosenberg 1972). Transience *causes* low levels of participation, which in turn *cause* an increased rate of delinquency. That is, participation is an *intervening variable* or *linking mechanism*

between transience and delinquency. When an intervening variable is controlled, the association between X and Y is reduced or vanishes.

Proposition 15: *Transience reduces levels of community surveillance.*

In areas abounding in newcomers, it will be difficult to know when someone doesn't live in a building he or she is entering. In stable neighborhoods, on the other hand, strangers are easily noticed and remembered.

Proposition 16: *Dense, poor, mixed-use, transient neighborhoods will also tend to be dilapidated.*

This is evident to anyone who visits these parts of cities. Housing is old and not maintained. Often these neighborhoods are very dirty and littered as a result of density, the predominance of renters, inferior public services, and a demoralized population (see Proposition 22).

Proposition 17: *Dilapidation is a social stigma for residents.*

It hardly takes a real estate tour of a city to recognize that neighborhoods not only reflect the status of their residents, but confer status upon them. In Chicago, for example, strangers draw favorable inferences about someone who claims to reside in Forest Glen, Beverly, or Norwood Park. But they will be leery of those who admit to living on the Near South Side. Granted, knowledge of other aspects of communities enters into these differential reactions, but simply driving through a neighborhood such as the South Bronx is vivid evidence that very few people would actually *want* to live there. During my days as a newspaper reporter, I discovered that to move just a block North, from West Oakland to Berkeley, greatly increased social assessments of individuals. This was underscored by the frequent number of times people told me they lived in Berkeley although the phone book showed them with an Oakland address. As Goffman (1963) discussed at length, stigmatized people will try to pass when they can.

Proposition 18: *High rates of neighborhood deviance are a social stigma for residents.*

Beyond dilapidation, neighborhoods abounding in crime and deviance stigmatize the moral standing of all residents. To discover that you are interacting with a person through whose neighborhood you would not drive is apt to influence the subsequent interaction in noticeable ways. Here is a person who lives where homicide, rape, and assault are common, where drug dealers are easy to find, where prostitutes stroll the sidewalks waving to passing cars, where people sell TVs, VCRs, cameras, and other such items out of the trunks of their cars. In this sense, place of residence can be a dirty, discreditable secret.

Proposition 19: *Living in stigmatized neighborhoods causes a reduction in an individual's stake in conformity.*

This is simply to note that people living in slums will see themselves as having less to risk by being detected in acts of deviance. Moreover, as suggested below in Propositions 25–28, the risks of being detected also are lower in stigmatized neighborhoods.

Proposition 20: *The more successful and potentially best role models will flee stigmatized neighborhoods whenever possible.*

Goffman (1963) has noted that in the case of physical stigmas, people will exhaust efforts to correct or at least minimize them—from plastic surgery to years of therapy. Presumably it is easier for persons to correct a stigma attached to their neighborhood than one attached to their bodies. Since moving is widely perceived as easy, the stigma of living in particular neighborhoods is magnified. Indeed, as we see below, some people do live in such places because of their involvement in crime and deviance. But, even in the most disorderly neighborhoods, *most* residents observe the laws and norms. Usually they continue to live there simply because they can't afford better. Hence, as people become able to afford to escape, they do. The result is a process of selection whereby the worst role models predominate.

Proposition 21: *More successful and conventional people will resist moving into a stigmatized neighborhood.*

The same factors that *pull* the more successful and conventional out of stigmatized neighborhoods *push* against the probability that conventional people will move into these neighborhoods. This means that only less successful and less conventional people *will* move there.

Proposition 22: *Stigmatized neighborhoods will tend to be overpopulated by the most demoralized kinds of people.*

This does not mean the poor or even those engaged in crime or delinquency. The concern is with persons unable to function in reasonably adequate ways. For here will congregate the mentally ill (especially since the closure of mental hospitals), the chronic alcoholics, the retarded, and others with limited capacities to cope (Faris and Dunham1939; Jones 1934).

Proposition 23: *The larger the relative number of demoralized residents, the greater the number of available "victims."*

As mixed use provides targets of opportunity by placing commercial firms within easy reach of neighborhood residents, the demoralized serve as human targets of opportunity. Many muggers begin simply by searching the pockets of drunks passed out in doorways and alleys near their residence.

Proposition 24: *The larger the relative number of demoralized residents, the lower will be residents' perception of chances for success, and hence they will have lower perceived stakes in conformity.*

Bag ladies on the corner, drunks sitting on the curbs, and schizophrenics muttering in the doorways are not advertisements for the American Dream. Rather, they testify that people in this part of town are losers, going nowhere in the system.

Proposition 25: *Stigmatized neighborhoods will suffer from more lenient law enforcement.*

This is one of those things that "everyone knows," but for which there is no firm evidence. However, evidence may not be needed, given the many obvious reasons why the police would let things pass in these neighborhoods that they would act on in better neighborhoods. First, the police tend to be reactive, to act upon complaints rather than seek out violations. People in stigmatized neighborhoods complain less often.

Moreover, people in these neighborhoods frequently are much less willing to testify when the police do act—and the police soon lose interest in futile efforts to find evidence. In addition, it is primarily vice that the police tolerate in these neighborhoods, and the police tend to accept the premise that vice will exist *somewhere*. Therefore, they tend to condone vice in neighborhoods from which they do not receive effective pressures to act against it (see Proposition 14). They may even believe that by having vice limited to a specific area they are better able to regulate it. Finally, the police frequently come to share the outside community's view of stigmatized neighborhoods— as filled with morally disreputable people, who deserve what they get.

Proposition 26: *More lenient law enforcement increases moral cynicism.*

Where people see the laws being violated with apparent impunity, they will tend to lose their respect for conventional moral standards.

Proposition 27: *More lenient law enforcement increases the incidence of crime and deviance.*

This is a simple application of deterrence theory. Where the probabilities of being arrested and prosecuted for a crime are lower, the incidence of such crimes will be higher (Gibbs 1975).

Proposition 28: *More lenient law enforcement draws people to a neighborhood on the basis of their involvement in crime and deviance.*

Reckless (1926:165) noted that areas of the city with "wholesome family and neighborhood life" will not tolerate "vice," but that "the decaying neighborhoods have very little resistance to the invasions of vice." Thus, stigmatized neighborhoods become the "soft spot" for drugs, prostitution, gambling, and the like. These are activities that require public awareness of where to find them, for they depend on customers rather than victims. Vice can function only where it is condoned, at least to some degree. In this manner, McKenzie (1926:146) wrote, the slum "becomes the hiding-place for many services that are forbidden by the mores but which cater to the wishes of residents scattered throughout the community."

Proposition 29: *When people are drawn to a neighborhood on the basis of their participation in crime and deviance, the visibility of such activities and the opportunity to engage in them increase.*

It has already been noted that vice must be relatively visible to outsiders in order to exist. Hence, to residents, it will be obvious. Even children not only will know *about* whores, pimps, drug dealers, and the like, they will *recognize* them. Back in 1840, Allison wrote of the plight of poor rural families migrating to rapidly growing English cities (p. 76):

> The extravagant price of lodgings compels them to take refuge in one of the crowded districts of the town, in the midst of thousands in similar necessitous circumstances with themselves. Under the same roof they probably find a nest of prostitutes, in the next door a den of thieves. In the room which they occupy they hear incessantly the revel of intoxication or are compelled to witness the riot of licentiousness.

In fact, Allison suggested that the higher social classes owed their "exemption from atrocious crime" primarily to the fact that they were not confronted by the temptations and seductions to vice that assail the poor. For it is the "impossibility of concealing the attractions of vice from the younger part of the poor in the great cities which exposes them to so many causes of demoralization."

Proposition 30: *The higher the visibility of crime and deviance, the more it will appear to others that these activities are safe and rewarding.*

There is nothing like having a bunch of pimps and bookies flashing big wads of money and driving expensive cars to convince people in a neighborhood that crime pays. If young girls ask the hookers on the corner why they are doing it, they will reply with tales of expensive clothes and jewelry. Hence, in some neighborhoods, deviants serve as role models that encourage residents to become "street wise." This is a form of "wisdom" about the relative costs and benefits of crime that increases the likelihood that a person will spend time in jail. The extensive recent literature on perceptions of risk and deterrence is pertinent here (Anderson 1979; Jenson, Erickson, and Gibbs 1978; Parker and Grasmick 1979).

CONCLUSION

A common criticism of the ecological approach to deviance has been that although many people live in bad slums, most do not become delinquents, criminals, alcoholics, or addicts. Of course not. For one thing, as Gans (1962), Suttles (1968), and others have recognized, bonds among human beings can endure amazing levels of stress and thus continue to sustain commitment to the moral order even in the slums. Indeed, the larger culture seems able to instill high levels of aspiration in people even in the worst ecological settings. However, the fact that most slum residents aren't criminals is beside the point to claims by human ecologists that aspects of neighborhood structure can sustain high rates of crime and deviance. Such propositions do not imply that residence in such a neighborhood is either a necessary or a sufficient condition for deviant behavior. There is conformity in the slums and deviance in affluent suburbs. All the ecological propositions imply is a substantial correlation between variations in neighborhood character and variations in crime and deviance rates. What an ecological theory of crime is meant to achieve is an explanation of why crime and deviance are so heavily concentrated in certain areas, and to pose this explanation in terms that do not depend entirely (or even primarily) on *compositional* effects—that is, on answers in terms of "kinds of people."

To say that neighborhoods are high in crime because their residents are poor suggests that controls for poverty would expose the spuriousness of the ecological effects. In contrast, the ecological theory would predict that the deviant behavior of the poor would vary as their ecology varied. For example, the theory would predict less deviance in poor families in situations where their neighborhood is less dense and more heterogeneous in terms of income, where their homes are less crowded and dilapidated, where the neighborhood is more fully residential, where the police are not permissive of vice, and where there is no undue concentration of the demoralized.

Finally, it is not being suggested that we stop seeking and formulating "kinds of people" explanations. Age and sex, for example, have powerful effects on deviant behavior that are not rooted in ecology (Gove 1985). What is suggested is that, although males will exceed females in terms of rates of crime and delinquency in all neighborhoods, males in certain neighborhoods will have much higher rates than will males in some other neighborhoods, and female behavior will fluctuate by neighborhood too. Or, to return to the insights on which sociology was founded, social structures are real and cannot be reduced to purely psychological phenomena.

REFERENCES

Allison, Archibald. 1840. *The Principles of Population and the Connection With Human Happiness.* Edinburgh: Blackwood.

Anderson, L.S. 1979. "The deterrent effect of criminal sanctions: Reviewing the evidence." In Paul J. Brantingham and Jack M. Kress (eds.), *Structure, Law and Power.* Beverley Hills: Sage.

Erickson, Maynard L. 1971. "The group context of delinquent behavior." *Social Problems* 19:114–129.

Faris, Robert E. L. and Warren Dunham. 1939. *Mental Disorder in Urban Areas.* Chicago: University of Chicago Press.

Frazier, E. Franklin. 1932. *The Negro in the United States.* New York: Macmillan.

Gans, Herbert J. 1962. *The Urban Villagers.* New York: Free Press.

Gibbs, Jack P. 1975. *Crime, Punishment, and Deterrence.* New York: Elsevier.

Goffman, Erving, 1959. *Presentation of Self in Everyday Life.* New York: Doubleday.

———. 1963. *Stigma.* Englewood Cliffs, NJ: Prentice Hall.

Gold, Martin. 1970. *Delinquent Behavior in an American City.* Belmont, CA: Brooks/Cole.

Gove, Walter R. 1985. "The effect of age and gender on deviant behavior: A biopsychological perspective." In Alice Rossi (ed.), *Gender and the Life Course.* New York: Aldine.

Gove, Walter R., Michael L. Hughes, and Omer R. Galle. 1979. Overcrowding in the home. *American Sociological Review* 44:59–80.

Guest, Avery M. 1984. "Robert Park and the natural area: A sentimental review." *Sociology and Social Research* 68:1–21.

Hayner, Norman S. 1942. Five cities of the Pacific Northwest. In Clifford Shaw and Henry McKay (eds.), *Juvenile Delinquency and Urban Areas*. Chicago: University of Chicago Press.

Hindelang, Michael J. 1973. Causes of delinquency: A partial replication and extension. *Social Problems* 20: 471–478.

Hindelang, Michael J., Travis Hirschi, and Joseph G. Weis. 1981. *Measuring Delinquency*. Beverly Hills: Sage.

Hirschi, Travis. 1969. *Causes of Delinquency*. Berkeley: University of California Press.

Hirschi, Travis and Michael J. Hindelang. 1977. "Intelligence and delinquency: A revisionist view." *American Sociological Review* 42:571–587.

Jensen, Gary F., Maynard L. Erickson, and Jack Gibbs. 1978. "Perceived risk of punishment and self-reported delinquency." *Social Forces* 57:57–58.

Jones, D. Caradog. 1934. *The Social Survey of Merseyside*. Vol. III. Liverpool: University Press of Liverpool.

Lazarsfeld, Paul F., Ann K. Pasanella, and Morris Rosenberg. 1972. *Continuities in the Language of Social Research*. New York: Free Press.

Lee, Barrett A., Ralph S. Oropesa, Barbara J. Metch, and Avery M. Guest. 1984. "Testing the decline-of-community thesis: Neighborhood organizations in Seattle, 1929 and 1979." *American Journal of Sociology* 89:1,161–1,188.

Levin, Yale and Alfred Lindesmith. 1937. "English Ecology and Criminology of the Past Century." *Journal of Criminal Law and Criminology* 27:801–816.

Mayhew, Heney. 1851. *London Labor and the London Poor*. London: Griffin.

McKenzie, Roderick. 1926. "The scope of human ecology." *Publications of the American Sociological Society* 20:141–154.

Minor, W. William and Joseph Harry. 1982. "Deterrent and experimental effects in perceptual deterrence research." *Journal of Research in Crime and Delinquency* 18:190–203.

Park, Robert E. 1952. *Human Communities: The City and Human Ecology*. New York: The Free Press.

Park, Robert E., Ernest W. Burgess, and Roderick McKenzie. 1925. *The City*. Chicago: University of Chicago Press.

Parker, J. and Harold G. Grasmick. 1979. "Linking actual and perceived certainty of punishment: An exploratory study of an untested proposition in deterrence theory." *Criminology* 17:366–379.

Reckless, Walter C. 1926. *Publications of the American Sociological Society* 20:164–176.

Shaw, Clifford R. and Henry D. McKay. 1942. *Juvenile Delinquency and Urban Areas*. Chicago: University of Chicago Press.

Simcha-Fagan, Ora and Joseph E. Schwartz. 1986. "Neighborhood and delinquency: An assessment of contextual effects." *Criminology* 24:667–699.

Stark, Rodney and William Sims Bainbridge. 1985. *The Future of Religion*. Berkeley: University of California Press.

Stark, Rodney, Daniel P. Doyle, and Jesse Lynn Rushing. 1983. "Beyond Durkheim: Religion and suicide." *Journal for the Scientific Study of Religion* 22:120–131.

Stark, Rodney and James McEvoy. 1970. "Middle class violence." *Psychology Today* 4:52–54, 110–112.

Suttles, Gerald. 1968. *The Social Order of the Slum*. Chicago: University of Chicago Press.

———. 1972. *The Social Construction of Communities*. Chicago: University of Chicago Press.

Thrasher, Frederick M. 1927. *The Gang*. Chicago: University of Chicago Press.

Tittle, Charles R., Wayne J. Villemez, and Douglas A. Smith. 1978. "The myth of social class and criminality: An empirical assessment of the empirical evidence." *American Sociological Review* 43: 643–656.

Toby, Jackson. 1957. "Social disorganization and stake in conformity: Complementary factors in the predatory behavior of hoodlums." *Journal of Criminal Law, Criminology and Police Science* 48:12–17.

Toby, Jackson and Marcia L. Toby. 1961. *Law School Status as a Predisposing Factor in Subcultural Delinquency*. New Brunswick: Rutgers University Press.

Welch, Kevin. 1983. "Community development and metropolitan religious commitment: A test of two competing models." *Journal for the Scientific Study of Religion* 22:167–181.

Wuthnow, Robert and Kevin Christiano. 1979. "The effects of residential migration on church attendance." In Robert Wuthnow (ed.), *The Religious Dimension*. New York: Academic Press.

READING 2-4

Broken Windows

James Q. Wilson and George L. Kelling

In the mid-1970s, the State of New Jersey announced a "Safe and Clean Neighborhoods Program," designed to improve the quality of community life in twenty-eight cities. As part of that program, the state provided money to help cities take police officers out of their patrol cars and assign them to walking beats. The governor and other state officials were enthusiastic about using foot patrol as a way of cutting crime, but many police chiefs were skeptical. Foot patrol, in their eyes, had been pretty much discredited. It reduced the mobility of the police, who thus had difficulty responding to citizen calls for service, and it weakened headquarters control over patrol officers.

Many police officers also disliked foot patrol, but for different reasons: it was hard work, it kept them outside on cold, rainy nights, and it reduced their chances for making a "good pinch." In some departments, assigning officers to foot patrol had been used as a form of punishment. And academic experts on policing doubted that foot patrol would have any impact on crime rates: it was, in the opinion of most, little more than a sop to public opinion. But since the state was paying for it, the local authorities were willing to go along.

Five years after the program started, the Police Foundation in Washington, D.C., published an evaluation of the foot-patrol project. Based on its analysis of a carefully controlled experiment carried out chiefly in Newark, the foundation concluded, to the surprise of hardly anyone, that foot patrol had not reduced crime rates. But residents of the foot-patrolled neighborhoods seemed to feel more secure than persons in other areas, tended to believe

From *The Atlantic Monthly* (March 1982): 29–83. Reprinted by permission of James Q. Wilson.

that crime had been reduced, and seemed to take fewer steps to protect themselves from crime (staying at home with the doors locked, for example). Moreover, citizens in the foot-patrol areas had a more favorable opinion of the police than did those living elsewhere. And officers walking beats had higher morale, greater job satisfaction, and a more favorable attitude toward citizens in their neighborhoods than did officers assigned to patrol cars.

These findings may be taken as evidence that the skeptics were right—foot patrol has no effect on crime; it merely fools the citizens into thinking that they are safer. But in our view, and in the view of the authors of the Police Foundation study (of whom Kelling was one), the citizens of Newark were not fooled at all. They knew what the foot-patrol officers were doing, they knew it was different from what motorized officers do, and they knew that having officers walk beats did in fact make their neighborhoods safer.

But how can a neighborhood be "safer" when the crime rate has not gone down—in fact, may have gone up? Finding the answer requires first that we understand what most often frightens people in public places. Many citizens, of course, are primarily frightened by crime, especially crime involving a sudden, violent attack by a stranger. This risk is very real, in Newark as in many large cities. But we tend to overlook or forget another source of fear—the fear of being bothered by disorderly people. Not violent people, nor, necessarily, criminals, but disreputable or obstreperous or unpredictable people: panhandlers, drunks, addicts, rowdy teenagers, prostitutes, loiterers, the mentally disturbed.

What foot-patrol officers did was to elevate, to the extent they could, the level of public order in these neighborhoods. Though the neighborhoods were predominantly black and the foot patrolmen were mostly white, this "order-maintenance" function of the police was performed to the general satisfaction of both parties.

One of us (Kelling) spent many hours walking with Newark foot-patrol officers to see how they defined "order" and what they did to maintain it. One beat was typical: a busy but dilapidated area in the heart of Newark, with many abandoned buildings, marginal shops (several of which prominently displayed knives and straight-edged razors in their windows), one large department store, and, most important, a train station and several major bus stops. Though the area was run-down, its streets were filled with people, because it was a major transportation center. The good order of this area was important not only to those who lived and worked there but also to many others, who had to move through it on their way home, to supermarkets, or to factories.

The people on the street were primarily black; the officer who walked the street was white. The people were made up of "regulars" and "strangers." Regulars included both "decent folk" and some drunks and derelicts who were always there but who "knew their place." Strangers were, well, strangers, and viewed suspiciously, sometimes apprehensively. The officer—call him Kelly—knew who the regulars were, and they knew him. As he saw his job, he was to keep an eye on strangers, and make certain that the disreputable regulars observed some informal but widely understood rules. Drunks and addicts could sit on the stoops, but could not lie down. People could drink on side streets, but not at the main intersection. Bottles had to be in paper bags. Talking to, bothering, or begging from people waiting at the bus stop was strictly forbidden. If a dispute erupted between a businessman and a customer, the businessman was assumed to be right, especially if the customer was a stranger. If a stranger loitered, Kelly would ask him if he had any means of support and what his business was; if he gave unsatisfactory answers, he was sent on his way. Persons who broke the informal rules, especially those who bothered people waiting at bus stops, were arrested for vagrancy. Noisy teenagers were told to keep quiet.

These rules were defined and enforced in collaboration with the "regulars" on the street. Another neighborhood might have different rules, but these, everybody understood, were the rules for this neighborhood. If someone violated them, the regulars not only turned to Kelly for help but also ridiculed the violator. Sometimes what Kelly did could be described as "enforcing the law," but just as often it involved taking informal or extralegal steps to help protect what the neighborhood had decided was the appropriate level of public order. Some of the things he did probably would not withstand a legal challenge.

A determined skeptic might acknowledge that a skilled foot-patrol officer can maintain order but still insist that this sort of "order" has little to do with the real sources of community fear—that is, with violent crime. To a degree, that is true. But two things must be borne in mind. First, outside observers should not assume that they know how much of the anxiety now endemic in many big-city neighborhoods stems from a fear of "real" crime and how much from a sense that the street is disorderly, a source of distasteful, worrisome encounters. The people of Newark, to judge from their behavior and their remarks to interviewers, apparently assign a high value to public order, and feel relieved and reassured when the police help them maintain that order.

Second, at the community level, disorder and crime are usually inextricably linked, in a kind of developmental sequence. Social psychologists and police officers tend to agree that if a window in a building is broken *and is left unrepaired,* all the rest of the windows will soon be broken. This is as true in nice neighborhoods as in run-down ones. Window-breaking does not necessarily occur on a large scale because some areas are inhabited by determined window-breakers whereas others are populated by window-lovers: rather, one unrepaired broken window is a signal that no one cares, and so breaking more windows costs nothing. (It has always been fun.)

Philip Zimbardo, a Stanford psychologist, reported in 1969 on some experiments testing the broken-window theory. He arranged to have an automobile without license plates parked with its hood up on a street in the Bronx and a comparable automobile on a street in Palo Alto, California. The car in the Bronx was attacked by "vandals" within ten minutes of its "abandonment." The first to arrive were a family—father, mother, and young son—who removed the radiator and battery. Within twenty-four hours, virtually everything of value had been removed. Then random destruction began—windows were smashed, parts torn off, upholstery ripped. Children began to use the car as a playground. Most of the adult "vandals" were well-dressed, apparently clean-cut whites. The car in Palo Alto sat untouched for more than a week. Then Zimbardo smashed part of it with a sledgehammer. Soon, passersby were joining in. Within a few hours, the car had been turned upside down and utterly destroyed. Again, the "vandals" appeared to be primarily respectable whites.

Untended property becomes fair game for people out for fun or plunder, and even for people who ordinarily would not dream of doing such things and who probably consider themselves law-abiding. Because of the nature of community life in the Bronx—its anonymity, the frequency with which cars are abandoned and things are stolen or broken, the past experience of "no one caring"—vandalism begins much more quickly than it does in staid Palo Alto, where people have come to believe that private possessions are cared for, and that mischievous behavior is costly. But vandalism can occur anywhere once communal barriers—the sense of mutual regard and the obligations of civility—are lowered by actions that seem to signal that "no one cares."

We suggest that "untended" behavior also leads to the breakdown of community controls. A stable neighborhood of families who care for their homes, mind each other's children, and confidently frown on unwanted intruders can change, in a few years or even a few months, to an inhospitable and frightening jungle. A piece of property is abandoned, weeds grow up, a window is smashed. Adults stop scolding rowdy children; the children, emboldened, become more rowdy. Families move out, unattached adults move in. Teenagers gather in front of the corner store. The merchant asks them to move; they refuse. Fights occur. Litter accumulates. People start drinking in front of the grocery; in time, an inebriate slumps to the sidewalk and is allowed to sleep it off. Pedestrians are approached by panhandlers.

At this point it is not inevitable that serious crime will flourish or violent attacks on strangers will occur. But many residents will think that crime, especially violent crime, is on the rise, and they will modify their behavior accordingly. They will use the streets less often, and when on the streets will stay apart from their fellows moving with averted eyes, silent lips, and hurried steps. "Don't get involved." For some residents, this growing atomization will matter little, because the neighborhood is not their "home" but "the place where they live." Their interests are elsewhere; they are cosmopolitans. But it will matter greatly to other people, whose lives derived meaning and satisfaction from local attachments rather than worldly involvement; for them, the neighborhood will cease to exist except for a few reliable friends whom they arrange to meet.

Such an area is vulnerable to criminal invasion. Though it is not inevitable, it is more likely that here, rather than in places where people are confident they can regulate public behavior by informal controls, drugs will change hands, prostitutes will solicit, and cars will be stripped. That the drunks will be robbed by boys who do it as a lark and the prostitutes' customers will be robbed by men who do it purposefully and perhaps violently. That muggings will occur.

Among those who often find it difficult to move away from this are the elderly. Surveys of citizens suggest that the elderly are much less likely to be the victims of crime than younger persons, and some have inferred from this that the well-known fear of crime voiced by the elderly is an exaggeration: perhaps we ought not to design special programs to protect older persons; perhaps we should even try to talk them out of their mistaken fears. This argument misses the point. The prospect of a confrontation with an obstreperous teenager or a drunken panhandler can be as fear-inducing for defenseless persons as the prospect of meeting an actual robber; indeed, to a defenseless person, the two kinds of confrontation are often indistinguishable. Moreover, the lower rate at which the elderly are victimized is a measure of the steps they have already taken—chiefly, staying behind locked doors—to minimize the risks they face. Young men are more frequently attacked than older women, not because they are easier or more lucrative targets but because they are on the streets more.

Nor is the connection between disorderliness and fear made only by the elderly. Susan Estrich, of the Harvard Law School, has recently gathered together a number of surveys on the sources of public fear. One, done in Portland, Oregon, indicated that three fourths of the adults interviewed cross to the other side of a street when they see a gang of teenagers; another survey, in Baltimore, discovered that nearly half would cross the street to avoid even a single strange youth. When an interviewer asked people in a housing project where the most dangerous spot was, they mentioned a place where young persons gathered to drink and play music, despite the fact that not a single crime had occurred there. In Boston public housing projects, the greatest fear was expressed by persons living in the buildings where disorderliness and incivility, not crime, were the greatest. Knowing this helps one understand the significance of such otherwise harmless displays as subway graffiti. As Nathan Glazer has written, the proliferation of graffiti, even when not obscene, confronts the subway rider with the "inescapable knowledge that the environment he must endure for an hour or more a day is uncontrolled and uncontrollable, and that anyone can invade it to do whatever damage and mischief the mind suggests."

In response to fear, people avoid one another, weakening controls. Sometimes they call the police. Patrol cars arrive, an occasional arrest occurs, but crime continues and disorder is not abated.

Citizens complain to the police chief, but he explains that his department is low on personnel and that the courts do not punish petty or first-time offenders. To the residents, the police who arrive in squad cars are either ineffective or uncaring; to the police, the residents are animals who deserve each other. The citizens may soon stop calling the police, because "they can't do anything."

The process we call urban decay has occurred for centuries in every city. But what is happening today is different in at least two important respects. First, in the period before, say, World War II, city dwellers—because of money costs, transportation difficulties, familial and church connections— could rarely move away from neighborhood problems. When movement did occur, it tended to be along public-transit routes. Now mobility has become exceptionally easy for all but the poorest or those who are blocked by racial prejudice. Earlier crime waves had a kind of built-in self-correcting mechanism: the determination of a neighborhood or community to reassert control over its turf. Areas in Chicago, New York, and Boston would experience crime and gang wars, and then normalcy would return, as the families for whom no alternative residences were possible reclaimed their authority over the streets.

Second, the police in this earlier period assisted in that reassertion of authority by acting, sometimes violently, on behalf of the community. Young toughs were roughed up, people were arrested "on suspicion" or for vagrancy, and prostitutes and petty thieves were routed. "Rights" were something enjoyed by decent folk, and perhaps also by the serious professional criminal, who avoided violence and could afford a lawyer.

This pattern of policing was not an aberration or the result of occasional excess. From the earliest days of the nation, the police function was seen primarily as that of a night watchman: to maintain order against the chief threats to order—fire, wild animals, and disreputable behavior. Solving crimes was viewed not as a police responsibility but as a private one. In the March, 1969, *Atlantic,* one of us (Wilson) wrote a brief account of how the police role had slowly changed from maintaining order to fighting crimes. The change began with the creation of private detectives (often ex-criminals), who worked on a contingency-fee basis for individuals who had suffered losses. In time, the detectives were absorbed into municipal police agencies and paid a regular salary; simultaneously, the responsibility for prosecuting thieves was shifted from the aggrieved private citizen to the professional prosecutor. This process was not complete in most places until the twentieth century.

In the 1960s, when urban riots were a major problem, social scientists began to explore carefully the order-maintenance function of the police, and to suggest ways of improving it—not to make streets safer (its original function) but to reduce the incidence of mass violence. Order-maintenance became, to a degree, coterminous with "community relations." But, as the crime wave that began in the early 1960s continued without abatement throughout the decade and into the 1970s, attention shifted to the role of the police as crime-fighters. Studies of police behavior ceased, by and large, to be accounts of the order-maintenance function and became, instead, efforts to propose and test ways whereby the police could solve more crimes, make more arrests, and gather better evidence. If these things could be done, social scientists assumed, citizens would be less fearful.

A great deal was accomplished during this transition, as both police chiefs and outside experts emphasized the crime-fighting function in their plans, in the allocation of resources, and in deployment of personnel. The police may well have become better crime fighters as a result. And doubtless they remained aware of their responsibility for order. But the link between order-maintenance and crime-prevention, so obvious to earlier generations, was forgotten.

That link is similar to the process whereby one broken window becomes many. The citizen who fears the ill-smelling drunk, the rowdy teenager, or the importuning beggar is not merely expressing his distaste for unseemly behavior, he is also giving voice to a bit of folk wisdom that happens to be a correct generalization—namely, that serious street crime flourishes in areas in which disorderly behavior goes unchecked. The unchecked panhandler is, in effect, the first broken window. Muggers and robbers, whether opportunistic or professional, believe they reduce their chances of being caught or even identified if they operate on streets where potential victims are already intimidated by prevailing conditions. If the neighborhood cannot keep a bothersome panhandler from annoying passersby, the thief may reason, it is even less likely to call the police to identify a potential mugger or to interfere if the mugging actually takes place.

Some police administrators concede that this process occurs, but argue that motorized-patrol officers can deal with it as effectively as foot-patrol officers. We are not so sure. In theory, an officer in a squad car can observe as much as an officer on foot; in theory, the former can talk to as many people as the latter. But the reality of police–citizen encounters is powerfully altered by the automobile. An officer on foot cannot separate himself from the street people; if he is approached, only his uniform and his personality can help him manage whatever is about to happen. And he can never be certain what that will be—a request for directions, a plea for help, an angry denunciation, a teasing remark, a confused babble, a threatening gesture.

In a car, an officer is more likely to deal with street people by rolling down the window and looking at them. The door and the window exclude the approaching citizen; they are a barrier. Some officers take advantage of this barrier, perhaps unconsciously, by acting differently if in the car than they would on foot. We have seen this countless times. The police car pulls up to a corner where teenagers are gathered. The window is rolled down. The officer stares at the youths. They stare back. The officer says to one, "C'mere." He saunters over, conveying to his friends by his elaborately casual style the idea that he is not intimidated by authority. "What's your name?" "Chuck." "Chuck who?" "Chuck Jones." "What'ya doing, Chuck?" "Nothing." "Got a P.O. [parole officer]?" "Nah." "Sure?" "Yeah." "Stay out of trouble, Chuckie." Meanwhile, the other boys laugh and exchange comments among themselves, probably at the officer's expense. The officer stares harder. He cannot be certain what is being said, nor can he join in and, by displaying his own skill at street banter, prove that he cannot be "put down." In the process, the officer has learned almost nothing, and the boys have decided the officer is an alien force who can safely be disregarded, even mocked.

Our experience is that most citizens like to talk to a police officer. Such exchanges give them a sense of importance, provide them with the basis for gossip, and allow them to explain to the authorities what is worrying them (whereby they gain a modest but significant sense of having "done something" about the problem). You approach a person on foot more easily, and talk to him more readily, than you do a person in a car. Moreover, you can more easily retain some anonymity if you draw an officer aside for a private chat. Suppose you want to pass on a tip about who is stealing handbags, or who offered to sell you a stolen TV. In the inner city, the culprit, in all likelihood, lives nearby. To walk up to a marked patrol car and lean in the window is to convey a visible signal that you are a "fink."

The essence of the police role in maintaining order is to reinforce the informal control mechanisms of the community itself. The police cannot, without committing extraordinary resources, provide a substitute for that informal control. On the other hand, to reinforce those natural forces the police must accommodate them. And therein lies the problem.

Should police activity on the street be shaped, in important ways, by the standards of the neighborhood rather than by the rules of the state? Over the past two decades, the shift of police from order-maintenance to law-enforcement has brought them increasingly under the influence of legal restrictions, provoked by media complaints and enforced by court decisions and departmental orders. As a consequence, the order-maintenance functions of the police are now governed by rules developed to control police relations with suspected criminals. This is, we think, an entirely new development. For centuries, the role of the police as watchmen was

judged primarily not in terms of its compliance with appropriate procedures but rather in terms of its attaining a desired objective. The objective was order, an inherently ambiguous term but a condition that people in a given community recognized when they saw it. The means were the same as those the community itself would employ, if its members were sufficiently determined, courageous, and authoritative. Detecting and apprehending criminals, by contrast, was a means to an end, not an end in itself; a judicial determination of guilt or innocence was the hoped-for result of the law-enforcement mode. From the first, the police were expected to follow rules defining that process, though states differed in how stringent the rules should be. The criminal-apprehension process was always understood to involve individual rights, the violation of which was unacceptable because it meant that the violating officer would be acting as a judge and jury—and that was not his job. Guilt or innocence was to be determined by universal standards under special procedures.

Ordinarily, no judge or jury ever sees the persons caught up in a dispute over the appropriate level of neighborhood order. That is true not only because most cases are handled informally on the street but also because no universal standards are available to settle arguments over disorder, and thus a judge may not be any wiser or more effective than a police officer. Until quite recently in many states, and even today in some places, the police make arrests on such charges as "suspicious person" or "vagrancy" or "public drunkenness"—charges with scarcely any legal meaning. These charges exist not because society wants judges to punish vagrants or drunks but because it wants an officer to have the legal tools to remove undesirable persons from a neighborhood when informal efforts to preserve order in the streets have failed.

Once we begin to think of all aspects of police work as involving the application of universal rules under special procedures, we inevitably ask what constitutes an "undesirable person" and why we should "criminalize" vagrancy or drunkenness. A strong and commendable desire to see that people are treated fairly makes us worry about allowing the police to rout persons who are undesirable by some vague or parochial standard. A growing and not-so-commendable utilitarianism leads us to doubt that any behavior that does not "hurt" another person should be made illegal. And thus many of us who watch over the police are reluctant to allow them to perform, in the only way they can, a function that every neighborhood desperately wants them to perform.

This wish to "decriminalize" disreputable behavior that "harms no one"—and thus remove the ultimate sanction the police can employ to maintain neighborhood order—is, we think, a mistake. Arresting a single drunk or a single vagrant who has harmed no identifiable person seems unjust, and in a sense it is. But failing to do anything about a score of drunks or a hundred vagrants may destroy an entire community. A particular rule that seems to make sense in the individual case makes no sense when it is made a universal rule and applied to all cases. It makes no sense because it fails to take into account the connection between one broken window left untended and a thousand broken windows. Of course, agencies rather than the police could attend to the problems posed by drunks or the mentally ill, but in most communities—especially where the "deinstitutionalization" movement has been strong—they do not.

The concern about equity is more serious. We might agree that certain behavior makes one person more undesirable than another, but how do we ensure that age or skin color or national origin or harmless mannerisms will not also become the basis for distinguishing the undesirable from the desirable? How do we ensure, in short, that the police do not become the agents of neighborhood bigotry?

We can offer no wholly satisfactory answer to this important question. We are not confident that there is a satisfactory answer, except to hope that by their selection, training, and supervision, the police will be inculcated with a clear sense of the outer limit of their discretionary authority. That limit, roughly, is this—the police exist to help regulate behavior, not to maintain the racial or ethnic purity of a neighborhood.

Consider the case of the Robert Taylor Homes in Chicago, one of the largest public-housing projects in the country. It is home for nearly 20,000 people, all black, and extends over ninety-two acres along South State Street. It was named after a distinguished black who had been, during the 1940s, chairman of the Chicago Housing Authority. Not long after it opened, in 1962, relations between project residents and the police deteriorated badly. The citizens felt that the police were insensitive or brutal; the police, in turn, complained of unprovoked attacks on them. Some Chicago officers tell of times when they were afraid to enter the Homes. Crime rates soared.

Today, the atmosphere has changed. Police–citizen relations have improved—apparently, both sides learned something from the earlier experience. Recently, a boy stole a purse and ran off. Several young persons who saw the theft voluntarily passed along to the police information of the identity and residence of the thief, and they did this publicly, with friends and neighbors looking on. But problems persist, chief among them the presence of youth gangs that terrorize residents and recruit members in the project. The people expect the police to "do something" about this, and the police are determined to do just that.

But do what? Though the police can obviously make arrests whenever a gang member breaks the law, a gang can form, recruit, and congregate without breaking the law. And only a tiny fraction of gang-related crimes can be solved by an arrest; thus, if an arrest is the only recourse for the police, the residents' fears will go unassuaged. The police will soon feel helpless, and the residents will again believe that the police "do nothing." What the police in fact do is to chase known gang members out of the project. In the words of one officer, "We kick ass." Project residents both know and approve of this. The tacit police–citizen alliance in the project is reinforced by the police view that the cops and the gangs are the two rival sources of power in the area, and that the gangs are not going to win.

None of this is easily reconciled with any conception of due process or fair treatment. Since both residents and gang members are black, race is not a factor. But it could be. Suppose a white project confronted a black gang, or vice versa. We would be apprehensive about the police taking sides. But the substantive problem remains the same: how can the police strengthen the informal social-control mechanisms of natural communities in order to minimize fear in public places? Law enforcement, per se, is no answer. A gang can weaken or destroy a community by standing about in a menacing fashion and speaking rudely to passersby without breaking the law.

We have difficulty thinking about such matters, not simply because the ethical and legal issues are so complex but because we have become accustomed to thinking of the law in essentially individualistic terms. The law defines *my* rights, punishes *his* behavior, and is applied by *that* officer because of *this* harm. We assume, in thinking this way, that what is good for the individual will be good for the community, and what doesn't matter when it happens to one person won't matter if it happens to many. Ordinarily, those are plausible assumptions. But in cases where behavior that is tolerable to one person is intolerable to many others, the reactions of the others—fear, withdrawal, flight—may ultimately make matters worse for everyone, including the individual who first professed his indifference.

It may be their greater sensitivity to communal as opposed to individual needs that helps explain why the residents of small communities are more satisfied with their police than are the residents of similar neighborhoods in big cities. Elinor Ostrom and her co-workers at Indiana University compared the perception of police services in two poor, all-black Illinois towns—Phoenix and East Chicago Heights—with those of three comparable all-black neighborhoods in Chicago. The level of criminal victimization and the quality of police–community relations appeared to be about the same in the towns and the Chicago neighborhoods. But the citizens living in their own villages were much more likely than those living in the Chicago neighborhoods to say that they do not stay at home for fear of crime, to agree that the local police have "the right to take any action necessary" to deal with problems, and to agree that the police "look out for the needs of the average citizen." It is possible that the residents and the police of the small towns saw themselves as engaged in a collaborative effort to maintain a certain standard of communal life, whereas those of the big city felt themselves to be simply requesting and supplying particular services on an individual basis.

If this is true, how should a wise police chief deploy his meager forces? The first answer is that nobody knows for certain, and the most prudent course of action would be to try further variations on the Newark experiment, to see more precisely what works in what kinds of neighborhoods. The second answer is also a hedge—many aspects of order-maintenance in neighborhoods can probably best be handled in ways that involve the police minimally, if at all. A busy, bustling shopping center and a quiet, well-tended suburb may need almost no visible police presence. In both cases, the ratio of respectable to disreputable people is ordinarily so high as to make informal social control effective.

Even in areas that are in jeopardy from disorderly elements, citizen action without substantial police involvement may be sufficient. Meetings between teenagers who like to hang out on a particular corner and adults who want to use that corner might well lead to an amicable agreement on a set of rules about how many people can be allowed to congregate, where, and when.

Where no understanding is possible—or if possible, not observed—citizen patrols may be a sufficient response. There are two traditions of communal involvement in maintaining order. One, that of the "community watchmen," is as old as the first settlement of the New World. Until well into the nineteenth century, volunteer watchmen, not policemen, patrolled their communities to keep order. They did so, by and large, without taking the law into their own hands—without, that is, punishing persons or using force. Their presence deterred disorder or alerted the community to disorder that could not be deterred. There are hundreds of such efforts today in communities all across the nation. Perhaps the best known is that of the Guardian Angels, a group of unarmed young persons in distinctive berets and T-shirts, who first came to public attention when they began patrolling the New York City subways but who claim now to have chapters in more than thirty American cities. Unfortunately, we have little information about the effect of these groups on crime. It is possible, however, that whatever their effect on crime, citizens find their presence reassuring, and that they thus contribute to maintaining a sense of order and civility.

The second tradition is that of the "vigilante." Rarely a feature of the settled communities of the East, it was primarily to be found in those frontier towns that grew up in advance of the reach of government. More than 350 vigilante groups are known to have existed; their distinctive feature was that their members did take the law into their own hands, by acting as judge, jury, and often executioner as well as policeman. Today, the vigilante movement is conspicuous by its rarity, despite the great fear expressed by citizens that the older cities are becoming "urban frontiers." But some community-watchmen groups have skirted the line, and others may cross it in the future. An ambiguous case, reported in *The Wall Street Journal,* involved a citizens' patrol in the Silver Lake area of Belleville, New Jersey. A leader told the reporter, "We look for outsiders." If a few teenagers from outside the neighborhood enter it, "we ask them their business," he said. "If they say they're going down the street to see Mrs. Jones, fine, we let them pass. But then we follow them down the block to make sure they're really going to see Mrs. Jones."

Though citizens can do a great deal, the police are plainly the key to order-maintenance. For one thing, many communities, such as the Robert Taylor Homes, cannot do the job by themselves.

For another, no citizen in a neighborhood, even an organized one, is likely to feel the sense of responsibility that wearing a badge confers. Psychologists have done many studies on why people fail to go to the aid of persons being attacked or seeking help, and they have learned that the cause is not "apathy" or "selfishness" but the absence of some plausible grounds for feeling that one must personally accept responsibility. Ironically, avoiding responsibility is easier when a lot of people are standing about. On streets and in public places, where order is so important, many people are likely to be "around," a fact that reduces the chance of any one person acting as the agent of the community. The police officer's uniform singles him out as a person who must accept responsibility if asked. In addition, officers, more easily than their fellow citizens, can be expected to distinguish between what is necessary to protect the safety of the street and what merely protects its ethnic purity.

But the police forces of America are losing, not gaining, members. Some cities have suffered substantial cuts in the number of officers available for duty. These cuts are not likely to be reversed in the near future. Therefore, each department must assign its existing officers with great care. Some neighborhoods are so demoralized and crime-ridden as to make foot patrol useless; the best the police can do with limited resources is respond to the enormous number of calls for service. Other neighborhoods are so stable and serene as to make foot patrol unnecessary. The key is to identify neighborhoods at the tipping point—where the public order is deteriorating but not unreclaimable, where the streets are used frequently but by apprehensive people, where a window is likely to be broken at any time, and must quickly be fixed if all are not to be shattered.

Most police departments do not have ways of systematically identifying such areas and assigning officers to them. Officers are assigned on the basis of crime rates (meaning that marginally threatened areas are often stripped so that police can investigate crimes in areas where the situation is hopeless) or on the basis of calls for service (despite the fact that most citizens do not call the police when they are merely frightened or annoyed). To allocate patrol wisely, the department must look at the neighborhoods and decide, from firsthand evidence, where an additional officer will make the greatest difference in promoting a sense of safety.

One way to stretch limited police resources is being tried in some public-housing projects. Tenant organizations hire off-duty police officers for patrol work in their buildings. The costs are not high (at least not per resident), the officer likes the additional income, and the residents feel safer. Such arrangements are probably more successful than hiring private watchmen, and the Newark experiment helps us understand why. A private security guard may deter crime or misconduct by his presence, and he may go to the aid of persons needing help, but he may well not intervene—that is, control or drive away—someone challenging community standards. Being a sworn officer—a "real cop"—seems to give one the confidence, the sense of duty, and the aura of authority necessary to perform this difficult task.

Patrol officers might be encouraged to go to and from duty stations on public transportation and, while on the bus or subway car, enforce rules about smoking, drinking, disorderly conduct, and the like. The enforcement need involve nothing more than ejecting the offender (the offense, after all, is not one with which a booking officer or a judge wishes to be bothered). Perhaps the random but relentless maintenance of standards on buses would lead to conditions on buses that approximate the level of civility we now take for granted on airplanes.

But the most important requirement is to think that to maintain order in precarious situations is a vital job. The police know this is one of their functions, and they also believe, correctly, that it cannot be done to the exclusion of criminal investigation and responding to calls. We may have encouraged them to suppose, however, on the basis of our oft-repeated concerns about serious, violent crime, that they will be judged exclusively on their capacity as crime-fighters. To the extent that this is the case, police administrators will continue to concentrate police personnel in the highest-crime areas (though not necessarily in the areas most vulnerable to criminal invasion), emphasize their training in the law and criminal apprehension (and not their training in managing street life), and join too quickly in campaigns to decriminalize "harmless" behavior (though public drunkenness, street prostitution, and pornographic displays can destroy a community more quickly than any team of professional burglars).

Above all, we must return to our long-abandoned view that the police ought to protect communities as well as individuals. Our crime statistics and victimization surveys measure individual losses, but they do not measure communal losses. Just as physicians now recognize the importance of fostering health rather than simply treating illness, so the police—and the rest of us—ought to recognize the importance of maintaining, intact, communities without broken windows.

ANOMIE THEORY

READING 2-5

Social Structure and Anomie

Robert K. Merton

The conceptual scheme to be outlined is designed to provide a coherent, systematic approach to the study of sociocultural sources of deviate behavior. Our primary aim lies in discovering how some social structures *exert a definite pressure* upon certain persons in the society to engage in nonconformist rather than conformist conduct. The many ramifications of the scheme cannot all be discussed; the problems mentioned outnumber those explicitly treated.

Among the elements of social and cultural structure, two are important for our purposes. These are analytically separable although they merge imperceptibly in concrete situations. The first consists of culturally defined goals, purposes, and interests. It comprises a frame of aspirational reference. These goals are more or less integrated and involve varying degrees of prestige and sentiment. They constitute a basic, but not the exclusive, component of what Linton aptly has called "designs for group living." Some of these cultural aspirations are related to the original drives of man, but they are not determined by them. The second phase of the social structure defines, regulates, and controls the acceptable modes of achieving these goals. Every social group invariably couples its scale of desired ends with moral or institutional regulation of permissible and required procedures for attaining these ends. These regulatory norms and moral imperatives do not necessarily coincide with technical or efficiency norms. Many procedures which from the standpoint of *particular individuals* would be most efficient in securing desired values, e.g., illicit oil-stock schemes, theft, fraud, are ruled out of the institutional area of permitted conduct.

From *American Sociological Review* 3 (October 1938), pp. 672–682.

The choice of expedients is limited by the institutional norms.

To say that these two elements, culture goals and institutional norms, operate jointly is not to say that the ranges of alternative behaviors and aims bear some constant relation to one another. The emphasis upon certain goals may vary independently of the degree of emphasis upon institutional means. There may develop a disproportionate, at times, a virtually exclusive, stress upon the value of specific goals, involving relatively slight concern with the institutionally appropriate modes of attaining these goals.

In no group is there an absence of regulatory codes governing conduct, yet groups do vary in the degree to which these folkways, mores, and institutional controls are effectively integrated with the more diffuse goals which are part of the culture matrix. Emotional convictions may cluster about the complex of socially acclaimed ends, meanwhile shifting their support from the culturally defined implementation of these ends. As we shall see, certain aspects of the social structure may generate countermores and antisocial behavior precisely because of differential emphases on goals and regulations. In the extreme case, the latter may be so vitiated by the goal-emphasis that the range of behavior is limited only by considerations of technical expediency. The sole significant question then becomes, which available means is most efficient in netting the socially approved value? The technically most feasible procedure, whether legitimate or not, is preferred to the institutionally prescribed conduct. As this process continues, the integration of the society becomes tenuous and anomie ensues.

Thus, in competitive athletics, when the aim of victory is shorn of its institutional trappings, and success in contests becomes construed as "winning the game" rather than "winning through circumscribed modes of activity," a premium is implicitly set upon the use of illegitimate but technically efficient means. The star of the opposing football team is surreptitiously slugged; the wrestler furtively incapacitates his opponent through ingenious but illicit techniques; university alumni covertly subsidize "students" whose talents are largely confined to the athletic field. The emphasis on the goal has so attenuated the satisfaction deriving from sheer participation in the competitive activity that these satisfactions are virtually confined to a successful outcome. Through the same process, tension generated by the desire to win in a poker game is relieved by successfully dealing oneself four aces, or, when the cult of success has become completely dominant, by sagaciously shuffling the cards in a game of solitaire. The faint twinge of uneasiness in the last instance and the surreptitious nature of public delicts indicate clearly that the institutional rules of the game *are known* to those who evade them, but that the emotional supports of these rules are largely vitiated by cultural exaggeration of the success-goal.[1] They are microcosmic images of the social macrocosm.

Of course, this process is not restricted to the realm of sport. The process whereby exaltation of the end generates a *literal demoralization,* i.e., a de-institutionalization, of the means is one which characterizes many[2] groups in which the two phases of the social structure are not highly integrated. The extreme emphasis upon the accumulation of wealth as a symbol of success in our own society militates against the completely effective control of institutionally regulated modes of acquiring a fortune.

Fraud, corruption, vice, crime, in short, the entire catalogue of proscribed behavior, becomes increasingly common when the emphasis on the *culturally induced* success-goal becomes divorced from a co-ordinated institutional emphasis. This observation is of crucial theoretical importance in examining the doctrine that antisocial behavior most frequently derives from biological drives breaking through the restraints imposed by society. The difference is one between a strictly utilitarian interpretation which conceives man's ends as random and an analysis which finds these ends deriving from the basic values of the culture.

Our analysis can scarcely stop at this juncture. We must turn to other aspects of the social structure if we are to deal with the social genesis of the varying rates and types of deviate behavior characteristic of different societies. Thus far, we have sketched three ideal types of social orders constituted by distinctive patterns of relations between culture ends and means. Turning from these types of *culture patterning,* we find five logically possible, alternative modes of adjustment or adaptation *by individuals* within the culture-bearing society or group. These are schematically presented in the following table, where ($+$) signifies "acceptance," ($-$) signifies "elimination," and ($\pm$) signifies "rejection and substitution of new goals and standards."

	Culture Goals	Institutionalized Means
I. Conformity	$+$	$+$
II. Innovation	$+$	$-$
III. Ritualism	$-$	$+$
IV. Retreatism	$-$	$-$
V. Rebellion[3]	$\pm$	$\pm$

Our discussion of the relation between these alternative responses and other phases of the social

---

[1] It is unlikely that interiorized norms are completely eliminated. Whatever residuum persists will induce personality tensions and conflict. The process involves a certain degree of ambivalence. A manifest rejection of the institutional norms is coupled with some latent retention of their emotional correlates. "Guilt feelings," "sense of sin," "pangs of conscience" are obvious manifestations of this unrelieved tension; symbolic adherence to the nominally repudiated values or rationalizations constitutes a more subtle variety of tensional release.

[2] "Many," and not all, unintegrated groups, for the reason already mentioned. In groups where the primary emphasis shifts to institutional means, i.e., when the range of alternatives is very limited, the outcome is a type of ritualism rather than anomie.

[3] This fifth alternative is on a plane clearly different from that of the others. It represents a *transitional* response which seeks to *institutionalize* new procedures oriented toward revamped cultural goals shared by the members of the society. It thus involves efforts to *change* the existing structure rather than to perform accommodative actions *within* this structure, and introduces additional problems with which we are not at the moment concerned.

structure must be prefaced by the observation that persons may shift from one alternative to another as they engage in different social activities. These categories refer to role adjustments in specific situations, not to personality in toto. To treat the development of this process in various spheres of conduct would introduce a complexity unmanageable within the confines of this paper. For this reason, we shall be concerned primarily with economic activity in the broad sense, "the production, exchange, distribution, and consumption of goods and services" in our competitive society, wherein wealth has taken on a highly symbolic cast. Our task is to search out some of the factors which exert pressure upon individuals to engage in certain of these logically possible alternative responses. This choice, as we shall see, is far from random.

In every society, Adaptation I (conformity to both culture goals and means) is the most common and widely diffused. Were this not so, the stability and continuity of the society could not be maintained. The mesh of expectancies which constitutes every social order is sustained by the modal behavior of its members falling within the first category. Conventional role behavior oriented toward the basic values of the group is the rule rather than the exception. It is this fact alone which permits us to speak of a human aggregate as comprising a group or society.

Conversely, Adaptation IV (rejection of goals and means) is the least common. Persons who "adjust" (or maladjust) in this fashion are, strictly speaking, *in* the society but not *of* it. Sociologically, these constitute the true "aliens." Not sharing the common frame of orientation, they can be included within the societal population merely in a fictional sense. In this category are *some* of the activities of psychotics, psychoneurotics, chronic autists, pariahs, outcasts, vagrants, vagabonds, tramps, chronic drunkards, and drug addicts.[4] These have relinquished, in certain

spheres of activity, the culturally defined goals, involving complete aim-inhibition in the polar case, and their adjustments are not in accord with institutional norms. This is not to say that in some cases the source of their behavioral adjustments is not in part the very social structure which they have in effect repudiated nor that their very existence within a social area does not constitute a problem for the socialized population.

This mode of "adjustment" occurs, as far as structural sources are concerned, when both the culture goals and institutionalized procedures have been assimilated thoroughly by the individual and imbued with affect and high positive value, but where those institutionalized procedures which promise a measure of successful attainment of the goals are not available to the individual. In such instances, there results a twofold mental conflict insofar as the moral obligation for adopting institutional means conflicts with the pressure to resort to illegitimate means (which may attain the goal) and inasmuch as the individual is shut off from means which are both legitimate *and* effective. The competitive order is maintained, but the frustrated and handicapped individual who cannot cope with this order drops out. Defeatism, quietism, and resignation are manifested in escape mechanisms which ultimately lead the individual to "escape" from the requirements of the society. It is an expedient which arises from continued failure to attain the goal by legitimate measures and from an inability to adopt the illegitimate route because of internalized prohibitions and institutionalized compulsives, *during which process the supreme value of the success-goal has as yet not been renounced.* The conflict is resolved by eliminating *both* precipitating elements, the goals and means. The escape is complete, the conflict is eliminated, and the individual is asocialized.

Be it noted that where frustration derives from the inaccessibility of effective institutional means for attaining economic or any other type of highly valued "success," that Adaptations II, III, and V (innovation, ritualism, and rebellion) are also possible. The result will be determined by the particular personality, and thus, the *particular* cultural

---

[4] Obviously, this is an elliptical statement. These individuals may maintain some orientation to the values of their particular differentiated groupings within the larger society or, in part, of the conventional society itself. Insofar as they do so, their conduct cannot be classified in the "passive rejection" category (IV).

background, involved. Inadequate socialization will result in the innovation response, whereby the conflict and frustration are eliminated by relinquishing the institutional means and retaining the success-aspiration; an extreme assimilation of institutional demands will lead to ritualism, wherein the goal is dropped as beyond one's reach but conformity to the mores persists; and rebellion occurs when emancipation from the reigning standards, due to frustration or to marginalist perspectives, leads to the attempt to introduce a "new social order."

Our major concern is with the illegitimacy adjustment. This involves the use of conventionally proscribed but frequently effective means of attaining at least the simulacrum of culturally defined success—wealth, power, and the like. As we have seen, this adjustment occurs when the individual has assimilated the cultural emphasis on success without equally internalizing the morally prescribed norms governing means for its attainment. The question arises, Which phases of our social structure predispose toward this mode of adjustment? We may examine a concrete instance, effectively analyzed by Lohman (1937), which provides a clue to the answer. Lohman has shown that specialized areas of vice in the near north side of Chicago constitute a "normal" response to a situation where the cultural emphasis upon pecuniary success has been absorbed, but where there is little access to conventional and legitimate means for attaining such success. The conventional occupational opportunities of persons in this area are almost completely limited to manual labor. Given our cultural stigmatization of manual labor, and its correlate, the prestige of white collar work, it is clear that the result is a strain toward innovational practices. The limitation of opportunity to unskilled labor and the resultant low income cannot compete *in terms of conventional standards of achievement* with the high income from organized vice.

For our purposes, this situation involves two important features. First, such antisocial behavior is in a sense "called forth" by certain conventional values of the culture *and* by the class structure involving differential access to the approved opportunities for legitimate, prestige-bearing pursuits of the culture goals. The lack of high integration between the means-and-end elements of the cultural pattern and the particular class structure combine to favor a heightened frequency of antisocial conduct in such groups. The second consideration is of equal significance. Recourse to the first of the alternative responses, legitimate effort, is limited by the fact that actual advance toward desired success-symbols through conventional channels is, despite our persisting open-class ideology,[5] relatively rare and difficult for those handicapped by little formal education and few economic resources. The dominant pressure of group standards of success is, therefore, on the gradual attenuation of legitimate, but by and large ineffective, strivings and the increasing use of illegitimate, but more or less effective, expedients of vice and crime. The cultural demands made on persons in this situation are incompatible. On the one hand, they are asked to orient their conduct toward the prospect of accumulating wealth, and on the other, they are largely denied effective opportunities to do so institutionally. The consequences of such structural inconsistency are psychopathological personality, and/or antisocial conduct, and/or revolutionary activities. The equilibrium between culturally designated means and ends becomes highly unstable with the progressive emphasis on attaining the prestige-laden ends by any means whatsoever. Within this context, Capone represents the triumph of amoral intelligence over morally prescribed "failure," when the channels of vertical mobility are

---

[5] The shifting historical role of this ideology is a profitable subject for exploration. The "office-boy-to-president" stereotype was once in approximate accord with the facts. Such vertical mobility was probably more common then than now, when the class structure is more rigid. The ideology largely persists, however, possibly because it still performs a useful function for maintaining the status quo. For insofar as it is accepted by the "masses," it constitutes a useful sop for those who might rebel against the entire structure, were this consoling hope removed. This ideology now serves to lessen the probability of Adaptation V. In short, the role of this notion has changed from that of an approximately valid empirical theorem to that of an ideology, in Mannheim's sense.

closed or narrowed *in a society which places a high premium on economic affluence and social ascent for all its members.*

The last qualification is of primary importance. It suggests that other phases of the social structure besides the extreme emphasis on pecuniary success must be considered if we are to understand the social sources of antisocial behavior. A high frequency of deviate behavior is not generated simply by "lack of opportunity" or by this exaggerated pecuniary emphasis. A comparatively rigidified class structure, a feudalistic or caste order, may limit such opportunities far beyond the point which obtains in our society today. It is only when a system of cultural values extols, virtually above all else, certain *common* symbols of success *for the population at large* while its social structure rigorously restricts or completely eliminates access to approved modes of acquiring these symbols *for a considerable part of the same population* that antisocial behavior ensues on a considerable scale. In other words, our egalitarian ideology denies by implication the existence of noncompeting groups and individuals in the pursuit of pecuniary success. The same body of success-symbols is held to be desirable for all. These goals are held to *transcend class lines,* not to be bounded by them, yet the actual social organization is such that there exist class differentials in the accessibility of these *common* success-symbols. Frustration and thwarted aspiration lead to the search for avenues of escape from a culturally induced intolerable situation; or unrelieved ambition may eventuate in illicit attempts to acquire the dominant values. The American stress on pecuniary success and ambitiousness for all thus invites exaggerated anxieties, hostilities, neuroses, and antisocial behavior.

This theoretical analysis may go far toward explaining the varying correlations between crime and poverty. Poverty is not an isolated variable. It is one in a complex of interdependent social and cultural variables. When viewed in such a context, it represents quite different states of affairs. Poverty as such, and consequent limitation of opportunity, are not sufficient to induce a conspicuously high rate of criminal behavior. Even the often mentioned "poverty in the midst of plenty" will not necessarily lead to this result. Only insofar as poverty and associated disadvantages in competition for the culture values approved for *all* members of the society are linked with the assimilation of a cultural emphasis on monetary accumulation as a symbol of success is antisocial conduct a "normal" outcome. Thus, poverty is less highly correlated with crime in southeastern Europe than in the United States. The possibilities of vertical mobility in these European areas would seem to be fewer than in this country, so that neither poverty per se nor its association with limited opportunity is sufficient to account for the varying correlations. It is only when the full configuration is considered, poverty, limited opportunity, and a commonly shared system of success symbols, that we can explain the higher association between poverty and crime in our society than in others where rigidified class structure is coupled with *differential class symbols of achievement.*

In societies such as our own, then, the pressure of prestige-bearing success tends to eliminate the effective social constraint over means employed to this end. "The-end-justifies-the-means" doctrine becomes a guiding tenet for action when the cultural structure unduly exalts the end and the social organization unduly limits possible recourse to approved means.

REFERENCE

Lohman, Joseph D. 1937. "The Participant Observer in Community Studies," *American Sociological Review* 2:890–98.

Anomie and Corporate Deviance

Nikos Passas

Although large corporations "may have other goals, such as the increase or maintenance of corporate power and prestige, along with corporate growth and stability, their paramount objectives are the *maximization of profits* and the general financial success of the corporation . . . " (Clinard 1983:18, emphasis added). So, it is not only that profits have to be made: the target is maximum possible profits.

Multiple and contradictory as organizational ends may often be, the goal of profit cannot be overlooked. Moreover, this goal may have to be attained *by all means,* particularly when the continuation of the corporation is at stake (cf. Scherer 1980:38; Box 1983:35).

Uncertainty, competition, technological improvements adding to the efficiency of other more powerful firms, and pursuit of parallel goals render the task formidable. In addition, anti-trust and other legislations disallow certain maneuvers. The state has been increasingly intervening by stipulating acceptable standards by which legitimate economic objectives should be pursued (Carson 1975:225) and official attitudes towards the regulation of the upper-world are recently changing (Levi 1987:15). As a result, the legally prescribed channels leading to the realization of corporate objectives are relatively restricted. The employment of deviant methods, therefore, may be the only possible way of dealing with problematic situations, or may be perceived as such.

Finney and Lesieur's conclusion, that "organizations . . . *commit crimes to achieve their objectives and solve their problems* and that commitment

to deviant courses of action involves normal processes of decision making under conditions of limited rationality" (Finney and Lesieur 1982:289; emphasis added), suggests that corporate deviance can be described in terms of organizational "innovation" (in the Mertonian sense). Box has also argued that, being a "goal-seeking entity" makes a corporation "inherently criminogenic, for it necessarily operates in an uncertain and unpredictable environment such that its purely *legitimate opportunities for goal achievement are sometimes limited and constrained*" (Box 1983:35, emphasis added). In these cases, there is a strain towards innovative solutions, ranging from acceptable practices to illegal "innovation" (cf. Box 1983:36).

The continuing uncovering of often planned and dangerous corporate illegalities in various industries indicates that they are, in fact, anything but rare (most presidents of the thousand top North-American manufacturing firms have supported this view) (cf. Green 1972:149–150 and 472). A study of a large number of trade violations has further indicated that they are related to the environmental scarcity of resources (Staw and Szwajkowski 1975). This highlights the fact that the pursuit of money (whether it represents a means or a goal in itself), can be regarded—in abstract—as a goal, the over-commitment to which is responsible for many a deviant act.

Under combined pressures, highly placed individuals may perpetrate offenses in their firm's interest. According to Gross, "persons who will engage in crime on behalf of the organization will most likely be . . . its top people" (Gross 1978:71). None the less, a large proportion of corporate deviance is actually committed by middle-range officials, and results from pressures from the top. That is, personal ambitions of those at the top as

From *Contemporary Crises* 14 (1990):157–178. Reprinted by permission of Kluwer Academic Publishers, © 1990.

well as organizational demands may create internal pressures on those less highly located, possibly independently from external pressures. A possible reaction of those in the middle, who strive for upward mobility within the corporation, is to break ethical and legal rules. Thus, Gross' argument that people violate the law, "should it seem to be required in order to enable the organization to attain its goals, to prosper, or, minimally, to survive" (Gross 1978:72), may be applied both to those at the top and to those who aspire to get there.

Upon a review of several studies, Box has argued that it is not only or simply that subordinates receive "offers they can't refuse," but that "corporate officials are frequently placed in a position where they are required to choose between impairing their career chances or being a loyal organizational person" (Box 1983:42). Under these circumstances, either because of fear to lose their jobs or because of a strong desire to "get ahead," the recipients of such pressures are likely to do "the dirty work." This is congruent with evidence cited by Box (1983:42–43).

In addition, here are the words of a cashier who broke the law without informing his superiors: "There is no doubt that I juggled the books, but I was under orders to balance the books *no matter what means*" (quoted in Cressey 1953:63, emphasis added). Among the details of a fraud known as the "Equity Funding Case" in the USA, which "resulted in losses estimated at $2 billion, the victims being the company's insurance customers," Clinard and his colleagues have reported that,

> *At company direction,* one computer specialist created fictitious insurance policies with a value of $430 million, with yearly premiums totalling $5.5 million. (Clinard et al. 1979:15, emphasis added)

A pharmaceutical executive has pointed out that, if a lower level executive goes to the president to consult him about the solution of a problem, and the president says,

> "Look, it's your concern to get around this problem the best way you can. *I don't want to know how you*

do it, but just get the job done," then the lower level executive will go and bend the rules. (Quoted in Braithwaite [1984], 1986:322, emphasis added)

As has been observed, sometimes

> *. . . goals are set too high or are simply unreasonable.* Then, an employee often confronts a hard choice— to risk being branded *incompetent* by telling superiors that they ask too much, *or to begin taking unethical or illegal shortcuts.* (Getschow 1979:1, emphasis added)

Clinard's survey has revealed that "middle management was clearly of the opinion that the very nature of top management's position and its actual behavior is largely responsible for unethical or illegal corporate behavior" and that it "sets the ethical tone of the corporation" (Clinard 1983:71, 89). According to Clinard's respondents, middle management works under many pressures, the most important being pressures to show profits and to keep costs in line, time pressures, and production and sales quotas (Clinard 1983:91). 90.6 percent of the executives said that "they felt such pressures do lead to unethical behavior within a corporation" (Clinard 1983:95). In brief, Clinard's subjects believed that, although external forces are not negligible, internal pressures, individual ethics and personal ambitions contribute greatly to corporate deviance.

Much of corporate deviance can be described as "non-conformity," in the sense that breach of legal norms constitutes, at the same time, behavior conforming to standards and procedures prevalent in the corporate world. Such standards may emerge out of efforts to deal with problematic situations and structurally generated strains. They may be further promoted and maintained, however, through processes of interaction leading to widespread rationalizations, which "excuse" or even "legitimize" illegal practices.

Rationalizations and systematized beliefs about the "business-like" way of dealing with things may come together and form deviant subcultures. While such subcultures or "ideologies" may come into existence—within a corporation or, more generally, among businesspeople—as a result of structural strains, they are also transmitted "as a generalization by phrases such as 'we are not in business for our health,' 'business is business,' or 'no business was ever built on the beatitudes'" (Sutherland [1949], 1961:240). As a consequence, their respect for, and commitment to, the law (or, more accurately, particular laws) is decreased. Anomic trends may then ensue, as the use of profitable and effective but illegal techniques becomes widespread and conveys the impression that successful business and law are sometimes imcompatible.

Business represents a legitimate activity and, to be sure, benefits society in many ways. But, when the cliché "business is business" is uttered in defense of law violations, the lines between what is legitimate and what is illegitimate get fuzzy. In anomic situations, offenders are in a better position to neutralize or rationalize their acts, and at the same time preserve their self-esteem. With weakened support for lawful behavior, considerations of cost and profit take precedence over others.

Sutherland has pointed out that, while perpetrators of "white-collar crime" do not see themselves as "conforming to the stereotype of 'criminal,' they do customarily think of themselves as 'law violators'" (Sutherland [1949], 1961:223). This is confirmed by a high-rank official of a distilling company, whose comment also indicates the degree of anomie and disrespect for legal standards: "We break the laws every day. *If you think I go to bed at night worrying about it, you're crazy. Everybody breaks the law*. The liquor laws are insane anyway" (quoted in Denzin 1977:919, emphasis added). The development of such attitudes intensifies existing anomic trends, and illegalities are perceived as an often indispensable part of the ordinary way of going about business. Once the degree of anomie has become comparatively acute, deviant acts may be committed even in absence of particular problems or pressures: "Carried to the extreme," Vaughan has remarked, "norm erosion might become so extensive within an organization that unlawful conduct occurs *regardless of resource scarcity*" (Vaughan [1983], 1985:61, emphasis added).

The anomic climate may be illustrated by some practices of large corporations, the complexity of which makes it difficult or impossible to identify concrete individuals as liable for corporate offenses. Corporate deviance, then, may be either directly or indirectly traceable to corporate élites. That is, deviance may be an *intended* or *unintended* consequence of the pursuit of high goals, as the responsibility for their achievement has been delegated to subordinates, who might bend the rules without informing the top officials (cf. Ermann and Lundman 1982:10–11). Furthermore, in big companies, as in all bureaucratic structures, the implementation of decisions involves several stages, tasks are fragmented and delegated to many different units, and people are separated from the ultimate consequences of their actions. In such criminogenic situations (Gross 1978; Jackal 1980), there may exist a long distance between the "criminal act" and the "criminal mind" (Braithwaite [1984], 1986:308). This, however, does not mean that corporate officials are unaware of the fact that illegal acts are being committed. Instead of establishing procedures and controls in order to prevent them, some companies not only tolerate them, but create a special post for a person to be blamed, in case serious offenses are discovered. It has been reported that the position of "vice-president responsible for going to jail" has existed in some companies, where

> Lines of accountability had been drawn in the organization such that if there were a problem and someone's head had to go on the chopping block, it would be that of the "vice-president responsible for going to jail." (Braithwaite [1984], 1986:308)

CONCLUSION

The processes leading to deviance, anomie and further deviance can be "thought," schematically, as follows: structurally induced problems and strains make for deviance; when situations calling for problem-solving departures from institutional norms persist, social interactions foster the development of deviant but effective patterns of action, along with (subcultural) rationalizations "justifying" them. Given the existence and "legitimation" of such practices, more of them can occur even in absence of any compelling pressures. Such interactions amplifying deviance could be disrupted and minimized through mechanisms of social control. Additional contradictions, however, leading to a relative immunity of upper-class individuals and legitimate corporations, sustain and perpetuate such an anomic climate affecting (at least, potentially) the whole society.

Corporate deviance is seen as a product of existing cultural, structural and economic demands and arrangements. Ironically, the forces enabling technological achievements, economic development, prosperity and growth are simultaneously conditions conducive to the commitment of harmful and, sometimes, frightful deviant acts. Highly valued objectives are frequently attained at the expense of other rightly cherished values and life-standards. Cases, such as illegal dumping of toxic and nuclear waste and pollution of the environment with disastrous short- and long-term effects, industrial accidents due to nonobservance of safety regulations, non-withdrawal of dangerous pharmaceutical products from the market, consumer frauds undermining public health, computer-related offenses, economic frauds upsetting the economic life, are regularly reported in the mass media, but represent only the tip of a multiply hazardous iceberg.

The fact that upper-world and corporate deviance is not always labelled and punished as criminal does not stop it from being economically and socially undesirable and costly. It is in view of these facts that official statistics and research showing higher rates of crime among the lower classes have to be considered (e.g., Braithwaite 1981). Data relative to what is labelled by the authorities as *crime* do not reflect rates of serious and consequential *deviant behavior*. We have seen that departures from institutional norms occur in all structural positions. It becomes clear that criminal statistics and research on crime are of limited value, when the object of study is deviance, rather than

an officially selected part of it. That is, the above sources may provide useful information and knowledge about the relationship between social strata and acts prohibited by the law and handled by criminal courts. However, they can do very little by way of highlighting the relationship between social strata and socially undesirable and harmful departures from institutional rules and norms. If their importance and significance is to be gauged by the social and economic cost to the society, the deviance of the powerful (however defined officially) is more dangerous and disquieting, as the rising levels of public sensitivity also testify. This is not to underplay the significance of predatory street-crime. It does represent a grave social problem and it has to be "fought against" (Wilson 1975; Lea and Young 1984; Kinsey et al. 1986). It appears, however, exaggerated to argue that it constitutes *the* crime problem and that it is "a far more serious matter than consumer fraud, anti-trust violations, etc." (Wilson 1975:xx). Because, meaningful humane communities are jeopardised also by such offenses: a study of "over 1,000 individuals found that more than 60 percent of those sampled felt that they were consistently being sold shoddy products and had little or no faith in the marketplace. They felt that no one really cared about the consuming public" (Bequai 1978:12).

From the preceding analysis it follows that corporate deviance *is* a very serious social problem. In spite of difficulties in controlling it effectively and the high costs of control itself to the society, our priorities may have to be re-evaluated. One has to pose and try to answer the pressing questions: what are the acceptable limits of tolerance? What means of control can be implemented (cf., for example, Braithwaite 1982 and [1984], 1986: chapter 9)? What are the available functional alternatives (i.e., realization of the prevailing cultural goals by means of alternative strategies)? What structural alternatives (radical re-shaping of existing structural and economic arrangements and revision of some of the cultural goals themselves, given the exorbitant price we have to pay for them) could be worked out realistically?

REFERENCES

Bequai, A. 1978. *White-Collar Crime: A Twentieth Century Crisis.* Lexington and Toronto: D.C. Heath.

Box, S. 1983. *Ideology, Crime and Mystification.* London and New York: Tavistock.

Braithwaite, J. 1981. "The Myth of Social Class and Criminality Reconsidered." *American Sociological Review* 46:36–57.

Braithwaite, J. 1982. "Enforced Self-Regulation: A New Strategy for Corporate Crime Control." *Michigan Law Review* 80:1466–1507.

Braithwaite, J. [1984], 1986. *Corporate Crime in the Pharmaceutical Industry.* London: Routledge & Kegan Paul.

Carson, W. G. [1971], 1975. "White-Collar Crime and the Enforcement of Factory Legislation." In W. G. Carson and P. Wiles (eds.), *The Sociology of Crime and Delinquency in Britain.* (London: Martin Robertson. Vol. 1, 220–236.

Clinard, M. B. 1983. *Corporate Ethics and Crime.* London: Sage.

Clinard, M. B., P. C. Yeager, J. Brissette, D. Petrashek and E. Harries. 1979. *Illegal Corporate Behavior.* Washington, D.C.: Law Enforcement Assistance Administration.

Cressey, D. R. 1953. *Other People's Money: A Study in the Social Psychology of Embezzlement.* Glencoe: The Free Press.

Denzin, N. K. 1977. "Notes on the Criminogenic Hypothesis: A Case Study of the American Liquor Industry." *American Sociological Review* 42:905–920.

Ermann, M. D. and R. J. Lundman. 1982. *Corporate Deviance.* New York: Holt, Rinehart & Winston.

Finney, H. C. and H. R. Lesieur. 1982. "A Contingency Theory of Organizational Crime." In S. B. Bacharach (ed.), *Research in the Sociology of Organizations.* Greenwich, CT: JAI Press.

Getschow, G. 1979 "Some Middle Managers Cut Corners to Achieve High Corporate Goals." *The Wall Street Journal*, Nov. 8:1.

Green, M. J. 1972. *The Closed Enterprise System: Ralph Nader's Study Group Report on Antitrust Enforcement.* New York: Grossman.

Gross, E. 1978. "Organisational Crime: A Theoretical Perspective." In N. Denzin (ed.), *Studies in Symbolic Interaction.* Greenwich: JAI Press, 55–85.

Kinsey, R., J. Lea and J. Young. 1986. *Losing the Fight Against Crime.* Oxford: Blackwell.

Lea, J. and J. Young. 1984. *What Is to Be Done about Law and Order?* Harmondsworth: Penguin.

Levi, M. 1987. *Regulating Fraud: White-Collar Crime and the Criminal Process.* London and New York: Tavistock.

Scherer, F. M. 1980. *Industrial Market Structure and Economic Performance.* Chicago: Rand McNally.

Staw, B. M. and E. Szwajkowski. 1975. "The Scarcity-Munificence Component of Organisational Environments and the Commission of Illegal Acts." *Administrative Science Quarterly* 203:345–354.

Sutherland, E. H. [1949], 1961. *White Collar Crime.* New York: Holt, Rinehart and Winston.

Vaughan, E. [1983], 1985. *Controlling Unlawful Organizational Behavior: Social Structure and Corporate Misconduct.* Chicago and London: The University of Chicago Press.

Wilson, J. Q. 1975. *Thinking About Crime.* New York: Vintage.

LEARNING THEORY

READING 2-7

Differential Association Theory

Edwin H. Sutherland

The following statement refers to the process by which a particular person comes to engage in criminal behavior.

1. *Criminal behavior is learned.* Negatively, this means that criminal behavior is not inherited, as such; also, the person who is not already trained in crime does not invent criminal behavior, just as a person does not make mechanical inventions unless he has had training in mechanics.

2. *Criminal behavior is learned in interaction with other persons in a process of communication.* This communication is verbal in many respects but includes also "the communication of gestures."

3. *The principal part of the learning of criminal behavior occurs within intimate personal groups.* Negatively, this means that the impersonal agencies of communication, such as picture shows and newspapers, play a relatively unimportant part in the genesis of criminal behavior.

4. *When criminal behavior is learned, the learning includes (a) techniques of committing the crime, which are sometimes very complicated, sometimes very simple; (b) the specific direction of motives, drives, rationalizations, and attitudes.*

5. *The specific direction of motives and drives is learned from definitions of the legal codes as favorable or unfavorable.* In some societies an individual is surrounded by persons who invariably define the legal codes as rules to be observed, while in others he is surrounded by persons whose definitions are favorable to the violation of the legal codes. In our American society these definitions are almost always mixed and consequently we have culture conflict in relation to the legal codes.

6. *A person becomes delinquent because of an excess of definitions favorable to violation of law over definitions unfavorable to violation of law.* This is the principle of differential association. It refers to both criminal and anti-criminal associations and has to do with counteracting forces. When persons become criminal, they do so because of contacts with criminal patterns and also because of isolation from anti-criminal patterns. Any person inevitably assimilates the surrounding culture unless other patterns are in conflict; a Southerner does not pronounce "r" because other Southerners do not pronounce "r." Negatively, this proposition of differential association means that associations which are neutral so far as crime is concerned have little or no effect on the genesis of criminal behavior. Much of the experience of a person is neutral in this sense, e.g., learning to brush one's teeth. This behavior has no negative or positive effect on criminal behavior except as it may be related to associations which are concerned with the legal codes. This neutral behavior is important especially as an occupier of the time of a child so that he is not in contact with criminal behavior during the time he is so engaged in the neutral behavior.

From Edwin H. Sutherland, *Principles of Criminology,* 4th ed., Chicago: J.B. Lippincott Co., 1947. Reprinted by pemission of Donald R. Cressey Estate.

7. *Differential associations may vary in frequency, duration, priority, and intensity.* This means that associations with criminal behavior and also associations with anti-criminal behavior vary in those respects. "Frequency" and "duration" as modalities of associations are obvious and need no explanation. "Priority" is assumed to be important in the sense that lawful behavior developed in early childhood may persist throughout life, and also that delinquent behavior developed in early childhood may persist throughout life. This tendency, however, has not been adequately demonstrated, and priority seems to be important principally through its selective influence. "Intensity" is not precisely defined but it has to do with such things as the prestige of the source of a criminal or anticriminal pattern and with emotional reactions related to the associations. In a precise description of the criminal behavior of a person these modalities would be stated in quantitative form and a mathematical ratio be reached. A formula in this sense has not been developed and the development of such a formula would be extremely difficult.

8. *The process of learning criminal behavior by association with criminal and anti-criminal patterns involves all of the mechanisms that are involved in any other learning.* Negatively, this means that the learning of criminal behavior is not restricted to the process of imitation. A person who is seduced, for instance, learns criminal behavior by association but this process would not ordinarily be described as imitation.

9. *While criminal behavior is an expression of general needs and values, it is not explained by those general needs and values since non-criminal behavior is an expression of the same needs and values.* Thieves generally steal in order to secure money, but likewise honest laborers work in order to secure money. The attempts by many scholars to explain criminal behavior by general drives and values, such as the happiness principle, striving for social status, the money motive, or frustration, have been and must continue to be futile since they explain lawful behavior as completely as they explain criminal behavior. They are similar to respiration, which is necessary for any behavior but which does not differentiate criminal from non-criminal behavior.

It is not necessary, at this level of explanation, to explain why a person has the associations which he has; this certainly involves a complex of many things. In an area where the delinquency rate is high a boy who is sociable, gregarious, active, and athletic is very likely to come in contact with the other boys in the neighborhood, learn delinquent behavior from them, and become a gangster; in the same neighborhood the psychopathic boy who is isolated, introvert, and inert may remain at home, not become acquainted with the other boys in the neighborhood, and not become delinquent. In another situation, the sociable, athletic, aggressive boy may become a member of a scout troop and not become involved in delinquent behavior. The person's associations are determined in a general context of social organization. A child is ordinarily reared in a family; the place of residence of the family is determined largely by family income; and the delinquency rate is in many respects related to the rental value of the houses. Many other factors enter into this social organization, including many of the small personal group relationships.

The preceding explanation of criminal behavior was stated from the point of view of the person who engages in criminal behavior. It is possible, also, to state theories of criminal behavior from the point of view of the community, nation, or other group. The problem, when thus stated, is generally concerned with crime rates and involves a comparison of the crime rates of various groups or the crime rates of a particular group at different times. One of the best explanations of crime rates from this point of view is that a high crime rate is due to social disorganization. The term "social disorganization" is not entirely satisfactory and it seems preferable to substitute for it the term "differential social organization." The postulate on which this theory is based, regardless of the name, is that crime is rooted in the social organization and is an expression of that social organization. A group may be organized for criminal behavior or organized against criminal behavior. Most communities are organized both for criminal and anti-criminal behavior and in that sense the crime rate is an expression of the differential group organization. Differential group organization as an explanation of a crime rate must be consistent with the explanation of the criminal behavior of the person, since the crime rate is a summary statement of the number of persons in the group who commit crimes and the frequency with which they commit crimes.

Becoming a Marihuana User

Howard S. Becker

The use of marihuana is and has been the focus of a good deal of attention on the part of both scientists and laymen. One of the major problems students of the practice have addressed themselves to has been the identification of those individual psychological traits which differentiate marihuana users from nonusers and which are assumed to account for the use of the drug. That approach, common in the study of behavior categorized as deviant, is based on the premise that the presence of a given kind of behavior in an individual can best be explained as the result of some trait which predisposes or motivates him to engage in the behavior (Marcovitz and Meyers 1944; Gaskill 1945; Charen and Perelman 1946).

This study is likewise concerned with accounting for the presence or absence of marihuana use in an individual's behavior. It starts, however, from a different premise: that the presence of a given kind of behavior is the result of a sequence of social experiences during which the person acquires a conception of the meaning of the behavior, and perceptions and judgments of objects and situations, all of which make the activity possible and desirable. Thus, the motivation or disposition to engage in the activity is built up in the course of learning to engage in it and does not antedate this learning process. For such a view it is not necessary to identify those "traits" which "cause" the behavior. Instead, the problem becomes one of describing the set of changes in the person's conception of the activity and of the experience it provides for him.

Fifty interviews with marihuana users from a variety of social backgrounds and present positions in society constitute the data from which the generalization was constructed and against which it was tested. The interviews focused on the history of the person's experience with the drug, seeking major changes in his attitude toward it and in his actual use of it and the reasons for these changes. The final generalization is a statement of that sequence of changes in attitude which occurred in every case known to me in which the person came to use marihuana for pleasure. Until a negative case is found, it may be considered as an explanation of all cases of marihuana use for pleasure. In addition, changes from use to nonuse are shown to be related to similar changes in conception, and in each case it is possible to explain variations in the individual's behavior in these terms.

From *American Journal of Sociology* 59 (November 1953), pp. 235–242. Reprinted by permission of the University of Chicago Press and the author.

This paper covers only a portion of the natural history of an individual's use of marihuana, starting with the person having arrived at the point of willingness to try marihuana. He knows that others use it to "get high," but he does not know what this means in concrete terms. He is curious about the experience, ignorant of what it may turn out to be, and afraid that it may be more than he has bargained for. The steps outlined below, if he undergoes them all and maintains the attitudes developed in them, leave him willing and able to use the drug for pleasure when the opportunity presents itself.

I

The novice does not ordinarily get high the first time he smokes marihuana, and several attempts are usually necessary to induce this state. One explanation of this may be that the drug is not smoked "properly," that is, in a way that insures sufficient dosage to produce real symptoms of intoxication. Most users agree that it cannot be smoked like tobacco if one is to get high:

> Take in a lot of air, you know, and . . . I don't know how to describe it, you don't smoke it like a cigarette, you draw in a lot of air and get it deep down in your system and then keep it there. Keep it there as long as you can.

Without the use of some such technique the drug will produce no effects, and the user will be unable to get high:

> The trouble with people like that [who are not able to get high] is that they're just not smoking it right, that's all there is to it. Either they're not holding it down long enough, or they're getting too much air and not enough smoke, or the other way around or something like that. A lot of people just don't smoke it right, so naturally nothing's gonna happen.

If nothing happens, it is manifestly impossible for the user to develop a conception of the drug as an object which can be used for pleasure, and use will therefore not continue. The first step in the sequence of events that must occur if the person is to become a user is that he must learn to use the proper smoking technique in order that his use of the drug

will produce some effects in terms of which his conception of it can change.

Such a change is, as might be expected, a result of the individual's participation in groups in which marihuana is used. In them the individual learns the proper way to smoke the drug. This may occur through direct teaching:

> I was smoking like I did an ordinary cigarette. He said, "No, don't do it like that." He said, "Suck it, you know, draw in and hold it in your lungs till you . . . for a period of time."
>
> I said, "Is there any limit of time to hold it?"
>
> He said, "No, just till you feel that you want to let it out, let it out." So I did that three or four times.

Many new users are ashamed to admit ignorance and, pretending to know already, must learn through the more indirect means of observation and imitation:

> I came on like I had turned on [smoked marihuana] many times before, you know. I didn't want to seem like a punk to this cat. See, like I didn't know the first thing about it—how to smoke it, or what was going to happen, or what. I just watched him like a hawk—I didn't take my eyes off him for a second, because I wanted to do everything just as he did it. I watched how he held it, how he smoked it, and everything. Then when he gave it to me I just came on cool, as though I knew exactly what the score was. I held it like he did and took a poke just the way he did.

No person continued marihuana use for pleasure without learning a technique that supplied sufficient dosage for the effects of the drug to appear. Only when this was learned was it possible for a conception of the drug as an object which could be used for pleasure to emerge. Without such a conception marihuana use was considered meaningless and did not continue.

II

Even after he learns the proper smoking technique, the new user may not get high and thus not form a conception of the drug as something which can be used for pleasure. A remark made by a user suggested the reason for this difficulty in getting high and pointed to the next necessary step on the road to being a user:

> I was told during an interview, "As a matter of fact, I've seen a guy who was high out of his mind and didn't know it."
>
> I expressed disbelief: "How can that be, man?"
>
> The interviewee said, "Well, it's pretty strange, I'll grant you that, but I've seen it. This guy got on with me, claiming that he'd never got high, one of those guys, and he got completely stoned. And he kept insisting that he wasn't high. So I had to prove to him that he was."

What does this mean? It suggests that being high consists of two elements: the presence of symptoms caused by marihuana use and the recognition of these symptoms and their connection by the user with his use of the drug. It is not enough, that is, that the effects be present; they alone do not automatically provide the experience of being high. The user must be able to point them out to himself and consciously connect them with his having smoked marihuana before he can have this experience. Otherwise, regardless of the actual effects produced, he considers that the drug has had no effect on him: "I figured it either had no effect on me or other people were exaggerating its effect on them, you know. I thought it was probably psychological, see." Such persons believe that the whole thing is an illusion and that the wish to be high leads the user to deceive himself into believing that something is happening when, in fact, nothing is. They do not continue marihuana use, feeling that "it does nothing" for them.

Typically, however, the novice has faith (developed from his observation of users who do get high) that the drug actually will produce some new experience and continues to experiment with it until it does. His failure to get high worries him, and he is likely to ask more experienced users or provoke comments from them about it. In such conversations he is made aware of specific details of his experience which he may not have noticed or may have noticed but failed to identify as symptoms of being high:

> I didn't get high the first time. . . . I don't think I held it in long enough. I probably let it out, you know,

you're a little afraid. The second time I wasn't sure, and he [smoking companion] told me, like I asked him for some of the symptoms or something, how would I know, you know. . . . So he told me to sit on a stool. I sat on—I think I sat on a bar stool—and he said, "Let your feet hang," and then when I got down my feet were real cold, you know.

> And I started feeling it, you know. That was the first time. And then about a week after that, sometime pretty close to it, I really got on. That was the first time I got on a big laughing kick, you know. Then I really knew I was on.

One symptom of being high is an intense hunger. In the next case the novice becomes aware of this and gets high for the first time:

> They were just laughing the hell out of me because like I was eating so much. I just scoffed [ate] so much food, and they were just laughing at me, you know. Sometimes I'd be looking at them, you know, wondering why they're laughing, you know, not knowing what I was doing. [Well, did they tell you why they were laughing eventually?] Yeah, yeah, I come back, "Hey, man, what's happening?" Like, you know, like I'd ask, "What's happening?" and all of a sudden I feel weird, you know. "Man, you're on, you know. You're on pot [high on marihuana]." I said, "No, am I?" Like I don't know what's happening.

The learning may occur in more indirect ways:

> I heard little remarks that were made by other people. Somebody said, "My legs are rubbery," and I can't remember all the remarks that were made because I was very attentively listening for all these cues for what I was supposed to feel like.

The novice, then, eager to have this feeling, picks up from other users some concrete referents of the term "high" and applies these notions to his own experience. The new concepts make it possible for him to locate these symptoms among his own sensations and to point out to himself a "something different" in his experience that he connects with drug use. It is only when he can do this that he is high. In the next case, the contrast between two successive experiences of a user makes clear the crucial importance of the awareness of the symptoms in being high and re-emphasizes the important role of interaction with other users in acquiring the concepts that make this awareness possible:

> [Did you get high the first time you turned on?] Yeah, sure. Although, come to think of it, I guess I really didn't. I mean, like that first time it was more or less of a mild drunk. I was happy, I guess, you know what I mean. But I didn't really know I was high, you know what I mean. It was only after the second time I got high that I realized I was high the first time. Then I knew that something different was happening.
>
> [How did you know that?] How did I know? If what happened to me that night would of happened to you, you would've known, believe me. We played the first tune for almost two hours—one tune! Imagine, man! We got on the stand and played this one tune, we started at nine o' clock. When we got finished I looked at my watch, it's a quarter to eleven. Almost two hours on one tune. And it didn't seem like anything.
>
> I mean, you know, it does that to you. It's like you have much more time or something. Anyway, when I saw that, man, it was too much. I knew I must really be high or something if anything like that could happen. See, and then they explained to me that that's what it did to you, you had a different sense of time and everything. So I realized that that's what it was. I knew then. Like the first time, I probably felt that way, you know, but I didn't know what's happening.

It is only when the novice becomes able to get high in this sense that he will continue to use marihuana for pleasure. In every case in which use continued, the user had acquired the necessary concepts with which to express to himself the fact that he was experiencing new sensations caused by the drug. That is, for use to continue, it is necessary not only to use the drug so as to produce effects but also to learn to perceive these effects when they occur. In this way marihuana acquires meaning for the user as an object which can be used for pleasure.

With increasing experience the user develops a greater appreciation of the drug's effects; he continues to learn to get high. He examines succeeding experiences closely, looking for new effects, making sure the old ones are still there. Out of this there grows a stable set of categories for experiencing the drug's effects whose presence enables the user to get high with ease.

The ability to perceive the drug's effects must be maintained if use is to continue; if it is lost, marihuana use ceases. Two kinds of evidence support this statement. First, people who become heavy users of alcohol, barbiturates, or opiates do not continue to smoke marihuana, largely because they lose the ability to distinguish between its effects and those of the other drugs. They no longer know whether the marihuana gets them high. Second, in those few cases in which an individual uses marihuana in such quantities that he is always high, he is apt to get this same feeling that the drug has no effect on him, since the essential element of a noticeable difference between feeling high and feeling normal is missing. In such a situation, use is likely to be given up completely, but temporarily, in order that the user may once again be able to perceive the difference.

III

One more step is necessary if the user who has now learned to get high is to continue use. He must learn to enjoy the effects he has just learned to experience. Marihuana-produced sensations are not automatically or necessarily pleasurable. The taste for such experience is a socially acquired one, not different in kind from acquired tastes for oysters or dry martinis. The user feels dizzy, thirsty; his scalp tingles; he misjudges time and distances; and so on. Are these things pleasurable? He isn't sure. If he is to continue marihuana use, he must decide that they are. Otherwise, getting high, while a real enough experience, will be an unpleasant one he would rather avoid.

The effects of the drug, when first perceived, may be physically unpleasant or at least ambiguous:

> It started taking effect, and I didn't know what was happening, you know, what it was, and I was very sick. I walked around the room, walking around the room trying to get off, you know; it just scared me at first, you know. I wasn't used to that kind of feeling.

In addition, the novice's naïve interpretation of what is happening to him may further confuse and frighten him, particularly if he decides, as many do, that he is going insane:

> I felt I was insane, you know. Everything people done to me just wigged me. I couldn't hold a conversation, and my mind would be wandering, and I was always thinking, oh, I don't know, weird things, like hearing music different. . . . I get the feeling that I can't talk to anyone. I'll goof completely.

Given these typically frightening and unpleasant first experiences, the beginner will not continue use unless he learns to redefine the sensations as pleasurable:

> It was offered to me, and I tried it. I'll tell you one thing. I never did enjoy it at all. I mean it was just nothing that I could enjoy. [Well, did you get high when you turned on?] Oh, yeah, I got definite feelings from it. But I didn't enjoy them. I mean I got plenty of reactions, but they were mostly reactions of fear. [You were frightened?] Yes, I didn't enjoy it. I couldn't seem to relax with it, you know. If you can't relax with a thing, you can't enjoy it, I don't think.

In other cases the first experiences were also definitely unpleasant, but the person did become a marihuana user. This occurred, however, only after a later experience enabled him to redefine the sensations as pleasurable:

> [This man's first experience was extremely unpleasant, involving distortion of spatial relationships and sounds, violent thirst, and panic produced by these symptoms.] After the first time I didn't turn on for about, I'd say, ten months to a year. . . . It wasn't a moral thing; it was because I'd gotten so frightened, bein' so high. An' I didn't want to go through that again, I mean, my reaction was, "Well, if this is what they call bein' high, I don't dig [like] it." . . . So I didn't turn on for a year almost, accounta that. . . .
>
> Well, my friends started, an' consequently I started again. But I didn't have any more, I didn't have that same initial reaction, after I started turning on again.
>
> [In interaction with his friends he became able to find pleasure in the effects of the drug and eventually became a regular user.]

In no case will use continue without such a redefinition of the effects as enjoyable.

This redefinition occurs, typically, in interaction with more experienced users who, in a number of ways, teach the novice to find pleasure in this experience which is at first so frightening (Charen and Perelman 1946). They may reassure him as to the temporary character of the unpleasant sensations and minimize their seriousness, at the same time calling attention to the more enjoyable aspects. An experienced user describes how he handles newcomers to marihuana use:

> Well, they get pretty high sometimes. The average person isn't ready for that, and it is a little frightening to them sometimes. I mean, they've been high on lush [alcohol], and they get higher that way than they've ever been before, and they don't know what's happening to them. Because they think they're going to keep going up, up, up till they lose their minds or begin doing weird things or something. You have to like reassure them, explain to them that they're not really flipping or anything, that they're gonna be all right. You have to just talk them out of being afraid. Keep talking to them, reassuring, telling them it's all right. And come on with your own story, you know: "The same thing happened to me. You'll get to like that after awhile." Keep coming on like that; pretty soon you talk them out of being scared. And besides they see you doing it and nothing horrible is happening to you, so that gives them more confidence.

The more experienced user may also teach the novice to regulate the amount he smokes more carefully, so as to avoid any severely uncomfortable symptoms while retaining the pleasant ones. Finally, he teaches the new user that he can "get to like it after awhile." He teaches him to regard those ambiguous experiences formerly defined as unpleasant as enjoyable. The older user in the following incident is a person whose tastes have shifted in this way, and his remarks have the effect of helping others to make a similar redefinition:

> A new user had her first experience of the effects of marihuana and became frightened and hysterical. She "felt like she was half in and half out of the room" and experienced a number of alarming physical symptoms. One of the more experienced users

present said, "She's dragged because she's high like that. I'd give anything to get that high myself. I haven't been that high in years."

In short, what was once frightening and distasteful becomes, after a taste for it is built up, pleasant, desired, and sought after. Enjoyment is introduced by the favorable definition of the experience that one acquires from others. Without this, use will not continue, for marihuana will not be for the user an object he can use for pleasure.

In addition to being a necessary step in becoming a user, this represents an important condition for continued use. It is quite common for experienced users suddenly to have an unpleasant or frightening experience, which they cannot define as pleasurable, either because they have used a larger amount of marihuana than usual or because it turns out to be a higher-quality marihuana than they expected. The user has sensations which go beyond any conception he has of what being high is and is in much the same situation as the novice, uncomfortable and frightened. He may blame it on an overdose and simply be more careful in the future. But he may make this the occasion for a rethinking of his attitude toward the drug and decide that it no longer can give him pleasure. When this occurs and is not followed by a redefinition of the drug as capable of producing pleasure, use will cease.

The likelihood of such a redefinition occurring depends on the degree of the individual's participation with other users. Where this participation is intensive, the individual is quickly talked out of his feeling against marihuana use. In the next case, on the other hand, the experience was very disturbing, and the aftermath of the incident cut the person's participation with other users to almost zero. Use stopped for three years and began again only when a combination of circumstances, important among which was a resumption of ties with users, made possible a redefinition of the nature of the drug:

It was too much, like I only made about four pokes, and I couldn't even get it out of my mouth, I was so high, and I got real flipped. In the basement, you know, I just couldn't stay in there anymore. My heart was pounding real hard, you know, and I was going out of my mind; I thought I was losing my mind completely. So I cut out of this basement, and this other guy, he's out of his mind, told me, "Don't, don't leave me, man. Stay here." And I couldn't.

I walked outside, and it was five below zero, and I thought I was dying, and I had my coat open; I was sweating, I was perspiring. My whole insides were all . . . , and I walked about two blocks away, and I fainted behind a bush. I don't know how long I laid there. I woke up, and I was feeling the worst, I can't describe it at all, so I made it to a bowling alley, man, and I was trying to act normal, I was trying to shoot pool, you know, trying to act real normal, and I couldn't lay and I couldn't stand up and I couldn't sit down, and I went up and laid down where some guys that spot pins lay down, and that didn't help me, and I went down to a doctor's office. I was going to go in there and tell the doctor to put me out of my misery . . . because my heart was pounding so hard, you know. . . . So then all week end I started flipping, seeing things there and going through hell, you know, all kinds of abnormal things. . . . I just quit for a long time then.

[He went to a doctor who defined the symptoms for him as those of a nervous breakdown caused by "nerves" and "worries." Although he was no longer using marihuana, he had some recurrences of the symptoms which led him to suspect that "it was all his nerves."] So I just stopped worrying, you know; so it was about thirty-six months later I started making it again. I'd just take a few pokes, you know. [He first resumed use in the company of the same user-friend with whom he had been involved in the original incident.]

A person, then, cannot begin to use marihuana for pleasure, or continue its use for pleasure, unless he learns to define its effects as enjoyable, unless it becomes and remains an object which he conceives of as capable of producing pleasure.

IV

In summary, an individual will be able to use marihuana for pleasure only when he goes through a process of learning to conceive of it as an object which can be used in this way. No one becomes a user without (1) learning to smoke the drug in a way which will produce real effects; (2) learning to recognize the effects and connect them with drug use (learning, in other words, to get high); and (3) learning to enjoy the sensations he perceives. In the course of this process he develops a disposition or motivation to use marihuana which was not and could not have been present when he began use, for it involves and depends on conceptions of the drug which could only grow out of the kind of actual experience detailed above. On completion of this process he is willing and able to use marihuana for pleasure.

He has learned, in short, to answer "Yes" to the question: "Is it fun?" The direction his further use of the drug takes depends on his being able to continue to answer "Yes" to this question and, in addition, on his being able to answer "Yes" to other questions which arise as he becomes aware of the implications of the fact that the society as a whole disapproves of the practice: "Is it expedient?" "Is it moral?" Once he has acquired the ability to get enjoyment out of the drug, use will continue to be possible for him. Considerations of morality and expediency, occasioned by the reactions of society, may interfere and inhibit use, but use continues to be a possibility in terms of his conception of the drug. The act becomes impossible only when the ability to enjoy the experience of being high is lost, through a change in the user's conception of the drug occasioned by certain kinds of experience with it.

In comparing this theory with those which ascribe marihuana use to motives or predispositions rooted deep in individual behavior, the evidence makes it clear that marihuana use for pleasure can occur only when the process described above is undergone and cannot occur without it. This is apparently so without reference to the nature of the individual's personal makeup or psychic problems.

Such theories assume that people have stable modes of response which predetermine the way they will act in relation to any particular situation or object and that, when they come in contact with the given object or situation, they act in the way in which their makeup predisposes them.

This analysis of the genesis of marihuana use shows that the individuals who come in contact with a given object may respond to it at first in a great variety of ways. If a stable form of new behavior toward the object is to emerge, a transformation of meanings must occur, in which the person develops a new conception of the nature of the object (Strauss 1952). This happens in a series of communicative acts in which others point out new aspects of his experience to him, present him with new interpretations of events, and help him achieve a new conceptual organization of his world, without which the new behavior is not possible. Persons who do not achieve the proper kind of conceptualization are unable to engage in the given behavior and turn off in the direction of some other relationship to the object or activity.

REFERENCES

Charen, Sol, and Luis Perelman. 1946. "Personality Studies of Marihuana Addicts." *American Journal of Psychiatry* 102:674–82.

Gaskill, Herbert S. 1945. "Marihuana, an Intoxicant." *American Journal of Psychiatry* 102:202–4.

Marcovitz, Eli, and Henry J. Meyers. 1944. "The Marihuana Addict in the Army." *War Medicine,* 6:382–91.

Strauss, Anselm. 1952. "The Development and Transformation of Monetary Meanings in the Child." *American Sociological Review* 17:275–86.

READING 2-9

The Training of House Prostitutes

Barbara Sherman Heyl

Although the day of the elaborate and conspicuous high-class house of prostitution is gone, houses still operate throughout the United States in a variety of altered forms. The business may be run out of trailers and motels along major highways, luxury apartments in the center of a metropolis or run-down houses in smaller, industrialized cities. Madams sometimes find themselves teaching young women how to become professional prostitutes. This paper focuses on one madam who trains novices to work at the house level. I compare the training to Bryan's (1965) account of the apprenticeship of call girls and relate the madam's role to the social organization of house prostitution.

Bryan's study of thirty-three Los Angeles call girls is one of the earliest interactionist treatments of prostitution. His data focus on the process of entry into the occupation of call girl and permit an analysis of the structure and content of a woman's apprenticeship. He concluded that the apprenticeship of call girls is mainly directed toward developing a clientele, rather than sexual skills (1965:288, 296–7). But while Bryan notes that pimps seldom train women directly, approximately half of his field evidence in fact derives from pimp-call girl apprenticeships. Thus, in Bryan's study (as well as in subsequent work on entry into prostitution as an occupation) there is a missing set of data on the more typical female trainer-trainee relationship and on the content and process of training at other levels of the business in nonmetropolitan settings. This paper attempts to fill this gap.

From *Social Problems* 24, No. 5 (June 1977), 539–55. Reprinted by permission of the University of California Press and the author. ©1977 by the Society for the Study of Social Problems.

ANN'S TURN-OUT ESTABLISHMENT

A professional prostitute, whether she works as a streetwalker, house prostitute, or call girl, can usually pick out one person in her past who "turned her out," that is, who taught her the basic techniques and rules of the prostitute's occupation. For women who begin working at the house level, that person may be a pimp, another "working girl," or a madam. Most madams and managers of prostitution establishments, however, prefer not to take on novice prostitutes, and they may even have a specific policy against hiring turn-outs (see Erwin [1960:204–5] and Lewis [1942:222]). The turn-out's inexperience may cost the madam clients and money; to train the novice, on the other hand, costs her time and energy. Most madams and managers simply do not want the additional burden.

It was precisely the madam's typical disdain for turn-outs that led to the emergence of the house discussed in this paper—a house specifically devoted to training new prostitutes. The madam of this operation, whom we shall call Ann, is forty-one years old and has been in the prostitution world twenty-three years, working primarily at the house level. Ann knew that pimps who manage women at this level have difficulty placing novices in houses. After operating several houses staffed by professional prostitutes, she decided to run a school for turn-outs partly as a strategy for acquiring a continually changing staff of young women for her house. Pimps are the active recruiters of new prostitutes, and Ann found that, upon demonstrating that she could transform the pimps' new, square women into trained prostitutes easily placed in professional houses, pimps would help keep her business staffed. Ann's house is a small operation in a middle-sized, industrial city (population 300,000), with a limited clientele of primarily working-class men retained as customers for ten to fifteen years and offered low rates to maintain their patronage.

Although Ann insists that every turn-out is different, her group of novices is remarkably homogeneous in some ways. Ann has turned out approximately twenty women a year over the six years while she has operated a training school. Exept for one Chicano, one black and one American Indian, the women were all white. They ranged in age from eighteen to twenty seven. Until three years ago, all the women she hired had pimps. Since then, more women are independent (so-called "outlaws"), although many come to Ann sponsored by a pimp. That is, in return for being placed with Ann, the turn-out gives the pimp a percentage of her earnings for a specific length of time. At present eighty percent of the turn-outs come to Ann without a long-term commitment to a pimp. The turn-outs stay at Ann's on the average of two to three months. This is the same average length of time Bryan (1965:290) finds for the apprenticeship in his callgirl study. Ann seldom has more than two or three women in training at any one time. Most turn-outs live at the house, often just a large apartment near the older business section of the city.

THE CONTENT OF THE TRAINING

The data for the following analysis are of three kinds. First, tape recordings from actual training sessions with fourteen novices helped specify the structure and content of the training provided. Second, lengthy interviews with three of the novices and multiple interviews with Ann were conducted to obtain data on the training during the novice's first few days at the house before the first group training sessions were conducted and recorded by Ann. And third, visits to the house on ten occasions and observations of Ann's interaction with the novices during teaching periods extended the data on training techniques used and the relationship between madam and novice. In addition, weekly contact with Ann over a four-year period allowed repeated review of current problems and strategies in training turn-outs.

Ann's training of the novice begins soon after the woman arrives at the house. The woman first chooses an alias. Ann then asks her whether she has ever "Frenched a guy all the way," that is, whether she has brought a man to orgasm during the act of fellatio. Few of the women say they have. By admitting her lack of competence in a specialized area, the novice has permitted Ann to assume the role of teacher. Ann then launches into instruction on performing fellatio. Such instruction is important to her business. Approximately eighty percent of her customers are what Ann calls "French tricks." Many men visit prostitutes to receive sexual services, including fellatio, their wives or lovers seldom perform. This may be particularly true of the lower- and working-class clientele of the houses and hotels of prostitution (Gagnon and Simon 1973:230). Yet the request for fellatio may come from clients at all social levels; consequently, it is a sexual skill today's prostitute must possess and one she may not have prior to entry into the business (Bryan 1965:293; Winick and Kinsie 1971:180, 207; Gray 1973:413).

Although Ann devotes much more time to teaching the physical and psychological techniques of performing fellatio than she does to any other sexual skill, she also provides strategies for coitus and giving a "half and half"—fellatio followed by coitus. The sexual strategies taught are frequently a mixture of ways for stimulating the client sexually and techniques of self-protection during the sexual acts. For example, during coitus, the woman is to move her hips "like a go-go dancer's" while keeping her feet on the bed and tightening her inner thigh muscles to protect herself from the customer's thrust and full penetration. Ann allows turn-outs to perform coitus on their backs only, and the woman is taught to keep one of her arms across her chest as a measure of self-defense in this vulnerable position.

After Ann has described the rudimentary techniques for the three basic sexual acts—fellatio, coitus, and "half and half"—she begins to explain the rules of the house operation. The first set of rules concerns what acts the client may receive for specific sums of money. Time limits are imposed on the clients, roughly at the rate of $1 per minute; the minimum rate in this house is $15 for any of the three basic positions. Ann describes in detail what will occur when the first client arrives: he will be admitted by either Ann or the maid; the women are to stand and smile at him, but not speak to him (considered "dirty hustling"); he will choose one of the women and go to the bedroom with her. Ann accompanies the turn-out and the client to the bedroom and begins teaching the woman how to check the man for any cuts or open sores on the genitals and for any signs of old or active venereal disease. Ann usually rechecks each client herself during the turn-out's first two weeks of work. For the first few days Ann remains in the room while the turn-out and client negotiate the sexual contract. In ensuing days Ann spends time helping the woman develop verbal skills to "hustle" the customer for more expensive sexual activities.

The following analysis of the instruction Ann provides is based on tape recordings made by Ann during actual training sessions in 1971 and 1975. These sessions took place after the turn-outs had worked several days but usually during their first two weeks of work. The tapes contain ten hours of group discussion with fourteen different novices. The teaching tapes were analyzed according to topics covered in the discussions, using the method outlined in Barker (1963) for making such divisions in the flow of conversation and using Bryan's analysis of the call girl's apprenticeship as a guide in grouping the topics. Bryan divides the content of the training of call girls into two broad dimensions, one philosophical and one interpersonal (1965:291–4). The first emphasizes a subcultural value system and sets down guidelines for how the novice *should* treat her clients and her colleagues in the business. The second dimension follows from the first but emphasizes actual behavioral techniques and skills.

The content analysis of the taped training sessions produced three major topics of discussion and revealed the relative amount of time Ann devoted to each. The first two most frequently discussed topics can be categorized under Bryan's dimension of interpersonal skills; they were devoted to teaching situational strategies for managing clients. The third topic resembles Bryan's value dimension (1965:291–2).

The first topic stressed physical skills and strategies. Included in this category were instruction on how to perfrom certain sexual acts and specification of their prices, discussion of particular clients, and instruction in techniques for dealing with certain categories of clients, such as "older men" or "kinky" tricks. This topic of physical skills also included discussion of, and Ann's demonstration of, positions designed to provide the woman maximum comfort and protection from the man during different sexual acts. Defense tactics, such as ways to get out of a sexual position and out of the bedroom quickly, were practiced by the novices. Much time was devoted to analyzing past encounters with particular clients. Bryan finds similar discussions of individual tricks among novice call girls and their trainers (1965:293). In the case of Ann's turn-outs these discussions were often initiated by a novice's complaint or question about a certain client and his requests or behavior in the bedroom. The novice always received tips and advice from Ann and the other women present on how to manage that type of bedroom encounter. Such sharing of tactics allows the turn-out to learn what Gagnon and Simon call "patterns of client management" (1973:231).

Ann typically used these discussions of bedroom difficulties to further the training in specific sexual skills she had begun during the turn-out's first few days at work. It is possible that the addition of such follow-up sexual training to that provided during the turn-out's first days at the house results in a more extensive teaching of actual sexual skills than that obtained either by call girls or streetwalkers. Bryan finds that in the call-girl training—except for fellatio—"There seems to be little instruction concerning sexual techniques as such, even though the previous sexual experience of the trainee may have been quite limited" (1965:293). Gray (1973:413) notes that her sample of streetwalker turn-outs were rarely taught specific work strategies:

> They learned these things by trial and error on the job. Nor were they schooled in specific sexual techniques: usually they were taught by customers who made the specific requests.

House prostitution may require more extensive sexual instruction than other forms of the business. The dissatisfied customer of a house may mean loss of business and therefore loss of income to the madam and the prostitutes who work there. The sexually inept streetwalker or call girl does not hurt business for anyone but herself; she may actually increase business for those women in the area should dissatisfied clients choose to avoid her. But the house depends on a stable clientele of satisfied customers.

The second most frequently discussed topic could be labeled: client management–verbal skills. Ann's primary concern was teaching what she calls "hustling." "Hustling" is similar to what Bryan terms a "sales pitch" for call girls (1965:292), but in the house setting it takes place in the bedroom while the client is deciding how much to spend and what sexual acts he wishes performed. "Hustling" is designed to encourage the client to spend more than the minimum rate.[1] The prominence on the teaching tapes of instruction in this verbal skill shows its importance in Ann's training of novices.

On one of the tapes Ann uses her own turning-out experience to explain to two novices (both with pimps) why she always teaches hustling skills as an integral part of working in a house.

Ann as a Turn-out[2]

Ann: Of course, I can remember a time when I didn't know that I was supposed to hustle. So that's why I understand that it's difficult to *learn* to hustle. When I turned out it was $2 a throw. They came in. They gave me their $2. They got a hell of a fuck.

And that was it. Then one Saturday night I turned *forty four* tricks! And Penny [the madam] used to put the number of tricks at the top of the page and the amount of money at the bottom of the page—she used these big ledger books. Lloyd [Ann's pimp] came in at six o'clock and he looked at that book and he just *knew* I had made all kinds of money. Would you believe I had turned forty-two $2 tricks and two $3 tricks—because two of 'em got generous and gave me an extra buck! [Laughs] I got my ass whipped. And I was so tired—I thought I was going to die—I was 15 years old. And I got my ass whipped for it. [Ann imitates an angry Lloyd:] "Don't you know you're supposed to ask for more money?!" No, I didn't. Nobody told me that. All they told me was it was $2. So that is learning it the *hard* way. I'm trying to help you learn it the *easy* way, if there is an easy way to do it.

In the same session Ann asks one of the turn-outs (Linda, age eighteen) to practice her hustling rap.

Learning the Hustling Rap

Ann: I'm going to be a trick. You've checked me. I want you to carry it from there. [Ann begins role-playing: she plays the client; Linda, the hustler.]
Linda: [mechanically] What kind of party would [you] like to have?
Ann: That had all the enthusiasm of a wet noodle. I really wouldn't *want* any party with that because you evidently don't want to give me one.
Linda: What kind of party would you *like* to have?
Ann: I usually take a half and half.
Linda: Uh, the money?
Ann: What money?
Linda: The money you're supposed to have! [loudly] 'Cause you ain't gettin' it for free!
Ann: [upset] Linda, if you *ever,* ever say that in my joint. . . Because that's fine for street hustling. In street hustling, you're going to *have* to hard-hustle those guys or they're not going to come up with anything. Because they're going to *try* and get it for free. But when they walk in here, they *know* they're not going to get it for free to begin with. So try another tack—just a little more friendly, not

---

[1] The term "hustling" has been used to describe a wide range of small-time criminal activities. Even within the world of prostitution, "hustling" can refer to different occupational styles; see Ross' description of the "hustler" who "is distinguished from ordinary prostitutes in frequently engaging in accessory crimes of exploitation," such as extortion or robbery (1959:16). The use of the term here is thus highly specific, reflecting its meaning in Ann's world.

[2] The sections "Ann as a Turn-out" and "Learning the Hustling Rap" are transcriptions from the teaching tapes. Redundant expressions have been omitted, and the author's comments on the speech tone or delivery are bracketed. Words underlined indicate emphasis by the speaker.

quite so hard-nosed. [Returning to role-playing:] I just take a half and half.

Linda: How about fifteen [dollars]?

Ann: You're leading into the money too fast, honey. Try: "What are you going to spend?" or "How much money are you going to spend?" or something like that.

Linda: How much would you like to spend?

Ann: No! Not "like." 'Cause they don't *like* to spend anything.

Linda: How much *would* you like to spend?

Ann: Make it a very definite, positive statement: "How much are you going to spend?"

Ann considers teaching hustling skills her most difficult and important task. In spite of her lengthy discussion on the tapes of the rules and techniques for dealing with the customer sexually, Ann states that it may take only a few minutes to "show a girl how to turn a trick." A substantially longer period is required, however, to teach her to hustle. To be adept at hustling, the woman must be mentally alert and sensitive to the client's response to what she is saying and doing and be able to act on those perceptions of his reactions. The hustler must maintain a steady patter of verbal coaxing, during which her tone of voice may be more important than her actual words.

In Ann's framework, then, hustling is a form of verbal sexual aggression. Referring to the problems in teaching novices to hustle, Ann notes that "taking the aggressive part is something women are not used to doing; particularly young women." No doubt, hustling is difficult to teach partly because the woman must learn to discuss sexual acts, whereas in her previous experience, sexual behavior and preferences had been negotiated nonverbally (see Gagnon and Simon 1973:228). Ann feels that to be effective, each woman's "hustling rap" must be her own—one that comes naturally and will strike the clients as sincere. All of that takes practice. But Ann is aware that the difficulty in learning to hustle stems more from the fact that it involved inappropriate sex-role behavior. Bryan concludes that it is precisely this aspect of

soliciting men on the telephone that causes the greatest distress to the novice call girl (1965:293). Thus, the call girl's income is affected by how much business she can bring in by her calls, that is, by how well she can learn to be socially aggressive on the telephone. The income of the house prostitute, in turn, depends heavily on her hustling skills in the bedroom. Ann's task, then, is to train the novice, who has recently come from a culture where young women are not expected to be sexually aggressive, to assume that role with a persuasive naturalness.

Following the first two major topics—client management through physical and verbal skills—the teaching of "racket" (prostitution world) values was the third-ranking topic of training and discussion on the teaching tapes. Bryan notes that the major value taught to call girls is "that of maximizing gains and minimizing effort, even if this requires transgressions of either a legal or moral nature" (1965:291). In her training, however, Ann avoids communicating the notion that the novices may exploit the customers in any way they can. For example, stealing or cheating clients is grounds for dismissal from the house. Ann cannot afford the reputation among her tricks that they risk being robbed when they visit her. Moreover, being honest with clients is extolled as a virtue. Thus, Ann urges the novices to tell the trick if she is nervous or unsure, to let him know she is new to the business. This is in direct contradiction to the advice pimps usually give their new women to hide their inexperience from the trick. Ann asserts that honesty in this case usually means that the client will be more tolerant of mistakes in sexual technique, be less likely to interpret hesitancy as coldness, and be generally more helpful and sympathetic. Putting her "basic principle" in the form of a simple directive, Ann declares: "Please the trick, but at the same time get as much money for pleasing him as you possibly can." Ann does not consider hustling to be client exploitation. It is simply the attempt to sell the customer the product with the highest profit margin. That is, she would defend hustling in terms familiar to the businessman or sales manager.

That Ann teaches hustling as a value is revealed in the following discussion between Ann and Sandy—a former hustler and long-time friend of Ann. Sandy, who married a former trick and still lives in town, has come over to the house to help instruct several novices in the hustling business.

Whores, Prostitutes and Hustlers

Ann: [To the turn-outs:] Don't get up-tight that you're hesitating or you're fumbling, within the first week or even the first five years. Because it takes that long to become a good hustler. I mean you can be a whore in one night. There's nothing to that. The first time you take money you're a whore.

Sandy: This girl in Midtown [a small, Midwestern city] informed me—I had been working there awhile—that I was a "whore" and she was a "prostitute." And I said: "Now what the hell does that mean?" Well the difference was that a prostitute could pick her customer and a whore had to take anybody. I said: "Well honey, I want to tell you something. I'm neither one." She said: "Well, you *work*." I said: "I know, but I'm a *hustler*. I make *money* for what I do."

Ann: And this is what I turn out—or try to turn out—hustlers. Not prostitutes. Not whores. But hustlers.

For Ann and Sandy the hustler deserves high status in the prostitution business because she has mastered a specific set of skills that, even with many repeat clients, earn her premiums above the going rate for sexual acts.

In the ideological training of call girls Bryan finds that "values such as fairness with other working girls, or fidelity to a pimp, may occasionally be taught" (1965:291–2); the teaching tapes revealed Ann's affirmation of both these virtues. When a pimp brings a woman to Ann, she supports his control over that woman. For example, if during her stay at the house, the novice breaks any of the basic rules—by using drugs, holding back money (from either Ann or the pimp), lying or seeing another man—Ann will report the infractions to the woman's pimp. Ann notes: "If I don't do that and the pimp finds out, he knows I'm not training her

right, and he won't bring his future ladies to me for training." Ann knows she is dependent on the pimps to help supply her with turn-outs. Bryan, likewise, finds a willingness among call-girls' trainers to defer to the pimps' wishes during the apprenticeship period (1965:290).

Teaching fairness to other prostitutes is particularly relevant to the madam who daily faces the problem of maintaining peace among competing women at work under one roof. If two streetwalkers or two call girls find they cannot get along, they need not work near one another. But if a woman leaves a house because of personal conflicts, the madam loses a source of income. To minimize potential negative feelings among novices, Ann stresses mutual support, prohibits "criticizing another girl," and denigrates the "prima donna"—the prostitute who flaunts her financial success before the other women.

In still another strategy to encourage fair treatment of one's colleagues in the establishment, Ann emphasizes a set of rules prohibiting "dirty hustling"—behavior engaged in by one prostitute that would undercut the business of other women in the house. Tabooed under the label of "dirty hustling" are the following: appearing in the line-up partially unclothed; performing certain disapproved sexual positions, such as anal intercourse; and allowing approved sexual extras without charging additional fees. The norms governing acceptable behavior vary from house to house and region to region, and Ann warns the turn-outs to ask about such rules when they begin work in a new establishment. The woman who breaks the work norms in a house, either knowingly or unknowingly, will draw the anger of the other women and can be fired by a madam eager to restore peace and order in the house.

Other topics considered on the tapes—in addition to physical skills, "hustling" and work values—were instruction on personal hygiene and grooming, role-playing of conversational skills with tricks on topics not related to sex or hustling ("living room talk"), house rules not related to hustling (such as punctuality, no perfume, no drugs), and guidelines for what to do during an arrest. There were specific suggestions on how to handle personal criticism, questions and insults from clients. In addition, the discussions on the tapes provided the novices with many general strategies for becoming "professionals" at their work, for example, the importance of personal style, enthusiasm ("the customer is always right"), and sense of humor. In some ways these guidelines resemble a beginning course in salesmanship. But they also provide clues, particularly in combination with the topics on handling client insults and the emphasis on hustling, on how the house prostitute learns to manage a stable and limited clientele and cope psychologically with the repetition of the clients and the sheer tedium of the physical work (Hughes 1971:342–5).

TRAINING HOUSE PROSTITUTES— A PROCESS OF PROFESSIONAL SOCIALIZATION

Observing how Ann trains turn-outs is a study in techniques to facilitate identity change (see also Davis 1971 and Heyl 1975, chapter 2). Ann uses a variety of persuasive strategies to help give the turn-outs a new occupational identity as a "professional." One strategy is to rely heavily on the new values taught the novice to isolate her from her previous life style and acquaintances. Bryan finds that "the value structure [taught to novice call girls] serves, in general, to create in-group solidarity and to alienate the girl from 'square' society" (1965:292). Whereas alienation from conventional society may be an indirect effect of values taught to call girls, in Ann's training of house prostitutes the expectation that the novice will immerse herself in the prostitution world ("racket life") is made dramatically explicit.

In the following transcription from one of the teaching tapes, the participants are Ann (age thirty-six at the time the tape was made), Bonnie (an experienced turn-out, age twenty-five) and Kristy (a new turn-out, age eighteen). Kristy has recently linked up with a pimp for the first time and volunteers to Ann and Bonnie her difficulty in adjusting to the racket rule of minimal contact with the square world—a rule her pimp is enforcing by not allowing Kristy to meet and talk with her old friends. Ann (A) and Bonnie (B) have listened to Kristy's (K) com-

plaints and are making suggestions. (The notation 'B-K' indicates that Bonnie is addressing Kristy.)

Kristy's Isolation from the Square World

B-K: What you gotta do is sit down and talk to him and weed out your friends and find the ones he thinks are suitable companions for you—in your new type of life.

K-B: None of them.

A-K: What about *his* friends?

K-A: I haven't met very many of his friends. I don't like any of 'em so far.

A-K: You are making the same mistake that makes me so goddamned irritated with square broads! You're taking a man and trying to train *him,* instead of letting the man train you.

K-A: What?! I'm not trying to train him, I'm just. . . .

A-K: All right, you're trying to force him to accept your friends.

K-A: I don't care whether he accepts them or not. I just can't go around not talking to anybody.

A-K: "Anybody" is your old man! He is your world. And the people he says you can talk to are the people that are your world. But what you're trying to do is force your square world on a racket guy. It's like oil and water. There's just no way a square and a racket person can get together. That's why when you turn out you've got to change your mind completely from square to racket. And you're still trying to hang with squares. You can't do it.

Strauss' (1969) concept of "coaching" illuminates a more subtle technique Ann employs as she helps the novice along, step by step, from "square" to "racket" values and life style. She observes carefully how the novice progresses, elicits responses from her about what she is experiencing, and then interprets those responses for her. In the following excerpt from one of the teaching tapes, Ann prepares two novices for feelings of depression over their newly-made decisions to become prostitutes.

Turn-out Blues

Ann: And while I'm on the subject—depression. You know they've got a word for it when you have a baby—it's called "postpartum blues." Now, I call it "turn-out blues." Every girl that ever turns out has 'em. And, depending on the girl, it comes about the third or fourth day. You'll go into a depression for no apparent reason. You'll wake up one morning and you'll say: "Why in the hell am I doing this? Why am I here? I wanna go home!" And I can't do a thing to help you. The only thing I can do is leave you alone and hope that you'll fight the battle yourself. But knowing that it will come and knowing that everybody else goes through it too, does help. Just pray it's a busy night! So if you get blue and you get down, remember: "turn-out blues"—everybody gets it. Here's when you'll decide whether you're going to stay or you're gonna quit.

Ann's description of "turn-out blues" is a good example of Strauss' account (1969:111–2) of how coaches will use prophesy to increase their persuasive power over their novices. In the case of "turn-out blues," the novice, if she becomes depressed about her decision to enter prostitution, will recall Ann's prediction that this would happen and that it happens to all turn-outs. This recollection may or may not end the woman's misgivings about her decision, but it will surely enhance the turn-out's impression of Ann's competence. Ann's use of her past experience to make such predictions is a form of positive leverage; it increases the probability that what she says will be respected and followed in the future.

In Bryan's study the call girls reported that their training was more a matter of observation than direct instruction from their trainer (1965:294). Ann, on the other hand, relies on a variety of teaching techniques, including lecturing and discussion involving other turn-outs who are further along in the training process and can reinforce Ann's views. Ann even brings in guest speakers, such as Sandy, the former hustler, who participates in the discussion with the novices in the role of the experienced resource person. "Learning the Hustling Rap," above, offers an example of role-playing—another teaching technique Ann frequently employs to help the turn-outs develop verbal skills. Ann may have to rely on more varied teaching approaches than the call-girl trainer because: (1) Ann herself is not working, thus her novices have fewer opportunities to watch their trainer interact with clients than do the call-girl novices; and (2) Ann's livelihood depends more directly on the success of her teaching efforts than does that of the call-girl trainer. Ann feels that if a woman under her direction does not "turn out well," not only will the woman earn less money while she is at her house (affecting Ann's own income), but Ann could also lose clients and future turn-outs from her teaching "failure."[3]

The dissolution of the training relationship marks the end of the course. Bryan claims that the sharp break between trainer and trainee shows that the training process itself is largely unrelated to the acquisition of a skill. But one would scarcely have expected the trainee to report "that the final disruption of the apprenticeship was the result of the completion of adequate training" (1965:296). Such establishments do not offer diplomas and terminal degrees. The present study, too, indicates that abrupt breaks in the training relationship are quite common. But what is significant is that the break is precipitated by personal conflicts exacerbated by both the narrowing of the skill-gap between trainer and trainee and the consequent increase in the novice's confidence that she can make it on her own. Thus, skill acquisition counts in such an equation, not in a formal sense ("completion of adequate training"), but rather in so far as it works to break down the earlier bonds of dependence between trainer and trainee.

THE FUNCTION OF TRAINING AT THE HOUSE LEVEL OF PROSTITUTION

Bryan concludes that the training is necessitated by the novice's need for a list of clients in order to work at the call-girl level and not because the actual

---

[3] These data bear only on the skills and values to which Ann *exposes* the turn-outs; confirmation of the effects of such exposure awaits further analysis and is a study in its own right. See Bryan's (1966) study of the impact of the occupational perspective taught by call-girl trainers on the individual attitudes of call girls. See Davis (1971:315) for a description of what constitutes successful "in-service training" for streetwalkers.

training is required to prepare her for such work. But turn-outs at the house level of prostitution do not acquire a clientele. The clients are customers of the house. In fact, the madam usually makes sure that only she has the names or phone numbers of her tricks in order to keep control over her business. If Ann's turn-outs (unlike call girls) do not acquire a clientele in the course of their training, why is the training period necessary?

Although Ann feels strongly that training is required to become a successful hustler at the house level, the function served by the training can be seen more as a spin-off of the structure of the occupation at that level: madams of establishments will often hire only trained prostitutes. Novices who pose as experienced hustlers are fairly easily detected by those proficient in the business working in the same house; to be found out all she need do is violate any of the expected norms of behavior: wear perfume, repeatedly fail to hustle any "over-money" or engage in dirty hustling. The exposure to racket values, which the training provides, may be more critical to the house prostitute than to the call girl. She must live and work in close contact with others in the business. Participants in house prostitution are more integrated into the prostitution world than are call girls, who can be and frequently are "independent"—working without close ties to pimps or other prostitutes. Becoming skilled in hustling is also less important for the call girl, as her minimum fee is usually high, making hustling for small increments less necessary. The house prostitute who does not know how to ask for more money, however, lowers the madam's income as well—another reason why madams prefer professional prostitutes.

The training of house prostitutes, then, reflects two problems in the social organization of house prostitution: (1) most madams will not hire untrained prostitutes; and (2) the close interaction of prostitutes operating within the confines of a house requires a common set of work standards and practices. These two factors differentiate house prostitution from call-girl and streetwalking operations and facilitate this madam's task of turning novices

into professional prostitutes. The teaching madam employs a variety of coaching techniques to train turn-outs in sexual and hustling skills and to expose them to a set of occupational rules and values. Hers is an effort to prepare women with conventional backgrounds for work in the social environment of a house of prostitution where those skills and values are expected and necessary.

REFERENCES

Barker, Roger G. (ed.). 1963. *The Stream of Behavior: Explorations of Its Structure and Content*. New York: Appleton-Century-Crofts.

Bryan, James H. 1965. "Apprenticeships in prostitution." *Social Problems* 12 (Winter):287–97.

———. 1966. "Occupational ideologies and individual attitudes of call girls." *Social Problems* 13 (Spring): 441–50.

Davis, Nanette J. 1971. "The prostitute: Developing a deviant identity." Pp. 297–332 in James M. Henslin (ed.), *Studies in the Sociology of Sex*. New York: Appleton-Century-Crofts.

Erwin, Carol. 1960. *The Orderly Disorderly House*. Garden City, N.Y.: Doubleday.

Gagnon, John H. and William Simon. 1973. *Sexual Conduct: The Social Sources of Human Sexuality*. Chicago: Aldine.

Gray, Diana. 1973. "Turning-out: A study of teenage prostitution." *Urban Life and Culture* 1 (January): 401–25.

Heyl, Barbara S. 1975. "The house prostitute: a case study." Unpublished Ph.D. dissertation, Department of Sociology, University of Illinois–Urbana.

Hughes, Everett C, 1971 "Work and self." Pp. 338–47 in *The Sociological Eye: Selected Papers*. Chicago: Aldine–Atherton.

Lewis, Gladys Adelina (ed.) 1942. *Call House Madam: The Story of the Career of Beverly Davis*. San Francisco: Martin Tudordale.

Ross, H. Laurence. 1959. "The 'Hustler' in Chicago." *Journal of Student Research* 1:13–19.

Strauss, Anselm L. 1969. *Mirrors and Masks: The Search for Identity*. San Francisco: Sociology Press.

Winick, Charles and Paul M. Kinsie. 1971. *The Lively Commerce: Prostitution in the United States*. Chicago: Quadrangle Books.

LABELING THEORY

READING 2-10

Outsiders

Howard S. Becker

[One] sociological view defines deviance as the infraction of some agreed-upon rule. It then goes on to ask who breaks rules, and to search for the factors in their personalities and life situations that might account for the infractions. This assumes that those who have broken a rule constitute a homogeneous category, because they have committed the same deviant act.

Such an assumption seems to me to ignore the central fact about deviance: it is created by society. I do not mean this in the way it is ordinarily understood, in which the causes of deviance are located in the social situation of the deviant or in "social factors" which prompt his action. I mean, rather, that *social groups create deviance by making the rules whose infraction constitutes deviance,* and by applying those rules to particular people and labeling them as outsiders. From this point of view, deviance is *not* a quality of the act the person commits, but rather a consequence of the application by others of rules and sanctions to an "offender." The deviant is one to whom that label has successfully been applied; deviant behavior is behavior that people so label (Tannenbaum 1951; Lement 1951; Kitsuse 1962).

Since deviance is, among other things, a consequence of the responses of others to a person's act, students of deviance cannot assume that they are dealing with a homogeneous category when they study people who have been labeled deviant. That

is, they cannot assume that these people have actually committed a deviant act or broken some rule, because the process of labeling may not be infallible; some people may be labeled deviant who in fact have not broken a rule. Furthermore, they cannot assume that the category of those labeled deviant will contain all those who actually have broken a rule, for many offenders may escape apprehension and thus fail to be included in the population of "deviants" they study. Insofar as the category lacks homogeneity and fails to include all the cases that belong in it, one cannot reasonably expect to find common factors of personality or life situation that will account for the supposed deviance.

What, then, do people who have been labeled deviant have in common? At the least, they share the label and the experience of being labeled as outsiders. I will begin my analysis with this basic similarity and view deviance as the product of a transaction that takes place between some social group and one who is viewed by that group as a rule-breaker. I will be less concerned with the personal and social characteristics of deviants than with the process by which they come to be thought of as outsiders and their reactions to that judgment.

The degree to which other people will respond to a given act as deviant varies greatly. Several kinds of variation seem worth noting. First of all, there is variation over time. A person believed to have committed a given "deviant" act may at one time be responded to much more leniently than he would be at some other time. The occurrence of "drives" against various kinds of deviance illustrates this clearly. At various times, enforcement officials may decide to make an all-out attack on some particular kind of deviance, such as gambling, drug addiction, or homosexuality. It is obviously much more dangerous to engage in one of these activities when a drive is on than at any other time.

The degree to which an act will be treated as deviant depends also on who commits the act and who feels he has been harmed by it. Rules tend to be applied more to some persons than others.

[These observations] support the proposition that deviance is not a simple quality, present in some kinds of behavior and absent in others. Rather, it is the product of a process which involves responses of other people to the behavior. The same behavior may be an infraction of the rules at one time and not at another; may be an infraction when committed by one person, but not when committed by another; some rules are broken with impunity, others are not. In short, whether a given act is deviant or not depends in part on the nature of the act (that is, whether or not it violates some rule) and in part on what other people do about it.

If we take as the object of our attention behavior which comes to be labeled as deviant, we must recognize that we cannot know whether a given act will be categorized as deviant until the response of others has occurred. Deviance is not a quality that lies in behavior itself, but in the interaction between the person who commits an act and those who respond to it.

It is not my purpose here to argue that only acts which are regarded as deviant by others are "really" deviant. But it must be recognized that this is an important dimension, one which needs to be taken into account in any analysis of deviant behavior. By combining this dimension with another—whether or not an act conforms to a particular rule—we can construct the following set of categories for the discrimination of different kinds of deviance.

Two of these types require very little explanation. *Conforming* behavior is simply that which obeys the rule and which others perceive as obeying the rule. At the other extreme, the *pure deviant* type of behavior is that which both disobeys the rule and is perceived as doing so.

TYPES OF DEVIANT BEHAVIOR

	Obedient Behavior	Rule-breaking Behavior
Perceived as deviant	Falsely accused	Pure deviant
Not perceived as deviant	Conforming	Secret deviant

The two other possibilities are of more interest. The *falsely accused* situation is what criminals often refer to as a "bum rap." The person is seen by others as having committed an improper action, although in fact he has not done so. False accusations undoubtedly occur even in courts of law, where the person is protected by rules of due process and evidence. They probably occur much more frequently in nonlegal settings where procedural safeguards are not available.

An even more interesting kind of case is found at the other extreme of *secret deviance*. Here an improper act is committed, yet no one notices it or reacts to it as a violation of the rules. As in the case of false accusation, no one really knows how much of this phenomenon exists, but I am convinced the amount is very sizable, much more so than we are apt to think.

In any case, being caught and branded as deviant has important consequences for one's further social participation and self-image. The most important consequence is a drastic change in the individual's public identity. Committing the improper act and being publicly caught at it place him in a new status. He has been revealed as a different kind of person from the kind he was supposed to be. He is labeled a "fairy," "dope fiend," "nut" or "lunatic," and treated accordingly.

In analyzing the consequences of assuming a deviant identity let us make use of Hughes' distinction between master and auxiliary status traits (Hughes 1945). Hughes notes that most statuses have one key trait which serves to distinguish those who belong from those who do not. Thus the doctor, whatever else he may be, is a person who has a certificate stating that he has fulfilled certain requirements and is licensed to practice medicine; this is the master trait. As Hughes points out, in our society a doctor is also informally expected to have a number of auxiliary traits: most people expect him to be upper middle class, white, male, and Protestant. When he is not there is a sense that he has in some way failed to fill the bill.

The same process occurs in the case of deviant statuses. Possession of one deviant trait may have a generalized symbolic value, so that people automatically assume that its bearer possesses other undesirable traits allegedly associated with it.

To be labeled a criminal one need only commit a single criminal offense, and this is all the term formally refers to. Yet the word carries a number of connotations specifying auxiliary traits characteristic of anyone bearing the label. A man who has been convicted of housebreaking and thereby labeled criminal is presumed to be a person likely to break into other houses; the police, in rounding up known offenders for investigation after a crime has been committed, operate on this premise. Further, he is considered likely to commit other kinds of crimes as well, because he has shown himself to be a person without "respect for the law." Thus, apprehension for one deviant act exposes a person to the likelihood that he will be regarded as deviant or undesirable in other respects.

There is one other element in Hughes' analysis we can borrow with profit: the distinction between master and subordinate statuses. Some statuses, in our society as in others, override all other statuses and have a certain priority (Hughes 1945). The status of deviant (depending on the kind of deviance) is this kind of master status. One receives the status as a result of breaking a rule, and the identification proves to be more important than most others. One will be identified as a deviant first, before other identifications are made. The question is raised: "What kind of person would break such an important rule?" And the answer is given: "One who is different from the rest of us, who cannot or will not

act as a moral human being and therefore might break other important rules." The deviant identification becomes the controlling one.

Treating a person as though he were generally rather than specifically deviant produces a self-fulfilling prophecy. It sets in motion several mechanisms which conspire to shape the person in the image people have of him (Ray 1961). In the first place, one tends to be cut off, after being identified as deviant, from participation in more conventional groups, even though the specific consequences of the particular deviant activity might never of themselves have caused the isolation had there not also been the public knowledge and reaction to it. For example, being a homosexual may not affect one's ability to do office work, but to be known as a homosexual in an office may make it impossible to continue working there. Similarly, though the effects of opiate drugs may not impair one's working ability, to be known as an addict will probably lead to losing one's job. In such cases, the individual finds it difficult to conform to other rules which he had no intention or desire to break, and perforce finds himself deviant in these areas as well. The homosexual who is deprived of a "respectable" job by the discovery of his deviance may drift into unconventional, marginal occupations where it does not make so much difference. The drug addict finds himself forced into other illegitimate kinds of activity, such as robbery and theft, by the refusal of respectable employers to have him around.

When the deviant is caught, he is treated in accordance with the popular diagnosis of why he is that way, and the treatment itself may likewise produce increasing deviance. The drug addict, popularly considered to be a weak-willed individual who cannot forego [sic] the indecent pleasures afforded him by opiates, is treated repressively. He is forbidden to use drugs. Since he cannot get drugs legally, he must get them illegally. This forces the market underground and pushes the price of drugs up far beyond the current legitimate market price into a bracket that few can afford on an ordinary salary. Hence the treatment of the addict's deviance places him in a position where it will probably be necessary to resort to deceit and crime in order to support his habit. The behavior is a consequence of the public reaction to the deviance rather than a consequence of the inherent qualities of the deviant act.

Put more generally, the point is that the treatment of deviants denies them the ordinary means of carrying on the routines of everyday life open to most people. Because of this denial, the deviant must of necessity develop illegitimate routines.

REFERENCES

Hughes, Everett C. 1945. "Dilemmas and Contradictions of Status." *American Journal of Sociology* 50:353–359.

Kitsuse, John. 1962. "Societal Reaction to Deviance: Problems of Theory and Method." *Social Problems* 9:247–256.

Lemert E. M. 1951. *Social Pathology.* New York: McGraw-Hill Book Co., Inc.

Marsh Ray. 1961. "The Cycle of Abstinence and Relapse Among Heroin Addicts." *Social Problems* 9:132–140.

Tannenbaum, Frank. 1951. *Crime and the Community.* (New York: McGraw Hill Book Co., Inc.

READING 2-11

Societal Reaction to Deviant Behavior

John I. Kitsuse

I propose to shift the focus of theory and research from the forms of deviant behavior to the *processes by which persons come to be defined as deviant by others*. Such a shift requires that the sociologist view as problematic what he generally assumes as given—namely, that certain forms of behavior are per se deviant and are so defined by the "conventional or conforming members of a group." This assumption is frequently called into question on empirical grounds when the societal reaction to behaviors defined as deviant by the sociologist is non-existent, indifferent, or at most mildly disapproving. For example, in his discussion of "ritualism" as a form of deviant behavior, Merton states that it is not that such behavior is treated by others as deviant which identifies it as deviant "since the overt behavior is institutionally permitted, though not culturally prescribed" (Merton 1957:150).

Reprinted from *Social Problems* 9, no. 3 (Winter 1962), 247–256.

Rather, the behavior is deviant because it "clearly represents a departure from the cultural model in which men are obliged to move onward and upward in the social hierarchy" (Merton 1957:150). The discrepancy between the theoretically hypothesized and empirically observable societal reaction is also noted by Lemert: "It is fairly easy to think of situations in which serious offenses against laws commanding public respect have only mild penalty or have gone entirely unpunished. Conversely, cases are easily discovered in which a somewhat minor violation of legal rules has provoked surprisingly stringent penalties" (Lemert 1951:55).

Clearly, the forms of behavior *per se* do not activate the processes of societal reaction which sociologically differentiate deviants from non-deviants. Thus, a central problem for theory and research in the sociology of deviance may be stated as follows: What are the behaviors which are defined by members of the group, community, or society as deviant, and how do those definitions organize and activate the societal reactions by which persons come to be differentiated and treated as deviants? In formulating the problem in this way, the point of view of those who interpret and define behavior as deviant must explicitly be incorporated into a sociological definition of deviance. Accordingly, deviance may be conceived as a process by which the members of a group, community, or society (1) interpret behavior as deviant, (2) define persons who so behave as a certain kind of deviant, and (3) accord them the treatment considered appropriate to such deviants. In the following pages, this conception of deviance and societal reaction will be applied to the processes by which persons come to be defined and treated as homosexuals.

SOCIETAL REACTIONS TO "HOMOSEXUAL BEHAVIOR"

As a form of deviant behavior, homosexuality presents a strategically important theoretical and empirical problem for the study of deviance. In the sociological and anthropological literature (Parsons and Bales 1955; Benedict 1938; Kardiner et al. 1945; Kirkpatrick 1955; Mead 1955), homosexual behavior and the societal reactions to it are conceptualized within the framework of ascribed sex statuses and the socialization of individuals to those statuses. The ascription of sex statuses is presumed to provide a complex of culturally prescribed roles and behaviors which individuals are expected to learn and perform. Homosexual roles and behaviors are conceived to be "inappropriate" to the individual's ascribed sex status, and thus theoretically they are defined as deviant.

With reference to American society, Allison Davis states: "Sex-typing of behavior and privileges is even more rigid and lasting in our society than is age-typing. Indeed, sexual status and color-caste status are the only life-long forms of rank. In our society, one can escape them in approved fashion only by death. Whereas sexual mobility is somewhat less rare today than formerly, sex-inappropriate behavior, social or physical, is still one of the most severely punished infractions of our

social code" (Davis 1941:350). In Lemert's (1951) terminology, norms concerning sex-appropriate behavior have a high degree of "compulsiveness" and social disapproval of violations is stringent and effective.

Such a view of homosexuality would lead one to hypothesize that "sex appropriate" (and conversely "sex-inappropriate") behaviors are unambiguously prescribed, deviations from those prescriptions are invariably interpreted as immoral, and the reactions of the conventional and conforming members of the society to such deviations are uniformly severe and effective. The evidence which apparently supports this hypothesis is not difficult to find, particularly with reference to the definition and treatment of male homosexuals. Individuals who are publicly identified as homosexuals are frequently denied the social, economic, and legal rights of "normal" males. Socially they may be treated as objects of amusement, ridicule, scorn, and often fear; economically they may be summarily dismissed from employment; legally they are frequently subject to interrogation and harassment by police.

In citing such evidence, however, it is important to note that the societal reaction to and the differentiation of homosexuals from the "normal" population is a consequence of the fact that the former are "known" to be homosexuals by some individuals, groups or agencies. Thus, within the framework of the present formulation of homosexuality as a form of deviant behavior, the processes by which individuals come to be "known" and treated as sexually deviant will be viewed as problematic and a problem for empirical investigation. I shall not be concerned here with the so-called "latent homosexual" unless he is so defined by others and differentially treated as a consequence of that definition. Nor will I be concerned with the variety of "internal" conflicts which may form the "clinical" picture of the homosexual except insofar as such conflicts are manifested in behavior leading others to conceive of him as a homosexual. In short, I shall proceed on the principle that it is only when individuals are defined and identified by others as homosexuals and accorded the treatment considered "appropriate" for individuals so defined that a homosexual "population" is produced for sociological investigation (Garfinkel 1956). With reference to homosexuality, then, the empirical questions are: What forms of behavior do persons in the social system consider to be "sex-inappropriate," how do they interpret such behaviors, and what are the consequences of those interpretations for their reactions to individuals who are perceived to manifest such behaviors?

In a preliminary attempt to investigate these questions, an interview schedule was constructed and administered to approximately seven hundred individuals, most of whom were college undergraduates. The sample was neither random nor representative of any specified population, and the generalizability of the interview materials is limited except insofar as they are relevant to the previously noted hypothesis that homosexual behavior is uniformly defined, interpreted, and negatively sanctioned. The interview materials will therefore be used for the purpose of illustrating the theory and method of the present conception of deviance and societal reaction.

The objectives of the interview were threefold: It attempted to document (1) the behavior forms which are interpreted as deviant, (2) the processes by which persons who manifest such behaviors are defined and (3) treated as deviant. Thus, in the construction of the interview schedule, what the interviewees considered to be "deviant" behavior, the interpretations of such behavior, and the actions of subjects toward those perceived as deviant were addressed as empirical questions. Labels such as alcoholic, illiterate, illegitimate child, and ex-convict were assumed to be categories employed by persons in everyday life to classify deviants, but the behavioral forms by which they identify individuals as deviants were treated as problematic. "Sexual deviant" was one of ten categories of deviants about which subjects were questioned in the interview. Among the more than seven hundred subjects interviewed, seventy-five stated they had "known" a homosexual and responded to questions concerning their experiences with such individuals. The data presented below are drawn from the protocols of interviews with this group of subjects.

The interview proceeded as follows:

The subject was asked "Have you ever known anyone who was a sexual deviant?" If he questioned the meaning of "deviant," the subject was asked to consider the question using his own meaning of "sexual deviant."

When the subject stated he had known a sexual deviant—a homosexual in this case—as he defined the term, he was asked to think about the most recent incident involving him in an encounter with such a person. He was then asked "When was the first time you noticed (found out) that this person was a homosexual?" followed by "What was the situation? What did you notice about him? How did he behave?" This line of questioning was focused on the interaction between the subject and the alleged deviant to obtain a detailed description of the situation which led the subject to define the person as homosexual. The subject's description of the person's behavior was systematically probed to clarify the terms of his description, particularly those which were interpretive rather than descriptive.

EVIDENCE OF HOMOSEXUALITY

Responses to the question "When was the first time you noticed (found out) that this person was homosexual?" and the related probes suggest that an individual's sexual "normality" may be called into question with reference to two broad categories of evidence. (a) *Indirect evidence* in the form of a rumor, an acquaintance's experience with the individual in question subsequently communicated to the subject, or general reputational information concerning the individual's behavior, associates, and sexual predelictions may be the occasion for suspecting him to be "different." Many subjects reported that they first "found out" or "knew" that the individuals in question were homosexuals through the reports of others or by "reputation."

Such information was generally accepted by the subjects without independent verification. Indeed, the information provided a new perspective for their retrospective as well as prospective observations and interpretations of the individuals' behaviors. An example of how hearsay organizes observation and interpretation is the following statement by a 35-year-old male (a draftsman):

I: Then this lieutenant was a homosexual?
S: Yes.
I: How did you find out about it?
S: The guy he approached told me. After that, I watched him. Our company was small and we had a bar for both enlisted men and officers. He would come in and try to be friendly with one or two of the guys.
I: Weren't the other officers friendly?
S: Sure, they would come in for an occasional drink; some of them had been with the company for three years and they would sometimes slap you on the back, but he tried to get over friendly.
I: What do you mean "over friendly"?
S: He had only been there a week. He would try to push himself on a couple of guys—he spent more time with the enlisted personnel than is expected from an officer.

(b) *Direct observation* by the subject of the individual's behavior may be the basis for calling the latter's sexual "normality" into question. The descriptions of behavior which subjects took to be indicative of homosexuality varied widely and were often vague. Most frequently the behaviors cited were those "*which everyone knows*" are indications of homosexuality. For example, a 20-year-old male subject reports an encounter with a stranger at a bar:

I: What happened during your conversation?
S: He asked me if I went to college and I said I did. Then he asked me what I was studying. When I told him psychology he appeared very interested.
I: What do you mean "interested"?
S: Well, you know queers really go for this psychology stuff.
I: Then what happened?
S: Ah, let's see. I'm not exactly sure, but somehow we got into an argument about psychology and to prove my point I told him to pick an area of study. Well, he appeared to be very pensive and after a great thought he said, "Okay, let's take homosexuality."

I: What did you make of that?
S: Well, by now I figured the guy was queer so I got the hell outta there.

The responses of other subjects suggest that an individual is particularly suspect when he is observed to behave in a manner which deviates from the *behaviors-held-in-common* among members of the group to which he belongs. For example, a behavior which is presumed to be held-in-common among sailors in the U. S. Navy is intense and active sexual activity. When a sailor does not affirm, at least verbally, his interest in such activity, his competence as a "male" may be called into question. A 22-year-old engineer, recently discharged from the Navy, responds to the "how did you first know" question as follows:

All of a sudden you just get suspicious of something. I began to wonder about him. He didn't go in for leave activities that most sailors go for. You know, girls and high times. He just never was interested and when you have been out at sea for a month or two, you're interested. That just wasn't Navy, and he was a career man.

Although the responses of our subjects indicate there are many behavioral gestures which "everyone knows" are indicators of homosexuality in males, there are relatively few such gestures that lead persons to suspect females of homosexuality. Following is an excerpt from a 21-year-old college co-ed whose remarks illustrate this lack of definite indicators *prior* to her labeling of an acquaintance as a homosexual:

I: When was the first time you noticed she was a deviant?
S: I didn't notice it. I thought she had a masculine appearance when I first saw her anyway.
I: What do you mean?
S: Oh, her haircut, her heavy eyebrows. She had a rather husky build.
I: Exactly when did you think she had a masculine appearance?
S: It was long after [the first meeting] that I found out that she was "one."
I: How do you define it?
S: Well, a lesbian. I don't know too much about them. It was ———— who told me about her.

I: Did you notice anything else about her [at the first meeting]?

S: No, because you really don't know unless you're looking for those things.

Unlike "effeminate" appearance and gestures in males, "masculine" appearance in females is apparently less likely to be immediately linked to the suspicion or imputation of homosexuality. The statements of the subject quoted above indicate that although "masculine appearance" is an important element in her conception of a lesbian, its significance did not become apparent to her until a third person told her the girl was homosexual. The remarks of other subjects in our sample who state they have "known" female homosexuals reveal a similar ambiguity in their interpretations of what they describe as indicators of sexual deviance.

A third form of evidence by direct observation is behaviors which the subjects interpreted to be *overt sexual propositions*. Descriptions of such propositions ranged from what the subjects considered to be unmistakable evidence of the person's sexual deviance to ambiguous gestures which they did not attempt to question in the situation. The following is an excerpt from an interview with a 24-year-old male school teacher who recounts an experience in a Korean Army barrack:

I: What questions did he [the alleged homosexual] ask?

S: "How long have you been in Korea?" I told him. "What do you think of these Korean girls?" which I answered, "Not too much because they are dirty." I thought he was probably homesick and wanted someone to talk to. I do not remember what he said then until he said, "How much do you have?" I answered him by saying, "I don't know, about average I guess." Then he said, "Can I feel it just once?" To this I responded with, "Get the hell out of here," and I gave him a shove when he reached for me as he asked the question.

In a number of interviews, the subjects' statements indicate that they interpreted the sequence of the alleged deviants' behavior as progressively inappropriate or peculiar in the course of their interaction with them. The link between such behavior and their judgment that a sexual proposition was being made was frequently established by the subjects' growing realization of its deviant character. A 21-year-old male subject recalls the following experience involving his high school tennis coach who had invited him to dinner:

S: Anyway, when I get there he served dinner, and as I think back on it—I didn't notice it at the time—but I remember that he did act sort of effeminate. Finally he got up to change a record and picked up some of my English themes. Then he brought them over and sat down beside me. He began to explain some of my mistakes in my themes, and in the meantime he slipped his arms around me.

I: Would you say that this was done in a friendly manner or with an intent of hugging you or something?

S: Well, no, it was just a friendly gesture of putting his arm around my shoulder. At that time, I didn't think anything of it, but as he continued to explain my mistakes, he started to rub my back. Then he asked me if I wanted a back rub. So I said, "No! I don't need one." At this time, I began thinking something was funny anyway. So I said that I had to go. . . .

THE IMPUTATION OF HOMOSEXUALITY

When a detailed description of the subject's evidence concerning the alleged homosexual was obtained, he was asked, "What did you make of that?" to elicit information about how he interpreted the person's observed or reported behavior. This line of questioning yielded data on the inferential process by which the subject linked his information about the individual to the deviant category "homosexual."

A general pattern revealed by the subjects' responses to this section of the interview schedule is that when an individual's sexual "normality" is called into question, by whatever form of evidence, the imputation of homosexuality is documented by *retrospective interpretations* of the deviant's behavior, a process by which the subject re-interprets the individual's past behavior in the light of the new information concerning his sexual deviance. This process is particularly evident in cases where the prior relationship between the subject and the alleged homosexual was more than a chance encounter or casual acquaintanceship. The subjects indicate that they reviewed their past interactions with the individuals in question, searching for subtle cues and nuances of behavior which might give further evidence of the alleged deviance. This retrospective reading generally provided the subjects with just such evidence to support the conclusion that "this is what was going on all the time."

Some of the subjects who were interviewed were themselves aware of their retrospective interpretations in defining individuals as sexually deviant. For example, a 23-year-old female graduate student states:

I: Will you tell me more about the situation?
S: Well, their relationship was a continuous one, although I think that it is a friendship now as I don't see them together as I used to; I don't think it is still homosexual. When I see them together, they don't seem to be displaying the affection openly as they did when I first realized the situation.
I: How do you mean "openly"?
S: Well, they would hold each other's hand in public places.
I: And what did you make of this?
S: Well, I really don't know, because I like to hold people's hands, too! I guess I actually didn't see this as directly connected with the situation. What I mean is that, if I hadn't seen that other incident [she had observed the two girls in bed together] I probably wouldn't have thought of it [i.e., hand-holding] very much. . . . Well, actually, there were a few things that I questioned later on that I hadn't thought really very much about. . . . I can remember her being quite affectionate towards me several times when we were in our room together, like putting her arm around my shoulder. Or I remember one time specifically when she asked me for a kiss. I was shocked at the time, but I laughed it off jokingly.

THE INTERACTIONAL CONTEXTS OF SOCIETAL REACTIONS

When the description of the alleged deviant's behavior and the subject's interpretations of that behavior were recorded, the subject was asked "What did you do then?" This question was directed toward documenting societal reactions to deviant behavior. Forms of behavior *per se* do not differ-

entiate deviants from non-deviants; it is the responses of the conventional and conforming members of the society who identify and interpret behavior as deviant which sociologically transform persons into deviants. Thus, in the formulation of deviance proposed here, if the subject observes an individual's behavior and defines it as deviant but does not accord him differential treatment as a consequence of that definition, the individual is not sociologically deviant.

The reactions of the subjects to individuals they defined as homosexuals ranged from immediate withdrawal from the scene of interaction and avoidance of further encounters with the alleged deviants to the maintenance of the prior relationship virtually unaltered by the imputation of deviance. The following responses to the question "What did you do then?" illustrate the variation in sanctions directed toward persons defined as homosexuals.

Explicit disapproval and immediate withdrawal: The most negatively toned and clearly articulated reaction reported by our subjects is that of the previously quoted Korean War veteran. It is interesting to note that extreme physical punishment as a reaction to persons defined as homosexuals, a reaction which is commonly verbalized by "normal" males as proper treatment of "queers," is not reported by any of the subjects. When physical force is used, it is invariably in response to the deviant's direct physical overtures, and even then it is relatively mild, e.g., "I gave him a shove when he reached for me."

Explicit disapproval and subsequent withdrawal: In the following excerpt, a 20-year-old male college student describes an encounter with a man whom he met in a coffee shop. In the course of their conversation, the man admitted his homosexuality to the subject. The two left the coffee shop and walked together to the subway station.

I: What happened then?
S: We got to the subway whereupon he suggested that he hail a cab and take me up to Times Square—a distance of almost 40 blocks.
I: Did you agree, and what did you think?

S: Yes, I thought he was just being very nice and I had no qualms about getting in a cab with a homosexual since I was quite sure I could protect myself against any advances in a cab.

I: What happened then?

S: When we had ridden a little distance, he put his hand on my knee, and I promptly removed it saying that it just wasn't right and that I wanted nothing of it. However, after a while, he put his hand back. This time I didn't take it away for a while because I was interested in what he would do. It was the funniest thing—he rubbed and caressed my knee the same way in which I would have done this to a girl. This time I took his hand and hit him across the chest with it, telling him to "cut it out." Finally, we got to Times Square, and I got out.

This example and that provided by the Korean War veteran's reaction to behavior interpreted as overt sexual propositions suggest the possibility that responses to persons suspected of homosexuality or defined as homosexuals on the basis of more indirect evidence of appearance, "confessions," hearsay, reputation, or association will vary within an even wider range of applied sanctions. Indeed, the statements of subjects concerning their responses to persons alleged to be deviant on such evidence indicate that the modal reaction is disapproval, implicitly rather than explicitly communicated, and a restriction of interaction through partial withdrawal and avoidance. It should be noted further that although the subject's silent withdrawal from an established relationship with an alleged deviant may represent a stronger disapproval than an explicitly communicated, physically enforced sanction against a stranger, moral indignation or revulsion is not necessarily communicated to the deviant. The subject's prior relationship with the alleged deviant and the demands of propriety in subsequent interactions with him qualify the form and intensity of the sanctions which are applied. Thus, when the organization of the subject's day-to-day activities "forces" him into interaction with the deviant, expressions of disapproval are frequently constrained and diffused by the rules of deference and demeanor (Goffman 1956). The following excerpts provide illustrations:

Implicit disapproval and partial withdrawal: A 20-year-old co-ed's reaction to a girl she concluded was a homosexual was expressed as follows:

Well, I didn't want to be alone with X [the homosexual] because the four of us had two connecting rooms and I was in the room with X. As much as I liked the girl and felt sorry for her, I knew she could really wring me through the wringer. So the rest decided that I should tell her that if she and Y wanted to be homos, to do it somewhere else and not in the room.

No disapproval and relationship sustained: The "live and let live" response to homosexuals, which is implied in the preceding reaction, was not uncommon among the subjects. Some subjects not only affirmed the right of the homosexual to "live his own life" but also reported that their knowledge of the deviance has had little or no effect upon their subsequent relationships with the deviants. In this regard, the mildest reaction, so mild that it might be considered no reaction at all, was that of a 19-year-old male college student:

I: What was your reaction to him?

S: My reactions to him have always been friendly because he seems like a very friendly person. Uh, and he has a very nice sense of humor and I've never been repelled by anything he's said. For one thing, I think he's tremendously interesting because he seems to have such a wide range for background. . . .

I: When was the last time you saw this person?

S: Last night. . . . I was sitting in a restaurant and he walked in with some friends . . . he just stopped in and said hello, and was his usual friendly self.

I: What in particular happened after that?

S: Actually, nothing. He sat down with his friends and we exchanged a few words about the records that were playing on the juke box. But nothing, actually. . . .

The theoretical significance of these data for the conception of deviance and societal reaction presented here is not that the subjects' information is of dubious accuracy or questionable relevance as evidence of homosexuality. Nor is it that the subjects' interpretations of them are unreasonable, unjustifiable, or spurious. They suggest rather that the conceptions of persons in everyday life concerning "sex-appropriate" or "sex-inappropriate" behavior may lead them to interpret a variety of behavioral forms as indications of the same deviation, and the "same" behavioral forms as indications of a variety of deviant as well as "normal" behavior. An individual's sexual "normality" may be made problematic by the interpretations and re-interpretations of his behavior by others, and the interpretive process may be activated by a wide range of situational behaviors which lend new significance to the individual's past and present behavior. His behavior with respect to speech, interests, dress, dating, or relations with other males are not *per se* significant in the deviant-defining process. The data suggest that the critical feature of the deviant-defining process is not the behavior of individuals who are defined as deviant, but rather the interpretations others make of their behaviors, whatever those behaviors may be.

With specific reference to homosexuality as a form of deviant behavior, the interview materials suggest that while reactions toward persons defined as homosexuals tend to be negatively toned, they are far from homogeneous as to the forms or intensity of the sanctions invoked and applied. Indeed, reactions which may appear to the sociological observer or to the deviant himself as negative sanctions, such as withdrawal or avoidance, may be expressions of embarrassment, a reluctance to share the burden of the deviant's problems, fear of the deviant, etc., as well as moral indignation or revulsion. In none of the interviews does the subject react with extreme violence, explicitly define or directly accuse the deviant of being a "queer," "fairy," or other terms of opprobrium, nor did any of them initiate legal actions against the deviant. In view of the extreme negative sanctions against homosexuality which are posited on theoretical grounds, the generally mild reactions of our subjects are striking.

The relative absence of extreme and overtly expressed negative sanctions against homosexuals among our subjects may, of course, reflect the higher than average educational level of the sample. A sample of subjects less biased toward the highly educated, middle-class segment of the population than was interviewed in this preliminary study may be expected to reflect a more definite pattern with reference to such negative reactions. We must, therefore, be cautious in generalizing the range of reactions among our subjects to the general population. It is equally important to note, however, that these data do indicate that reactions to homosexuals in American society are not *societal* in the sense of being uniform within a narrow range; rather, they are significantly conditioned by sub-cultural as well as situational factors. Thus, not only are the processes by which persons come to be defined as homosexuals contingent upon the interpretations of their behavior by others, but also the sanctions imposed and the treatment they are accorded as a consequence of that definition vary widely among conventional members of various subcultural groups.

REFERENCES

Benedict, Ruth. 1938. "Continuities and Discontinuities in Cultural Conditioning." *Psychiatry* 1:161–167.

Davis, Allison. 1941. "American Status Systems and the Socialization of the Child." *American Sociological Review* 6.

Garfinkel, Harold. 1956. "Some Sociological Concepts and Methods for Psychiatrists." *Psychiatric Research Reports* 6:181–195.

Goffman, Erving. 1956. "The Nature of Deference and Demeanor." *American Anthropologist* 58:473–502.

Kardiner, Abram, et al. 1945. *Psychological Frontiers of Society*. New York: Columbia University Press.

Kirkpatrick, Clifford. 1955. *The Family*. New York: Ronald Press.

Lemert, Edwin N. 1951. *Social Pathology*. New York: McGraw-Hill.

Mead, Margaret. 1955. *Sex and Temperament*. New York: William Morrow.

Merton, Robert K. 1957. *Social Theory and Social Structure,* revised. Glencoe: Free Press.

Parsons, Talcott, and Robert F. Bales. 1955. *Family Socialization and Interaction Process*. Glencoe: Free Press.

Labeling the CIA Deviant

William B. Waegel
M. David Ermann
Alan M. Horowitz

With few exceptions, the study of deviance has been biased overwhelmingly toward individual deviance while almost completely excluding the deviance of organizations.

Our contention is that greater research effort should be devoted to understanding deviance by powerful organizations. In part, this research should stress efforts of organizational spokesmen to negotiate and re-define the meaning of controversial organizational actions. Large organizations to a greater extent than individuals, typically possess resources, such as ready access to the mass media, which afford them the opportunity to promote vigorously counterdefinitions of their activities. The ability to defend therefore must be accorded a central place in the analysis of deviance. In this regard, Schur (1971:56) has noted: "As imputation of deviant character inevitably incorporates some exercise of power . . . it is not surprising that various forms of negotiation and bargaining have been found to be a crucial element in labeling."

We propose that *organizational deviance exists to the extent that observed or imputed actions are perceived by parties in sanctioning positions as violating standards of proper conduct and are attributed to an organization.* This definition differs from past definitions in its simultaneous specification of the actors perceived as deviant and those holding this perception (cf., Ermann and Lundman, 1978a, 1978b:56–58). Deviance thus is viewed as a socially constructed category, resulting from the efforts of parties imputing deviance and the reactions of the party to whom deviance is being imputed. Our emphasis in this paper is on responses in a case where the party reacting is powerful and enjoys the aid of powerful allies.

Accounts provided to defend the Central Intelligence Agency (CIA) against imputations of deviance provide our empirical focus. We view the CIA as a unified entity because rarely have its internal factions become visible in the process whereby it manages its public image. Throughout, we deal with situations where competing external definitions of the agency and its actions have been proffered and the definitions that might become accepted were problematic.

METHODOLOGY

Our data collection relied on coverage of CIA activities in *The New York Times Index* (NYTI) from 1947–1975, and the twenty-five yearly indexes on *Administration of the Internal Security Act and Other Internal Security Laws* for 1951–1975 (published by the Senate Judiciary Committee, Subcommittee on Intelligence). The researchers read every reference to the CIA in the NYTI and systematically recorded incidents involving allegations of agency wrongdoing and responses by any parties to such allegations. We then referred back to articles that dealt with efforts to control the CIA, interorganizational relations involving the CIA, allegations of CIA wrongdoing, and most importantly, responses by the CIA to such allegations. When Congressional or other governmental documents were relevant, we read and abstracted from the original documents.

From *The Sociological Quarterly* 22 (Winter 1981):43–55. Reprinted by permission of the University of California Press and William Waegel. ©1981 by The Sociological Quarterly.

Finally, we used available popular and journalistic accounts (e.g., Marchetti and Marks 1974; Agee 1975; Stone 1976; Wise and Ross 1964). Through this procedure, patterns of Congressional and public reaction to CIA activities emerged. At the same time parties acting in defense of the CIA were identified and the types of responses made to counter allegations of wrongdoing were recorded.

Our experience indicates that the *Times* functioned suitably as a "newspaper of record." The editorial biases of the established press recording only the statements of "respectable" public figures does not appear to be a problem for our analysis, because our research concerns only public behaviors of established groups. Because our focus is on public definitions of agency activities and the agency's responses to various allegations, our concern is with the visible definitional work that was performed by various parties. Such information appears to have been thoroughly reported by the *Times*. A comparison with other written records indicates that public statements regarding the CIA were accurately reported in the *Times*.

IMPUTATIONS OF ORGANIZATIONAL DEVIANCE

The data indicate three distinct periods when concerted efforts were undertaken to define the CIA as deviant. For each period, our examination will focus on the accounts offered by the CIA and its supporters, and the factors that contributed to the widespread acceptance of those accounts. For reasons of space and readability, citations for minor quotations are omitted here but are available from the authors.

I. Communists in the CIA.   Attempts to assign a deviant status to the CIA first mobilized significant resources during the McCarthy "red scare" of the early 1950s, when the Cold War climate prompted influential parties to attempt to define a communist-infiltrated CIA as a threat and promote a public definition of the agency as deviant. Even the outgoing head of the agency publicly stated that he believed "there are Communists in my organization." Two

years later Senator Joseph McCarthy, the most influential figure in the red scare, declared that the CIA was the country's "worst situation" from the standpoint of Communist infiltration.

The agency itself did not respond to these allegations, but a strong defense was provided by other influential parties. President Eisenhower, as Truman had done before him, praised the CIA for performing an important national service. Eisenhower was widely quoted as being strongly committed to protecting the agency, and advised that he would not let its employees respond to subpoenas from the McCarthy Committee. Nominally, this position was taken to protect the secrecy of agency operations, but its effect was to deny to the parties imputing deviance information they might have used to support their claims. The agency was never subjected to Congressional hearings during this time, partly because this strategic use of executive power reduced the ability of the McCarthy forces to obtain information relevant to their claims.

A second strategy employed by agency supporters involved vigorously promoting a counter-definition that would carry the full weight of the executive branch. Two different executive commissions were established, and both reported that the agency was not guilty of the allegations of communist infiltration. The thrust of the Doolittle Commission report in October of 1954 was to promote a positive counter-definition; it directed attention away from the agency's domestic problems and focused on the success of its foreign operations. Doolittle's report was a positive appraisal of the agency and a legitimation of its authority and structure:

> With respect to the Central Intelligence Agency in general we conclude: (a) that its place in the overall organization of the government is proper; (b) that the laws under which it operates are adequate; (c) that the established procedures for its financial support are sufficient to meet its current operational needs; (d) that in spite of the limitations imposed by its relatively short life and rapid expansion it is doing a creditable job; (e) that it is gradually improving its capabilities; and (f) that it is exercising care to insure the loyalty of its personnel.

In summary attributions of deviance were effectively neutralized through the efforts of powerful third parties. In fact, the furor probably resulted in the construction of a more positive public image than had previously existed, one which proposed that minor internal problems should not be allowed to detract from the overwhelmingly positive functions the CIA performed for the nation.

II. The CIA as an Invisible Government. During the following decade, the dominant definition of CIA activities remained largely unchanged. Around the year 1966, however, qualitative change began to appear. Growing numbers of influential Congressmen and segments of the press began to define the CIA as deviant based on the belief that it was no longer playing a neutral role, but was exceeding its statutory authority by making national policy as well as carrying it out. They charged that the CIA was in effect making foreign policy and thus usurping the roles of President and Congress, and that under existing arrangements it was answerable only to itself. In 1967, Senator Mansfield charged that agency penetration into various domestic groups such as the National Student Association and labor organizations represented a move toward "big brotherism." Senator Fulbright stated that CIA policy and operations were "undermining democracy," and Senator Young declared: "The CIA has gradually taken on the character of an invisible government, answerable only to itself."

In essence, the change was from a view of the CIA as benign to a definition of it as threatening. A central element in this emerging image was the belief that the agency had come to represent a threat by encroaching on traditional policy-making procedures. Symbolic of the more general redefinition outside the Congress was the wide attention given to a book on the CIA entitled *The Invisible Government* (Wise and Ross 1964).

Critics also pointed out that over the CIA's 19-year existence, 150 resolutions for tighter Congressional control of the agency had been introduced but none implemented. Related charges included: the CIA had provided the information to the committees that were supposed to control it; the committees exercised no real control because they were either not informed of agency operations or informed after the fact; a handful of senior members of oversight committees did not so much control the CIA as shield it; and the agency had great influence in selection of oversight committee members.

The activities which precipitated this re-evaluation apparently had existed for some time, and had been vocally pointed out by leftist students and other critics. It was a cumulation of information and the attachment of new interpretations to it, rather than specific dramatic disclosures, that brought about this new definition of the CIA.

A powerful coalition of supporters of the agency attempted to deflect and neutralize the "invisible government" image, with members of the oversight committees almost without exception among the most vocal defenders. Several accounts were offered in defense of the agency, and counter-definitions of its activities and its role in policy-making were promoted. Defenders argued that critics ignored the "overwhelming number of constructive acts performed in defense of the United States" and that criticism would impair the effectiveness of the agency and thus harm national security. As the controversy escalated, the President and the Secretary of State entered the debate to support the argument that the agency did not initiate policy and that its operations were of great value.

The promotion of competing definitions continued for the next year as further revelations of controversial agency activities surfaced. Again, the CIA and its defenders employed the deflection and neutralization strategies which had proven effective in the past. A member of the Senate oversight committee argued that, "The policies of the CIA are not set by the CIA," and the Secretary of State pronounced that the agency was merely following orders from above in penetrating private domestic organizations. A special White House report and CIA Director Helms both asserted that the activities being criticized were essentially normal practices, having been carried out in this country since the Truman Administration and by "the enemy" for a like period.

The Administration defended the practices as necessary to offset communist influence, and suggested that CIA financing of private organizations was only a fraction of what the enemy spent. It was reiterated that the agency was indispensable to national security. And, finally, the chair of the oversight committee defined the recent wave of disclosures as significantly impairing agency effectiveness.

In summary, the primary accounts offered in defense of the CIA were as follows: (1) it only acts in accord with orders from above; (2) in light of what "the enemy" is doing, we must do the same, and these practices are essentially business as usual; (3) unfortunately, these practices create some problems in a free society but must be tolerated for our own good; and (4) criticism is impairing the effectiveness of an important tool of government which has performed invaluable functions in the past by being given a free rein.

III. The CIA as an Uncontrollable Menace. By the early 1970s, Congressional perception of the CIA as an organization constituting a threat to certain democratic values appears to have been largely neutralized by a rather successful redefinition of agency practices. Earlier perceptions reemerged in the events surrounding Watergate, however, particularly with regard to the revelations of widespread domestic spying. With them came renewed attempts to label the CIA deviant. Those promoting this definition now pointed to activities which were clearly and directly in violation of charter. Despite the legislative provision that the CIA have no internal security functions, it was widely reported and believed that the agency conducted massive, illegal domestic spying operations against anti-war and other dissident groups. For instance, reports indicated that as much as one-third of the officially listed work force of 18,000 was involved in political operations, and that over 250 domestic groups had been infiltrated.

By this time, strategies and tactics for deflecting and neutralizing imputations of deviance had become refined and somewhat routinized. Top-level agency officials, members of the Administration, and entrenched Congressional supporters were well-coordinated and strategically located for this purpose. As one observer noted: "The Republican White House and the Democratic Old Guard in the Senate are in a bipartisan alliance against any real reform. A similar coalition (exists) in the House. . . ."

The most visible formal response to these allegations was again the establishment of special investigative bodies in the executive and legislative branches. Each of these served as a forum for promoting a specific definition, and their final reports sponsored competing definitions of the agency and the legitimacy of its activities. A House Special Subcommittee on Intelligence, which was not dominated by either the "Old Guard" or critics, concluded that the CIA had allowed itself to be used for "improper purposes" for which there was "no support in law or reason." In contrast, the Rockefeller Commission report concluded that there was no widespread pattern of illegal activity, and that allegations of massive domestic spying were unfounded—with one or two exceptions. It was emphasized that there was no vast network of uncontrolled domestic operations; the CIA's transgressions were defined as relatively minor. Vice-President designate Ford declared that if he became President he would insist on careful supervision to counter the image of the agency as an "uncontrollable octopus."

Imputations of deviance were countered with a number of strategies and techniques. The argument was advanced that the CIA itself did not bear responsibility for objectionable activities, because it was not customary for the agency to question orders from executive branch officials. There were attempts to promote a counter-definition of the extent and (what is perhaps more revealing) the importance of the domestic spying operations; Director Colby defined the critics' charges as exaggerated, and domestic operations as involving "some violations of rights, but nothing earth-shattering."

An attempt to neutralize Congressional criticism may also be seen in the 1973 announcement of cut-backs in agency personnel as well as in clandestine military and domestic operations. The implicit suggestion was that the objectionable agency activities could be controlled effectively through internal means. Shortly thereafter, Secretary of State Kissinger argued for the vital necessity of an autonomous CIA, accountable only to selected members of the executive branch of government.

Another deflection strategy involved replacing the director when the agency came under heavy criticism. This had occurred during previous periods of mounting criticism and calls for tighter Congressional control, and served to sponsor the impression that objectionable policies and practices could be controlled with the installation of a new director.

Bolder tactics were pursued involving counter-labeling of critics in an effort to discredit them and their interpretations of agency activities. The most prominent case concerned Daniel Schorr, a CIA critic who had disseminated classified information. It was argued that Schorr's action jeopardized the safety of agency personnel, and he was vehemently denounced by former Director Helms as the irresponsible "Killer Schorr." Similarly, attempts were made to discredit one of the more vocal critics in the House (Michael Harrington) for his role in disclosing secret testimony. Analytically, this strategy not only may discredit labelers but intimidate them as well. If sponsoring a deviant definition of a powerful organization can be seen as entailing the risk of significant personal costs, others may be less willing to undertake such an enterprise in the future.

SUCCESS OF CIA RESPONSES

Defense against imputations of deviance to the CIA have been quite successful. This success may be indexed by the virtual absence of constraints imposed on the agency by the relevant sanctioning body, the U.S. Congress. The structure, operational authority, and autonomy of the agency have remained essentially unchanged. The account most widely used in defense of the agency held that the broad range of activities engaged in by an organization as complex as the CIA must be viewed in terms of a "balance sheet"; a few aberrations should not be permitted to taint the agency and detract from the otherwise positive, valuable, and necessary

functions it has performed. Our analysis indicates that historically there have been powerful and strategically placed third parties willing to throw their full influence behind vigorous identity work on behalf of the agency. In the following section we will discuss the importance of these coalitions and the specific negotiation tactics used.

ORGANIZATIONAL RESPONSE OPTIONS

Concerted attempts by influential parties to label an organization deviant typically elicit adaptive responses by the labeled organization. The management of the public identity of the organization becomes a center of heightened activity. Parties concerned with the viability of the organization will attempt to prevent the negative definition from gaining widespread acceptance and promote a competing definition centering around positive aspects of the organization. Several distinct responses are available to an organization following attempts to define it as deviant.

Cessation. The organization may respond by discontinuing the objectionable action. In the face of actual or threatened sanctions, it may acknowledge its deviance and even assume a repentant role; it may promise that the offensive action will not recur and engage in overt measures which may be pointed to as indicating a serious commitment to prevent a recurrence. Trice and Roman (1969) have argued for the general availability and acceptability of such a repentant role in our culture. The probable outcome in the case of large, powerful organizations would be publicly displayed modifications of organizational conduct intended to normalize its public image. The extended controversy and ultimate recall of Firestone tires implicated in highway fatalities and the identity work evidenced in Firestone's subsequent advertising campaign represent an example of this mode of response. Another example is found in the public pronouncements of spokesmen for the Hooker Chemical Company (responsible for the dumping of toxic chemicals in the Love Canal in Niagara, New York) that the organization would "assume its responsibility as a good citizen" by attempting to remedy the situation.

Repudiation. An organization may reject as untrue the definition of itself or its activities as deviant. The feasibility of this response is enhanced where (a) there is considerable dissensus concerning the evaluation of the organization's action, (b) the organization has some ability to restrict the flow of information regarding its activities, and (c) the organization is able to enlist other interested parties in support of its position. Under these circumstances, the actions defined as deviant may continue but the identity of the organization remains a topic of contention.

Re-definition. Where outright repudiation is unfeasible or unsuccessful, organizations may attempt to negotiate the meaning of controversial activities. As with individuals (Scott and Lyman 1968, 1970), negotiation by organizations involves the offering of accounts to justify or excuse untoward conduct. Negotiation is a commonly available response because the meaning of social action is frequently problematic; a variety of interpretations often can be attached to the same event. The ultimate outcome of the negotiation process is largely a function of the organization's ability to enter into strategic coalitions. Just as moral entrepreneurs who impute deviance typically pursue the strategy of forming coalitions with other interested parties to strengthen their claims (Becker 1963; Gusfield 1963), coalition formation is also a typical strategy employed in attempts to resist or counter imputations of deviance.

The CIA's primary response to imputations of deviance has been re-definition. This type of response involves a consistent rejection of the deviant label, and is successful "when that which was previously called deviant comes to be called normative" (Rogers and Buffalo 1974:113). During periods when the legitimacy of CIA activities has been called into question and its public identity rendered problematic, a coalition of Congressional supporters and members of the executive branch has thrown its full weight behind a positive definition of the agency and its activities.

RE-DEFINITION TECHNIQUES

Like the accounts offered by individuals, organizational accounts follow socially approved vocabularies for neutralizing untoward action. Organizational accounts can be sub-classified, paralleling the Scott and Lyman (1970) distinction, as justifications and excuses.

Justifications are statements that acknowledge responsibility for an act, and place a positive value on it in the face of contrary claims. They typically state that the act was appropriate or even necessary under the circumstances, although under most circumstances it would not have been. Excuses, in contrast, deny responsibility while acknowledging an act's negative character; they protect the organization by divorcing it from the act.

The most common justification for controversial agency activities centered around the contention that such activities were acceptable or even necessary because they served national interests in the "fight against the enemy." A recurrent theme in defense of CIA actions is that distasteful practices are engaged in by "both sides" and constitute business as usual. Agency efforts to "destabilize" the Allende government in Chile, for example, were defined by Secretary of State Kissinger as necessary on national security grounds. The uncertainties and conflicting interpretations of the world political situation provided a fertile context for the acceptability of this justification.

Controversial activities were also justified by minimizing the injury they entailed. Agency supporters contended that penetration into and surveillance of domestic groups, while technically in violation of charter, did not involve significant harm or victimization. This justification is seen in the argument that only "minor violations of civil rights" resulted from CIA domestic actions. Target groups were defined as a significant threat to internal political stability; the monitoring of their activities was justified as a legitimate and warranted response to what the then director Colby labeled as an "upsurge of extreme radicalism." The success of the account minimizing the harm of the agency's activities was enhanced by the inability of critics to gather concrete information documenting the details or the total number of actual incidents involving controversial domestic activities.

Justification may be more successful on the part of organizations because, unlike individuals, they can exhibit a set of official goals that place alleged transgressions in a larger context of organizational performance. If these official goals are accepted and it is believed that the organization in question is needed to perform important goals, the successful justification of infractious activity is more easily accomplished. Organizational spokesmen and supporters are thus in a position to claim that they must be held to different standards of social accountability than individuals.

Excusing accounts were repeatedly offered as a technique for defusing and neutralizing criticism of CIA activities. The most successful excuses alluded to the character of and constraints on complex organizations such as the CIA, or involved the mystification of controversial activities.

The excuse that organizations experience constraints not imposed on individuals directs attention to external factors which are said to limit the organization's options and therefore limit its responsibility for certain improper actions. Organizations located within a legally based hierarchy of authority relations are in a unique position to claim that responsibility for wrongdoing resides in parties external to the organization. The "following orders from above" excuse has been one of the most successful defenses of the CIA, and has a surface plausibility which has been difficult to undermine. This account was prominent during the Invisible Government controversy and again when it was claimed that the agency was merely following executive orders in the Watergate events and other domestic incidents. McHugh (1972) argues that attributions of deviance rest heavily on a belief in the actor's responsibility for the wrongdoing. Accordingly, a common excusing account in our culture centers around the idea of shifting the locus of responsibility. In essence, the "constraint on organization" excuse assigns responsibility to others outside the organization. The frequent acceptance of this account has occurred because cultural definitions are ambiguous with regard to the free will and responsibility that can be associated with organizational conduct.

Another widely used excuse relates to the character of organization, either pointing to the limitations inherent in any complex organization or to the fact that the CIA formally has been delegated functions which occasionally entail rather sordid behavior. The former is illustrated during the Red Scare period by statements that the CIA was doing the best any organization could be expected to do to keep communists out, and that all things considered it was doing a creditable job. The latter is illustrated by the Rockefeller Commission's portrayal of agents as "heroes doing dangerous work," and its suggestion that the CIA must be understood in terms of the value of its activities for national security. In these and other cases, defenders of the agency claimed that the activities at issue were understandable and excusable given the special nature of human organizations and the peculiar mission assigned to the Central Intelligence Agency.

Efforts were also made to excuse CIA conduct by what may be termed mystification. Here the organization contends that the whole story is not out and probably will not be forthcoming, but if it were it would serve to exonerate. Organizations vested with the responsibility of carrying out official goals are in a position to claim credit for, in the words of one defender, "an overwhelming number of constructive acts performed in defense of the United States," while at the same time arguing that supportive evidence cannot be disclosed. Such an excuse is plausible regarding areas of action far removed from everyday social matters where an argument emphasizing particular organizational expertise might strike a responsive chord. It may be noted that the same form of excuse was used many times to defend controversial actions during the Vietnam War. Mystification relies on the acceptability of official secrecy and thus has been quite successful for the CIA.

CONCLUSIONS

This paper has focused on organizational response processes. It has identified several attempts to label the CIA as deviant, and has used these cases to analyze techniques to neutralize imputations of deviance and avoid sanctioning. The CIA (as well as other large organizations) are not passive recipients of deviant labels. Rather, the CIA and its supporters responded vigorously in ways which were intended to strike a responsive chord among relevant audiences.

When allegations of wrongdoing are sponsored by influential parties, the public identity of an organization becomes a matter of heightened concern. Unless neutralized, such allegations may result in new constraints being imposed on organizational activities or a loss of confidence by consumers or other organizational clients.

Organizations are able to fashion a variety of accounts justifying and excusing their conduct, some of which are similar to accounts used by individuals and others which are uniquely available to organizations. The most successful organizational accounts refer to the special characteristics of and constraints on complex organizations which act to reduce or displace responsibility for wrongdoing.

The ability to restrict public access to potentially discrediting information and thus mystify the nature of an organization's activities represents another available technique. Through this technique, organizational responsibility and intentionality are obfuscated. The CIA used this strategy successfully to promote an alternative definition of controversial activities. Police departments frequently respond in similar fashion to allegations of citizen abuse. Organizations which are less able to restrict access to discrediting information are considerably more vulnerable to successful labeling.

The ultimate success of efforts to justify and excuse problematic organizational action is contingent upon the relative power of the parties making competing claims. Within the deviance literature as a whole, there is substantial agreement regarding the centrality of the power dimension in deviance outcomes. We suggest that the power dimension in the case of organizations can be usefully conceptualized in terms of the ability to enter into and maintain coalitions with strategically located third parties. With regard to the CIA, such coalitions were critical to its success in deflecting attributions of deviance and avoiding the consequences of such labeling.

REFERENCES

Agee, Philip. 1975. *Inside the Company: CIA Diary.* London: Penguin Books.

Becker, Howard S. 1963. *Outsiders.* New York: Free Press.

Ermann, M. David and Richard J. Lundman. 1978a. *Corporate and Governmental Deviance: Problems of Organizational Behavior in Contemporary Society.* New York: Oxford.

———. 1978b. "Deviant acts by complex organizations: deviance and social control at the organizational level of analysis." *The Sociological Quarterly* 19:55–67.

Gusfield, Joseph R. 1963. *Symbolic Crusade.* Urbana, Illinois: University of Illinois Press.

McHugh, Peter. 1972. "A common-sense conception of deviance." Pp. 312–29 in Jack D. Douglas (ed.), *Deviance and Respectability.* New York: Basic Books.

Marchetti, Victor and John D. Marks. 1974. *The CIA and the Cult of Intelligence.* New York: Alfred Knopf.

New York Times Index: A Book of Record. 1947–1975. New York: The New York Times Company.

Rogers, Joseph W. and M. D. Buffalo. 1974. "Fighting back: nine modes of adaptation to a deviant label." *Social Problems* 22:101–18.

Schur, Edwin M. 1971. *Labeling Deviant Behavior.* Englewood Cliffs, N.J.: Prentice Hall.

Scott, Marvin B. and Stanford M. Lyman. 1968. "Accounts." *American Sociological Review* 33:46–62.

———. 1970. "Accounts, deviance, and social order." Pp. 89–119 in Jack D. Douglas (ed.), *Deviance and Respectability.* New York: Basic Books.

Stone, I. F. 1976. "How the CIA is winning." *The New York Review of Books,* May 27:3–4.

Trice, Harrison M. and Paul Roman. 1969. "Delabeling, relabeling, and alcoholics anonymous." *Social Problems* 17:536–48.

U.S. Senate, Judiciary Committee, Subcommittee on Intelligence. 1951–1975. "Administration of the internal security act and other internal security laws." Washington, D.C.: Government Printing Office.

Wise, David and Thomas B. Ross. 1964. *The Invisible Government.* New York: Random House.

CONFLICT THEORY

READING 2-13

Capitalism, Class, and Crime in America

David M. Gordon

It seems important to emphasize, first of all, that crime is ubiquitous in the United States. Our laws are so pervasive that one must virtually retire to hermitage in order to avoid committing a crime. According to a national survey conducted in 1965 by the President's Crime Commission (1967), 91 percent of all adult Americans "admitted that they had committed acts for which they might have received jail or prison sentences." The Crime Commission also found that in 1965 "more than two million Americans were received in prisons or juvenile training schools, or placed on probation"— well over 2 percent of the labor force. Criminal behavior, it appears, is clearly a norm and not an aberration.[1]

Given that ubiquity, it seems equally important to emphasize our extraordinary selectivity in our attention to the problem of crime. We focus all our nearly paranoid fears about "law 'n' order" and "safe streets" on a limited number of crimes while we altogether ignore many other kinds of crime, equally serious and of much greater economic importance.

One can sketch the dimensions of this selectivity quite easily. The crimes on which the public *does* concentrate its fears and cannons are often lumped together as "urban" or "violent" crimes.

These crimes can be usefully summarized by those for which the FBI accumulates a general statistical index. Seven "Index Crimes" are traced in the Bureau's periodic Crime Report: willful homicide, forcible rape, aggravated assault, robbery, burglary, larceny (of more than $50), and motor vehicle theft. Together, these seven crimes encompass the raging fire in fear of which we hide inside our homes.

The crimes to which the public and the media choose to pay almost no attention seem just as obvious. Many kinds of relatively hidden profitable crimes, most of them called "white-collar" crimes, occur with startling frequency. Tax evasion, price fixing, embezzlement, swindling, and consumer fraud capture billions of dollars every year.

> Illicit gains from white-collar crime far exceed those of all other crime combined. . . . One corporate price-fixing conspiracy criminally converted more money each year it continued than all of the hundreds of thousands of burglaries, larcenies, or thefts in the entire nation during those same years. Reported bank embezzlements cost ten times more than bank robberies each year. (Clark 1970:38)

The selectivity of public opinion is matched, moreover, by the biases of our governmental system for the enforcement and administration of justice, which prosecutes and punishes some crimes and criminals heavily while leaving others alone. Some defenders of the system occasionally argue that it concentrates most heavily on those crimes of the greatest magnitude and importance, but the data do not support this view: the Index Crimes on which the system focuses account for small proportions of the total personal harm and property loss resulting from crime in the United States. For example,

---

[1] One should add, of course, that these figures refer only to those harmful acts which actually violate some law. Many other tangibly harmful acts, like faulty manufacture of automobiles or certain kinds of pollution, have not yet been declared illegal.

Reprinted from *Crime and Delinquency* 19, no. 2 (April 1973), 163–84. Reprinted by permission of Sage Publications.

deaths resulting from "willful homicide" are one-fifth as frequent as deaths from motor vehicle accidents; although many experts ascribe nearly half of motor vehicle accidents to mechanical failure, the system rarely pays attention to those liable for that failure. The economic loss attributable to Index Crimes against property—robbery, burglary, and so on—are one-fifth the losses attributable to embezzlement, fraud, and unreported commercial theft, and yet the system concentrates almost exclusively on the former.

One can much more reasonably argue, as many have in other contexts, that the selectivity of our police, courts, and prisons corresponds most closely to the relative *class status* of those who perpetrate different crimes. We seem to have a dual system of justice in this country, as both the Crime Commission and Goldfarb have most clearly shown. The public system concentrates on crimes committed by the poor, while crimes by the more affluent are left to private auspices. Our prisons function, as Goldfarb notes, like a "national poor-house," swallowing the poor, chewing them up, and occasionally spitting them back at the larger society. When the more affluent get in trouble, in contrast, private psychiatric and counseling assistance supplant prosecution: "In the classes of offenses committed by rich and poor *equally,* it is rarely the rich who end up behind bars" (Goldfarb 1969:312).

COMPETITIVE CAPITALISM AND RATIONAL CRIME

Capitalist societies depend, as radicals often argue, on basically competitive forms of social and economic interaction and upon substantial inequalities in the allocation of social resources. Without inequalities, it would be much more difficult to induce workers to work in alienating environments. Without competition and a competitive ideology, workers might not be inclined to struggle to improve their relative income and status in society by working harder. Finally, although rights of property are protected, capitalist societies do not guarantee economic security to most of its individual members. Individuals must fend for themselves, finding the best available opportunities to provide for themselves and their families. At the same time, history bequeaths a corpus of laws and statutes to any social epoch which may or may not correspond to the social morality of that epoch. Inevitably, at any point in time, many of the "best" opportunities for economic survival open to different citizens will violate some of those historically determined laws. Driven by the fear of economic insecurity and by a competitive desire to gain some of the goods unequally distributed throughout the society, many individuals will eventually become "criminals." As Adam Smith himself admitted, "Where there is no property, . . . civil government is not so necessary" (Smith 1937:670).

In that respect, therefore, radicals argue that nearly all crimes in capitalist societies represent perfectly *rational* responses to the structure of institutions upon which capitalist societies are based. Crimes of many different varieties constitute functionally similar responses to the organization of capitalist institutions for those crimes help provide a means of survival in a society within which survival is never assured. Three different kinds of crime in the United States provide the most important examples of this functionally similar rationality among different kinds of crime: ghetto crime, organized crime, and corporate (or "white-collar") crime.[2]

It seems especially clear, first of all, that ghetto crime is committed by people responding quite reasonably to the structure of economic opportunities available to them. Only rarely, it appears, can ghetto criminals be regarded as raving, irrational,

---

[2] This is not meant to imply, obviously, that there would be no crime in a communist society in which perfectly secure equal support was provided for all. It suggests, quite simply, that one would have to analyze crime in such a society with reference to a different set of ideas and a different set of institutions.

antisocial lunatics (Brown 1965; Cleaver 1969; Jackson 1970; Malcolm X 1964; Shaw and McKay 1969; Wolfgang and Ferracuti 1967). The "legitimate" jobs open to many ghetto residents, especially to young black males, typically pay low wages, offer relatively demeaning assignments, and carry the constant risk of layoff. In contrast, many kinds of crime "available" in the ghetto often bring higher monetary return, offer even higher social status, and—at least in some cases like numbers running—sometimes carry relatively low risk of arrest and punishment. Given those alternative opportunities, the choice between "legitimate" and "illegitimate" activities is often quite simple. As Arthur Dunmeyer, a black hustler from Harlem, has put it:

> In some cases this is the way you get your drug dealers and prostitutes and your numbers runners. . . . They see that these things are the only way that they can compete in the society, to get some sort of status. They realize that there aren't any real doors open to them, and so, to commit crime was the only thing to do, they can't go back. (Brown and Dunmeyer 1971:292)

In much the same way, organized crime represents a perfectly rational kind of economic activity (Cressey 1969; Morris and Hawkins 1969). Activities like gambling and prostitution are illegal for varieties of historical reasons, but there is a demand for those activities nonetheless. As Donald Cressey writes: "The American confederation of criminals thrives because a large minority of citizens demands the illicit goods and services it has for sale" (Cressey 1969:294). Clark makes the same point, arguing that organized crimes are essentially "consensual crimes . . . , desired by the consuming public" (Clark 1970:68). The simple fact that they are both illegal and in great demand provides a simple explanation for the secrecy, relative efficiency, and occasional violence of those who provide them. In nearly every sense the organization of the heroin industry, for example, bears as rational and reasonable a relationship to the nature of the product as the structures of the tobacco and alcoholic beverages industries bear to the nature of their own products.[3]

Finally, briefly to amplify the third example, corporate crime also represents a quite rational response to life in capitalist societies. Corporations exist to protect and augment the capital of their owners. If it becomes difficult to perform that function one way, corporate officials will quite inevitably try to do it another. When Westinghouse and General Electric conspired to fix prices, for instance, they were resorting to one of many possible devices for limiting the potential threat of competition to their price structures. Similarly, when Ford and General Motors proliferate new car model after new car model, each differing only slightly from its siblings, they are choosing to protect their price structures by what economists call "product differentiation." In one case, the corporations were using oligopolistic power quite directly; in the other, they rely on the power of advertising to generate demand for the differentiated products. In the context of the perpetual and highly competitive race among corporations for profits and capital accumulation, each response seems quite reasonable. Sutherland made the same points about corporate crime and linked the behavior of corporations to lower-class criminality:

> I have attempted to demonstrate that businessmen violate the law with great frequency . . . . If these conclusions are correct, it is very clear that the criminal behavior of businessmen cannot be explained by poverty, in the usual sense, or by bad housing or lack of recreational facilities or feeble-mindedness or emotional instability. Business leaders are capable, emotionally balanced, and in no sense pathological. . . . The assumption that an offender must have some such pathological distortion of the intellect or the emotions seems to me

---

[3] As Cressey (1969) points out, for instance, it makes a great deal of sense in the heroin industry for the supplier to seek a monopoly on the source of the heroin but to permit many individual sellers of heroin at its final destination, usually without organization backing, because the risks occur primarily at the consumers' end.

absurd, and if it is absurd regarding the crimes of businessmen, it is equally absurd regarding the crimes of persons in the lower economic class. (Sutherland 1971:310)

CLASS INSTITUTIONS AND DIFFERENCES AMONG CRIMES

If most crime in the United States in one way or another reflects the same kind of rational response to the insecurity and inequality of capitalist institutions, what explains the manifold differences among different kinds of crimes? Some crimes are much more violent than others, some are much more heavily prosecuted, and some are much more profitable. Why?

As a first step in explaining differences among crimes, I would apply the general radical perspective in a relatively straightforward manner and argue quite simply that many of the most important differences among different kinds of crime in this country are determined by the *structure of class institutions* in our society and by the *class biases* of the State. That argument has two separate components.

First, I would argue that many of the important differences among crimes in this society derive quite directly from the different socio-economic classes to which individuals belong. Relatively affluent citizens have access to jobs in large corporations, to institutions involved in complicated paper transactions involving lots of money, and to avenues of relatively unobtrusive communication. Members of those classes who decide to break the law have, as Clark puts it, "an easier, less offensive, less visible way of doing wrong" (Clark 1970:38). Those raised in poverty, on the other hand, do not have such easy access to money. If they are to obtain it criminally, they must impinge on those who already have it or direct its flow. As Robert Morgenthau, a former federal attorney, has written, those growing up in the ghetto "will probably never have the opportunity to embezzle funds from a bank or to promote a multimillion dollar stock fraud scheme. The criminal ways which we encourage [them] to choose will be those closest at hand—from vandalism to mugging to armed robbery" (Morgenthau 1969:20).

Second, I would argue that the biases of our police, courts, and prisons *explain* the relative violence of many crimes—that many of the differences in the degree of violence among different kinds of crime do not cause the selectivity of public concern about those crimes but *are* in fact *caused by* that selectivity. For a variety of historical reasons, as I noted above, we have a dual system of justice in this country; the police, courts, and prisons pay careful attention to only a few crimes. It is only natural, as a result, that those who run the highest risks of arrest and conviction may have to rely on the threat or commission of violence in order to protect themselves. Many kinds of ghetto crimes generate violence, for instance, because the participants are severely prosecuted for their crimes and must try to protect themselves however they can. Other kinds of ghetto crimes, like the numbers racket, are openly tolerated by the police, and those crimes rarely involve violence. It may be true, as Clark argues, that "violent crime springs from a violent environment" (Clark 1970:39), but violent environments like the ghetto do not always produce violent crimes. Those crimes to which the police pay attention usually involve violence, while those which the police tend to ignore quite normally do not. In similar ways, organized crime has become violent historically, as Cressey (1969) especially argues, principally because its participants are often prosecuted. As long as that remains true, the suppliers of illegal goods require secrecy, organization, and a bit of violence to protect their livelihood. Completely in contrast, corporate crime does not require violence because it is ignored by the police; corporate criminals can safely assume they do not face the threat of jail and do not therefore have to cover their tracks with the threat of harming those who betray them. When Lockheed Aircraft accountants and executives falsified their public reports in order to disguise cost overruns on the C-5A airplane in 1967 and 1968, for instance, they did not have to force Defense Department officials at knifepoint to play along with their falsifications. As Robert Sherrill (1970:43) reports in his investigation of the Lockheed affair, the Defense Department officials were entirely willing to cooperate. "This sympathy," he writes, "was reflected in orders from top Air Force officials to withhold information regarding Lockheed's dilemma from all reports that would be widely circulated." If only local police were equally sympathetic to the "dilemmas" of street corner junkies, the violent patterns of drug-related crimes might be considerably transformed.

In short, it seems important to view some of the most important differences among crimes—differences in their violence, their style, and their impact—as fundamental outgrowths of the class structure of society and the class biases of our major institutions, including the State and its system of enforcement and administration of justice. Given that argument, it places a special burden on attempts to explain the historical sources of the duality of the public system of justice in this country, for that duality, coupled with the class biases of other institutions, plays an important role in determining the patterns of American crime.

THE SOURCES OF DUALITY

One can explain the duality of our public system of justice quite easily, it seems to me, if one is willing to view the State through the radical perspective. The analysis involves answers to two separate questions. First, one must ask why the State ignores certain kinds of crimes, especially white-collar crimes and corporate crimes. Second, given that most crimes among the poor claim the poor as their victims, one must ask why the State bothers to worry so incessantly about those crimes.

The answer to the first question draws directly from the radical theory of the State. According to the radical theory, the government in a capitalist society like the United States exists primarily to preserve the stability of the system which provides, preserves, and protects returns to the owners of capital. As long as crimes among the corporate class tend in general to harm members of other classes, like those in the "consuming" class, the State will not spontaneously move to prevent those crimes from taking place. On the other hand, as Paul Sweezy (1968) has especially argued, the State may be pressured to prosecute the wealthy if their criminal practices become so egregiously offensive that their victims may move to overthrow the system itself. In those cases, the State may punish individual members of the class in order to protect the interests of the entire class. Latent opposition to the practices of corporations may be forestalled, to pick several examples, by token public efforts to enact and enforce antitrust, truth-in-lending, antipollution, industrial safety, and auto safety legislation. As James Ridgeway (1970) has most clearly shown in the case of pollution, however, the gap between the enactment of the statutes and their effective enforcement seems quite cavernous.[4]

The answer to the second question seems slightly more complicated historically. Public responses to crime among the poor have changed periodically throughout American history, varying according to changes in the patterns of the crimes themselves and to changes in public morality. The subtlety of that historical process would be difficult to trace in this kind of discussion. But some patterns do seem clear.

Earlier in American history, as Clark (1970) has pointed out, we intended to ignore many crimes among the poor because those crimes

---

[4] This rests on an assumption, of course, that one learns much more about the priorities of the state by looking at its patterns of enforcement than by noting the nature of its statutes. This seems quite reasonable. The statutory process is often cumbersome, whereas the patterns of enforcement can sometimes be changed quite easily. Furthermore, as many radicals would argue, the State in democratic societies can often support the capitalist class most effectively by selective enforcement of the laws rather than by selective legislation. For varieties of relatively complicated historical reasons, selective enforcement of the law seems to arouse less fear for the erosion of democratic tradition than selective legislation itself. As long as we have statutes which nominally outlaw racial inequality, for instance, inadequate enforcement of those laws seems to cause relatively little furor; before we had such laws in this country, protests against the selective statutes could ultimately be mounted.

rarely impinged upon the lives of the more affluent. Gambling, prostitution, dope, and robbery seemed to flourish in the slums of the early twentieth century, and the police rarely moved to intervene. More recently, however, some of the traditional patterns of crime have changed. Two dimensions of change seem most important. On the one hand, much of the crime has moved out of the slums: "Our concern arose when social dynamics and population movements brought crime and addiction out of the slums and inflicted it on or threatened the powerful and well-to-do" (Clark 1970:55). On the other hand, the styles in which ghetto criminals have fulfilled their criminal intent may have grown more hostile since World War II.

Out of frustration, some of the crime among younger ghetto-born blacks may be more vengeful now, more concerned with sticking it to whitey. Coupled with the spread of ghetto crime into other parts of the city, this symbolic expression of vengefulness undoubtedly heightens the fear that many affluent citizens feel about ghetto crime. Given their influence with the government, they quite naturally have moved toward increasing public attention to the prevention and punishment of crimes among the poor.

THE IMPLAUSIBILITY OF REFORM

One needs to ask, finally, whether these patterns can be changed and the trends reversed. Can we simultaneously eradicate the causes of crime and reform our dual system of justice? At the heart of that question lies the question posed at the beginning of this essay, for it simultaneously raises the necessity of explaining the failures of our present system to prevent the crime it seeks most systematically to control.

I would argue, quite simply, that reform is implausible unless we change the basic institutions upon which capitalism in the United States depends. We cannot legitimately expect to eradicate the initial causes of crime for two reasons. First,

capitalism depends quite substantially on the preservation of the conditions of competition and inequality. Those conditions, as I argue above, will tend to lead quite inevitably to relatively pervasive criminal behavior; without those conditions, the capitalist system would scarcely work at all. Second, as many have argued, the general presence of racism in this country, though capitalists may not in fact have created it, tends to support and maintain the power of the capitalists as a class by providing cheap labor and dividing the working class. Given the substantial control of capitalists over the policies and priorities of the State, we cannot easily expect to prod the State to eliminate the fundamental causes of racism in this country. In that respect, it seems likely that the particular inequalities facing blacks and their consequent attraction to the opportunities available in crime seem likely to continue.

Given expectations that crime will continue, it seems equally unlikely that we shall be able to reform our systems of prosecution and punishment in order to mitigate their harmful effects on criminals and to equalize their treatment of different kinds of crime. First and superficially, as I noted above, several important and powerful vested interests have acquired a stake in the current system and seem likely to resist efforts to change it. Second and more fundamentally, the cumulative effect of the patterns of crime, violence, prosecution, and punishment in this country plays an important role in helping legitimize and stabilize the capitalist system. Although capitalists as a class may not have created the current patterns of crime and punishment, those patterns currently serve their interests in several different ways. We should expect that the capitalists as a class will hardly be able to push reform of the system. Given their relative reluctance to reform the system, we should expect to be able to push reform only in the event that we can substantially change the structure of power to which the State responds.

The current patterns of crime and punishment support the capitalist system in three different ways.

First, the pervasive patterns of selective enforcement seem to reinforce a prevalent ideology in this society that individuals, rather than institutions, are to blame for social problems. Individuals are criminally prosecuted for motor accidents because of negligent or drunken driving, for instance, but auto manufacturers are never criminally prosecuted for the negligent construction of unsafe cars or for their roles in increasing the likelihood of death through air pollution. Individual citizens are often prosecuted and punished for violence and for resisting arrest, equally, but those agents of institutions, like police and prison guards, or institutions themselves, like Dow Chemical, are never prosecuted for inflicting unwarranted violence on others. These patterns of selectivity reinforce our pervasive preconceptions of the invulnerability of institutions, leading us to blame ourselves for social failure; this pattern of individual blame, as Edwards and MacEwan (1970) have especially argued, plays an important role in legitimizing the basic institutions of this kind of capitalist society.

Second, and critically important, the patterns of crime and punishment manage "legitimately" to neutralize the potential opposition to the system of many of our most oppressed citizens. In particular, the system serves ultimately to keep thousands of men out of the job market or trapped in the secondary labor market by perpetuating a set of institutions which serves functionally to feed large numbers of blacks (and poor whites) through the cycle of crime, imprisonment, parole, and recidivism. The system has this same ultimate effect in many different ways. It locks up many for life, first of all, guaranteeing that those potentially disaffected souls keep "out of trouble." As for those whom it occasionally releases, it tends to drive them deeper into criminality, intensifying their criminal and violent behavior, filling their heads with paranoia and hatred, keeping them perpetually on the run and unable, ultimately, to organize with others to change the institutions which pursue them. Finally, it blots their records with the stigma of criminality and, by denying them many decent employment opportunities, effectively precludes the reform of even those who vow to escape the system and to go "straight."

If the system did not effect this neutralization, if so many of the poor were not trapped in the debilitating system of crime and punishment, they might gather the strength to oppose the system that reinforces their misery. Like many other institutions in this country, the system of crime and punishment serves an important function for the capitalist class by dividing and weakening those who might potentially seek to overthrow the capitalist system. Although the capitalists have not created the system, in any direct sense, they would doubtlessly hate to have to do without it.

The third and perhaps most important functionally supportive role of the current patterns of crime and punishment is that those patterns allow us to ignore some basic issues about the relationships in our society between institutions and individuals. By treating criminals as animals and misfits, as enemies of the state, we are permitted to continue avoiding some basic questions about the dehumanizing effects of our social institutions. We keep our criminals out of sight, so we are never forced to recognize and deal with the psychic punishment we inflict on them. Like the schools and the welfare system, the legal system turns out, upon close inspection, to be robbing most of its "clients" of the last vestiges of their personal dignity. Each one of those institutions, in its own way, helps us forget about the responsibilities we might alternatively assume for providing the best possible environment within which all of us could grow and develop as individuals. Cleaver sees this "role" of the system quite clearly:

> Those who are now in prison could be put through a process of real rehabilitation before their release. . . . By rehabilitation I mean they would be trained for jobs that would not be an insult to their dignity, that would give them some sense of security, that would allow them to achieve some brotherly connection with their fellow man. But for

this kind of rehabilitation to happen on a large scale would entail the complete reorganization of society, not to mention the prison system. It would call for the teaching of a new set of ethics, based on the principle of cooperation, as opposed to the presently dominating principle of competition. It would require the transformation of the entire moral fabric. . . . (Cleaver 1969:179, 182)

By keeping its victims so thoroughly hidden and rendering them so apparently inhuman, our system of crime and punishment allows us to forget how sweeping a "transformation" of our social ideology we would require in order to begin solving the problem of crime. The more we forget, the more protected the capitalists remain from a thorough re-examination of the ideological basis of the institutions upon which they depend.

REFERENCES

Brown, Claude. 1965. *Manchild in the Promised Land.* New York: Macmillan.

Brown, Claude and Arthur Dunmeyer. 1971. "A Way of Life in the Ghetto." p. 292 in D. Gordon (ed.), *Problems in Political Economy.* Lexington, MA: D.C. Heath.

Clark, Ramsey. 1970. *Crime in America.* New York: Simon and Schuster.

Cleaver, Eldridge. 1969. *Post-Prison Writings and Speeches.* New York: A Ramparts Book by Random House.

Cressey, Donald. 1969. *Theft of the Nation: The Structure and Operations of Organized Crime.* New York: Harper & Row.

Edwards, Richard and Arthur MacEwen. 1970. "A Radical Approach to Economics." *American Economic Review* (May).

Goldfarb, Ronald. 1969. "Prison: The National Poorhouse." *New Republic,* November:312.

Jackson, George. 1970. *Soledad Brother.* New York: Bantam Books.

Malcolm X. 1964. *Autobiography.* New York: Grove Press.

Morgenthau, Robert. 1969. "Equal Justice and the Problem of White Collar Crime." *The Conference Board Record* (August):20.

Morris, Norval and Gordon Hawkins. 1969. *The Honest Politician's Guide to Crime Control.* Chicago: University of Chicago Press.

President's Commission on Law Enforcement and Administration of Justice. 1967. *The Challenge of Crime in a Free Society.* Washington, D.C.: U.S. Government Printing Office.

Ridgeway, James. 1970. *The Politics of Ecology.* New York: Dutton.

Shaw, Clifford and Henry McKay. 1969. *Juvenile Delinquency and Urban Areas.* Chicago: University of Chicago Press.

Sherrill, Robert. 1970. "The Convenience of Being Lockheed." *Scanlan's Monthly* (August):43.

Smith, Adam. 1937. *The Wealth of Nations.* New York: Modern Library.

Sutherland, Edwin H. 1971. "The Crime of Corporations" in D. Gordon (ed.), *Problems in Political Economy.* Lexington, MA: D.C. Heath.

Sweezy, Paul. 1968. *The Theory of Capitalist Development.* New York: Monthly Review Press.

Wolfgang, Marvin E. and Franco Ferracuti. 1967. *The Subculture of Violence.* New York: Barnes and Noble.

The Police and the Black Male

Elijah Anderson

The police, in the Village–Northton [neighborhood] as elsewhere, represent society's formal, legitimate means of social control (see Rubenstein 1973; Wilson 1968; Fogelson 1977; Reiss 1971; Bittner 1967; Banton 1964). Their role includes protecting law-abiding citizens from those who are not law-abiding, by preventing crime and by apprehending likely criminals. Precisely how the police fulfill the public's expectations is strongly related to how they view the neighborhood and the people who live there. On the streets, color-coding often works to confuse race, age, class, gender, incivility, and criminality, and it expresses itself most concretely in the person of the anonymous black male. In doing their job, the police often become willing parties to this general color-coding of the public environment, and related distinctions, particularly those of skin color and gender, come to convey definite meanings. Although such coding may make the work of the police more manageable, it may also fit well with their own presuppositions regarding race and class relations, thus shaping officers' perceptions of crime "in the city." Moreover, the anonymous black male is usually an ambiguous figure who arouses the utmost caution and is generally considered dangerous until he proves he is not.

There are some who charge—perhaps with good reason—that the police are primarily agents of the middle class who are working to make the area more hospitable to middle-class people at the expense of the lower classes. It is obvious that the police assume whites in the community are at least middle class and are trustworthy on the streets. Hence the

police may be seen primarily as protecting "law-abiding" middle-class whites against anonymous "criminal" black males.

To be white is to be seen by the police—at least superficially—as an ally, eligible for consideration and for much more deferential treatment than that accorded blacks in general. This attitude may be grounded in the backgrounds of the police themselves.[1] Many have grown up in Eastern City's "ethnic" neighborhoods. They may serve what they perceive as their own class and neighborhood interests, which often translates as keeping blacks "in their place"—away from neighborhoods that are socially defined as "white." In trying to do their job, the police appear to engage in an informal policy of monitoring young black men as a means of controlling crime, and often they seem to go beyond the bounds of duty. The following field note shows what pressures and racism young black men in the Village may endure at the hands of the police:

> At 8:30 on a Thursday evening in June I saw a police car stopped on a side street near the Village. Beside the car stood a policeman with a young black man. I pulled up behind the police car and waited to see what would happen. When the policeman released the young man, I got out of my car and asked the youth for an interview.
>
> "So what did he say to you when they stopped you? What was the problem?" I asked. "I was just coming around the corner, and he stopped me, asked me what was my name, and all that. And what I had in my bag. And where I was coming from. Where I lived, you know, all the basic stuff, I guess. Then he

From Elijah Anderson, *Streetwise* (Chicago: University of Chicago Press, 1990). Reprinted by permission of the University of Chicago Press and the author.

[1] For an illuminating typology of police work that draws a distinction between "fraternal" and "professional" codes of behavior, see Wilson (1968).

searched me down and, you know, asked me who were the supposedly tough guys around here? That's about it. I couldn't tell him who they are. How do I know? Other gang members could, but I'm not from a gang, you know. But he tried to put me in a gang bag, though." "How old are you?" I asked. "I'm seventeen, I'll be eighteen next month." "Did he give any reason for stopping you?" "No, he didn't. He just wanted my address, where I lived, where I was coming from, that kind of thing. I don't have no police record or nothin'. I guess he stopped me on principle, 'cause I'm black." "How does that make you feel?" I asked. "Well, it doesn't bother me too much, you know, as long as I know that I hadn't done nothin', but I guess it just happens around here. They just stop young black guys and ask 'em questions, you know. What can you do?"

On the streets late at night, the average young black man is suspicious of others he encounters, and he is particularly wary of the police. If he is dressed in the uniform of the "gangster," such as a black leather jacket, sneakers, and a "gangster cap," if he is carrying a radio or a suspicious bag (which may be confiscated), or if he is moving too fast or too slow, the police may stop him. As part of the routine, they search him and make him sit in the police car while they run a check to see whether there is a "detainer" on him. If there is nothing, he is allowed to go on his way. After this ordeal the youth is often left afraid, sometimes shaking, and uncertain about the area he had previously taken for granted. He is upset in part because he is painfully aware of how close he has come to being in "big trouble." He knows of other youths who have gotten into a "world of trouble" simply by being on the streets at the wrong time or when the police were pursuing a criminal. In these circumstances, particularly at night, it is relatively easy for one black man to be mistaken for another. Over the years, while walking through the neighborhood I have on occasion been stopped and questioned by police chasing a mugger, but after explaining myself I was released.

Many youths, however, have reason to fear such mistaken identity or harassment, since they might be jailed, if only for a short time, and would have to post bail money and pay legal fees to extricate themselves from the mess (Anderson 1986). When law-abiding blacks are ensnared by the criminal justice system, the scenario may proceed as follows. A young man is arbitrarily stopped by the police and questioned. If he cannot effectively negotiate with the officer(s), he may be accused of a crime and arrested. To resolve this situation he needs financial resources, which for him are in short supply. If he does not have money for an attorney, which often happens, he is left to a public defender who may be more interested in going along with the court system than in fighting for a poor black person. Without legal support, he may well wind up "doing time" even if he is innocent of the charges brought against him. The next time he is stopped for questioning he will have a record, which will make detention all the more likely.

Because the young black man is aware of many cases when an "innocent" black person was wrongly accused and detained, he develops an "attitude" toward the police. The street word for police is "the man," signifying a certain machismo, power, and authority. He becomes concerned when he notices "the man" in the community or when the police focus on him because he is outside his own neighborhood. The youth knows, or soon finds out, that he exists in a legally precarious state. Hence he is motivated to avoid the police, and his public life becomes severely circumscribed.

To obtain fair treatment when confronted by the police, the young man may wage a campaign for social regard so intense that at times it borders on obsequiousness. As one streetwise black youth said: "If you show a cop that you nice and not a smartass, they be nice to you. They talk to you like the man you are. You gonna get ignorant like a little kid, they gonna get ignorant with you." Young black males often are particularly deferential toward the police even when they are completely within their rights and have done nothing wrong. Most often this is not out of blind acceptance or respect for the "law," but because they know the police can cause them hardship. When confronted or arrested, they adopt a particular style of behavior to get on the policeman's good side. Some simply "go limp" or politely ask, "What seems to be the trouble, officer?" This pose requires a deference that is in sharp contrast with the youth's more usual image, but many seem to take it in stride or not even to realize it. Because they are concerned primarily with staying out of trouble, and because they perceive the police as arbitrary in their use of power, many defer in an equally arbitrary way. Because of these pressures, however, black youths tend to be especially mindful of the police and, when they are around, to watch their own behavior in public. Many have come to expect harassment and are inured to it; they simply tolerate it as part of living in the Village–Northton.

After a certain age, say twenty-four, a black man may no longer be stopped so often, but he continues to be the object of policy scrutiny. As one twenty-seven-year-old black college graduate speculated:

> I think they see me with my little bag with papers in it. They see me with penny loafers on. I have a tie on, some days. They don't stop me so much now. See, it depends on the circumstances. If something goes down, and they hear that the guy had on a big black coat, I may be the one. But when I was younger, they could just stop me, carte blanche, any old time. Name taken, searched, and this went on endlessly. From the time I was about twelve until I was sixteen or seventeen, endlessly, endlessly. And I come from a lower-middle-class black neighborhood, OK, that borders a white neighborhood. One neighborhood is all black, and one is all white. OK, just because we were so close to that neighborhood, we were stopped endlessly. And it happened even more when we went up into a suburban community. When we would ride up and out to the suburbs, we were stopped every time we did it.
>
> If it happened today, now that I'm older, I would really be upset. In the old days when I was younger, I didn't know any better. You just expected it, you knew it was gonna happen. Cops would come up, "What you doing, where you coming from?" Say things to you. They might even call you nigger.

Such scrutiny and harassment by local police makes black youths see them as a problem to get beyond, to deal with, and their attempts affect their overall behavior. To avoid encounters with "the man," some streetwise young men camouflage themselves, giving up the urban uniform and emblems that identify them as "legitimate" objects of police attention. They may adopt a more conventional presentation of self, wearing chinos, sweat suits, and generally more conservative dress. Some youths have been known to "ditch" a favorite jacket if they see others wearing one like it, because wearing it increases their chances of being mistaken for someone else who may have committed a crime.

But such strategies do not always work over the long run and must be constantly modified. For instance, because so many young ghetto blacks have begun to wear Fila and Adidas sweat suits as status symbols, such dress has become incorporated into the public image generally associated with young black males. These athletic suits, particularly the more expensive and colorful ones, along with high-priced sneakers, have become the leisure dress of successful drug dealers, and other youths will often mimic their wardrobe to "go for bad" in the quest for local esteem. Hence what was once a "square" mark of distinction approximating the conventions of the wider culture has been adopted by a neighborhood group devalued by that same culture. As we saw earlier, the young black male enjoys a certain power over fashion: whatever the collective peer group embraces can become "hip" in a manner the wider society may not desire (see Goffman 1963). These same styles then attract the attention of the agents of social control.

THE IDENTIFICATION CARD

Law-abiding black people, particularly those of the middle class, set out to approximate middle-class whites in styles of self-presentation in public, including dress and bearing. Such middle-class emblems, often viewed as "square," are not usually embraced by young working-class blacks. Instead, their connections with and claims on the institutions of the wider society seem to be symbolized by the identification card. The common identification card associates its holder with a firm, a corporation, a school, a union, or some other institution of substance and influence. Such a card, particularly from a prominent establishment, puts the police and others on notice that the youth is "somebody," thus creating an important distinction between a black man who can claim a connection with the wider society and one who is summarily judged as "deviant." Although blacks who are established in the middle class might take such cards for granted, many lower-class blacks, who continue to find it necessary to campaign for civil rights denied them because of skin color, believe that carrying an identification card brings them better treatment than is meted out to their less fortunate brothers and sisters. For them this link to the wider society, though often tenuous, is psychically and socially important. The young college graduate continues:

> I know [how] I used to feel when I was enrolled in college last year, when I had an ID card. I used to hear stories about the blacks getting stopped over by the dental school, people having trouble sometimes. I would see that all the time. Young black male being stopped by the police. Young black male in handcuffs. But I knew that because I had that ID card that I would not be mistaken for just somebody snatching a pocketbook, or just somebody being where maybe I wasn't expected to be. See, even though I was intimidated by the campus police—I mean, the first time I walked into the security office to get my ID they all gave me the double-take to see if I was somebody they were looking for. See, after I got the card, I was like, well, they can think that now, but I have this [ID card]. Like, see, late at night when I be walking around, and the cops be checking me out, giving me the looks, you know. I mean, I know guys, students, who were getting stopped all the time, sometimes by the same officer, even though they had the ID. And even they would say, "Hey, I got the ID, so why was I stopped?"

The cardholder may believe he can no longer be treated summarily by the police, that he is no longer likely to be taken as a "no count," to be prejudicially confused with that class of blacks "who are always causing trouble on the trolley." Furthermore, there is a firm belief that if the police stop a person

who has a card, they cannot "do away with him without somebody coming to his defense." This concern should not be underestimated. Young black men trade stories about mistreatment at the hands of the police; a common one involves policemen who transport youths into rival gang territories and release them, telling them to get home the best way they can. From the youth's perspective, the card signifies a certain status in circumstances where little recognition was formerly available.

"DOWNTOWN" POLICE AND LOCAL POLICE

In attempting to manage the police—and by implication to manage themselves—some black youths have developed a working connection of the police in certain public areas of the Village–Northton. Those who spend a good amount of their time on these corners, and thus observing the police, have come to distinguish between the "downtown" police and the "regular" local police.

The local police are the ones who spend time in the area; normally they drive around in patrol cars, often one officer to a car. These officers usually make a kind of working peace with the young men on the streets; for example, they know the names of some of them and may even befriend a young boy. Thus they offer an image of the police department different from that displayed by the "downtown" police. The downtown police are distant, impersonal, and often actively looking for "trouble." They are known to swoop down arbitrarily on gatherings of black youths standing on a street corner; they might punch them around, call them names, and administer other kinds of abuse, apparently for sport. A young Northton man gave the following narrative about his experiences with the police.

> And I happen to live in a violent part. There's a real difference between the violence level in the Village and the violence level in Northton. In the nighttime it's more dangerous over there.
>
> It's so bad now, they got downtown cops over there now. They doin' a good job bringin' the highway

patrol over there. Regular cops don't like that. You can tell that. They even try to emphasize to us the certain category. Highway patrol come up, he leave, they say somethin' about it. "We can do our job over here." We call [downtown police] Nazis. They about six feet eight, seven feet. We walkin', we jump out. "You run, and we'll blow your nigger brains out." I hate bein' called a nigger. I want to say somethin' but get myself in trouble.

When a cop do somethin', nothing happen to 'em. They come from downtown. From what I heard some of 'em don't even wear their real badge numbers. So you have to put up with that. Just keep your mouth shut when they stop you, that's all. Forget about questions, get against the wall, just obey 'em. "Put all that out right there"—might get rough with you now. They snatch you by the shirt, throw you against the wall, pat you hard, and grab you by the arms, and say, "Get outta here." They call you nigger this and little black this, and things like that. I take that. Some of the fellas get mad. It's a whole different world.

Yeah, they lookin' for trouble. They gotta look for trouble when you got five, eight police cars together and they laughin' and talkin', start teasin' people. One night we were at a bar, we read in the paper that the downtown cops comin' to straighten things out. Same night, three police cars, downtown cops with their boots on, they pull the sticks out, beatin' around the corner, chase into bars. My friend Todd, one of 'em grabbed him and knocked the shit out of him. He punched 'im, a little short white guy. They start a riot. Cops started that shit. Everybody start seein' how wrong the cops was—they start throwin' bricks and bottles, cussin' 'em out. They lock my boy up; they had to let him go. He was just standin' on the corner, they snatch him like that.

One time one of 'em took a gun and began hittin' people. My boy had a little hickie from that. He didn't know who the cop was, because there was no such thing as a badge number. They have phony badge numbers. You can tell they're tougher, the way they dress, plus they're bigger. They have boots, trooper pants, blond hair, blue eyes, even black [eyes]. And they seven feet tall, and six foot six inches and six foot eight inches. Big! They are the rough cops. You don't get smart with them or they beat the shit out of you *in front of everybody,* they don't care.

We call 'em Nazis. Even the blacks among them. They ride along with 'em. They stand there and watch a white cop beat your brains out. What takes me out is the next day you don't see 'em. Never see 'em again, go down there, come back, and they ride right back downtown, come back, do their little dirty work, go back downtown, and put their real badges on. You see 'em with a forty-five or fifty-five number: "Ain't no such number here, I'm sorry, son." Plus, they got unmarked cars. No sense takin' 'em to court. But when that happened at that bar, another black cop from the sixteenth [local] district, ridin' a real car, came back and said, "Why don't y' all go on over to the sixteenth district and file a complaint? Them musclin' cops was wrong. Beatin' people." So about ten people went over there; sixteenth district knew nothin' about it. They come in unmarked cars, they must have been downtown cops. Some of 'em do it. Some of 'em are off duty, on their way home. District commander told us they do that. They have a patrol over there, but them cops from downtown have control of them cops. Have bigger ranks and bigger guns. They carry .357s and regular cops carry little .38s. Downtown cops are all around. They carry magnums.

Two cars the other night. We sittin' on the steps playing cards. Somebody called the cops. We turn around and see four regular police cars and two highway police cars. We drinkin' beer and playin' cards. Police get out and say you're gamblin'. We say we got nothin' but cards here, we got no money. They said all right, got back in their cars, and drove away. Downtown cops dressed up like troopers. That's intimidation. Damn!

You call a cop, they don't come. My boy got shot, we had to take him to the hospital ourselves. A cop said, "You know who did it?" We said no. He said, "Well, I hope he dies if y'all don't say nothin'." What he say that for? My boy said, "I hope your mother die," he told the cop right to his face. And I was grabbin' another cop, and he made a complaint about that. There were a lot of witnesses. Even the nurse behind the counter said the cop had no business saying nothin' like that. He said it loud, "I hope he dies." Nothin' like that should be comin' from a cop.

Such behavior by formal agents of social control may reduce the crime rate, but it raises questions about social justice and civil rights. Many of the old-time liberal white residents of the Village view the police with some ambivalence. They want their streets and homes defended, but many are convinced that the police manhandle "kids" and mete out an arbitrary form of "justice." These feelings make many of them reluctant to call the police when they are needed, and they may even be less than completely cooperative after a crime has been committed. They know that far too often the police simply "go out and pick up some poor black kid." Yet they do cooperate, if ambivalently, with these agents of social control.

In an effort to gain some balance in the emerging picture of the police in the Village–Northton, I interviewed local officers. The following edited conversation with Officer George Dickens (white) helps place in context the fears and concerns of local residents, including black males:

> I'm sympathetic with the people who live in this neighborhood [the Village–Northton], who I feel are victims of drugs. There are a tremendous number of decent, hardworking people who are just trying to live their life in peace and quiet, not cause any problems for their neighbors, not cause any problems for themselves. They just go about their own business and don't bother anyone. The drug situation as it exists in Northton today causes them untold problems. And some of the young kids are involved in one way or another with this drug culture. As a result, they're gonna come into conflict even with the police they respect and have some rapport with.
>
> We just went out last week on Thursday and locked up ten young men on Cherry Street, because over a period of about a week, we had undercover police officers making drug buys from those young men. This was very well documented and detailed. They were videotaped selling the drugs. And as a result, right now, if you walk down Cherry Street, it's pretty much a ghost town; there's nobody out. [Before, Cherry Street was notorious for drug traffic.] Not only were people buying drugs there, but it was a very active street. There's been some shock value as a result of all those arrests at one time.
>
> Now, there's two reactions to that. The [television] reporters went out and interviewed some people who said, "Aw, the police overreacted, they locked up innocent people. It was terrible, it was harassment." One of the neighbors from Cherry Street called me on Thursday, and she was outraged. Because she said,

> "Officer, it's not fair. We've been working with the district for well over a year trying to solve some of the problems on Cherry Street." But most of the neighbors were thrilled that the police came and locked all those kids up. So you're getting two conflicting reactions here. One from the people that live there that just wanta be left alone, alright? Who are really being harassed by the drug trade and everything that's involved in it. And then you have a reaction from the people that are in one way or another either indirectly connected or directly connected, where they say, "You know, if a young man is selling drugs, to him that's a job." And if he gets arrested, he's out of a job. The family's lost their income. So they're not gonna pretty much want anybody to come in there to make arrests. So you've got contradicting elements of the community there. My philosophy is that we're going to try to make Northton livable. If that means we have to arrest some of the residents of Northton, that's what we have to do.
>
> You talk to Tyrone Pitts, you know the group that they formed was formed because of a reaction to complaints against one of the officers of how the teenagers were being harassed. And it turned out that basically what he [the officer] was doing was harassing drug dealers. When Northton against Drugs actually formed and seemed to jell, they developed a close working relationship with the police here. For that reason, they felt the officer was doing his job.
>
> I've been here eighteen months. I've seen this neighborhood go from . . . let me say, this is the only place I've ever worked where I've seen a rapport between the police department and the general community like the one we have right now. I've never seen it any place else before coming here. And I'm not gonna claim credit because this happened while I happened to be here. I think a lot of different factors were involved. I think the community was ready to work with the police because of the terrible situation in reference to crack. My favorite expression when talking about crack is "crack changed everything." Crack changed the rules of how the police and the community have to interact with each other. Crack changed the rules about how the criminal justice system is gonna work, whether it works well or poorly. Crack is causing the prisons to be overcrowded. Crack is gonna cause the people that do drug rehabilitation to be overworked. It's gonna cause a wide variety of things. And I think the reason the rapport between the police and the community in Northton developed at the time it

did is very simply that drugs to a certain extent made many areas in this city unlivable.

In effect the officer is saying that the residents, regardless of former attitudes, are now inclined to be more sympathetic with the police and to work with them. And at the same time, the police are more inclined to work with the residents. Thus, not only are the police and the black residents of Northton working together, but different groups in the Village and Northton are working with each other against drugs. In effect, law-abiding citizens are coming together, regardless of race, ethnicity, and class. He continues:

> Both of us [police and the community] are willing to say, "Look, let's try to help each other." The nice thing about what was started here is that it's spreading to the rest of the city. If we don't work together, this problem is gonna devour us. It's gonna eat us alive. It's a state of emergency, more or less.

In the past there was significant negative feeling among young black men about the "downtown" cops coming into the community and harassing them. In large part these feelings continue to run strong, though many young men appear to "know the score" and to be resigned to their situation, accommodating and attempting to live with it. But as the general community feels under attack, some residents are willing to forgo certain legal and civil rights and undergo personal inconvenience in hopes of obtaining a sense of law and order. The officer continues:

> Today we don't have too many complaints about police harassment in the community. Historically there were these complaints, and in almost any minority neighborhood in Eastern City where I ever worked there was more or less a feeling of that [harassment]. It wasn't just Northton; it was a feeling that the police were the enemy. I can honestly say that for the first time in my career I don't feel that people look at me like I'm the enemy. And it feels nice; it feels real good not to be the enemy, ha-ha. I think we [the police] realize that a lot of problems here [in the Village–Northton] are related to drugs. I think the neighborhood realizes that too. And it's a matter of "Who are we gonna be angry with? Are we gonna be angry with the police because we feel like they're this army of occupation, or are we gonna argue with these

people who are selling drugs to our kids and shooting up our neighborhoods and generally causing havoc in the area? Who deserves the anger more?" And I think, to a large extent, people of the Village–Northton decided it was the drug dealers and not the police.

> I would say there are probably isolated incidents where the police would stop a male in an area where there is a lot of drugs, and this guy may be perfectly innocent, not guilty of doing anything at all. And yet he's stopped by the police because he's specifically in that area, on that street corner where we know drugs are going hog wild. So there may be isolated incidents of that. At the same time, I'd say I know for a fact that our complaints against police in this division, the whole division, were down about 45 percent. If there are complaints, if there are instances of abuse by the police, I would expect that our complaints would be going up. But they're not; they're dropping.

Such is the dilemma many Villagers face when they must report a crime or deal in some direct way with the police. Stories about police prejudice against blacks are often traded at Village get-togethers. Cynicism about the effectiveness of the police mixed with community suspicion of their behavior toward blacks keeps middle-class Villagers from embracing the notion that they must rely heavily on the formal means of social control to maintain even the minimum freedom of movement they enjoy on the streets.

Many residents of the Village, especially those who see themselves as the "old guard" or "old-timers," who were around during the good old days when antiwar and antiracist protest was a major concern, sigh and turn their heads when they see the criminal justice system operating in the ways described here. They express hope that "things will work out," that tensions will ease, that crime will decrease and police behavior will improve. Yet as incivility and crime become increasing problems in the neighborhood, whites become less tolerant of anonymous blacks and more inclined to embrace the police as their heroes.

Such criminal and social justice issues, crystallized on the streets, strain relations between the newcomers and many of the old guard, but in the present context of drug-related crime and violence in the Village–Northton, many of the old-timers are adopting a "law and order" approach to crime and public safety, laying blame more directly on those they see as responsible for such crimes, though they retain some ambivalence. Newcomers can share such feelings with an increasing number of old-time "liberal" residents. As one middle-aged white woman who has lived in the Village for fifteen years said:

> When I call the police, they respond. I've got no complaints. They are fine for me. I know they sometimes mistreat black males. But let's face it, most of the crime is committed by them, and so they can simply tolerate more scrutiny. But that's them.

Gentrifiers and the local old-timers who join them, and some traditional residents continue to fear, care more for their own safety and well-being than for the rights of young blacks accused of wrong-doing. Yet reliance on the police, even by an increasing number of former liberals, may be traced to a general feeling of oppression at the hands of street criminals, whom many believe are most often black. As these feelings intensify and as more yuppies and students inhabit the area and press the local government for services, especially police protection, the police may be required to "ride herd" more stringently on the youthful black population.

Thus young black males are often singled out as the "bad" element in an otherwise healthy diversity, and the tensions between the lower-class black ghetto and the middle- and upper-class white community increase rather than diminish.

REFERENCES

Anderson, Elijah. 1986. "Of old heads and young boys: Notes on the urban black experience." Unpublished paper commissioned by the National Research Council, Committee on the Status of Black Americans.

Banton, Michael. 1964. *The policeman and the community*. New York: Basic Books.

Bittner, Egon. 1967. "The police on Skid Row." *American Sociological Review* 32 (October):699–715.

Fogelson, Robert. 1977. *Big city police*. Cambridge: Harvard University Press.

Goffman, Erving. 1963. *Behavior in public places*. New York: Free Press.

Reiss, Albert J. 1971. *The police and the public*. New Haven: Yale University Press.

Rubinstein, Jonathan. 1973. *City police*. New York: Farrar, Straus and Giroux.

Wilson, James Q. 1968. "The police and the delinquent in two cities." In *Controlling delinquents,* ed. Stanton Wheeler. New York: John Wiley.

READING 2-15

Fraternities and Rape on Campus

**Patricia Yancey Martin and
Robert A. Hummer**

Many rapes, far more than come to the public's attention, occur in fraternity houses on college and university campuses, yet little research has analyzed fraternities at American colleges and

From *Gender & Society* 3, No. 4, 1989. Reprinted by permission of Sage Publications, Inc. © 1989 by Sociologists for Women in Society.

universities as rape-prone contexts (cf. Ehrhart and Sandler 1985).

Ehrhart and Sandler (1985) identify over 50 cases of gang rapes on campus perpetrated by fraternity men, and their analysis points to many of the conditions that we discuss here. Their analysis is unique in focusing on conditions in fraternities that make gang rapes of women by fraternity men both feasible and probable. They identify excessive alcohol use, isolation from external monitoring, treatment of women as prey, use of pornography, approval of violence, and excessive concern with competition as precipitating conditions to gang rape (also see Merton 1985; Roark 1987).

The study reported here confirmed and complemented these findings by focusing on both conditions and processes. We examined dynamics associated with the social construction of fraternity life, with a focus on processes that foster the use of coercion, including rape, in fraternity men's relations with women. Our examination of men's social fraternities on college and university campuses as groups and organizations led us to conclude that fraternities are a physical and sociocultural context that encourages the sexual coercion of women. We make no claims that all fraternities are "bad" or that all fraternity men are rapists. Our observations indicated, however, that rape is especially probable in fraternities because of the kinds of organizations they are, the kinds of members they have, the practices their members engage in, and a virtual absence of university or community oversight. Analyses that lay blame for rapes by fraternity men on "peer pressure" are, we feel, overly simplistic (cf. Burkhart 1989; Walsh 1989). We suggest, rather, that fraternities create a sociocultural context in which the use of coercion in sexual relations with women is normative and in which the mechanisms to keep this pattern of behavior in check are minimal at best and absent at worst. We conclude that unless fraternities change in fundamental ways, little improvement can be expected.

METHODOLOGY

Our goal was to analyze the group and organizational practices and conditions that create in fraternities an abusive social context for women. We developed a conceptual framework from an initial case study of an alleged gang rape at Florida State University that involved four fraternity men and an 18-year-old coed. The group rape took place on the third floor of a fraternity house and ended with the

"dumping" of the woman in the hallway of a neighboring fraternity house. According to newspaper accounts, the victim's blood-alcohol concentration, when she was discovered, was .349 percent, more than three times the legal limit for automobile driving and an almost lethal amount. One law enforcement officer reported that sexual intercourse occurred during the time the victim was unconscious: "She was in a life-threatening situation" (*Tallahassee Democrat* 1988b). When the victim was found, she was comatose and had suffered multiple scratches and abrasions. Crude words and a fraternity symbol had been written on her thighs (*Tampa Tribune* 1988). When law enforcement officials tried to investigate the case, fraternity members refused to cooperate. This led, eventually, to a five-year ban of the fraternity from campus by the university and by the fraternity's national organization.

In trying to understand how such an event could have occurred, and how a group of over 150 members (exact figures are unknown because the fraternity refused to provide a membership roster) could hold rank, deny knowledge of the event, and allegedly lie to a grand jury, we analyzed newspaper articles about the case and conducted open-ended interviews with a variety of respondents about the case and about fraternities, rapes, alcohol use, gender relations, and sexual activities on campus. Our data included over 100 newspaper articles on the initial gang rape case; open-ended interviews with Greek (social fraternity and sorority) and non-Greek (independent) students (N = 20); university administrators (N = 8, five men, three women); and alumni advisers to Greek organizations (N = 6). Open-ended interviews were held also with judges, public and private defense attorneys, victim advocates, and state prosecutors regarding the processing of sexual assault cases. Data were analyzed using the grounded theory method (Glaser 1978; Martin and Turner 1986). In the following analysis, concepts generated from the data analysis are integrated with the literature on men's social fraternities, sexual coercion, and related issues.

FRATERNITIES AND THE SOCIAL CONSTRUCTION OF MEN AND MASCULINITY

Our research indicated that fraternities are vitally concerned—more than with anything else—with masculinity (cf. Kanin 1967). They work hard to create a macho image and context and try to avoid any suggestion of "wimpishness," effeminacy, and homosexuality. Valued members display, or are willing to go along with, a narrow conception of masculinity that stresses competition, athleticism, dominance, winning, conflict, wealth, material possessions, willingness to drink alcohol, and sexual prowess vis-à-vis women.

Practices of Brotherhood

Practices associated with fraternity brotherhood that contribute to the sexual coercion of women include a preoccupation with loyalty, group protection and secrecy, use of alcohol as a weapon, involvement in violence and physical force, and an emphasis on competition and superiority.

Loyalty, Group Protection, and Secrecy Loyalty is a fraternity preoccupation. Members are reminded constantly to be loyal to the fraternity and to their brothers. Among other ways, loyalty is played out in the practices of group protection and secrecy. The fraternity must be shielded from criticism. Members are admonished to avoid getting the fraternity in trouble and to bring all problems "to the chapter" (local branch of a national social fraternity) rather than to outsiders. Fraternities try to protect themselves from close scrutiny and criticism by the Interfraternity Council (a quasi-governing body composed of representatives from all social fraternities on campus), their fraternity's national office, university officials, law enforcement, the media, and the public. Protection of the fraternity often takes precedence over what is procedurally, ethically, or legally correct. Numerous examples were related to us of fraternity brothers' lying to outsiders to "protect the fraternity."

Group protection was observed in the alleged gang rape case with which we began our study. Except for one brother, a rapist who turned state's evidence, the entire remaining fraternity membership was accused by university and criminal justice officials of lying to protect the fraternity. Members consistently failed to cooperate even though the alleged crimes were felonies, involved only four men (two of whom were not even members of the local chapter), and the victim of the crime nearly died. According to a grand jury's findings, fraternity officers repeatedly broke appointments with law enforcement officials, refused to provide police with a list of members, and refused to cooperate with police and prosecutors investigating the case (*Florida Flambeau* 1988).

Secrecy is a priority value and practice in fraternities, partly because full-fledged membership is premised on it (for confirmation, see Ehrhart and Sandler 1985; Longino and Kart 1973; Roark 1987). Secrecy is also a boundary-maintaining mechanism, demarcating in-group from out-group, us from them. Secret rituals, handshakes, and mottoes are revealed to pledge brothers as they are initiated into full brotherhood. Since only brothers are supposed to know a fraternity's secrets, such knowledge affirms membership in the fraternity and separates a brother from others. Extending secrecy tactics from protection of private knowledge to protection of the fraternity from criticism is a predictable development. Our interviews indicated that individual members knew the difference between right and wrong, but fraternity norms that emphasize loyalty, group protection, and secrecy often overrode standards of ethical correctness.

Alcohol as Weapon Alcohol use by fraternity men is normative. They use it on weekdays to relax after class and on weekends to "get drunk," "get crazy," and "get laid." The use of alcohol to obtain sex from women is pervasive—in other words, it is used as a weapon against sexual reluctance. According to several fraternity men whom we interviewed, alcohol is the major tool used to gain sexual mastery over women (cf. Adams and Abarbanel 1988; Ehrhart and Sandler 1985). One fraternity man, a 21-year-old senior, described alcohol use to gain sex as follows: "There are girls that you know will fuck, then some you have to put some effort into it. . . . You have to buy them drinks or find out if she's drunk enough."

A similar strategy is used collectively. A fraternity man said that at parties with Little Sisters: "We provide them with 'hunch punch' and things get wild. We get them drunk and most of the guys end up with one." " 'Hunch punch,' " he said, "is a girls' drink made up of overproof alcohol and powdered Kool-Aid, no water or anything, just ice. It's very strong. Two cups will do a number on a female." He had plans in the next academic term to surreptitiously give hunch punch to women in a "prim and proper" sorority because "having sex with prim and proper sorority girls is definitely a goal." These women are a challenge because they "won't openly consume alcohol and won't get openly drunk as hell." Their sororities have "standards committees" that forbid heavy drinking and easy sex.

In the gang rape case, our sources said that many fraternity men on campus believed the victim had a drinking problem and was thus an "easy make." According to newspaper accounts, she had been drinking alcohol on the evening she was raped; the lead assailant is alleged to have given her a bottle of wine after she arrived at his fraternity house. Portions of the rape occurred in a shower, and the victim was reportedly so drunk that her assailants had difficulty holding her in a standing position (*Tallahassee Democrat,* 1988a). While raping her, her assailants repeatedly told her they were members of another fraternity under the apparent belief that she was too drunk to know the difference. Of course, if she was too drunk to know who they were, she was too drunk to consent to sex (cf. Allgeier 1986; Tash 1988).

One respondent told us that gang rapes are wrong and can get one expelled, but he seemed to see nothing wrong in sexual coercion one-on-one. He seemed unaware that the use of alcohol to obtain sex from a woman is grounds for a claim that a rape occurred (cf. Tash 1988). Few women on campus (who also may not know these grounds) report date rapes, however; so the odds of detection and punishment are slim for fraternity men who use

alcohol for "seduction" purposes (cf. Byington and Keeter 1988; Merton 1985).

Violence and Physical Force Fraternity men have a history of violence (Ehrhart and Sandler 1985; Roark 1987). Their record of hazing, fighting, property destruction, and rape has caused them problems with insurance companies (Bradford 1986; Pressley 1987). Two university officials told us that fraternities "are the third riskiest property to insure behind toxic waste dumps and amusement parks." Fraternities are increasingly defendants in legal actions brought by pledges subjected to hazing (Meyer 1986; Pressley 1987) and by women who were raped by one or more members. In a recent alleged gang rape incident at another Florida university, prosecutors failed to file charges but the victim filed a civil suit against the fraternity nevertheless (*Tallahassee Democrat* 1989).

Competition and Superiority Interfraternity rivalry fosters in-group identification and out-group hostility. Fraternities stress pride of membership and superiority over other fraternities as major goals. Interfraternity rivalries take many forms, including competition for desirable pledges, size of pledge class, size of membership, size and appearance of fraternity house, superiority in intramural sports, highest grade-point averages, giving the best parties, gaining the best or most campus leadership roles, and, of great importance, attracting and displaying "good looking women." Rivalry is particularly intense over members, intramural sports, and women (cf. Messner 1989).

FRATERNITIES' COMMODIFICATION OF WOMEN

In claiming that women are treated by fraternities as commodities, we mean that fraternities knowingly, and intentionally, *use* women for their benefit. Fraternities use women as bait for new members, as servers of brothers' needs, and as sexual prey.

Women as Bait Fashionably attractive women help a fraternity attract new members. As one fraternity man, a junior, said, "They are good bait." Beautiful, sociable women are believed to impress the right kind of pledges and give the impression that the fraternity can deliver this type of woman to its members. Photographs of shapely, attractive coeds are printed in fraternity brochures and videotapes that are distributed and shown to potential pledges. The women pictured are often dressed in bikinis, at the beach, and are pictured hugging the brothers of the fraternity. One university official says such recruitment materials give the message: "Hey, they're here for you, you can have whatever you want," and, "We have the best looking women. Join us and you can have them too." Another commented: "Something's wrong when males join an all-male organization as the best place to meet women. It's so illogical."

Fraternities compete in promising access to beautiful women. One fraternity man, a senior, commented that "the attraction of girls [i.e., a fraternity's success in attracting women] is a big status symbol for fraternities." One university official commented that the use of women as a recruiting tool is so well entrenched that fraternities that might be willing to forgo it say they cannot afford to unless other fraternities do so as well. One fraternity man said, "Look, if we don't have Little Sisters, the fraternities that do will get all the good pledges." Another said, "We won't have as good a rush [the period during which new members are assessed and selected] if we don't have these women around."

In displaying good-looking, attractive, skimpily dressed, nubile women to potential members, fraternities implicitly, and sometimes explicitly, promise sexual access to women. One fraternity man commented that "part of what being in a fraternity is all about is the sex" and explained how his fraternity uses Little Sisters to recruit new members:

We'll tell the sweetheart [the fraternity's term for Little Sister], "You're gorgeous; you can get him."

We'll tell her to fake a scam and she'll go hang all over him during a rush party, kiss him, and he thinks he's done wonderful and wants to join. The girls think it's great too. It's flattering for them.

Women as Servers The use of women as servers is exemplified in the Little Sister program. Little Sisters are undergraduate women who are rushed and selected in a manner parallel to the recruitment of fraternity men. They are affiliated with the fraternity in a formal but unofficial way and are able, indeed required, to wear the fraternity's Greek letters. Little Sisters are not full-fledged fraternity members, however; and fraternity national offices and most universities do not register or regulate them. Each fraternity has an officer called Little Sister Chairman who oversees their organization and activities. The Little Sisters elect officers among themselves, pay monthly dues to the fraternity, and have well-defined roles. Their dues are used to pay for the fraternity's social events, and Little Sisters are expected to attend and hostess fraternity parties and hang around the house to make it a "nice place to be." One fraternity man, a senior, described Little Sisters this way: "They are very social girls, willing to join in, be affiliated with the group, devoted to the fraternity." Another member, a sophomore, said: "Their sole purpose is social—attend parties, attract new members, and 'take care' of the guys."

Our observations and interviews suggested that women selected by fraternities as Little Sisters are physically attractive, possess good social skills, and are willing to devote time and energy to the fraternity and its members. One undergraduate woman gave the following job description for Little Sisters to a campus newspaper:

It's not just making appearances at all the parties but entails many more responsibilities. You're going to be expected to go to all the intramural games to cheer the brothers on, support and encourage the pledges, and just be around to bring some extra life to the house. [As a Little Sister] you have to agree to take on a new responsibility other than studying to maintain your grades and managing to keep your checkbook from bouncing. You have to make time to be a part of the fraternity and support the brothers in all they do. (*The Tomahawk* 1988)

The title of Little Sister reflects women's subordinate status; fraternity men in a parallel role are called Big Brothers. Big Brothers assist a sorority primarily with the physical work of sorority rushes, which, compared to fraternity rushes, are more formal, structured, and intensive. Sorority rushes take place in the daytime and fraternity rushes at night so fraternity men are free to help. According to one fraternity member, Little Sister status is a benefit to women because it gives them a social outlet and "the protection of the brothers." The gender-stereotypic conceptions and obligations of these Little Sister and Big Brother statuses indicate that fraternities and sororities promote a gender hierarchy on campus that fosters subordination and dependence in women, thus encouraging sexual exploitation and the belief that it is acceptable.

Women as Sexual Prey Little Sisters are a sexual utility. Many Little Sisters do not belong to sororities and lack peer support for refraining from unwanted sexual relations. One fraternity man (whose fraternity has 65 members and 85 Little Sisters) told us they had recruited "wholesale" in the prior year to "get lots of new women." The structural access to women that the Little Sister program provides and the absence of normative supports for refusing fraternity members' sexual advances may make women in this program particularly susceptible to coerced sexual encounters with fraternity men.

Access to women for sexual gratification is a presumed benefit of fraternity membership, promised in recruitment materials and strategies and through brothers' conversations with new recruits. One fraternity man said: "We always tell the guys that you get sex all the time, there's always new girls. . . . After I became a Greek, I found out I could be with females at will." A university official told us that, based on his observations, "no one [i.e., fraternity men] on this campus wants to have 'relationships.' They just want to have fun [i.e., sex]." Fraternity men plan and execute strategies aimed at obtaining sexual gratification, and this occurs at both individual and collective levels.

Individual strategies include getting a woman drunk and spending a great deal of money on her. As for collective strategies, most of our undergraduate interviewees agreed that fraternity parties often culminate in sex and that this outcome is planned. One fraternity man said fraternity parties often involve sex and nudity and can "turn into orgies." Orgies may be planned in advance, such as the Bowery Ball party held by one fraternity. A former fraternity member said of this party:

> The entire idea behind this is sex. Both men and women come to the party wearing little or nothing. There are pornographic pinups on the walls and usually porno movies playing on the TV. The music carries sexual overtones. . . . They just get schnockered [drunk] and, in most cases, they also get laid.

When asked about the women who come to such a party, he said: "Some Little Sisters just won't go. . . . The girls who do are looking for a good time, girls who don't know what it is, things like that."

Other respondents denied that fraternity parties are orgies but said that sex is always talked about among the brothers and they all know "who each other is doing it with." One member said that most of the time, guys have sex with their girlfriends "but with socials, girlfriends aren't allowed to come and it's their [members'] big chance [to have sex with other women]." The use of alcohol to help them get women into bed is a routine strategy at fraternity parties.

CONCLUSIONS

In general, our research indicated that the organization and membership of fraternities contribute heavily to coercive and often violent sex. Fraternity houses are occupied by same-sex (all men) and same-age (late teens, early twenties) peers whose maturity and judgment are often less than ideal. Yet fraternity houses are private dwellings that are mostly off-limits to, and away from scrutiny of, university and community representatives, with the result that fraternity house events seldom come to the attention of outsiders. Practices associated with the social construction of fraternity brotherhood emphasize a macho conception of men and masculinity, a narrow, stereotyped conception of women and femininity, and the treatment of women as commodities. Other practices contributing to coercive sexual relations and the cover-up of rapes include excessive alcohol use, competitiveness, and normative support for deviance and secrecy (cf. Bogal-Allbritten and Allbritten 1985; Kanin 1967).

Some fraternity practices exacerbate others. Brotherhood norms require "stricking together" regardless of right or wrong; thus rape episodes are unlikely to be stopped or reported to outsiders, even when witnesses disapprove. The ability to use alcohol without scrutiny by authorities and alcohol's frequent association with violence, including sexual coercion, facilitates rape in fraternity houses. Fraternity norms that emphasize the value of maleness and masculinity over femaleness and femininity and that elevate the status of men and lower the status of women in members' eyes undermine perceptions and treatment of women as persons who deserve consideration and care (cf. Ehrhart and Sandler 1985; Merton 1985).

Androgynous men and men with a broad range of interests and attributes are lost to fraternities through their recruitment practices. Masculinity of a narrow and stereotypical type helps create attitudes, norms, and practices that predispose fraternity men to coerce women sexually, both individually and collectively (Allgeier 1986; Hood 1989; Sanday 1981, 1986). Male athletes on campus may be similarly disposed for the same reasons (Kirshenbaum 1989; Telander and Sullivan 1989).

Research into the social contexts in which rape crimes occur and the social constructions associated with these contexts illumine rape dynamics on campus. Blanchard (1959) found that group rapes almost always have a leader who pushes others into the crime. He also found that the leader's latent homosexuality, desire to show off to his peers, or fear of failing to prove himself a man is frequently an impetus. Fraternity norms and practices contribute to the approval and use of sexual coercion

as an accepted tactic in relations with women. Alcohol-induced compliance is normative, whereas, presumably, use of a knife, gun, or threat of bodily harm would not be because the woman who "drinks too much" is viewed as "causing her own rape" (cf. Ehrhart and Sandler 1985).

Our research led us to conclude that fraternity norms and practices influence members to view the sexual coercion of women, which is a felony crime, as sport, a contest, or a game (cf. Sato 1988). This sport is played not between men and women but between men and men. Women are the pawns or prey in the interfraternity rivalry game; they prove that a fraternity is successful or prestigious. The use of women in this way encourages fraternity men to see women as objects and sexual coercion as sport. Today's societal norms support young women's right to engage in sex at their discretion, and coercion is unnecessary in a mutually desired encounter. However, nubile young women say they prefer to be "in a relationship" to have sex while young men say they prefer to "get laid" without a commitment (Muehlenhard and Linton 1987). These differences may reflect, in part, American puritanism and men's fears of sexual intimacy or perhaps intimacy of any kind. In a fraternity context, getting sex without giving emotionally demonstrates "cool" masculinity. More important, it poses no threat to the bonding and loyalty of the fraternity brotherhood (cf. Farr 1988). Drinking large quantities of alcohol before having sex suggests that "scoring" rather than intrinsic sexual pleasure is a primary concern of fraternity men.

Unless fraternities' composition, goals, structures, and practices change in fundamental ways, women on campus will continue to be sexual prey for fraternity men. As all-male enclaves dedicated to opposing faculty and administration and to cementing in-group ties, fraternity members eschew any hint of homosexuality. Their version of masculinity transforms women, and men with womanly characteristics, into the out-group. "Womanly men" are ostracized; feminine women are used to demonstrate members' masculinity. Encouraging renewed emphasis on their founding values (Longino and Kart 1973), service orientation and activities

(Lemire 1979), or members' moral development (Marlowe and Auvenshine 1982) will have little effect on fraternities' treatment of women. A case for or against fraternities cannot be made by studying individual members. The fraternity qua group and organization is at issue. Located on campus along with many vulnerable women, embedded in a sexist society, and caught up in masculinist goals, practices, and values, fraternities' violation of women—including forcible rape—should come as no surprise.

REFERENCES

Adams, Aileen, and Gail Abarbanel. 1988. *Sexual Assault on Campus: What Colleges Can Do*. Santa Monica, CA: Rape Treatment Center.

Allgeier, Elizabeth. 1986. "Coercive versus Consensual Sexual Interactions." G. Stanley Hall Lecture to American Psychological Association Annual Meeting, Washington, DC, August.

Blanchard, W. H. 1959. "The Group Process in Gang Rape." *Journal of Social Psychology* 49:259–66.

Bogal-Allbritten, Rosemarie B., and William L. Allbritten. 1985. "The Hidden Victims: Courtship Violence Among College Students." *Journal of College Student Personnel* 43:201–4.

Bradford, Michael. 1986. "Tight Market Dries Up Nightlife at University." *Business Insurance* (March 2):2, 6.

Burkhart, Barry. 1989. Comments in Seminar on Acquaintance/Date Rape Prevention: A National Video Teleconference, February 2.

Byington, Diane B., and Karen W. Keeter. 1988. "Assessing Needs of Sexual Assault Victims on a University Campus." In *Student Services: Responding to Issues and Challenges* (pp. 23–31). Chapel Hill: University of North Carolina Press.

Ehrhart, Julie K., and Bernice R. Sandler. 1985. *Campus Gang Rape: Party Games?* Washington, DC: Association of American Colleges.

Farr, K. A. 1988. "Dominance Bonding through the Good Old Boys Sociability Network." *Sex Roles* 18:259–77.

Florida Flambeau. 1988. "Pike Members Indicted in Rape." (May 19):1, 5.

Glaser, Barney G. 1978. *Theoretical Sensitivity: Advances in the Methodology of Grounded Theory*. Mill Valley, CA: Sociology Press.

Hood, Jane. 1989. "Why Our Society Is Rape-Prone." *New York Times,* May 16.

Kanin, Eugene J. 1967. "Reference Groups and Sex Conduct Norm Violations." *The Sociological Quarterly* 8:495–504.

Kirshenbaum, Jerry. 1989. "Special Report, an American Disgrace: A Violent and Unprecedented Lawlessness Has Arisen Among College Athletes in All Parts of the Country." *Sports Illustrated* (February 27): 16–19.

Lemire, David. 1979. "One Investigation of the Stereotypes Associated with Fraternities and Sororities." *Journal of College Student Personnel* 37: 54–57.

Longino, Charles F., Jr., and Cary S. Kart. 1973. "The College Fraternity: An Assessment of Theory and Research." *Journal of College Student Personnel* 31: 118–25.

Marlowe, Anne F., and Dwight C. Auvenshine. 1982. "Greek Membership: Its Impact on the Moral Development of College Freshmen." *Journal of College Student Personnel* 40:53–57.

Martin, Patricia Yancey, and Barry A. Turner. 1986. "Grounded Theory and Organizational Research." *Journal of Applied Behavioral Science* 22:141–57.

Merton, Andrew. 1985. "On Competition and Class: Return to Brotherhood." *Ms.* (September):60–65, 121–22.

Messner, Michael. 1989. "Masculinities and Athletic Careers." *Gender & Society* 3:71–88.

Meyer, T. J. 1986. "Fight Against Hazing Rituals Rages on Campuses." *Chronicle of Higher Education* (March 12):34–36.

Muehlenhard, Charlene L., and Melaney A. Linton. 1987. "Date Rape and Sexual Aggression in Dating Situations: Incidence and Risk Factors." *Journal of Counseling Psychology* 34:186–96.

Pressley, Sue Anne. 1987. "Fraternity Hell Night Still Endures." *Washington Post* (August 11):B1.

Roark, Mary L. 1987. "Preventing Violence on College Campuses." *Journal of Counseling and Development* 65:367–70.

Sanday, Peggy Reeves. 1981. "The Sociocultural Context of Rape: A Cross-Cultural Study." *Journal of Social Issues* 37:5–27.

———. 1986. "Rape and the Silencing of the Feminine." In *Rape,* edited by S. Tomaselli and R. Porter (pp. 84–101). Oxford: Basil Blackwell.

Sato, Ikuya. 1988. "Play Theory of Delinquency: Toward a General Theory of 'Action.' " *Symbolic Interaction* 11:191–212.

Tallahassee Democrat. 1988a. "FSU Fraternity Brothers Charged." (April 27):1A, 12A.

———. 1988b. "FSU Interviewing Students About Alleged Rape." (April 24):1D.

———. 1989. "Woman Sues Stetson in Alleged Rape." (March 19):3B.

Tampa Tribune. 1988. "Fraternity Brothers Charged in Sexual Assault of FSU Coed." (April 27):6B.

Tash, Gary B. 1988. "Date Rape." *The Emerald of Sigma Pi Fraternity* 75(4):1–2.

Telander, Rick, and Robert Sullivan. 1989. "Special Report, You Reap What You Sow." *Sports Illustrated* (February 27):20–34.

The Tomahawk. 1988. "A Look Back at Rush, A Mixture of Hard Work and Fun" (April/May):3D.

Walsh, Claire. 1989. Comments in Seminar on Acquaintance/Date Rape Prevention: A National Video Teleconference, February 2.

READING 2-16

The Manufacture of Deviance in the Soviet Purge

Walter D. Connor

This study concerns itself with a modern instance of the manufacture of deviance—the Stalinist purge, the Soviet "Great Terror" of 1936–1938. The lessons derived from it may point to a need to rethink some contemporary ideas about deviance. Centuries, and deep historical, cultural and ideological differences separate the purge from the campaigns against witches and heretics in England, Europe and Puritan Massachusetts; yet important similarities argue the value of examining the purge, its mechanics and outcome, within a comparative framework which includes the earlier anti-deviance campaigns. Each of these campaigns recruited masses of persons to deviant status, the majority of whom were in fact innocent of the acts with which they were charged. And in each, deviance-invention had more or less traumatic effects on the society in which it took place.

The remaining sections of this paper will describe and analyze a single case of "epidemic deviance"—the purge—in an attempt to support the following propositions:

1. that the limits on the amount of deviance a society can "afford to recognize" rather than being constant over time are, in fact, quite elastic under certain circumstances, and allow for rapid increase in the number of deviants recognized;

2. that the critical circumstance under (1) is the existence of a repressive control system, as exemplified by the Inquisition and the Soviet system in the 1930's (Erikson [1966] focuses on a set of cases involving a relatively restrained control system—a focus which precludes examining the behavior of repressive systems);

3. that the elasticity of a repressive control system may be (as in the Soviet case) amplified by a deployment pattern which appears to reduce the costs of recruiting and maintaining a deviant population through setting up camps rather than prisons, removing deviants to geographically remote areas, and trying to maintain their contribution to the economy through forced labor, all of which allow rapid expansion in the intake of deviants.

Finally, two additional themes run through what is to follow: first, the tendency of the deviant-detection activities of repressive control systems to

From *American Sociological Review* 37 (August 1972), 403–413. Reprinted by permission of the American Sociological Association and the author.

snowball, almost randomly recruiting deviants, and second, the irrelevance, under certain circumstances, of prior community support, or the lack thereof, for the progress of the purge. As we shall see, even its victims, once in the interrogation phase, often found it in their interest, as they saw it, to cooperate in expanding the purge.

THE VICTIMS

Many authors have tried to estimate the scope of the purge, to number its victims. Their figures—admittedly loose and tentative approximations—have one thing in common: they reflect a social upheaval probably unmatched in modern peacetime history.

Since this study is a discussion of sociological questions raised by the purge (and since space constraints preclude it), no lengthy description of the victim population is offered here. Extended treatments of it are available in other sources (Beck and Godin 1951:86–170; Conquest 1968:276 ff.). For present purposes, it may suffice to note that the victim population was diverse, reflecting many subgroups in Soviet society, and at the same time, special. Beyond the most visible victims—the high party and state officials who appeared in the dock at the Moscow trials—party and state bureaucrats at the provincial and district levels were hard hit. Rank-and-file old Bolsheviks, as well as members of other defunct revolutionary parties, perished in large numbers. Industrial managers, engineers, transport officials and others with responsible posts in large organizations contributed to the victim group in numbers greatly disproportionate to their share of the population, as did the Soviet officer corps, from marshals on down. Citizens with relatives abroad, or other foreign contacts (many if not most of them legal, in trade, tourist, or cultural organizations), as well as foreign Communists who had emigrated to the USSR, were arrested in large numbers. Other target groups included relatives of those arrested, and members of Soviet ethnic minorities residing in cities outside their own areas.

While diverse, this population, heavily composed of better-educated urban groups, was less diverse than Soviet society itself. It included in large numbers members of the new Soviet elite, persons whose careers had been made primarily in the years since the revolution. The purge fell less heavily on those at the bottom of Soviet society—the lower working strata, the collective farm peasantry. All victims were, however, united in facing situations of presumed and nonrebuttable guilt after their arrest.

PROCESSING AND CONFESSION

Where offenses do not lend themselves easily to proof by eyewitness testimony (as in the witch's pact with the devil, the conspiracies of counterrevolutionaries, and any offense which has not actually been committed), confession must play a major role in establishing guilt. Victims of the Soviet purge were in fact required to confess not only their own guilt, but also the guilt of others, to their interrogators. Confessions were critical to the purge, for many reasons.

First, the Stalin regime encountered a large public relations problem in the purge. The Soviet Union was, by the mid-1930's, held to have left behind the Red terror, the "class justice" of its earlier years. Thus, to admit that a prophylactic purge, and not the uncovering of a vast network of political deviants, was taking place would have compromised the Soviet Union too much in the eyes of both enemies and admirers. Confessions at the Moscow trials convinced many foreigners and Soviet citizens that, however implausible, old Bolsheviks were in truth selling out the nation, and that the Soviet Union was indeed infested with active plotters and saboteurs. The accusations were untrue, but given the commitment made to ferreting out deviants, they had to be proven nonetheless. Where evidence cannot be convincing (since it does not exist), confessions may fill the gap.

Second, the success of individual interrogators of the NKVD in extracting confessions indicated their vigilance, and in part guaranteed their own safety.

Accusations of insufficient vigilance changed many an interrogator into an accused, while a high "productivity index" was some disproof of leniency. As the purge intensified, the spectacle of interrogators following those they processed to the camps was not uncommon (see Beck and Godin 1951:238; Ginzburg 1967:139, 388–390; Weissberg 1951:298).

Third, each confessing deviant, in naming his recruiters, and those whom he had recruited to anti-state activity, supplied an important input. The more persons, and the more important the persons, who could thus be detected, the more credible the vigilance and effectiveness of the entire NKVD.

Many accused, reluctant to implicate other innocents, filled their recruit quota with those beyond reach. Experienced prisoners often provided new arrivals with names of the dead or arrested who could be recruited with impunity. But others were convinced that the key to ending the purge, and to their own release, lay in reducing the process to complete absurdity. These sought to drive the purge to its limits by implicating all those in responsible positions still at large. Military officers implicated their whole units, officials denounced everyone in their organizations, academics their colleagues (see Weissberg 1951:314–317; Beck and Godin 1951:188, 194–200).

Confessions, of course, were seldom voluntary. They were the product of interrogation, and the speed and fullness of confession depended on the mechanics of the interrogation process. Except in the cases of some special victims such as military and NKVD officers, early in the purge little physical violence seems to have been used on the accused. More often, the first stage of interrogation was to persuade the prisoner that the NKVD already knew everything, that only one's official confession, identification of recruits, and minor details were lacking.[1] In return for cooperation, light sentences were often promised. Persistence in denying guilt led to threats of heavier sentences or death penalties as well as arrest or exile for relatives still at large.

Those who refused to cooperate, were subjected to the "conveyor"—a lengthy, sleepless interrogation by a succession of well-rested interrogators (see, e.g., Beck and Godin 1951:53–54; Weissberg 1951:53–54, 238 ff.; Ginzberg 1967:83 ff.).

But the conveyor was time-consuming. A speedier, more efficient method of processing was needed. (The amount of time between arrest and formal dispatch to a camp varied. For workers and peasants, whose confessions were expected to be simple, only a few months generally elapsed. Members of the intelligentsia typically took longer) (see Beck and Godin 1951:75). The "breakthrough" for permission to use systematic beatings and other torture, came in August, 1937 (Conquest 1968:307). Thereafter, the purge moved toward its peak.

In essence, then, one became a deviant upon arrest. Practically speaking, one could not prove his innocence.

> [A] person whose work had always been above reproach was undoubtedly covering up counterrevolutionary activities. But should there have been any instance of trouble or any accident in the defendant's place of work, that was proof of his sabotaging activities. If the defendent admitted having observed anything suspicious in the private or professional life of a superior who was also under indictment, he was guilty of a lack of revolutionary alertness. If a woman repudiated her husband once he was arrested, she thereby admitted that she thought him a counterrevolutionary and was therefore guilty for having lived with him. If she did not renounce him, she was guilty of questioning the infallibility of the NKVD. (Lipper 1951:38)

Such guides for behavior interpretation are strikingly similar to those used to detect witches centuries earlier.

> If the accused was found to be in good repute among the populace, he or she was clearly a witch, since witches invariably sought to be highly thought of; if in bad repute, then he or she was also clearly a witch,

---

[1] However, one was often not told what one's offense was. This had to be invented by the accused himself. As the prison culture became more aware of what the interrogators sought, experienced prisoners could often help newcomers with inventing their legends. (See Conquest 1968:304–305).

since no one approves of witches. If the accused was especially regular in worship or morals, it was argued that the worst witches made the greatest show of piety. (Currie 1968:15)

THE VIGILANCE INDUSTRY

Explaining the growth and acceleration of the purge involves examining the purge machinery—the Soviet secret police or NKVD—which, in the period that concerns us, amply satisfied Currie's three criteria of repressive control systems.

Invulnerability to Restraint As a practical matter, the NKVD was invulnerable to all external restraints, save those imposed by the top leadership: essentially, Stalin himself.[2] Beyond this, the NKVD was unrestrained, as the toll of victims among the top Party, government, economic and military leadership shows. By and large, the leadership of other social institutions found cooperation with the NKVD in rooting out deviants in their midst the only course that offered a modicum of safety. Attempts at restraint were *prima facie* evidence of counterrevolutionary or subversive intent.

Extraordinary Powers The powers granted the NKVD in coping with deviants vastly exceeded the normal Soviet criminal law, substantive and procedural. First, a contamination principle operated, whereby not only the presumptive deviant, but his friends and acquaintances, and *their* friends, might also be arrested on an assumption of, at worst, their complicity and at best, their "lack of vigilance" (see Conquest 1968:260, 300). Second, physical beating, while probably used in many criminal interrogations, was not officially sanctioned: after August, 1937, its application to "politicals" received official sanction. Third, the trial mode of political deviants diverged markedly from that of regular criminals: trials *in absentia,* trials by special three-man boards rather than people's

courts, the lack of any provisions for a defense—all these gave the NKVD extraordinary processing powers over those marked for removal.

Structured Interests The Soviet seige mentality of the 1920's and 1930's, coupled with the impact of Stalin's own personality, gave the secret police a large role to play, and conferred a privileged status on its members. As a control institution, the NKVD had interests in maintaining itself and acquiring powers and resources—interest it could promote by detecting (or inventing) growing members of deviants. In this sense, at least, there were positive rewards to be gained.

Yet such a view minimizes the degree to which, in 1937–1938, the NKVD was a mechanism whose motive force Stalin largely supplied. Within this mechanism, individual workers had another sort of interest: sparing themselves from the fate of deviants. Some, of course, pursued promotion, etc., within the NKVD. But it seems doubtful that such rewards offered as much stimulus as enrichment from confiscating witches' property offered the Renaissance inquisitors (Currie 1968:21–24).

The NKVD was, simultaneously, both a source and target of the pressures for ever-increasing vigilance, pressures with which early in the purge many officers over-complied, creating the momentum that would characterize it at its peak. Thus, it appears, the terror extended beyond any targets Stalin himself might have seen as "rational." As an organization, the NKVD could not pull back from its activities. While many interrogators may have doubted the deviants' guilt, "they were caught in their own system. It was impossible for them not to arrest a man who had been denounced as an agent of Hitler" (Conquest 1968:465). Nor could NKVD administrations at the provincial and district level safely restrict their output of arrests: many, indeed, received orders from Moscow specifying "target figures," indicating that so many nameless thousands of wreckers or saboteurs lived in their jurisdictions who should be identified and apprehended (see Petrov and Petrov 1956:73; Medvedev 1971:284).

---

[2] Indeed, in running its course, the purge consumed the two chief purgers—NKVD heads Yagoda and Yezhov.

Opportunities arose for self-aggrandizement by the unscrupulous, who denounced others out of enmity, ambition, or covetousness. Some sought their superior's job, others more room in a crowded communal apartment. For some, denunciations became a quasi-racket. Two men in Kiev denounced over 169 people. A party member in Odessa denounced 230, and another in Poltava his entire party organization. One industrious denouncer applied for a free vacation, claiming he had spent his strength struggling with the enemy (Conquest 1968:280).

Added to these amateurs were the "secret collaborators" of the NKVD, or *seksots*. *Seksots* were both voluntary and involuntary. The voluntary were those who enjoyed the work of denunciation, or felt they were serving the cause. The latter delivered denunciations for fear of their own arrest or in hopes of improving the lot of arrested relatives. These soon found themselves entangled in a system interested only in incriminating information. When none existed, self-interest dictated its manufacture: "the *seksot* who failed to produce information was himself automatically suspect" (Conquest 1968:281; see also Beck and Godin 1951:164–166).

THE PURGE IN REVIEW

Many questions about the purge are, and will probably remain unanswered. As Dallin and Breslauer (1970:5) note, both "the purposes and functions of political terror are many." The latter may be, however, somewhat clearer than the former. The purge's results, at least, are observable. As to the purposes of the purge as a species of political terror, the present author agrees with Dalin and Breslauer that "we can do little more than guess." Purpose, however clear it may have been in Stalin's mind initially, cannot well account for the purge's scale, cannot easily explain its reaching a point at which the "NKVD . . . had files proving that almost every leading official everywhere was a spy" (Conquest 1968: 316). As the purge developed from an operationally rational desire by Stalin to eliminate all potential sources of opposition and potential support for that opposition, it reached a point

where a "spillover of victimization" occurred (see Dallin and Breslauer 1970:27–28). Arrests by quota, even when ordered from Moscow, probably partly resulted from NKVD over-compliance, rather than clear political purpose. But arrests by quota, and other elements contributing to the spillover, did reflect the repressive character of the NKVD—a system whose very characteristics made for constant growth in the volume of deviance it encountered. Eventually, the purge reached its limits, but they were the limits characteristic of a repressive, rather than a restrained control system.

> The first substantial question an interrogator asked was "Who are your accomplices?" So from each arrest several other arrests more or less automatically followed. But if this had gone on for a few more months and each new victim named only two or three accomplices, the next wave would have struck at 10 to 15 percent of the population, and soon after that at 30 to 45 percent . . . we can see that the extreme limits had been reached. To have gone on would have been impossible economically, politically—and even physically, in that interrogators, prisons and camps, already grotesquely overloaded, could not have managed it. (See Conquest 1968:316–317)

Though it had reached its limits, the purge did not "collapse under its own weight." It came to an end by a decision which reflected the realities: not a formal decree, but a decision communicated in cues too obvious to be ignored. In late 1938, selective prosecutions of regional NKVD heads (see Conquest 1968:466–467) for "abuse of authority," "unjustified arrest" and similar charges, signalled the change, and were further confirmed by the dismissal of the national NKVD head, Yezhov, in December, 1938. He disappeared in February, 1939. The purge had run its course.

THE ELASTICITY OF LIMITS

The purge, as we have seen, was marked by rapid growth, rather than stability, in the number of deviants detected. That such rapid growth occurred, a product of the repetitive cycle of arrests, confessions and denunciations, does not refute the claim that such processes have limits, nor contravene the observation that societies can afford to recognize only so much deviance: rather, the purge illustrates how far such processes may go, how many can be removed from society before the costs are recognized, the limits reached. The rapid growth indicates an elasticity, rather than constancy, in the amount of deviance that can be afforded over the short term at least.

To return to the issues raised earlier: what factors present in the purge could account for the elasticity of its limits? First, the very nature of repressive control systems involves a strain toward detecting and processing deviants in increasing numbers, including a broadening of the definition of deviance, and the recruitment of even the innocent to the status of "deviants." The concern of the NKVD rank and file for their safety guaranteed their vigilance. At higher levels, the NKVD leadership could well understand that its place in the system depended on continuing combat against the opposition: the more dangerous the opposition, the more secure the place of the secret police, and hence the strain toward exaggerating (and inventing) that opposition (see Brzezinski 1956:20–23). In its demand for more and more evidence of political deviation the NKVD was open to exploitation by those who sought job advancement, more living space or other goods through denunciations. The NKVD's mode of operation was supported by the top and bottom of Soviet society: Stalin's suspicion, which gave the initial push, was borne out by the deviance the NKVD uncovered, and encouraged an intensified hunt, while at the bottom *seksots* and racketeering denouncers responded to the atmosphere, supplying more denunciations. Finally, those already arrested, who sensed that the purge could be pushed to its limits and hopefully reversed thereby, contributed still more denunciations.

Of interest is the rapid growth of the purge in the absence of any substantial prior community support for an operation of the scope it was to assume. While the mobilization of previously-weak anti-deviance sentiments among the broader public by interested parties may be observed in many types of societies, and millions of Soviet citizens may have come to believe that the victims were, indeed, "enemies of the people" (Medvedev 1971:365–367), the purge case seems extreme in this regard. Here we may be dealing with a corollary of those modern social systems in which repressive control can flourish: a radical asymmetry of power, and, by implication, an extremely narrow monopoly on decisions about what constitutes deviance, its proofs, and how society will proceed against it. The idea that societies do not define deviance, but that groups or persons with specific interests and the requisite resources do construct such definitions and make them stick, is not new (Becker 1963:15, 17 and ff.; Merton 1966:784–785). Characteristic of the Soviet Union was a radical monopoly of such powers—their concentration in the hands of Stalin and a handful close to him. His own personality, rather than the collective interests and apprehensions of the Soviet upper elite (many of whom were purge victims), shaped the purge to a large degree. In such situations, over the short run at least, community sentiment counts little, and leadership decisions more.

Continental witch persecutions likewise seem to have halted only when monarchs or officials who were well-insulated themselves from charges of witchcraft applied restrictions on torture and confiscation of property (Currie 1968:22, 24). As Dallin and Breslauer (1970:83) argue, "terror as an instrument of purposive policy does not erode or wither 'on its own' . . . The decline in its use requires active or passive, explicit or tacit, decision-making." One might add that, as the purge demonstrates, even when the terror launched by a repressive control system *outgrows* purposive policy, its halt still seems to require such decision-making. The purge went beyond any limits community sentiment could have imposed. As Brzezinski (1956:31) observes, the ability to recruit deviants on the scale of the purge already demonstrates a radical monopoly of power. "The purge is an expression of the regime's power, not an effort to achieve it."

Much like the Inquisition, which shared its characteristics of repressive control, the NKVD created its own opportunities, invented the deviance it was to repress. In a relatively short period, it "recognized" millions of previously-hidden political deviants. The total number of deviants increased, with no evident displacement of non-political deviants.[3] The degree of elasticity in the limits, then, seems strongly related to the nature of the control system: restrained and repressive systems behave differently, with different results. The distinction is critical, and one cannot generalize to the behavior of all control systems by investigating the behavior of one type.

A final factor—the Soviet deployment pattern— seems critical in two ways: first, it amplified the recruitment and containment capabilities of an already repressive control system, and second, it represents an alternative to the model of a relatively fixed-capacity containment system, on which the notion of limits on the recognizable quantity of deviance seems to depend.

The Soviet deployment pattern was one in which some of the problems of expense in controlling and containing deviant populations—recruiting personnel, constructing detention facilities, losing the labor capacities of the confined—all seemed, at least, less pressing than in other systems.

The secret police were, despite (or perhaps because of) the nature of their work, a favored group in Soviet society. The privileges and high salary of an NKVD officer were, for some, enough incentive to minimize recruitment problems. Even before the purge, the NKVD was a large, quasi-military body, with thousands of troops—a pool from which convoy detachments, guards, etc. could be drawn (see Medvedev 1971: 392).

Perhaps more important was the question of "brick and mortar"; for while these are expensive, little of either was used for long-term containment

of purge victims. The prisons of the large cities were grotesquely crowded in 1938, cells holding ten times the number for which they had been intended. To construct new stone or brick prisons to hold the millions arrested would, indeed, have been a task awesome enough to create new limits. Such limits were not inherent in the course actually taken: recommissioning disused buildings— churches, monasteries, hotels, etc.—as prisons, and, more important, containing prisoners in camps— wood buildings, barbed wire "walls." Such a solution was less capital-intensive by far than the alternatives. When, as was often the case, a train containing thousands of prisoners ended its eastward journey in a desolate area of Siberia or Central Asia, and the prisoners, under armed guard, constructed most of the camp facilities themselves, considerable short-term savings resulted. It was in such camps that the vast majority of prisoners were held: the simplicity of construction and materials, the ready labor supply guaranteed, for a considerable time, that the containment capacity of the Soviet system was not fixed, but indefinitely expandable. Sending the prisoners to remote, relatively unpopulated areas enabled the regime to avoid the problems that might arise from containing massive numbers of convicts in or near population centers.

Another critical element of the Soviet deployment pattern (and one which distinguishes it from the other historical examples noted here) was convict involvement in forced labor. This is not the place for a full discussion of the forced labor theory, but the opportunities inherent in convict labor perhaps contributed to the scope of the purges. The costs of maintaining large numbers in confinement can be reduced by retaining the confined as part of the active labor force. Even in the pre-Soviet period, Russia had a tradition of using convict labor in jobs unattractive to free labor. In the earlier Soviet period, forced labor was used heavily in construction, lumbering, and extractive industries. Such was the fate of purge victims. They were not retired from economic production, nor was their labor "make-work."

---

[3] In fact, some persons apparently sought definition as nonpolitical deviants (through commission of, and jailing for, minor criminal offenses) in order to preempt identification as "politicals" (see, *e.g.*, Beck and Godin 1951:96–97). Residence in a local jail on a nonpolitical charge was one way of sitting out the peak of the purge.

This does not mean that it was economically rational. Removing millions of citizens, many highly skilled and educated, from their normal work clearly bespeaks irrationality. But using their labor power may, given deviant recruitment, have been seen as more economical than confining them in prisons (see Medvedev 1971:394). In any case, to many the whole enterprise probably appeared rational. In retrospect the purges make little economic sense. The critical break-through in industrialization had been reached by 1935; the extractive industries in remote sections of the country could probably have been maintained by positive incentives; the arrest and disappearance of skilled technicians and managers harmed the economy. Whether all this was understood in the 1930's, we cannot tell. But to some, at least, forced labor in unattractive industries in remote areas seemed a rational way to deploy the millions of deviants arrested in 1936–1938.

Thus, it seems that the idea that all societies experience a relative stability in the number of deviants they encounter, a stability rooted in relatively stable containment and control capacities, needs modifying. As with all single cases, the Soviet experience is, presumably, not to be duplicated completely. But some of its elements may be (or may have been), and thereby deserve consideration when one examines the generalizations about social control activities discussed here. The experience of the purge suggests that the limits on deviant-recruitment vary greatly in elasticity with the type of control system involved, and that they can be broad indeed. It also indicates the sort of economic, physical and geographic circumstances under which repressive control systems can recruit rapidly increasing numbers of deviants to permanent service at the borders of society, without assessing the effects as too expensive to be borne.

Beyond these issues, the purge is of more general interest to students who view deviance through "conflict" or "functionalist" perspectives. Many purge characteristics support a conflict interpretation. The mode of securing confessions and denunciations, the quotas, the size of the enterprise, all point to the importance of the radical disparity in power between rulers and ruled (the latter including most of the elite itself) in the Soviet case. It is hard to argue the validity of a functionalist interpretation, in a strict sense: that the purge showed the Soviet social order generating the deviance it needed to define its boundaries. Neither Soviet society, nor the Soviet elite, needed the purge. The deviance was "generated," but for the most part in a very special sense: it was invented. The victims' crimes were not acts engaged in, *then* defined as deviance: they were acts that had not taken place. The purge, in its general traumatic impact on Soviet life (especially among the military) was, in fact, more evidently dysfunctional in light of the next large challenge the Soviet system would face—the German invasion of 1941. Indeed, as the record of wartime collaboration between some nationalities and the Nazis demonstrates, it had not managed, despite its massive intake, to remove all potential "traitors" from circulation.

REFERENCES

Beck, F. and W. Godin (pseuds.). 1951. *Russian Purge and the Extraction of Confession.* New York: The Viking Press.

Becker, Howard S. 1963. *Outsiders: Studies in the Sociology of Deviance.* New York: Free Press.

Brzezinski, Zbigniew K. 1956. *The Permanent Purge: Politics in Soviet Totalitarianism.* Cambridge: Harvard University Press.

Conquest, Robert. 1968. *The Great Terror: Stalin's Purge of the Thirties.* New York: The Macmillan Company.

Currie, Elliott P. 1968. "Crime without criminals: witchcraft and its control in Renaissance Europe." *Law and Society Review* 3 (October):7–32.

Dallin, Alexander and George W. Breslauer. 1970. *Political Terror in Communist Systems.* Stanford: Stanford University Press.

Erikson, Kai T. 1966. *Wayward Puritans: A Study in the Sociology of Deviance.* New York: John Wiley and Sons.

Ginsburg, Evgeniia Semenovna. 1967. *Journey into the Whirlwind.* New York: Harcourt, Brace & World.

Lipper, Elinor. 1951. *Eleven Years in Soviet Prison Camps.* Chicago: Regnery.

Medvedev, Roy. 1971. *Let History Judge: The Origins and Consequences of Stalinism.* New York: Knopf.

Merton, Robert K. 1966. "Social problems and sociological theory." Pp. 775–823 in Robert K. Merton and Robert A. Nisbet (eds.), *Contemporary Social Problems*. (2nd edition). New York: Harcourt, Brace & World.

Petrov, Vladimir and Evdokia Petrov. 1956 *Empire of Fear*. New York: Praeger.

Weissberg, Alexander. 1951. *The Accused*. New York: Simon and Schuster.

STUDY QUESTIONS

1. According to Kai Erikson, what are the positive functions for society of deviance and its control?

2. How do Maria Grabe's findings on television crime programs support functionalist theory?

3. What types of deviance are best explained by Rodney Stark's propositions, and what types of deviance are not easily explained by his propositions?

4. What are the potential advantages of James Q. Wilson and George Kelling's proposals if implemented in a community?

5. What kinds of criticisms might be leveled against Wilson and Kelling's proposals?

6. Using Robert Merton's goals–means model of deviance, identify three types of highly valued goals (other than monetary success) that may lead people facing blocked opportunities to engage in deviant behavior to achieve the goal.

7. What motivates corporate executives to engage in deviant behavior, according to Nicos Passas?

8. Describe the research methods used by Howard Becker in his study of marijuana users and by Barbara Heyl in her article on brothel prostitutes.

9. What kinds of behaviors and beliefs were learned by the marijuana users studied by Becker and the brothel prostitutes studied by Heyl?

10. Is Howard Becker's concept of "secret deviance" (in his article, "Outsiders") fully consistent with the tenets of labeling theory?

11. Critically evaluate the use of "direct observation" and "indirect evidence" in labeling someone deviant, as described by John Kitsuse.

12. What does Kitsuse mean by "retrospective interpretation"?

13. Drawing on Waegel, Ermann, and Horowitz's article on the CIA, what did members of Congress hope to accomplish by imputing deviant behavior to the CIA?

14. In what ways do the patterns of deviant behavior or social control depicted in the articles by David Gordon, Elijah Anderson, and Patricia Martin and Robert Hummer illustrate the importance of power and inequality for understanding the dynamics of deviance and control?

15. Describe the negative consequences for Soviet society of Stalin's purges as discussed by Walter Connor.

16. What aspects of the purge, according to Connor, made it so easy for people to be falsely accused and punished?

PART THREE

RESEARCHING DEVIANCE

Introduction to Researching Deviance

Accurate knowledge about deviance is important for many reasons. First, many members of the public hold misconceptions or stereotypes about deviant people. Carefully conducted studies are therefore needed to improve our understanding of the motivations for engaging in deviant behavior and of the life experiences of deviant individuals. Second, some deviant behavior is clearly harmful to deviant actors, to their victims, and to society at large. Research can provide reliable information that can be used to aid policy makers, criminal justice agents, and practitioners who work with offenders.

Social scientists use several standard research methods in studying deviance and control, each of which has unique advantages as well as certain disadvantages. This section of the book examines some of the data sources and research methods commonly used to study deviance and social control.

A great deal of deviant behavior is studied from a distance, by researchers who mine datasets produced by government agencies and social service organizations. Data of this kind can be found in police crime reports, case histories of mental patients, reports of drug-related emergency room visits, or other kinds of information gathered by officials. One of the best known and frequently used sources on crime is the Uniform Crime Reports produced annually by the FBI. This source presents figures on the number and rate of crimes reported to the police throughout the country, and allows us to track changes in crime rates over time. Official data of this kind are invaluable but not without problems: the Uniform Crime Reports, for instance, have been criticized for presenting information on only some kinds of crime, and for being vulnerable to police underreporting or miscategorization of some crimes, including the deliberate manipulation of figures to serve the interests of the organization collecting the data (e.g., a police department that downgrades certain offenses in order to show that serious crime is not increasing). Official statistics may also reflect the changing priorities and enforcement efforts of control agencies, rather than actual changes in the amount of crime. Still, such data are widely used by criminologists and other social scientists. In the chapter on "Measuring Crime," Joseph Senna and Larry Siegel describe the strengths and weaknesses of the FBI's Uniform Crime Reports.

Survey research is frequently used to study deviance. Surveys are conducted in order to:

- measure the *prevalence* of deviant behavior through either victimization surveys that ask respondents whether they have been a victim of crime (e.g., the Justice Department's annual National Crime Victimization Survey) or "self-report" instruments that ask subjects whether they have been personally involved in various deviant acts (e.g., the National Institute of Drug Abuse annual survey on personal use of illegal drugs); Senna and Siegel's chapter examines both victimization and self-report methods;

- determine the level of public agreement or disagreement in evaluations of various deviant acts by asking respondents to rank the *seriousness* of specific behaviors (subjects score each behavior on a scale from "most serious" to "least serious"); or
- tap *public opinion* on deviance or public preferences on how best to control it (respondents have been asked, for instance, whether a given behavior is immoral or harmful, whether it should be punished more harshly, or whether it should be legalized; other surveys measure public evaluations of the police, courts, and prisons).

Surveys on sensitive issues raise obvious questions about the accuracy of the findings: When it comes to questions about one's personal involvement in deviant or criminal acts, or one's victimization by others, how many respondents tell the truth? Some of the most problematic statistics on personal involvement in deviance are yielded by surveys on illegal drug use. In the article, "Number Jumble Clouds Judgment of Drug War," Jeff Leen highlights several methodological problems in such surveys, as well as in other official statistics on drug use, such as emergency room visits and drug tests of persons arrested for crimes. The last study featured in this section deals with victimization surveys. Michael Smith ("Improving Surveys on Violence Against Women") discusses some of the distinctive problems with conventional surveys on domestic violence, and he proposes a fresh approach. Smith's article is important because it highlights both the strengths and weaknesses of survey research on deviant behavior.

Qualitative research is an alternative to the quantitative approaches of large-scale surveys and the analysis of official statistics. The two main qualitative methods are in-depth interviews and participant-observation in the field. Many of the selections in this text are based on in-depth interviews with deviants or with some audience, where the subjects are asked open-ended questions and encouraged to speak at length about their views and experiences. The value of this method should become clear once you read the selections based on in-depth interviewing. Here, I focus on the other main qualitative research technique: *participant-observation*. Participant-observation puts the researcher in direct contact with deviant individuals and groups, or with agents of control, in their natural settings: researchers observe deviants or control agents and actively participate in at least some of their activities. The main advantage of field research in natural settings is that it allows social scientists to observe deviant behavior as it is *enacted* and to observe deviants *interacting* among themselves and with others—something not possible in in-depth interviewing, which is one step removed from actors' lived experiences. Participant-observation gives the researcher unique data on how deviance is performed and what it means to actors. Jack Douglas makes a strong case for using this method: "Sociologists must be involved as participants in the everyday lives of deviant groups if they wish to observe the social meanings of things to those deviants. This is the only way to get valid information on social meanings, especially those shared by deviants" (Douglas 1972:27).

Participant-observation on deviants has been used to gather data on the ways in which deviants experience and justify their deviant acts, the social organization of deviant groups, the socialization of new members, operational strategies for engaging in deviant activities and avoiding detection by the authorities or other people, and ways in which they control and sanction members who violate the group's own norms.

Some of the main challenges facing participant-observers involve the problems of gaining access, maintaining the confidence of deviants once access has been achieved, determining what kinds of activities the researcher will and will not participate in, and evaluating the information provided by deviant informants as to its validity and reliability. In order to gain access and acceptance within such groups, the researcher must get group members to define him as a "right square"—someone who is not deviant but who can be trusted not to "blow the whistle" and inform the authorities, who is tolerant and nonjudgmental of the deviants under study, who tells the truth, and who can be counted on by group members when they need something the researcher is able and willing to provide (Irwin 1972; Polsky 1969). Gaining trust is absolutely vital: it is "essential that the researcher in some way convince the people he wants to study that he does not represent the officials and that his future statements about the group will in no way be of value to officials in controlling that group" (Douglas 1972: 12). The level of participation and the roles researchers play in the setting vary from one person to another: some researchers involve themselves in only some of the group's activities while others participate more fully. This is partly a function of what the researcher is allowed to do and partly a function of what he or she feels comfortable doing. If participant-observation offers unique opportunities for the social scientist to observe criminal and other deviant acts *in progress,* it can also have a downside insofar as observing unseemly acts raises ethical questions, particularly if the deviant acts cause serious harm to others.

At this point, the reader may be wondering why any deviant individual or group would allow themselves to be studied by a social scientist. Aren't the risks of being identified, compromised, or reported to the authorities or others much too high? Perhaps the "researcher" is an undercover cop or someone else with ulterior motives! These are indeed overriding fears for many people involved in criminal and other deviant activity, people who would never consider allowing themselves to be observed while engaged in such activity. But others believe they have something to gain from being studied. As Douglas writes, "Like most people, deviants are interested in themselves and see themselves as people who others would find interesting. . . . But, unlike people defined as 'normal,' deviants experience a profound public relations problem and are often anxious to have somebody study them, especially if such study will result in a book. In addition to their desire for the world to see what they are like, they also often want to justify themselves to the world or to show that they are superior to those who consider them 'deviants'" (Douglas 1972:13). Some deviants, in other words, *want* to be studied in the hope that the researchers' writings will correct popular misunderstandings about them or to provide the outside world with justifications for their deviant conduct. You can imagine a pimp, for example, who feels that pimps have been unfairly maligned by almost everyone in society, and who might therefore welcome the chance to "set the record straight" to demonstrate that he is not a parasite who exploits prostitutes but is instead involved in a worthy enterprise.

This discussion of participant-observation suggests that researching deviants in their natural settings is by no means easy. There are problems inherent in studying any highly discredited individuals up close: First, it may be extremely difficult to gain access to these individuals because they fear others discovering that they are involved in stigmatized conduct (prostitutes' customers and drug users, for example). Second, even if access is achieved, the researcher may have difficulty winning and maintaining the confidence of group members and getting accurate information from them; they may have some residual suspicions of the researcher's motives or fears about what may be done with the information gathered. Studying deviants in their natural settings is thus a delicate operation, but it has been done very successfully in numerous settings. Gangs, drug dealers, cults, prostitutes, and many other types of deviance have been studied using this method. Observational research is featured later in the book in three chapters: Joshua Gamson conducted observations on stigmatized individuals who appear on television talk shows like Jerry Springer; Carole Vance observed hearings of a government commission on pornography; and D. L. Rosenhan studied several mental institutions by having himself and several colleagues committed to the hospitals as "pseudo-patients."

An alternative strategy to observation of deviance in the field is to study deviants outside their natural settings, those who have been incarcerated in a correctional facility, a mental institution, or some other facility. Problems with this research method are well known. Inmates are not a representative sample of the population of deviants. Only those who have been filtered out of the population—by being apprehended and incarcerated—are studied under this approach, and findings from such nonrandom samples cannot be used to generalize to the population at large. A second problem has to do with the validity of the information provided by inmates: what they tell an interviewer may be distorted by the very fact that they are being questioned in an institution. They may conceal information that might embarrass or compromise them—out of fear that it might be communicated to the staff—or they might offer researchers a "sad tale" about their lives in order to elicit sympathy from the researcher and perhaps obtain a break from staff members, if the inmate believes the researcher might convey this information to the staff (McCall 1978:27).

Nevertheless, researchers have gathered important data by observing and interviewing inmates in prisons, mental hospitals, and other kinds of correctional institutions. Diana Scully and Joseph Marolla's study of incarcerated rapists, featured later in the book, is a good example of this approach. Some researchers have entered institutions not to study the inmates but instead to study the institution itself. D. L. Rosenhan's investigation of mental hospitals, which appears later in the book, is one of the most famous studies in this genre.

REFERENCES

Douglas, Jack D. 1972. "Observing Deviance," in J. Douglas (ed.), *Research on Deviance*. New York: Random House.

Irwin, John. 1972. "Participant Observation of Criminals," in J. Douglas (ed.), *Research on Deviance*. New York: Random House.

McCall, George J. 1978. *Observing the Law*. New York: Free Press.

Polsky, Ned. 1969. *Hustlers, Beats, and Others*. Chicago: University of Chicago Press.

Measuring Crime

Joseph J. Senna and Larry J. Siegel

Each source of crime data collection helps criminal justice experts understand the nature and extent of criminal behavior in the United States and to measure crime trends and patterns. Usually, three separate measures are used: official record data, victim survey data, and self-report crime survey data. Each source can be used independently, but taken together they provide a detailed picture of the crime problem. The data provided by these three sources of crime data diverge in many key areas, but they have enough similarities to enable crime experts to draw some conclusions about crime in the United States. Each method is discussed in detail in the following sections.

OFFICIAL CRIME DATA: THE UNIFORM CRIME REPORTS

The Federal Bureau of Investigation's UCR is the best known and most widely cited source of aggregate criminal statistics (FBI 1998). The FBI receives and compiles records from over seventeen thousand police departments serving a majority of the U.S. population. Its major unit of analysis involves *index crimes:* criminal homicide, forcible rape, robbery, aggravated assault, burglary, larceny/theft, motor vehicle theft, and arson. The FBI tallies and annually publishes the number of reported offenses by city, county, standard metropolitan statistical area, and geographical divisions of the United States. Besides these statistics, the UCR shows the number and characteristics (age, race, and gender) of individuals who have been

arrested for these and all other crimes—*nonindex crimes*—except traffic violations.

Data on the number of clearances involving the arrest of only juvenile offenders, data on the value of property stolen and recovered in connection with index offenses, and detailed information pertaining to criminal homicide are also reported. Traditionally, slightly more than 20 percent of all reported index crimes are cleared by arrest each year. Violent crimes are more likely to be solved than property crimes because police devote more resources to the more serious acts. For these types of crimes, witnesses (including the victim) are frequently available to identify offenders, and in many instances the victim and offender were previously acquainted.

The UCR uses three methods to express crime data. First, the number of crimes reported to the police and arrests made are expressed as raw figures (e.g., 18,209 murders occurred in 1998). Second, crime rates per 100,000 people are computed. That is, when the UCR indicates that the murder rate was 6.3 in 1998, it means that about 6 people in every 100,000 were murdered between January 1 and December 31 of 1998. Third, the FBI computes changes in the number and rate of crime over time. For example, murder rates declined 7.4 percent between 1997 and 1998.

How Accurate is the UCR? Despite criminologists' continued reliance on the UCR, its accuracy has been suspect. Some criminologists claim that victims of many serious crimes do not report these incidents to police; therefore, these crimes do not become part of the UCR. The reasons for not reporting vary. Some victims do not trust the police or have confidence in their ability to solve crimes. Others do not have property insurance and therefore

From Joseph J. Senna and Larry J. Siegel, *Essentials of Criminal Justice,* 3rd ed., Wadsworth, 2001. Reprinted by permission of the Wadsworth Group, a division of Thomson Learning.

believe it is useless to report theft. In other cases, victims fear reprisals from an offender's friends or family. According to surveys of crime victims, less than 40 percent of all criminal incidents are reported to the police (Chappell, Geis, Schafer, and Siegel 1971). The way police departments record and report criminal and delinquent activity also affects the validity of UCR statistics. Some departments may define crimes loosely—for example, reporting a trespass as a burglary or an assault on a woman as an attempted rape—whereas others pay strict attention to FBI guidelines. These reporting practices may help explain interjurisdictional differences in crime.

Some local police departments make systematic errors in UCR reporting. Some count an arrest only after a formal booking procedure, although the UCR requires arrests to be counted if the suspect is released without a formal charge. More serious allegations claim that in some cases police officials may deliberately alter reported crimes to improve their department's public image (Sherman and Glick 1984). Police administrators interested in lowering the crime rate may falsify crime reports by, for example, classifying a burglary as a nonreportable trespass (Seidmar and Couzens 1974). Exhibit 2.1 lists other issues that have been raised about the UCR's validity.

VICTIM SURVEYS

The second source of crime data is surveys that ask crime victims about their encounters with criminals. The NCVS is conducted by the U.S. Bureau of the Census in cooperation with the Bureau of Justice Statistics of the U.S. Department of Justice (Rennison 1999). In these national surveys, samples of housing units are selected, using a complex, multistage sampling technique. Each year data are obtained from a nationally representative sample of roughly forty-five thousand households that includes more than ninety-four thousand persons. They are asked to report on the frequency, characteristics, and consequences of criminal victimization in the United States. The victims are surveyed on the number of sexual assaults, robberies, assaults, thefts, household

---

EXHIBIT 2.1

Factors Affecting the Validity of the Uniform Crime Report

1. No federal crimes are reported.
2. Reports are voluntary and vary in accuracy and completeness.
3. Not all police departments submit reports.
4. The FBI uses estimates in its total crime projections.
5. If an offender commits multiple crimes, only the most serious is recorded. Thus, if a narcotic addict rapes, robs, and murders a victim, only the murder is recorded. Consequently, many lesser crimes go unreported.
6. Each act is listed as a single offense for some crimes but not for others. If a person robbed six people in a bar, the offense is listed as one robbery; but if he assaulted or murdered them, it is listed as six assaults or six murders.
7. Incomplete acts are grouped together with completed ones.
8. Important differences exist between the FBI's definition of certain crimes and those used in a number of states.
9. Victimless crimes such as drug sales often go undetected.
10. Many cases of child abuse and family violence are unreported.

Source: Leonard Savitz, "Official Statistics," *Contemporary Criminology*, ed. Leonard Savitz and Norman Johnston (New York: Wiley, 1982), 3–15. Updated 1999, with data from the FBI.

---

burglaries, and motor vehicle thefts they experienced. The total sample is interviewed twice a year about victimization during the preceding six months. Households remain in the sample for about three years, and new homes rotate into the sample continually. The NCVS reports that the interview completion rate in the national sample is usually more than 90 percent in any given period. Because of the care with which the samples are drawn and the high completion rate, NCVS data are considered a relatively unbiased, valid estimate of all victimizations for the target crimes included in the survey.

The number of crimes accounted for by the NCVS (about 31 million) is considerably larger than the number of crimes reported to the FBI. For example, whereas the UCR shows that about 446,000 robberies occurred in 1998, the NCVS estimates that about 886,000 actually occurred. Victims seem to report to the police only crimes that involve considerable loss or injury. If we are to believe NCVS findings, the official UCR statistics do not provide an accurate picture of the crime problem because many crimes go unreported to the police.

Is The NCVS Valid? Like the UCR, the NCVS may also suffer from some methodological problems. As a result, its findings must be interpreted with caution. Among the potential problems are these:

- Overreporting due to victims' misinterpretation of events. For example, a lost wallet may be reported as stolen, or an open door may be viewed as a burglary attempt.
- Underreporting due to the embarrassment of reporting crime to interviewers, fear of getting in trouble, or simply forgetting an incident.
- Inability to record the personal criminal activity of those interviewed, such as drug use or gambling; murder is also not included for obvious reasons.
- Sampling errors, which produce a group of respondents who do not represent the nation as a whole.
- Inadequate question format that invalidates responses. Some groups, such as adolescents, may be particularly susceptible to error because of question format (Wells and Rankin 1995).

SELF-REPORT SURVEYS

The problems associated with official statistics have led many criminologists to seek alternative sources of information in assessing the true extent of crime patterns. In addition, official statistics do not say much about the personality, attitudes, and behavior of individual criminals. They also are of little value in charting the extent of substance abuse in the population because relatively few abusers

are arrested. Criminologists have therefore sought additional sources to supplement and expand official data. One frequently employed alternative to official statistics is the *self-report survey.* These surveys allow participants to reveal information about their violations. Most often, self-report surveys are administered to groups of subjects through a mass distribution of questionnaires. Although the surveys might ask for the subjects' names, more commonly the responses remain anonymous. The basic assumption of self-report surveys is that anonymity and confidentiality will be ensured, which encourages people to accurately describe their illegal activities. Self-reports are viewed as a mechanism to get at the "dark figures of crime," the figures missed by official statistics.

Most self-report studies have focused on juvenile delinquency and youth crime, for two reasons (Porterfield 1946; Hardt and Bodine 1965; Murphy, Shirley, and Witner 1946). First, the school setting makes it convenient to test thousands of subjects simultaneously because they all have the means to respond to a research questionnaire (pens, desks, and time). Second, because school attendance is universal, a school-based self-report survey represents a cross section of the community. However, self-reports are not restricted to youth crime. They are also used to examine the offense histories of prison inmates, drug users, and other segments of the population. They can be used to estimate the number of criminal offenders who have previously been unknown to the police. These respondents represent many criminals who have never figured in official crime statistics, some of whom may even be serious or *chronic offenders* (Dunford and Elliott 1983). In sum, self-reports provide an appreciable amount of information about offenders that cannot be found in official statistics.

In general, self-reports indicate that the number of people who break the law is far greater than the number projected by official statistics. Almost everyone questioned is found to have violated some law (Gold 1966; Short and Nye 1958; Hindelang 1973). Furthermore, self-reports dispute the notion that criminals and delinquents specialize in one type of crime or another; offenders seem to engage in a "mixed bag" of crime and deviance (Osgood, Johnston, O'Malley, and Bachman 1988).

Self-report surveys indicate that the most common offenses are truancy, alcohol abuse, use of a false ID, shoplifting or larceny under $50, fighting, marijuana use, and damage to the property of others. It is not unusual for self-reports to find combined substance abuse, theft, violence, and damage rates of more than 50 percent among suburban, rural, and urban high school youths. What is surprising is the consistency of these findings in samples taken around the United States. A national survey of thousands of high school seniors, one of the most important sources of self-report data, shows a widespread yet stable pattern of youth crime since 1978 (Johnston, O'Malley, and Bachman 1991; Flanagan and Maguire 1990). Young people self-report a great deal of crime: About 31 percent of high school seniors now report stealing in the last twelve months, almost 20 percent said they were involved in a gang fight, about 13 percent injured someone so badly that the victim had to see a doctor, about 30 percent admitted shoplifting, and almost 25 percent engaged in breaking and entering. The facts that so many—at least 33 percent—of all U.S. high school students engaged in theft and almost 19 percent committed a serious violent act during the past year show that criminal activity is widespread and is not restricted to a few "bad apples."

Are Self-Reports Valid? Although self-report data have profoundly affected criminological inquiry, some important methodological issues have been raised about their accuracy. Critics of self-report studies frequently suggest that it is unreasonable to expect people to candidly admit illegal acts. They have nothing to gain, and the ones taking the greatest risk are the ones with official records who may be engaging in the most criminality. On the other hand, some people may exaggerate their criminal acts, forget some of them, or be confused about what is being asked. Some surveys contain an overabundance of trivial offenses, such as shoplifting small amounts of items or using false identification, often lumped together with serious crimes to form a total crime index. Consequently, comparisons between groups can be highly misleading.

Although many criminologists believe in the reliability of self-reports, nagging questions still remain about their validity (Hindelang, Hirschi, and Weis 1981). Even if 90 percent of a school population voluntarily participates in a self-report survey, researchers can never be sure whether the few who refuse to participate or are absent that day comprise a significant portion of the school's population of persistent, high-rate offenders (Simon 1995). It is also unlikely that the most serious chronic offenders in the teenage population are the most willing to cooperate with university-based criminologists administering self-report tests (Cernkovich, Giordano, and Pugh 1985). For example, persistent substance abusers tend to underreport the frequency of their drug use (Wish, Gray, and Levine 1996; Gray and Wish 1993).

REFERENCES

Cernkovich, Stephen, Peggy Giordano, and Meredith Pugh. 1985. "Chronic Offenders: The Missing Cases in Self-Report Delinquency." *Criminology* 76:705–32.

Chappell, Duncan, Gilbert Geis, Stephen Schafer, and Larry Siegel. 1971. "Forcible Rape: A Comparative Study of Offenses Known to the Police in Boston and Los Angeles." In *Studies in the Sociology of Sex,* ed. James Henslin. New York: Appleton-Century-Crofts, 169–93.

Dunford, Franklyn, and Delbert Elliott. 1983. "Identifying Career Criminals Using Self-Reported Data." *Journal of Research in Crime and Delinquency* 21: 57–86.

Federal Bureau of Investigation. 1999. *Crime in the United States, 1998.* Washington, D.C.: Government Printing Office.

Flanagan, Timothy, and Kathleen Maguire. 1990. *Sourcebook of Criminal Justice Statistics, 1989.* Washington, D.C.: Government Printing Office.

Gold, Martin. 1966. "Undetected Delinquent Behavior." *Journal of Research in Crime and Delinquency* 3:27–46.

Gray, Thomas, and Eric Wish. 1993. *Maryland Youth at Risk: A Study of Drug Use in Juvenile Detainees.* College Park, Md.: Center for Substance Abuse Research.

Hardt, Robert, and George Bodine. 1965. *Development of Self-Report Instruments in Delinquency Research: A Conference Report.* Syracuse, N. Y.: Syracuse University Youth Development Center.

Hindelang, Michael. 1973. "Causes of Delinquency: A Partial Replication and Extension." *Social Problems* 20:471–87.

Hindelang, Michael, Travis Hirschi. and Joseph Weis. 1981. *Measuring Delinquency.* Beverly Hills: Sage.

Johnston, Lloyd, Patrick O'Malley, and Jerald Bachman. 1991. *Monitoring the Future, 1990.* Ann Arbor: University of Michigan, Institute for Social Research.

Murphy, Fred, Mary Shirley, and Helen Witner. 1946. "The Incidence of Hidden Delinquency." *American Journal of Orthopsychology* 16:686–96.

Osgood, D. Wayne, Lloyd Johnston, Patrick O'Malley, and Jerald Bachman. 1988. "The Generality of Deviance in Late Adolescence and Early Adulthood." *American Sociological Review* 53:81–93.

Porterfield, A. L. 1946. *Youth in Trouble.* Fort Worth, Tex.: Leo Potishman Foundation.

Rennison, Callie Marie. 1999. *Criminal Victimization 1998 Changes 1997–98 with Trends 1993–98.* Washington, D.C.: Bureau of Justice Statistics.

Seidman, David, and Michael Couzens. 1974. "Getting the Crime Rate Down: Political Pressure and Crime Reporting." *Law and Society Review* 8:457.

Sherman, Lawrence, and Barry Glick. 1984. "The Quality of Arrest Statistics." *Police Foundation Reports* 2:1–8.

Short, James, and F. Ivan Nye. 1958. "Extent of Undetected Delinquency, Tentative Conclusions." *Journal of Criminal Law, Criminology and Police Science* 49:296–302.

Simon, Leonore. 1995. "Validity and Reliability of Violent Juveniles: A Comparison of Juvenile Self-Reports with Adult Self-Reports." Paper presented at the meeting of the American Society of Criminology, Boston.

Wells, L. Edward, and Joseph Rankin. 1995. "Juvenile Victimization: Convergent Validation of Alternative Measurements." *Journal of Research in Crime and Delinquency* 32:287–307.

Wish, Eric, Thomas Gray, and Eliot Levine. 1996. *Recent Drug Use in Female Juvenile Detainees: Estimates from Interviews, Urinalysis and Hair Analysis.* College Park, Md.: Center for Substance Abuse Research.

READING 3-2

Number Jumble Clouds Judgment of Drug War

Jeff Leen

As the election season began gearing up in late 1991, President George Bush got an unsettling bit of front-page news:

The number of habitual cocaine users in the United States had jumped an astounding 29 percent in a single year, from 662,000 to 855,000, according to the National Institute on Drug Abuse (NIDA). Bush had aggressively pushed his administration's anti-drug effort. Now, he had little to show for it.

But the bad news, widely reported by newspapers across the country, was wrong. NIDA had miscounted in its annual National Household Survey on

Reprinted by permission from *The Washington Post* (Jan. 2, 1998), pp. A01, A20. © 1998 The Washington Post.

Drug Abuse, one of the nation's "leading drug indicators." A year later, without fanfare, the number of habitual users was revised back down to 625,000.

"Problems with statistical imputation," the General Accounting Office concluded in a 1993 report on the miscalculation that received little public attention. "We certainly think that more adequate quality control procedures could have caught findings of such significant policy relevance."

The 1991 cocaine mistake stands out as just one example of the tenuous grasp scientists, politicians, the media and the public have in evaluating America's 25-year crusade against drugs. Different methods of calculating the number of drug users continue to produce widely gyrating estimates, including those contained in the 1997 White House drug strategy report that variously gives the number of habitual cocaine users as 582,000 and 2.2 million.

In spending a proposed $16 billion on the federal drug war in 1998—a 400 percent increase since 1986—lawmakers will rely on reams of data that often attempt to impose statistical order on a chaotic social problem that defies easy analysis. Extensive federally funded efforts to accurately assess the subterranean drug world have led to contradictory findings and occasional statistical curiosities, such as a 79-year-old female respondent whose avowed heroin usage in one survey resulted in a projection of 142,000 heroin users, 20 percent of the national total.

"It's clear that these things are badly mismeasured and nobody cares about it," said Peter Reuter, the former co-director of drug research for the nonprofit RAND think tank and now a University of Maryland professor. "That's because drug policy isn't a very analytically serious business."

Measuring the drug war with any precision is a daunting task. Hard-core drug users are hard to find, much less question, and people frequently lie on drug-use surveys—one study shows two-thirds of teenagers giving deceptive answers. Since surveys typically receive only a small number of positive responses, analysts risk making substantial errors in creating projections for the entire nation. Survey results sometimes include warnings acknowledging these obstacles, such as "subject to large sampling error" or "great caution should be taken."

But the caveats often are downplayed or ignored, either by those issuing the data or by journalists and others promulgating the information. In reporting the apparent 1991 jump in habitual cocaine use, for example, the White House's Office of Drug Control Policy noted that the statistics were both "cause for concern" and "highly unreliable."

The difficulty in measuring and evaluating the nation's illegal drug problem made it harder to set policy, stoked partisan rhetoric and confused the public, drug analysts say. Many experts, for example, believe cocaine and crack use are in decline, and the federal household survey indicates that overall drug use is down 49 percent from its peak of 25 million monthly users in 1979; yet many Americans still perceive the drug war as perennially lost.

"You really can't tell from the big debate that goes on in public what the big picture is," said David Musto, a Yale University medical historian who has studied drug trends for three decades. "When I tell people about it, they're completely surprised by the fact there has been a decline since 1980."

That big picture can be obscured by drug statistics that are "often incomplete, erratic and contradictory," in the words of two RAND researchers funded by the government to measure cocaine consumption. The first problem of drug war analysis is the sheer number of measurements—there are more than 50 federal drug-related "data systems" with hundreds of "drug variables" produced by an array of federal agencies.

For cocaine alone there are national statistics on casual use (at least once a year), current use (at least once a month), frequent or habitual use (at least once a week), crack use and use broken down by age, race and sex. There are stats on tonnage consumed, purity, price per gram, price per kilo, patients reporting cocaine problems in emergency rooms, patients seeking treatment and so forth.

"It's not that one thing is better than the other," said Eric Wish, director of the Center for Substance Abuse Research at the University of Maryland.

"They all give a different piece of the puzzle, and they need to be put together. But because of federal turf issues, it's more of an adversarial process than a collaborative relationship."

Reuter said he has pointed out discrepancies in the habitual cocaine-use figures in the national strategy report in the past, but the discordant numbers keep appearing. On page 11 of the 1997 strategy, the count of habitual cocaine users is given as 582,000, a number that "has not changed markedly since 1985." But in a chart on page 227 of the strategy's budget summary, the number of such users is given as 2,238,000.

"I can't seem to get the machinery that cranks out these reports to pay attention to these inconsistencies," Reuter said.

An official with the Office of National Drug Control Policy blamed the 1997 inconsistency on "sloppy writing." But the precise reasoning behind it gives a glimpse into the problem of gauging the drug war. The warring numbers in this case come out of different measuring methodologies—one based on the household survey, the other on urine tests of jail inmates—that give radically different results.

"The truth is probably somewhere in the middle," said Joe Gfroerer, who manages the household survey for the federal Substance Abuse and Mental Health Services Administration (SAMHSA). "It's just a difficult thing to estimate."

Jared Hermalin, the GAO project manager who uncovered the 1991 cocaine mistake, said: "There's every reason to believe that maybe the numbers are not absolutely correct but the trends are correct. That's the main thing we need to know."

In recognition of the need for better analysis, the office of national drug policy director Barry R. McCaffrey has proposed a comprehensive Performance Measurement System intended, for the first time, to standardize measurement of the drug war.

"Facts should drive policy, but they haven't until very, very lately, with McCaffrey," Sen. Joseph R. Biden Jr. (D-Del.), a longtime critic of the household survey's measurement of hard-core cocaine use, said in an interview.

The proposed system shows just how complex measuring the drug war is. It contains one mission statement with five goals, 32 objectives and 99 "targets" that will be tracked by more than 111 "measures."

Even when the data is not marred by obvious statistical flaws, the sheer profusion of it can baffle those looking for simple answers on whether the drug war has been a success or failure. There is consensus that overall drug use, as well as marijuana and cocaine use specifically, have [sic] declined dramatically since the 1970s. But that clarity soon clouds when researchers delve deeper.

For example, according to the household survey, current (monthly) cocaine use decreased in the 1980s—and was often cited as a sign of success; but, also according to the household survey, hard-core (weekly) use did not drop, and that was cited as a sign of failure. More recently, even as the household survey shows that the overall number of cocaine users has declined (success), emergency room data shows that the number of people seeking medical treatment for cocaine problems is rising (failure) as chronic addicts age and their health deteriorates. And the household survey may show that overall drug use is down (success), but a high school survey shows that teenage marijuana use is up (failure).

For the past 25 years, the nation's most prominent gauge of illegal drug use has been the national household survey, begun by NIDA in 1972 and taken over by SAMHSA in 1992. Government workers annually conduct one-hour, in-person interviews with a randomly selected sample of 18,000 people, age 12 and up. From the answers, statisticians extrapolate the size of the nation's drug-taking population.

The second most-publicized measurement is the NIDA-sponsored, 22-year-old "Monitoring the Future" survey. Each year, more than 51,000 high school students at more than 400 public and private schools are polled about their drug use.

In the 1970s and 1980s, the household and high school surveys were treated as national news on the state of the drug war, particularly in tracking the rise of marijuana and cocaine.

"I've been looking at the household survey and the high school survey for years and years," said Eric Sterling, a former House Judiciary Committee staff counsel now with the Criminal Justice Policy Foundation. "They have an effect like electric shock on a dead frog's leg. There's a spasm people have when they get this data. People, certainly on Capitol Hill, look to respond."

In the mid-1980s, the advent of crack played havoc with the existing measurement system. Simply put, there was no measurement in place for crack use—crack was so new that the household survey did not start asking about it until 1987.

Faced with an unprecedented national outcry after the overdose death of University of Maryland basketball star Len Bias on June 19, 1986, Congress rushed through a law punishing crack cocaine possession at a rate 100 times that of powder cocaine. Without hard data, lawmakers relied heavily on high-pitched media accounts, some of which "were not supported by data at the time and in retrospect were simply incorrect," the U.S. Sentencing Commission later concluded in a comprehensive study on "Cocaine and Federal Sentencing Policy."

"It was really the opposite of science," said Sterling, who wrote the draft version of the crack law when he served with the Judiciary Committee. "It was mythology-driven. It was said repeatedly that there were 3,000 new crack addicts every day. These kinds of numbers would get thrown out and repeated without anybody doing the arithmetic or asking: 'How does this number relate to anything we know about the usage?' "

The lawmakers believed—erroneously, it would later turn out—that crack had killed Bias. (Testimony from someone who was with Bias when he died pointed to powder cocaine.) Congress reacted so strongly to crack in part because it believed it was dealing with a rapidly spreading "crack epidemic."

Yet the household survey eventually estimated that crack use stabilized almost immediately and never approached the levels that powder cocaine had—crack stood at 668,000 monthly users in 1996 compared with more than 5 million for powder cocaine in 1985, according to survey figures.

But the statistical data eventually provoked just as much criticism as the absence of data did. Crack use turned out to be harder to measure than powder cocaine use. Like heroin, crack quickly concentrated among poor urban addicts. Many of them lived on the streets, where they would not be counted by the household survey.

"The household survey and the school survey are pretty useless for measuring hard drug use in the population," said Wish, the University of Maryland research center director.

By the late 1980s, drug researchers like Wish thought that the nation's cocaine problem was breaking into two distinct groups: mainly white suburbanites who used cocaine casually on weekends and mainly black urban addicts who used crack or cocaine daily. For casual users, Bias's death seemed to have the effect of scaring millions off cocaine; the household survey indicated that after 1985 the number of monthly cocaine users plummeted 70 percent.

Yet the trend in hard-core usage is still being sorted out.

In 1990, just as the Bush administration had begun touting the decline in casual use, then-Senate Judiciary Committee Chairman Biden produced a report counting habitual cocaine users at 2.2 million. That was nearly triple the household survey's estimate.

Biden's numbers had come from what would eventually emerge as a third leading indicator of the nation's drug use—the Justice Department's Drug Use Forecasting (DUF) program, started in 1987. The DUF program collects voluntary urine samples from 30,000 jail inmates in 23 cities across the country each year to test for cocaine and other drugs. Biden's figures were extrapolations from these urine tests.

Mark Kleiman, a Harvard researcher who supervised the Biden committee's work, subsequently acknowledged that the methodology was "not precise." But he said conservative assumptions were used to come up with numbers that gave a clearer picture of the nation's cocaine use.

But the GAO and household study researchers like Gfroerer say that the DUF urine tests cannot be used to extrapolate larger numbers because they are not part of a randomly selected scientific sample.

"DUF really isn't representative of anything," Gfroerer said. "The way it's collected, you can't project it out to any population."

Although the household survey is based on a randomly selected sample, it also has limitations, according to some researchers. Only a tiny percentage of people admit to heroin and cocaine use, and they must then become the basis for projections into the millions of users. For example, of 32,594 people surveyed in 1991, only 127 admitted to using heroin in the past year, according to the GAO. From this number the survey projected 701,000 heroin users nationwide.

Thus, small errors in the way the survey is carried out can be magnified. That means yearly shifts of a few hundred thousand in a projected user population of a million are statistically insignificant because they could be explained by possible errors in sampling, reporting or extrapolation, Gfroerer said.

The GAO found such problems in the 1991 cocaine and heroin figures. For heroin, further investigation revealed that 53 of the 127 users counted in the survey were inappropriately "imputed"—researchers made a subjective decision to count them even though they gave contradictory answers. When the error was later corrected, the number of heroin users dropped 46 percent to 381,000.

Moreover, of the 701,000 annual heroin users originally estimated in 1991, 142,000 were derived from the survey response of a lone 79-year-old white woman. Her answer was weighted in an effort to make the survey result more representative of the nation's population; but the resulting statistical projection accounted for one-fifth of all the estimated heroin users in the United States that year, according to the GAO.

"The bottom line is [that] to make projections from the household survey to the number of heroin users in the country is probably not a good idea," said Hermalin, the GAO project manager. "Cocaine [estimation] is dangerous, too."

In 1994, the household survey was revamped to make it more accurate at counting hard-core drug use, but Gfroerer said the difficulty was "only partially" corrected.

"The basic issue of understating of hard-core drug use, those problems are exactly as they have been," Gfroerer said. "We still feel it's important to collect these data as part of the survey. The real issue is how you report them."

READING 3-3

Improving Surveys on Violence Against Women

Michael D. Smith

A major methodological problem in victimization surveys on the physical and sexual abuse of women is the underreporting of abuse. An abused woman may not reveal her victimization to an interviewer for a variety of reasons. She may feel that the subject is too personal to discuss, she may be embarrassed or ashamed, she may fear reprisal by her abuser should he find out about the interview, she may misunderstand the question, or she may think the abuse was too minor to mention. She may even

From *Gender & Society* 8 (March 1994), 109–27. © 1994 Sociologists for Women in Society. Reprinted by permission of Sage Publications.

have forgotten about it, particularly if it was minor and happened long ago. If the abuse was especially traumatic, she may not want, or be able, to recall it. If she does disclose that she has been abused, she may not respond fully and honestly to followup questions about the experience. No one knows the exact extent to which survey respondents understate their victimization, but feminist and mainstream researchers agree that the problem is significant especially when the abuser is a male intimate (Brush 1990; Hanmer and Saunders 1984; Koss 1992; Sessar 1990; Stark and Flitcraft 1988; Straus 1990b; Weis 1989).

The consequences of massive underreporting are serious. Indeed, without a reasonably accurate measure of victimization, an entire survey is put in jeopardy, for one cannot know if those women who disclosed having been abused are representative of all victims in the sample. Underreporting also has negative implications for social policy: the greater the degree of underreporting, the lower the estimates of abuse, and the lower the probability of mobilizing resources to combat the problem. Policymakers pay attention to large numbers.

Feminist research points to a number of methodological strategies for improving the accuracy of survey data on this delicate subject. I tried to implement these strategies in a survey of Toronto women conducted in 1987 (Smith 1987). My goal was to draw out data that did some justice to the sensitivity and complexity of the subject matter and at the same time attend to the chief concerns of established survey research—getting a representative sample and generating valid and reliable data.

FEMINIST APPROACHES TO DATA GATHERING

Broad Definitions

Not surprisingly, the broader the definition of violence, the higher the reported level of victimization, all else being equal. Thus, most national crime surveys, which define violence in narrow legalistic terms, uncover very low levels of violence against women, particularly by male intimates. There are other reasons for these low levels. One is that many women may not think of such violence as "criminal" and thus may not report it in a "crime" survey. Feminist surveys, on the other hand, that define violence on the basis of women's subjective experiences of violence, including noncriminal and marginally criminal acts, uncover very high levels of violence (e.g., Hanmer and Saunders 1984; Radford 1987; Russell 1982). Other surveys usually obtain results that fall in between these two extremes.

To illustrate the point, the 1982 British Crime Survey (BCS) found that less than 2 percent of all women in the sample were victims of an actual or threatened crime of violence (robbery, wounding, assault, indecent assault, rape) during the survey year (Hough and Mayhew 1983). One year later, feminist researcher Radford (1987) found that almost *all* women in the London borough of Wandsworth had experienced some sort of male violence during the preceding 12 months. In the Wandsworth survey, violence included racial and sexual assault and harassment, threatened or actual attacks in public places, threatened or actual attacks by a stranger in the respondent's home, threatened or actual attacks by a man the respondent was living with, obscene phone calls, sexual harassment at work, seeing another woman threatened or attacked, and knowing well another woman who was attacked. Of the respondents, 44 percent actually suffered a personal victimization. Of course, this comparison ignores the fact that the risk of victimization *is* much higher in inner-city Wandsworth than in the country as a whole, but it seems unlikely that this could account for the huge discrepancy in reported rates.

As Radford (1987) points out, the BCS investigated "crime"; the Wandsworth survey explored "violence against women." What the law defines as serious, and thus as criminal, does not necessarily coincide with women's real-life experiences; for example, in Britain a husband still cannot be found guilty of raping his wife. It seems appropriate that a survey on violence against women take women's subjective experiences seriously. A compromise is to take into account respondents' subjective experiences and legal (or other) categories of violence. Whereas feminist research takes seriously the perceptions and interpretations of women, some degree of standardization is also important if one wishes to compare the results of different studies. Accordingly, definitions can be developed from women's accounts of their own victimization and then organized as much as possible on the basis of legal or other criteria. It is important to emphasize, however, that such definitions should encompass experiences, such as routine street harassment, that are only marginally illegal but that nevertheless sometimes provoke fear, even terror, in the recipient (McNeil 1987).

Lifetime Prevalence

The majority of representative sample surveys dealing wholly or partly with physical or sexual violence against women have produced estimates of annual victimization rates. A smaller number of such surveys have reported data on lifetime or "ever" rates: the proportion of women in the sample who have ever been victimized, if not in their entire lifetime, in their adult lifetime, or within marriage or some other unbounded period of time. Annual rates have their uses, of course, including monitoring trends over time, but data on lifetime prevalence are equally if not more important.

Focusing only on annual rates can lead to a false sense of security by obscuring the real scope of the violence. For example, the U.S. National Crime Survey (NCS) annual statistics indicate that the likelihood of a woman suffering a rape in any given year is roughly 16 per 10,000 women. Yet, Koppel (1987) calculates, on the basis of NCS annual statistics averaged over a 10-year period (1975–84) and life tables published by the National Center for Health Statistics, that a woman's lifetime (a "lifetime" begins at age 12) chances of suffering a rape are in the neighborhood of 8 out of 100! Using the same data sources, Koppel estimates that about 3 of every 4 females currently 12 years of age will be victims of a violent crime (completed or attempted assault, robbery, or rape) at some time in

their lives. Koppel computed these lifetime likelihoods of personal victimization from the probabilities of victimization at the various ages that constitute a lifetime. Even these figures are underestimates, of course, because they are derived from NCS annual data, which greatly underestimate the real amount of violence against women, especially wife abuse and sexual abuse (Koss 1992; Stark and Flitcraft 1988).

From the researcher's point of view, obtaining estimates of lifetime or "ever" rates (as opposed solely to annual rates), usually increases the size of the sample of reported victims, sometimes dramatically. In a German survey, 86 percent of the rapes reported took place *before* the 12 months leading up to the study (Sessar 1990). A larger sample of victims allows for more meaningful and statistically reliable comparisons among victim and abuser subgroups. It also provides a surer footing for investigating the causes and consequences of victimization because it avoids the biasing effects of turning victims into nonvictims simply because they were victimized prior to the traditional 12-month reference period (Sessar 1990).

To be sure, there are problems associated with measuring the prevalence of violence within a long recall period, including forgetting by victims, particularly of minor incidents that took place long ago (Skogan 1986; Van Dijk, Mayhew, and Killias 1990; Weis 1989). On the other hand, Killias (1990) found, on the basis of interviews with 95 victims of serious crime and a matched sample of nonvictims in the Swiss Crime Survey, that inaccuracies in the categorization of respondents as victims or nonvictims, with no time limit on the recall period, were minimal; inaccuracies in the frequency and kinds of victimizations were more problematic. Russell (1982) argues that an abused woman may disclose incidents that occurred in the distant past more readily than recent incidents because the former are less emotionally painful to recall. Whatever the case, we should not forget that women's experiences of male violence accumulate over a lifetime and that the psychological effects of a single episode may remain for years (Stanko 1990; Koss,

Gidycz, and Widniewski 1987). It makes little sense to exclude a woman as a victim of violence simply because she did not report having been assaulted during the 12 months immediately prior to the survey.

Multiple Measures

Methodologists have long advocated the use of multiple measures as a way of enhancing the reliability and validity of social variables (e.g., Bohrnstedt 1983). But most mainstream survey researchers seem to have paid scant attention to this advice when it comes to estimating the extent of violence against women. Indeed, some have computed such estimates on the basis of a single question (e.g., Bland and Orn 1986; Fergusson et al. 1986).

Feminist studies underline the importance of asking respondents about their possible involvement in violence more than once, in different ways, and at different points in the survey. Hanmer and Saunders (1984), in a community survey of violence to women in inner-city Leeds, Yorkshire, found that some women mentioned having been victimized, not when the interviewer first broached the subject, but only toward the end of the interview, usually while answering another, related question. In an earlier analysis of data from the Toronto survey (Smith 1987), a significant number of respondents who initially denied having been abused by their husbands or partners revealed that they had indeed been victimized when asked again in different words later in the interview (see also Junger 1987, 1990; Kelly 1988; Roberts 1989).

Presumably, as an interview progresses, such respondents either remember a previously forgotten incident or have second thoughts about their initial decision not to disclose. In the latter case, those who are ambivalent about divulging such personal information probably engage in a quick mental calculus of the costs (e.g., shame or embarrassment) and benefits (e.g., the therapeutic value of sharing a painful memory with a sympathetic listener) of doing so. Some may decide at the outset not to disclose but have mixed feelings about the decision. Given time to think about their initial negative

response as the interview goes on and a second or third opportunity to disclose, some of these respondents then reveal having been victimized. It is also possible, of course, that the prior question may not describe some women's particular experiences, at least as the women define those experiences.

Open Questions

Most conventional surveys on violence against women have used closed questions almost exclusively to ask about violent experiences. It seems that mainstream researchers have either assumed that this type of question elicits the most valid and reliable responses, or decided that open questions are too difficult, too time consuming, and ultimately too costly to process.

Time and money aside, a case can be made for both formats (Sheatsley 1983). Open questions, however, appear to be superior in one vital area: building interviewer-respondent rapport. For one thing, an open format may reduce the threat of a question on violence, because it allows the respondent to qualify her response, to express exact shades of meaning, rather than forcing her to choose from a number of possibly threatening alternatives. For another, open questions may reduce the power imbalance inherent in the interview situation (the relationship between researcher and researched parallels the hierarchical nature of traditional male-female relationships) because open questions encourage interaction and collaboration between interviewer and respondent (Hanmer and Saunders 1984; Hoff 1990). The less threatening the question and the more equal the power relationship, the greater the probability of rapport and, in turn, of eliciting an honest answer to a sensitive question on violence. In any event, feminist scholars reject as exploitive the treatment of respondents merely as "subjects" to be analyzed by an "objective" interviewer (Hoff 1990). Not surprisingly, feminist surveys have made extensive use of open questions to ask whether or not respondents have been victimized and, if so, about the details of the experience (Gordon and Riger 1989; Hanmer and Saunders 1984; Radford 1987; Russell 1982).

Given a disclosure of abuse, no matter how elicited, when the interviewer asks the respondent to describe the event and its aftermath in her own words, preconceived distinctions between private and public places, strangers and nonstrangers, minor and severe violence, and the like tend to blur. This is especially apparent when trying to determine the severity of the violence. As several studies have found, some women, especially those with a long history of victimization by an intimate, initially play down the severity of even the most horrific violence; they may dismiss whatever injuries they have suffered, for instance, as trifling. Only in the course of providing an in-depth account of the abuse in their own words do these women reveal, typically in an offhand remark, the true nature of the violence (Hanmer and Saunders 1984; Junger 1987; Kelly 1988; Stanko 1990). Hanmer and Saunders speculate that such minimizing serves to shore up the victim's crumbling sense of security about her relationship with the abuser. It may also be a way of coping with the popular notion that there must be something wrong with her, the victim. The point is, open questions are best able to elicit the sort of detail that results in a rendition of the violent event that at least approximates the lived experience of the victim. As we shall see, these renditions lead to a considerable reorganization and recoding of victimizations originally categorized on the basis of quantitative measures.

Effective Interviewers

Brush (1990) argues that the most important factor in producing accurate data on woman abuse through surveys is the quality of the interaction between interviewer and interviewee, in particular, the ability of the interviewer to infuse a sense of "trust, safety, and intimacy" into the interviewing relationship (p. 65). But there are few systematic analyses of the characteristics of effective interviewers in the survey literature on violence against women. In fact, research on interviewers generally is in short supply (Fowler and Mangione 1990). In most of the handful of feminist surveys on woman abuse, however, the investigators have gone to great pains to

identify and select the best interviewers available and to train them with particular care. Apparently on the assumption that only a woman can get "inside the culture" of another woman (Oakley 1981), the interviewers invariably have been female.

Take Russell's (1982) survey on wife rape. Russell chose the 33 interviewers employed in this study on the basis of their interviewing skills and "empathetic attitudes" to rape victims. The interviewers received more than 65 hours of paid training (much more than is usual). The training included "consciousness raising" about rape and incest and the "defining and desensitizing" of sexual words so as to make the interviewers as comfortable as possible with whatever vocabulary respondents might employ. In the Leeds study, Hanmer and Saunders (1984) recruited "feminist interviewers" who would behave in a "sensitive manner" and convey a "feeling of warmth and unflappability" in interviews. The interviewers also had to be familiar with local women's organizations that offered support to victims of violence and to be motivated to work on the survey because they wanted to know more about woman abuse in general. Gordon and Riger (1989), in their survey on rape, brought in specialists from rape crisis intervention teams at local hospitals and police departments to instruct interviewers on how to recognize the "less obvious signs of emotional upset and postrape trauma" (p.198). The generally illuminating results of these studies suggest that the majority of the interviewers were adept at establishing rapport and evoking candid responses to threatening questions about physical and sexual victimization.

THE TORONTO SURVEY: METHOD

Sample and Interviews

The data on which this analysis is based are from a telephone survey of Toronto women conducted in 1987. Using a method of random digit dialing that maximizes the probability of selecting a working residential number and at the same time a simple random sample (Tremblay 1981), a sample of telephone numbers was generated from a list of all telephone exchanges in the Census Metropolitan Area of Toronto. Over 99 percent of Toronto households have at least one phone (Statistics Canada 1986).

Female interviewers working for the Institute for Social Research, located at York University, then conducted telephone interviews, averaging 23 minutes, with 604 currently or formerly married or cohabiting women between the ages of 18 and 50. The formerly married or cohabiting respondents had to have ended their marriage or relationship within the last two years to be eligible for the survey. The interviews took place in January and February, 1987.

The survey response rate, defined as the number of completed interviews divided by the number of estimated eligible respondents, was 56.4 percent. Details regarding the calculation of this rate, sampling decisions, and other technical aspects of the study have been reported at length elsewhere (Smith 1987, 1989).

Definitions

I defined violence as any threatened, attempted, or completed assault or sexual assault on a woman by a male stranger or nonstranger. Assaults range from the threat of bodily harm to an actual physical attack resulting in injury. Sexual assaults range from indecent exposure (flashing) to rape and include any unwanted physical contact of a sexual nature. (In this article, I use the terms violence, assault, and abuse more or less synonymously.) These definitions emerged out of women's accounts of their own experiences, which were then organized as much as possible on the basis of legal criteria in the Canadian Criminal Code (Verdun-Jones 1989).

As for victim-offender relationships, I classified an incident as stranger violence if the woman did not see or recognize the offender, knew him only by sight, or knew him only by hearsay. If the victim and offender were intimates, related to, well known to, or casually acquainted with one another, the incident was classified as nonstranger violence.

These definitions are similar to those used in the NCS (U.S. Department of Justice 1990).

In this study, lifetime prevalence of violence refers to either the number or percentage of women in the sample who disclosed having been assaulted or sexually assaulted one or more times since the age of approximately 16.

Measures

A wide range of closed and open questions was used to ask about possible experiences as a victim of violence. The first question was about stranger abuse in public places:

> For this survey, abuse means being pushed, grabbed, slapped, punched, kicked, beaten up, attacked with a weapon, or physically attacked in any other way. Since you were 16 years of age, has any male stranger abused you, or tried to abuse you, in public?

A second set of victimization questions and the principal measure of abuse by a present or former husband or male partner was a somewhat reworded rendition of the Conflict Tactics Scales. The last 9 CTS items describe acts of violence. If the respondent indicated that she had ever been the recipient of any of these acts of violence "in the whole time you've been (were) together," she was counted as a victim.

Three supplementary questions followed. These questions broadened the scope of the inquiry to include other men besides the respondent's current husband or partner. The first supplementary question was as follows:

> Have you had *any* (any *other*) experiences as a victim of abuse by a husband or partner, a boyfriend or date, or any man you are, or were, having a relationship with that I have not asked about?

The second supplementary question was on sexual abuse:

> Have you ever been sexually assaulted? By that I mean forced to have sex against your will by a husband, partner, boyfriend, or date?

The third supplementary question was the last question of the interview:

We realize that this topic is very sensitive and that many women are reluctant to talk about their own experiences. But we're also a bit worried that we haven't asked the right questions. So now that you have had a chance to think about the topic, can you tell me anything (anything more) from your own experience that may help us understand this problem?

The interviewer followed up a positive response to any of these questions by asking how many times the abuse occurred. She then asked the respondent to describe the experience, or if more than one, the "worst" experience, in her own words, probing as necessary for details about motives, social context, physical and psychological consequences, and the like. In the case of a revelation of sexual abuse, the interviewer was instructed to determine if the sexual abuse was part of an episode that the respondent had already described in answer to an earlier question. Only previously unreported sexual assaults are included in this analysis; no incident or victim was counted twice. The interviewer recorded the victim's responses verbatim as much as possible. The resulting qualitative data were then transcribed, content analyzed, and coded according to the definitions earlier set forth.

RESULTS

The following results are intended more as an illustration of the value of a feminist approach to data collection in surveys on violence against women than as estimates of the prevalence of such violence. Nevertheless, it is worth noting that the woman-centered approach employed in the Toronto survey produced much higher rates of victimization than have most conventional surveys (Smith 1987). It also revealed more about the range and complexity of such experiences, though these dimensions receive only limited attention here. For ease of presentation, I shall deal first with stranger violence and second with nonstranger violence.

Stranger Violence

Twenty-one percent of the respondents initially reported that a male stranger had physically abused,

or tried to abuse, them in public since the age of 16. Five other women answered the question on male strangers negatively but subsequently revealed, in response to the question on sexual abuse, that a male stranger had sexually molested them in a manner that fell within the definition of violence used in this article. The addition of these women brought the proportion of victims of stranger violence to 22 percent. By the same token, 8 women who responded affirmatively to the question on stranger abuse subsequently indicated when asked to describe the event that their attackers were more like casual acquaintances than strangers, specifically, her friend's brother, her brother's friend, a carpenter working in the house, a man she met in a bar, a man she met at a party, her husband's business acquaintance, and two unspecified male acquaintances. Subtracting these cases reduced the proportion of victims of stranger violence to 20 percent of the sample of 604 women, as shown in Table 3.1. Of these victims, 42 percent were either sexually or physically and sexually abused.

When asked to describe the incident, or the worst incident, approximately 29 percent of the victims described a threatened assault (i.e., one with no actual physical contact). Most of these were flashings:

- I was walking down the street and a man stopped his car and did filthy things.
- A man called me over to his car for directions and he had his pants open.

A few women described being followed or chased (e.g., "When I got off the bus, a strange man followed me. When I ran, he ran"). Three women described threats that were purely verbal (e.g., "I was mistaken as a prostitute. A man propositioned me. I was scared").

Most victims (71.3 percent) described an attempted or completed assault, that is, an assault involving some degree of physical contact. The majority of these incidents were unwanted touchings, often, but not always, of a sexual nature. The following accounts are illustrative:

- I was standing in front of a bus stop and a man came up behind me and started touching my bottom.

TABLE 3-1

THE PREVALENCE OF PHYSICAL AND SEXUAL VIOLENCE

Violence	Number of women	% of victims	% of sample	% victims sexually abused
By strangers				
Threatened	35	28.7	5.8	
Attempted/completed	87	71.3	14.4	
Total	122	100.0	20.2	42.6
By nonstrangers				
Husband/partner	180	74.4	29.8	
Boyfriend/date	40	16.5	6.6	
Other relative/acquaintance	22	9.1	3.6	
Total	242	100.0	40.1	29.3
Grand total	299*	100.0	49.5	38.5

*The grand total is less than the sum of the column totals because some women reported violence by a stranger *and* a nonstranger.

- I was going into an elevator in an apartment building and a man grabbed my face and held my cheeks and tried to kiss me. Fortunately the elevator doors closed and I was safe.
- I was going home on the subway, and this guy would push up against me and make it extremely uncomfortable for me. I couldn't move or do anything.

The other attempted or completed assaults involved physical force of varying levels of severity. For example:

- I was leaving a bar with my girlfriend. We were walking towards the car. A drunk man was leaning against the wall. He tried to kiss me. He kept walking behind me, then he punched me, and knocked me down. His friends ran up to me and helped me up. They said he'd been drinking.
- A neighbor called me at 6 a.m. to say that her husband was going to beat her up. So I went over to her place. He hit me with his fists, punched me black and blue.

It should be emphasized that although the original question referred to strangers and public places, not all respondents interpreted these terms in the same way. As already noted, some strangers were not total strangers but rather casual acquaintances of the victim. Also, some women related incidents that occurred not in public but in semipublic locations (e.g., at work) and even (in two cases) the victim's home. (As long as the woman did not know the offender, such incidents remained coded as stranger violence.) These inconsistencies underline the importance of asking questions that allow for the possibility that responses may not fall neatly into the survey researcher's preestablished categories.

Nonstranger Violence

Table 3-1 shows that 40 percent of all women in the study revealed that they had ever suffered physical violence as an adult (i.e., since the age of 16) at the hands of a husband, partner, boyfriend, date, other male family member, or male acquaintance. I derived this result from the eight recoded cases noted in the previous section plus the responses to four measures of nonstranger violence (1) the nine-item CTS violence index; (2) the question regarding any, or any other, abuse by a male intimate; (3) the question on sexual assault, and (4) the final question of the survey inviting the respondent to discuss anything from her own experience that might shed light on the problem. Each of the last three items, besides eliciting additional accounts of nonstranger violence from women who had already disclosed having been victimized by an intimate or known man, produced a substantial number of "new" victims. These were women who denied having been abused when asked earlier either because they did not remember, were unwilling to disclose, misinterpreted the question, thought that their experience was outside the scope of the prior question, or denied having been abused for some other reason.

All of the nonstranger assaults in Table 3-1 involved physical contact; no woman described a solely visual or verbal episode (i.e., threat). Slightly over 29 percent of the assaults also involved sexual abuse, although this figure may be low. Unlike most of the stranger-abuse victims, some women who suffered an assault by a known male made it clear that they did not wish to provide a detailed account of the episode, an episode that may or may not have had a sexual element to it; in fact, a handful of women declined to provide any details whatsoever. Still other physical attacks were sex-related but not described explicitly as sexual abuse and thus not coded as such (e.g., "My ex-boyfriend wanted me to get into the car and have sex with him. I wouldn't, so he beat me up"). In short, Table 3-1 probably underestimates the proportion of women who were physically and sexually abused by a male nonstranger.

Table 3-1 also shows that one out of every two women in the sample experienced violence at least once as an adult at the hands of either an unknown or known male. Roughly 39 percent of these incidents were sexual attacks, in whole or in part. In deriving these figures, no respondent was counted as a victim more than once; although many women suffered abuse by a stranger and a nonstranger, the table shows only one of those victimizations.

It must be emphasized that the data in the subtotals rows of Table 3-1 resulted in part from descriptions of the "worst" incident provided by women who reported more than one victimization. Had the interviewers asked these women about the most recent incident, the results may have been some-what different. In any case, the importance of the findings lies more in how the information was elicited than in the numbers themselves.

REFERENCES

Bland, R., and H. Orn. 1986. "Family violence and psychiatric disorder." *Canadian Journal of Psychiatry* 31:129–35.

Bohrnstedt, G. W. 1983. "Measurement." In *Handbook of Survey Research,* edited by P. H. Rossi, J. D. Wright, and A. B. Anderson. New York: Academic Press.

Brush, L. D. 1990. "Violent acts and injurious outcomes in married couples: Methodological issues in the national survey of families and households." *Gender & Society* 4:56–67.

Fergusson, D. M., L. J. Horwood, K. L. Kershaw, and F. T. Shannon. 1986. "Factors associated with reports of wife assault in New Zealand." *Journal of Marriage and the Family* 48:407–12.

Fowler, F. J., and T. W. Mangione. 1990. *Standardized Survey Interviewing: Minimizing Interviewer Related Error.* Newbury Park, CA: Sage.

Gordon, M. T., and S. Riger. 1989. *The Female Fear.* New York: Free Press.

Hanmer, J., and S. Saunders. 1984. *Well-Founded Fear: A Community Study of Violence to Women.* London: Hutchinson.

Hoff, L. 1990. *Battered Women as Survivors.* London: Routledge.

Hough, M., and P. Mayhew. 1983. *The British Crime Survey.* Home Office Research Study No. 76. London: Her Majesty's Stationery Office.

Junger, M. 1987. "Women's experiences of sexual harassment: Some implications for their fear of crime." *British Journal of Criminology* 27:358–83.

———. 1990. "The measurement of sexual harassment: Comparison of the results of three different instruments." *International Review of Victimology* 1:231–39.

Kelly, L. 1988. *Surviving Sexual Violence,* Minneapolis: University of Minnesota Press.

Killias, M. 1990. "New methodological perspectives for victimization surveys: The potentials for computer-assisted telephone surveys and some related innovations." *International Review of Victimology* 1:153–57.

Koppel, M. 1987. *Lifetime Likelihood of Victimization.* Bureau of Justice statistics technical report. Washington, DC: U.S. Department of Justice.

Koss, M. 1992. "The underdetection of rape: Methodological choices influence incidence estimates." *Journal of Social Issues* 48:61–75.

Koss, M., C. Gidycz, and N. Widniewski. 1987. "The scope of rape: Incidence and prevalence of sexual aggression and victimization in a national sample of students in higher education." *Journal of Consulting and Clinical Psychology* 55:162–70.

McNeill. S. 1987. "Flashing: Its effect on women." In *Women, Violence and Social Control,* edited by J. Hanmer and M. Maynard. Atlantic Highlands, NJ: Humanities Press International.

Oakley, A. 1981. "Interviewing women: A contradiction in terms." In *Doing Feminist Research,* edited by H. Roberts. London: Routledge & Kegan Paul.

Radford, J. 1987. "Policing male violence-policing women." In *Women, Violence and Social Control,* edited by J. Hanmer and M. Maynard. Atlantic Highlands, NJ: Humanities Press International.

Roberts, C. 1989. *Women and Rape.* New York: New York University Press.

Russell, D.E.H. 1982. *Rape in Marriage.* New York: Macmillan.

Sessar, K. 1990. "The forgotten nonvictim." *International Review of Victimology* 1:113–32.

Sheatsley, P. 1983. "Questionnaire construction and item writing." In *Handbook of Survey Research,* edited by P. Rossi, J. Wright, and A. Anderson. New York: Academic Press.

Skogan, W. G. 1986. "Methodological issues in the study of victimization." In *From Crime Policy to Victim Policy: Reorienting the Justice System,* edited by E. A. Fattah. London: Macmillan.

Smith, M. D. 1987. "The incidence and prevalence of woman abuse in Toronto." *Violence and Victims* 2:33–47.

———. 1989. "Woman abuse: The case for surveys by telephone." *Journal of Interpersonal Violence* 4:80–98.

———. 1990. "Sociodemographic risk factors in wife abuse: Results from a Toronto survey." *Canadian Journal of Sociology* 15:39–58.

Stanko, E. 1990. *Everyday Violence: How Women and Men Experience Sexual and Physical Danger.* London: Pandora.

Stark, E. and A. Flitcraft. 1988. "Violence among intimates: An epidemiological review." In *Handbook of Family Violence,* edited by V. B. Van Hasselt, R. D. Morrison, A. S. Bellack, and M. Herson. New York: Plenum.

Statistics Canada. 1986. Household Facilities and Equipment Survey, Household Surveys Divisions. Unpublished data, Table C3. Ottawa: Ministry of Supply and Services.

Straus, M. A. 1990a. "Measuring intrafamily conflict and violence: The Conflict Tactic (CT) scales." In *Physical Violence in American Families: Risk Factors and Adaptations to Violence in 8,145 Families,* edited by M. A. Straus and R. J. Gelles. New Brunswick, NJ: Transaction.

———. 1990b. "The Conflict Tactics scales and its critics: An evaluation and new data on validity and reliability." In *Physical Violence in American Families: Risk Factors and Adaptations to Violence in 8,145 Families,* edited by M. A. Straus and R. J. Gelles. New Brunswick, NJ: Transaction.

Tremblay, V. 1981. "Study of telephone sampling techniques." *New Surveys* 6:8–13.

U.S. Department of Justice. 1990. National crime surveys: National sample, 1986–1989. Ann Arbor, MI: Inter-University Consortium for Political and Social Research.

Van Dijk, J., P. Mayhew, and M. Killias. 1990. *Experiences of Crime across the World: Key Findings from the 1989 International Crime Survey.* Deventer, The Netherlands: Kluwer.

Verdun-Jones, S. 1989. *Criminal Law in Canada: Cases, Questions and the Code.* Toronto: Harcourt Brace Jovanovich.

Weis, J. G. 1989. "Family violence research methodology and design." In *Family Violence,* edited by L. Ohlin and M. Tonry. Chicago and London: University of Chicago Press.

STUDY QUESTIONS

1. What are the strengths and weaknesses of the Uniform Crime Reports, as outlined by Joseph Senna and Larry Siegel?
2. What are the main problems with the different data sources on drug use as described in Jeff Leen's article?
3. According to Michael Smith, what are the main deficiencies of mainstream victimization surveys on family violence?
4. Identify the corrective steps Smith proposes to improve survey research on this topic.

PART FOUR

INSTITUTIONAL CONTEXTS

DEVIANCE IN THE MEDIA AND ON THE INTERNET

Introduction

The mass media are filled with reports on crime and other types of deviance, and for most people the media are the main source of information and conceptions about deviant behavior. Popular perceptions are strongly influenced by the ways in which the media portray deviant individuals and types of deviance. The media do not simply report on deviance and control, but sometimes also construct trends where the evidence is thin or identify new, frightening forms of deviance ("road rage," satanism, school shootings, etc.) that may be much more isolated and rare than the impression left with the viewing audience (Best 1999). Vincent Sacco explores the media's role and influence on popular perceptions of deviance in his chapter, "Media Constructions of Crime."

Joshua Gamson ("Deviants on Talk Shows") argues that tabloid talk shows on television—such as Jerry Springer and Rikki Lake—may serve to demonize deviant people. At the same time, such shows can serve as an arena in which deviants can try to proclaim their identities and justify their lifestyles, which may help to humanize them in the eyes of some viewers. In other words, these shows provide a forum for both further degradation and stigmatization of such behavior *and* the empowerment of discredited individuals and potential normalization of certain types of deviant behavior.

The Internet has opened up new channels of communication about many kinds of deviance, as well as new opportunities for individuals to engage in deviance. The very anonymity of the Internet facilitates deviance that might not be engaged in outside cyberspace, such as networking with rightwing hate groups or learning how to build bombs. "Cybersex," the Internet equivalent of telephone sex, is a new form of behavior that some people regard as deviant, even if it is engaged in by consenting adults; pedophiles cruise the net in search of young girls and boys for sexual banter, sometimes leading to an illicit rendezvous; the Internet provides an additional and growing medium for the distribution of pornography; and Internet chatrooms and bulletin boards offer novel ways for individuals to meet, learn about, and support deviants like themselves. America Online, for example, features chatrooms for alcoholics, transgenders, marijuana users, and the obese—to mention but a few. Because of the anonymity and sheer volume of traffic on the Internet, the growth of deviance via computer presents new problems for those who seek to control deviance. But the Internet also offers the authorities some new opportunities for surveillance and social control. The FBI has launched a war against cyber pedophiles, for instance. And police agencies throughout the country now routinely secure warrants to search for incriminating evidence in the e-mail of suspects who are customers of major service providers such as AOL. Keith Durkin and Clifton Bryant's article, "Log on to Sex," examines sexual deviance and control on the Internet. They point out that deviant sexual subcultures are growing with the help of the Internet, which offers a learning environment for novices, an easy way of networking with like-minded deviants, and information and opportunities for individuals to act on their deviant sexual fantasies. The Internet is a mammoth technological innovation that, Durkin and Bryant write, provides tremendous opportunities for "creating, imitating, enhancing, and extending deviant sexual behavior."

REFERENCE

Best, Joel. 1999. *Random Violence*. Berkeley: University of California Press.

READING 4-1

Media Constructions of Crime

Vincent F. Sacco

Central to the interplay between individuals' private troubles with crime and the social issue of crime are the mass media. The news media, in particular, provide an important forum in which private troubles are selectively gathered up, invested with a broader meaning, and made available for public consumption.

FROM PRIVATE TROUBLE . . .

Analyses of media content demonstrate that the news provides a map of the world of criminal events that differs in many ways from the one provided by official crime statistics. Variations in the volume of news about crime seem to bear little relationship to variations in the actual volume of crime between places or over time (Davis 1952; Skogan and Maxfield 1981). Whereas crime statistics indicate that most crime is nonviolent, media reports suggest, in the aggregate, that the opposite is true (Garofalo 1981; Skogan and Maxfield 1981; Schlesinger, Tumber, and Murdock 1991). While crime news tends to provide only sparse details about victims and offenders, that which is provided is frequently at odds with the official picture. Both offenders and victims, for instance, appear less youthful in media reports than they do in statistical records (Gordon and Riger 1989:70; Lotz 1991). In addition, news content does not reflect and frequently even reverses the relationship that, according to much social scientific evidence, exists

between minority group membership and criminal offending (Lotz 1991:114).[1] With respect to gender, however, both crime statistics and crime news portray offending as predominantly a male activity (Bortner 1984).

News reports also distort the relationship between crime and legal control. In the news, the police appear to be more effective in apprehending offenders than police data would suggest they are (Marsh 1991; Roshier 1973). Moreover, while the activities of the police are prominently featured, the functioning of other actors in the criminal justice system is much less visible (Gorelick 1989). This probably reflects a professional judgment that criminal events are most newsworthy immediately following their occurrence and thus when they are in the early stages of justice system processing, when police activity is prominent (Sherizen 1978:203–24).

These images of crime, the criminal, and the victim that appear with patterned regularity in print and broadcast news emerge quite logically from the organizational processes of news production. News stories are most useful to news organizations when they are gathered easily from credible sources; for this reason, policing agencies have become the principal suppliers of these stories (Chibnall 1977; Fisherman 1981; Ericson 1989). In short, relationships involving news organizations and policing agencies allow the collection of news about common crime to be

From *Annals of the American Academy of Political and Social Science* 539 (May 1995), 141–154. © 1995 American Academy of Political and Social Science. Reprinted by permission of Sage Publications.

[1] Lotz (1991) found, for instance, that in newspapers in New York, Miami, and Philadelphia, white offenders outnumbered black offenders by 7 to 1 in those news reports that allowed for the identification of race.

routinized in a manner that uses the resources of news agencies efficiently.[2] In addition, the public view of the police as apolitical crime experts imbues police-generated crime news with authority and objectivity.

Ease of access to authoritative news is not the only advantage that police-generated crime stories offer, since such stories are consistent with several other professional values that structure the news production process. Much of what we call news consists of reports of specific incidents that have occurred since the publication of the previous day's newspaper or the airing of the previous night's newscast. As discrete incidents that occur at particular times and places, individual crimes conform closely to this requirement of periodicity.

Stories about individual crimes—with their characteristic portrayals of villains and victims—also have dramatic value. The dramatic potential is heightened when the victim or offender is a celebrity, when the incident is of a very serious nature, or when the circumstances of the offense are atypical. In addition, the routine crime story is a rather uncomplicated matter, and it is unnecessary for news workers to assume that readers or viewers require an extensive background in order to appreciate the story. The lack of factual complexity associated with the ordinary individual crime story generally means that it can be easily written and edited by news workers whose professional activities are consistently regulated by rigid deadlines.

The elastic character of the crime news supply offers a further advantage. On any given day, particularly in large metropolitan areas, there is an almost limitless supply of crimes that could be the object of media attention. However, from day to day, or from week to week, the demand of the news agency for crime news may vary due to other events that are seen to demand coverage. Depending on the size of the news hole, crime coverage may be expanded or contracted in compensatory fashion. A study by Sanford Sherizen of crime news in Chicago newspapers found, for instance, that crime reports were often located on the obituary pages so that layout difficulties resulting from the inability to plan these pages could be overcome through the use of crime news filler (Sherizen 1978:221).

Over the last several years, a number of changes in local and national media environments have altered the nature and extent of crime coverage. The growth of cable stations, for instance, has increased the carrying capacity for news generally and for crime news specifically. More stories can be covered, and those that are judged to be particularly newsworthy can be covered in greater detail. The live television coverage of court proceedings—as in the case of the Menendez brothers, Lorena Bobbit, or O. J. Simpson—has become commonplace. The increasing sophistication of news gathering, surveillance, and home video technologies has meant that it is no longer unusual to capture thefts, robberies, or even homicides on tape. One consequence of the diffusion of these technologies has been to raise to national prominence stories with no real national significance. Crime stories that would have been a purely local affair in an earlier period now attract much wider attention because a videotape of the incident is available for broadcast.

The last two decades have also witnessed a redefinition of what can be considered an appropriate subject for news reporting. Changes in mores relating to public discussion of sex and violence have allowed respectable media outlets to report crimes that would have previously been seen as taboo and to do so at a level of detail that would once have been considered lurid. At the same time, the politicization of crimes such as sexual assault and domestic violence has broadened the range of

---

[2] In comparison to interpersonal crimes like homicide or robbery, corporate crimes are covered with greater difficulty. Generally, corporate crimes are more complex and more difficult to personalize, and well-established source-reporter relationships do not exist for corporate crime as they do for common crimes. Coverage of corporate, white-collar, and organized crime is more common, however, than is sometimes thought (Randall 1987).

crime stories that, it can be argued, legitimately require coverage (Soothill and Walby 1991:6).

Programmatic developments in commercial broadcast media have magnified the impact of these changes. The proliferation of news magazines, daytime talk shows, docudramas, and various other forms of infotainment has ushered in a programming cycle that is heavily dependent on crime news and victim accounts. The frequent reliance of many of these programs on dramatic reenactments of real events and their mixing of factual reports with rumor and speculation blurs the basic distinctions that analysts of crime content have traditionally drawn between news and entertainment media (Newman 1990).

. . . TO PUBLIC ISSUES

Public issues grow up around private troubles when the experiences of individuals are understood as exemplifying a larger social problem, and the news media play a vital role in the construction of such problems (Best 1989a; Gusfield 1989; Schneider 1985). Most notably, professional judgments of newsworthiness and the selective use of news sources allow some groups, rather than others, the opportunity to express a view about what is and what is not a problem and how any such problem should be managed. By implication, the relationships that link the police to news agencies serve law enforcement as well as media interests. The police role as the dominant gatekeeper means that crime news is often police news and that the advancement of a police perspective on crime and its solution is facilitated (Fishman 1981; Ericson 1989). It has been argued that this results in the adoption of an uncritical posture with respect to the police view of crime and the measures necessary to control it (Ericson 1991; Zatz 1987). More generally, the frame of reference offered by a government bureaucracy or other recognized authority with respect to crime problems may only infrequently be called into question and, as a consequence, competing perspectives may become marginalized.

This tendency may be no less true of in-depth issue coverage than of routine news reporting. Henry Brownstein maintains that during the 1980s, there was relatively little reporting that took issue with the official version of the drug problem constructed by government experts (Brownstein 1991). In a similar way, Philip Jenkins has noted how experts of the Federal Bureau of Investigation were able to present themselves as the authorities on the subject of serial murder and how they made themselves available to journalists who reciprocated with favorable coverage of the agency (Jenkins 1994:212–213).

It would be incorrect, however, to suggest that news media are merely the passive conveyors of the claims about problems offered up by government bureaucracies, political candidates, or other self-interested groups, since any such claims must be transformed to meet the requirements of the medium in question. In an analysis of television network news coverage of threats to children, Joel Best argued that "inevitably, network news stories distort the problems they explore" (Best 1989b:277) in large part because news conventions impose severe constraints on how stories are covered. Stories must be told in a few minutes, frequently by reporters who may have little more than a surface familiarity with the complexities of the problem at hand. Moreover, the topic must be viewed as serious enough and as visual enough to be chosen over competing issues. Best found, in the case of child victimization, that the stories used frightening and dramatic examples to typify the problem and that they emphasized the existence of a consensus among knowledgeable experts regarding its scope and seriousness.

In other instances, news media may more actively engage in problem construction. Investigative reporting, or the coverage of an event judged to be especially newsworthy, may contribute to the establishment of a media agenda that finds expression in the reporting of further stories or in more detailed features. A study by David L. Protess and his colleagues revealed how one Chicago newspaper set its own media agenda after an extensive investigative series on rape (Protess 1985). The researchers found that while the series did not appear to have a substantial impact on the perceptions of policymakers or the general public, there were significant changes in the extent and depth of rape coverage after the series ended, even though police reports of rape were unchanged. In a related way, during the summer of 1994, the O. J. Simpson case provided an opportunity for sidebar stories relating to the prevalence and causes of domestic violence, the inadequacy of justice system responses, and pending federal and state legislation. Such coverage contextualized the original incident in a way that helped construct the social issue of violence against women at the same time that it legitimated continuing, detailed attention to the original story.

The Content of Crime Problems

Media constructions of crime problems address both the frequency and the substance of private trouble with crime. Rhetoric regarding both of these dimensions serves to impress on readers and viewers the gravity of particular crime problems and the need to confront them in particular ways.

Large numbers of problems provide convincing evidence that problems exist. This is perhaps most evident in the case of crime waves, when it is argued that crime is becoming more frequent. A study by Steven Gorelick, for instance, of an anticrime campaign sponsored by a New York daily newspaper found that crime in the city was frequently described as a "mushrooming cloud," a "floodtide," a "spreading cancer," or in similar terms (Gorelick 1989:429). Sometimes these claims about the numbers of people affected have greater specificity in that some particular segment of the population is claimed to be experiencing rapidly increasing risks of offending or victimization (Cook and Skogan 1990).

Yet, with respect to many crime waves, it is the belief that crime is increasing, rather than crime itself, that is really on the rise (Baker 1983). A study by Mark Fishman of a 1976 New York crime wave against the elderly described how crime waves may be "things of the mind" (Fishman 1978). Fishman found that there was no compelling evidence to indicate that the criminal victimization of the elderly actually increased during the study period. Instead, the crime wave originated in the efforts of journalists to organize individual crime stories around a compelling news theme. The theme of crime against the elderly was elaborated as competing news organizations responded to each other's coverage of the issue. In addition, the police, in their role as gatekeepers of crime news, reacted to the increased media interest by making available more stories that reflected and reinforced the crime-against-the-elderly theme.

A more recent example of a journalistic construction of rapidly rising crime is provided by James D. Orcutt and J. Blake Turner (1993). Their analysis focused on the way in which graphic artists in the national print media transformed survey data, which showed modest yearly changes in drug use, into evidence of a "coke plague." While the numbers were real, their graphical presentation in the weekly periodical under study was misleading. As in the case described by Fishman, the dynamics of competitive journalism created a media feeding frenzy that found news workers "snatching at shocking numbers" and "smothering reports of stable or decreasing use under more ominous headlines" (Orcutt and Turner 1993:203).

Claims about statistical frequency are not restricted to reports about how the numbers are increasing, however. With respect to the problem of violence against women, for instance, it is argued that the numbers have always been very high but that the failure to police such incidents, the stigma associated with victimization, and an institutional unwillingness to believe the accounts of victims have resulted in statistical counts that dramatically underestimate the problem. Thus, whether or not the numbers are going up is defined as less salient than the observation that they have always been higher than we have thought.

According to Neil Gilbert (1994), outrageous claims about the prevalence of problems sometimes make their way into news reports in part because of journalists' general inability to evaluate the data supplied to them. Too often, they lack the technical sophistication to critically assess claims about the frequency of crime or victimization in an independent fashion. Instead, they collect and validate information by talking to experts who are expected to offer informed opinions. However, in the case of emergent problems, it is often the problem advocate, interested in advancing a particular point of view, who may be among the first to collect and publicize empirical evidence. As a result, the estimates yielded by advocacy research may be the only ones available at the earliest stages of problem development. Philip Jenkins has argued that the emergence of serial murder as a social issue in the early 1980s was spurred by "epidemic estimates" that placed the number of serial murder victims at between 20 and 25 percent of American homicides (Jenkins 1994:22). While such numbers continue to circulate through popular and journalistic accounts, more reasoned analysis suggests that the number of serial murder victims is closer to 2 percent of American homicides.

The emergence of crime problems is related not only to claims about the frequency of criminal events but also to claims about their character. Exactly what types of events such incidents are thought to be and who is thought to be typically involved in them matter as much as does the rate at which they are thought to occur.

Any particular social problem can be framed in many ways, and these various frames imply different causal attributions and prospective solutions (Gusfield 1989; Schneider 1985). Because they are able to legitimate some views and to marginalize others, the news media are an important part of this framing process. Depending on the sources accessed or the type of coverage, rape can be framed as a sex crime or as a crime of violence; the "drug problem" as a product of pushers who hook their victims or as an example of the overreach of criminal law; and violence on the part of youths as a condition necessitating either swift punishment or comprehensive community development.

More generally, when private troubles are constructed as a crime problem of any sort, they are framed in ways that assign primary responsibility

for their solution to the criminal justice system. Joel Best (1991) has shown how crime problem interpretations of the 1987 freeway shooting incidents in California competed in the relevant news coverage with other interpretations of the incidents. Whereas the crime problem frame implied the need for increased patrols, better investigation, and more effective prosecution, other definitions of the issue—as a gun problem, a traffic problem, or a courtesy problem—suggested other solutions.

In a related way, the social distributional character of victimization is frequently ignored by news coverage that stresses the random character of victimization. While the best social science literature indicates that the risks of crime, like the risks of other misfortunes, are not equally shared, media images often convey a different message. According to Brownstein, for instance, much of the coverage of the drug issue in New York City between 1986 and 1990 emphasized the random character of drug violence even though police statistics indicated that the risks of such violence were extremely low (Brownstein 1991:95). Themes relating to randomness serve the interests of both news workers and others who seek to frame crime problems. News stories about random crimes have great dramatic value, as the media frenzies that surround serial murders illustrate. Moreover, the advocates to whom news workers have access during the early stages of problem development often stress the random nature of a particular form of victimization since problems must be seen as more urgent when everyone is threatened.

While much routine crime reporting can be understood as maintaining established crime problem frames, new problems are always being discovered as old problem paradigms expand or as novel elements come together with established news themes. The discovery of new problems provides a journalistic opportunity to tell a story that has not been told before, but such stories are told most effectively when they resonate with existing cultural themes. In the 1970s, the problem of crime against the elderly brought together in one package an already familiar concern about crime in the streets and victims' rights with an emerging concern about the aging population (Cook and Skogan 1990). The problem of satanic crime, which received extensive media coverage in the 1980s, combined familiar news themes relating to religious cults, child abuse, and juvenile crime (Crouch and Damphousse 1992; Jenkins and Maier-Katkin 1992). Media attention to date rape and stalking extends earlier news themes relating to violence against women.

The transition from private troubles to public issues is not always a linear process since media interest in particular crime problems can vary in intensity or decline over time. The 1987 shootings on California freeways never became a well-established problem, despite a strong start (Best 1991). In the case of crimes against the elderly, Fay Lomax Cook and Wesley Skogan (1990) observe that while the issue achieved a prominent position on media and other agendas during the early 1970s, by the decade's end, it had declined precipitously. On the other hand, Fishman has argued that as long as police departments are the routine sources of crime news, the media will reinforce a climate of opinion that keeps the attention of the police focused on "crime in the streets." He concludes that while social problems may come and go, "law-and-order news is here to stay" (Fishman 1981:389).

CONCLUSION

If the news business is concerned with the production of crime problems, then the private troubles of criminal offenders and crime victims are the raw materials. These troubles are not simply reported on, however, since they are fundamentally transformed by the news-gathering process. Screened through a law enforcement filter, contextualized by advocacy claims and culturally resonant news themes, and shaped and molded by the conventions and requirements of commercial media, these private troubles become public issues.

Some critics argue that the police perspective implicit in so much crime news reporting dramatically restricts the parameters of discussion and debate about the problem of crime. As a consequence, the causes of offending are individualized and the relationships that link crime to broader social forces are left largely unexplored (Gorelick 1989; Humphries 1981). Correspondingly, traditional law-and-order responses are reaffirmed as the most efficient way to manage crime problems. A study of media coverage of attacks against women in Toronto found that explanations of the phenomenon tended to focus attention on the ways in which victims placed themselves in conditions of risk, on offender pathology, and on the need for a more coercive criminal justice response (Voumvakis and Ericson 1984). The authors note that while these terms of reference were not unreasonable, the attention they received left little room for alternative interpretations of the problem, particularly those interpretations that link the victimization of women to structures of gender inequality.

As news workers observe and influence each other, and as the line between news and entertainment becomes more confused, public discussion of crime problems reflects and reinforces this consensus, and popular views of these problems begin to assume a taken-for-granted character. Inevitably, but regrettably, the emergence of such a consensus relegates to the margins the search for alternative ways of thinking about crime and its solution.

REFERENCES

Baker, Mary Holland, et al. 1983. "The Impact of a Crime Wave: Perceptions, Fear, and Confidence in the Police." *Law and Society Review* 17:317–34.

Best, Joel, ed. 1989a. *Images of Issues: Typifying Social Problems.* Hawthorne, NY: Aldine de Gruyter.

———. 1989b. "Secondary Claims-Making: Claims about Threats to Children on the Network News." *Perspectives on Social Problems* 1:277.

———. 1991. " 'Road Warriors' on 'Hair-Trigger Highways': Cultural Resources and the Media's Construction of the 1987 Freeway Shootings Problem." *Sociological Inquiry* 61:327–45.

Bortner, M. A. 1984. "Media Images and Public Attitudes toward Crime and Justice." In *Justice and the Media,* ed. Ray Surette. Springfield, IL: Charles C Thomas.

Brownstein, Henry H. 1991. "The Media and the Construction of Random Drug Violence." *Social Justice* 18:85–103.

Chibnall, Steve. 1977. *Law-and-Order News: An Analysis of Crime Reporting in the British Press* London: Tavistock.

Cook, Fay Lomax, and Wesley G. Skogan. 1990. "Agenda Setting and the Rise and Fall of Policy Issues: The Case of Criminal Victimization of the Elderly." *Environment and Planning C: Government and Policy,* 8:395–415.

Crouch, Ben M., and Kelly R. Damphousse. 1992. "Newspapers and the Antisatanism Movement: A Content Analysis." *Sociological Spectrum* 12:1–20.

Davis, James. 1952. "Crime News in Colorado Newspapers." *American Journal of Sociology,* 57:325–30.

Ericson, Richard V. 1989. "Patrolling the Facts: Secrecy and Publicity in Police Work." *British Journal of Sociology* 40:205–26.

———. 1991. "Mass Media, Crime, Law and Justice." *British Journal of Sociology* 31:219–49.

Fishman, Mark. 1978. "Crime Waves as Ideology." *Social Problems* 25:531.

———. 1981. "Police News: Constructing an Image of Crime." *Urban Life* 9:371–94.

Garofalo, James. 1981. "Crime and the Mass Media" *Journal of Research in Crime and Delinquency* 18:319–50.

Gilbert, Neil. 1994. "Miscounting Social Ills." *Society* 31:24–25.

Gordon, Margaret T., and Stephanie Riger. 1989. *The Female Fear.* New York: Free Press.

Gorelick, Steven M. 1989. " 'Join Our War': The Construction of Ideology in a Newspaper Crimefighting Campaign." *Crime and Delinquency* 35:421–36.

Gusfield, Joseph. 1989. "Constructing the Ownership of Social Problems: Fun and Profit in the Welfare State." *Social Problems* 36:431–41.

Humphries, Drew. 1981. "Serious Crime, News Coverage and Ideology: A Content Analysis of Crime Coverage in a Metropolitan Newspaper." *Crime and Delinquency* 27:191–205.

Jenkins, Philip. 1994. *Using Murder: The Social Construction of Serial Homicide.* Hawthorne, NY: Aldine de Gruyter.

Jenkins, Philip, and Daniel Maier-Katkin. 1992. "Satanism: Myth and Reality in a Contemporary Moral Panic." *Crime, Law and Social Change* 17:53–75.

Lotz, Roy Edward. 1991. *Crime and the American Press.* New York: Praeger.

Marsh, Harry L. 1991. "A Comparative Analysis of Crime Coverage in Newspapers in the United States and Other Countries from 1960 to 1989: A Review of the Literature." *Journal of Criminal Justice* 19:67–80.

Newman, Graeme R. 1990. "Popular Culture and Criminal Justice: A Preliminary Analysis." *Journal of Criminal Justice* 18:261–74.

Orcutt, James D., and J. Blake Turner. 1993. "Shocking Numbers and Graphic Accounts: Quantified Images of Drug Problems in the Print Media." *Social Problems* 40:190–206.

Protess, David L., et al. 1985. "Uncovering Rape: The Watchdog Press and the Limits of Agenda Setting." *Public Opinion Quarterly* 49:19–37.

Randall, Donna. 1987. "The Portrayal of Business Malfeasance in the Elite and General Public Media." *Social Science Quarterly* 68:281–93.

Roshier, Bob. 1973. "The Selection of Crime News by the Press." In *The Manufacture of News: Social Problems, Deviance and the Mass Media,* ed. Stanley Cohen and Jock Young. London: Constable.

Schlesinger, Philip, Howard Tumber, and Graham Murdock. 1991. "The Media of Politics, Crime and Criminal Justice." *British Journal of Sociology* 42:397–420.

Schneider, Joseph W. 1985. "Social Problems Theory: The Constructionist View." *Annual Review of Sociology* 11:209–29.

Sherizen, Sanford. 1978. "Social Creation of Crime News: All the News Fitted to Print." In *Deviance and Mass Media,* ed. Charles Winick Beverly Hills, CA: Sage.

Skogan, Wesley G., and Michael G. Maxfield. 1981. *Coping with Crime: Individual and Neighborhood Reactions.* Beverly Hills, CA: Sage.

Soothill, Keith, and Sylvia Walby. 1991. *Sex Crime in the News.* London: Routledge.

Voumvakis, Sophia E., and Richard V. Ericson. 1984. *News Accounts of Attacks on Women: A Comparison of Three Toronto Newspapers.* Toronto: University of Toronto, Centre of Criminology.

Zatz, Marjorie S. 1987. "Chicano Youth Gangs and Crime: The Creation of a Moral Panic." *Contemporary Crises* 11:129–58.

READING 4-2

Deviants on Talk Shows

Joshua Gamson

On television talk shows, you are begged and coached and asked to tell, tell, tell. Here you are testifying, dating, getting laughs, being made over, screaming, performing, crying, not just talking but talking back, and you are doing these things in front of millions of people. The last few years have seen shows on "lipstick lesbians," gay teens, gay cops, lesbian cops, cross-dressing hookers, transsexual call girls, gay and lesbian gang members, straight go-go dancers pretending to be gay, people who want their relatives to stop cross-dressing, lesbian and gay comedians, gay people in love with straight ones, women who love gay men, same-sex marriage, drag queen makeovers, drag kings, same-sex sexual harassment, homophobia, lesbian mothers, gay twins, gay beauty pageants, transsexual beauty pageants, people who are fired for not being gay, gay men reuniting with their high school sweethearts, bisexual teens, bisexual couples, bisexuals in general, gays in the military, same-sex crushes, hermaphrodites, boys who want to be girls, female-to-male transsexuals, male-to-female transsexuals and their boyfriends, and gay talk shows—to mention just a few. Watching all this, be it tap-dancing drag queens or married gay bodybuilders or self-possessed bisexual teenagers, I sometimes get choked up. For people whose life experience is so heavily tilted toward invisibility, whose nonconformity, even when it looks very much like conformity, discredits them and disenfranchises them, daytime TV talk shows are a big shot of visibility and media accreditation. It looks, for a moment, like you own this place.

From Joshua Gamson. *Freaks Talk Back: Tabloid Talk Shows and Sexual Nonconformity* (Chicago: The University of Chicago Press, 1998). Reprinted by permission of the University of Chicago Press and the author.

Indeed, listening closely to the perspectives and experiences of sex and gender nonconformists—people who live, in one way or another, outside the boundaries of heterosexual norms and gender conventions—sheds a different kind of light on talk shows. Dangers begin to look like opportunities, spotlights start to feel like they're burning your flesh. Exploiting the need for visibility and voice, talk shows provide them, in distorted but real, hollow but gratifying, ways. They have much to tell about those needs and those contradictions, about the weird and changing public sphere in which people are talking. Just as important for my purposes, talk shows shed a different kind of light on sex and gender conformity. They are spots not only of visibility but of the subsequent redrawing of the lines between the normal and the abnormal. They are, in a very real sense, battlegrounds over what sexuality and gender can be in this country: in them we can see most clearly the kinds of strategies, casualties, and wounds involved, and we can think most clearly about what winning these kinds of battles might really mean. These battles over media space allow us to get a grip on the ways sex and gender conformity is filtered through the daily interactions between commercial cultural industries and those making their lives within and around media culture.

DEFECATING IN PUBLIC

It is a long, twisted road that takes us toward insight, but the controversy over the talk show genre in general—a genre itself largely composed of controversy and conflict—is a promising first step. On the one side, cultural critics, both popular and scholarly, point adamantly toward the dangers of exploitation, voyeurism, pseudotherapy, and the "defining down" of deviance, in which the strange and unacceptable are made to seem ordinary and fine. On the other side, defenders both within and outside the television industry argue that talk shows are democracy at work—flawed democracy but democracy nonetheless—giving voice to the socially marginalized and ordinary folks, providing rowdy commonsense counterpoints to elite authority in mass-mediated culture. Beneath each position, and in the space between them, is a piece of the puzzle.

The list of dangers is well worth considering. There is, to begin with, concern for the people who go on the shows, who are offered and accept a deal with the devil. They are manipulated, sometimes lied to, seduced, used, and discarded; pick 'em up in a limo, producers joke, send 'em home in a cab. They are sometimes set up and surprised—"ambushed," as critics like to call it—which can be extremely damaging, even to the point of triggering lawsuits and murderous impulses, as in the case of Scott Amedure, who revealed his secret crush for Jonathan Schmitz on a never-aired *Jenny Jones Show,* including his fantasy of tying Schmitz up in a hammock and spraying him with whipped cream and champagne. Amedure was murdered several days later by Schmitz, who, after receiving an anonymous love note, went to his admirer's trailer home near Detroit and shot him at close range with a 12-gauge shotgun. Schmitz complained that the show had set him up to be humiliated. "There was no ambush," a spokeswoman for *Jenny Jones* owner Warner Brothers said; "that's not our style." Amedure, Schmitz proclaimed, had "fucked me on national TV" (Bull and Gallagher 1995; Signorile 1995; Green 1995).

Although most survive without bodily harm, guests often do considerable damage to themselves and others. They are offered airfare and a hotel room in New York, Los Angeles, or Chicago, a bit of television exposure, a shot of attention and a microphone, some free "therapy." In exchange, guests publicly air their relationship troubles, deep secrets, and intimate life experiences, usually in the manners most likely to grab ratings: exaggerated, loud, simplified, and so on. Even more disturbing, perhaps, it is those who typically do not feel entitled to speak, or who cannot afford or imagine therapy, who are most vulnerable to the seduction of television. This is, critics suggest, not a great deal for the guests, since telling problems and secrets in front of millions of people is a poor substitute for actually working them out. Not to mention, critics often add, a bit undignified. "Therapy is not a spectator sport," says sociologist and talk show critic-at-large Vicki Abt. Telling secrets on television is "like defecating in public" (Kaplan 1995:12).

While it is worth challenging the equation of talking and defecating, all this, we will see, is basically the case. But it is also the easy part: talk shows are show business, and it is their mission to exploit. They commodify and use talkers to build an entertainment product, which is then used to attract audiences, who then are sold to advertisers, which results in a profit for the producers. Exploitation thus ought to be the starting point for analysis and not, as it so often is, its conclusion. The puzzling thing is not the logic of commercial television, which is well documented, well understood, and extremely powerful, but why so many people, many of them fully aware of what's expected of them on a talk show, make the deal.

Yet it is not really the guests, generally dismissed as dysfunctional losers on display, who concern talk show critics most centrally. It is the audience, either innocent or drawn in by appeals to their most base interests, that preoccupies critics the most. For some, the problem is the model of problem solving offered. Psychologists Jeanne Heaton and Nona Wilson argue in *Tuning in Trouble,* for instance, that talk shows provide "bad lessons in mental health," offer "bad advice and no resolutions for problems," and wind up "reinforcing stereotypes rather than defusing them." "Credible therapeutic practice aimed at catharsis or confrontation," they point out, "is quite different from the bastardized Talk TV version." Indeed, they suggest that viewers avoid "the temptation to apply other people's problems or solutions to your own life," avoid using "the shows as a model for how to communicate" or as tools for diagnosing friends and relatives, and so on (Heaton and Wilson 1995:129, 144, 252–258). The advice is sound, if a bit elementary: talk shows are not a smart place to look for either therapy or problem solving.

Beyond the worry that audiences will adopt therapeutic technique from daytime talk, critics are even more troubled by the general social effects of talk shows. Here and there, a critic from the Left, such as Jill Nelson writing in *The Nation,* assails the casting of "a few pathological individuals" as representatives of a population, distracting from social, political, and economic conditions in favor of stereotypes such as "stupid, sex-addicted, dependent, baby-makers, with an occasional castrating bitch thrown in" (women of all colors) and "violent predators out to get you with their penis, their gun, or both" (young black men) (Nelson 1995:801). More commonly, though, critics make the related argument that talk shows indulge voyeuristic tendencies that, while perhaps offering the opportunity to feel superior, are ugly. "*Exploitation, voyeurism, peeping Toms, freak shows,* all come to mind in attempting to characterize these happenings," write Vicki Abt and Mel Seesholtz (1994:206), for instance. "For the audience," *Washington Post* reporter Howard Kurtz adds in *Hot Air,* "watching the cavalcade of deviant and dysfunctional types may serve as a kind of group therapy, a communal exercise in national voyeurism" (Kurtz 1996:62). These "fairground-style freak shows" are just a modern-day version of throwing Christians to the lions, psychologists Heaton and Wilson assert: in place of Christians we have "the emotionally wounded or the socially outcast," in place of lions are "psychic demons," in place of blood there is psychological damage, in place of crowds yelling "Kill, kill, kill!" we have crowds yelling "Why don't you cut his balls off?" (Heaton and Wilson 1995:127–128). Even if such events serve to unite the Romans among us, offering what Neal Gabler calls "the reassurance of our superiority over the guests and over the programs themselves" (Gabler 1995:m1), they do so

at significant costs. "Perhaps the sight of so many people with revolting problems makes some folks feel better about their own rather humdrum lives," Kurtz argues, but "we become desensitized by the endless freak show" (Kurtz 1996:62).[1] Talk shows are pruriently addictive, the argument goes, like rubbernecking at car wrecks: daytime talk shows are to public information what pornography is to sexual intimacy.

I will have more to say about the ceaseless characterization of talk shows as "freak shows," but for now it is enough to note that the lines are drawn so starkly: between Christians and Romans, between "deviant and dysfunctional types" and "some folks," the guests and "us," between "the fringes of society, those who break rules" and "law-abiding, privacy-loving, ordinary people who have had reasonably happy childhoods and are satisfied with their lives." These are important lines, and plainly political ones, and the ones critics most fiercely act to protect. And as one who falls both within and outside the lines, I find the confidence with which critics draw them in need of as much careful consideration as the genre's alarming exploitations.

In fact, the lines of difference and normality are the centerpiece of the arguments against talk shows: talk shows, critics repeat over and over, redefine deviance and abnormality, and this is not a good thing. "The lines between what is bizarre and alarming and what is typical and inconsequential are blurred," point out psychologists Heaton and Wilson; talk shows "exaggerate abnormality" by suggesting that "certain problems are more common than they are, thus exaggerating their

---

[1] My own use of the word *freaks* is meant to call attention to rather than reproduce the stigmatization of sex and gender non-conformists, and to complicate the notion that talk shows can simply be understood as freak shows. I use the word as neither a pejorative nor a description of how people see themselves—most people seen as freaks, it's safe to assume, view themselves as human rather than as curiosities—but as a description of a stigmatized social status, a label put on certain populations of people who, in radical ways, do not fit what is at any given time perceived as the natural order.

frequency," and by embellishing "the symptoms and outcomes of problems, thus exaggerating their consequences." Viewers are left with images of "drag queens getting makeovers and transsexuals' surprising transformations blended together with normal adolescent development" (Heaton and Wilson 1995:131–32, 163). Kurtz, himself a regular on political talk shows, is a little less clinical in his assessment: "This is more than just harmless diversion. It is, all too often, a televised exercise in defining deviancy down. By parading the sickest, the weirdest, the most painfully afflicted before an audience of millions, these shows bombard us with sleaze to the point of numbness. The abnormal becomes ordinary, the pathetic merely another pause in our daily channel surfing" (Kurtz 1996:63).

This boundary between the normal and the abnormal, tightly linked to those between decent and vulgar, sacred and profane, healthy and unhealthy, and moral and immoral, is the key not only for critics in journalism, but for those in politics as well. "This is the world turned upside down," former secretary of education William Bennett complained of daytime talk (Empower America 1995). "We've forgotten that civilization depends on keeping some of this stuff under wraps" (Dowd 1995:A25). As a reminder, Bennett offered his own tamer, secularized version of the Mother Teresa versus the freaks argument: this place is owned by perverts, and decent people must retrieve it. Launching a campaign to "clean up" the "cultural rot" of daytime TV, pressuring advertisers to withdraw from shows that "parade perversity into our living rooms" (Dupree 1995:4), Bennett, with Connecticut senator Joseph Lieberman and the public-interest group Empower America, emphasized the degenerative moral impact of talk shows, which "increasingly make the abnormal normal, and set up the most perverse role models for our children and adults." The entertainment industry, Lieberman told a press conference, is "degrading our culture and ultimately threatening our children's future," through both "sexual deviancy" and "constant hyperemotional

confrontations." "The reality is that these shows are at the, at the front lines," he continued, echoing the *Post*'s Kurtz nearly word for word, "of distorting our perceptions of what is normal and acceptable," adding to "the tendency of our country to define deviancy down" (Empower America 1995). Our living rooms, our children, our normality, all under threat.

The interesting thing here is not just that talk shows are seen as a threat to norms and normality—as we will see, they are indeed just that, and the fight is often between those who think this is a good thing and those who think it is not—but just who threatens whom here, who is "us" and who is "them." Sexual nonconformists are only the most obvious specter. Consider the common strategy of listing topics to demonstrate the degraded status of talk shows: "Maury Povich has done women who leave husbands for other women, student-teacher affairs, and a woman who says she was gang-raped at fourteen. Geraldo Rivera has done transsexuals and their families, teen prostitutes, mud-wrestling women, swinging sexual suicide, power dykes, girls impregnated by their stepfathers, serial killers, kids who kill, and battered women who kill" (Kurtz 1996:52). One need not deny the prurience and sensationalism of talk shows to see the connections being made by critics. Serial killers and bisexual women, transsexuals and mud wrestlers, dykes and battered women: "the sickest, the weirdest, the most painfully afflicted." New York *Daily News* columnist Linda Stasi, not shy about telling us what she really thinks, provides a further, complicating hint of the threatening categories: talk shows, she says, have become "a vast, scary wasteland where the dregs of society—sociopaths, perverts, uneducated lazy scum who abuse their children and sleep with anyone who'll have them—become stars for fifteen minutes" (Kurtz 1996:67). That list is a typical and fascinating mix: perverts and those lacking education, lazy people and people who have a lot of sex. Kurtz backs up Stasi, for instance, asserting that, "after all, middle-class folks who work hard and raise their children in a reasonable fashion don't get invited on *Donahue* or *Geraldo.* They do not exist on daytime television. Instead we are bombarded with negative images of the sort of losers most of us would avoid at the local supermarket" (Kurtz 1996:63).

Just as exploitation is an obvious component of talk shows, so is democratization. Where critics choose one Greco-Roman analogy, defenders tout another: in place of the Christian-eating spectacle, they see, although not always so simply, a democratic forum. Where critics see "freaks" and "trash," defenders see "have-nots" and "common people." These are important counterpoints, and raise important questions suppressed by critics of voice, visibility, and inclusion. But this line of thinking, too, on its own tends to run in an unhelpful direction, simplifying the conditions of visibility, the distortions of voice, and the restrictions on inclusion that daytime talk involves. Just because people are talking back does not mean we are witnessing democratic impulses and effects.

This populist defense of talk shows, familiar from arguments about popular culture in general, is taken many steps beyond the shoulder-shrugging "it's a free country" line. Talk shows, defenders claim, give voice to common folks and visibility to invisible folks, and it is this characteristic that elicits such hostility. Indeed, Donahue and others assert, the talk show genre was and is a "revolutionary" one. "It's called democracy," Donahue argues, "but [before my program] there were no shows that—every day, let just folks stand up and say what-for. I'm proud of the democracy of the show" (ABC News 1996). Ellen Willis, writing in *The Nation,* makes a similar, although much more complex, point: "Social conservatives have been notably unsuccessful at stemming the democratization of culture, the breakdown of those class, sex and race-bound conventions that once reliably separated high from low, 'news' from 'gossip,' public from unspeakably private, respectable from deviant. Talk shows are a product of this democratization; they let people who have been largely excluded from

the public conversation appear on national TV and talk about their sex lives, their family fights, sometimes their literal dirty laundry. . . . On talk shows, whatever their drawbacks, the proles get to talk"(Willis 1996:22–23). When the proles get the microphone, when the excluded become included, there is always a fight. The nastiness of critics toward talk shows, the argument goes, is simply a veiled anxiety about cultural democratization—and especially about the assertive, rowdy space taken on talk shows by usually silent classes of people. Talk shows "operate at the level of everyday life, where real people live and breathe," Donna Gaines writes. "Bennett's morality squad may see talk shows as carnival freak shows, but all that means is that the shows have the power to drag us statistical outcasts in from the margins" (Gaines 1995:21).

What critics and defenders, both inside my brain and outside of it, agree upon is that talk shows are consumed with blurring old distinctions (while often reaffirming them), with making differences harder to tell (while often asserting them with ease): the deviant isn't readily distinguished from the regular person, class stereotypes melt into the hard realities on which they rest, what belongs in private suddenly seems to belong in front of everybody, airing dirty laundry looks much like coming clean. Talk shows wreak special havoc with the "public sphere," moving private stuff into a public spotlight, arousing all sorts of questions about what the public sphere can, does, and should look like. In doing so, they mess with the "normal," giving hours of play and often considerable sympathy to stigmatized populations, behaviors, and identities, and at least partly muddying the waters of normality. And since those brought into the public sphere of TV talk are increasingly distant from the white middle-class guests of earlier years, talk shows wind up attaching class difference to the crossing of public/private and normal/abnormal divides. It is around this stirred pot, in which humdrum and freaky, off-limits and common property, high status and low, sane and crazed, all brew together, that the anxious flies swarm. This seething brew, and not just the talk shows themselves, is what is so powerful and intriguing, and it is this brew on which I myself am feeding, using the close study of TV talk to investigate the broader, linked activities of line-drawing between public and private, classy and trashy, normal and abnormal.

I have long been especially interested in how the lines between normal and abnormal sexual beings are drawn and redrawn: the ways those lines restrict me personally, from the question of whom I can touch to the question of where I can work; the dilemmas confronted by social movements trying to gain rights by claiming the mantle of normality, even as they are also celebrating their "queer" difference and criticizing the oppressive constraints imposed by a hetero-as-normal society (Gamson 1995, 1996); the ways sexual categories intersect with others (race, class, gender) with their own hierarchies of natural and defective people, and the permutations of perversion pile up and multiply (Cohen 1996; Murray 1995; Lorde 1984; Hemphill 1991; Allison 1994). The mass media are plainly very central to these processes of sexual meaning-making, and talk shows are hot spots for the processes, and so my attention is driven toward them.

Jenny Jones is interviewing lesbian teenagers. She and the audience probe in all sorts of ways: Jenny wants to know how it felt to have sex with boys ("boring, pretty gross," says Kimberly), audience members want to know "why do you always try to look like guys if you're attracted to the female thing?" and so on. The show proceeds according to plan, with one screaming match, a proud mother, self-possessed young women, and a beautiful young woman named Amy crying as she explains her suicide attempts. At first, she talks as she must have in the preinterview. "I just couldn't be myself," she explains. "But it's dangerous to come out," Jones suggests, and again, Amy begins with tame emotion, acting the coming-out poster child. "I feel so much better," she says. "I'm so much happier, I mean, all those people who stand up and say 'I hate you' "—and suddenly, as she

begins to mimic the people who hate her, some of whom have just stood up in the audience, it is as if a switch is flipped. She speaks with hatred, pointing her finger at her imaginary self, and the camera operator, recognizing the sudden intensity, zooms in. "All those people who stand up and say, 'I hate you, because you're a homosexual I hate you, because you like a girl, because you do this, because you do that, because you're different.' That's wrong. And I will be who I want to be," she says, her voice strong but breaking, "and I'm proud to be gay." The fact that the producers undoubtedly saw the moment in terms of its usefulness, that they cynically did what they could to increase the possibility of provoking deep feeling, does not alter its intensity; for a moment, watching Amy, you could actually *feel* what it meant to be hated, *feel* what the poster-child rhetoric conveys more safely, the pain in which lesbian pride resides (Jenny Jones Show 1993).

Talk shows leave openings, sometimes tiny, sometimes rather gaping, but typically more than elsewhere in mass culture, for honest expressions like these to burst through, little shots of something like the truth, through the walls of distortion. These appear at first like insignificant flashes, especially given the machinations that surround them; but it is exactly because they are so rare elsewhere in media culture, because they are wrapped in the falseness and control to which television has made us accustomed, that they are powerful. And when it is *your* identity being cried over or loathed or exalted, these emotion bolts can sometimes bring a lump to your throat that you thought you had long since swallowed.

The assertion that we all have sexual cores to which we must be true does not work nearly as sympathetically for transgendered people as for gay ones. While gay people are asked to bring their lives into line with their "real" essence, transgendered people are typically programmed in ways that emphasize anatomy as the only *true* gender marker, and thus any dissonance between genital status and gender identity as a sign of inauthenticity. Transsexualism, for instance, is often framed as a monstrous secret to be revealed to nontranssexuals—what would you do if you found out your girlfriend was a man?—and transsexuals not so much as gender-crossers but as *gender-liars.* "You're terrible. You're fooling people. You're deceiving people," one audience member tells a transsexual woman on *Sally,* although there has been no evidence of deception presented. "I mean, that would be very scary. Let's say you go to a bar, a disco, wherever you go, and all of a sudden, you got out to the parking lot, you escort this girl wherever you're going to go. All of a sudden, surprise! I mean, you know" (Multimedia Entertainment 1995). The story of Brandon Teena, a young transgendered person who lived as a man for a period before being raped and murdered, is programmed by *Geraldo* as one of several "secret lives revealed" (Investigative News Group 1996). In another program called "bizarre" over and over by its host, Dona, married for two years to Bobby, a man who "turned out to be a woman," describes what Geraldo calls "the terrible day when you discovered that the man you married was, in fact, a woman." "My world collapsed. When she dropped her pants—and I don't mean to be crude—when a man takes his penis out, I don't care how big or little it is, they take it out, they don't do this. My world went black. I was looking at my own death. It was the most disgusting, vile, filthy, degrading thing that's ever happened to me in my life. I'd rather been raped by a herd of donkeys. . . . Her whole life is a lie, every single day." Later, asked by an audience member if she can trust enough to love again, Dona assures the audience that "I have a wonderful boyfriend, and he's all man. I checked his plumbing out, I'll guarantee you that," she says, as the audience applauds (Investigative News Group 1994).

As on the shows about married homosexuals, an underlying dichotomous "truth" is protected: there are only gay and straight, male and female. But in contrast to the way "living a lie" themes play out on shows about married homosexuals—come out so you don't hurt people, in short—with

transgendered people, it is the *transgender status itself,* not just whether or not it is revealed, that appears as deception. Often, in fact, transsexuals insist that there is nothing misleading about their behavior, since they live in accordance with their gender identity; the host and the audience insist that current (or sometimes even prior) genital status outranks all others, and that to operate otherwise is to lie. Introducing Conrad to the audience for her tellingly titled show "I Was Fooled," for instance, Sally Jessy Raphael says he "has been living a lie for the last 13 years," and announces that he will now be confronted by some women who "can't really forgive the fact that Connie, dressed as a man, seduced them into a romantic relationship that included sex." All of these ex-girlfriends, and Sally herself, refer to Conrad using male pronouns, while he argues that "all I'm doing is being myself." Yet the show is structured as an argument between the deceiver and the deceived, and there is little that can take it off course. "The whole point," as one ex-girlfriend put it, "is you're not who you pretended to be" (Multimedia Entertainment 1994). Similarly, on a *Jerry Springer* episode called "My Boyfriend Turned Out to Be a Girl," 19-year-old Sean, whom Springer announces "was masquerading as a boy so he could date young girls," explains that to him it was never a masquerade. "I'm not sitting there saying, 'Oh, yeah, I'm going to trick her. I'm going to trick her,' you know. It's a matter of, you know, I'm sitting there, living my life as a boy. . . . I never thought about it, you know. To me, it was just a boy-and-girl relationship. That's it." While his ex-girlfriend and others continue to refer to him as "he" ("It's way beyond me that underneath him he's got the same parts I do, you know," ex-girlfriend Andrea says), a series of guests are brought on to denounce the "masquerade," including his ex-best friend Justin ("What am I going to tell my kids?" he asks, apparently very confused; " 'I grew up and my best friend was a faggot'? See, I wouldn't have minded if he was a girl and he knew he was gay"), Andrea's mother ("There's a lot of people that's had a tough life, okay, but they don't go out and perpetrate other people"), and Justin's father ("You don't know exactly what people are all about anymore") (Multimedia Entertainment 1994). In these "masquerade" themed shows, it is the very existence of an inconsistency between genitals and gender presentation that gets framed as deception: to be transsexual is to *be* dishonest. Indeed, it is the rare sort of talk show revelation that may only go to show that some secrets are best kept, that rape by a herd of donkeys may be preferable to this kind of "truth."

While the rhetoric of truth-telling corresponds closely to the ideology of coming out, the push built into talk show practice toward multiple, individual truths coincides with another queer practice: dislodging the confidence in a natural, universal order to all things sexual. For populations whose oppression has been so closely tied to assertions of a single order of the normal, who have been told that their bodies and desires are against God and nature, talk shows' suspicion of traditional authority and disinterest in the normal can be a refreshing invitation to bring forward new, disruptive, destabilizing experiences. On talk shows, the authoritative voices of the natural order—religious and scientific authorities, primarily—are just so many in a pile of claims about how things really are. In fits and starts, through a foggy veil, important pieces of lives *as they are lived by the stigmatized* come through, different and startling versions of the truths of sex and gender. They come through details and vocabularies: *pre-op* and *post-op, gaydar* and *fag hag.* They come through in simple, extraordinary visuals: here are two African American men in tuxes exchanging wedding vows, here is a Latina lesbian construction worker and her African American bartender lover yelling at a white doctor-man in a suit, here is a transsexual man crying with his parents, a bisexual woman who looks like the housewife she once was. They come through even more in the ongoing testimony of all kinds of people, the individual storytelling that remains the most common talk show format: here is what it was like for me to come out in Tennessee, here is what testosterone does to your clitoris, here

is what it means to me to be bisexual and committed to a relationship. Often, the show is not just a spectacle of difference but a spectacle of talking back, in which the different duke it out with those who judge, label, and dismiss them.

Talk shows have made it at least quite a bit more difficult to hold onto a single framework—a true world order of sexuality and gender—into which all of these words and images and testimonies can be fit. There is no single story, and different truths pop up one after another; none is the truest, none is demonstrably false.

REFERENCES

ABC News. 1996. *Nightline* ("Phil Donahue"), January 26.

Abt, Vicki, and Mel Seesholtz. 1994. "The Shameless World of Phil, Sally, and Oprah: Television Talk Shows and the Deconstructing of Society." *Journal of Popular Culture*: 206.

Allison, Dorothy. 1994. *Skin: Talking about Sex, Class, and Literature.* Ithaca, NY: Firebrand Books.

Bull, Chris, and John Gallagher. 1995. "Talked to Death." *Advocate,* April 18.

Cohen, Cathy. 1996. "Contested Membership: Black Gay Identities and the Politics of AIDS." In *Queer Theory/Sociology,* ed. Steven Seidman. Cambridge, MA: Blackwell.

Dowd, Maureen. 1995. "Talk Is Cheap." *New York Times,* October 26.

Dupree, Scotty. 1995. "Targeting Talk TV." *Mediaweek,* October 30.

Empower America. 1995. "Press Conference." Washington, DC: Federal Document Clearing House, October 26.

Gabler, Neal. 1995. "Audience Stays Superior to the Exploitalk Shows." *Los Angeles Times,* March 19.

Gaines, Donna. 1995. "How Jenny Jones Saved My Life." *Village Voice,* November.

Gamson, Joshua. 1995. "Must Identity Movements Self-Destruct? A Queer Dillemma." *Social Problems* 42:390–407.

———. 1996. "The Organizational Shaping of Collective Identity: The Case of Lesbian and Gay Film Festivals in New York." *Sociological Forum* 11:231–62.

Green, Michelle. 1995. "Fatal Attraction." *People,* March 27.

Heaton, Jeanne, and Nona Wilson. 1995. *Tuning in Trouble: Talk TV's Destructive Impact on Mental Health.* San Francisco: Jossey-Bass.

Hemphill, Essex, ed. 1991. *Brother to Brother: New Writings by Black Gay Men.* Boston: Alyson.

Investigative News Group. 1994. *Geraldo* ("You're Not the Man I Married"), February 14.

———. 1996. *Geraldo* ("Secret Lives Revealed"), August 21.

Jenny Jones Show. 1993. *The Jenny Jones Show* ("Teenage Lesbians Defend Their Orientation"), February 23.

Kaplan, Janice. 1995. "Are Talk Shows out of Control?" *TV Guide,* April 1.

Kurtz, Howard. 1996. *Hot Air: All Talk, All the Time.* New York: Times Books.

Lorde, Audre. 1984. *Sister Outsider.* Trumansburg, NY: Crossing Press.

Multimedia Entertainment. 1994a. *Sally Jessy Raphael* ("I Was Fooled"), May 17.

———. 1994b. *The Jerry Springer Show* ("My Boyfriend Turned Out to Be a Girl"), December 27.

———. 1995. *Sally Jessy Raphael* ("My Teen Son Wants to Be a Woman"), June 27.

Murray, Stephen O. 1995. *Latin American Male Homosexualities.* Albuquerque: University of New Mexico Press.

Nelson, Jill. 1995. "Talk Is Cheap." *The Nation,* June 5.

Signorile, Michelangelo. 1995. "The *Jenny Jones* Murder: What Really Happened?" *OUT,* June.

Willis, Ellen. 1996. "Bring In the Noise," *The Nation,* April 1.

Log on to Sex: Erotic Cyberspace as a New Frontier

Keith F. Durkin and Clifton D. Bryant

New forms of deviancy, including sexual deviancy, are not entirely the invention of the fertile imagination. More often, new opportunities in the pursuit of deviancy are provided by innovations in technology. Such opportunities, in turn, invite or occasionally even drive exploration and experimentation in using the technology, with the result that new, and sometimes ingenious residual functions and latent uses of the technology relevant to deviancy are discovered. Thus, novel configurations of deviant behavior, including sexual deviancy, may evolve in a kind of serendipitous fashion from technological invention.

From *Deviant Behavior* 16: 179–200. © 1995 Taylor & Francis. Reprinted by permission of Taylor and Francis, Inc.

TECHNOLOGY AND DEVIANT BEHAVIOR

Behavioral scientists have long recognized that emerging technology has a powerful influence on human behavior, although frequently there is a delay or lag between the emergence of the technology and the social behavioral adaptation to it (Ogburn 1964). The social response to technology often takes the form of *technicways,* or normative and patterned behavioral configurations (Odum 1937; Bryant 1984). Whereas technicways generally assume functional dimensions, they may also mutate and take on dysfunctional or even deviant parameters. These deviant technicways often encompass sexually proscribed behavior. Furthermore, deviant sexual technicways would appear to divide and multiply in an entropic fashion.

Some examples of technology and sexually deviant adaptation include the automobile, which was intended as a means of transportation but has also proved to be a splendid platform for private assignation and fornication, as well as a major "vehicle" for a wide variety of clandestine sexual misconduct; and Edison's motion picture projector, which was intended for wholesome vicarious entertainment but has also proved to be extremely effective in affording vicarious carnal gratification in the form of pornographic films. The telephone also has served to generate a multitude of opportunities for carnal gratification. Its capacity for anonymous communication has made possible the obscene phone call. It has also afforded the opportunity for the telephone masturbator to use a telephone conversation with a female as the basis for sexual fantasy and carnal stimulation, incorporating the autoerotic activity into the fantasy. The effectiveness of this practice has been exploited in recent years by so-called "dial-a-porn" services,[1] which offer sexually explicit conversation for salacious purposes on a commercial basis. Undoubtedly, in time many others will grasp the deviant efficacy of the telephone and perceive additional innovative uses.

The citizens-band (CB) radio is another case in point. The CB radio initially appealed to persons who sought a convenient and efficient means for communicating in emergencies and in other inopportune circumstances. Truck drivers proved to be an enthusiastic customer group, using the CB radio to contact other truckers. Prostitutes also found truck drivers to be an enthusiastic customer group for their sexual services, and for some prostitutes, using the CB radio, which proved to be an expedient way to contact truckers, became a standard mode of soliciting customers (Klein 1981; Luxenburg and Klein 1983). Like legitimate businesspeople, deviant commercial enterprises are often quick to take advantage of new technology to improve efficiency and maximize profits. For example, rather than the bordello prostitute of times past, the prostitute contacted by telephone—the "call girl"—is now the norm in some locales. Prostitutes in some resort cities, such as Las Vegas, are said to carry beepers, in order to be able to respond quickly to telephone requests for sexual services.

The near explosion of technological advances in recent decades, in such fields as electronics, photography, and communications, to mention but a few, has deluged society with a cornucopia of devices and appliances, compelling in their novelty and application, but ominous in their latent deviant capabilities. Numerous instruments and mechanisms ranging from the Polaroid camera to the camcorder have been shown to have suitable utility for the facilitation of sexual deviance. Of the most recent technological products, the computer promises to open enormous new frontiers of opportunity for the proliferation and enhancement of sexual deviance, to have an applicability for carnal behavior that is socially volatile in both its perversity and import.

THE COMPUTER, CYBERSPACE, AND DEVIANT INFORMATION

The computer, although intended primarily as a mechanism for extremely rapid, extraordinarily complex, computational purposes, quickly came to be seen also as a communication device. The computer paired with modern telephone technology has come to serve as a highly efficient means of contacting persons and corporate entities all over the world. On-line bulletin board systems, known

---

[1] For those of less imaginative bent, the telephone has enabled the offering of "dirty" stories, obscene language, and salacious conversation from a female as part of a commercial service. Alleged to have originated in Japan (*Parade* 1976:20), the so-called "dial-a-porn" services have become big business in the United States. The individual with a lascivious aural appetite can dial an advertised telephone number and be carnally entertained, either by a conversation with a paid female performer, or by listening to a prerecorded message (see Borna, Chapman, and Menezes 1993; Glascock and LaRose 1993). In either instance, the caller hears sexually explicit talk or sounds and is billed for the time on the line, on his or her monthly telephone bill (U.S. Department of Justice 1986:1428–1436). (Although primarily used by males, women do use these services.)

as BBSs, are essentially modern-day, high-tech, electronic "party lines," by which users can send and receive messages, engage in conversations, and upload and download files. The electronic entity or domain that encompasses bulletin boards and all of the other communicative potential of computers has become known as "cyberspace" (Gibson 1989). By linking up with a particular, specialized BBS, one can use a computer to contact individuals with mutual interests anywhere in the world. In 1987, there were 4,000 BBSs; by 1992, there were 44,000. Periodicals such as *Boardwatch* or *Computer Shopper* list and describe the array of available BBSs (see *New York Times* 1989:38). On-line services such as CompuServe, Prodigy, America Online, and Delphi offer the computer user immediate access to all sorts of information, such as news, weather, travel services, and stock market quotes, as well as access to all kinds of specialized interest bulletin boards and the means to send and receive private messages. On-line services thus permit people to contact and communicate with persons who share similar interests and avocations, which may involve such disparate topics as cooking, cats, and chess (see *U.S. News and World Report* 1985:59).

Because the on-line services reach an unknown multitude of computer users (inasmuch as institutional computers are used by vast numbers of individuals for purposes not related to their work, the actual number of persons who can access BBSs cannot be accurately calculated), there is the potential for an enormous range of interests to be addressed, including deviant interests. Aware of this market, entrepreneurs of all stripes are rising to the need and offering unique BBSs to satisfy even the most exotic requirements. A relatively superficial exploration of available bulletin boards reveals a diverse array of nonsexual, deviant variants seeking subscribers, or interested persons who might like to share information. Included among this genre of BBS is one that collects and distributes all sorts of law-enforcement radio codes, including generic codes and frequencies as well as special codes for specific law enforcement agencies. While these codes are made available ostensibly to help computer users better "enjoy" and understand the radio traffic on a police scanner, it is patently obvious that this master list of police codes could easily find miscreant uses. Additionally, this bulletin board provides a compendium of information concerning plants and substances that have psychotropic properties but are technically not illegal to possess at this time. It also contains relatively detailed information about automatic teller machine (ATM) fraud, which would no doubt be quite instructive to a would-be ATM thief. The same bulletin board gives advice on how to cause vandalistic damages, including lists of useful vandalism tools (wire cutter, BB gun, etc.) and appealing sites to be vandalized, such as the showroom windows of automobile dealerships.

In addition to bulletin boards that deliberately provide deviant information, some bulletin boards are used by individuals seeking technical advice for deviant acts. Several years ago, for example, a 10-year-old youngster in the Midwest placed an ad seeking instructions for making a time bomb on a bulletin board devoted to scientific interests. Someone with the necessary expertise did provide the information, and the boy subsequently blew up a mailbox using a bomb that he had constructed (Jackson 1989:20).

The Carnal Computer and Cybersex

Sometimes the interest being catered to by a bulletin board may be sex, particularly esoteric variations of sex that frequently are deviant and sometimes illegal. This potential use of bulletin boards has not escaped the notice of relevant U.S. governmental agencies. The Attorney General's Commission on Pornography (U.S. Department of Justice 1986: 1437), for example, has stated:

> The personal home computer provides individuals with an extraordinary new form of communication and information access. Providers of sexually explicit materials have taken advantage of this new technology by making computer subscription services the most recent advance in "sexually explicit communications."

Although the computer can be used to communicate directly with specific individuals in other locales using E-mail and other modes of communication, initial and subsequent contacts involving "erotic entertainment" are often made through intermediate computer networks, in the form of sexually oriented bulletin boards.[2] Because it allows "two users to exchange intimacies in private" (*Time* 1984:83), the computer bulletin board, particularly when used for erotic purposes, can perhaps best be likened to the Valentine box in grammar or middle school into which students could put anonymous Valentine messages to be taken out and read by those to whom they were addressed. The box could also be used to respond privately. The sexually oriented computer bulletin board permits users to trade pseudonymous messages.

The initial anonymity of these bulletin boards may give way to a more intimate and personalized (albeit guarded) form of carnal interaction. One newspaper account (Markoff 1992:5), for example, describes this process:

> One recent evening, users of the America Online network had the opportunity to visit a series of "rooms" offering, for example, "Naughty Girls," "Romance Connection" and a "Gay Room." After meeting electronically in the public room—actually a window in which comments from many users scroll by—new friends adjourned to private rooms for intimate conversations, often using noms de plume or "handles."

---

[2] Both a computer and a modem (a telecommunicational device for computers) are a prerequisite for gaining access to these sexually orientated bulletin boards. To access these services, users dial the bulletin board's inbound phone number. Some of these numbers may be obtained from advertisements in computer or pornographic magazines, others by word-of-mouth. Moreover, once one bulletin board is accessed, information about other boards can readily be obtained from that service. When people initially call one of these bulletin boards, they typically have to complete a registration process. Users normally have to indicate that they are older than 18 or 21, and that they are not an employee of any law enforcement agency. Also, users normally have to pay a registration fee. Although this payment may be made by mail, many services allow users to make the payment on line by credit card. After this process is complete, users can readily access the sexually explicit services offered.

Exchanging erotic verbal chit-chat via computer has been labeled as a new form of "erotic entertainment in which consenting computer owners exchange X-rated messages over the telephone lines" (*Time* 1984:83). Allegedly, some couples who meet over the computer and exchange erotic pleasantries sometimes move on to exchange names, telephone numbers, and pictures; they may even arrange dates. Some have gotten married (*Time* 1984:83). Media accounts have even reported a new formalized or institutionalized bond between computer daters that represents a step in commitment that is short of marriage but perhaps more analogous to an engagement. Some computer partners enter into a "cyber-wedding," an electronic bond that lets the individuals "pledge their love while looking ahead to a future that could include real-life marriage—if they hit it off [when they later meet in person]" (Haight 1994:1).

A few years back, erotic exchange by computer was said to be "mostly lighthearted flirting" (*Time* 1984:83). Recently, however, computer sex has been moving in more intimate and compelling directions. On-line socializing with a member of the opposite sex that has moved beyond lighthearted flirting has been termed "hot chatting" (Tamosaitis 1994:56). The anonymity that computer interaction affords provides self-confidence, allows the individual to assume almost any identity (e.g., become any age, take on any appearance, and effect any persona), and promotes inspiration. A person can interact with a "computer pal," develop a symbolic sexual intimacy, share erotic fantasies, talk "dirty," and in the process, experience a "tonic" for his or her real-life sex. Hot chatting in cyberspace appears to help energize the libido of persons who have a jaded sex relationship with their regular partner. As one 45-year-old attorney was reported to have revealed (Tamosaitis 1994:68):

> I've been married for 15 years and sex with my wife has grown routine. But after I've spent some time in erotic banter with a sensitive female online, I bring new enthusiasm and desire back into my bedroom.

Such an erotic process would seem to be functional, provided the individual does not become unduly preoccupied with his or her cyberspace "lover." Such a preoccupation could conceivably lead to marital friction.

While hot chatting may be a developmental process, with the interaction moving in incremental fashion to more intense levels of salacious conversation, it appears that participants' intentions often are obvious from the outset, as evidenced by the computer names they select. One researcher (Matek 1988:120–121) has observed, for example, that

> [O]bscene content is not always a part of this chatter, but the names of "handles" chosen by many of these participants divulge a sexual implication: Honey Blonde, Priapus Rex, Wet End, Love for Tender, Bilady Jugs. At times the "conversation" too is suggestive, and occasionally the computer screens read like a pornographic novel, as two or more strangers engage in "computer sex" with each of the participants describing successive steps in their fantasy encounter.

Obviously, some individuals derive carnal enjoyment from the mutual use of sexual words with a person of the opposite sex, and the computer handily affords the opportunity with both convenience and anonymity.

The Computer and Sexual Deviancy

The computer bulletin board system can provide an enormous, and extremely rapid, contact network for persons of related interests, including those interested in sexual deviancy. Individuals can seek, identify, and communicate with fellow deviants of similar carnal persuasion across the country, and even around the world. Information from deviant subcultures can be broadly disseminated, and interested new persons can be recruited. Individuals can learn of formal meeting sites, and infomal gathering places, and can even arrange a personal rendezvous.

The sexual computer network offers a high degree of anonymity, protection, and secrecy. Individuals can, through their personal computer, verbalize their sexual fantasies, and, in some instances, go

on to operationalize them. The sexual bulletin boards operate at varying levels of lasciviousness. Some are hardly more than "naughty," while others are disturbingly degenerate, even to the point of being pathological. As in an onion, when each layer of carnality is peeled back, another deeper and more perverse layer is revealed. There are ominous signs in this phenomenon. There are reported to be instances in which attempts were made to solidify contacts with teenagers or children who had inadvertently discovered some of the bulletin boards while playing with a computer (*Los Angeles Times* 1989:20–21). One newspaper account (Markoff 1992:E5) reports:

> Last fall, a 42-year-old man in Fremont, California, using a nationwide computer conferencing system, posed as a 13-year-old homosexual boy. He said he was electronically approached by someone identifying himself as a 50-year-old New Yorker who tried to arrange a meeting. In Massachusetts in January, a man was indicted for raping a 12-year-old boy whom he befriended through a computer bulletin board.

In a case that occurred several years ago, law enforcement authorities from California arrested two men in Virginia who were trying to locate a 12-year-old child to molest and then to murder as the subject matter for a "snuff" film (Jackson 1989:20–21). The authorities discovered the plot through an ad placed by the two men on a computer bulletin board seeking other people with a sexual interest in children. In a telephone conversation with an undercover detective, one of the men indicated that he recognized the risk involved in kidnapping a youngster and then murdering him, but that "the pleasure of doin' it would be worth it." When arrested, one of the men had a supply of muriatic acid to apply to the youngster's corpse.

Apparently these are not isolated incidents. A press release from the U.S. Department of Justice issued on Tuesday, August 31, 1993, reported that "people who use computers to obtain child pornography are being arrested and charged by federal prosecutors" (p. 1). The press release went on to say that since May, six persons had been charged or indicted, and nine more cases were to be filed in September. In these cases, the Justice Department had obtained information about a child pornography bulletin board in Aalborg, Denmark, known as BAMSE. They had learned that several hundred Americans were using this bulletin board and were paying fees to download graphic images, text, and computer games dealing with child and hard-core pornography. The U.S. authorities asked the Danish police to search the home of the Danish national who operated the bulletin board. The Danish police did so and seized the computer system records and a large number of pornographic pictures of children. A few months later, at the request of U.S. authorities, Danish police raided another home and obtained the computer records of another child pornography bulletin board known as SCREW-DRIVER. U.S. Customs Service officials traveled to Denmark to copy the computer records. After examining the records, they discerned that a number of Americans had been "importing" child pornography by computer. A massive federal law enforcement effort called "Operation Long Arm" served 31 search warrants in 15 states and 30 cities. The various indictments reported in the press release resulted from that operation. According to the release, the searches, arrests, and indictments were possible because, "since each purchase had to be made by electronic messaging, detailed records were obtainable" (U.S. Department of Justice, August 13, 1993:2).

Agents of various law enforcement agencies, such as U.S. postal inspectors, routinely explore sexually oriented bulletin boards with the intention of catching offenders who are transmitting child pornography or looking to exploit or victimize children. In 1989, after exploring on-line services, a group of postal inspectors, Illinois state police, Chicago police, and Cook County (Illinois) deputy sheriffs arrested 90 people on charges of trafficking in child pornography and child molestation (Jackson 1989:20).

Reports of children encountering the dangers of sexual deviancy as they explore cyberspace are becoming more numerous. One recent newspaper account (Schwartz 1993:26), for example, relates that "an 8-year-old girl [inadvertently was] attempting computer conversations with a group of transvestites." The little girl, according to the newspaper report, was "using her computer and modem to make new friends through a service called America On-line" (Schwartz 1993:1) and discovered an electronic discussion group called "TV chat," which stood for "transvestite chat." The little girl thought it meant "television chat." An adult who happened to be monitoring the interaction fortunately steered the youngster to a more suitable discussion group. The same newspaper account told of a mother who discovered that her "telecomputing 13-year-old son [had] started getting messages full of sexual innuendo from adult women" (Schwartz 1993:26). The same mother also was appalled when "her 11-year-old son was approached on line recently by a woman in her 30s who invited him to do it, perhaps not knowing his age." A Massachusetts prosecutor asserted, "Instead of hanging around the playground looking for the loneliest kid, potential child molesters merely have to log on" (Kantrowitz et al. 1994:40).

The hazards of cybersex do not pertain only to children. Electronic erotica may also come to be a "rival" in a marriage. In another newspaper report (Garreau 1993:A-10), the author reveals:

> One woman wrote *The Washington Post* complaining that her husband, who had been in therapy for his sexual problems, found affirmation, acceptance and ultimately physical companionship in the bondage and discipline conference on CompuServe, one of several large switching systems on which subscribers can order merchandise, make airline reservations, check the weather and talk dirty. The pair is now divorcing.

There is yet another danger in cyberspace. Females are more sought after than men for computer talk. As a result, some users resort to "gender bending"—a person of one sex (usually a man) portraying himself as the opposite sex. According to a newspaper report, "male wallflowers have learned, however, that if they sign on as women they are instantly flocked to" (Garreau 1993:A-10).

Sometimes gender bending can become quite elaborate, and even sinister. One such instance was the case of "Joan," a gregarious computer user who used the handle "Talkin Lady" and became something of an electronic celebrity (see Van Gelder 1985:94). "Joan" claimed to be a New York neuropsychologist in her late 20s who was confined to a wheelchair because of a serious automobile accident that had killed her boyfriend and left her severely disfigured and with multiple physical handicaps. "Joan" had many computer friends and fans. One of her fans, a married woman, developed such affectionate ties to her as a sexual confidant and vicarious "lover" that she almost left her husband. In reality, "Joan" was a prominent New York psychiatrist named Alex in his 50s who made a hobby out of his computer deception. On one occasion, "Joan" introduced a woman "she" met through the computer to the real-life Alex, who went on to have an affair with her. It was traumatic to many of "her" contacts when "Joan's" true identity was revealed.

This type of occurrence, coupled with the reported attempts (sometimes successful) on the part of some individuals to lure juveniles into meetings for sexual purposes, raises the possibility of "gender bending" as a device for developing a misrepresented relationship with a woman via computer and luring her into a meeting for perverse purposes.

The use of cyberspace for criminal intent with a sexual dimension sometimes assumes convoluted parameters. It has been reported, for example, that authorities have uncovered that a "violence-prone organization" called the Aryan Brotherhood Youth Movement had established electronic bulletin boards in three different states in order to compile lists of suspected homosexuals for the intended purpose of assaulting them (Jackson 1989:20).

Computer Guides to Sexual Deviance

Whereas there are numerous bulletin boards that address nonsexual deviancy, a significant number also have a sexual orientation. These are available in great variety. Some are like travel guides, in that they provide information about the sexual services (and prices) available in different cities in the United States, Mexico, various countries in Europe, and so forth. Sometimes, specific establishments are mentioned, and some bulletin boards even provide an estimate of mugging risk in each city or place of business.

Some of these travel guide bulletin boards deal essentially with prostitution services; others provide details about other sexual commodities, including erotic dancing, stripping, table dancing, lap dancing, nude showering on stage, dancers having sex with each other, being able to inspect the genital areas of nude dancers ("some women will give you a view of spots only her gynecologist sees," advises one bulletin board), and being allowed to touch or fondle the performers. Given today's tolerant standards, the on-line travel guides to erotic establishments are relatively tame.

Computer Bulletin Boards and Sexual Deviancy "Menus"

Some on-line bulletin board services make direct appeals for individuals of more perverse appetites. A lengthy exploration of the diversity of bulletin boards available in cyberspace reveals an amazing inventory of sexual interests, carnal activities, and exotic enterprises. A bulletin board can be accessed for almost any sexual appetite or persuasion. The topics discussed on these boards range from erotic enemas to zoophilia and include such singular subject matter as ritual genital mutilation, naming the penis, semen speed at ejaculation, having sex with a tiger, breast size versus IQ, pubic hair removal techniques, and a "pop-up" Kama Sutra book. In fact, there have been recent postings from *ampotemnophiles,* or persons with an "erotic obsession or fetish for amputated limbs or digits" (Money et al. 1977). One of these individuals had a leg amputated some years ago and now wished to have the other leg amputated as well (presumably for erotic reasons). This person was seeking a medical professional to perform the procedure, and also wished to contact others of similar desires.

It is also not uncommon to find individuals attempting to sell pornographic tapes, some of which deal with the most bizarre sexual practices (e.g., urolinga and coprophilia), through on-line bulletin boards. In the area of homosexual behavior, one service lists more than 400 gay and lesbian bulletin boards with highly unique names. Among the more active are those concerned with sadism and masochism (S/M). Some of the boards emphasize interest in sexual bondage, self-bondage, sexual spankings, electric shocks, and so on. There seems to be considerable personal E-mail traffic, and some of the messages involve invitations to get together for shopping or dinner when next visiting a particular city, suggesting a long-term network of individuals. Other messages have referred to a "whipping demonstration" to be held in a large East Coast city on a certain date and invited those interested to attend. The existence of elaborate S/M subcultures, complete with consciousness-raising groups, sex clubs, specialized periodicals, and theatrical companies, has been reported by various researchers (e.g., Weinberg and Falk 1980), but the computer appears to expand greatly the geographical boundaries of such subcultures, and dramatically facilitate communication among members and between members and interested individuals.

Perhaps one of the most unusual of the many sexual bulletin boards are those that concern bestiality (i.e., sexual activities with animals). Some of the information offered on such bulletin boards is so outlandish that one might at first assume it is an elaborate hoax, and, if not a hoax, then perhaps the meanderings of someone's fertile fantasy life. The files from some of the bulletin boards, however, are simply too extensive and too detailed to represent a hoax; it is highly doubtful that someone would go to that much trouble to perpetrate a joke! One bulletin board did suggest that it began as a joke but soon attracted a sincere and dedicated following of persons with a genuine interest.) Furthermore, the information appears to grow at a rate greater than an individual's fantasy could generate.

The information available on these bulletin boards includes question and answer files that provide both an introduction and an orientation to bestiality. Some provide graphics files that, according to the editor of the service, "should tell you everything you need to know." Numerous animal-related sex concerns are discussed. Also available are detailed reviews of films and videotapes allegedly portraying sexual activity between humans and animals. Clearly, the market for this type of materials is such that their production is justified. There is every reason to believe that the bestiality subculture will grow and that the number of persons involved will proliferate; the computer bulletin board supports such expansion by facilitating contact and communication among persons with such bizarre erotic interests, even when they are geographically separated by vast distances.

In fact, there is every reason to believe that many, if not most, of the deviant sexual subcultures will expand, become more elaborate, and involve more people because of the on-line bulletin boards. In the past, such subcultures were most frequently limited to particular geographical areas, such as large metropolitan areas along the East or West Coasts. Now those subcultures can readily network with individuals across the nation, or even worldwide. Even persons who reside in small towns in the heartland can more readily contact other individuals with similar sexual interests in their general vicinity and interact with them via computer. If conditions of mutual trust can be met, meetings can be arranged; and, in time, larger groupings can be formed.

There is the possibility that bulletin board users may be inspired by other users to attempt convoluted erotic gratification through, for example, sexual asphyxia (see Lowery and Wetli 1982) or other anti-social or violent sexual practices. The hazard inherent in carnal scenarios of these varieties, of course, is that they may be harmful or dangerous to self or others, especially the youthful computer user.

Some of the sexual themes featured on bulletin boards are merely the sexually exotic. Others are grotesque in their singularity. Still others are redolent of pathology. Some cross the line of illegality.

Most if not all, however, would be of interest to the sexologist or the researcher of deviant behavior.

THE PROGNOSIS FOR COMPUTER SEX RESEARCH

Whether the computer is simply a glorified pornography communication device or whether it has the potential to motivate and initiate deviancy remains to be seen. Given the increasing computer precociousness of many adolescents, there is genuine reason for apprehension in regard to the latter. In regard to both possibilities, only the tip of the iceberg has revealed itself thus far. There is an enormous range of opportunities for systematic research of computer sex. The phenomenon is easily accessed, the participants are only a keyboard away, and those individuals who are involved appear to be eager to communicate with interested parties. In effect, the computer constitutes an electronic survey research mechanism with enormous potential for innovative investigation of deviancy, although some sampling limitations need to be resolved. Just as the computer has begun to revolutionize social life, it will revolutionize crime and deviancy, especially the parameters of deviant sexual behavior; in fact, it is doing so already. The computer may well also revolutionize research addressing crime and deviant behavior. Regardless of the outcome, however, the computer is today's Pandora's Box, and the lid is already open.

REFERENCES

Borpa, Shaheen, Joseph Chapman, and Dennis Menezes. 1993. "Deceptive Nature of Dial-a-Porn Commercials and Public Policy Alternatives." *Journal of Business Ethics* 12:503–509.

Bryant, Clifton D. 1984. "Odum's Concept of the Technicways: Some Reflections on an Underdeveloped Sociological Nation." *Sociological Spectrum* 4:115–142.

Garreau, Joel. 1993, November 29. "Bawdy Bytes: The Growing World of Cybersex." *The Washington Post*, pp. 1, A10.

Glascock, Jack, and Robert LaRose. 1993. "Dial-a-Porn Recordings: The Role of the Female Participant in Male Sexual Fantasies." *Journal of Broadcasting and Electronic Media* 39:313–324.

Haight, Kathy. 1994, March 7. "Love: Couples Are Meeting, Courting, Getting Married On-Line." *Roanoke Times and World-News* (Extra Section), pp. 1, 3.

Horvitz, Robert. 1989. "The USENET Underground." *Whole Earth Review* (Winter):111–115.

Jackson, Robert L. 1989, October 1. "Computer-Crime Sleuths Go Underground." *Los Angeles Times*, p. 20.

Kantrowitz, Barbara, Patricia King, and Debra Rosenberg. 1994, April 18. "Child Abuse in Cyberspace." *Newsweek*, p. 40.

Klein, Lloyd. 1981. "Sex Solicitation by Short-Wave Radio." *Creative Sociology* 9:61–68.

Los Angeles Times. 1989, October 1. "Child Molesters Use Electronic Networks: Computer-Crime Sleuths Go Undercover." Pp. 20–21.

Lowery, Sharon A., and Charles V. Wetli. 1982. "Sexual Asphyxia: A Neglected Area of Study." *Deviant Behavior* 4:19–40.

Luxenburg, Joan, and Lloyd Klein. 1984. "CB Radio Prostitution: Technology and the Displacement of Deviance." *Journal of Offender Counseling, Services, and Rehabilitation* 9(Fall/Winter):71–87.

Markoff, John. 1992, March 22. "Sex by Computer: The Latest Technology Fuels the Oldest of Drives." *New York Times*, p. 5.

Money, John, Russell Jobaris, and Gregg Furth. 1977. "Ampotemnophilia: Two Cases of Self-Demand Amputation as a Paraphilia." *Journal of Sex Research* 13:115–125.

The New York Times. 1989, April 2. "As Computer Bulletin Boards Grow: If It's Out There It's Posted Here." P. B38.

Odum, Howard W. 1937. "Notes on the Technicways in Contemporary Society." *American Sociological Review* 2:336–346.

Ogburn, William F. 1964. *On Culture and Social Change*. Chicago: University of Chicago Press.

Parade. 1976, July 4. "Dirty-Story Time." P. 20.

Schwartz, John. 1993, November 28. "Caution: Children at Play on the Information Highway (Access to Adult Networks Holds Hazards)." *The Washington Post*, pp. 1, 26.

Tamosaitis, Nancy. 1994. "Modem Sex: Can Online Fantasies Rev Up Your Libido?" *Longevity:* 56, 68.

Time. 1984, May 14. "X-Rated: The Joys of Compusex." P. 83.

U.S. Department of Justice. 1986. *The Attorney General's Commission on Pornography, Final Report.* Washington, DC: U.S. Government Printing Office.

———. 1993, August 31. "Feds Crack Down on Computer Importation of Child Pornography." Press release.

U.S. News and World Report. 1985, June 3. "For Every Taste a Bulletin Board." P. 59.

Van Gelder, Lindsey. 1985, October. "The Strange Case of the Electronic Lover." *Ms.* pp. 94, 99, 101–104, 117, 123–124.

Vander Zanden, James W. 1993. *Sociology: The Core,* 2nd ed. New York: McGraw-Hill.

Weinberg, Thomas S., and Gerhard Falk. 1980. "The social organization of sadism and masochism." *Deviant Behavior* 1:379–394.

STUDY QUESTIONS

1. In what ways do the media distort the reality of crime in America, as described in Vincent Sacco's chapter?
2. Drawing on Joshua Gamson's essay, describe the ways individuals who appear on tabloid talk shows attempt to justify and normalize their deviant behavior.
3. Which theory of deviance could be used to further our understanding of the larger societal role of the talk shows analyzed by Gamson?
4. According to Keith Durkin and Clifton Bryant, in what ways is the Internet a medium for the emergence of new types of deviance and new forms of communication among deviant populations?

MEDICINE AND PSYCHIATRIC INSTITUTIONS

Introduction

Some types of behavior that were considered abnormal and punished just a few generations ago have become less stigmatized in recent years (e.g., premarital sex, masturbation), while other behaviors that were once considered normal are now labeled deviant by many people and increasingly sanctioned (e.g., cigarette smoking). And just as behaviors may be redefined as normal or as deviant with the passage of time, so the alleged causes of the behavior, and its appropriate treatment, may undergo change. What was once regarded as sinful or patently immoral may be redefined as symptomatic of some other kind of disorder. A major example of this is what Peter Conrad and Joseph Schneider call the "medicalization" of deviance. When conduct is medicalized, the cause of the behavior is attributed to an illness, disease, or disorder that requires medical or psychiatric treatment rather than punishment. Alcoholism, for example, is now considered a "disease" rather than a manifestation of a person's lack of self-control or moral poverty. The medical profession has been heavily involved in the redefinition of certain kinds of deviance under the rubrics of illness, disease, addiction, and disorder. Conrad and Schneider point out that the net effects of this trend have been, first, to relieve actors of accountability for their deviance (now seen as "beyond their control") and, second, an intensification and expansion of control on the part of the medical establishment.

D. L. Rosenhan's chapter, "On Being Sane in Insane Places," demonstrates how the labeling process works in the context of mental institutions, which Rosenhan and his colleagues studied incognito. The researchers were readily admitted to a dozen mental hospitals after they complained of hearing voices. These "pseudopatients" remained in the hospitals for some time, observing interactions between staff and inmates and recording detailed fieldnotes on what they observed. Rosenhan argues that once a person has been labeled, say, "schizophrenic," it is almost impossible to convince hospital psychiatrists that one is "sane." Rosenhan claims that his findings cast doubt on the notion that we can distinguish "sane" from "insane" people. His study also illustrates the importance of institutional context—in this case, mental hospitals—on the labeling and treatment of deviance, including falsely accused deviance.

READING 4-4

Medicine as an Institution of Social Control

Peter Conrad and Joseph W. Schneider

In our society we want to believe in medicine, as we want to believe in religion and our country; it wards off collective fears and reduces public anxieties (see Edelman 1977). In significant ways medicine, especially psychiatry, has replaced religion as the most powerful extralegal institution of social control. Physicians have been endowed with some of the charisma of shamans. In the 20th century the medical model of deviance has ascended with the glitter of a rising star, expanding medicine's social control functions.

MEDICAL COLLABORATION

Medicine acts not only as an independent agent of social control, but frequently medical collaboration with other authorities serves social control functions. Such collaboration includes roles as information provider, gatekeeper, institutional agent, and technician. These interdependent medical control functions highlight the extent to which medicine is interwoven in the fabric of society. Historically, medical personnel have reported information on gunshot wounds and venereal disease to state authorities. More recently this has included reporting "child abuse" to child welfare or law enforcement agencies (Pfohl 1977).

The medical profession is the official designator of the "sick role." This imbues the physician with authority to define particular kinds of deviance as illness and exempt the patient from certain role obligations. These are general gatekeeping and social control tasks. In some instances the physician functions as a specific gatekeeper for special exemptions from conventional norms; here the exemptions are authorized because of illness, disease, or disability. A classic example is the so-called insanity defense in certain crime cases. Other more commonplace examples include competency to stand trial, medical deferment from the draft or a medical discharge from the military, requiring physicians' notes to legitimize missing an examination or excessive absences in school, and, before abortion was legalized, obtaining two psychiatrists' letters testifying to the therapeutic necessity of the abortion. Halleck (1971) has called this "the power of medical excuse." In a slightly different vein, but still forms of gatekeeping and medical excuse, are medical examinations for disability or workman's compensation benefits. Medical reports required for insurance coverage and employment or medical certification of an epileptic as seizure free to obtain a driver's license are also gatekeeping activities.

Physicians in total institutions have one of two roles. In some institutions, such as schools for the retarded or mental hospitals, they are usually the administrative authority; in others, such as in the military or prisons, they are employees of the administration. In total institutions, medicine's role as an agent of social control (for the institution) is more apparent. In both the military and prisons, physicians have the power to confer the sick role and to offer medical excuse for deviance (see Daniels 1969; Waitzkin & Waterman 1974). For example, discharges and sick call are available medical designations for deviant behavior. Since physicians are both hired and paid by the

From Peter Conrad and Joseph W. Schneider, "Medicine as an Institution of Social Control: Consequences for Society," pp. 241–260 in *Deviance and Medicalization: From Badness to Sickness* (Philadelphia: Temple Univ. Press, 1992). © 1992 by Temple University. Reprinted by permission of Temple University Press.

institution, it is difficult for them to be fully an agent of the patient, engendering built-in role strains. An extreme example is in wartime when the physician's mandate is to return the soldier to combat duty as soon as possible. Under some circumstances physicians act as direct agents of control by prescribing medications to control unruly or disorderly inmates or to help a "neurotic" adjust to the conditions of a total institution. In such cases "captive professionals" (Daniels 1969) are more likely to become the agent of the institution than the agent of the individual patient (Szasz 1965; see also Menninger 1967).

Under rather rare circumstances physicians may become "mere technicians," applying the sanctions of another authority who purchase[s] their medical skills. An extreme example would be the behavior of the experimental and death physicians in Nazi Germany. A less heinous but nevertheless ominous example is provided by physicians who perform court-ordered sterilizations (Kittrie 1971). Perhaps one could imagine sometime in the future, if the death penalty becomes commonplace again, physicians administering drugs as the "humanitarian" and painless executioners.[1]

MEDICAL IDEOLOGY

Medical ideology is a type of social control that involves defining a behavior or condition as an illness primarily because of the social and ideological benefits accrued by conceptualizing it in medical terms. These effects of medical ideology may benefit the individual, the dominant interests in the society, or both. They exist independently of any organic basis for illness or any available treatment. Howard Waitzkin and Barbara Waterman (1974) call one latent function of medicalization "secondary gain," arguing that assumption of the

sick role can fulfill personality and individual needs (e.g., gaining nurturance or attention or legitimizing personal failure (Shuval & Antonovsky 1973).[2] One of the most important functions of the disease model of alcoholism and to a lesser extent drug addiction is the secondary gain of removing blame from, and constructing a shield against condemnation of, individuals for their deviant behavior. Alcoholics Anonymous, a nonmedical quasireligious self-help organization, adopted a variant of the medical model of alcoholism independent of the medical profession. One suspects the secondary gain serves their purpose well.

Disease designations can support dominant social interests and institutions. A poignant example is prominent 19th-century New Orleans physician S. W. Cartwright's antebellum conceptualization of the disease drapetomania, a condition that affected only slaves. Its major symptom was running away from their masters (Cartwright 1851). Medical conceptions and controls often support dominant social values and morality: the 19th-century Victorian conceptualization of the illness of and addiction to masturbation and the medical treatments developed to control this disease make chilling reading in the 1970s (Comfort 1967; Englehardt 1974). The recent Soviet labeling of political dissidents as mentally ill is another example of the manipulation of illness designations to support dominant political and social institutions (Conrad 1977). These examples highlight the sociopolitical nature of illness designations in general (Zola 1975).

In sum, medicine as an institution of social control has a number of faces. The three types of medical social control discussed here do not necessarily exist as discrete entities but are found in combination with one another. For example, court-ordered sterilizations or medical prescribing of drugs to unruly nursing home patients combines both technological and collaborative aspects of medical control; legitimating

---

[1] It is worth noting that in the recent Gary Gilmore execution a physician was involved; he designated the spot where the heartbeat was loudest and measured vital signs during the execution ceremony. A few states have actually passed death penalty legislation specifying injection of a lethal drug as the means of execution.

[2] Although Waitzkin and Waterman suggest that such secondary gain functions are latent (i.e., unintended and unrecognized), the cases we have discussed here show that such "gains" are often intentionally pursued.

disability status includes both ideological and collaborative aspects of medical control; and treating Soviet dissidents with drugs for their mental illness combines all three aspects of medical social control. It is clear that the enormous expansion of medicine in the past 50 years has increased the number of possible ways in which problems could be medicalized. In the next section we point out some of the consequences of this medicalization.

SOCIAL CONSEQUENCES OF MEDICALIZING DEVIANCE

Jesse Pitts (1968), one of the first sociologists to give attention to the medicalization of deviance, suggests that "medicalization is one of the most effective means of social control and that it is destined to become the main mode of *formal* social control" (p. 391, emphasis in original). Although his bold prediction is far-reaching (and, in light of recent developments, perhaps a bit premature), his analysis of a decade ago was curiously optimistic and uncritical of the effects and consequences of medicalization. Nonsociologists, especially psychiatric critic Thomas Szasz (1961, 1963, 1970, 1974) and legal scholar Nicholas Kittrie (1971), are much more critical in their evaluations of the ramifications of medicalization. Szasz's critiques are polemical and attack the medical, especially psychiatric, definitions and treatments for deviant behavior. Szasz's analyses, although path breaking, insightful, and suggestive, have not been presented in a particularly systematic form. Both he and Kittrie tend to focus on the effects of medicalization on individual civil liberties and judicial processes rather than on social consequences. Their writings, however, reveal that both are aware of sociological consequences.

In this section we discuss some of the more significant consequences and ramifications of defining deviant behavior as a medical problem. We must remind the reader that we are examining the *social* consequences of medicalizing deviance, which can be analyzed separately from the validity of medical definitions or diagnoses, the effective-

ness of medical regimens, or their individual consequences. These variously "latent" consequences inhere in medicalization itself and occur *regardless* of how efficacious the particular medical treatment or social control mechanism is. As will be apparent, our sociological analysis has left us skeptical of the social benefits of medical social control. We separate the consequences into the "brighter" and "darker" sides of medicalization. The "brighter" side will be presented first.

Brighter Side

The brighter side of medicalization includes the positive or beneficial qualities that are attributed to medicalization. We review briefly the accepted socially progressive aspects of medicalizing deviance. They are separated more for clarity of presentation than for any intrinsic separation in consequence.

First, medicalization is related to a longtime *humanitarian* trend in the conception and control of deviance. For example, alcoholism is no longer considered a sin or even a moral weakness; it is now a disease. Alcoholics are no longer arrested in many places for "public drunkenness"; they are now somehow "treated," if only to be dried out for a time. Medical treatment for the alcoholic can be seen as a more humanitarian means of social control. It is not retributive or punitive, but at least ideally, therapeutic. Troy Duster (1970:10) suggests that medical definitions increase tolerance and compassion for human problems and they "have now been reinterpreted in an almost nonmoral fashion." (We doubt this, but leave the morality issue for a later discussion.) Medicine and humanitarianism historically developed concurrently and, as some have observed, the use of medical language and evidence increases the prestige of human proposals and enhances their acceptance (Wootton 1959; Zola 1975). Medical definitions are imbued with the prestige of the medical profession and are considered the "scientific" and humane way of viewing a problem. This is especially true if an apparently "successful" treatment for controlling the behavior is available, as with hyperkinesis.

Second, medicalization allows for the extension of the *sick role* to those labeled as deviants. Many of the perceived benefits of the medicalization of deviance stem from the assignment of the sick role. Some have suggested that this is the most significant element of adopting the medical model of deviant behavior (Sigler & Osmond 1974). By defining deviant behavior as an illness or a result of illness, one is absolved of responsibility for one's behavior. It diminishes or *removes blame* from the individual for deviant actions. Alcoholics are no longer held responsible for their uncontrolled drinking, and perhaps hyperactive children are no longer the classroom's "bad boys" but children with a medical disorder. There is some clear secondary gain here for the individual. The label "sick" is free of the moral opprobrium and implied culpability of "criminal" or "sinner." The designation of sickness also may reduce guilt for drinkers and their families and for hyperactive children and their parents. Similarly, it may result in reduced stigma for the deviant. It allows for the development of more acceptable accounts of deviance: a recent film depicted a child witnessing her father's helpless drunken stupor; her mother remarked, "It's okay. Daddy's just sick."[3]

The sick role allows for the "confidential legitimation" of a certain amount of deviance, so long as the individual fulfills the obligations of the sick role.[4] As Renée Fox (1977:15) notes:

> The fact that the exemptions of sickness have been extended to people with a widening arc of attitudes, experiences and behaviors in American society means

primarily that what is regarded as "conditionally legitimated deviance" has increased. . . . So long as [the deviant] does not abandon himself to illness or eagerly embrace it, but works actively on his own or with medical professionals to improve his condition, he is considered to be responding appropriately, even admirably, to an unfortunate occurrence. Under these conditions, illness is accepted as legitimate deviance.

The deviant, in essence, is medically excused for the deviation. But, as Talcott Parsons (1972) has pointed out, "the conditional legitimation is bought at a price," namely, the recognition that illness itself is an undesirable state, to be recovered from as expeditiously as possible" (p. 108). Thus the medical excuse for deviance is only valid when the patient-deviant accepts the medical perspective of the inherent undesirability of his or her sick behavior and submits to a subordinate relationship with an official agent of control (the physician) toward changing it. This, of course, negates any threat the deviant may pose to society's normative structure, for such deviants do not challenge the norm; by accepting deviance as sickness and social control as "treatment," the deviant underscores the validity of the violated norm.

Third, the medical model can be viewed as portraying an *optimistic* outcome for the deviant. Pitts (1968) notes, "the possibility that a patient may be exploited is somewhat minimized by therapeutic ideology, which creates an optimistic bias concerning the patient's fate" (p. 391). The therapeutic ideology, accepted in some form by all branches of medicine, suggests that a problem (e.g., deviant behavior) can be changed or alleviated if only the proper treatment is discovered and administered. Defining deviant behavior as an illness may also mobilize hope in the individual patient that with proper treatment a "cure" is possible (Frank 1974). Clearly this could have beneficial results and even become a self-fulfilling prophecy. Although the medical model is interpreted frequently as optimistic about individual change, under some circumstances it may lend itself to pessimistic interpretations. The attribution of physiological cause coupled with the lack of effective treatment

---

[3] It should be noted, however, that little empirical evidence exists for reduced stigmatization. Derek Phillips' (1963) research suggests that people seeking medical help for their personal problems are highly at risk for rejection and stigmatization. Certain illnesses carry their own stigma. Leprosy, epilepsy, and mental illness are all stigmatized illnesses (Gussow & Tracy 1968); Susan Sontag (1978) proposes that cancer is highly stigmatized in American society. We need further research on the stigma-reducing properties of medical designations of deviance; it is by no means an automatic result of medicalization.

[4] On the other hand, Paul Roman and Harrison Trice (1968:248) contend that the sick role of alcoholic may actually reinforce deviant behavior by removing responsibility for deviant drinking behavior.

engendered a somatic pessimism in the late 19th-century conception of madness.

Fourth, medicalization lends the *prestige of the medical profession* to deviance designations and treatments. The medical profession is the most prestigious and dominant profession in American society (Friedson 1970). As just noted, medical definitions of deviance become imbued with the prestige of the medical profession and are construed to be the "scientific" way of viewing a problem. The medical mantle of science may serve to deflect definitional challenges. This is especially true if an apparently "successful" treatment for controlling the behavior is available. Medicalization places the problem in the hands of healing physicians. "The therapeutic value of professional dominance, from the patient's point of view, is that it becomes the *doctor's* problem" (Ehrenreich & Ehrenreich 1975:156, emphasis in original). Physicians are assumed to be beneficent and honorable. "The medical and paramedical professions," Pitts (1968) contends, "especially in the United States, are probably more immune to corruption than are the judicial and parajudicial professions and relatively immune to political pressure" (p. 391).

Darker Side

There is, however, another side to the medicalization of deviant behavior. Although it may often seem entirely humanitarian to conceptualize deviance as sickness as opposed to badness, it is not that simple. There is a "darker" side to the medicalization of deviance.

Dislocation of Responsibility   As we have seen, defining behavior as a medical problem removes or profoundly diminishes responsibility from the individual. Although affixing responsibility is always complex, medicalization produces confusion and ambiguity about who is responsible. Responsibility is separated from social action; it is located in the nether world of biophysiology or psyche. Although this takes the individual officially "off the hook," its excuse is only a partial one. The individual, the putative deviant, and the undesirable conduct are still associated. Aside from where such conduct is "seated," the sick deviant is the medium of its expression.

With the removal of responsibility also comes the lowering of status. A dual-class citizenship is created: those who are deemed responsible for their actions and those who are not. The not-completely responsible sick are placed in a position of dependence on the fully responsible nonsick (Parsons 1975:108). Kittrie (1971:347) notes in this regard that more than half the American population is no longer subject to the sanctions of criminal law. Such persons, among others, become true "second-class citizens."

Assumption of the Moral Neutrality of Medicine

Cloaked in the mantle of science, medicine and medical practice are assumed to be objective and value free. But this profoundly misrepresents reality. The very nature of medical practice involves value judgment. To call something a disease is to deem it undesirable. Medicine is influenced by the moral order of society—witness the diagnosis and treatment of masturbation as a disease in Victorian times—yet medical language of disease and treatment is assumed to be morally neutral. It is not, and the very technological-scientific vocabulary of medicine that defines disease obfuscates this fact.

Defining deviance as disease allows behavior to keep its negative judgment, but medical language veils the political and moral nature of this decision in the guise of scientific fact. There was little public clamor for moral definitions of homosexuality as long as it remained defined an illness, but soon after the disease designation was removed, moral crusaders (e.g., Anita Bryant) launched public campaigns condemning the immorality of homosexuality. One only needs to scratch the surface of medical designations for deviant behavior to find overtly moral judgments.

Thus, as Zola (1975:86) points out, defining a problem as within medical jurisdiction

is not morally neutral precisely because in establishing its relevance as a key dimension for action, the moral issue is prevented from being squarely faced and occasionally from even being raised. By the acceptance of a specific behavior as an undesirable state the issue becomes not whether to treat an individual problem but how and when.

Defining deviance as a medical phenomenon involves moral enterprise.

Domination of Expert Control   The medical profession is made up of experts; it has a monopoly on anything that can be conceptualized as an illness. Because of the way the medical profession is organized and the mandate it has from society, decisions related to medical diagnosis and treatment are controlled almost completely by medical professionals.

Conditions that enter the medical domain are not ipso facto medical problems, whether we speak of alcoholism, hyperactivity, or drug addiction. When a problem is defined as medical, it is removed from the public realm, where there can be discussion by ordinary people, and put on a plane where only medical people can discuss it. As Janice Reynolds (1973:220–221) succinctly states,

> The increasing acceptance, especially among the more educated segments of our populace, of technical solutions—solutions administered by disinterested and morally neutral experts—results in the withdrawal of more and more areas of human experience from the realm of public discussion. For when drunkenness, juvenile delinquency, sub par performance and extreme political beliefs are seen as symptoms of an underlying illness or biological defect the merits and drawbacks of such behavior or beliefs need not be evaluated.

The public may have their own conceptions of deviant behavior, but those of the experts are usually dominant. Medical definitions have a high likelihood for dominance and hegemony: they are often taken as the last scientific word. The language of medical experts increases mystification and decreases the accessibility of public debate.

Medical Social Control   Defining deviant behavior as a medical problem allows certain things to be done that could not otherwise be considered; for example, the body may be cut open or psychoactive medications given. As we elaborated above, this treatment can be a form of social control.

In regard to drug treatment, Henry Lennard (1971) observes: "Psychoactive drugs, especially those legally prescribed, tend to restrain individuals from behavior and experience that are not complementary with the requirements of the dominant value system" (p. 57). These forms of medical social control presume a prior definition of deviance as a medical problem. Psychosurgery on an individual prone to violent outbursts requires a diagnosis that something is wrong with his brain or nervous system. Similarly, prescribing drugs to restless, overactive, and disruptive schoolchildren requires a diagnosis of hyperkinesis. These forms of social control, what Stephan Chorover (1973) has called "psychotechnology," are powerful and often efficient means of controlling deviance. These relatively new and increasingly popular forms of medical control could not be used without the prior medicalization of deviant behavior. As is suggested from the discovery of hyperkinesis and to a lesser extent the development of methadone treatment of opiate addiction, if a mechanism of medical social control seems useful, then the deviant behavior it modifies will be given a medical label or diagnosis. We imply no overt malevolence on the part of the medical profession; rather, it is part of a larger process, of which the medical profession is only a part. The larger process might be called the individualization of social problems.

Individualization of Social Problems   The medicalization of deviance is part of a larger phenomenon that is prevalent in our society: the individualization of social problems. We tend to look for causes and solutions to complex social problems in the individual rather than in the social system. William Ryan (1971) has identified this process as "blaming the victim": seeing the causes of the problem in individuals (who are usually of low status) rather than as endemic to the society. We seek to change the "victim" rather than the society. The medical practice of diagnosing an illness in an individual lends itself to the individualization of social problems. Rather than seeing certain deviant behaviors as symptomatic of social conditions, the medical perspective focuses on the individual, diagnosing and treating the illness itself and generally ignoring the social situation.

Hyperkinesis serves as a good example of this. Both the school and parents are concerned with the child's behavior; the child is difficult at home and disruptive in school. No punishments or rewards seem consistently effective in modifying the behavior, and both parents and school are at their wits' end. A medical evaluation is suggested. The diagnosis of hyperkinetic behavior leads to prescribing stimulant medications. The child's behavior seems to become more socially acceptable, reducing problems in school and home. Treatment is considered a medical success.

But there is an alternative perspective. By focusing on the symptoms and defining them as hyperkinesis, we ignore the possibility that the behavior is not an illness but an adaptation to a social situation. It diverts our attention from the family or school and from seriously entertaining the idea that the "problem" could be in the structure of the social system. By giving medications, we are essentially supporting the existing social and political arrangements in that it becomes a "symptom" of an individual disease rather than a possible "comment" on the nature of the present situation. Although the individualization of social problems aligns well with the individualistic ethic of American culture, medical intervention against deviance makes medicine a de facto agent of dominant social and political interests.

Depoliticization of Deviant Behavior Depoliticization of deviant behavior is a result of both the process of medicalization and the individualization of social problems. Probably one of the clearest recent examples of such depoliticization occurred when political dissidents in the Soviet Union were declared mentally ill and confined to mental hospitals (Conrad 1977). This strategy served to neutralize the meaning of political protest and dissent, rendering it (officially, at least) symptomatic of mental illness.

The medicalization of deviant behavior depoliticizes deviance in the same manner. By defining the overactive, restless, and disruptive child as hyperkinetic, we ignore the meaning of the behavior in the context of the social system. If we focused our analysis on the school system, we might see the child's behavior as a protest against some aspect of the school or classroom situation, rather than symptomatic of an individual neurological disorder. Similar examples could be drawn of the opiate addict in the ghetto, the alcoholic in the workplace, and others. Medicalizing deviant behavior precludes us from recognizing it as a possible intentional repudiation of existing political arrangements.

There are other related consequences of the medicalization of deviance beyond the six discussed. The medical ideal of early intervention may lead to early labeling and secondary deviance (see Lemert 1972). The "medical decision rule," which approximates "when in doubt, treat," is nearly the converse of the legal dictum "innocent until proven guilty" and may unnecessarily enlarge the population of deviants (Scheff 1963). Certain constitutional safeguards of the judicial system that protect individuals' rights are neutralized or bypassed by medicalization (Kittrie 1971). Social control in the name of benevolence is at once insidious and difficult to confront. Although these are all significant, we wish to expand on still another consequence of considerable social importance, the exclusion of evil.

EXCLUSION OF EVIL

Evil has been excluded from the imagery of modern human problems. We are uncomfortable with notions of evil; we regard them as primitive and nonhumanitarian, as residues from a theological era.[5] Medicalization contributes to the exclusion of

---

[5] Writing in the early 1970s, Kittrie (1971) noted, "Ours is increasingly becoming a society that views punishment as a primitive and vindictive tool and is therefore loath to punish" (p. 347). Some recent scholarship in penology and the controversy about the death penalty has slightly modified this trend.

concepts of evil in our society. Clearly medicalization is not the sole cause of the exclusion of evil, but it shrouds conditions, events, and people and prevents them from being confronted as evil. The roots of the exclusion of evil are in the Enlightenment, the diminution of religious imagery of sin, the rise of determinist theories of human behavior, and the doctrine of cultural relativity. Social scientists as well have excluded the concept of evil from their analytic discourses (Wolff 1969).

Although we cannot here presume to identify the forms of evil in modern times, we would like to sensitize the reader to how medical definitions of deviance serve to further exclude evil from our view. It can be argued that regardless of what we construe as evil (e.g., destruction, pain, alienation, exploitation, oppression), there are at least two general types of evil: evil intent and evil consequence. Evil intent is similar to the legal concept mens rea, literally, "evil mind." Some evil is intended by a specific line of action. Evil consequence is, on the other hand, the result of action. No intent or motive to do evil is necessary for evil consequence to prevail; on the contrary, it often resembles the platitude "the road to hell is paved with good intentions." In either case medicalization dilutes or obstructs us from seeing evil. Sickness gives us a vocabulary of motive (Mills 1940) that obliterates evil intent. And although it does not automatically render evil consequences good, the allegation that they were products of a "sick" mind or body relegates them to a status similar to that of "accidents."

For example, Hitler orchestrated the greatest mass genocide in modern history, yet some have reduced his motivation for the destruction of the Jews (and others) to a personal pathological condition. To them and to many of us, Hitler was sick. But this portrays the horror of the Holocaust as a product of individual pathology; as Thomas Szasz frequently points out, it prevents us from seeing and confronting man's inhumanity to man. Are Son of Sam, Charles Manson, the assassins of King and the Kennedys, the Richard Nixon of Watergate, Libya's Muammar Kaddafi, or the all-too-common

child beater sick? Although many may well be troubled, we argue that there is little to be gained by deploying such a medical vocabulary of motives.[6] It only hinders us from comprehending the human element in the decisions we make, the social structures we create, and the actions we take. Hannah Arendt (1963), in her exemplary study of the banality of evil, contends that Nazi war criminal Adolph Eichmann, rather than being sick, was "terribly, terrifyingly normal."

Susan Sontag (1978) has suggested that on a cultural level, we use the metaphor of illness to speak of various kinds of evil. Cancer, in particular, provides such a metaphor: we depict slums and pornography shops as "cancers" in our cities; J. Edgar Hoover's favorite metaphor for communism was "a cancer in our midst"; and Nixon's administration was deemed "cancerous," rotting from within. In our secular culture, where powerful religious connotations of sin and evil have been obscured, cancer (and for that matter, illness in general) is one of the few available images of unmitigated evil and wickedness. As Sontag (1978:85) observes:

> But how to be . . . [moral] in the late twentieth century? How, when . . . we have a sense of evil but no longer the religious or philosophical language to talk intelligently about evil. Trying to comprehend "radical" or "absolute" evil, we search for adequate metaphors. But the modern disease metaphors are all cheap shots . . . Only in the most limited sense is any historical event or problem like an illness. It is invariably an encouragement to simplify what is complex.

Thus we suggest that the medicalization of social problems detracts from our capability to see and confront the evils that face our world.

---

[6] We *do not* suggest that these individuals or any other deviants discussed in this book are or should be considered evil. We only wish to point out that medicalization on a social level contributes to the exclusion of evil. To the extent that evil exists, we would argue that social structures and specific social conditions are the most significant cause of evil.

REFERENCES

Cartwright, S. W. 1851. "Report on the diseases and physical peculiarities of the negro race." *N.O. Med. Surg. J* 7:691–715.

Chalfant, P. 1977. "Professionalization and the medicalization of deviance: The case of probation officers." *Offender Rehabilitation* 2:77–85.

Chorover, S. 1973. "Big Brother and psychotechnology." *Psychol. Today* 7:43–54.

Comfort, A. 1967. *The Anxiety Makers*. London: Thomas Nelson & Sons.

Conrad, P. 1975. "The discovery of hyperkinesis: notes on the medicalization of deviant behavior." *Social Prob.* 23:12–21.

———. 1977. "Soviet dissidents, ideological deviance, and mental hospitalization." Presented at Midwest Sociological Society Meetings, Minneapolis.

Daniels, A. K. 1969. "The captive professional: Bureaucratic limitation in the practice of military psychiatry." *J. Health Soc. Behav.* 10:255–265.

Ehrenreich, B., and Ehrenreich, J. 1975. "Medicine and social control." In B. R. Mandell (Ed.), *Welfare in America: Controlling the "Dangerous" Classes*. Englewood Cliffs, N.J.: Prentice Hall.

Englehardt, H. T., Jr. 1974. "The disease of masturbation: values and the concept of disease." *Bull. Hist. Med.* 48:234–248.

Fox, Renée. 1977. "The medicalization and demedicalization of American society." *Daedalus,* 106:9–22.

Frank, J. 1974. *Persuasion and Healing*. Rev. ed. New York: Schocken Books, Inc.

Kittrie, N. 1971. *The Right to Be Different: Deviance and Enforced Therapy*. Baltimore: Johns Hopkins University Press. Copyright the Johns Hopkins Press, 1971.

Lemert, E. M. 1972. *Human Deviance, Social Problems and Social Control,* 2nd ed. Englewood Cliffs, N.J.: Prentice Hall.

Lyman, S. 1978. *The Seven Deadly Sins: Society and Evil*. New York: St. Martin's Press.

Menninger, W. C. 1967. *A Psychiatrist for a Troubled World*. B. H. Hall (Ed.). New York: Viking Press.

Mills, C. W. 1940. "Situated actions and vocabularies of motive." *Am. Sociol. Rev.* 6:904–913.

Parsons, T. 1972. "Definitions of illness and health in light of American values and social structure." In E. G. Jaco (Ed.), *Patients, Physicians and Illness,* 2nd ed. New York: The Free Press.

Pfohl, S. J. 1977. "The 'discovery' of child abuse." *Social Prob.* 24:310–323.

Pitts, J. 1968. "Social control: The concept." In D. Sills (Ed.), *International Encyclopedia of Social Sciences.* Vol. 14. New York: Macmillan Publishing.

Reynolds, J. M. 1973. "The medical institution: The death and disease-producing appendage." In L. T. Reynolds & J. M. Henslin (Eds.), *American Society: A Critical Analysis.* New York: David McKay.

Scheff, T. J. 1963. "Decision rules, types of errors, and their consequences in medical diagnosis." *Behav. Sci.* 8:97–107.

Shuval, J. T., & Antonovsky, A. 1973. "Illness: A mechanism for coping with failure." *Soc. Sci. Med.* 7:259–265.

Sigler, M., & Osmond, H. 1974. *Models of Madness, Models of Medicine.* New York: Macmillan Publishing.

Sontag, S. 1978. *Illness as Metaphor.* New York: Farrar, Straus & Giroux.

Szasz, T. 1961. *The Myth of Mental Illness.* New York: Hoeber-Harper.

———. 1963. *Law, Liberty and Psychiatry.* New York: Macmillan Publishing.

———. 1965. "Legal and moral aspects of homosexuality." In J. Marmor (Ed.), *Sexual Inversion: The Multiple Roots of Homosexuality.* New York: Basic Books.

———. 1970. *The Manufacture of Madness.* New York: Harper & Row.

———. 1974. *Ceremonial Chemistry.* New York: Anchor Books.

Waitzkin, H. K., & Waterman, B. 1974. *The Exploitation of Illness in Capitalist Society.* Indianapolis: Bobbs-Merrill.

Zola, I. K. 1972. "Medicine as an institution of social control." *Sociological Rev.* 20:487–504.

———. 1975. In the name of health and illness: on some socio-political consequences of medical influence." *Soc. Sci. Med.* 9:83–87.

On Being Sane in Insane Places

D. L. Rosenhan

If sanity and insanity exist, how shall we know them?

The question is neither capricious nor itself insane. However much we may be personally convinced that we can tell the normal from the abnormal, the evidence is simply not compelling. It is commonplace, for example, to read about murder trials wherein eminent psychiatrists for the defense are contradicted by equally eminent psychiatrists for the prosecution on the matter of the defendant's sanity. More generally, there are a great deal of conflicting data on the reliability, utility, and meaning of such terms as "sanity," "insanity," "mental illness," and "schizophrenia" (Ash 1949; Beck 1962; Boisen 1938; Keitman 1961). Finally, as early as 1934, Benedict (1934) suggested that normality and abnormality are not universal. What is viewed as normal in one culture may be seen as quite aberrant in another. Thus, notions of normality and abnormality may not be quite as accurate as people believe they are.

At its heart, the question of whether the sane can be distinguished from the insane (and whether degrees of insanity can be distinguished from each other) is a simple matter: Do the salient characteristics that lead to diagnoses reside in the patients themselves or in the environments and contexts in which observers find them?

Gains can be made in deciding which of these is more nearly accurate by getting normal people (that is, people who do not have, and have never suffered, symptoms of serious psychiatric disorders) admitted to psychiatric hospitals and then determining whether they were discovered to be sane and, if so, how. If the sanity of such pseudopatients were always detected, there would be prima facie evidence that a sane individual can be distinguished from the insane context in which he is found. Normality (and presumably abnormality) is distinct enough that it can be recognized wherever it occurs, for it is carried within the person. If, on the other hand, the sanity of the pseudopatients were never discovered, serious difficulties would arise for those who support traditional modes of psychiatric diagnosis. Given that the hospital staff was not incompetent, that the pseudopatient had been behaving as sanely as he had been outside of the hospital, and that it had never been previously suggested that he belonged in a psychiatric hospital, such an unlikely outcome would support the view that psychiatric diagnosis betrays little about the patient but much about the environment in which an observer finds him.

This article describes such an experiment. Eight sane people gained secret admission to 12 different hospitals.[1]

PSEUDOPATIENTS AND THEIR SETTINGS

The eight pseudopatients were a varied group. One was a psychology graduate student in his twenties. The remaining seven were older and "established."

From *Science* 179, no. 4070 (Jan. 19, 1973), pp. 250–258. Reprinted by permission of the American Association for the Advancement of Science. © 1973 by the AAAS.

[1] Data from a ninth pseudopatient are not incorporated in this report because, although his sanity went undetected, he falsified aspects of his personal history, including his marital status and parental relationships. His experimental behaviors therefore were not identical to those of the other pseudopatients.

Among them were three psychologists, a pediatrician, a psychiatrist, a painter, and a housewife. Three pseudopatients were women, five were men. All of them employed pseudonyms, lest their alleged diagnoses embarrass them later. Those who were in mental health professions alleged another occupation in order to avoid the special attentions that might be accorded by staff, as a matter of courtesy or caution, to ailing colleagues.[2] With the exception of myself (I was the first pseudopatient and my presence was known to the hospital administrator and chief psychologist and, so far as I can tell, to them alone), the presence of pseudopatients and the nature of the research program was not known to the hospital staffs.[3]

The settings were similarly varied. In order to generalize the findings, admission into a variety of hospitals was sought. The 12 hospitals in the sample were located in five different states on the East and West Coasts. Some were old and shabby, some were quite new. Some were research-oriented, others not. Some had good staff-patient ratios, others were quite understaffed. Only one was a strictly private hospital. All of the others were supported by state or federal funds or, in one instance, by university funds.

After calling the hospital for an appointment, the pseudopatient arrived at the admissions office complaining that he had been hearing voices. Asked what the voices said, he replied that they were

often unclear, but as far as he could tell they said "empty," "hollow," and "thud." The voices were unfamiliar and were of the same sex as the pseudopatient. The choice of these symptoms was occasioned by their apparent similarity to existential symptoms. Such symptoms are alleged to arise from painful concerns about the perceived meaninglessness of one's life. It is as if the hallucinating person were saying, "My life is empty and hollow." The choice of these symptoms was also determined by the *absence* of a single report of existential psychoses in the literature.

Beyond alleging the symptoms and falsifying name, vocation, and employment, no further alterations of person, history, or circumstances were made. The significant events of the pseudopatient's life history were presented as they had actually occurred. Relationships with parents and siblings, with spouse and children, with people at work and in school, consistent with the aforementioned exceptions, were described as they were or had been. Frustrations and upsets were described along with joys and satisfactions. These facts are important to remember. If anything, they strongly biased the subsequent results in favor of detecting sanity, since none of their histories or current behaviors were seriously pathological in any way.

Immediately upon admission to the psychiatric ward, the pseudopatient ceased simulating *any* symptoms of abnormality. In some cases, there was a brief period of mild nervousness and anxiety, since none of the pseudopatients really believed that they would be admitted so easily. Indeed, their shared fear was that they would be immediately exposed as frauds and greatly embarrassed. Moreover, many of them had never visited a psychiatric ward; even those who had, nevertheless had some genuine fears about what might happen to them. Their nervousness, then, was quite appropriate to the novelty of the hospital setting, and it abated rapidly.

Apart from that short-lived nervousness, the pseudopatient behaved on the ward as he "normally" behaved. The pseudopatient spoke to patients and staff as he might ordinarily. Because there is uncommonly little to do on a psychiatric ward,

---

[2] Beyond the personal difficulties that the pseudopatient is likely to experience in the hospital, there are legal and social ones that, combined, require considerable attention before entry. For example, once admitted to a psychiatric institution, it is difficult, if not impossible, to be discharged on short notice, state law to the contrary notwithstanding. I was not sensitive to these difficulties at the outset of the project, nor to the personal and situational emergencies that can arise, but later a writ of habeas corpus was prepared for each of the entering pseudopatients and an attorney was kept "on call" during every hospitalization. I am grateful to John Kaplan and Robert Bartels for legal advice and assistance in these matters.

[3] However distasteful such concealment is, it was a necessary first step to examining these questions. Without concealment, there would have been no way to know how valid these experiences were; nor was there any way of knowing whether whatever detections occurred were a tribute to the diagnostic acumen of the staff or to the hospital's rumor network. Obviously, since my concerns are general ones that cut across individual hospitals and staffs, I have respected their anonymity and have eliminated clues that might lead to their identification.

he attempted to engage others in conversation. When asked by staff how he was feeling, he indicated that he was fine, that he no longer experienced symptoms. He responded to instructions from attendants, to calls for medication (which was not swallowed), and to dining-hall instructions. Beyond such activities as were available to him on the admissions ward, he spent his time writing down his observations about the ward, its patients, and the staff. Initially these notes were written "secretly," but as it soon became clear that no one much cared, they were subsequently written on standard tablets of paper in such public places as the dayroom. No secret was made of these activities.

The pseudopatient, very much as a true psychiatric patient, entered a hospital with no foreknowledge of when he would be discharged. Each was told that he would have to get out by his own devices, essentially by convincing the staff that he was sane. The psychological stresses associated with hospitalization were considerable, and all but one of the pseudopatients desired to be discharged almost immediately after being admitted. They were, therefore, motivated not only to behave sanely, but to be paragons of cooperation. That their behavior was in no way disruptive is confirmed by nursing reports, which have been obtained on most of the patients. These reports uniformly indicate that the patients were "friendly," "cooperative," and "exhibited no abnormal indications."

THE NORMAL ARE NOT DETECTABLY SANE

Despite their public "show" of sanity, the pseudopatients were never detected. Admitted, except in one case, with a diagnosis of schizophrenia,[4] each was discharged with a diagnosis of schizophrenia "in remission." The label "in remission" should in no way be dismissed as a formality, for at no time during any hospitalization had any question been

raised about any pseudopatient's simulation. Nor are there any indications in the hospital records that the pseudopatient's status was suspect. Rather the evidence is strong that, once labeled schizophrenic, the pseudopatient was stuck with that label. If the pseudopatient was to be discharged, he must naturally be "in remission"; but he was not sane, nor, in the institution's view, had he ever been sane.

The uniform failure to recognize sanity cannot be attributed to the quality of the hospitals, for, although there were considerable variations among them, several are considered excellent. Nor can it be alleged that there was simply not enough time to observe the pseudopatients. Length of hospitalization ranged from 7 to 52 days, with an average of 19 days. The pseudopatients were not, in fact, carefully observed, but this failure clearly speaks more to traditions within psychiatric hospitals than to lack of opportunity.

Finally, it cannot be said that the failure to recognize the pseudopatients' sanity was due to the fact that they were not behaving sanely. While there was clearly some tension present in all of them, their daily visitors could detect no serious behavioral consequences—nor, indeed, could other patients. It was quite common for the patients to "detect" the pseudopatients' sanity. During the first three hospitalizations, when accurate counts were kept, 35 of a total of 118 patients on the admissions ward voiced their suspicions, some vigorously. "You're not crazy. You're a journalist, or a professor [referring to the continual note-taking]. You're checking up on the hospital." While most of the patients were reassured by the pseudopatient's insistence that he had been sick before he came in but was fine now, some continued to believe that the pseudopatient was sane throughout his hospitalization.[5] The fact that the patients often recognized normality when staff did not raises important questions.

---

[4] Interestingly, of the 12 admissions, 11 were diagnosed as schizophrenic and one, with the identical symptomatology, as manic-depressive psychosis. This diagnosis has a more favorable prognosis, and it was given by the only private hospital in our sample.

[5] It is possible, of course, that patients have quite broad latitudes in diagnosis and therefore are inclined to call many people sane, even those whose behavior is patently aberrant. However, although we have no hard data on this matter, it was our distinct impression that this was not the case. In many instances, patients not only singled us out for attention, but came to imitate our behaviors and styles.

Failure to detect sanity during the course of hospitalization may be due to the fact that physicians operate with a strong bias toward what statisticians call the type 2 error. This is to say that physicians are more inclined to call a healthy person sick (a false positive, type 2) than a sick person healthy (a false negative, type 1). The reasons for this are not hard to find: It is clearly more dangerous to misdiagnose illness than health. Better to err on the side of caution, to suspect illness even among the healthy.

But what holds for medicine does not hold equally well for psychiatry. Medical illnesses, while unfortunate, are not commonly pejorative. Psychiatric diagnoses, on the contrary, carry with them personal, legal, and social stigmas (Cumming and Cumming 1965; Farina and Ring 1965; Freeman and Simmons 1963; Johannsen 1969; Linksy 1970). It was therefore important to see whether the tendency toward diagnosing the sane insane could be reversed. The following experiment was arranged at a research and teaching hospital whose staff had heard these findings but doubted that such an error could occur in their hospital. The staff was informed that at some time during the following 3 months, one or more pseudopatients would attempt to be admitted into the psychiatric hospital. Each staff member was asked to rate each patient who presented himself at admissions or on the ward according to the likelihood that the patient was a pseudopatient. A 10-point scale was used, with a 1 and 2 reflecting high confidence that the patient was a pseudopatient.

Judgments were obtained on 193 patients who were admitted for psychiatric treatment. All staff who had had sustained contact with or primary responsibility for the patient—attendants, nurses, psychiatrists, physicians, and psychologists—were asked to make judgments. Forty-one patients were alleged, with high confidence, to be pseudopatients by at least one member of the staff. Twenty-three were considered suspect by at least one psychiatrist. Nineteen were suspected by one psychiatrist *and* one other staff member. Actually, no genuine pseudopatient (at least from my group) presented himself during this period.

The experiment is instructive. It indicates that the tendency to designate sane people as insane can be reversed when the stakes (in this case, prestige and diagnostic acumen) are high. But what can be said of the 19 people who were suspected of being "sane" by one psychiatrist and another staff member? Were these people truly "sane," or was it rather the case that in the course of avoiding the type 2 error the staff tended to make more errors of the first sort—calling the crazy "sane"? There is no way of knowing. But one thing is certain: Any diagnostic process that lends itself so readily to massive errors of this sort cannot be a very reliable one.

THE STICKINESS OF PSYCHODIAGNOSTIC LABELS

Beyond the tendency to call the healthy sick—a tendency that accounts better for diagnostic behavior on admission than it does for such behavior after a lengthy period of exposure—the data speak to the massive role of labeling in psychiatric assessment. Having once been labeled schizophrenic, there is nothing the pseudopatient can do to overcome the tag. The tag profoundly colors others' perceptions of him and his behavior.

From one viewpoint, these data are hardly surprising, for it has long been known that elements are given meaning by the context in which they occur. Gestalt psychology made this point vigorously, and Asch (1946, 1952) demonstrated that there are "central" personality traits (such as "warm" versus "cold") which are so powerful that they markedly color the meaning of other information in forming an impression of a given personality. "Insane," "schizophrenic," "manic-depressive," and "crazy" are probably among the most powerful of such central traits. Once a person is designated abnormal, all of his other behaviors and characteristics are colored by that label. Indeed, that label is so powerful that many of the pseudopatients' normal behaviors were overlooked entirely or profoundly misinterpreted.

All pseudopatients took extensive notes publicly. Under ordinary circumstances, such behavior would have raised questions in the minds of observers, as, in fact, it did among patients. Indeed, it seemed so certain that the notes would elicit suspicion that elaborate precautions were taken to remove them from the ward each day. But the precautions proved needless. The closest any staff member came to questioning these notes occurred when one pseudopatient asked his physician what kind of medication he was receiving and began to write down the response. "You needn't write it," he was told gently. "If you have trouble remembering, just ask me again."

If no questions were asked of the pseudopatients, how was their writing interpreted? Nursing records for three patients indicate that the writing was seen as an aspect of their pathological behavior. "Patient engages in writing behavior" was the daily nursing comment on one of the pseudopatients who was never questioned about his writing. Given that the patient is in the hospital, he must be psychologically disturbed. And given that he is disturbed, continuous writing must be a behavioral manifestation of that disturbance, perhaps a subset of the compulsive behaviors that are sometimes correlated with schizophrenia.

The notes kept by pseudopatients are full of patient behaviors that were misinterpreted by well-intentioned staff. Often enough, a patient would go "berserk" because he had, wittingly or unwittingly, been mistreated by, say, an attendant. A nurse coming upon the scene would rarely inquire even cursorily into the environmental stimuli of the patient's behavior. Rather, she assumed that his upset derived from his pathology, not from his present interactions with other staff members. Occasionally, the staff might assume that the patient's family (especially when they had recently visited) or other patients had stimulated the outburst. But never were the staff found to assume that one of themselves or the structure of the hospital had anything to do with a patient's behavior. One psychiatrist pointed to a group of patients who were sitting outside the cafeteria entrance half an hour before lunchtime. To a group of young residents he indicated that such behavior was characteristic of

the oral-acquisitive nature of the syndrome. It seemed not to occur to him that there were very few things to anticipate in a psychiatric hospital besides eating.

A psychiatric label has a life and an influence of its own. Once the impression has been formed that the patient is schizophrenic, the expectation is that he will continue to be schizophrenic. When a sufficient amount of time has passed, during which the patient has done nothing bizarre, he is considered to be in remission and available for discharge. But the label endures beyond discharge, with the unconfirmed expectation that he will behave as a schizophrenic again. Such labels, conferred by mental health professionals, are as influential on the patient as they are on his relatives and friends, and it should not surprise anyone that the diagnosis acts on all of them as a self-fulfilling prophecy. Eventually, the patient himself accepts the diagnosis, with all of its surplus meanings and expectations, and behaves accordingly.

The inferences to be made from these matters are quite simple. Much as Zigler and Phillips (1961) have demonstrated that there is enormous overlap in the symptoms presented by patients who have been variously diagnosed, so there is enormous overlap in the behaviors of the sane and the insane. The sane are not "sane" all of the time. We lose our tempers "for no good reason." We are occasionally depressed or anxious, again for no good reason. And we may find it difficult to get along with one or another person—again for no reason that we can specify. Similarly, the insane are not always insane. Indeed, it was the impression of the pseudopatients while living with them that they were sane for long periods of time—that the bizarre behaviors upon which their diagnoses were allegedly predicated constituted only a small fraction of their total behavior. If it makes no sense to label ourselves permanently depressed on the basis of an occasional depression, then it takes better evidence than is presently available to label all patients insane or schizophrenic on the basis of bizarre behaviors or cognitions. It seems more useful, as Mischel (1968) has pointed out, to limit our discussions to *behaviors,* the stimuli that provoke them, and their correlates.

THE EXPERIENCE OF PSYCHIATRIC HOSPITALIZATION

The term "mental illness" is of recent origin. It was coined by people who were humane in their inclinations and who wanted very much to raise the station of (and the public's sympathies toward) the psychologically disturbed from that of witches and "crazies" to one that was akin to the physically ill. And they were at least partially successful, for the treatment of the mentally ill *has* improved considerably over the years. But while treatment has improved, it is doubtful that people really regard the mentally ill in the same way that they view the physically ill. A broken leg is something one recovers from, but mental illness allegedly endures forever.[6] A broken leg does not threaten the observer, but a crazy schizophrenic? There is by now a host of evidence that attitudes toward the mentally ill are characterized by fear, hostility, aloofness, suspicion, and dread (Sarbin and Mancuso 1970; Sarbin 1967; Nunnally 1961). The mentally ill are society's lepers.

That such attitudes infect the general population is perhaps not surprising, only upsetting. But that they affect the professionals—attendants, nurses, physicians, psychologists, and social workers—who treat and deal with the mentally ill is more disconcerting, both because such attitudes are self-evidently pernicious and because they are unwitting. Most mental health professionals would insist that they are sympathetic toward the mentally ill, that they are neither avoidant nor hostile. But it is more likely that an exquisite ambivalence characterizes their relations with psychiatric patients, such that their avowed impulses are only part of their entire attitude. Negative attitudes are

there too and can easily be detected. Such attitudes should not surprise us. They are the natural offspring of the labels patients wear and the places in which they are found.

Consider the structure of the typical psychiatric hospital. Staff and patients are strictly segregated. Staff have their own living space, including their dining facilities, bathrooms, and assembly places. The glassed quarters that contain the professional staff, which the pseudopatients came to call "the cage," sit out on every dayroom. The staff emerge primarily for caretaking purposes—to give medication, to conduct a therapy or group meeting, to instruct or reprimand a patient. Otherwise, staff keep to themselves, almost as if the disorder that afflicts their charges is somehow catching.

So much is patient-staff segregation the rule that, for four public hospitals in which an attempt was made to measure the degree to which staff and patients mingle, it was necessary to use "time out of the staff cage" as the operational measure. While it was not the case that all time spent out of the cage was spent mingling with patients (attendants, for example, would occasionally emerge to watch television in the dayroom), it was the only way in which one could gather reliable data on time for measuring.

The average amount of time spent by attendants outside of the cage was 11.3 percent (range, 3 to 52 percent). This figure does not represent only time spent mingling with patients, but also includes time spent on such chores as folding laundry, supervising patients while they shave, directing ward clean-up, and sending patients to off-ward activities. It was the relatively rare attendant who spent time talking with patients or playing games with them. It proved impossible to obtain a "percent mingling time" for nurses, since the amount of time they spent out of the cage was too brief. Rather, we counted instances of emergence from the cage. On the average, daytime nurses emerged from the cage 11.5 times per shift, including instances when they left the ward entirely (range, 4 to 39 times). Late afternoon and night nurses were

---

[6] The most recent and unfortunate instance of this tenet is that of Senator Thomas Eagleton.

even less available, emerging on the average 9.4 times per shift (range, 4 to 41 times). Data on early morning nurses, who arrived usually after midnight and departed at 8 a.m., are not available because patients were asleep during most of this period.

Physicians, especially psychiatrists, were even less available. They were rarely seen on the wards. Quite commonly, they would be seen only when they arrived and departed, with the remaining time being spent in their offices or in the cage. On the average, physicians emerged on the ward 6.7 times per day (range, 1 to 17 times). It proved difficult to make an accurate estimate in this regard, since physicians often maintained hours that allowed them to come and go at different times.

POWERLESSNESS AND DEPERSONALIZATION

The data I have presented do not do justice to the rich daily encounters that grew up around matters of depersonalization and avoidance. I have records of patients who were beaten by staff for the sin of having initiated verbal contact. During my own experience, for example, one patient was beaten in the presence of other patients for having approached an attendant and told him, "I like you." Occasionally, punishment meted out to patients for misdemeanors seemed so excessive that it could not be justified by the most radical interpretations of psychiatric canon. Nevertheless, they appeared to go unquestioned. Tempers were often short. A patient who had not heard a call for medication would be roundly excoriated, and the morning attendants would often wake patients with, "Come on, you m .... f .... s, out of bed!"

Neither anecdotal nor "hard" data can convey the overwhelming sense of powerlessness which invades the individual as he is continually exposed to the depersonalization of the psychiatric hospital. It hardly matters *which* psychiatric hospital—the excellent public ones and the very plush private hospital were better than the rural and shabby ones

in this regard, but, again, the features that psychiatric hospitals had in common overwhelmed by far their apparent differences.

Powerlessness was evident everywhere. The patient is deprived of many of his legal rights by dint of his psychiatric commitment (Wexler and Scoville 1971). He is shorn of credibility by virtue of his psychiatric label. His freedom of movement is restricted. He cannot initiate contact with the staff, but may only respond to such overtures as they make. Personal privacy is minimal. Patient quarters and possessions can be entered and examined by any staff member, for whatever reason. His personal history and anguish is available to any staff member (often including the "gray lady" and "candy striper" volunteer) who chooses to read his folder, regardless of their therapeutic relationship to him. His personal hygiene and waste evacuation are often monitored. The water closets may have no doors.

At times, depersonalization reached such proportions that pseudopatients had the sense that they were invisible, or at least unworthy of account. Upon being admitted, I and other pseudopatients took the initial physical examinations in a semi-public room, where staff members went about their own business as if we were not there.

On the ward, attendants delivered verbal and occasionally serious physical abuse to patients in the presence of other observing patients, some of whom (the pseudopatients) were writing it all down. Abusive behavior, on the other hand, terminated quite abruptly when other staff members were known to be coming. Staff are credible witnesses. Patients are not.

A nurse unbuttoned her uniform to adjust her brassiere in the presence of an entire ward of viewing men. One did not have the sense that she was being seductive. Rather, she didn't notice us. A group of staff persons might point to a patient in the dayroom and discuss him animatedly, as if he were not there.

One illuminating instance of depersonalization and invisibility occurred with regard to medications. All told, the pseudopatients were administered nearly 2,100 pills, including Elavil, Stelazine, Compazine, and Thorazine, to name but a few. (That such a variety of medications should have been administered to patients presenting identical symptoms is itself worthy of note.) Only two were swallowed. The rest were either pocketed or deposited in the toilet. The pseudopatients were not alone in this. Although I have no precise records on how many patients rejected their medications, the pseudopatients frequently found the medications of other patients in the toilet before they deposited their own. As long as they were cooperative, their behavior and the pseudopatients' own in this matter, as in other important matters, went unnoticed throughout.

THE CONSEQUENCES OF LABELING AND DEPERSONALIZATION

We continue to label patients "schizophrenic," "manic-depressive," and "insane," as if in those words we had captured the essence of understanding. The facts of the matter are that we have known for a long time that diagnoses are often not useful or reliable, but we have nevertheless continued to use them. We now know that we cannot distinguish insanity from sanity. It is depressing to consider how that information will be used.

Not merely depressing, but frightening. How many people, one wonders, are sane but not recognized as such in our psychiatric institutions? How many have been needlessly stripped of their privileges of citizenship, from the right to vote and drive to that of handling their own accounts? How many have feigned insanity in order to avoid the criminal consequences of their behavior, and, conversely, how many would rather stand trial than live interminably in a psychiatric hospital—but are wrongly thought to be mentally ill? How many have been stigmatized by well-intentioned, but nevertheless erroneous, diagnoses? On the last point, recall again that a "type 2 error" in psychiatric diagnosis does not have the same consequences it does in medical diagnosis. A diagnosis of cancer that has been found to be in error is cause

for celebration. But psychiatric diagnoses are rarely found to be in error. The label sticks, a mark of inadequacy forever.

Finally, how many patinets might be "sane" outside the psychiatric hospital but seem insane in it—not because craziness resides in them, as it were, but because they are responding to a bizarre setting, one that may be unique to institutions which harbor nether people? Goffman calls the process of socialization to such institutions "mortification"—an apt metaphor that includes the processes of depersonalization that have been described here. And while it is impossible to know whether the pseudopatients' responses to these processes are characteristic of all inmates—they were, after all, not real patients—it is difficult to believe that these processes of socialization to a psychiatric hospital provide useful attitudes or habits of response for living in the "real world."

SUMMARY AND CONCLUSIONS

It is clear that we cannot distinguish the sane from the insane in psychiatric hospitals. The hospital itself imposes a special environment in which the meanings of behavior can easily be misunderstood. The consequences to patients hospitalized in such an environment—the powerlessness, depersonalization, segregation, mortification, and self-labeling—seem undoubtedly counter-therapeutic.

I do not, even now, understand this problem well enough to perceive solutions. But two matters seem to have some promise. The first concerns the proliferation of community mental health facilities, of crisis intervention centers, of the human potential movement, and of behavior therapies that, for all of their own problems, tend to avoid psychiatric labels, to focus on specific problems and behaviors, and to retain the individual in a relatively non-perjorative environment. Clearly, to the extent that we refrain from sending the distressed to insane places, our impressions of them are less likely to be distorted. (The risk of distorted perceptions, it seems to me, is always present, since we are much more sensitive to an individual's behaviors and verbalizations than we are to the subtle contextual stimuli that often promote them. At issue here is a matter of magnitude. And, as I have shown, the magnitude of distortion is exceedingly high in the extreme context that is a psychiatric hospital.)

I and the other pseudopatients in the psychiatric setting had distinctly negative reactions. We do not pretend to describe the subjective experiences of true patients. Theirs may be different from ours, particularly with the passage of time and the necessary process of adaptation to one's environment. But we can and do speak to the relatively more objective indices of treatment within the hospital. It could be a mistake, and a very unfortunate one, to consider that what happened to us derived from malice or stupidity on the part of the staff. Quite the contrary, our overwhelming impression of them was of people who really cared, who were committed and who were uncommonly intelligent. Where they failed, as they sometimes did painfully, it would be more accurate to attribute those failures to the environment in which they, too, found themselves than to personal callousness. Their perceptions and behavior were controlled by the situation, rather than being motivated by a malicious disposition. In a more benign environment, one that was less attached to global diagnosis, their behaviors and judgments might have been more benign and effective.

REFERENCES

Asch, S. E. 1946. *J. Abnorm. Soc. Psychol.* 41:258.
———. 1952. *Social Psychology.* 1949. New York: Prentice Hall.
Ash, P. 1949. *Abnorm. Soc. Psychol.* 44:272.
Beck, A. T. 1962. *Amer. J. Psychiat.* 119:210.
Benedict, R. 1934. *J. Gen. Psychol.* 10:59.
Boisen, A. T. 1938. *Psychiatry* 2:233.
Cumming, J., and E. Cumming. 1965. *Community Ment. Health* 1:135.
Farina, A., and K. Ring. 1965. *J. Abnorm. Psychol.* 70:47.
Freeman, H. E., and O. G. Simmons. 1963. *The Mental Patient Comes Home.* New York: Wiley.
Freudenberg, R. K., and J. P. Robertson. 1956. *A.M.A. Arch. Neurol. Psychiatr.* 76:14.
Johannsen, W. J. 1969. *Ment. Hygiene* 53:218.
Kreitman, N. 1961. *J. Ment. Sci.* 107:876.
Linsky, A. S. 1970. *Soc. Psychiat.* 5:166.
Mischel, W. 1968. *Personality and Assessment.* New York: Wiley.
Nunnally, J. C., Jr. 1961. *Popular Conceptions of Mental Health.* New York: Holt, Rinehart & Winston.
Sarbin, T. R., and J. C. Mancuso. 1970. *J. Clin. Consult. Psychol.* 35:159.
Schmitt, H. O., and C. P. Fonda. 1956. *J. Abnorm. Soc. Psychol.* 52:262.
Seeman, W. 1953. *J. Nerv. Ment. Dis.* 118:541.
Wexler, D. B., and S. E. Scoville. 1971. *Ariz. Law Rev.* 13:1.
Zigler, E., and L. Phillips. 1961. *J. Abnorm. Soc. Psychol.* 63:69.
Zubin, J. 1967. *Annu. Rev. Psychol.* 18:373.

STUDY QUESTIONS

1. Drawing on the article by Peter Conrad and Joseph Schneider, discuss the main consequences of the medicalization of deviance—for the deviant individuals, for how these deviants are perceived by others, and for the medical profession itself.
2. Whose interests are served by medicalizing deviance, according to Conrad and Schneider?
3. In what ways does D. L. Rosenhan's research on mental hospitals lend support to labeling theory?
4. Are Rosenhan's conclusions about insanity fully convincing, or could other conclusions be reached on the basis of his observations?

POLITICS AND THE CONTROL OF DEVIANCE

Introduction

Deviance and control are routinely fought over in the political arena. One day the U.S. Supreme Court issues a ruling on abortion, sparking denunciation from the losing side. The next day, Congress rejects the president's gun control legislation, and the White House criticizes the legislators for being handmaidens of the National Rifle Association. The tobacco industry is increasingly vilified by the federal government; Mothers Against Drunk Driving lobby the halls of Congress for tougher drunk driving legislation; and police involvement in "racial profiling" of African Americans has become a national controversy. These are but a few examples that reveal how *contested* deviance and control can be and why it is crucial to study the political arena for a full understanding of the topic. The articles featured in this section show how political variables shape perceptions of deviant behavior as well as changes over time in policies regarding the control of deviance.

American drug policy has always been highly politicized, but policies have changed over time. The "zero-tolerance" policy of universal enforcement against all drug offenders, popular in America since the mid-1980s, stands in contrast to some alternative approaches that date back just a few decades. In 1972 a blue-ribbon commission appointed by President Richard Nixon recommended the decriminalization of marijuana possession (National Commission 1972). Nixon rejected the recommendation, but 11 states subsequently decriminalized the possession of small quantities of marijuana. In "Politics of Marijuana Decriminalization" Albert DiChiara and John Galliher examine the political dynamics of decriminalization. They examine why marijuana possession laws were relaxed in some states and not in others in the 1970s, and why drug penalties grew harsher in the 1980s.

Carole Vance observed the proceedings of the 1986 Commission on Pornography, which was created by Attorney General Edwin Meese. In her article, "The Meese Commission on the Road," she faults the commission for approaching the subject with strong biases and for its lack of fairness during its hearings. The commission produced a report that had a far-reaching impact on the porn industry in America, and it demonstrates how quickly and radically government policy can change with respect to the sex industry. The Reagan administration accepted the commission's recommendations and the Justice Department implemented many of them (Weitzer 2000).

Prostitution is another form of deviance that has generated controversy in recent years, at the local level rather than the national level.

Alternatives have been proposed to the prevailing policy of criminalization. Ronald Weitzer's article, "Prostitution Control in America," evaluates the policies of legalization and decriminalization, and argues that a third alternative (a "two-track policy") may be superior to the others. Guided by the principle of harm reduction, the two-track policy would involve different approaches to street prostitution and indoor prostitution.

REFERENCES

National Commission on Marijuana and Drug Abuse. 1972. *Marijuana: A Signal of Misunderstanding.* Washington, DC: Government Printing Office.

Weitzer, Ronald. 2000. "Why We Need More Research on Sex Work." In R. Weitzer (ed.), *Sex for Sale: Prostitution, Pornography, and the Sex Industry.* New York: Routledge.

Politics of Marihuana Decriminalization

Albert DiChiara and John F. Galliher

Many have observed that the 1970s was a period when a wide variety of deviant groups and their supporters began to mobilize to challenge popular stereotypes and to demand an end to discriminatory treatment (see, e.g., Weitzer 1991). The decriminalization of marihuana represents one part of this pattern. Previous research on the origins of criminal laws justifiably has been criticized for analysis of isolated case studies of one particular law, which Hagan (1980) claims has resulted in confusion in attempts to explain a law's passage. The study reported here attempts to avoid this problem by analysis of the legislative process in 11 states which, over a five-year period, removed jail

From *Law and Society Review* 28, No. 1 (1994). pp. 41–77. ©1994 by The Law and Society Association. Reprinted by permission of the Law and Society Association.

sentences for possession of small amounts of marihuana. These laws, sometimes collectively referred to as "decriminalization," often specify that offenders are to be issued summons like those for traffic offenses rather than being taken into custody.

We demonstrate that while decriminalization laws resolved certain conflicts, the legislation produced additional conflicts or moral dissonance all its own when behavior considered by some to be immoral was no longer severely punished, thereby setting the stage for the stalling of the movement toward decriminalization. Our view is that decriminalization as a policy alternative, and marihuana decriminalization in particular, represented a unique historical moment in the evolution of criminal sanctions. The ideological, social, and political basis for decriminalization opened a narrow and tenuous "policy window," and thus the viability of this policy was limited and quickly supplanted by de facto decriminalization. We also demonstrate that the effects of these laws were primarily symbolic, and thus it should not be surprising that another type of symbolic response, de facto decriminalization, was a commonly accepted alternative that addressed conflicting social-class and political interests more adequately than statutory change. According to these formulations, a theory of decriminalization and its consequent contradictions must include consideration of the national mood, political leadership, concerns of interest groups, especially law enforcement and drug users, as well as public opinion.

ESTABLISHING MORAL DISSONANCE

During the first half of the 20th century, marihuana use was concentrated among Latin Americans (LaGuardia Commission on Marihuana 1944), African Americans, the Greenwich Village "beat" community, and jazz musicians (Polsky 1967). These usage patterns are of great significance, for research on alcohol prohibitions (Gusfield 1963), opium laws (Morgan 1978), and other drug legislation (Musto 1973; Helmer 1975) indicates that the most severe punishment is reserved for those instances where a substance is publicly associated with a threatening minority group. During the 1960s, however, patterns of marihuana use began to change. By 1970 Goode reported survey data indicating that marihuana smokers were likely to be urban, college graduates in their early 20s. By 1977, 60% of those aged 18–25 had used this substance (Abelson & Fishburne 1977). A survey in 1979 (Fishburne et al.) indicated that 68% of those aged 18–25 reported that they had used marihuana. In addition, 69% of whites, 62% of all others, and 73% of those with college training had used the drug. These figures indicate not only that marihuana use increased dramatically during the 1970s among those 18–25, but that the increase especially occurred among middle-class, college-educated whites—a totally different picture from what existed during the 1930s. These demographic changes in the typical marihuana user provided the key social context for the reform of marihuana laws.

Given what is known about the relationship between patterns of drug use and penalty structures, it was not completely surprising that, coincident with these changing patterns of marihuana use, several states reduced marihuana possession penalties to misdemeanor levels, among them Nebraska (Galliher et al. 1974) and Utah (Galliher & Basilick 1979). The increasing risks of arrest for affluent young people were critical ingredients in the passage of these new laws, especially in homogeneous states where drug use was not associated with any local minority group (Galliher et al. 1974; Galliher & Basilick 1979). A statewide survey in Utah revealed widespread marihuana use by young people of nearly all ages and all social classes (Galliher & Basilick 1979:291): "Economic status is no deterrent to obtaining drugs and youngsters of all economic levels are involved," the survey concluded. An attorney who supported reduction in drug penalties explained to the Utah state senate: "These are your kids, after all." Another attorney involved in the lobbying effort said: "We also pointed out that the courts would be reluctant to convict in marihuana possession cases since the marihuana problem was hitting middle-class families and Mormon youth."

PUBLIC OPINION AND AGENDA SETTING

Over all, public opinion is not necessarily the most important consideration (Kingdon 1984). Those most intensely interested are specialists in a given policy arena, who often emphasize "equity and efficiency" (p. 140). Assuming the significance of moral dissonance in the enforcement of marihuana laws, the relevant values and beliefs were those of political leaders, since the general public has been divided about evenly on this issue and thereby stalemated. For example, the 1977 Gallup Poll found 53% supported decriminalization; in 1980, 52% favored the idea; in 1985, 46% did so. This deep division of opinion may reflect an ambivalence arising from a recognition that while use of marihuana may be immoral and may represent a health hazard, incarceration of marihuana users is not a reasonable response. Thus public opinion can be said to have made marihuana decriminalization a legitimate issue, but did not ensure its legislative success.

Conservative columnist William F. Buckley (1972) was among the first nationally prominent figures to endorse decriminalization. More significantly, prestigious groups and people associated with law enforcement such as the American Bar Association (MacKenzie 1973), U.S. Attorney General William Saxbe,[1] and FBI Director Clarence Kelley[2] lent their support to decriminalization. The reasons included the massive costs to law enforcement, the impossibility of deterring marihuana use, and the social cost of ruining a person's future employment opportunities with an arrest. Kelley said it might be better "not to prosecute for possession of marihuana, but spend greater attention and time on those who sell" marihuana and other drugs. First President Ford, and then President Carter, lent the prestige of their office to the cause of decriminalization, claiming that their primary motivation came from their children. President Ford claimed: "More people are hurt by criminal laws against marihuana use than are hurt by the drug itself."[3] Later President Carter asked the Congress to decriminalize marihuana possession (Wooten 1977).[4] No longer could it be said that marihuana was simply a minority-linked drug, and these changes in attitude and usage patterns were to play a role in future attempts to alter the method of its legal control. Both U.S. senators and representatives argued that middle- and upper-class college students, on the road to professional careers, should not be incarcerated for

marihuana possession because such users would lose respect for a law their experience tells them is incommensurate with the danger of the drug (Peterson 1985).

A POLICY WINDOW OPENS

Beginning in the 1960s policymakers increasingly began to view deviance as being magnified by official reactions (Empey 1978). Thus a series of programs designed to limit the negative effects of official sanctions were enacted (Olson-Raymer 1984). Among these were laws to abolish the indeterminate sentence (Dershowitz 1976), as well as laws to decriminalize status offenses in California and New York (Rubin 1985). And official opinion on marihuana reflected in government reports also began to change. Initially, during the early 1960s, and before, when the effects of marihuana were studied by government agencies, its users were often described as was stated in the President's Advisory Commission on Narcotics and Drug Abuse (1963) as "frustrated, hopeless, maladjusted" and as exhibiting "psychological dependence" (pp. 1, 4). But by the late 1960s, we see evidence of the beginnings of moral dissonance when marihuana was described by the President's Commission on Law Enforcement and Administration of Justice (1968:13) as merely a "mild hallucinogen" and by the 1970s a federal commission described the marihuana user as "essentially indistinguishable from their non-marihuana-using peers by any fundamental criterion other than their marihuana use" (National Commission on Marihuana & Drug Abuse [NCMDA] 1972:41). The Comprehensive Drug Abuse and Prevention Act of 1970 reduced the federal marihuana possession penalty to a misdemeanor and also required reports to Congress on marihuana and other drugs.

In accordance with the latter provision of this legislation, in 1972 the NCMDA, drawing on advice from experts in a variety of fields appointed by President Nixon, released its report. It minimized the health risks of marihuana use and urged that public possession of one ounce or less of marihuana (the usual purchase amount) be

---

[1] "Pot Statement Expected," *Columbus Evening Dispatch*, 15 Nov. 1974, p. B9.

[2] "Get Sellers, Kelley Says," *Atlanta Constitution*, 24 June 1975, p. 6A.

[3] *Columbus Evening Dispatch*, 15 Nov. 1974 (cited in note 1).

[4] "Carter Asks Congress to Decriminalize Marihuana Possession; Cocaine Law Is Studied," *New York Times*, 15 March 1977, sec. 1, p. 15; "Administration Urges Marihuana Decriminalization," *South Mississippi Sun* (Biloxi-Gulfport), 15 March 1977.

TABLE 6-1

PROVISIONS OF STATE MARIHUANA POSSESSION DECRIMINALIZATION LAWS

State	Year	Title of Law	Maximum Penalty	Amount of Marihuana
Oregon	1973	Violation	Up to $100—1st offense	Up to 1 oz.
Alaska	1975	Misdemeanor	Up to $100	Up to 1 oz. (in public)
Maine	1975	Civil violation	Up to $200	"Usable Amount"
Colorado	1975	Petty offense	Up to $100	Up to 1 oz.
California	1975	Misdemeanor	Up to $100	Up to 1 oz.
Ohio	1975	Minor misdemeanor	Up to $100	Up to 100 grams
Minnesota	1976	Petty misdemeanor	Up to $100—1st offense	"Small Amount"
Mississippi	1977	Noncriminal	$100–$250—1st offense	Up to 1 oz.
New York	1977	Violation	Up to $100—1st offense	Up to 25 grams
N. Carolina	1977	Misdemeanor	Up to $100—1st offense	Up to 1 oz.
Nebraska	1978	Civil offense	$100—1st offense	Up to 1 oz.

decriminalized, subject only to confiscation, and that public use remain a criminal offense punishable by a $100 fine. Surveys conducted by the commission found that only a minority of prosecutors and judges viewed marihuana possession penalties as a deterrent and that police seldom attempted to seek out such law violators. Instead these surveys found that law enforcement viewed such prohibitions as too costly, claimed they created discrimination in enforcement, and ruined the lives of those arrested. At this point there seemed to be no difference between the demands of affluent marihuana users and the requirements of law enforcement efficiency. Much as the 1931 report of the Wickersham commission was instrumental in discrediting national prohibition of alcohol by describing the law as both ineffective and the source of political corruption (Kerr 1985), the key triggering event in decriminalization was the 1972 NCMDA Report. Beginning the next year and extending into 1978, 11 states passed laws modeled closely after its recommendations (Table 6-1).

DATA SOURCES

We reviewed all issues of a major daily newspaper in each state we studied for a year prior to, and immediately after, the passage of the decriminalization law to assess the type of political environment in which each law passed. In addition, we secured numerous articles that dealt with marihuana and marihuana offenses from private collections and library holdings in the states involved. We also explored legislative records of floor debate and/or public hearings. The quality and amount of such information available varied greatly across the states, but at least some such information was available for all states. In Mississippi and North Carolina we conducted interviews with key informants to supplement our analysis of existing records that appeared to give an incomplete picture of the legislative process. In addition, we contacted the legislatures in all states that did not decriminalize marihuana to locate existing records of the introduction of relevant bills, as well as committee hearings and floor debate on any marihuana reforms.

THE PUZZLING PATTERNS OF MARIHUANA DECRIMINALIZATION

A survey of some of the earliest of these marihuana laws found great variation in the legislative process of decriminalization from state to state, with no apparent logic to the pattern (National Governors' Conference 1977). Decriminalization in Maine, California, and Ohio was preceded by extensive legislative staff research, but such research was also conducted in New Jersey where the legislation failed. In Ohio and Maine decriminalization was part of an overall criminal code revision that diverted attention, to a degree, from the marihuana penalty changes. But in Colorado and California successful decriminalization bills stood alone, and in Iowa and New Jersey decriminalization bills failed despite being part of a general criminal code revision. In Minnesota, Ohio, and California, the survey reported an individual or interest group was of primary importance, but in other states they were not important factors. The press was typically supportive of decriminalization, but this was true in states that passed, as well as those that did not pass, such laws. The severity of existing penalties was an important influence in California and Colorado, but in Minnesota experience with previous penalty reductions made decriminalization more palatable. In none of these states did the National Organization for the Reform of Marihuana Laws (NORML), the only national organization lobbying for decriminalization, make a visible and constructive contribution to the decriminalization process. The limited significance of this organization is apparently a result of the ineptitude of its leadership (Anderson 1981). Interest groups cannot always control the course of the debate; in addition, the efforts of opposing interest groups often cancel each other out (Kingdon 1984).

The states that passed decriminalization laws had quite diverse political, cultural, and demographic characteristics. Some of these states (Minnesota, Oregon, and New York) are well-known liberal enclaves. But some are conservative (e.g., Nebraska, Mississippi, and North Carolina). And every region of the nation is represented: the West (California, Oregon, Colorado, and Alaska); the East (Maine and New York); the Middle West (Nebraska, Minnesota, and Ohio); and the South (Mississippi and North Carolina). There are populous states (Ohio, California, and New York) as well as sparsely populated states (Maine, Nebraska, and Alaska). Some of the states have heterogeneous populations, with

sizable numbers of African Americans or Hispanics (among them New York, California, Mississippi, and North Carolina). Some states are relatively homogeneous (e.g., Oregon, Minnesota, Nebraska, and Maine; U.S. Bureau of the Census 1980). These variations in the demographic characteristics of decriminalization states are curious because some research leads us to believe that the demographic characteristics of a state will, to a considerable extent, determine the local response to drug use (Musto 1973; Galliher et al. 1974; Galliher & Basilick 1979). These puzzling patterns parallel the variations across the states in the process by which decriminalization laws were passed.

DECRIMINALIZATION HISTORIES

Routine Policy Change

The decriminalization policy window was open only five years and ultimately ended with a significant shift in the national mood and change in presidential administrations. Nonetheless, the legislation begun in the early 1970s seemed full of promise for providing significant policy changes. Oregon was the first state to pass a decriminalization law—in 1973. Before the law was changed, conviction for possession of less than one ounce of marihuana was a misdemeanor and could be punished with a $1,000 fine, a one-year sentence, or both.[5] Possessing more than one ounce was a felony, and could incur a $2,500 fine and/or a 10-year sentence. However, these penalties existed only on the statute books, and a local paper noted many instances in which they were not actually enforced, particularly against juveniles.[6] The conservative Republican hog-farmer legislator who introduced the bill in the state legislature compared

---

[5] "Obvious, Subtle Effects of Pot Using Described," *Eugene Register-Guard,* 6 Oct. 1972, p. 4A.
[6] "Marihuana Costs Man $200 Fine," *Eugene Register-Guard,* 7 March 1973, p. 4D; "Youth Pays Fine for Possessing Pot," *Eugene Register-Guard,* 9 March 1973, p. 5A; "Court Dismisses Marihuana Case," *Eugene Register-Guard,* 18 March 1973, p. 3A; "Drug Sentence Put Off One Year," *Eugene Register-Guard,* 3 April 1973, p. 4A.

marihuana's dangers and penalties with that of alcohol and other drugs:

> "Having explored all the basic components of the marihuana situation, I am convinced we could and should take steps to decriminalize its use. Prohibition was not the answer to our alcohol problem in 1919, nor is it the answer to the marihuana problem in 1973." He sat down amid an ovation (Anderson 1981:122).

Later the legislator noted that public views toward marihuana were changing and that he had received very few letters objecting to his position, while the great majority supported his stand.[7] A local prosecuting attorney announced that less emphasis would be placed on marihuana enforcement and more on hard drugs and drug trafficking. He ordered local law enforcement authorities to begin issuing citations to marihuana users instead of putting them in jail.[8] This apparently involved no political risk, as no opposition to his ideas surfaced. Later, the prosecutor testified in support of such legislation in at least four other states (Alaska, Maine, Ohio, and Minnesota), and was greeted warmly in all four.

In Ohio, the Oregon prosecutor assured legislators that decriminalization had caused no perceptible increase in the use of the drug.[9] An Ohio federal court overturned a marihuana *sale* sentence of 20–40 years as cruel and unusual, and therefore "unconstitutional" (*Downey v. Perini* 1975).[10] This court decision provided a legal mandate for new Ohio marihuana legislation. A physician was quoted as saying: "We just want to end the agony of arrest records for teenagers found with small amounts of marihuana."[11] A former police chief of

Toledo declared that the money spent on marihuana arrests was wasted.[12]

Along with U. S. Attorney General Saxbe, a Republican and an Ohio native, who as we noted above supported decriminalization,[13] there were other similar proponents in Ohio. A wealthy Republican whose family owned a Columbus (the state capital) newspaper, several television and radio stations, hotels, and much of Ohio's largest bank eventually supported the bill. He had easy access to every state official, and he drew on it when necessary. He showed a film to the state legislature about a young marihuana smoker whose parents had found some marihuana in his room. Horrified, they called the police and had him arrested to save him from the drug. He was in fact sentenced to prison where he was soon gang-raped. Then he hanged himself in his cell (Anderson 1981:166). After this presentation the bill had no trouble passing.

In Colorado the state attorney general indicated that he supported reduced marihuana penalties because marihuana cases were clogging the courts and wasting money.[14] A split state supreme court "reluctantly" upheld the conviction of four defendants for selling marihuana. Two justices asserted that when marihuana is misclassified as a narcotic, "the classification lacks a fundamental rational basis and is unreasonable and is constitutionally offensive" (*People v. Summit* 1974:855 (Lee, J., dissenting)). A *Denver Post* editorial strongly endorsed the legislative efforts to lower the marihuana penalties by reclassifying marihuana as a "dangerous drug" rather than a "narcotic."[15] The Colorado legislation was supported by conservatives, and an ultra-conservative in the senate even proposed total legalization.[16] In the senate, the

---

[7] "Drug Penalty Bill Passed by House," *Eugene Register-Guard,* 22 June 1973, p. 13A.
[8] "Hard Drug Crackdown Set," *Eugene Register-Guard,* 15 March 1973, p. 1C.
[9] "Marihuana Legislation Subject of Panel at Fair," *Columbus Evening Dispatch,* 1 Sept. 1974, p. A2.
[10] "Pot Case—Alleged Vendetta by Police Here Led to Overturning Ohio Statutes," *Cleveland Plain Dealer,* 28 July 1975, p. 14A.
[11] *Columbus Evening Dispatch,* 1 Sept. 1974 (cited in note 9).

---

[12] Ibid.
[13] *Columbus Evening Dispatch,* 15 Nov. 1974 (cited in note 1).
[14] "Marihuana Law Change Viewed—MacFarlane Supports Leniency," *Denver Post,* 16 Dec. 1974, p. 30.
[15] "Moderating Marihuana Laws" (Editorial), *Denver Post,* 27 Feb. 1975, p. 26.
[16] "Decriminalization Effort—Conservatives Back 'Pot' Proposals," *Denver Post,* 10 April 1975, p. 2.

Republican sponsor of the bill to decriminalize possession summarized the prevailing mood, admitting that marihuana was dangerous, but "any person has the right to go to hell any way he chooses so long as he doesn't hurt anybody else."[17]

In April 1975 under a new city ordinance, the Denver prosecutor started giving tickets for marihuana possession rather than making arrests. During house hearings, another Colorado prosecutor said: "We simply can no longer in the criminal justice system expend taxpayers' money and lawyers' and investigators' time chasing the pot smoker around the dormitory" (debate in the Colorado House, 20 Feb. 1975). The Denver prosecutor's office reported that in 1972–73 only 7 marihuana cases in the city ended with sentences to prison out of 2,200 marihuana-related cases, at a total cost of $1,650,000. A deputy district attorney observed that the law was selectively enforced and was "the single most destructive force in society—in terms of turning our children against the system."[18]

In Maine, the Oregon prosecutor testified once again about his state's decriminalization law in legislative hearings:

> [S]tudies indicate that use of marihuana has not increased in the state since then. Tremendous amounts of time and money have been spent trying to enforce the marihuana laws. . . . As a law enforcement officer, I am vitally concerned with the best use of the limited resources of the criminal justice system.[19]

Others testifying in favor of the revised code included a mother of seven who said several of her children had "problems because of marihuana use, but she wouldn't want to see them jailed."[20] A state legislator noted that in 1974 a total of 1,700 were arrested in the state for possession of marihuana.[21]

A former Republican state attorney general, head of a criminal code revision commission, put decriminalization in the new code. He defended a statement in the new code that marihuana was less harmful to our society than tobacco and alcohol, declaring that the latter two drugs cause many more deaths and havoc in people's lives than marihuana.[22] According to the local paper, the new code was an attempt to restrict the law "to instances where enforcement is to be encouraged and the prohibitions to be taken as representative of community judgments that are widely and strongly held . . . . Otherwise the already badly overextended law tends to squander . . . law enforcement and court resources."[23] A house member also noted that it would be easier to prove possession under this code because a civil offense is not subject to the same strict rules of evidence as are crimes.[24]

A 28 March 1975 *Kennebec Journal* editorial supported the efforts of the commission to abolish the criminal penalty for marihuana possession, "a move we have supported in the past and do again."[25]

> What hypocrites we can be without even conscious thought! We shy away from decriminalizing marihuana possession because it carries the name drug, and hug to our bosoms the cocktail hour because its image is social. Yet there are 450,000 under-21 alcoholics in this country; alcohol is responsible for one-half of traffic fatalities, accounts for one-third of all suicides and has some part in one-half of the 5,500,000 arrests made yearly. The marihuana cigarette will never match those figures, but we're afraid to look truth in the eye.[26]

---

[17] "Liberalized Laws—Senators Debate Bill on Marihuana," *Denver Post,* 2 May 1975, p. 3.

[18] "Testimony Favors Easing 'Pot' Law—Senate Judiciary Hearing," *Denver Post,* 9 April 1975, p. 18.

[19] "Pot Decriminalization Aired," *Kennebec Journal,* 28 March 1975, p. 1.

[20] Ibid., p. 2.

[21] Ibid.

[22] "Lund Defends Marihuana Decriminalization," *Kennebec Journal,* 26 March 1975, p. 25.

[23] "Criminal Code Revision: A New Balance," *Kennebec Journal,* 3 March 1975, p. 1.

[24] "Bigelow Bill Dies in House," *Kennebec Journal,* 10 June 1975, p. 10.

[25] "A Polarizing Issue" (Editorial), *Kennebec Journal,* 28 March 1975, p. 4.

[26] Ibid.

We should recall that the Governors' Conference Report on state marihuana laws observed in 1977 that previous penalty reductions made decriminalization a relatively easy process in Minnesota. A 1973 law had made the maximum penalty 90 days in jail and a $300 fine. A decriminalization bill sponsor was quoted as saying: "There are a lot of young people in my district who smoke pot. . . . Enforcement of the present law involves an awful lot of expense, and . . . people who otherwise lead perfectly normal lives go to jail."[27] Another sponsor had "seen kids subjected to the criminal justice process, seen the disruption of their lives and the threat of jail hanging over them."[28] A legislative supporter concluded:

> My main interest is to put out accurate information to the public. We've got to give them the truth. . . . We've been putting out untruthful stuff the past 100 years—so much so that kids don't believe anything. I mean we've been telling people that pot-smoking will shrink your brain and turn you into a rapist.[29]

A local judge testified at the senate hearings that he favored decriminalization because of the time it would save the courts (Minnesota Senate Judiciary Committee 1975a). And a district attorney claimed: "As a prosecutor it is my feeling that the efforts of our police departments could be better utilized in investigating more serious crimes" (Minnesota House Judiciary Committee 1975). A Minnesota sheriff agreed: "I am against marihuana, however I feel the enforcement is not always constant. The new law, the way it's set up, could be more consistent . . . I don't have a large department . . . things could be speeded up" (Minnesota Senate Judiciary Committee 1975b). And a senator observed that police look the other way "from the use of marihuana by kids" (ibid.). Also, a 1973 study discovered that only 21 perons were confined in the state for marihuana

possession, even though 40% to 50% of all Minnesota high school students had used the drug (Minnesota Senate Debate 1975).[30]

Nebraska was one of the pioneers in lowering marihuana possession penalties with a 1969 law that reduced the penalty for first-offense possession of marihuana to a maximum seven-day jail sentence; on subsequent offenses the sentence merely doubled (Galliher et al. 1974). Thus, like Minnesota's decriminalization, the move to decriminalization was not a major legislative step. A Nebraska state senator reasoned that a massive amount of police time could be saved by decriminalization: "A policeman, for the same amount of time, effort and money, could be dealing with ten or twelve individuals" (Nebraska Senate 1978). The Nebraska supreme court acknowledged that the costs of enforcing the marihuana laws exceeded the benefits (*State v. Kells* 1977).[31] A survey of rural Hall County found 57% favored decriminalization.[32] The people, the press, and the legislature in Nebraska showed little interest in this law. As one state senator argued: "Particularly [if] a minor or young person has done wrong smoking marihuana, you don't destroy their career for the rest of their life" (Nebraska Senate 1978).

Alaska was the first state to enact misdemeanor marihuana possession penalties in 1968. Alcohol and alcoholism were widely recognized as the main social problem in the state. This was true even though a local attorney estimated that half the school children in the Anchorage area had used marihuana.[33] The Republican governor claimed that he opposed legalization of marihuana, but said, "I can certainly appreciate the hypocrisy in the manner we treat booze and, by comparison,

---

[27] "Present Law Held Useless," *St. Paul Dispatch,* 21 April 1975, pp. 19, 21.
[28] "Knoll Says Law Has 'Bad Effects,' " *St. Paul Dispatch,* 21 April 1975, pp. 19, 21.
[29] Ibid.

[30] "Marihuana Law Isn't Enforced, Study Says," *St. Paul Dispatch,* 21 April 1975, pp. 19, 21.
[31] "Marihuana Arrest in Home Legal, Nebraska Supreme Court Rules," *Lincoln Journal,* 2 Nov. 1977, pp. 1, 17.
[32] "Laxer Pot Laws Said Favored," *Lincoln Journal,* 24 Feb. 1978, p. 7.
[33] "Supreme Court Receives Case on Marihuana," *Anchorage Daily Times,* 16 Oct. 1974, p. 2.

marihuana."[34] The attorney general was also quoted as favoring the bill. The Commissioner of Public Safety in Alaska said in endorsing decriminalization: "Nobody in law enforcement objects to lessening the penalty for the possession of small amounts for an individual for his own use. [I have] no objection to doing away with jail time and lowering the fine" (Alaska House 1975). He admitted that such a change would save his resources, but said that even without the change his officers did not attempt to seek out marihuana users.

But the Anchorage newspaper bitterly opposed the decriminalization bill and published seven editorials in the year prior to decriminalization attacking the bill and its supporters. One editorial referred to it as "the odious measure," "the ugly mess," and "the garbage in the door."[35] The paper and the Republican candidate for the U.S. senate attempted to make this the key issue in the election,[36] but few apparently listened and the Republican lost the election by a wide margin.

Shortly after the state legislature had passed the decriminalization bill, the Alaska supreme court ruled that private use and possession of marihuana were a constitutional right:

> There is no adequate justification for the state's intrusion into the citizen's right to privacy by its prohibition of possession of marihuana for personal consumption in the home. . . . The state cannot impose its own notions of morality, propriety, or fashion on individuals when the public has no legitimate interest in the affairs of those individuals. . . . It appears that the use of marihuana, as it is presently used in the United States today, does not constitute a public health problem of any significant dimensions. It is, for instance, far more innocuous in terms of psychological and social damage than alcohol or tobacco.[37]

In North Carolina, in 1977, a liquor-by-the-drink bill was hotly debated in the state legislature, thoroughly covered by the press, and ultimately defeated. By comparison, the marihuana decriminalization bill that passed that same year was covered in only seven news reports. Even so, editorial opinion on decriminalization in the local press was sharply divided.[38] As early as the mid-1960s it was reported that drug use was increasing in the state's colleges,[39] and that marihuana use in particular was even more common among whites than among African Americans.[40] The press reported on what was called "High Noon" at the University of North Carolina in Chapel Hill. Several hundred students routinely gathered at noon to smoke marihuana at the campus bell tower.[41] A senate supporter recalled in an interview:

> There was tremendous disparity from Chapel Hill to Rose Hill. In Rose Hill you can make corn liquor but with a joint you're going to jail for two years. After football games in the Bell Tower at Chapel Hill as many as 15,000 smoked marihuana with the State Bureau of Investigation, local and county police watching. Do the same thing in Anderson, North Carolina, in the mountains and you were gone.

Another senator commented: "Last summer my nephew was busted for smoking marihuana . . . and due to the fact that maybe I've got somebody with clout over there, this kid got off fairly easily" (North Carolina Senate 1977). By contrast he cited the case of another "young boy" who was sentenced to prison for marihuana possession and murdered while there. Another senator observed: "I do not believe that the majority of the people of North Carolina support the concept that fifty or sixty kids

[34] "Marihuana Bill Moves to Vote," *Anchorage Daily Times,* 13 April 1975, p. A7.

[35] "No Marihuana Veto: Double-Dealing" (Editorial), *Anchorage Daily Times,* 24 May 1975, p. 4.

[36] "Gravel Hits Lewis, Press," *Anchorage Daily Times,* 3 Oct. 1974, p. 2.

[37] "Court Dilutes Pot Law: Ruling Says Constitution Protects Use in Home," *Anchorage Daily Times,* 27 May 1975, pp. 1, 2, referring to *Ravin v. State* (1975).

[38] "No Glib Solutions Needed," *Fayetteville Times,* 9 March 1977; "Rufus Shouldn't Let 'Young Kids' Fool Him," *Goldsboro News-Argus,* 4 March 1977; "Decriminalization?" *Shelby Star,* 7 March 1977.

[39] "Drug Usage May Be on Rise at State's Colleges," *News & Observer* (Raleigh), 19 Dec. 1965.

[40] "A Profile of Users of Hard, Soft Drugs," *News & Observer* (Raleigh), 24 March 1974.

[41] "'High Nooners' Photographed," *News & Observer* (Raleigh), 16 Jan. 1975.

in North Carolina ought to be imprisoned for doing what thousands of others have done without any punishment at all" (ibid.).

The director of corrections noted the state's prison overcrowding and asserted that there should be no imprisonment for alcohol and drug violations.[42] Soon a state commission confirmed that the state prisons were too crowded and therefore faced the threat of federal court intervention and control.[43] The threat was real since such intervention had already occurred in Mississippi. Another article noted that North Carolina led all states in the percentage of its population in prison.[44] A local judge was quoted as saying: "When drug use was restricted to young hippies, we could talk about THEM. When it hits the neighbor down the street, it's US. It's not what we can do about THEM, now it's what we can do for US."[45]

On the basis of such concerns, a liberal Democratic state representative began pressing the attorney general to support a decriminalization bill. In July 1977 the attorney general finally supported the bill and justified it as a means of concentrating on hard drug sales, of relieving prison crowding, and of avoiding placing kids in prison with "professional felons." Just prior to the passage of the marihuana law, there were several stories of arrests in North Carolina involving massive amounts of drugs, including one case involving 25 tons of marihuana,[46] making it apparent that the local criminal justice system had its hands full with major dealers.

Various law enforcement representatives in all these states expressed support for decriminalization laws both to ensure the most efficient use of law enforcement resources and to protect the young. The list of supporters included prosecutors, state and federal judges, attorneys general, and the police. As Polsby (1984) has predicted, legislation passed quickly if those who would enforce new legislation also supported it. Although there were some differences across the states, decriminalization was never elevated to a critical political issue because the existing marihuana laws were not routinely enforced. There was widespread opinion among those directly involved that marihuana was not that dangerous, at least when compared to heroin, alcohol, or even tobacco. Since the drug was increasingly being used by affluent youngsters, it seemed rational that law enforcement should be explicitly freed to concentrate on more serious offenses, including more potent drugs. Much as Lempert (1974) predicted, decriminalization in these states was associated with "moral dissonance" stemming from widespread "dissonant behavior," leading in turn to obvious problems in law enforcement. In only two of these states could we locate evidence of opposition from the press. Missing was evidence of intense political conflict. This collective experience demonstrates Kingdon's (1984:176) point that "when the issue has a serious chance of legislative or other action, then advocates become more flexible, bargaining from their previously rigid positions, compromising in order to be in the game." It also illustrates Jacob's (1988) contention that a routine legislative process is easier to achieve if the initiative is narrowly defined: the successfull bills all called for decriminalization of only possession, and only possession of small amounts of the drug, and most bills only called for this on the first offense. Instead of conflict, there were often-stated concerns that went unchallenged about the impact of law enforcement on the lives of the young.

Protracted Political Conflict

In a minority of the states that were successful in passing marihuana decriminalization bills, the legislative process involved sometimes rancorous political conflict. The fact that the process of

---

[42] "Prison Aid Is Urged by Jones," *News & Observer* (Raleigh), 21 July 1976, p. 11.

[43] "Prisons Face Threat of Federal Control," *News & Observer* (Raleigh), 8 Feb. 1977, p. 19.

[44] "N.C. Prison Rate Highest in Nation," *News & Observer* (Raleigh), 23 May 1977, p. 19.

[45] "Pot in N.C.: It's Becoming No Big Deal," *News & Observer* (Raleigh), 4 July 1977.

[46] "N.C. Now Major Importing Point for Pot Smugglers," *Durham Sun,* 12 Jan. 1976.

decriminalization was so protracted and difficult, as well as so seldom successful, demonstrates that routinization was the key to success. Later we will demonstrate that when marihuana reforms were not presented in a routine manner, the initiatives always failed. No better example of protracted conflict can be found than in Mississippi where there were increasing numbers of arrests of young people for marihuana possession during the mid-1970s. Middle-class youths were sometimes convicted of marihuana possession, with some judges giving no prison sentences and some giving the maximum possible penalty of one to three years. The senate sponsor of the decriminalization bill said: "We're putting children in jail and ruining their lives,"[47] and "your children and your neighbor's children are in severe jeopardy."[48]

One state legislator who was often associated with the Far Right supported decriminalization because of this disparity. In two separate cases in January 1977, involving the smuggling of tons of marihuana into Mississippi, ten out-of-state men were fined but given no jail sentences.[49] This prompted a flood of editorials and letters to the editor in papers across the state and included references to the obvious disparity in the handling of young people in the state compared with that for major drug dealers.[50] This harshness was especially outrageous because the state prison had been under federal court order since 1975 to reduce its crowding. This was a special problem for Mississippi because it is such a poor state and could not easily afford to build new prisons. A county sheriff, who was president of the Mississippi Sheriff's Association, agreed with the idea of decriminalization,

and he said that his office "already concentrates on drug pushers rather than users. . . . If we were to round up everybody in [this] county who has smoked marihuana and send them to prison, . . . I don't know that we would have enough left to hold Sunday school."[51] Still, law enforcement and legislators were deeply divided on this issue.[52]

Mississippi was one of the first states to adopt prohibition of alcohol in 1908 and did not repeal it until 1966. From the lessons learned from alcohol prohibition, a young, conservative Republican president of a family-owned insurance company concluded that it was grossly unfair to treat young marihuana users differently from those who had used alcohol openly in Mississippi during prohibition. He traveled around the state speaking to individuals and groups, including state legislators, and also arranged hearings on decriminalization bills in 1975, 1976, and 1977. He displayed little concern about his personal reputation, which was sometimes under attack. For example, he was accused of being a drug dealer,[53] and a local newspaper implied that he had a financial interest in plans to manufacture marihuana cigarettes once the drug was legalized.[54]

But this business executive strategically mentioned that he was not in favor of marihuana use but only opposed to putting young marihuana users in prison. In a "Letter to Parents" he wrote: "We do not advocate or encourage the use of marihuana. . . . We do advocate a non-criminal, civil fine or citation approach to possession of small amounts."[55] He also emphasized the long list of conservatives and establishment organizations

---

[47] "Bill to Reduce Penalty to Be Debated," *Mississippi Press* (Pascagoula), 9 Feb. 1977.

[48] "Bill Reducing Marihuana Penalty Dealt Crushing Blow by Senate," *Natchez Democrat,* 10 Feb. 1977.

[49] "Officials Fear Mild Punishments Will Deter Drug Crackdown Efforts," *South Mississippi Sun* (Biloxi-Gulfport), 14 Jan. 1977; "11 Tons of Pot Seized in Giant Coast 'Bust,' " *Jackson Daily News,* 4 Oct. 1976.

[50] See, e.g., "Letter to Editor," *Daily Herald"* (Biloxi-Gulfport), 10 Feb. 1977.

[51] "Marihuana Penalty Revision Draws Mixed Reviews," *Daily Journal* (Tupelo), 3 March 1977.

[52] Ibid.; "State Marihuana Law May Come before Senators," *Enterprise Journal,* 11 Feb. 1977; "One Down, One Still to Come," *Jackson Daily News,* 11 Feb. 1977; "House Approves Bill to Relax Pot Laws," *Mobile* (Alabama) *Register,* 11 Feb. 1977; "Senate Approves Marihuana Reform," *South Mississippi Sun* (Biloxi-Gulfport), 11 March 1977.

[53] "Slander and Worse," *Delta Democrat Times* (Greenville), 5 May 1975.

[54] "Playboy and Pot," *New Albany* (Miss.) *Gazette,* 12 June 1975.

[55] *George County Times,* 24 April 1975.

supporting decriminalization and eventually convinced the director of the Mississippi Bureau of Narcotics to publicly support the bill. The latter told the state legislature (Mississippi Joint Judiciary Hearings 1977): "It is a bill that we could live with. . . . Our major thrust today is toward heroin, cocaine, amphetamines, barbiturates. . . . I personally feel that alcohol is much more physically damaging to the body than marihuana." After defeats in 1975 and 1976 a decriminalization law was finally passed in 1977. This third bill was no doubt helped by the light sentences given to major drug smugglers earlier that year, but the big difference appears to have been the support of the top drug enforcement official in the state. In an interview the young executive recalled his protracted negotiations with the leaders of the state Bureau of Narcotics:

> I spent several hours on many occasions at the Mississippi Bureau of Narcotics Office talking with the Director and his division heads. They kept saying they didn't arrest kids for possession and I kept saying, let's make your policy into law. After several drafts of the proposed bill, the Director said he could live with it except for the wording "civil offense." He crossed out the "civil" and put in "misdemeanor." I crossed out "misdemeanor" and said let's just leave it an offense. That is how the final draft came about.

Here we have a first-hand account of the process of selling decriminalization to law enforcement.

In California prior to decriminalization, state law provided for penalties of up to 10 years for simple possession. From the outset, the *Los Angeles Times* favored marihuana reform, giving it a great deal of coverage in dozens of articles. The 25 June 1974 paper presented a strong editorial urging senate passage of the assembly bill.[56] The chiefs of police from San Diego and San Francisco indicated that the law merely codified what they had been doing all along—that for years they had only given citations to marihuana users.[57] Prosecutors

in Colorado and Oregon had made similar admissions. But the Los Angeles police chief referred to supporters of decriminalization as "irresponsible, no-good sons of bitches" and "pot peddlers,"[58] and " 'it is obvious that a 15 percent philosophical minority who believe in a licentious and libertine existence are going to force it on all of us, even if it kills us.' He predicted that the new law will lead to a doubling of the number of heroin addicts in the state within a year."[59] Earlier, then Governor Ronald Reagan had vetoed decriminalization bills on several occasions because he felt that reducing the penalty would give the "impression to young people that it isn't to be feared. They're going to seize on this as encouragement."[60]

In 1972 there were 73,000 arrested and 150 in prison for marihuana offenses in California—at an annual cost of $100 million (California Senate Select Committee on Control of Marijuana 1974:92, 96, 123). In May 1975 the assembly defeated a decriminalization bill but narrowly passed it in June. All Republicans voted against the bill both times and tried to make it a major partisan issue. The conflict was intense, and the charge was even made before a legislative committee that funding for proreform witnesses came from communists.[61] An assembly Republican told the press: "If the Democrats want to pass that bill and foster San Francisco morals on California, . . . they ought to get full credit for it. Ring it around their necks."[62] The Republicans saw what they regarded as a good political issue. Said their leader in the assembly: "Republicans ought not to be a party to taking the first step toward the legalization of marihuana."[63] Four previous attempts

[56] "Reducing the Marihuana Penalty" (Editorial), *Los Angeles Times,* 25 June 1974, pt. 2, p. 6.

[57] "Police Differ on Possible Impact of Marihuana Law," *Los Angeles Times,* 26 Dec. 1975, pt. 2, pp. 1, 2.

[58] "Davis Predicts Outcry on 'Pot,' " *Los Angeles Times,* 2 May 1975, pt. 2, p. 1.

[59] "Davis Hits Signing of 'Pot' Bill, Predicts Crime Wave," *Los Angeles Times,* 11 July 1975, pt. 1, p. 3.

[60] "Reagan Warns against Easier 'Pot' Penalties," *Los Angeles Times,* 5 Dec. 1974, pt. 1, p. 32.

[61] "Bill to Ease State Marihuana Penalties Clears Key Panel," *Los Angeles Times,* 12 Feb. 1975, pt. 1, pp. 1, 25.

[62] "Bill to Ease 'Pot' Law Moves to Assembly Floor," *Los Angeles Times,* 30 April 1975, pt. 2, pp. 1, 3.

[63] "Bill to Relax 'Pot' Law Hits Roadblock," *Los Angeles Times,* 8 May 1975, pt. 1, pp. 3, 31.

had failed: statewide referendum attempts in 1972 and 1974 and vetoes of decriminalization bills by Reagan in 1973 and 1974. It was not until Governor Reagan left office that a bill passed the state legislature and was signed into law.

In New York by 1977, according to a survey of New York City judges, it had become clear that the notoriously tough Rockefeller drug laws passed in 1973 had not deterred illegal drug use (Raab 1977). A congressional committee studied New York City's public schools and found a marked increase in all drug use, including marihuana (Burks 1977). During the assembly debate there were dire predictions for the chain smoker of marihuana: "One year of cannabis smoking, 20 cigarettes a day, can produce sinusitis, pharyngitis, bronchitis and emphysema and other respiratory conditions" (New York Assembly 1977a). All these alleged horrors were just too much for one member of the assembly to endure in silence: "It really bothers me to hear somebody talk about recreational drugs. You might as well talk about recreational cancer because the debilitating effect of drugs are far worse" (ibid.). The small Conservative party nearly killed the bill by bullying conservative Republicans into joining their opposition, but then backed away after criticism by William F. Buckley for its "unthinking traditionalism."[64]

New York assembly members claimed: "No judge is convicting, no jury is convicting, the law is not working" (New York Assembly 1977a); "One judge that I know of in Upstate New York . . . refused to impose the penalties and publicly stated it. And, all the people in the 7th Judicial District knew that he refused to impose the penalties, and they elected him to the supreme court of this state" (New York Assembly 1977b). A member of the New York assembly who was also a police officer reported:

In ten years in the New York City Police Department I never experienced or met anybody that had mugged somebody to get the money to buy marihuana. I never found anybody that was addicted to marihuana. . . . Forcing a police officer to go out and lock somebody up for having marihuana causes them to be hypocritical because he knows that if the case is brought to court that the probability of anybody being prosecuted is practically nil. (New York Assembly 1977a)

In the New York Senate it was reported that there were 27,644 marihuana possession arrests in the state in 1975 and 20,961 in 1976—at a total cost of $52 million (New York Senate 1977). An editorial on 30 April 1977 stated, "The imperatives for reform are clear."[65]

In both New York and California it was obvious that marihuana possession penalties did not deter marihuana use even though massive numbers of arrests were made at great expense. The question was, could young people be protected from the law and could law enforcement be protected from collapse? Yet the bills were the subject of protracted conflict and nearly failed to pass because in both states the opposition to decriminalization was represented by an organized interest group. In California and Mississippi there were deep divisions of opinion among local law enforcement. In Mississippi the legislation took three years of intensive lobbying in spite of the obvious problems of crowded prisons and hanging judges, and was ultimately passed only when the director of the Mississippi Bureau of Narcotics was convinced to support the bill. In these three states we again see the law enforcement problems and widespread dissonant behavior Lempert (1974) predicted, but here we also see the intense political conflict that he imagined would be associated with all such legal changes. In these three states concern for young people was not prominently mentioned and, in any case, did not immobilize opposition to decriminalization. The importance of including in our analysis the total cohort of decriminalization states, avoiding isolated case studies as cautioned by Hagan (1980), now becomes apparent. By including the total group of

---

[64] "Justice Done, Undone, Done in: No Pot Luck," *New York Times,* 29 May 1977, sec. 4, p. 14.

[65] "Melting the Marihuana Glacier" (Editorial), *New York Times,* 30 April 1977, pt. 4, p. 20.

decriminalization states, we can distinguish between conditions that are incidental to marihuana decriminalization and those that are essential.

THE FAILURE TO PASS DECRIMINALIZATION BILLS DURING THE 1970s

In 1978 the eminent criminologist Jerome Skolnick confidently predicted: "It is conceivable that in the next ten years marihuana will be virtually decriminalized in this country" and that some states would do the same with heroin and cocaine (Skolnick & Dombrink 1978:194). But by 1979 the movement to decriminalize marihuana had come to an end. Just as Kingdon (1984) claimed, the policy window closed just as quickly as it had opened. In 1973 a writer in *Harper's* had expressed certainty that marihuana would be *legalized* in Iowa by 1980, preceded by decriminalization in 1976, as this was an idea "whose time had come" (Bourjaily 1973:13). But the effort to pass a decriminalization bill failed in Iowa (National Governors' Conference 1977). In 1976 it was predicted that Illinois and New Jersey would decriminalize marihuana possession (Post 1976). Illinois never passed such a law, and developments in New Jersey provide an example of how quickly the situation changed. By 1978 proponents of decriminalization in New Jersey had the support of legislative leaders, the state's governor, and attorney general, as well as the endorsement of a legislative study commission (Sullivan 1974; Waldron 1978). Even so, such legislation got nowhere in the 1979 legislature or thereafter.

Records of floor debate and committee hearings indicate that many of the 39 states which did not pass marihuana decriminalization bills never seriously considered marihuana reform legislation. For example, decriminalization legislation was not even introduced in some states, among them Texas (National Governors' Conference 1977), Alabama (Adams 1993), Florida (Helms 1993), Kentucky (Cummins 1993), Idaho (Silvers 1993), Delaware (Gross 1993), Montana (Foley 1993), Arizona

(Muir 1993) and Nevada (Galliher & Cross 1983). In other states, decriminalization bills never got out of committee and left no record of public hearings or floor debate. For example, in Maryland decriminalization bills were introduced in 1973, 1974, and 1976, but the closest a bill came to being reported out of committee was a 4–4 deadlock in the Senate Judiciary Committee in 1978 (Garland 1981).

In some areas failure of marihuana reforms seems to have been a consequence of how the issue was originally framed because legal change seemed to require a specific formula for success. No matter what the traditions of the local political culture, if the bills proposed violated the narrow boundaries of successful decriminalization legislation, the initiatives inevitably failed. For example, in Virginia a legislative subcommittee recommended removing jail terms for marihuana possession and *cultivation* (Edwards 1979). The proposal got nowhere. Suggesting that cultivation be treated the same as simple possession apparently was beyond the bounds of possible reform. In Maryland one bill introduced in the Senate Judiciary Committee in 1974 would have "eliminated all penalties" for possession of marihuana (Barker & Walsh 1974). Marihuana reform bills introduced thereafter were all scuttled, including a 1977 initiative to study legislation to "fully legalize marihuana" (Baker 1977). In Seattle in 1974 voters rejected by a 2 to 1 margin an initiative that would have legalized marihuana possession.[66] All subsequent attempts at marihuana reform in Washington State were stalled. In Louisiana a 1972 "proposal was introduced . . . to study the feasibility of *legalization* or decriminalization of marijuana" (emphasis added), which failed by more than a 2 to 1 margin (National Governors' Conference 1977:pt. I, p. 215). Subsequent 1976 decriminalization bills in both the house and the senate died in committee. The only marihuana reform bill reported out of committee was debated

---

[66] "Around the Nation," *Washington Post,* 28 March 1974, p. A10.

in the senate and amended to include jail terms; thus the concept of decriminalization was dead (National Governors' Conference 1977).

Other states had similar experiences. A 1977 Oklahoma bill (H.B. 1268) providing for the "*legal possession of four ounces or less*" died in committee (emphasis added). In Washington, D.C., a task force appointed by the mayor advised legalizing marihuana use and possession (Claiborne 1973), and thereafter marihuana reforms were stymied in spite of support from the D.C. Medical Society (Feinberg 1973). A 1972 Michigan bill would have *legalized* use of marihuana in a private residence (H. 6051). Similar bills were reintroduced in Michigan in 1973/74, 1975/76, and 1977/78, with no success. A *Chicago Tribune* headline reported on a "Stormy Session on Marihuana Bill" where a proposal to *legalize* possession of marihuana in private residences was defeated in the Illinois House Judiciary Committee.[67] Thereafter several decriminalization bills were introduced, but all failed. In 1974 the Massachusetts state senate approved plans for a public referendum to "legalize marihuana" that got nowhere.[68] In addition that year, bills that would have *legalized* possession and *sale* of marihuana in Massachusetts were introduced (H. 3406, H. 3587). In subsequent years decriminalization bills failed, even though there was support from law enforcement (Buckley 1975) and 54% of those polled in the state in 1978 supported decriminalization (Clark University Department of Government 1978). If *legalization* seemed to be one word to avoid, *sale* of marihuana was another.

In some states, failure of decriminalization initiatives appeared to result not only from the terms originally used to propose marihuana reforms but also as a consequence of who was sponsoring the legislation. In Kansas the *Topeka Journal* reported about a bill that would have decriminalized possession of less than two ounces of marihuana, sponsored by a Democratic legislator from Lawrence, the home of

the University of Kansas.[69] The paper reported that in past sessions the legislator had "attempted outright legalization, and much broader decriminalization" measures. His picture appeared with the article, showing him with shoulder-length hair and a heavy beard. Given his historical support for more sweeping marihuana proposals as well as his appearance, it was not surprising that this and his later even more modest decriminalization proposals failed.[70]

In Wisconsin multiple, wide-ranging marihuana reform bills were introduced in 1971, 1973, 1975, 1977, and 1979. All these bills would have eliminated prohibitions for possession and use as well as *sale* of the drug. The sponsor of these bills was a liberal African American, Democratic house member whom the press described as "outrageous" and as one who "loved to shock the system."[71] Early in the marihuana debate he argued: "[i]f a person wants to take a joint to make life more palatable, we shouldn't say he can't."[72] This line of reasoning predictably triggered angry responses, including one from a house colleague who said: "As far as I'm concerned intoxication is a sin."[73] Along with marihuana reform, the maverick legislator defended the legalization of all drugs, prostitution, gay rights, and abortion on demand. The *Milwaukee Journal* noted with considerable understatement that the "mortality rate of such unorthodox bills is high."[74] This legislator, however, remained undeterred, for he felt that even if his bills were not passed, their mere introduction was "educational."[75] Like the legislator in Kansas, he seemed to be the wrong messenger, with the wrong message. The difference in his approach and that of the conservative Republican in Mississippi who said he did

---

[67] 23 April 1975, p. 1A.
[68] "Marihuana Vote Urged," *New York Times,* 26 April 1974, p. 31.

[69] "Marihuana Law Revision Proposed," *Topeka Journal,* 26 Jan. 1977.
[70] "Pot Backers Go for 6th Try," *Wichita Eagle,* 11 March 1979.
[71] "The OUTRAGEOUS Mr. Barbee," *Milwaukee Journal, Insight Magazine,* 16 April 1972, pp. 24, 25.
[72] "Barbee Presents Case for Legalization of Marihuana," *Capital Times* (Madison, WI), 29 April 1971, p. 19.
[73] Ibid.
[74] *Milwaukee Journal, Insight Magazine,* 16 April 1972, p. 25 (cited in note 71).
[75] "Barbee Calls His "Far-out' Bills Educational," *Capital Times,* 28 June 1973, p. 15.

not "advocate or encourage the use of marihuana" could not have been greater. Not only was the marihuana policy window open for a short period, but it only allowed for narrowly circumscribed reforms. It did not extend to sale of marihuana and did not include the legalization of possession. Successful reforms also required some maintenance of the message that marihuana use was improper.

THE DEMISE OF DECRIMINALIZATION IN THE 1980s

If the 1972 NCMDA Report provided the form as well as the timing of the states' decriminalization laws, perhaps we should again look to the federal level to understand why only 11 states passed such laws and why none did so after 1978. What seems important, if not essential, to this legislation is federal leadership. That leadership was briefly available during the Ford administration and early in the Carter administration, but missing prior to that time and thereafter. Until his resignation in 1974, President Nixon had consistently opposed decriminalization of marihuana, even after the publication of his commission's report, which he rejected.[76] After Nixon left office and until 1978 there was considerable agreement among national political leaders on the desirability of marihuana decriminalization. However, this changed after marihuana use by Carter White House staff was reported. Carter was besieged by further charges of drug use among senior White House staff being leaked to the press. The Republican Senate minority leader called for an official investigation by the Justice Department into drug use among White House staff (Smith 1978). President Carter gave no support to decriminalization thereafter, undoubtedly in part because partisan political conflict with Republican opposition had not been the usual path to success, and Carter could have been expected to know that a partisan political conflict on marihuana decriminalization without whole-hearted Republican support would be hard to win.

[76] "Transcript of the President's News Conference on Foreign and Domestic Matters," *New York Times,* 25 March 1972, p. 12.

Even as early as the late 1970s, the views political leaders expressed began to change. In 1977 Dr. Robert DuPont, the former drug-policy advisor to the Nixon and Ford administrations, reversed his earlier support for decriminalization and advocated de facto decriminalization in its place.

> On the substantive merits of the issue, everybody is for decriminalization. But the real issue is symbolic. Nobody wants to have anyone, young or old, go to jail for possession of small amounts of marihuana. But being in favor of decriminalization is seen by the majority of the public as being in favor of pot. . . . It is possible to eliminate jail as a threat for simple possession of marihuana without favoring decriminalization. That is the way out! In fact, as a nation we have already done that. . . . Those who now go to jail are the sellers of marihuana. (Anderson 1981:312)

De facto decriminalization has the added advantage of being a means of avoiding the rancorous conflict that surrounded decriminalization bills in New York, California, and Mississippi.

Additional evidence concerning de facto decriminalization emerges when government records of incarceration and arrest are compared with survey data on frequency of marihuana use. If it is assumed, as some respondents argued, that the primary concern in decriminalization hinges on the issue of incarceration, then it is necessary to determine the levels at which incarceration is actually used. In 1984 questionnaires were mailed to all state departments of correction asking for the number of inmates in the state prison system whose most serious crime was marihuana possession. The 43 states responding reported a total of 2,729 prisoners, for an average of about 65 per state. Given such small numbers, one can understand why a sense of urgency or widespread dissonance was missing.

The incarceration figures can also be compared with arrest figures. The *FBI Uniform Crime Reports* between 1977 and 1992 indicate that total drug arrests nearly doubled, while marihuana possession arrests have declined by nearly a third. In 1977 marihuana possession arrests accounted for 61% of all drug arrests; in 1986, 36% of all drug arrests; by 1992 this figure had dropped to 25%. These figures show that the police no longer are swamped primarily by marihuana possession cases, and that over these three decades there has been a steady decrease in the emphasis on marihuana possession enforcement compared to other drugs. Thus the sense of urgency regarding the bureaucratic benefits flowing from marihuana reform has vanished. Still, compared with the about 300,000 marihuana possession arrests made annually, the numbers incarcerated for marihuana possession are minuscule and give real evidence of de facto decriminalization.

The relatively constant number of marihuana possession arrests is mirrored by levels of marihuana use that remained relatively stable between the 1970s and the 1980s. For example, in 1976 approximately 52% of high school seniors had ever used marihuana. In 1980 the figure had increased to 60% but had dropped again by 1985 to 54%, about the same level as found in 1976 (Bachman et al. 1986). One possible explanation for the decreasing support for the decriminalization movement is that states passing such laws might have routinely experienced consequent increases in marihuana use. No such evidence exists. There were similar patterns in the frequency of marihuana use in decriminalization states compared with those without such laws (Johnston et al. 1981). The decreased proportions of all drug arrests involving marihuana and scant use of incarceration cannot be attributed to there being far fewer marihuana users or much less marihuana in circulation. Given the widespread use of marihuana reflected in survey results, these arrest and incarceration figures suggested some de facto decriminalization. Yet they also indicated that the process was not quite complete, contrary to the claims of DuPont.

If de facto decriminalization indicates *how* the legislative reform has been stalled, the question that remains is *why* it occurred and at this particular time. Himmelstein (1986) has observed that by the 1980s, or even earlier, local parents' groups concerned about marihuana began to form, the New Right emerged as a major antimarihuana force, and federal officials no longer supported decriminalization. He concluded: "Which is cause and effect is hard to say" (p. 10). The 1980s ushered in a new conservative Republican administration. In 1986 President Reagan attempted to initiate a "national crusade" to combat the drug epidemic, which he said was "a repudiation of everything America is" (Pasztor 1986). This crusade is consistent with Reagan's opposition to decriminalization while he was governor of California, given his fear of sending the wrong message to potential users. To this was added Mrs. Reagan's cant, "Just Say No to Drugs." More recently, the Bush administration's director of drug control policy, William Bennett, joined the crusade in criticizing skeptics like economist Milton Friedman and former Secretary of State George Shultz for their observations that the nation's drug control policies were not enforceable. Bennett was unswayed by these difficulties. "I remain an ardent defender of our nation's laws against illegal drug use and our attempts to enforce them because I believe drug use is wrong" (Bennett 1989). When a federal judge called for legalization due to his first-hand observations of the collapse of drug law enforcement, Bennett responded by asserting that this argument was as "morally atrocious as it ever was."[77] Bennett, like DuPont, apparently preferred unenforced legislation as opposed to actual decriminalization because of the symbolic power criminal penalties provide even if unenforced. The cornerstone of the Bush administration's efforts to control illegal drugs is found in its voluminous *National Drug Control Strategy,* published in 1989. No mention was made there of decriminalization of marihuana, and only feeble recommendations were made for marihuana control, including increased intelligence in foreign drug-producing countries and stepped-up crop eradication.

SUMMARY: THE CONTINUING CONTRADICTIONS OF MARIHUANA CONTROL

The problem addressed here concerns the origins of marihuana decriminalization, both its inception and its lapse into de facto decriminalization. Two factors

---

[77] "Bennett Says 'No' to Drugs," *Kansas City Star,* 14 Dec. 1989, p. 1.

seem important—bureaucratic, law enforcement problems and moral dissonance. The first played a major role in decriminalization, while the second was a factor both in the origins of decriminalization legislation and in the symbolic form this reform eventually took in de facto decriminalization, which avoids jail terms without formal legal change. Marihuana decriminalization provided what initially seemed to be an ideal resolution to the conflict between the drug use of affluent Americans and the requirements of law enforcement.

As early as 1974 it had become clear that even while most opponents of decriminalization agreed that marihuana users should not be imprisoned, they preferred de facto decriminalization and "a minimum penalty . . . to make it clear to young people that society . . . does not approve of [marihuana] use" (Himmelstein 1983:105). The problem with decriminalization as a solution to these practical problems, as Ronald Reagan had said while he was still governor of California, was that it indicated that marihuana was not really a dangerous drug. Since the consequences of marihuana decriminalization were primarily symbolic, another type of symbolic policy was seen as the required response. De facto decriminalization offered an ideal resolution of this additional conflict that developed as a consequence of the decriminalization laws themselves. In the final analysis the real differences for law enforcement and, for most marihuana users, in the consequences of de facto versus de jure decriminalization are not that great. De facto decriminalization is an effective means of reducing the moral dissonance inherent in the arrest of high-status individuals while still retaining the presence of criminal penalties. Since law enforcement has only finite resources, if legislatures refuse to set law enforcement priorities, police will do it for them. Legislators are seldom interested in taking political risks. Thus the obvious symbolic advantages of de facto decriminalization tip the balance.

REFERENCES

Abelson, Herbert I., and Patricia M. Fishburne. 1977. *National Survey on Drug Abuse.* Rockville, MD: National Institute on Drug Abuse.

Adams, Anne. 1993. "Report of Legislative Analyst." Alabama Legislative Reference Service, Montgomery, AL, 16 March.

Alaska. 1975. House Judiciary Committee, S.B. 350, 1 May.

Anderson, Patrick. 1981. *High in America: The True Story behind NORML and the Politics of Marijuana.* New York: Viking Press.

Bachman, Jerald G., Lloyd D. Johnston, Patrick M. O'Malley, and Ronald H. Humphrey. 1986. "Changes in Marihuana Use Linked to Changes in Perceived Risks and Disapproval." Monitoring the Future, Occasional Paper No. 19. Ann Arbor, MI: Institute for Social Research, Univ. of Michigan.

Baker, Donald P. 1977. "Md. Delegate Backs Study on Easing Marijuana Law." *Washington Post,* 23 Feb., p. C7.

Barker, Karlyn, and Edward Walsh. 1974a. "Md. Senate Unit Kills 2 Bills to Cut Marijuana Penalties." *Washington Post,* 1 March, p. B10.

Bennett, William S. 1989. "A Response to Milton Friedman." *Wall Street Journal,* 19 Sept., p. A30.

Bourjaily, Vance. 1973. "Marijuana Politics: Iowa, 1973." *Harper's Magazine,* August, p. 12.

Boyko, Edgar Paul. 1990. "Showdown over Pot-Smoking in Anchorage, Alaska." *Donahue Show,* 16 Nov.

Buckley, John J. 1975. Remarks of Middlesex County Sheriff before the Human Services and Elderly Affairs Committee, 13 March, Massachusetts State Legislature.

Buckley, William F., Jr. 1972. "The Spirit of the Law." *National Rev.,* 8 Dec., p. 1348.

Burks, Edward C. 1977. "House Panel Finds Big Rise in Drug Use in New York's Schoolchildren." *New York Times,* 8 Feb., sec. 1, p. 15.

California Senate Select Committee on Control of Marijuana. 1974. *Understanding the Social Costs of Marijuana.* Sacramento: California Legislature.

CBS News. 1991. "60 Minutes," 1 Dec.

Claiborne, William L. 1973. "Mayor's Task Force Advises Legalizing Marijuana Here." *Washington Post,* 6 March, p. A1.

Clark University Department of Government. 1978. "Majority Supports Decriminalization of Marihuana." Released July 14, State Library of Massachusetts.

Colorado. 1975. House Judiciary Committee, H.B. 1027, 20 Feb.

Cummins, Leslie. 1993. "Report of Legislative Research Commission." Frankfort, KY, 24 Feb.

Dershowitz, Alan M. 1976. "Criminal Sentencing in the United States: An Historical and Conceptual Overview." *Annals of the American Academy of Political and Social Science* 423:117.

Edelman, Murray. 1964. *The Symbolic Uses of Politics.* Urbana: Univ. of Illinois Press.

Edwards, Paul G. 1979. "Reduced Pot Penalties Asked." *Washington Post,* 20 Jan., p. B2.

Empey, LaMar T. 1978. *American Delinquency: Its Meaning and Construction.* Homewood, IL: Dorsey Press.

Federal Bureau of Investigation. 1977–92. *Uniform Crime Reports.* Washington, DC: GPO.

Feinberg, Lawrence. 1973. "D.C. Doctors: Legalize Use of Marijuana." *Washington Post,* 21 Nov., p. C2.

Fishburne, Patricia M., Herbert I. Abelson, and Ira H. Cisin. 1979. *National Survey on Drug Abuse: Main Findings.* Rockville, MD: National Institute on Drug Abuse.

Foley, Jodie Ann. 1993. "Report of Archival Technician." Montana Historical Society, Helena, MT, 6 April.

Galliher, John F., and Linda Basilick. 1979. "Utah's Liberal Drug Laws: Structural Foundations and Triggering Events." *Social Problems* 26:284.

Galliher, John F., James L. McCartney, and Barbara E. Baum. 1974. "Nebraska's Marijuana Law: A Case of Unexpected Legislative Innovation." *Law and Society Rev.* 8:441.

Gallup Poll. 1977. "Public Would Not Legalize Marijuana Now, but Decriminalization Wins Support." *Gallup Opinion Index,* Report No. 143 (June).

———. 1980. "Opposition to Legalization of Marijuana Unchanged." *Gallup Opinion Index,* Report No. 179 (July).

———. 1985. "Public Resists More Liberal Marijuana Laws." *Gallup Report,* Report No. 241 (Oct.).

Garland, Eric. 1981. "Legal Marihuana: An Idea Going Up in Smoke." *Baltimore Magazine,* Jan., p. 63.

Goode, Erich. 1970. *The Marijuana Smokers.* New York: Basic Books.

Gross, Randy L. 1993. "Report of Archivist Supervisor." Bureau of Archives and Records Management, Delaware Department of State, Dover, DE, 2 April.

Hagan, John. 1980. "The Legislation of Crime and Delinquency: A Review of Theory, Method, and Research." *Law and Society Rev.* 14:603.

Helmer, John. 1975. *Drugs and Minority Oppression.* New York: Seabury Press.

Helms, James. 1993. "Report of Division of Library and Information Services." Florida Department of State, Tallahassee, 15 March.

Himmelstein, Jerome L. 1983. *The Strange Career of Marihuana: Politics and Ideology of Drug Control in America.* Westport, CT: Greenwood Press.

———. 1986. "The Continuing Career of Marihuana: Backlash . . . within Limits." *Contemporary Drug Problems* 13:1.

Johnston, Lloyd D., Patrick M. O'Malley, and Jerald G. Bachman. 1981. *Marihuana Decriminalization: The Impact on Youth, 1975–1980.* Monitoring the Future, Occasional Paper, No. 13. Ann Arbor: Institute for Social Research, Univ. of Michigan.

Kerr, K. Austin. 1985. *Organized for Prohibition: A New History of the Anti-Saloon League.* New Haven, CT: Yale Univ. Press.

Kingdon, John W. 1984. *Agendas, Alternatives, and Public Policies.* Boston: Little, Brown and Co.

LaGuardia Commission on Marihuana. 1944. *The Marihuana Problem in the City of New York: Sociological, Medical, Psychological, and Pharmacological Studies.* New York: LaGuardia Commission on Marihuana, New York City.

Lempert, Richard. 1974. "Toward a Theory of Decriminalization." *Et Al.* 3:1.

MacKenzie, John P. 1973. "Bar Moves on Drug, Sex Laws." *Washington Post,* 9 Aug., pp. Al, A12.

Minnesota House Judiciary Committee. 1975. Hearings on H.F. 749, 1 April.

Minnesota Senate Judiciary Committee. 1975a. Hearings on H.F. 749, 21 March.

———. 1975b. Hearings on H.F. 749, 11 April.

Minnesota Senate. 1975. Debate, H.F. 749, 12 May.

Mississippi Joint Judiciary Committee. 1977. Hearings on Controlled Substances Act, 1 Feb.

Morgan, Patricia A. 1978. "The Legislation of Drug Law: Economic Crisis and Social Control," *J. of Drug Issues* 8:53.

Muir, Louise. 1993. "Report of Library, Archives and Public Records." Phoenix, AZ, 8 April.

Musto, David F. 1973. *The American Disease: Origins of Narcotic Control.* New Haven, CT: Yale Univ. Press.

National Commission on Marihuana & Drug Abuse. 1972. *Marihuana: A Signal of Misunderstanding.* Washington, DC: GPO.

National Governors' Conference Center for Policy Research & Analysis. 1977. *Marijuana: A Study of*

State Policies and Penalties. Washington, DC: U.S. Department of Justice.

NBC News. 1990. "Showdown over Pot-Smoking in Anchorage, Alaska." *Donahue Show,* 16 Nov.

Nebraska Senate. 1978. Debate, L.B. 808, 7 April.

New York Assembly. 1977a. Debate, 16 May.

———. 1977b. Debate, 27 June.

New York Senate. 1977. Debate, 28 June.

North Carolina Senate. 1977. Debate, H.B. 1325, January 29.

Olson-Raymer, Gayle. 1984. "National Juvenile Justice Policy: Myth or Reality." In S. H. Decker, ed., *Juvenile Justice Policy: Analyzing Trends and Outcomes.* Beverly Hills, CA: Sage Publications.

Pasztor, Andy. 1986. "Reagans Issue Call for Crusade against Drugs." *Wall Street Journal,* 15 Sept., p. 64.

Peterson, Ruth D. 1985. "Discriminatory Decision Making at the Legislative Level: An Analysis of the Comprehensive Drug Abuse Prevention and Control Act of 1970." *Law and Human Behavior* 9:243.

Polsby, Nelson W. 1984. *Political Innovation in America: The Politics of Policy Initiation.* New Haven, CT: Yale Univ. Press.

Polsky, Ned. 1967. *Hustlers, Beats, and Others.* Chicago: Aldine Publishing Co.

Post, Penny. 1976. "Joint Effort." *Seventeen,* Feb., p. 30.

President's Advisory Commission on Narcotics and Drug Abuse. 1963. *Final Report.* Washington, DC: GPO (Nov.).

President's Commission on Law Enforcement & Administration of Justice. 1968. *Task Force Report: Narcotics and Drug Abuse.* Washington, DC: GPO.

Raab, Selwyn. 1977. "Stiff Antidrug Laws Held No Deterrent." *New York Times,* 2 Jan., sec. 1, p. 1.

Rubin, H. Ted. 1985. *Juvenile Justice: Policy, Practice and Law.* 2d ed. New York: Random House.

Silvers, Carol. 1993. "Report of State Documents Coordinator." Idaho State Library, Boise, Idaho, 26 Feb.

Skolnick, Jerome. 1978. *House of Cards: The Legalization and Control of Casino Gambling.* Boston: Little Brown and Co.

Skolnick, Jerome H., and John Dombrink. 1978. "The Legalization of Deviance." *Criminology* 16:193.

Smith, Terence. 1978. "Carter Orders White House Staff to Follow Drug Laws or Resign." *New York Times,* 25 July, p. A1.

Sullivan, Ronald. 1974. "Study Asks Easing of Marijuana Law." *New York Times,* 12 Oct., p. 67.

Time. 1990. "Alaska: Mowing the Grass." 19 Nov., p. 47.

U.S. Bureau of the Census. 1980. *Census of Population: General Population Characteristics.* Washington, DC: GPO.

U.S. Office of National Drug Control Policy. 1989. *National Drug Control Strategy.* Executive Office of the President. Washington, DC: GPO, September.

Waldron, Martin. 1978. "Trenton Topics." *New York Times,* 21 March p. 75.

Weitzer, Ronald. 1991. "Prostitutes' Rights in the United States: The Failure of a Movement." *Sociological Q.* 32:23.

Wooten, James T. 1977. "Carter Seeks to End Marijuana Penalty for Small Amounts." *New York Times,* 3 Aug., pp. A1.

CASES CITED

People v. Summit, 183 Col. 421, 517 P.2d 850 (1974).

Downey v. Perini, 518 F.2d 1288 (1975).

Drug Enforcement Administration, U.S. Department of Justice. Opinion and Recommended Ruling, Findings of Fact, Conclusions of Law and Decision of Administrative Judge: In the Matter of Marihuana Rescheduling Petition. Docket No. 86–22, 6 Sept. 1988.

State v. Kells, 199 Neb. 374, 259 N.W.2d 19 (1977).

Ravin v. State, 537 P.2d 494 (1975).

LEGISLATION CITED

Alaska Statutes. "Depressant, Hallucinogenic and Stimulant Drugs," Ch. 12, p. 21, October 1975.

California, Statutes of. Ch. 248, p. 641, 9 July 1975.

Colorado, Session Laws of. Ch. 115, pp. 433–437, 1 July 1975.

Oklahoma. H.B. 1268 (1977).

Massachusetts. H. 3406, "Penalty Removal for Possession," Social Welfare Committee (1974).

Massachusetts. H. 3587, "Legalize Sale of Marihuana," Social Welfare Committee (1974).

Maine, Laws of. Ch. 499 at 1368, effective 1 March 1976 (1975).

Michigan. H.B. 6051, "Permits Private [Marihuana] Use in Residence" (1972).

Minnesota, Laws of. Ch. 42, p. 101, 11 March 1976.

Mississippi, Laws of. Ch. 482, p. 922, 1 July 1977.

Nebraska, Laws of. Legislative Bill 808, 20 April 1978, p. 817.

New York, Laws of. Ch. 360, 29 June 1977.
North Carolina, Laws of. Ch. 862, p. 1178 (1 July 1977).
Ohio, Laws of. H.B. No. 300, p. 2324, 1 July 1976 (1975).
Oregon, Laws. Ch. 680, p. 1521, 22 July 1973.

South Dakota, Laws of. Ch. 158, p. 227, 1 April 1976.
South Dakota, Laws of. Ch. 188, p. 233, 24 March 1977.
U.S. Congress. 1970. Comprehensive Drug Abuse Prevention and Control Act of 1970, Public Law 91-513, 84 Stat. 1236 (1970), vol. 1, pp. 1236–96.

READING 4-7

The Meese Commission on the Road

Carole S. Vance

The report of the Attorney General's Commission on Pornography, released on July 9, recommends a repressive agenda for controlling sexual images and texts: vigorous enforcement of existing obscenity laws and the passage of draconian new measures. If the Meese commission gets its way, it will be because it has launched a novel propaganda offensive that superficially uses the rhetoric of social science and feminism—though not their substance—to disguise the traditional right-wing moral agenda. As part of its ideological warfare the commission uses vague but powerful words—"degrading," "violent pornography," "harm"—to unite what it hopes is a broad constituency in an unthinking but culturally overdetermined reaction that links sexuality and its surrogate, sexual images, with harm to women and death.

The commission's 300-plus hours of public hearings and business meetings featured zany, if unintended, comedy: vice cops, born-again Christians and prosecutors thundering indictments of pornography and its progeny—divorce, premarital sex, sexual "deviation" and family destruction—in a 1950s-style epiphany of prurient righteousness. But its ninety-two recommendations, backed up by a substantial Federal, state and local apparatus already in place, pose a serious threat to free expression.

From *The Nation* 243, No. 3 (August 2, 1986), pp. 65, 76–82. Reprinted by permission of *The Nation.*

Appointed by Attorney General Edwin Meese 3d in May 1985 to find "new ways to control the problem of pornography," the panel was hardly intended to be an open-ended inquiry. It was chaired by Henry Hudson, a vigorous anti-vice prosecutor from Arlington, Virginia, who had been praised by President Reagan for closing down every adult bookstore in his district. Hudson was assisted by executive director Alan Sears, who has a reputation in the U.S. Attorney's Office in the Western District of Kentucky as a tough opponent of obscenity, and his staff of vice cops and attorneys. Their schedule called for six public hearings, with preselected topics, in Washington (general), Chicago (law enforcement), Houston (social science), Los Angeles (production and distribution), Miami (child pornography) and New York (organized crime).

Prior to convening, seven of the eleven commissioners had taken public stands opposing pornography and supporting obscenity law as a means to control it. James Dobson heads the fundamentalist organization Focus on the Family. "I have a personal dislike for pornography and all it implies," he told *The Washington Post.* Judge Edward Garcia, recently appointed by Reagan to Federal District Court in California, prosecuted obscenity cases before becoming a judge. Diane Cusack, a member of the Scottsdale, Arizona, City

Council, urged residents to take photographs and license numbers of patrons entering the local adult theater. Father Bruce Ritter, a Franciscan priest, directs Covenant House, a home for runaways in New York's Times Square area, and is an outspoken critic of pornography. Attorney Harold (Tex) Lezar played an instrumental role in setting up the commission as an aide to Reagan's first Attorney General, William French Smith. Frederick Schauer, a law professor at the University of Michigan, has written extensively on obscenity. He argues that forms of expression intended to be sexually arousing are less like speech and more like dildos, and are thus exempt from First Amendment protection: "The prototypical pornographic item on closer analysis shares more of the characteristics of sexual activity than the communicative process."

The four members of the panel with no public positions on pornography included Park Elliott Dietz, a psychiatrist at the University of Virginia and a consultant to the Federal Bureau of Investigation Academy, who specializes in the subject of sexual deviations ("paraphilias"); Judith Becker, a Columbia University psychologist known for her research on rapists and rape victims; Ellen Levine, a vice president of CBS and the editor of *Woman's Day;* and Deanne Tilton, head of the California Consortium of Child Abuse Councils. As events unfolded, those four, joined occasionally by Schauer, constituted the commission's moderate bloc. The three moderate women frequently resisted the staff's conservative agenda. They signed a statement that, while abhorring "the exploitation of vulnerable people" in pornography, rejected "judgemental and condescending efforts to speak on women's behalf as though they were helpless, mindless children." In the end Becker and Levine wrote a devastating eighteen-page dissent as their introduction to the report.

THE SHOW TRIAL

Any pretense of objectivity that the commission might have wished to claim was dispelled by its glaring and persistent biases in gathering and evaluating evidence. The list of witnesses invited to testify was no more open than the commissioners' minds: 77 percent supported greater control, if not elimination, of sexually explicit material. Heavily represented were law-enforcement officers and members of vice squads (68 of 208 witnesses), politicians, and spokespersons for conservative antipornography groups like Citizens for Decency through Law and the National Federation for Decency.

Of the "victims" of pornography, many told tales of divorce, promiscuity, masturbation and child abuse—all, in their view, caused by sexually explicit material. For these born-again victims, the remedy for complex social problems was found in renouncing pornography and sexual sin. The vice cops on the staff energetically recruited the alleged victims to testify, assisted by antipornography groups and prosecutors. The same zeal was not applied to the search for people who had positive experiences.

Witnesses appearing before the commission were treated in a highly uneven manner. Commissioners accepted virtually any claim made by antipornography witnesses as true, asking few probing questions and making only the most cursory requests for evidence or attempts to determine witness credibility. Those who did not support more restriction of sexually explicit speech were often met with rudeness and hostility, and their motives for testifying were impugned. The panelists asked social scientist Edward Donnerstein if pornographers had tried to influence his research findings or threatened his life. They asked actress Colleen Dewhurst, testifying for Actors' Equity about the dangers of censorship in the theater, if persons convicted of obscenity belonged to the union, and if the union was influenced by organized crime. They questioned her at length about the group's position on child pornography.

The commission flagrantly violated ordinary rules of fair procedure. In the most publicized case it sent a letter on Justice Department letterhead to twenty-three large bookstore chains, booksellers and convenience stores, stating that the panel had "received testimony alleging that your company is involved in the sale or distribution of pornography," and that the final report would list "identified distributors." (The anonymous allegations came from the testimony of the Rev. Donald Wildmon, executive director of the National Federation for Decency.) "Failure to respond," the letter concluded, "will necessarily be accepted as an indication of no objection." Southland Corporation, owner of the 7-Eleven chain which Wildmon singled out as one of "the leading retailers of porn magazines in America," decided after receiving the commission's letter that it would no longer carry *Playboy* and *Penthouse.* The magazines and the American Booksellers Association filed suit. On July 3, Federal District Court Judge John Garrett Penn ruled against the commission in the *Playboy* case, giving the Justice Department five days to write to all the companies it contacted and explain that the original letter did not mean to imply their publications were obscene or to threaten a blacklist. The commission was also prohibited from publishing Wildmon's accusations in its final report.

Another lawsuit against the commission—to counter the staff's attempt to withhold a draft of the report and all its working papers, available to the public under the Federal Advisory Committee Act—was filed by the American Civil Liberties Union. The commission's staff backed off its claim that possession of these documents in the hands of organized crime might constitute a threat to itself, and settled before getting to court.

All of these defects, as well as the serious constitutional questions raised by the panel's recommendations, are reviewed in *Polluting the Censorship Debate,* a 200-page summary and critique prepared by A.C.L.U. legislative counsel Barry Lynn, an articulate and effective critic.

The commission's heavy-handed procedures raised the hackles of some of its own members as well as outsiders. The law-enforcement recommendations were discussed and voted on before the hearings were half over, leading some commissioners to ask if the panel could logically favor stricter penalties before establishing harm. Commissioners were even asked to vote in favor of a pending Senate bill that they had never seen. Hudson and Sears persisted in ramming through recommendations that ignored commissioners' input, eventually angering moderates and inspiring them to resist. The "vibrator bill" was a prime example, a model statute that would ban as obscene "any device designed or marketed as useful primarily for the stimulation of human genital organs." When Becker, Levine and Tilton strongly objected, the chair deferred the bill rather than risk losing a vote, but then he brought it up again twice.

Battles were also fought over the report's text, which by March had swollen to more than a thousand pages of disputed prose, putting forth adventurous legal theories and recommendations that even some commissioners found excessive. Schauer, "extremely disturbed" by the report, began to write his own, first billed as a dissent. His 214-page essay—cohesive, professional and more persuasive in marshaling feminist and social science arguments—made its debut at the final work session in April. The expected showdown between the staff and Schauer was averted when commissioners adopted both reports. Inspection of the complete table of contents reveals two reports, each covering similar topics. The Schauer draft, although admittedly more moderate, provides a liberal gloss to a conservative set of recommendations. Many readers, journalists included, never get beyond the Schauer essay, and conclude that the document is not as right wing as they had expected.

THE TESTIMONY

If these were the McCarthy hearings of sex, they were scripted by the cast of *Saturday Night Live.* The atmosphere throughout the hearings was one of excited repression: witnesses alternated between chronicling the negative effects of pornography and making sensationalized presentations of "it." Taking a lead from women's antipornography groups, everyone had a slide show: the F.B.I., the U.S. Customs Service, the U.S. Postal Service and sundry vice squads. The material shown was hardly mainstream fare; it was unconventional, difficult for the average viewer to relate to and likely to be upsetting. Becker and Levine characterized it as "very violent and extremely degrading."

The report lists in alphabetical order the titles of materials found in sixteen adult bookstores in six cities: 2,370 films, 725 books and 2,325 magazines, beginning with *A Cock Between Friends* and ending with *69 Lesbians Munching*. A detailed plot summary is given for the book *The Tying Up of Rebecca,* along with descriptions of sex aids advertised in the books, their cost and how to order them. Videos like "Debbie Does Dallas" and "Biker Slave Girls" were described in loving detail. Were there not some question about the applicability of copyright law to arguably obscene material, the many pages of direct quotation might prompt a serious copyright claim.

Witnesses made their unique contributions. Judith Trevillian, from Citizens Against Pornography, Michigan, brought a portable tape recorder to reproduce for the audience "the chilling horror I felt in my kitchen after my first encounter with Dial-a-Porn." "Suck on my boobs. I'm coming all over my hand," boomed the tape, as the audience sat in attentive silence. In Miami a patient of a local therapist appeared as a victim of pornography. "At age 12, I was a typically normal, healthy boy and my life was filled with normal activities and hobbies," he stated. But that changed when he found a deck of "hard core" pornographic playing cards, depicting penetration, fellatio and cunnilingus. "By the age of 16, after a steady diet of *Playboy, Penthouse, Scandinavian Children,* perverted paperback books and sexology magazines, I had to see a doctor for neuralgia of the prostate." He went on to promiscuous sex with two women, but eventually found Christ. He concluded, "If it weren't for my faith in God and the forgiveness in Jesus Christ, I would now possibly be a pervert, an alcoholic or dead."

The Meese commission conducted a show trial in which pornography was found guilty. But producing an updated discourse about pornography and sex proved difficult, despite the staff's tight control over witnesses, topics and rules of evidence.

The chief supporters and beneficiaries of the commission were conservatives and fundamentalists, whose main objection to pornography is its depiction—and, they believe, advocacy—of sex outside of marriage and procreation. The Justice Department knew that this position would no longer sell outside the right wing. The attack on sexually explicit material had to be modernized by couching it in more contemporary and persuasive arguments, drawn chiefly from social science and feminism. So the preeminent harm that pornography was said to cause was not sin and immorality but violence.

Conservatives have been gunning for the 1970 report of the President's Commission on Obscenity and Pornography, a major obstacle to their social agenda on sex, because that exhaustive review found no evidence that sexually explicit material caused antisocial behavior. The report recommended that restrictive laws governing adults' access to sexual materials be repealed and that the government undertake massive sex-education programs for adults and young people. The goal of the Meese commission was to overturn the 1970 panel's findings, and so it has. A mirror image, the Meese report finds that pornography causes harm—individual, social, moral and ethical. It recommends restrictive legal measures, but it declines to support sex-education programs. The conservative tenor and goals of the report can hardly be disguised.

UPDATING THE HARMS OF PORNOGRAPHY

Conservatives found it harder than they expected to enlist social science in their cause. With $500,000, in contrast to the 1970 commission's $2 million (in 1967 dollars), the Meese commission was unable to fund any research and had but one part-time social scientist as a consultant. So it reviewed research conducted by other investigators. However, the staff either did not understand or else willfully ignored the nuances of social science research. Star witnesses Edward Donnerstein and Neil Malamuth, who have conducted many of the interesting new experiments on sexually explicit images, testified with care. Aggressive imagery and mainstream media are more worrisome than sexual imagery and X-rated channels, they said. Caution is required in interpreting the necessarily artificial laboratory findings to naturalistic settings and to populations other than college boys. Causal inference to actual behavior like rape is unwarranted. Not all the social science testimony was so disappointing. Dolf Zillmann, a communications researcher from Indiana University, testified that nonviolent images of consensual sex have negative effects, including greater acceptance of extramarital sex, and his collaborator, Jennings Bryant, thundered that when porn comes into your life, "forget trust, forget family, forget commitment, forget love, forget marriage!"

Social scientists on the commission became critical, particularly Judith Becker. She insisted that the panel use the customary term "negative effects" when describing social science results rather than the loaded term "harm," and she plainly stated, "There is no social science evidence linking pornography with violence."

When it became clear that social science would not provide the indictment of pornography that he wanted, Hudson announced that harm should be evaluated according to two additional tiers of evidence: "the totality of the evidence," which included victim testimony, anecdotal evidence, expert opinion, personal experience and common sense; and "moral, ethical and cultural values." Pornography could thus still be convicted on two out of three tiers.

Sears is candid in admitting that "much of the evidence that was considered was anecdotal." This signals an abrupt departure from standard practice in social science and public health research. By the 1950s it had become clear that scientific theories based on anecdotal report or even expert opinion were often unreliable and wrong, overturned by the results of more objective and standardized research methods. The mind boggles at what other anecdotal "findings" a carefully selected witness list might prove: working mothers are responsible for delinquency; abortion leads to nervous breakdown; white bread causes insanity.

The report's section on harms—written by Frederick Schauer—overstates the evidence, leaps to unsupported conclusions about what might be "reasonably assumed" in social science, cites no research to support statements and appears to misunderstand what causality means in social science. The panel's conclusion that violent pornography causes sexual violence, reached "unanimously and confidently," required "assumptions not found exclusively in the experimental evidence," Schauer wrote. "We see no reason, however, not to make these assumptions." The rules of evidence spelled out here are casual, not causal.

The commission fared much better in its attempt to coopt the language of antipornography feminists. One would think it was a difficult undertaking, since Hudson, Sears and the conservative cohort were no feminists. Hudson usually addressed female commissioners as "ladies." He transmuted the term used by women's antipornography groups, "the degradation of women," into "the degradation of femininity," which conjured up visions of Victorian womanhood dragged from the pedestal. Beyond language, conservatives consistently opposed proposals that feminists universally support—for sex education, for example.

However, witnesses provided by women's antipornography groups proved more useful than social scientists. They were eager to cast their personal experiences of incest, childhood sexual abuse, rape and sexual coercion in terms of the "harm" and "degradation" caused by pornography. Some were willing to understate, and most to omit mentioning, their support for those cranky feminist demands so offensive to conservative ears: abortion, birth control, lesbian and gay rights. Other feminist groups, including COYOTE, the U.S. Prostitutes Collective, the A.C.L.U. Women's Rights Project and the Feminist Anti Censorship Task Force (FACT, of which I am a member), criticized the panel's simple-minded attempt to link violence against women with sexual images and noted the irony of the Attorney General's concern for women at a time when the Administration has seriously cut back on women's programs. Protests were organized in conjunction with hearings in Los Angeles and New York.

The notion that pornography degrades women proved to be a particularly helpful unifying term, floating in and out of fundamentalist as well as antipornography feminist testimony. Speakers didn't notice, or chose not to, that the term "degradation" has very different meanings in each community. For antipornography feminists, pornography degrades women when it depicts or glorifies sexist sex: images that put men's pleasure first or indicate that women's lot in life is to serve men. For fundamentalists, degrading sexual images show sex outside marriage, including many behaviors considered acceptable, even desirable, by feminist thinkers, such as masturbation and egalitarian lesbian sex.

Although the commission happily assimilated the rhetoric of antipornography feminists, it decisively rejected their remedies. Conservative men pronounced the testimony of Andrea Dworkin "eloquent" and "moving" and insisted on including her remarks in the final report. But antipornography feminists had argued against obscenity laws and in favor of ordinances, such as those developed for Minneapolis and Indianapolis by Dworkin and Catharine MacKinnon, which outlaw pornography as a violation of women's civil rights. The commission never seriously entertained the idea that obscenity laws should be repealed; given its conservative constituency and agenda, it couldn't have.

Even more startling were MacKinnon and Dworkin's statements to the press that the commission "has recommended to Congress the civil rights legislation women have sought," and this comment by Dorchen Leidholdt, founder of Women Against Pornography: "I'm not embarrassed at being in agreement with Ed Meese." (She also supported the panel's efforts to publish Donald Wildmon's list of "businesses that traffic in pornography.") The only plausible explanation is that each group is strategizing how best to use the other. The Meese commission used feminist language to justify its conservative agenda, while antipornography feminist groups used the Meese commission to gain public recognition and legitimacy.

THE DEFINITION

If orchestrating the new discourse was taxing, defining pornography was even harder. Having spent one year and a half-million dollars, the commission failed to define pornography. Two definitions came and went, one so broad that it included virtually all sexually explicit material. One critic joked, taking off from Justice Potter Stewart's remark, "Apparently they don't know it when they see it, but they don't want anybody to see it anyway."

The commissioners were unable to define pornography, but Jesuitical discussions that consumed two days of their Scottsdale, Arizona, business meeting produced a novel taxonomy that drew on the antipornography feminist vocabulary. Sexually explicit images, the panel decided, could be divided into four classes: violent (I), not violent but degrading (II), not violent and not degrading (III), not sexually explicit but portraying nudity (IV). Class I pornography was "an offense against humanity," whereas Class II was an offense to "profound human dignity."

A free-for-all erupted when commissioners specified what they meant by degrading sexual images. Nominations for Class II included oral sex, anal sex, group sex and masturbation. A discussion ensued on the concept of "homosexual degradation," which for some commissioners appeared to include any sexually explicit image of homosexuality. "Homosexual activity, contrary to appropriate purposes of human sexuality, is not a good thing," one panelist intoned.

Full-scale war broke out when the commissioners reached the category of nondegrading, nonviolent sexual images. The name itself is curious, suggesting an inability to characterize such images in a positive way. Moderates, citing the evidence from social science research, suggested that they cause little or no harm. For conservatives, anecdotal evidence and common sense proved that even these images were harmful. Moderates cringed at the unabashedly moralistic tone, but conservatives were apoplectic at the possibility that the commission might tell the American public that any sexually explicit image—heterosexual and homosexual, inside and outside marriage—is harmless.

The chair faced the prospect of a badly split vote. Commissioners could agree on virtually nothing about this class of material. Hudson decided to let each commissioner contribute an essay to the report expressing his or her personal view about Class III. But citizens will not have the same opportunity to make up their own minds if new obscenity laws sweep Class III material from the shelves and screens.

In the end the commission was unwilling to find any category of sexual images harmless. They even cast a dubious eye on nudity. It could be "dangerous" and "provocative," that is, provoke people to have sex. Statues like *David* and *Aphrodite* are great works of art, but imagine thousands of such statues lining a highway, one commissioner mused. It did give one pause.

Two important points emerge from this definitional swamp. First is the finding that all sexual images cause harm. On that one the conservatives won. The second is the invention of the category of violent pornography. This category is problematic, but moderates have accepted it as blindly as have conservatives. The reasons for this uncritical response are complex: a genuine concern about violence, particularly against women; a willingness to believe that depictions of violence or coercion in sexual images cause literal imitation; an ignorance and fear of sexually stigmatized behavior, particularly sadomasochism.

What falls into the category of violent pornography? Some material is suggested by recent social psychology laboratory experiments on "aggressive" and "nonaggressive" sexually explicit materials. ("Violent pornography" is not a social science term.) The studies commonly use specially made shorts depicting a woman's rape: in one version she resists to the end; in the other she gives in and "enjoys" it. The negative attitudinal effects found with the second scenario—quite apart from questions of the duration of effects and generalizability—have

been attributed to a much broader range of material. To indict pornography this broadening is necessary because the rape scenario appears in only a small fraction of commercial pornography. The commission's own content analysis of April 1986 top-selling pornographic magazines found an extraordinarily low rate of pictures showing "force, violence, or weapons": 0.6 percent, or 3 out of 512. This analysis and supporting data, which were included in early drafts, mysteriously disappeared from the final report.

But the commission used the term "violent pornography," defined as "actual or unmistakably simulated or unmistakably threatened violence presented in a sexually explicit fashion," to cover a wide range of other materials. Leading the pack was the snuff film, a movie in which a real woman is purportedly killed. The snuff film was the hearings' unicorn: much talked about, long searched for but never found. Legions of vice cops testified that an actual snuff film had never been identified, despite diligent investigations. Some R-rated Hollywood movies were also candidates for Class I. "Slice and dice" films such as *The Texas Chainsaw Massacre* offer scenes of eroticized violence, but they are not pornography because they are not sexually explicit.

The remaining candidate for inclusion in this category, then, was sadomasochistic imagery, of which the commission saw a great deal and found deeply upsetting. During the course of their discussions, S&M migrated from the "degrading" to the "violent" class, more by a process of osmosis than decision. The commission called no witnesses to discuss the nature of S&M, either professional experts or typical participants. They ignored a small but increasing body of literature that documents important features of S&M sexual behavior, namely consent and safety. Typically, the conventions we use to decipher ordinary images are suspended when it comes to S&M images. When we see war movies, for example, we do not leave the theater believing that the carnage we saw was real or that the performers were injured making the films. But the commissioners assumed that images of domination and submission were both real and coerced.

The exceptional status of S&M images was heightened by testimony about coerced performances in any and all pornography, such as Linda Marchiano's account of how her husband abused her in the making of *Deep Throat.* Although coercion could exist in the making of any image— sexual or nonsexual, S&M or non-S&M—popular prejudice transformed concern about coercion into another indictment of S&M images. A critique of coercion should have focused on working conditions, not images. It helped that the images shown to the panelists were carefully selected so that the preponderance portrayed female submission and male dominance, thus framing sadomasochism in the context of gender inequality. Reverse images of male submission, common in the genre, or homosexual images, were rarely shown.

THE RESULTS

The most tangible results of the Meese commission's recommendations will be increased prosecutions under existing obscenity laws and the passage of new ones. Federal actions that require only administrative approval are likely to begin right away: appointment of special task forces and Justice Department directives to Federal prosecutors to increase enforcement. It is likely that new legislation will be passed at the Federal, state and local levels, following the commission's specific recommendations.

The commission's endorsement of citizen action groups is significant because it extends the report's recommendations far beyond legally obscene materials to include materials that "some citizens may find dangerous or offensive or immoral." The report provides a detailed plan describing how citizens can canvass local bookstores and newsstands for offensive items, report to the police, monitor prosecutions and sentencing, and organize demonstrations and boycotts. The creation of a "network of sex spies," to use Barry Lynn's term, could prove more important than prosecution in making

sexually explicit material unavailable in many areas of the country. Emboldened by the recent successes of the Rev. Jerry Falwell's boycotts, these groups may step beyond sexually explicit material to police other offensive images and texts.

Another legacy of the Meese commission must be seen in terms of what it failed to do. It only reluctantly approved of programs to educate schoolchildren about sexual abuse, for fear that this would be misread as an endorsement of sex education or an encouragement to children to make hysterical accusations against male relatives. It refused even to consider decriminalizing work in the sex industry and prostitution, preferring arrest and worsened working conditions for the participants, overwhelmingly female.

The most far-reaching and dangerous effect of the Meese commission's work may be its impact on judicial interpretation and application of obscenity laws. It is possible that the rhetoric about the harms of pornography—disseminated via simplistic headlines like "Pornography Breeds Violence, U.S. Panel Says"—may alter the cultural atmosphere in which judges and juries make necessarily subjective judgments about sexually explicit material. The commission's recommendations also contradict the assumptions of our legal system, which regulates bad actions rather than the books, speech or political theories that might arguably cause them. But Alan Sears inveighs against sexually related materials because they lead to "improper or bad attitudes." The genius of the Meese commission lies in its ability to make plausible in regard to sexual words and images a standard that is totally implausible in any other sphere.

The commission's chances of success—despite internal dissent, criticism by social scientists and widely publicized lawsuits by *Playboy* and *Penthouse*—remain high. The commission has with uncanny intuition gone to the heart of our culture's symbolic infrastructure about sex: sex degrades women; sex and violence are intimately linked, perhaps identical. To the extent that the commission has tapped fears usually expressed in conservative terms and has repackaged them in contemporary language, its findings will have appeal.

A total return to the sexual landscape of the 1950s is improbable. Too many changes have occurred in sex roles, families and sexual expression to permit the rollback conservatives have in mind.

Yet sexual liberalization is enormously fragile, in part because it is so dependent on other social changes now under heavy assault from the right, in part because even progressives perceive sexuality as still too shameful and private an issue for which to mobilize a vigorous public defense.

Prostitution Control in America

Ronald Weitzer

PROBLEMS WITH CURRENT POLICY

Prostitution control in America involves the commitment of substantial criminal justice resources—with little impact on the sex trade or on collateral problems such as victimization of prostitutes and effects on host communites.

Criminal Justice System Costs

There are approximately 90,000 annual arrests in the United States for violations of prostitution laws (Bureau of Justice Statistics annual), in addition to an unknown number of arrests of prostitutes under disorderly conduct or loitering statutes. The fiscal costs are substantial. A study of the country's sixteen largest cities found that they spent a total of $120 million in 1985 enforcing prostitution laws (Pearl 1987). Data are unavailable on the costs of prostitution control nationwide, but extrapolating from the above figure on just a few cities, there is no question that the total expenditure is considerable.

What are the benefits of these expenditures? A San Francisco Crime Committee (1971: 20) concluded in

From *Crime, Law & Social Change* 32, no.1 (1999), pp.83–102. © 2000 Kluwer Academic Publishers. Reprinted by permission of Kluwer Academic Publishers.

1971 that spending on prostitution control "buys essentially nothing of a positive nature," and Atlanta's Task Force on Prostitution (1986) concluded that this spending was a "waste" that burdened the courts and lowered police morale. Moreover, law enforcement has little effect on the amount of prostitution, offers little protection to prostitutes at risk, and gives little relief to communities besieged by street prostitution. At best, the problem is *contained* within a particular area where prostitutes are occasionally subjected to the revolving door of arrest, fines, brief jail time, and release, or *displaced* into another locale, begetting the same revolving-door dynamic. Containment is the norm throughout the United States; displacement requires sustained police intervention, which is rare. Instead, law enforcement typically consists of periodic arrests and occasional, sweeping crackdowns on prostitutes. Containment may be acceptable to residents of neighborhoods free of street prostitution, but is aggravating to many residents of prostitution zones.

Victimization

Street prostitutes are at considerable risk of violence from customers, exploitation from pimps, and drug and health problems. A survey of 200 street prostitutes in San Francisco found that two-thirds had been assaulted by customers and pimps and 70 percent had been raped by customers (Silbert and Pines 1982). Other studies report similar rates of victimization among street prostitutes (Barnard 1993; Davis 2000; Farley and Barkan 1998; James and Meyerling 1977). However, all of these studies relied on convenience samples (women who contacted service agencies or were interviewed in jail or on the streets), not random samples, which likely skews the results toward that part of the population experiencing the most victimization. This means that the high victimization rates reported are probably lower for street prostitutes as a whole. Having said that, all evidence indicates that street prostitutes are indeed vulnerable to abuse and that prevailing methods of prostitution control in most cities offer little protection against such victimization.

Workers involved in upscale prostitution, such as escorts and call girls, are relatively free of victimization (Perkins 1991:290). They are not immune to violence, but it is not the occupational hazard that it is for street workers.

Community Impact

It is street prostitution—not the more clandestine, indoor varieties of sex work—that generates the lion's share of citizen complaints about prostitution in America. A wide variety of sources (e.g., Clark 1993; Persons 1996) and my extensive search of newpaper articles in Lexis/Nexis (Weitzer 2000) identified a set of common claims made by residents of neighborhoods with street prostitution.

Unlike the antiprostitution reformers of the 19th and early 20th centuries, who made much of the immorality and sinfulness of prostitution as well as the exploitation of "fallen" women (Hobson 1987; Pivar 1973), neighborhood groups in contemporary America are driven less by moral indignation than by *overt street behavior* on the part of prostitutes, pimps, and customers. Stress is placed on the *tangible environmental effects* of sexual commerce on the street.

The degree to which prostitutes, pimps, and customers cause commotion in public places varies across time and place. Still, the public visibility of the enterprise increases the likelihood that it will have some adverse effect on the surrounding community. Similarities across cities in the manifestation of street prostitution produce similar complaints among residents. Standard complaints center on conduct such as streetwalkers' brazen flagging down of customers' cars, arguing and fighting with people on the street, visible drug use, performing sex acts in public, and littering with used condoms and syringes (both unsightly trash and a public health hazard). Children are frequently mentioned in the litany of grievances: they witness transactions and sex acts being consumated; they sometimes discover discarded condoms and syringes; and they are occasionally approached by prostitutes or customers.

Customers are scorned in these communities as much as the prostitutes (Persons 1996). Not only do they contribute to traffic congestion in their ritual cruising of prostitution strolls, they also harass and proposition women whom they mistake for prostitutes. Many communities have targeted the customers (by recording their license plate numbers, videotaping, etc.) more than the prostitutes, because the johns are seen as more vulnerable to public identification and shaming.

Residents define street prostitution not as a mere nuisance or "victimless crime" but instead as eroding the quality of life and contributing to neighborhood decay and street disorder (cf. Kelling and Coles 1996; Skogan 1990; Wilson and Kelling 1982). As a coalition of twenty-eight neighborhood and business groups in San Francisco declared, street prostitution "poses a very serious threat to the integrity of San Francisco's business and residential communities" (Coalition 1996).

No data exist on the magnitude of the problems due to street prostitution in American cities (aside from arrest rates and residents' claims that the problem is serious), but the literature on this topic indicates that street prostitution can present a real problem for host communities.

ALTERNATIVE POLICIES

Soliciting for purposes of prostitution, pimping, and other prostitution-related activities are crimes throughout the United States, and this criminalization policy is seldom questioned. Rarely have policy makers shown a willingness to rethink the status quo and experiment with novel approaches.[1] No national commission of inquiry has examined prostitution, with the result that almost no public debate has taken place. Alternatives to the current policy of blanket criminalization are evaluated below.

Decriminalization

[Total] decriminalization would remove criminal penalties and result in a laissez-faire approach in which prostitution would be left unregulated. Prostitutes' rights groups, like COYOTE (Call Off Your Old Tired Ethics),[2] favor full decriminalization of adult prostitution because they define it as work, like any other work, and because decriminalization is the only policy that recognizes prostitutes' "right" to use their bodies as they wish. Regulations are opposed because they would allow government interference with this right and because they would only perpetuate the stigmatization of prostitutes (e.g., if restricted to brothels or red light districts).

There is virtually no public support for decriminalization. A 1983 survey found that only 7 percent of the public thought "there should be no laws against prostitution" (Merit 1983). Policy makers are almost universally opposed to decriminalization, making this a nonstarter in any serious discussion of policy alternatives (Parnas 1981). Moreover, the logic behind decriminalization is shaky. Freed of regulation, prostitutes arguably

would enjoy advantages unavailable to purveyors of other commercial services (Skolnick and Dombrink 1978:201; Decker 1979:463). A major Canadian commission held that prostitution should enjoy no special immunity from the law: "it is difficult to see how some degree of regulation could be avoided" in light of "the special risks inherent in the activity of prostitution" (Special Committee 1985:518). Taken to its extreme, decriminalization would permit prostitutes and their customers to engage in sexual exchanges without restriction, except for extant prohibitions on public nudity and sex.

Although decriminalization is roundly dismissed by the American public and policy makers, its advocates sometimes manage to get it onto the public agenda. A recent example illustrates the fate of a decriminalization proposal, in a city known for its tolerance. A Task Force on Prostitution was formed by San Francisco's Board of Supervisors in 1994 to explore alternatives to existing methods of prostitution control. Members included representatives of community and business groups, the National Lawyer's Guild, National Organization for Women, prostitutes' rights groups, the police department, and the district attorney's office. From the beginning, the prostitutes' advocates and their sympathizers set the agenda and dominated the proceedings, which led to chronic infighting. Supervisor Terence Hallinan was the driving force behind the panel but unsatisfied with the result: "I didn't ride herd on this task force. I would have liked a better balance . . . Instead of coming up with good, practical solutions, they spent months fighting about decriminalization and legalization."[3] After a majority of the members voted to recommend a policy of decriminalization in January 1995,[4] the six community and business representatives resigned. One of the latter later proclaimed that the departure of community members

---

[1] There has been more debate in official circles in Britain and Canada, where a number of cities have considered legalization.
[2] Founded in 1973 by former prostitute Margo St. James, COYOTE is the premier prostitutes' rights group in the United States, and is affiliated with several lesser known organizations (Weitzer 1991). Although COYOTE claims to represent all prostitutes, it has been closely aligned with upper-echelon call girls, not streetwalkers.

---

[3] *San Francisco Examiner,* December 6, 1995.
[4] "The Task Force therefore recommends that the City stop enforcing and prosecuting prostitution crimes" (San Francisco Task Force 1996: 6).

shredded the legitimacy of the panel and troubled the remaining members: "They were upset as hell because the task force lost credibility without the citizens' groups participating."[5] While the comment is not made from a disinterested position, the task force report itself expresses regret that consensus was not achieved on its main recommendation.

The panel's endorsement of decriminalization reflected the interests of prostitutes' advocates and their allies and doomed the report's prospect for serious consideration in official circles. The city's Board of Supervisors promptly shelved the report. It is possible, however, that a less radical recommendation would have been received more favorably by city officials; Supervisor Hallinan and even some community leaders had floated the possibility of legalization (zoning into red light areas) when the task force was first proposed.

Legalization

Legalization spells *regulation* of some kind: licensing or registration, confining prostitutes to red light districts, state-restricted brothels, mandatory medical exams, special business taxes, etc. Implicit in the idea of legalization is the principle of harm reduction: that is, that regulation is necessary to reduce some of the problems associated with prostitution. The American public is divided on the issue, with support for legalization ranging from a quarter to half the population in most polls (Gallup 1991, 1996; Harris 1978, 1990; Merit 1983; Weitzer 2000). This support has not, however, translated into popular pressure for legal change anywhere in the country, in part because most citizens see it as far removed from their personal interests and because policy makers are largely silent on the issue (Weitzer 1991).

Some advocates of legalization cite with approval Nevada's legal brothels. Confined to small-scale operations in rural areas of the state (and prohibited in Las Vegas and Reno due to opposition from the gambling industry), this model hardly solves the problem of street prostitution in urban areas. Streetwalkers flourish in Las Vegas and Reno, despite the existence of legal brothels in counties adjacent to these cities. What is needed is some kind of specifically urban solution to an essentially urban problem.

Since Nevada legalized brothels in 1971, no other state has seriously considered legalization. Legislators fear being branded as "condoning" prostitution, and see no political advantages in any kind of liberalization. The exceptions seem to prove the rule of futility. For example, bills to permit licensing of prostitutes and brothels were introduced in the California State Assembly in the 1970s, to no avail (Jennings 1976; Parnas 1981). In 1992 New York City Councilor Julia Harrison offered a resolution for licensing prostitutes, restricting legal brothels to certain parts of the city, and requiring HIV tests of the workers. The purpose was "to eliminate the pestilence of street activity in residential neighborhoods," as the resolution declared. Harrison told me that she got the "highest praise from the community" in her district, Flushing, but her proposal met with stiff opposition in the city council and never made it out of committee.[6]

A major determinant of the success of legalization is the willingness of prostitutes to comply with the regulations. Those who have pimps may not be allowed to work in most regulated systems, particularly if it means a dilution of the pimps' control over their employees. Where legalization includes stipulations as to who can and cannot engage in the sex trade, certain types of individuals will be excluded from the legal regime, forcing them to operate illicitly. Where underage or diseased or migrant prostitutes are ineligible, they would have no recourse but to work in the shadows of the regulated system. Moreover, every conceivable form of legalization would be rejected by some or many eligible prostitutes, who would see no benefits in abiding by the new restrictions and would resent the infringement on their freedom. It is precisely on these grounds that prostitutes' rights groups

---

[5] Interview, April 29, 1997.

[6] Interview, June 7, 1993.

denounce licensing, mandatory health checks, and legal brothel systems. A possible exception would be zoning street prostitution into a suitable locale: away from residential areas but in places that are safe and unintimidating for prostitutes and customers alike. Many streetwalkers would be satisfied with this kind of arrangement, but others would not. Red light districts in industrial zones have been proposed, but most streetwalkers would reject confinement to these areas because they typically lack places of refuge and sustenance, such as restaurants, coffee shops, bars, parks, and cheap hotels—all of which are facilitative of street prostitution (Cohen 1980). Even if an acceptable locale could be found, there is no guarantee that street prostitution would be confined to that area; market saturation in the designated zone would push some workers into less competitive locales. Moreover, while zoning presumably would remove street prostitution from residential areas, it would not necessarily remedy other problems associated with street work, such as violence and drug abuse.

Would a system of legal prostitution attract an influx of prostitutes into the host city? If limited to one or a few cities in the United States, the answer would be affirmative. Were it more widespread, each locale would hold less attraction to outside workers.

More fundamentally, would legalization, in any of its forms, institutionalize and officially condone prostitution and make it more difficult for workers to leave the business? Government officials, feminists, and prostitutes' rights advocates alike object to legalization on precisely these grounds. Whether legalization would indeed make it more difficult for workers to leave prostitution than is the case under criminalization would depend in part on whether the workers were officially labeled as prostitutes— via registration, licensing, special commercial taxes, a registry for mandatory health checks—or whether their identities would remain unknown to the authorities, as might be the case if legalization took the form of zoning.

A final consideration is the willingness and capacity of municipal authorities to actively regulate

the sex trade and compel compliance with the rules. American officials are almost universally unprepared to assume this responsibility. Why would any American city assume the added burden of planning, launching, and managing a system of legal prostitution when the benefits are doubtful and when the logistical, resource, and moral costs would be envisioned as unacceptably high? Whatever the possible merits (health, safety, etc.) of any particular model of legalization, it is therefore imperative to consider its feasibility in the United States. Advocates face almost impossible odds trying to marshall support from legislators and the wider population. Proposals for legalization, while occasionally floated, will remain nonstarters in this country for the foreseeable future. A third policy alternative may have broader appeal.

A Two-Track Model

Policy makers often fail to draw the crucial distinction between street and off-street prostitution, partly because both types are criminalized by law throughout the United States. But since prostitution manifests itself in fundamentally different ways on the street and in indoor venues, it is only sensible to treat the two differently. One model would (1) *target resources exclusively toward the control of street prostitution* and (2) *relax controls on indoor prostitution* such as escort agencies, massage parlors, call girls, and brothels. A few blue-ribbon panels have recommended changes either consistent with or close to this two-track model. A San Francisco commission noted that whereas street prostitution has significant adverse consequences for public order and public health, the situation is quite the opposite for indoor prostitution—a situation warranting a dual approach (San Francisco Committee 1971). An Atlanta task force went a step further in recommending that law enforcement be directed against street prostitution rather than off-street prostitution and that city officials provide more assistance to neighborhoods affected by prostitution, in the form of greater liaison between neighborhood associations and the authorities and redevelopment of communities to discourage street prostitution and other crime (Atlanta Task Force 1986). And a landmark Canadian commission argued that abating street prostitution would require legislation allowing prostitutes to work somewhere else. It recommended (1) allowing unobtrusive street solicitation, (2) punishment of obnoxious behavior by streetwalkers (offensive language, disturbing the peace, disrupting traffic), and (3) permitting one or two prostitutes to work out of their residence (Special Committee 1985). (The third proposal was endorsed by a recent Canadian task force [Working Group 1998:71]). Indoor work by one or two prostitutes was seen as preferable to work on the streets or in brothels since it gives the workers maximum autonomy and shields them against exploitation by pimps and other managers. The commission also recommended giving provincial authorities the option of legalizing small, nonresidential brothels, subject to appropriate controls.

In all three cases, government officials rejected the recommendations—without explanation in San Francisco and Atlanta, and in Canada on the grounds that it would condone prostitution. Some Australian states, however, have recently implemented the two-track approach, i.e., decriminalizing brothels and increasing enforcement against street prostitution (Sullivan 1997).

Track One: Indoor Prostitution Some cities already have an informal policy of de facto decriminalization of indoor prostitution—essentially ignoring call girls, escort agencies, and massage parlors unless a complaint is made, which is seldom. Police in other cities, however, devote substantial time and resources to this side of the sex trade, where it accounts for as much as half the prostitution arrests or consumes up to half the vice budgets. One study of sixteen cities found that indoor prostitution accounted for between a quarter and a third of all prostitution arrests in Baltimore, Memphis, and Milwaukee, and half the arrests in Cleveland.[7] Some cities (like Houston and Philadelphia) have shifted their emphasis

from the street to indoor prostitution, ostensibly to go after the "big fish."[8] Some other police departments devote an entire branch to combatting outcall and escort services, e.g., the Pandering Unit in Detroit and the Ad Vice Unit in Los Angeles.

Efforts against indoor prostitution typically involve elaborate, time-consuming undercover operations to entrap the women. Such stings require considerable planning, and large-scale operations can last a year or two, becoming rather costly affairs. The Heidi Fleiss case in Los Angeles is only the most notorious recent example. There have been some federal actions as well. In 1990, for example, federal agents launched raids on more than forty upscale escort agencies in twenty-three cities. The sting was the culmination of a two-year undercover investigation, costing $2.5 million.[9]

An officer attached to the Ad Vice unit in Los Angeles justified his work with rather twisted logic: "We're trying to keep it from becoming rampant on our streets" (A&E 1997). In fact, crackdowns on indoor prostitution can have the opposite result—increasing the number of streetwalkers—thus unintentionally exacerbating the most obtrusive side of the prostitution trade. Closures of massage parlors and other indoor venues have had precisely this effect in some cities (Cohen 1980: 81; Larsen 1992; Lowman 1992; Pearl 1985), and a New Orleans vice officer noted that, "Whenever we focus on indoor investigations, the street scene gets insane."[10]

The success of a policy of nonenforcement regarding indoor prostitution would require that it be implemented without fanfare. A public announcement that a city had decided to take a "hands off" approach to this variety of sex work might serve as a magnet drawing legions of indoor workers and clients into the locale. But in cities where it is not already standard practice, an unwritten policy of nonenforcement might be a sensible innovation. It would

---

[7] Julie Pearl study, on file with *Hastings Law Journal.*

[8] Interviews with vice officers in these cities by Julie Pearl; transcripts on file with *Hastings Law Journal.*

[9] *San Francisco Chronicle,* April 6, 1990.

[10] Vice sergeant interviewed by Julie Pearl, May 1985; transcript on file at *Hastings Law Journal.*

free up resources for the more pressing problems on the street, and might have the effect of pushing some streetwalkers indoors, as one commission reasoned: "Keeping prostitutes off the streets may be aided by tolerating them off the streets" (San Francisco Committee 1971:44). Such an effect is far from certain, however. As a general rule, there is little mobility between the different ranks of prostitution (Benson and Matthews 1995; Heyl 1979), and each type has unique attractions to the workers. Advantages of street work include greater flexibility in working conditions than the more restrictive indoor work, rapid turnover of customers and lower time-commitment per trick, and the freedom and excitement of street hustling. Regarding the latter, "Many prostitutes say they prefer the constant action on the street . . . They enjoy the game aspect of the transaction and the intensity of life as a streetwalker, in contrast to work in a massage parlor or house" (James 1973:148). Some clients also prefer streetwalkers: advantages include easy access, anonymity, low cost, choice of women, and the thrill of cruising for sex on the streets—though other clients are attracted to indoor venues because they are safer and more discreet (Campbell 1998). Moreover, indoor work may not be an option for those streetwalkers who lack the social skills and physical attractiveness that may be required by such establishments or their clients. Indoor and outdoor prostitution serve different markets (Reynolds 1986). Having said that, greater police intervention on the street has at least some potential to induce some streetwalkers indoors, perhaps into massage parlors.

Compared to street prostitution, there is relatively little public opposition to indoor prostitution, provided it remains inconspicuous. Escort agencies and call girls are typically ignored by community groups, and even massage parlors and brothels arouse little concern relative to streetwalking—again, provided they remain discreet. In San Francisco, a leader of the neighborhood group Save Our Streets told me that most residents of his community would not be bothered by indoor prostitution: "My gut feeling is that, yes, that would be OK. No one has voiced concern over massage parlors"

in the area.[11] And a Washington, DC, neighborhood activist remarked that "people wouldn't be too upset if prostitution went indoors."[12] Community groups rarely mobilize against indoor prostitution, and it appears that the general population is less concerned about this side of the trade. A 1988 survey of residents of Toledo, Ohio (a conservative, working-class city) found that 28 percent supported legal "government-controlled brothels" and 19 percent supported decriminalization of "private call-girl prostitution" (McCaghy and Cernkovich 1991). No national public opinion polls have asked about specific types of prostitution; instead, they ask vague questions about "legalization" or legal "regulation." Findings of a national Canadian survey may approximate American patterns: while only 11 percent of the population found street prostitution acceptable, a higher number accepted designated red light districts (28 percent), brothels (38 percent), escort and call girl services (43 percent), and prostitution on private premises (45 percent) (Peat Marwick 1984). Clearly, the *visibility* of prostitution shapes its public acceptability.

Is there a class bias in the two-track approach? Does it favor the higher class, indoor sector and unfairly target the lower-echelon streetwalkers? Inherent in any two-track approach are disparate effects on actors associated with each track, and with respect to prostitution there are legitimate grounds for differential treatment: (1) certain other types of commercial enterprise are prohibited on the streets, and there is no compelling reason why street prostitution should be permitted and (2) "this kind of policy may not be considered too inequitable if the costs inflicted on society by the street prostitutes are greater . . . than from those working in hotels" and other indoor venues (Reynolds 1986:194). The legal principle on which this proposal rests is that the criminal law should not interfere with the conduct of consenting adults, provided that this conduct does not *harm* the legally protected interests of others. Whereas street prostitution often involves violence

---

[11] Interview, July 9, 1993.
[12] Interview, July 27, 1993.

against prostitutes, ancillary crime, disorderly behavior in public, and other adverse effects on host neighborhoods, indoor prostitution is in accord with the harm-reduction principle (Caughey 1974; Comment 1977). As the San Francisco Committee on Crime (1971:38) flatly concluded, "continued criminalization of private, non-visible prostitution cannot be warranted by fear of associated crime, drug abuse, venereal disease, or protection of minors." The Canadian commission (1985:515) agreed: "The concern with the law is not what takes place in private, but the public manifestation of prostitution." Similarly, harms to prostitutes themselves are pronounced for street workers but much less so for workers in brothels and massage parlors and call girls and escorts (Bryan 1966; Exner et al. 1977; Farley and Davis 1978; Reynolds 1986). As a recent Canadian task force noted, "the two objectives of harm reduction and violence prevention could most likely occur if prostitution was conducted indoors" (Working Group 1998:35). The policy implication is clear: "reassign police priorities to those types of prostitution that inflict the greatest costs" (Reynolds 1986:192), namely, street prostitution.

Track Two: Restructuring Street Prostitution Control One advantage of the two-track model is that resources previously devoted to the control of indoor prostitution can be transferred to where they are most needed: the street-level sex trade. Under this model, a policy of *more frequent arrests* of streetwalkers and johns would replace the current norm of sporadic, half-hearted enforcement. This is just the first step, however. What happens after arrest is equally important.

Most prostitution arrests in the United States require that offenders be caught in the act of solicitation, a labor-intensive form of control that limits enforcement efforts. In this legal context it would be naive to think that the "oldest profession" can be wholly eradicated from any major American city. The costs to the prostitute (fines, jail time) could be enhanced, but not dramatically for a misdemeanor offense. Moreover, stiffer penalties have the unfortunate side-effect of forcing prostitutes back onto the streets to recoup their losses, essentially becoming an added cost of doing business. Other, very different approaches are worth considering. A San Diego Task Force (1993), a British parliamentary committee (Benson and Matthews 1996), and the Association of Chief Police Officers in Britain (Bennetto 1996) have called for community service sanctions for prostitutes, and New York City has recently experimented with this penalty. If the policy of fining prostitutes simply encourages reoffending to recover losses, community service may open up avenues for a different line of work for at least some of the individuals who truly aspire to reintegration into conventional society. *Community service sanctions are superior to fines or incarceration for this population,* and any policy of intensified arrests should be coupled with a shift toward community service sanctions.

A third reform in the control of street-level prostitution is the need for a more *comprehensive program of meaningful job training and other needed services for those who want to leave prostitution* but eschew low-paying, dead-end jobs. It is not known what percentage of street prostitutes want to leave prostitution, but for those who do, resources are scarce (and even scarcer for sex workers who do not want to leave the industry, but need services). Services to women in the sex industry are woefully inadequate (Weiner 1996; Seattle Women's Commission 1995). For example, in Seattle,

> Existing services are not prepared to deal with the unique issues of sex industry women [e.g., stigma, sexual trauma, emotional problems] . . . Nor do women have the backup resources of family and education needed to reorganize their lives. (Boyer, Chapman, and Marshall 1993:20)

Getting prostitutes off the streets requires positive incentives and assistance in the form of housing, job training, counseling, and drug treatment, but the dominant approach is overwhelmingly coercive rather than rehabilitative. Past experience abundantly shows the failure of narrowly punitive intervention. Without meaningful alternatives to prostitution there is little opportunity for a career change.

What about the customers? Traditionally, the act of patronizing a prostitute was not a crime in the United States. This was largely due to the tremendous status disparity between male clients and "women of ill repute." Prostitutes were outcasts whereas patrons were seen as valuable members of society, even if they occasionally dabbled in deviant sexual liaisons. As Abraham Flexner wrote in 1920, the customer "discharges important social and business relations, is a father or brother responsible for the maintenance of others, has commercial or industrial duties to meet. He cannot be imprisoned without damaging society" (quoted in Little 1995: 38–39). This justification for gender discrimination persists in some quarters today. The renowned Model Penal Code reflects this double standard: The code stipulates that prostitution should be treated as a misdemeanor, while patronizing a prostitute should be punished as a mere violation—an infraction punishable by a fine rather than incarceration. The disparity was defended even as late as 1980, in the official commentary on the code:

> Authorization of severe penalties [jail time] for such misconduct [patronizing] is wholly unrealistic. Prosecutors, judges, and juries would be prone to nullify severe penalties in light of the common perception of extramarital intercourse as a widespread practice. . . . This level of condemnation [a violation and fine] would seem far more in keeping with popular understanding than would more severe sanctions. Furthermore, the lenient treatment of customers reflects the orientation of the offense toward the merchandizers of sexual activity. (American Law Institute 1980:468)

The prevalence of extramarital sex, a "popular understanding" favoring the clients, and the notion that the law should target sellers, not buyers, of vice are all invoked to justify lenient treatment of clients. Most state penal codes now treat patronizing as a misdemeanor, not a mere violation as the Model Penal Code recommended.

Since the 1960s, the act of patronizing or soliciting a prostitute has been criminalized by all states, though many state laws continue to punish patronizing less severely than prostitution (Posner and Silbaugh 1996:156). And in most cities, enforcement against customers is either sporadic or lacking altogether. Although the double standard has eroded to some extent, it is still only in the exceptional jurisdiction where prostitutes and their patrons are treated equally. Elsewhere, gender bias persists in both arrest rates and penalties (Bernat 1985; Lowman 1990). Nationally, of the approximately 90,000 prostitution arrests every year, roughly one-third are males (Bureau of Justice Statistics annual), which breaks down to about 20 percent male prostitutes and 10 percent male customers. In light of the fact that customers greatly outnumber prostitutes, the gender disparity in arrests appears even more disproportional. Gender bias is also evident in sanctions. In Seattle from 1991 to 1993, for example, 2,508 prostitutes were arrested for solicitation while only 500 customers were arrested for patronizing (Seattle Women's Commission 1995). And in 1993, 69 percent of the prostitutes charged with solicitation were convicted whereas only 9 percent of the customers were convicted, largely because they were offered pre-trial diversion. Indeed, in most cities first-time arrested customers are routinely offered diversion rather than prosecution. And those customers who are prosecuted and convicted are less likely than prostitutes to receive fines or jail time (Lowman 1990). In Vancouver between 1991 and 1995, for example, only 0.5 percent of convicted customers were jailed and 9 percent fined; the remainder received absolute or conditional discharges. Convicted prostitutes were treated more harshly: 29 percent were jailed and 32 percent were given suspended sentences (Atchison et al. 1998).

An argument can be made for paying more attention to the *demand side* of prostitution. First, sheer numbers would seem to justify greater control of the customers, who are far more numerous than prostitutes. A major 1992 survey found that 16 percent of American men ages 18–59 said they had ever paid for sex (Laumann et al. 1994). A question on something as stigmatized as one's personal involvement in prostitution is likely to yield some underreporting; still, it is clear that a significant proportion of the male population has had such encounters.

Second, demand-side prostitution controls can pay much higher dividends than supply-side controls. Prostitutes are dependent on this work for their livelihood and not easily deterred by sanctions. Customers, who have a greater stake in conventional society, are more fearful of arrest and punishment and more vulnerable than prostitutes to public shaming and stigmatization (Persons 1996). A British study found that arrested customers were unconcerned about fines but very worried about damage to their reputations if their activities were made public (Matthews 1993:14–15). A corrolary is that customers are much less likely to recidivate after their first arrest. For example, in Washington, D.C., only 7 percent of the 563 males (mostly customers, some male prostitutes) arrested for prostitution offenses from 1990 to 1992 had previously been arrested for such an offense, whereas this was true of 47 percent of the 847 females arrested for prostitution offenses.[13] Similar findings were reported in Vancouver, Canada: 2 percent of the arrested customers and 49 percent of the arrested prostitutes were recidivists (Lowman 1990).

The large number of patrons and their greater susceptibility to deterrence are arguably good grounds for intensifying enforcement against them. Indeed, the customers may be uniquely qualified for deterrence:

> It is exactly in such situations, when the perpetrator is enmeshed in society and where the act is not central and integrated in his way of life, that punishment and deterrence have a positive effect . . . With a unilateral criminalization of the customers, we believe that a portion of the prostitution market will disappear. (Finstad and Hoigard 1993:222)

Others claim that cracking down on customers may even eradicate prostitution from a locale: "If communities really desire to eliminate prostitution, and not its side effects, customer control

would be an obvious strategy to pursue" (Boles and Tatro 1978:76). And there appears to be substantial public support for targeting customers in some fashion, including public shaming. A 1995 national poll found that half of the public believed the media should disseminate the names and pictures of men convicted of soliciting prostitutes (*Newsweek* 1995). Residents of neighborhoods with street prostitution are especially likely to favor such controls (Weitzer 2000). As a member of one civic association noted, "These guys are the weak link in this chain. He's the one with the most to lose; that's why he's got to be kept out" (Gray 1991:25).

Though most cities continue to target their enforcement efforts against prostitutes rather than their customers, a few cities have begun to redirect control efforts toward the customers. One particularly innovative program is the "johns' school"—a program designed to educate and rehabilitate arrested customers. Since 1995, when San Francisco launched its First Offenders Prostitution Program for customers, several other cities have followed suit, including Buffalo, Las Vegas, Nashville, St. Paul, and some Canadian and British cities. San Francisco's school is a joint effort by the district attorney's office, the police department, the public health department, community leaders, and former prostitutes. The men avoid an arrest record and court appearance by paying a $500 fee, attending the school, and not reoffending for one year after the arrest. Every aspect of the all-day course is designed to *shame, educate, and deter* the men from future contact with prostitutes. The lectures are designed for maximum shock value: the men are frequently asked how they would feel if their mothers, wives, or daughters were "prostituted," and why they were "using" and "violating" prostitutes by patronizing them. The audience is also exposed to a graphic slide show on sexually transmitted diseases, horror stories about the wretched lives of prostitutes and their oppression by pimps, and information about the adverse impact of street prostitution on neighborhoods.

---

[13] Figures provided by the U.S. Attorney's Office, Washington, DC.

Unlike other shaming sanctions—such as printing customers' names or photos in local newspapers or on cable TV shows—where humiliation or "stigmatizing shaming" (Braithwaite 1989) of the offender is a goal, shaming in the johns' schools occurs in the context of a day of reeducation about the various harms of prostitution. This is closer to the "reintegrative shaming" model (Braithwaite 1989) linking punishment to rehabilitation, though this ends once the class concludes. A measure of rehabilitation is recidivism: of the nearly 2,200 graduates of San Francisco's school from March 1995 to February 1999, only eighteen were subsequently rearrested for solicitation. Toronto's program reports low recidivism as well.[14]

Low recidivism, or "specific deterrence" among the graduates of the johns' schools does not necessarily mean that the program is also having a larger "general deterrent" effect (on the never-arrested population of prospective johns), since in most cities with johns' schools, the number of johns on the streets is thus far unabated. Moreover, it is difficult to tell whether non-recidivism is due to the school experience per se or to the arrest. Official statistics show low recidivism among previously arrested customers generally (including those who had not attended a johns' school), suggesting that the arrest is the decisive deterrent.

Customers are also the focus of another innovative program. Inspired by drug forfeiture laws, a growing number of cities have passed ordinances empowering police to confiscate customers' cars when caught in the act of soliciting sexual favors on the street. Portland, Detroit, New York, Chicago, Washington, San Diego, Milwaukee, and Philadelphia are only a few of the cities where such laws have been enacted. After a car is seized a civil hearing is held to determine if there are grounds for forfeiture. Forfeited cars are sold at auction or retained as city property.

The laws vary substantially. Some are lenient with first-time offenders; others treat first-timers and repeat offenders the same. Most cities eventually return the car if the arrested driver is not the owner—if the car belongs to the driver's wife, employer, or a rental company. But some cities confiscate vehicles even if the owner was uninvolved in the crime. In St. Paul, Minnesota, for instance, an auto dealer's car taken on a test drive was used to solicit a prostitute and was seized by the police. (The Supreme Court ruled in *Bennis v. Michigan* in March 1996 that confiscation of property, even if the owner was not involved in the crime, is not unconstitutional.) Finally, in some cities (Oakland, California, Portland, Oregon, Washington, D.C.), a person may be acquitted of the criminal offense of soliciting a prostitute but lose his car in the civil case (where the standard of proof is lower), while in other cities the policy is to return the car if the criminal case fails.

Portland's 1989 forfeiture law has been the inspiration for other cities. Police seized 1,089 vehicles from 1990 through 1993, 52 of which (5 percent) were eventually forfeited; more recently, police have seized around 350 cars per year, only a few of which have been forfeited.[15] Most were first-time arrestees, who were allowed to sign a release agreement stipulating that they would refrain from any future street solicitation or automatically forfeit their car. The result is that the number of repeat offenders is almost nil. Between 1989 and May 1993, only 1 percent of the arrestees had been rearrested.[16]

The benefits of forfeiture laws may not be limited to their deterrent value but may also provide revenue for the police department. In Detroit, for instance, the proceeds have been used to buy police equipment and pay for officers' overtime. And even when cars are returned to their owners, some cities (e.g., Portland) recover the costs of police time,

---

[14] Personal communication from Sergeant Doug Mottram, Metropolitan Toronto Police, August 7, 1997.

[15] Interview with Sergeant Steve Larson, Portland Police Department, September 24, 1997.

[16] *Newsday,* May 12, 1993.

towing, and storage by charging a fee for the returned car. This is tantamount to a fine levied on all seized cars, whether or not the drivers are found guilty.

The forfeiture policy raises some obvious problems. Loss of a car penalizes not only the perpetrator but other family members who depend on it, and the punishment may not fit the crime. Permanent loss of a car worth perhaps thousands of dollars seems disproportionately harsh for a misdemeanor offense, and arguably violates the Eighth Amendment's prohibition on excessive fines. Moreover, there is a wide disparity in the value of the cars seized, from the worthless to the expensive. Such unequal punishment may violate the equal protection clause of the Fourteenth Amendment.

The car seizure policy and the johns' schools show that some cities (albeit a minority) have begun to take customers more seriously than in the past. Moreover, the two programs are more imaginative than the arrest-and-fine approach and put more emphasis on deterring arrestees from recidivating. It remains to be seen whether sustained efforts to attack the demand for street prostitutes will pay dividends in reducing demand, as some analysts claim. But even if it does not have this effect, it can be justified by the principle that law enforcement should be gender neutral.

CONCLUSION

The two-track model outlined here has advantages over both the current policy of blanket criminalization and the alternatives of decriminalization and legalization. It is arguably superior to the other approaches in satisfying key tests: public preferences regarding the proper focus of law enforcement, efficient use of criminal justice resources, and the harm-reduction principle. Essential ingredients of the policy include (1) redirecting control efforts from indoor to street prostitution, (2) gender-neutral law enforcement, and (3) providing support services and assistance for persons who want to leave prostitution. Most effective implementation of the policy would require changes in all three areas simultaneously.

REFERENCES

A&E [Arts and Entertainment Network]. 1997. "Red Light Districts," Videotape.

American Law Institute. 1980. *Model Penal Code and Commentaries, Part II, Sections 240.0 to 251.4.* Philadelphia: American Law Institute.

Atchison, C., L. Fraser, and J. Lowman. 1988. "Men Who Buy Sex." In J. Elias, V. Bullough, V. Elias, and G. Brewer (eds.), *Prostitution.* Amherst: Prometheus.

Atlanta Task Force on Prostitution. 1986. *Findings and Recommendations.* Mayor's Office: Atlanta, Georgia.

Barnard, M. 1993. "Violence and Vulnerability: Conditions of Work for Street Working Prostitutes." *Sociology of Health and Illness* 15:683–705.

Bennetto, J. 1996. "Community Work the Best Penalty for Vice, say Police." *The Independent* [London], October 21.

Benson, C. and R. Matthews. 1995. "Street Prostitution: Ten Facts in Search of a Policy." *International Journal of the Sociology of Law* 23:395–415.

Benson, C., and R. Matthews. 1996. *Report of the Parliamentary Group on Prostitution.* London: Middlesex University.

Bernat, F. 1985. "New York State's Prostitution Statute: Case Study of the Discriminatory Application of a Gender Neutral Law." In C. Schweber and C. Feinman (eds.), *Criminal Justice Politics and Women.* New York: Haworth.

Boles, J., and C., Tatro. 1978. "Legal and Extralegal Methods of Controlling Female Prostitution: A Cross-Cultural Comparison." *International Journal of Comparative and Applied Criminal Justice* 2:71–85.

Boyer, D., L. Chapman, and B. Marshall. 1993. *Survival Sex in King County: Helping Women Out.* Report submitted to the King County Women's Advisory Board, March.

Braithwaite, J. 1989. *Crime, Shame, and Reintegration.* Cambridge: Cambridge University Press.

Bryan, J. 1996. "Occupational Ideologies and Individual Attitudes of Call Girls." *Social Problems* 13:441–450.

Bureau of Justice Statistics. Annual. *Sourcebook of Criminal Justice Statistics.* Washington, D.C.: Government Printing Office.

Campbell, R. 1988. "Invisible Men: Making Visible Male Clients of Female Prostitutes in Merseyside." In J. Elias, V. Bullough, V. Elias, and G. Brewer (eds.), *Prostitution.* Amherst: Prometheus.

Caughey, M. 1974. "The Principle of Harm and Its Application to Laws Criminalizing Prostitution." *Denver Law Journal* 51:235–262.

Clark, C. 1993. "Prostitution." *Congressional Quarterly Researcher* 3:505–527.

Coalition of San Francisco Business and Neighborhood Communities Impacted by Prostitution. 1996. *Resolution.*

Comment. 1977. "Privacy and Prostitution." *Iowa Law Review* 63:248–265.

Cohen, B. 1980. *Deviant Street Networks: Prostitution in New York City.* Lexington, MA: Lexington.

Davis, N. J. 2000. "From Victims to Survivors: Working with Recovering Street Prostitutes." In R. Weitzer (ed.), *Sex for Sale: Prostitution, Pornography, and the Sex Industry.* New York: Routledge.

Decker, J. 1979. *Prostitution: Regulation and Control.* Littleton, CO: Rothman.

Exner, J. E., J. Wylie, A. Leura, and T. Parrill. 1977. "Some Psychological Characteristics of Prostitutes." *Journal of Personality Assessment* 41:474–485.

Farley, F., and S. Davis. 1978. "Masseuses, Men, and Massage Parlors." *Journal of Sex and Marital Therapy* 4:219–225.

Farley, M., and H. Barkan. 1998. "Prostitution, Violence, and Posttraumatic Stress Disorder." *Women and Health* 27:37–49.

Finstad, L., and C. Hoigard. 1993. "Norway." In N. Davis (ed.), *Prostitution: An International Handbook on Trends, Problems, and Policies.* Westport, CT: Greenwood.

Gallup Organization. 1991. *Gallup Poll Monthly.* No. 313. October.

———. 1996. Public Opinion Online, Lexis/Nexis. Gallup poll, May 28–29.

Gray, K. 1991. "Prostitution Opponents Aim to Seize Johns' Cars." *Newsday,* December 5, p. 25.

Harris Poll. 1978. Public Opinion Online, Lexis/Nexis. N = 1,513, November 30–December 10.

———. 1990. Public Opinion Online, Lexis/Nexis. N = 2,254, January 11–February 11.

Heyl, B. 1979. "Prostitution: An Extreme Case of Sex Stratification." In F. Adler and R. Simon (eds.), *The Criminology of Deviant Women.* Boston: Houghton Mifflin.

Hobson, B. M. 1987. *Uneasy Virtue.* New York: Basic Books.

James, J. 1973. "Prostitute-Pimp Relationships." *Medical Aspects of Human Sexuality* 7:147–160.

Jennings, M. A. 1976. "The Victim as Criminal: A Consideration of California's Prostitution Law." *California Law Review* 64:1235–1284.

Kelling, G., and C. Coles. 1996. *Fixing Broken Windows.* New York: Free Press.

Larsen, E. N. 1992. "The Politics of Prostitution Control: Interest Group Politics in Four Canadian Cities." *International Journal of Urban and Regional Research* 16:169–189.

Laumann, E., J. Gagnon, R. Michael, and S. Michaels. 1994. *The Social Organization of Sexuality: Sexual Practices in the United States.* Chicago: University of Chicago Press.

Little, C. 1995. *Deviance and Control.* Itasca, IL: Peacock.

Lowman, J. 1990. "Notions of Formal Equality Before the Law: The Experience of Street Prostitutes and Their Customers." *Journal of Human Justice* 1:55–76.

———. 1992. "Street Prostitution Control." *British Journal of Criminology* 32:1–17.

McCaghy, C., and S. Cernkovich. 1991. "Changing Public Opinion toward Prostitution Laws." Paper presented at the World Congress of Sexology, Amsterdam.

Matthews, R. 1993. *Kerb-Crawling, Prostitution, and Multi-Agency Policing.* Paper no. 43. London: Home Office.

Merit Audits and Surveys. 1983. *Merit Report.* October 15–20.

Milman, B. 1980. "New Rules for the Oldest Profession: Should We Change Our Prostitution Laws?" *Harvard Women's Law Journal* 3:1–82.

Newsweek poll. 1995. Public Opinion Online. Lexis/ Nexis. N = 753, January 26–27.

Pearl, J. 1987. "The Highest Paying Customer: America's Cities and the Costs of Prostitution Control." *Hastings Law Journal* 38:769–800.

Peat Marwick and Partners. 1984. *A National Population Study of Prostitution and Pornography.* Report no. 6. Ottawa: Department of Justice.

Perkins, R. 1991. *Working Girls.* Canberra: Australian Institute of Criminology.

Persons, C. 1996. "Sex in the Sunlight: The Effectiveness, Efficiency, Constitutionality, and Advisability of Publishing Names and Pictures of Prostitutes' Patrons." *Vanderbilt Law Review* 49:1525–1575.

Pivar, D. 1973. *Purity Crusade.* Westport, CT: Greenwood.

Posner, R., and K. Silbaugh. 1996. *A Guide to America's Sex Laws.* Chicago: University of Chicago Press.

Reynolds, H. 1986. *The Economics of Prostitution.* Springfield: Charles Thomas.

San Diego Prostitution Task Force. 1993. *Report.* San Diego City Council, October.

San Francisco Committee on Crime. 1971. *A Report on Non-Victim Crime in San Francisco. Part 2: Sexual Conduct, Gambling, Pornography.* Mayor's Office.

San Francisco Task Force on Prostitution. 1996. *Final Report.* San Francisco Board of Supervisors, March.

Seattle Women's Commission. 1995. *Project to Address the Legal, Political, and Service Barriers Facing Women in the Sex Industry.* Report to the Mayor and City Council. Seattle: July.

Silbert, M., and A. Pines. 1982. "Victimization of Street Prostitutes." *Victimology* 7:122–133.

Skogan, W. 1990. *Disorder and Decline.* New York: Free Press.

Skolnick, J., and J. Dombrink. 1978. "The Legalization of Deviance." *Criminology* 16:193–208.

Special Committee on Pornography and Prostitution. 1985. *Pornography and Prostitution in Canada.* Ottawa: Dept. of Supply and Services.

Sullivan, B. 1997. *The Politics of Sex: Prostitution and Pornography in Australia since 1945.* New York: Cambridge University Press.

Weiner, A. 1996. "Understanding the Social Needs of Streetwalking Prostitutes." *Social Work* 41:97–105.

Weitzer, R. 1991. "Prostitutes' Rights in the United States: The Failure of a Movement." *Sociological Quarterly* 32:23–41.

———. 2000. "The Politics of Prostitution in America." In R. Weitzer (ed.), *Sex for Sale: Prostitution, Pornography, and the Sex Industry.* New York: Routledge.

Wilson, J. Q., and G. Kelling. 1982. "Broken Windows." *Atlantic Monthly,* March, 29–38.

Working Group [Federal/Provincial Territorial Working Group on Prostitution]. 1998. *Report and Recommendations in Respect of Legislation, Policy, and Practices Concerning Prostitution-Related Activities.* Ottawa: Department of Justice.

STUDY QUESTIONS

1. Drawing on the article by Albert DiChiara and John Galliher, why did some states pass legislation decriminalizing marijuana possession?
2. What do DiChiara and Galliher mean by "de facto decriminalization"?
3. In what ways did the Meese commission on pornography demonstrate its lack of impartiality, as documented by Carole Vance?
4. Based on the analysis of prostitution policy by Ronald Weitzer, identify the main problems with the policies of criminalization, legalization, and decriminalization of prostitution in the United States.
5. What are the potential advanteages of the "two-track policy" outlined by Weitzer?

PART FIVE

IDENTITY, INTERACTION, AND RESISTANCE

BECOMING DEVIANT: IDENTITY AND BEHAVIORAL CHANGE

Introduction

Becoming deviant refers to the process whereby a person comes to engage in deviant behavior and to acquire a deviant identity. This process is fluid, and often unfolds gradually. The individual may "drift" into deviance, experiment with it for a while, and then resume normal behavior (Matza 1964). Becoming deviant, in the full sense, may involve a series of stages, each contingent on a number of variables. Richard Troiden ("Becoming Homosexual") found that the process of "becoming homosexual" is gradual—fraught with initial ambivalence, uncertainty, or confusion over one's sexual orientation. His study shows that individuals move through a series of stages, though some individuals never progress to the next stage while others "drift away" from homosexuality after deciding that it is not for them.

The contingent nature of becoming deviant is also documented in the article "Drifting into Drug Dealing," by Sheigla Murphy, Dan Waldorf, and Craig Reinarman. Researchers interviewed ex-cocaine sellers, whose initial entry into dealing was tentative, but who later became more committed to selling as a job. Persons who become dealers experience some transformation in their identities. The "dealer identity" is grafted onto, rather than replaces, their more conventional identities.

Deviant jobs like drug dealing and prostitution have documented effects on actors' self-conceptions, but this is even more profound for people whose deviance is not occupational but rather identity-based, an essential part of who they are. Job-related deviance is one form of *instrumental deviance*—deviance as a means to a material end, such as income—whereas identity-based nonconformity is referred to as *expressive deviance*—deviance that reflects the actor's core self. Examples of expressive deviants include nudists, hermits, and transgenders. "Transgender" refers to people who wish to live, at least part of the time, outside the dominant gender system of male and female roles (a "third gender") or who wish to live within that system but want to be seen as the opposite sex to their birth sex. The latter wish to be seen as that which they have been denied because of their genitalia. Transgenders range from occasional cross-dressers to persons who identify with the opposite sex so strongly that they have surgery to alter their sexual makeup (via hormone injections, breast implants, electrolysis, or genital removal or reconstruction). Perhaps more so than any other type of deviants, transgenders who undergo a sex change operation, or sex reassignment surgery, are involved in radical identity transformation, embracing a new gender and anatomical identity. The selection by Patricia Gagné, Richard Tewksbury, and Deanna McGaughey ("Coming Out as a Transgendered Person") is a fascinating study of the process of becoming transgendered. The authors document the difficulties faced by people who challenge binary assumptions about sex and gender and who try to establish an alternative gender.

REFERENCE

Matza, David. 1964. *Delinquency and Drift.* New York: John Wiley.

Drifting into Drug Dealing

Sheigla Murphy, Dan Waldorf, and Craig Reinarman

For decades the predominant image of the illicit drug dealer was an older male reprobate sporting a long, shabby overcoat within which he had secreted a cornucopia of dangerous consciousness-altering substances. This proverbial "pusher" worked school yards, targeting innocent children who would soon be chemically enslaved repeat customers. The newer villains have been depicted as equally vile but more violent. Old or new, the ideal-typical "drug dealer" is motivated by perverse greed and/or his own addiction, and has crossed a clearly marked moral boundary, severing most ties to the conventional world.

The cocaine sellers we interviewed, on the other hand, had more varied and complex motives for selling cocaine. Moreover at least within their subcultures, the moral boundaries were both rather blurry and as often wandered along as actually crossed. Their life histories reminded us of Matza's later but related discussion of the *overlap* between deviance and conventionality:

> Overlap refers to . . . the marginal rather than gross differentiation between deviant and conventional folk and the considerable though variable interpenetration of deviant and conventional culture. Both themes sensitize us to the regular exchange, traffic, and flow— of persons as well as styles and precepts—that occur among deviant and conventional worlds. (1969:68)

Our subjects were already seasoned users of illicit drugs. For years their drug use coexisted comfortably with their conventional roles and activities; having a deviant dimension to their identities appeared to cause them little strain. In fact, because

their use of illicit drugs had gone on for so long, was so common in their social worlds, and had not significantly affected their otherwise normal lives, they hardly considered it deviant at all.

Thus, when they began to sell cocaine as well as use it, they did not consider it a major leap down an unknown road but rather a series of short steps down a familiar path. It was not as if ministers had become mobsters; no sharp break in values, motives, world views, or identities was required. Indeed, few woke up one morning and made a conscious decision to become sellers. They did not break sharply with the conventional world and actively choose a deviant career path; most simply drifted into dealing by virtue of their strategies for solving the problems entailed in using a criminalized substance, and only then developed additional deviant motives centering on money.

SAMPLE AND METHODS

The sample consists of 80 ex-sellers who sold cocaine in the San Francisco Bay Area. We interviewed them in 1987 and 1988. Most had stopped selling before crack sales peaked in this area. Only five of the eighty had sold crack or rock. Of these five, two had sold on the street and two had sold in "rock party houses"[1] as early as 1978. It is important to note, therefore, that the sellers we describe

---

[1] Rock party houses are distinct from "rock houses" or "crack houses." In the former, sellers invite only selected customers to their homes to smoke rock and "party." Unlike crack houses, where crack is sold to all comers, outsiders are never invited to rock party houses, and the arrangement is social and informal. Proprietors of both types, however, charge participants for the cocaine.

From *Qualitative Sociology* 13, No. 4, 1990, pages 321–343. Reprinted by permission of Kluwer Academic Publishers and the authors.

are very likely to be different from street crack dealers in terms of the product type, selling styles, visibility, and thus the risks of arrest and attendant violence.

To be eligible for the study our respondents had to have sold cocaine steadily for at least a year and to have stopped selling for at least 6 months. We designed the study to include only *former* sellers so that respondents would feel free to describe all their activities in detail without fear that their accounts could somehow be utilized by law enforcement authorities.

They spoke of six different levels or types of sellers: smugglers, big dealers, dealers, sellers (unspecified), bar dealers, and street dealers. The social organization of cocaine sales probably varies in other areas. We located and interviewed ex-sellers from the full range of these dealer-identified sales levels, but we have added two categories in order to provide a more detailed typology. Our eight levels of sales were defined according to the units sold rather than the units bought. So, for example, if a seller bought quarters or eighths of ounces and regularly sold grams, we categorized him or her as a gram dealer rather than a part-ounce dealer.

Levels of Sales	Number of Interviews
Smugglers	2
Kilograms/pounds	13
Parts of kilos and pounds	6
Ounce dealers	18
Part-ounce dealers	13
Gram dealers	12
Part-gram dealers	11
Crack dealers	5
Total	80

Unlike most other studies of dealing and the now infamous street crack dealers, the majority of our respondents sold cocaine hydrochloride (powder) in private places. There are a number of styles of selling drugs—selling out of homes, selling out of rock houses and shooting galleries, selling out of party houses, selling out of rented "safe houses"

and apartments, delivery services (using telephone answering, answering machines, voice mail and telephone beepers), car meets,[2] selling in bars, selling in parks, and selling in the street. Within each type there are various styles. For example, in some African-American communities in San Francisco a number of sellers set up business on a street and respond to customers who come by on foot and in automobiles. Very often a number of sellers will approach a car that slows down or stops to solicit customers; drugs and money are exchanged then and there. Such sales activities are obvious to the most casual observers; even television camera crews often capture such transactions for the nightly news. On certain streets in the Mission District, a Latino community in San Francisco, street drug sales are less blatant. Buyers usually walk up to sellers who stand on the street among numerous other people who are neither buyers nor sellers. There, specific transactions rarely take place on the street itself; the participants generally retreat to a variety of shops and restaurants. Buyers seldom use cars for transactions and sellers tend not to approach a car to solicit customers.

Despite the ubiquity of street sales in media accounts and the preponderance of street sellers in arrest records, we set out to sample the more hidden and more numerous sellers who operate in private. Most users of cocaine hydrochloride are working- or middle-class. They generally avoid street sellers both because they want to avoid being observed and because they believe that most street sellers sell inferior quality drugs (Waldorf et al. 1991). Further, we found that people engaged in such illegal and furtive transactions tend to prefer dealing with people like themselves, people they know.

We located our respondents by means of chain referral sampling techniques (Biernacki and Waldorf 1981; Watters and Biernacki 1989). This is a method

---

[2] Car meets are transactions that take place in cars. Arrangements are made over the telephone in advance and both buyer and seller arrange to meet at parking lots, usually at busy shopping centers, and exchange drugs and money. Each arrives in his or her own car and leaves separately.

commonly used by sociologists and ethnographers to locate hard-to-find groups and has been used extensively in qualitative research on drug use (Lindesmith 1947; Becker 1953; Feldman 1968; Preble and Casey 1969; Rosenbaum 1981; Biernacki 1986). We initiated the first of our location chains in 1974–75 in the course of a short-term ethnography of cocaine use and sales among a small friendship network (Waldorf et al. 1977). Other chains were developed during a second study of cocaine cessation conducted during 1986–1987 (Reinarman et al. 1988; Macdonald et al. 1988; Murphy et al. 1989; Waldorf et al. 1991). Another three chains were developed during the present study. We located the majority of our respondents via referral chains developed by former sellers among their previous customers and suppliers. Initial interviewees referred us to other potential respondents whom we had not previously known. In this way we were able to direct our chains into groups of ex-sellers from a variety of backgrounds.

We employed two interview instruments: an open-ended, exploratory interview guide designed to maximize discovery of new and unique types of data, and a more structured survey designed to gather basic quantifiable data on all respondents. The open-ended interviews were tape-recorded, transcribed, and content-analyzed. These interviews usually took from 2 to 4 hours to complete, but when necessary we conducted longer and/or follow-up interviews (e.g., one woman was interviewed for 10 hours over three sessions). The data analyzed for this paper was drawn primarily from the tape-recorded depth interviews.

There is no way to ascertain if this (or any similar) sample is representative of all cocaine sellers. Because the parameters of the population are unknowable, random samples on which systematic generalizations might be based cannot be drawn. We do know that, unlike other studies of drug sellers, we placed less emphasis on street sellers and included dealers at all levels.

TABLE 1-1

DEMOGRAPHICS (N = 80)

Age: Range = 18–60 years
   Mean = 37.1
   Median = 35.4

	Number	**Percent**
Sex:		
Male	54	67.5
Female	26	32.5
Ethnicity:		
African-American	28	35.0
White	44	58.8
Latino(a)	4	5.0
Asian	1	1.2
Education:		
Less than high school grad	11	13.8
High school graduate	18	22.5
Some college	31	38.8
B.A. or B.S. degree	12	15.0
Some graduate	3	3.8
Graduate degree	5	6.3

[Percentages may not equal 100% due to rounding]

DEALERS

Dealers are people who are "fronted" (given drugs on consignment to be paid for upon sale) and/or who buy quantities of drugs for sale. Further, in order to be considered a dealer by users or other sellers a person must: 1) have one or more reliable connections (suppliers); 2) make regular cocaine purchases in amounts greater than a single gram (usually an eighth of an ounce or greater) to be sold in smaller units; 3) maintain some consistent supplies for sale; and 4) have a network of customers who make purchases on a regular basis. Although the stereotype of a dealer holds that illicit drug sales are a full-time occupation, many dealers, including members of our sample, operate part-time and supplement income from a legal job.

As we noted in the introduction, the rather average, ordinary character of the respondents who fit this definition was striking. In general, without prior knowledge or direct observation of drug sales, one would be unable to distinguish our respondents from other, non-dealer citizens. When telling their career histories, many of our respondents invoked very conventional, middle-class American values to explain their involvement in dealing (e.g., having children to support, mortgages or rent to pay in a high-cost urban area, difficulty finding jobs which paid enough to support a family). Similarly, their profits from drug sales were used in "normal" ways—to buy children's clothes, to make house or car payments, to remodel a room. Moreover, like Matza's delinquents, most of our respondents were quite law-abiding, with the obvious exception of their use and sales of an illicit substance.

When they were not dealing, our respondents engaged in activities that can only be described as mainstream American. For example, one of our dealers, a single mother of two, found herself with a number of friends who used cocaine and a good connection. She needed extra income to pay her mortgage and to support her children, so she sold small amounts of cocaine within her friendship network. Yet while she sold cocaine, she worked at a full-time job, led a Girl Scout troop, volunteered as a teacher of cardio-pulmonary resuscitation (CPR) classes for young people, and went to Jazzercize classes. Although she may have been a bit more civic-minded than many others, her case served to remind us that cocaine sellers do not come from another planet.

MODES OF ENTREE INTO DEALING

Once they began selling cocaine, many of our respondents moved back and forth between levels in the distribution hierarchy. Some people dealt for short periods of time and then quit, only to return several months later at another level of sales.[3] The

---

[3] These movements back and forth among different levels of involvement in dealing were different from the "shifts and oscillations" found among the cocaine dealers studied by Adler (1985:133–141). She studied a circle of high-level dealers over an extended period of field work and found that the stresses and strains of dealing at the top of the pyramid often led her participants to attempt to get out of the business. While many of our interviewees felt similar pressures later in their careers and subsequently quit, our focus here is on becoming a cocaine seller.

same person may act as a broker on one deal, sell a quarter gram at a profit to a friend on another, and then pick up an ounce from an associate and pass it on to another dealer in return for some marijuana in a third transaction. In a few instances each of these roles were [sic] played by the same person within the same twenty-four hour period. But whether or not a dealer/respondent moved back and forth in this way, s/he usually began selling in one of five distinct ways. All five of these modes of entree pre-suppose an existing demand for cocaine from people known to the potential dealers. A person selling any line of products needs two things, a group of customers and a product these customers are interested in purchasing. Cocaine sellers are no different. In addition to being able and willing to pay, however, cocaine customers must also be trustworthy because these transactions are illegal.

The first mode of entree, *the go-between*, is fairly straightforward. The potential seller has a good cocaine connection and a group of friends who place orders for cocaine with him/her. If the go-between's friends use cocaine regularly enough and do not develop their own connections, then a period of months or even years might go by when the go-between begins to spend more and more time and energy purchasing for them. Such sellers generally do not make formal decisions to begin dealing; rather, opportunities regularly present themselves and go-betweens gradually take advantage of them. For example, one 30 year-old, African-American who became a gram dealer offered this simple account of his passage from go-between to seller:

> Basically, I first started because friends pressured me to get the good coke I could get. I wasn't even making any money off of it. They'd come to me and I'd call up my friend who had gotten pretty big selling a lot of coke. (Case# E-5)

This went on for six months before he began to charge his friends money for it. Then his connection started fronting him eighths of ounces at a time, and he gradually became an official dealer, regularly selling drugs for a profit. Others who began in this way often took only commissions-in-kind (a free snort) for some months before beginning to charge customers a cash mark-up.

Another African-American male began selling powdered cocaine to snorters in 1978, and by the mid-eighties had begun selling rock cocaine (crack) to smokers. He described his move from go-between to dealer as follows:

> Around the time I started indulging [in cocaine] myself, people would come up and say, "God, do you know where I can get some myself?" I would just say, 'Sure, just give me your money,' I would come back and either indulge with them or just give it to them depending on my mood. I think that's how I originally set up my clientele. I just had a certain group of people who would come to me because they felt that I knew the type of people who could get them a real quality product.
>
> And pretty soon I just got tired of, you know, being taken out of situations or being imposed upon . . . I said that it would be a lot easier to just do it myself. And one time in particular, and I didn't consider myself a dealer or anything, but I had a situation one night where 5 different people called me to try to get cocaine . . . not from me but it was like, "Do you know where I can get some good cocaine from?" (Case# E-11)

Not all go-betweens-cum-dealers start out so altruistically. Some astute businessmen and women spot the profit potential early on and immediately realize a profit, either in-kind (a share of the drugs purchased) or by tacking on a surcharge to the purchase price. The following respondent, a 39 year old African-American male, described this more profit-motivated move from go-between to formal seller:

> Well, the first time that I started it was like I knew where to get good stuff . . . and I had friends that didn't know where to get good stuff. And I knew where to get them really good stuff and so I would always put a couple of dollars on it, you know, if I got it for $20 I would sell it to them for $25 or $30 or whatever.
>
> It got to be where more and more people were coming to me and I was going to my man more and I would be there 5 or 6 times a day, you know. So he would tell

me, "Here, why don't you take this, you know, and bring me x-amount of dollars for it." So that's how it really started. I got fronted and I was doing all the business instead of going to his house all the time, because he had other people that were coming to his house and he didn't want the traffic. (Case# E-13)

The second mode of entree is the *stash dealer*, or a person who becomes involved in distribution and/or sales simply to support or subsidize personal use. The name is taken from the term "stash," meaning a personal supply of marijuana (see Fields 1985, on stash dealers in the marijuana trade). This forty-one year-old white woman who sold along with her husband described her start as a stash dealer this way:

> (Q) So what was your motivation for the sales?
> (A) To help pay for my use, because the stuff wasn't cheap and I had the means and the money at the time in order to purchase it, where our friends didn't have that amount of money without having to sell something . . . Yeah, friendship, it wasn't anything to make money off of, I mean we made a few dollars . . . (Case# E-7)

The respondents who entered the dealing world as stash dealers typically started out small (selling quarter and half grams) and taking their profits in product. However, this motivation contributed to the undoing of some stash dealers in that it led to greater use, which led to the need for greater selling, and so on. Unless they then developed a high-volume business that allowed them to escalate their cocaine use and still make profits, the reinforcing nature of cocaine tempted many of them to use more product than was good for business.

Many stash dealers were forced out of business fairly early on in their careers because they spent so much money on their own use they were financially unable to "re-cop" (buy new supplies). Stash dealers often want to keep only a small number of customers in order to minimize both the "hassle" of late-night phone calls and the risk of police detection, and they do not need many customers since they only want to sell enough to earn free cocaine. Problems arise, however, when their small group of customers do not buy the product promptly. The longer stash dealers had cocaine in their possession, the more opportunities they had for their own use (i.e., for profits to "go up your nose"). One stash dealer had an axiom about avoiding this: "It ain't good to get high on your own supply" (Case# E-57). The predicament of using rather than selling their product often afflicts high-level "weight dealers" as well, but they are better able to manage for longer periods of time due to larger volumes and profit margins.

The third mode of entry into cocaine selling had to do with users' desire for high-quality, unadulterated cocaine. We call this type the *connoisseur.* Ironically, the motivation for moving toward dealing in this way is often health-related. People who described this mode of entree described their concerns, as users, about the possible dangers of ingesting the various adulterants or "cuts" commonly used by dealers to increase profits. User folklore holds that the larger the quantity purchased, the purer the product. This has been substantiated by laboratory analysis of the quality of small amounts of street drugs (typically lower) as opposed to larger police seizures (typically higher).

The connoisseur type of entry, then, begins with the purchase of larger quantities of cocaine than they intend to use in order to maximize purity. Then they give portions of the cocaine to close friends at a good price. If the members of the network start to use more cocaine, the connoisseurs begin to make bigger purchases with greater regularity. At some point they begin to feel that all this takes effort and that it makes sense to buy large quantities not only to get purer cocaine but to make some money for their efforts. The following 51 year-old, white business executive illustrated the connoisseur route as follows:

> I think the first reason I started to sell was not to make money or even to pay for my coke, because I could afford it. It was to get good coke and not to be snorting a lot of impurities and junk that people were putting into it by cutting it so much. So I really think that I started to sell it or to get it wholesale so that I would get the good stuff. And I guess my first, . . . what I did with it in the beginning, because I couldn't

use all that I had to buy to get good stuff, I sold it to some of my friends for them to sell it, retail it. (Case# E-16)

Connoisseurs, who begin by selling unneeded quantities, often found they unlearned certain attitudes when they moved from being volume buyers looking for quality toward becoming dealers looking for profit. It was often a subtle shift, but once their primary motivation gradually changed from buying-for-purity to buying-to-sell they found themselves beginning to think and act like dealers. The shift usually occurred when connoisseurs realized that the friends with whom they had shared were in fact customers who were eager for their high quality cocaine and who often made demands on their time (e.g., friends seeking supplies not merely for themselves, but for other friends a step or two removed from the original connoisseur). Some connoisseurs also became aware of the amount of money that could be made by becoming business-like about what had been formally friendly favors. At such points in the process they began to buy-to-sell, for a profit, as well as for the purpose of obtaining high-quality cocaine for personal use. This often meant that, rather than buying sporadically, they had to make more regular buys; for a successful businessperson must have supplies when customers want to buy or they will seek another supplier.

The fourth mode of entree into cocaine selling is an *apprenticeship.* Like the other types, apprentices typically were users who already had loosened conventional normative strictures and learned deviant motives by interacting with other users and with dealers; and they, too, drifted into dealing. However, in contrast to the first three types, apprentices moved toward dealing less to solve problems inherent in using a criminalized substance than to solve the problems of the master dealer. Apprenticeships begin in a personal relationship where, for example, the potential seller is the lover or intimate of a dealer. This mode was most often the route of entry for women, although one young man we interviewed learned to deal from his father. Couples often start out with the man doing the dealing—picking up the product, handling the money, weighing and packaging, etc. The woman gradually finds herself acting as an unofficial assistant—taking telephone messages, sometimes giving people pre-packaged cocaine and collecting money. Apprentices frequently benefit from being involved with the experienced dealer in that they enjoy both supplies of high-quality cocaine and indirect financial rewards of dealing.

Some of our apprentices moved into official roles or deepened their involvement when the experienced dealer began to use too much cocaine to function effectively as a seller. In some such cases the abuse of the product led to an end of the relationship. Some apprentices then left dealing altogether while others began dealing on their own. One thirty-two year-old African-American woman lived with a pound dealer in Los Angeles in 1982. Both were freebasers (cocaine smokers) who sold to other basers. She described her evolution from apprentice to dealer this way:

> I was helping him with like weighing stuff and packaging it and I sort of got to know some of the people that were buying because his own use kept going up. He was getting more out of it, so I just fell into taking care of it partly because I like having the money and it also gave me more control over the situation, too, for awhile, you know, until we both got too out of it. (Case# E-54)

The fifth mode of entree into cocaine selling entailed the *expansion of an existing product line.* A number of the sellers we interviewed started out as marijuana salespersons and learned many aspects of the dealers' craft before they ever moved to cocaine. Unlike in the other modes, in this one an existing marijuana seller already had developed selling skills and established a network of active customers for illicit drugs. Expansion of product line (in business jargon, horizontal integration) was the route of entry for many of the multiple-ounce and kilo cocaine dealers we interviewed. The combination of the availability of cocaine through their marijuana connection and their marijuana customers' interest in purchasing cocaine, led many marijuana sellers to add cocaine to their product line.

Others who entered dealing this way also found that expanding from marijuana to cocaine solved some problems inherent in marijuana dealing. For example, cocaine is far less bulky and odoriferous than marijuana and thus did not present the risky and costly shipping and storage problems of multiple pounds of marijuana. Those who entered cocaine selling via this product line expansion route also recognized, of course, that there was the potential for higher profits with cocaine. They seemed to suggest that as long as they were already taking the risk, why shouldn't they maximize the reward? Some such dealers discontinued marijuana sales altogether and others merely added cocaine to their line. One white, 47 year-old mother of three grown children described how she came to expand her product line:

> (Q) How did you folks [she and her husband] get started dealing?
> (A) The opportunity just fell into our lap. We were already dealing weed and one of our customers got this great coke connection and started us onto dealing his product. We were selling him marijuana and he was selling us cocaine.
> (Q) So you had a network of weed buyers, right? So you could sell to those . . . ?
> (A) There was a shift in the market. Yeah, because weed was becoming harder [to find] and more expensive and a bulkier product. The economics of doing a smaller, less bulkier product and more financially rewarding product like cocaine had a certain financial appeal to the merchant mentality. (Case# E-1)

CONSCIOUS DECISION TO SELL

As noted earlier, the majority of our sample were middle class wholesalers who, in the various ways just described, drifted into dealing careers. The few street sellers we interviewed did not drift into sales in the same way. We are obliged to note again that the five modes of entry into cocaine selling we have identified should not be taken as exhaustive. We have every reason to believe that for groups and settings other than those we have studied there are other types of entree and career trajectories. The five cases of street sellers we did examine suggest that entree into street-level sales was more of a conscious decision of a poor person who decided to enter an underground economy, not an effort to solve a user's problems. Our interviews with street sellers suggest that they chose to participate in an illicit profit-generating activity largely because licit economic opportunities were scarce or nonexistent. Unlike our other types, such sellers sold to strangers as well as friends, and their place of business was more likely to be the street corner rather than homes, bars, or nightclubs. For example, one 30 year-old Native American ex-prostitute described how she became a street crack dealer this way:

> I had seen in the past friends that were selling and stuff and I needed extra money so I just one day told one of my friends, you know, if he could help me, you know, show me more or less how it goes. So I just went by what I seen. So I just started selling it. (Case# E-AC 1)

A few higher level dealers also made conscious decisions to sell (see Adler 1985), particularly when faced with limited opportunity structures. Cocaine selling, as an occupation, offers the promise of lavish lifestyle, otherwise unattainable to most ghetto youth and other impoverished groups. Dealing also provides an alternative to the low paying, dead-end jobs typically available to those with little education and few skills. A 55-year-old African-American man who made his way up from grams to ounce sales described his motivation succinctly: "The chance presented itself to avoid the 9 to 5" (Case# E-22).

Street sellers and even some higher-level dealers are often already participating in quasi-criminal lifestyles; drug sales are simply added to the repertoire of illicit activities. The perceived opportunity to earn enormous profits, live "the good life," and set your own work schedule are powerful enticements to sell. From the perspective of people with few life chances, dealing cocaine may be seen as their only real chance to achieve the "American Dream" (i.e., financial security and disposable

income). Most of our sample were not ghetto dwellers and/or economically disadvantaged. But for those who were, there were different motivations and conscious decisions regarding beginning sales. Popular press descriptions of cocaine sellers predominantly portray just such street sellers. Although street sellers are the most visible, our data suggest that they represent what might be called the tip of the cocaine dealing iceberg.

LEVELS OF ENTRY

The levels at which a potential dealer's friends/connections were selling helped determine the level at which the new dealer entered the business. If the novitiate was moving in social scenes where "big dealers" are found, then s/he is likely to begin by selling grams and parts of grams. When supplies were not fronted, new dealers' personal finances, i.e., available capital, also influenced how much they could buy at one time.

Sellers move up and down the cocaine sales ladder as well as in and out of the occupation (see Adler 1985). Some of our sellers were content to remain part-ounce dealers selling between a quarter and a half an ounce a week. Other sellers were more ambitious and eventually sought to become bigger dealers in order to increase profits. One interviewee reported that her unusually well organized suppliers had sales quotas, price fixing, and minimum purchase expectations which pushed her toward expansion. The levels of sales and selling styles of the new dealer's suppliers, then, interacted with personal ambitions to influence eventual sales careers.

Another important aspect of beginning to sell cocaine is whether the connection is willing to "front" the cocaine (risk a consignment arrangement) rather than requiring the beginner to pay in full. Having to pay "up front" for one's inventory sometimes slowed sales by tying up capital, or even deterred some potential dealers from entering the business. Fronted cocaine allowed people with limited resources to enter the occupation. Decisions to front or not to front were based primarily on the connection's evaluation of the new seller's ability to "move" the product. This was seen as a function of the potential volume of business the beginning seller could generate among his/her networks of friends and/or customers. The connection/fronter also evaluates the trustworthiness of the potential dealer, as well as their own capability of absorbing the loss should the deal "go bad" and the frontee be unable to pay. The judgement of the fronter is crucial, for a mistake can be very costly and there is no legal recourse.

LEARNING TO DEAL

In the go-between, stash, and connoisseur modes of entree, novices gradually learn the tricks of the trade by observing the selling styles of active dealers, and ultimately by doing. Weighing, packaging, and pricing the product are basic techniques. A scale, preferably a triple-beam type which are [sic] accurate to the tenth of a gram, is a necessary tool. In the last ten years answering machines, beepers, and even cellular phones have become important tools as well. Learning how to manage customers, and to establish selling routines and rules of procedure are all essential skills that successful dealers must master.

The dealers who enter sales through the apprenticeship and product line expansion modes have the advantage of their own or their partner/seller's experience. Active marijuana sellers already have a network of customers, scales, familiarity with metric measures, and, most important, a connection to help them move into a new product line. Apprentices have lived with and/or observed the selling styles of their dealer/mentors and have access to their equipment, connections and customers. Both apprentices and marijuana dealers who have expanded into cocaine also know how to "maintain a low profile" and avoid any kind of attention that might culminate in arrest. In this way they were able to reduce or manage the paranoia that often inheres in drug dealing circles.

Many sellers learn by making mistakes, often expensive mistakes. These include: using too much cocaine themselves, fronting drugs to people who do not pay for them, and adding too much "cut" (usually an inactive adulterant such as vitamin B) to their product so they develop a reputation for selling inferior cocaine and sometimes have difficulty selling the diluted product. One thirty-two year-old African American male made one such error in judgment by fronting to too many people who did not "come through." It ended up costing him $15,000:

> It was because of my own recklessness that I allowed myself to get into that position. There was a period where I had a lot of weight that I just took it and just shipped it out to people I shouldn't have shipped it out to . . . I did this with 10 people and a lot of them were women to be exact. I had a lot of women coming over to my house and I just gave them an ounce apiece one time . . . So when maybe 6 of those people didn't come through . . . there was a severe cramp in my cash flow. This made me go to one of the family members to get the money to re-cop. (Case# E-11)

Business Sense/People Sense

Many people have a connection, the money to make the initial buy, a reputation for being reliable, and a group of friends interested in buying drugs, but still lack the business sense to be a successful dealer. Just because a person drifts into dealing does not mean that he or she will prosper and stay in dealing. We found a variety of ways in which people initially became dealers, few of which hinged on profits. But what determined whether they continued dealing was their business sense. Thus even though a profit orientation had little to do with becoming a dealer, the ability to consistently realize profits had a major influence over who remained a dealer. In this sense, cocaine selling was like any other capitalist endeavor.

According to our respondents, one's ability to be a competent dealer depended on being able to separate business from pleasure. Success or failure at making this separation over time determined whether a profit was realized. Certain business practices were adopted by prosperous dealers to assist them in making this important distinction. For example, prepackaging both improves quality control and helps keep inventory straight; establishing rules for customers concerning when they can purchase and at what prices reduces the level of hassle; limiting the amount of fronting can reduce gross sales volume, but it also reduces financial risk and minimizes the amount of debt collection work; and limiting their own personal use keeps profits from disappearing up one's nose or in one's pipe.

Being a keen judge of character was seen as another important component of being a skilled dealer. Having the "people skills" to judge whether a person could be trusted to return with the money for fronted supplies, to convince people to pay debts that the dealer had no legal mechanisms for collecting, and to engender the trust of a connection when considerable amounts of money were at stake, are just a few of the sophisticated interpersonal skills required of a competent dealer.

Adler also discusses the importance of a "good personal reputation" among upper level dealers and smugglers:

> One of the first requirements for success, whether in drug trafficking, business enterprise broadly, or any life undertaking, is the establishment of a good personal reputation. To make it in the drug world, dealers and smugglers had to generate trust and likability (1985:100).

Adler's general point applies to our respondents as well, although the experiences of some of our middle and lower level dealers suggested a slight amendment: A likable person with a good reputation could sell a less than high quality product, but an unlikable person, even one with a bad reputation, could still do a considerable amount of business if s/he had an excellent product. One forty-seven year-old white woman described her "difficult" husband/partner, "powder keg Paul":

> He would be so difficult, you couldn't believe it. Somebody [this difficult] better have a super primo product to make all this worthwhile . . . He's the kind

of guy you don't mind buying from because you know you'll get a good product, but he's the kind of guy you never want to sell to . . . he was that difficult. (Case# E-1)

High quality cocaine, in other words, is always at a premium in this subculture, so even without good people skills a dealer or connection with "good product" was tolerated.

FROM USER TO DEALER: THE TRANSFORMATION OF IDENTITY

In each of our respondents' deviant careers there occurred what Becker referred to as a change in self conception. Among our respondents, this took the form of a subtle shift in identity from a person who *has* a good connection for cocaine to a person who *is* a good connection for cocaine. There is a corresponding change in the meaning of, and the motives for, selling. The relationship between the seller and the customer undergoes a related transformation, from "picking up something for a friend" to conducting a commercial transaction. In essence, dealing becomes a business quite like most others, and the dealer gradually takes on the professional identity of a business person. Everett Hughes, writing on the sociology of work, urged social scientists to remember that when we look at work,

> We need to rid ourselves of any concepts which keep us from seeing that the essential problems of men at work are the same whether they do their work in the laboratories of some famous institution or in the messiest vat of a pickle factory. (1951:313)

When they had fully entered the dealer role, our respondents came to see selling cocaine as a job— work, just like other kinds of work save for its illegality. For most, selling cocaine did not mean throwing out conventional values and norms. In fact, many of our respondents actively maintained their conventional identities (see Broadhead 1983). Such identities included those of parents legally employed workers, neighbors, churchgoers and softball players, to list just a few. Dealer identities tended not to replace former, "legitimate" identities but were added to a person's repertoire of more conventional identities.

Like everyone else in modern life, sellers emphasized one or another dimension of their identities as appropriate to the situation. In his study of heroin addicts Biernacki notes that, "The arrangement of identities must continuously be managed in such a way as to stress some identities at certain points in particular social worlds and situations, and at the same time to de-emphasize others" (1986:23). Our sellers, too, had to become adept at articulating the proper identity at the proper time. By day, one woman dealer was a concerned mother at her daughter's kindergarten field trip, and that same evening she was an astute judge of cocaine quality when picking up an ounce from her connection. At least for our interviewees, selling cocaine rarely entailed entirely terminating other social roles and obligations.

Yet, at some point in all of our sellers' careers, they found themselves transformed from someone who has a good connection to someone who is a good connection, and they gradually came to accept the identity of dealer as a part of their selves. Customers began to treat them like a salesperson, expecting them to be available to take calls and do business and even for services such as special off-hour pick-ups and deliveries or reduced rates for volume purchases. When dealers found themselves faced with such demands, they typical began to feel *entitled* to receive profits from selling. They came to be seen as dealers by others, and in part for this reason, came to see themselves as dealers. As Becker's (1963) model suggests, selling *behavior* usually preceded not only motivation but also changes in attitude and identity. As one 38-year-old white woman put it,

> I took over the business and paid all my husband's debts and started to make some money. One day I realized I was a coke dealer . . . It was scary, but the money was good. (Case# E-75)

Acceptance of the dealer identity brings with it some expectations and values shared by dealers and customers alike. Customers have the expectation that the dealer will have a consistent supply of cocaine for sale. Customers also expect that the dealer will report in a fairly accurate manner the quality of his/her present batch of drugs within the confines of the *caveat emptor* philosophy that informs virtually all commercial activities in market societies. Buyers do not expect sellers to denigrate their product, but they do not expect the dealer to claim that their product is "excellent" if it is merely "good." Customers assume the dealer will make a profit, but dealers should not be "too greedy." A greedy dealer is one who makes what is estimated by the buyer to be excessive profits. Such estimations of excessiveness vary widely among customers and between sellers and buyers. But the fact that virtually all respondents spoke of some unwritten code of fairness suggests that there is, in E. P. Thompson's (1971) phrase, a "moral economy" of drug dealing that constrains the drive for profit maximization even within an illicit market.[4]

For their part, dealers expect that customers will act in a fashion that will minimize their chances of being arrested by being circumspect about revealing their dealer status. One simply did not, for example, bring to a dealer's house friends whom the dealer had not met. Dealers want customers to appreciate the risks undertaken to provide them with cocaine. And dealers come to feel that such risks deserve profits. After all, the seller is the one who takes the greatest risks; s/he could conceivably receive a stiff jail sentence for a sales conviction. While drifting into dealing and selling mostly to friends and acquaintances mitigated the risks of arrest and reduced their paranoia, such risks remained omnipresent.

In fact, the growing realization of such risks—and the rationalization it provided for dealing on a for-profit basis—was an integral part of becoming

---

[4] In addition to lore about "righteous" and "rip off" dealers, there were present other norms that suggested the existence of such an unwritten code or moral economy, e.g., refusing to sell to children or to adults who "couldn't handle it" (i.e., had physical, financial, familial, or work-related problems because of cocaine use).

a cocaine seller. As our 38 year-old white woman dealer put it, "When it's all said and done, I'm the one behind bars, and I had better have made some money while I was selling or why in the hell take the risk?" (Case# E-75).

REFERENCES

Adler, P. 1985. *Wheeling and Dealing: An Ethnography of an Upper-Level Drug Dealing Community.* New York: Columbia University Press.

Becker, H. S. 1953. "Becoming a marijuana user." *American Journal of Sociology* 59:235–242.

Becker, H. S. 1986. *Pathways from Heroin Addiction.* Philadelphia: Temple University Press.

Biernacki, P., and D. Waldorf. 1981. "Snowball sampling: Problems and techniques of chain referral sampling." *Sociological Methods and Research* 10:141–163.

Broadhead, R. 1983. *The Private Lives and Professional Identity of Medical Students.* New Brunswick, NJ: Transaction Books.

Feldman, H. W. 1968. "Ideological supports to becoming and remaining a heroin addict." *Journal of Health and Social Behavior* 9:131–139.

Fields, A. 1985. "Weedslingers: A study of young black marijuana dealers." *Urban Life* 13:247–270.

Goldstein, P., H. Brownstein, P. Ryan, and P. Belucci. 1989. "Crack and homicide in New York City, 1988." *Contemporary Drug Problems* 16:651–687.

Grinspoon, L., and J. Bakalar. 1976. *Cocaine: A Drug and Its Social Evolution.* New York: Basic Books.

Hughes, E. 1951. "Work and the self." In John Rohrer and Muzafer Sherif (eds.), *Social Work at the Crossroads.* New York: Harper and Brothers, 313–323.

Lindesmith, A. 1947. *Addiction and Opiates.* Chicago: Aldine Press.

Macdonald, P., D. Waldorf, C. Reinarman, and S. Murphy. 1988. "Heavy cocaine use and sexual behavior." *Journal of Drug Issues* 18:437–455.

Murphy, S., C. Reinarman, and D. Waldorf. 1989. "An eleven year follow-up of a network of cocaine users." *British Journal of the Addictions* 84:427–436.

Matza, D. 1964. *Delinquency and Drift.* New York: Wiley.

———. 1969. *Becoming Deviant.* Englewood Cliffs, NJ: Prentice Hall.

Morales, E. 1988. *Cocaine: The White Gold Rush in Peru.* Tucson, AZ: University of Arizona Press.

Preble, E., and J. H. Casey, Jr. 1969. "Taking care of business: The heroin user's life on the streets." *The International Journal of the Addictions* 4:1–24.

Reinarman, C., D. Waldorf, and S. Murphy. 1988. "Scapegoating and social control in the construction of a public problem: Empirical and critical findings on cocaine and work." *Research in Law, Deviance and Social Control* 9:37–62.

Reuter, P. 1990. *Money from Crime: The Economics of Drug Dealing.* Santa Monica, CA: Rand Corporation.

Rosenbaum, M. 1981. *Women on Heroin.* New Brunswick, NJ: Rutgers University Press.

Thompson, E. P. 1971. "The moral economy of the English crowd in the eighteenth century." *Past and Present* 50:76–136.

Waldorf, D., C. Reinarman, S. Murphy and B. Joyce. 1977. *Doing Coke: An Ethnography of Cocaine Snorters and Sellers.* Washington, D.C.: Drug Abuse Council.

Waldorf, D., C. Reinarman, and S. Murphy. 1991. *Cocaine Changes.* Philadelphia: Temple University Press.

Watters, J. K., and P. Biernacki. 1989. "Targeted sampling: Options for the study of hidden populations." *Social Problems* 36:416–430.

Becoming Homosexual

Richard R. Troiden

According to Warren's (1972) informants, the concept of gay identity contains the components of same-sex sexual activity, same-sex sexual attraction, self-identification as homosexual, involvement in the homosexual subculture, and same-sex romantic attachments. Here, these identities are viewed as being acquired in four stages: sensitization, dissociation and signification, coming out, and commitment.

METHOD

As a means of ascertaining the ways in which gay men come to realize and decide they are gay, I undertook an interview study of a sample of male homosexuals. The sample was collected by means of the "snowball" technique: contacting men known to me, interviewing them, and then asking each to supply the names of other men willing to be interviewed. Using this technique, 150 men were interviewed, 50 in each of three areas: New York City, Suffolk County (a suburban to semirural area about 50 miles from New York), and Minneapolis, Minnesota. All of the respondents were white. All were between the ages of 20 and 40; slightly more than half ($N = 77$) were in their 20s, and the remainder ($N = 73$) were in their 30s (or exactly 40 years old). Over a third (36%) had no college education; a third (34%) had attended college; and roughly a third (30%) had at least some graduate school experience. Since many studies of homosexual populations have concentrated on men who frequent gay bars, I sought to incorporate non-gay-bar-goers into the sample. Roughly half ($N = 78$) were bar-goers, and half ($N = 72$) were not. A

From *Psychiatry: Journal for the Study of Interpersonal Processes* 42 (November 1979), pp. 362–373. Reprinted by permission of Guilford Publications.

bar-goer was defined as someone who went to a gay bar for sexual and/or social purposes more than once per month during the previous year.

THE MODEL

Stage 1: Sensitization

As the name *sensitization* implies, it is during this stage that men gain experiences which *later* serve as sources for interpreting their feelings as homosexual. The stage is divided into an early (prior to age 13) and a late (age 13–17) phase, and its hallmark is a sense of apartness from more conventional peers.

Most informants reported that during the early part of the stage they were only dimly aware, if aware at all, of the nature of their sexual orientation. Altman (1971) suggests that prior to adolescence many boys gain certain types of experiences that may later serve as sources for interpreting their sexual feelings as homosexual. Plummer (1975) singles out for special attention events located in social, genital, and emotional spheres as predisposing young men to later self-identification of themselves as homosexual. Unfortunately, Plummer does not specify exactly when those experiences are gained.

Data will be presented which indicate that experiences in these areas produced a sense of difference during childhood (prior to age 13) that crystallized into a distinct sense of *sexual* dissimilarity during high school, usually before informants reached age 17. It is not so much childhood experiences themselves, then, but the *meanings* which later came to be attributed to them that are important in the acquisition of gay identities. These results also indicate that a majority of the sample recalled engaging in their first homosexual contacts to orgasm during the latter part of this stage.

Of the interviewees, 72% experienced a sense of apartness during preadolescence. The following comments convey the content of this stage:

A Student: I never felt as if I fit in. I don't know why for sure. I felt different. I thought it was because I was more sensitive.

A College Instructor: I felt different due to my interest in school, ineptness at sports, and the like.

A Minister: I felt intimidated by my peers . . . I envied their athletic skills.

A Waiter: I was fascinated by the male body and decided that I wanted to be a dancer. My friends often teased me about it but it didn't upset me all that much because I was good at other sports, too. On a certain level, however, I felt that my fascination with the male body was somehow wrong, but I couldn't tell you why I felt this way.

The comments of all informants are summarized in Table 2-1. As the table indicates, the most frequently recalled sources of a childhood sense of difference were: alienation, reasons unknown (22%); feelings of gender inadequacy (19%); and warmth and excitement in the presence of other males (15%). The references to alienation and gender inadequacy show that childhood *social* experiences played a greater role

in sensitizing a person for subsequent self-definition as homosexual than did preadolescent experiences gained in the spheres of *genitality* (same-sex relations) and *emotionality* (warmth and excitement).

However, this is not to say that feelings of alienation, gender inadequacy, or warmth and excitement either cause or are indicative of homosexuality. Nor is the claim being made that homosexuality causes the emergence of such feelings. Moreover, the assertion is *not* made that a childhood sense of difference is experienced only by persons who later become homosexual, or that differences need necessarily exist between the overt behavior of young males who later acquire gay identities and those who do not. It is quite possible that during their childhood many males who later develop *heterosexual* commitments also feel estranged, for various reasons, from other males.

What *is* suggested here is that homosexual and heterosexual males may differ in terms of the *meanings* they later come to attribute to a childhood sense of apartness. The same childhood feelings which the adolescent heterosexual may come to redefine as the initial signs of, for instance, artistic sensitivity may be reinterpreted by the teen-aged male who later becomes homosexual as the first stirrings of

TABLE 2-1

IN WHAT WAYS DID YOU FEEL DIFFERENT DURING YOUR CHILDHOOD YEARS?[1]

	Responses	
	%	No.
A general sense of alienation; no specific reason	22	30
A sense of gender inadequacy	19	27
Experiences warmth and excitement in presence of other males	15	21
Did not share many interests in common with male age-mates	14	20
Effeminacy	9	13
Awareness of and fascination with male body	6	8
A medical or physical disability	6	8
Was a self-designated homosexual	4	6
Experienced guilt over sexual activity with other males	2	3
Other	2	3
	99	139[2]

[1]As used here, "childhood" refers to the time prior to the 13th birthday.
[2]Responses were obtained from the 108 informants who experienced a sense of difference during childhood. In this and the following tables, the number of responses exceeds the number of informants because of multiple responses.

homosexual interest. Childhood experiences gained in social, emotional, and genital realms, then, came to be *invested* with homosexual meanings when informants were adolescents. Thus, the reinterpretation of past events as indicating a homosexual potential appears to be a necessary condition for the eventual adoption of a gay identity.

In the later phase of the sensitization stage, during their high school years, usually prior to their 17th birthday, almost all—99%—of the males experienced a sense of *sexual* difference. Informants recollected that a global sense of apartness during childhood crystallized into a subjectively experienced sense of sexual difference during middle adolescence. Reasons offered by informants for this solidification are listed in Table 2-2. Unlike the childhood sense of difference that mainly grew out of *social* experiences, the grounds for feelings of sexual difference during adolescence stemmed primarily from the spheres of *emotionality* and *genitality:* less opposite-sex interest than other males (40%), undue interest—as defined by informants—in other young men (14%), sexual activity with other males (11%), and gender inadequacy (11%) were the most frequently cited. These

responses are significant considering that nearly two-thirds, or 98 of the 150 interviewees, engaged in their first homosexual activity to orgasm during this stage, at a mean age of 14.9. This indicates that an important aspect of the process of becoming homosexual involves learning to recognize and define one's feelings as homosexual.

Stage 2: Dissociation and Signification

The hallmark of this stage—*dissociation*—consists of the partitioning in consciousness of sexual feelings and/or activity from sexual identity. Rather than diminishing a growing awareness of "possible" homosexual tendencies, dissociation has the ironic effect of *signifying* these feelings. That is, the very act of dissociation serves to *re-present* to those who practice it that which they are attempting to dissociate—namely, the implications which their same-sex sexual interest or activity may hold regarding the fundamental character of their sexual orientations.

The suspicion that one "might" be homosexual is used to mark the outset of the stage, a point suggested in Plummer's thesis on "becoming" homosexual. The mean age at which participants in

---

TABLE 2-2

IN WHAT WAYS DID YOU FEEL DIFFERENT DURING YOUR HIGH SCHOOL YEARS?[1]

	Responses	
	%	No.
Less interested than peers in members of the opposite sex	40	71
Felt "unduly" interested in persons of the same sex	14	25
As a consequence of sexual activity with other males	11	19
A sense of gender inadequacy	11	20
Opposite-sex sexual relations were somewhat unsatisfying; something seemed to be missing	9	16
Was a self-designated homosexual	4	7
Alienation	3	6
Homosexual activity was more satisfying than heterosexual activity	2	4
Other	5	9
	99	177[2]

[1]As used here, "high school years" refers to events which occurred between a person's 13th birthday and graduation from high school.
[2]Responses were obtained from the 149 informants who felt a sense of difference during their adolescence.

this study started questioning their heterosexuality—that is, could no longer take their "straightness" as given—was 17.1. Of the 150 informants, 148 remembered having passed through a period in their lives when they thought they "might" be homosexual but could not tell for sure.

The following comments are fairly representative of the forms dissociation assumed for these men:

A Hotel Desk Clerk: I went into service at 17, mainly to get away from home. That's where I finished high school. Anyway, when I was in service I started to realize that I felt a sexual attraction for other men, that I was as strongly attracted to men as I was to women. I was engaged to be married at the time, so I passed the attraction off as being due to the circumstances—the loneliness and the lack of female companionship. I rationalized my feelings as indicating feelings of deep friendship. But I couldn't seem to stop thinking about it. The possibility that I might be gay terrified me.

A Waiter: Before I was publicly labeled a faggot, I realized that I wasn't very interested in women. I had had enough experiences with girls to realize that while I was aroused by them, I was also aroused by males and wanted to have sex with

them. However, I thought this was something I'd outgrow in time, something that would straighten itself out as I matured.

An Auto Mechanic: I had a sexual experience with a neighbor. We got drunk together and we ended up masturbating each other. I felt guilty and ashamed. I knew that the activity was homosexual, but I refused to label myself as gay. I rationalized it away as sexual experimentation and curiosity. Even so, I still worried about it. I didn't like to think that I could enjoy homosexual activity, which suggested homosexual inclinations. I decided that I'd try not to think about my attraction toward men, that if I didn't think about it, it might go away.

Dissociation or the separation of identity from activity and/or feelings is reflected in the examples presented above, where there is a seeming need to explain ("something I'd outgrow"), excuse ("due to . . . loneliness and the lack of female companionship"), or justify ("sexual experimentation and curiosity") the implications which one's acts or feelings have regarding the nature and direction of one's sexual identity.

Table 2-3 summarizes the circumstances that led informants to question the nature of their sexual

TABLE 2-3

WHAT LED YOU TO QUESTION THE NATURE OF YOUR SEXUAL ORIENTATION?

	Responses	
	%	No.
Becoming sexually aroused by another male or beginning to view other males in sexual terms	24	40
A physically enjoyable homosexual experience or homosexual fantasies	23	39
The desire to repeat a homosexual experience	18	31
Reading or learning about homosexuality	16	28
Heterosexual interests or emotional involvements seemed less strong than those exhibited by male peers	11	19
Developing a "crush" on or an emotional attachment for another male	7	12
Other	1	1
	100	170*

*Responses were obtained from the 148 informants who reported that for a time in their lives they thought that they might be homosexual but couldn't tell for sure.

feelings. Sexual doubts were prompted by experiences subjects defined as more explicitly homosexual than those which had earlier led them to believe they were merely sexually different. Events most frequently reported as having provided grounds for suspecting homosexual interests were: becoming sexually aroused by another male (24%) and physically enjoyable homosexual experiences or fantasies (23%). Although the homosexual component in these feelings and behavior was recognized during this stage, no degree of permanence was attributed to it. Put somewhat differently, even though informants questioned their sexual feelings, they neither effortlessly nor immediately defined them as decidedly homosexual. Most males attributed a temporary status to the sensations, as a glance at Table 2-4 will show. Sexual attractions were not labeled as definitely homosexual because they were interpreted as a phase of development that would eventually pass (54%), or because interviewees believed they shared little or nothing in common with homosexuals as a group (22%). In short, the idea that one might possibly be homosexual was ego-dystonic for these men at this point in their lives.

Stage 3: Coming Out

The events included within the stage of *coming out* occur relatively close together. Thus, for heuristic purposes, the decision to label one's sexual feelings as definitely homosexual is used to mark the outset of this stage. Self-definition as homosexual, initial involvement in the homosexual subculture, and redefinition of homosexuality as a positive and viable lifestyle alternative are viewed as making up the content of this stage. While the commencement of homosexual activity on a regular basis (one or more times per week) is associated with the stage (the mean age was 21.0), a majority of the sample (68%) experienced homosexual contacts to orgasm one or more times prior to labeling themselves as homosexual. For this reason, changes in the conception of one's identity and of one's view of homosexuality and homosexuals—rather than homosexual behavior—are seen as crucial to this stage.

Some disagreement exists among both social scientists and members of the gay community as to what is meant by the term "coming out." The ways in which participants in this study defined "coming out" are presented in Table 2-5. Some disagreement

---

TABLE 2-4

WHEN YOU THOUGHT YOU MIGHT BE GAY, WHAT KEPT YOU FROM LABELING YOUR FEELINGS AS SUCH?

	Responses	
	%	No.
Viewed feelings as indicating a phase	54	89
Inaccurate knowledge regarding homosexuality led to believe that little was shared in common with homosexuals as a group	22	36
Did not reciprocate sexually (e.g., was passive partner in fellatio) or viewed homosexual activity as an expedient means of sexual release	7	12
No history of homosexual experience or a history of heterosexual experience	8	13
Viewed feelings as indicating tendencies	3	5
Viewed feelings as indicating bisexuality	2	4
Other	3	5
	99	164*

*Responses were obtained from the 148 informants who did not label these feelings as gay even though they suspected they "might" be homosexual.

TABLE 2-5

WHAT DOES THE TERM "COMING OUT" MEAN?*

	Responses	
	%	No.
To admit to oneself a homosexual preference, or decide that one is, essentially, homosexual	31	77
To admit to oneself a homosexual preference *and* to begin to practice homosexual activity	27	41
To start actively seeking out other males as sexual partners	9	13
First homosexual experience as a young adult (i.e., after middle teens)	8	12
A homosexual experience that triggers self-designation as homosexual	1	2
Other	3	5
	99	150

*Informants were asked to define what the term "coming out" meant to them—that is, how they would use the term.

existed among interviewees about the meaning of coming out, with 51% maintaining that coming out refers to the act of defining oneself to oneself as homosexual. This definition is used here.

The decision to label sexual feelings as definitely homosexual is used to mark the transition to this stage; the mean age at which this occurred was 19.7. However, approximately two-thirds of the interviewees ($N = 93$) *did not* designate themselves as homosexual—that is, arrive at homosexual self-definitions—at the time they designated their feelings as such. The reasons for labeling sexual feelings but not sexual identities as homosexual are listed in Table 2-6. The most frequently cited

TABLE 2-6

WHEN YOU LABELED YOUR FEELINGS AS HOMOSEXUAL, WHAT KEPT YOU FROM LABELING YOURSELF AS SUCH?

	Responses	
	%	No.
Viewed feelings as indicating a phase	34	35
Viewed feelings as indicating bisexuality	28	29
Viewed feelings as indicating tendencies	13	14
Inaccurate knowledge regarding homosexuality led to belief that little was shared in common with homosexuals as a group	12	12
No history of homosexual experience or a history of heterosexual experience	7	7
Did not reciprocate sexually (e.g., was passive partner in fellatio) or viewed homosexual activity as an expedient means of sexual release	5	5
Other	2	2
	101	104*

*Responses were obtained from the 93 informants who did not label themselves as homosexual at the same time they labeled their sexual feelings as homosexual.

reasons for not labeling sexual identities as homosexual were: Homosexual attractions were seen as a phase (34%), as indicating bisexuality (28%), or as a manifestation of homosexual tendencies or inclinations (13%). Thus, these data indicate that many respondents recalled having experienced at least some degree of confusion regarding the nature of their sexual identities in the twilight of their teens. It will be shown that this uncertainty was for the most part eliminated once these men were able to gain accurate knowledge regarding homosexuals and homosexuality.

The mean age at which homosexual self-designation occurred was 21.3. The following comment illustrates the types of circumstances that encouraged self-definition as homosexual:

A Waiter: I met a straight guy when I was in college. He also was studying dance. As our friendship developed, I realized that I was falling in love with him and that I had never cared for anyone as deeply as I cared for him. I think he suspected the way I felt for him but I'm not sure. One night we were out drinking with a bunch of guys at a college bar. We both got rather high and when we returned to the dorm I went with him to his room. It

was the beginning of a very beautiful night. I walked over to him, put my arms around him, and kissed him. He reciprocated. We eventually mutually masturbated each other. He is now married and has a family. This incident led a fateful resignation on my part that I was irrevocably gay. Due to the beauty of the experience, however, I was able to rid myself of any doubts I had regarding my being a homosexual as negating the possibility of being a good person.

The circumstances in which informants arrived at homosexual self-definitions are summarized in Table 2-7. Meeting other gay men was the most common circumstance leading to homosexual self-definition. Males who "tested" themselves differed from males who concluded they were homosexual after a meaningful homophile experience. The former decided to determine their sexual preferences after undergoing an intense psychological struggle, often of protracted duration, during which they attempted to suppress their homosexual feelings. Over time, however, these men decided that any form of sexual identity—heterosexual, bisexual, or homosexual—would be preferable to the sexual ambiguity and confusion they were experiencing.

TABLE 2-7

WHAT CIRCUMSTANCES SURROUNDED YOUR DECISION TO LABEL YOURSELF AS BEING ESSENTIALLY HOMOSEXUAL?

	Responses	
	%	No.
Knowing or meeting other gays socially	33	65
Deciding to put oneself to the "test" by seeking out homosexual contacts to see if this was what was "really" desired	17	33
A physically or emotionally enjoyable homosexual experience	17	34
Fell in love with another male	16	31
A chance homosexual experience or chance entry into a gay social contact such as a homosexual bar	8	16
Realizing that the label "homosexual" applied to oneself as a consequence of reading about or learning of the existence of homosexuals	6	12
Reciprocated sexually	3	6
Other	2	3
	102	200

Accordingly, they put themselves to the test—that is, they actively sought out homosexual experiences in order to determine whether or not their inclinations were in fact homosexual. The sense of urgency or need to decide once and for all who and what they were sexually was for the most part absent in the life histories of those men who decided they were homosexual as a consequence of a chance homosexual encounter which they found fulfilling. When these men—as young adults—had the opportunity to engage in homosexual activity, they simply did so, decided they liked it, and consequently defined themselves as homosexual.

The findings presented here partially replicate the results obtained in Dank's (1971) study of homosexual identity. He also found the mean age of self-designation as homosexual to be 21. In addition, males who took part in this study tended to arrive at homosexual self-definitions in social contexts quite similar to those reported by Dank's respondents. However, these results differ from Dank's with respect to the role played by love as a generating force to homosexual self-definition. Falling in love rather than initiating a love affair with another male enabled a number of informants in this study to arrive at homosexual self-definitions.

Initial involvement in the homosexual subculture also occurred during this stage. When asked, "Which came first, beginning to think of yourself as homosexual or associating with other homosexuals?," 52% of the informants stated both occurred at roughly the same time, 41% said homosexual self-definition took place at least six months prior to interactions with other gays, and 7% claimed they had associated with other gays at least six months before self-labeling.

Once again, this finding is quite similar to Dank's results. Of his respondents, 50% defined themselves as homosexual when they began associating with other homosexuals. The mean age at which participants in this research started associating with other gays—that is, started to involve themselves in the homosexual subculture—was 21.8, in comparison with the mean age for self-designation as homosex-

ual, 21.3. Thus, self-definition and initial subcultural involvement took place quite closely together. However, following the interactionist tradition of George H. Mead, Dank and Warren point out that the real significance of subcultural exposure resides in the impact it has on an individual's sense of identity and his attitudes toward homosexuality.

The opportunity to gain information about homosexuality that runs contrary to society's stereotypes led the men who took part in this study to see both themselves and homosexuality in a positive light. According to self-reports, 87% changed their attitudes about themselves roughly one year after becoming self-defined homosexuals. Self-conceptions were reportedly altered by 6% at approximately the same time as self-designation. Only 11 males experienced no change at all. Of the men who experienced attitude change, 46% viewed the change as positive, leading to a firmer sense of identity, 20% maintained they achieved higher levels of self-acceptance and happiness, and 11% claimed they felt less guilty or anxious about their sexual-emotional preferences. The change in self-image was related by 44% to exposure to the gay world or making a gay friend(s).

In addition to changes in self-image and identity, time spent in the gay world altered the views these men held toward homosexuality. The meaning of the cognitive category *homosexual* was transformed (Dank). Before arriving at homosexual self-definitions, nearly all—94%—of the respondents recalled having viewed homosexuality as a form of mental illness. When interviewed, only two men looked upon homosexuality as a "sickness." The rest saw it as a variation from the norm. When asked how these changes in attitudes were brought about, the vast majority (88%) claimed their favorable views stemmed from gaining the opportunity to meet homosexuals with interests and attitudes similar to their own—men who, like themselves, appear to be heterosexual. In short, differential association elicited and reinforced a positive sense of identity and served as a barrier to and/or neutralized the highly negative images of homosexuals held by dominant groups in American society.

Stage 4: Commitment

Following Warren, the taking of a lover—that is, the fusion of gay sexuality and emotionality into a meaningful whole—was used to signify the outset of the stage of *commitment*. Commitment is indicated when homosexuality is adopted as a way of life—that is, when men express contentment with their life situations, see no reason to change, or believe nothing is to be gained by choosing bisexuality or heterosexuality.

The taking of a lover *confirms* gay identity. In terms of the perspective of Warren's informants, an individual whose sexual activity is exclusively homosexual, who has been sexually active with other males for an extended period of time, say 20 or 30 years, but who has never entered a love relationship with another male or interacted with other gays socially, would be viewed as possessing a *homosexual* rather than gay identity. Without a romantic involvement—that is, never having had a lover and social interaction with other gays—the individual is defined as lacking a *gay* identity:

> The romantic-sexual act fusion . . . serves as a highly significant benchmark symbol of converted self-identity for many . . . members [of the gay community] who . . . indicate that [the linking] of romantic-sex acts . . . differentiates the "true" homosexual from the one who is simply experimenting. (Warren 1972:223)

The assertion that love relationships are usually initiated in the post-coming-out period has a basis in fact. Current evidence (Gagnon and Simon 1973) suggests that large numbers of male homosexuals are more likely to enter into love relations after, rather than at the same time as, they label themselves as homosexual. Gagnon and Simon suggest that once familiar with the sexual side of the gay scene, many homosexual men may begin to personalize their sexual encounters, seeking persons from whom social, emotional, and intellectual as well as sexual gratification can be obtained. The data derived from this research bear out this suggestion. When asked, "At the present time do you want a lover (given your own definition of the term)?," 91% replied yes. Further, 76% of the informants answered yes to the question, "Have you ever had a lover?," and an additional 12% indicated they had been in love with another man and would have gladly entered into a love relationship had the other person been willing. The men who initiated one or more love relationships entered their first love affair at a mean age of 23.9—approximately $2\frac{1}{2}$ years *after* the mean age of homosexual self-definition.

Contrary to Warren's conception, however, the process of becoming committed to homosexuality as a way of life is seen here as involving more than the taking of a lover. Although a foundation for commitment is laid during the coming-out stage, when men redefine homosexuality as a legitimate life-style alternative, they can still see heterosexuality or bisexuality as more viable and rewarding. In a similar vein, while many men may come to accept a gay identity, they may still place a higher premium on heterosexual or bisexual identities. That is, men may vary in the extent to which they are satisfied with their identities.

Therefore, one's present identity has implications for the future, since today's identity can provide the foundation for tomorrow's interactions. In fact, the degree of satisfaction an individual expresses about his present identity as a future identity is a measure of his commitment to that identity (Hammersmith and Weinberg 1973). Thus *commitment* to identity differs from *acceptance,* in that commitment presupposes a reluctance to abandon the identity even if given the opportunity to do so. When asked, "To what extent would you say you are accepting of and comfortable with your homosexuality?," 88% of the sample said they were accepting, 11% replied they were somewhat accepting, and only one person stated he was somewhat unaccepting. No one claimed to be completely unaccepting.

When asked, "At this time would you say you are more, less, or about as happy as you were prior to arriving at a homosexual self-definition?," 91%

indicated they were more happy, 8% stated they were about as happy, and only one person said he was less happy. Gaining a sense of identity (47%) and a clearer sense of what is desired both sexually and emotionally (13%) were the most frequently mentioned reasons for higher levels of happiness. Thus, perceived levels of happiness increased with the crystallization of a sense of identity.

An increased sense of identity, however, does not necessarily guarantee commitment to that identity. Similarly, increased happiness resulting from a firmer sense of identity does not warrant the presupposition that the newly acquired identity is necessarily the most highly valued one for that person. A compromise might well be involved. In certain instances, *any* conception of identity might be viewed as an improvement over no sense of identity, or over feelings of ambiguity and uncertainty regarding an identity. Some males could feel happier after defining themselves as homosexual and yet remain convinced they would be even more contented living as heterosexuals. Therefore, to be judged as committed, the homosexual should value homosexuality at least as much as, and perhaps more than, the bisexual or heterosexual alternatives, and elect to remain homosexual if faced with the opportunity to abandon his homosexuality.

When respondents were asked if they would choose to remain homosexual if given the chance to abandon the homosexual option, 91% stated they would not become heterosexual even if they knew of a proven method to accomplish this change; 10 indicated they would change; and 3 replied they didn't know what they would do.

The most frequently mentioned reasons for not becoming heterosexual were: contentment and happiness with a homosexual preference (52%); the belief that nothing would be gained by a change of sexual orientation (24%); and a clearly expressed preference for the gay life (14%). These data, then, seem to show that the majority of the males who participated in this research endeavor saw homosexuality as more personally meaningful

and rewarding than heterosexuality. One could, therefore, conclude that most of these males are committed homosexuals. In short, given the definition presented here, the vast majority of these men could be described as having acquired gay identities.

When informants were asked, "In what ways do you think homosexuals are similar to and different from heterosexuals?," they most frequently saw homosexuals as differing from heterosexuals only in sexual behavior and preference (65%).

CONCLUSIONS

A number of comments are in order on the model of gay identity development outlined and supported in this paper. First, gay identities are not viewed as being acquired in an absolute, fixed, or final sense. One of the main assumptions of this model is that identity is never fully acquired, but is always somewhat incomplete, forever subject to modification.

Nor is the model meant to convey the idea that gay identity development is inevitable for those who experience the first stages. Rather, each stage is viewed as making the acquisition of a gay identity more probable, but not as an inevitable determinant. As some persons progress through these stages, some steps may be merged or glossed over, bypassed, or realized simultaneously. A kind of shifting effect is probably involved, with some males "drifting away" at various points prior to stage four. It is quite possible that as adolescents, young adults, or even as adults, a relatively large number of males consciously "test" the extent to which they may be sexually attracted to other men. As a consequence of such sexual experimentation, a substantial number of males may decide that homosexuality is not for them and choose to leave the scene entirely. It is therefore quite likely that only a tiny portion of American males who practice homosexual behavior ever take on gay identities. Those who do acquire them exhibit the following characteristics: homosexual behavior, homosexual attractions, homosexual self-conceptions, social as well as sexual affiliations with the gay world, and same-sex romantic attachments.

Perhaps the most striking conclusion that can be drawn regarding the process of acquiring a gay identity is its tenuous character. For a majority of the sample, the route to gay identity was fraught with ambiguity, confusion, and uncertainty. For only a small minority was the gay identity taken on rapidly.

REFERENCES

Altman, D. 1971. *Homosexual.* London: Outerbridge and Dienstfrey.
Dank, B. M. 1971. "Coming Out in the Gay World." *Psychiatry* 34:180–197.
Plummer, K. 1975. *Sexual Stigma.* London: Routledge and Kegan Paul.
Warren, C. A. B. 1974. *Identity and Community in the Gay World.* Wiley-Interscience (doctoral dissertation, University of Southern California).

Coming Out as a Transgendered Person

Patricia Gagné, Richard Tewksbury, and Deanna McGaughey

Coming out is a term generally used to refer to the processes whereby gay men, lesbians, or bisexuals inform others of their sexual identity. Despite this popularized notion, the social scientific literature has shown coming out to be a broader and more complex process whereby people recognize and accept their sexual preference, adopt a sexual identity, inform others of their sexual orientation, and become involved in relationships with others of similar sexual identity (Cass 1979, 1984; Coleman 1981–82; Isay 1990; Trolden and Goode 1980; Weinberg 1978).

In Western societies, gender identity has been largely dictated by external genitalia, the initial signifier of "sex," and other reproductive anatomy (see Laqueur 1990). With the rise of technology, reduced infant mortality, greater life expectancy,

contraception, infant feeding formula, and the feminist movement, the immutable relationship between sex and gender has been questioned (see Huber 1989; Huber and Spitze 1983). Nonetheless, the expression of alternative forms of gender has been largely limited to the expansion of existing norms and roles—a liberal form of social change. Ironically, those hoping to freely express alternative gender identities have largely reacted against the binary system and thus have been restricted by it. Gender becomes something one must "confess" through social signifiers that may only be interpreted within the existing social order (see Foucault [1978] 1990). Falling in "between" the gender binary will often result in assumptions of homosexuality, as in the case of the feminine man or the masculine woman. Expressions of gender that fall "outside" the dominant gender system make social presentations of gender undecipherable. Frequently, those who fall outside or between the gender binary are encouraged to conform to the dominant system.

From *Gender & Society* 11, No. 4, August 1997, 478–508. © 1997 Sociologists for Women in Society. Reprinted by permission of Sage Publications.

Those who cannot or will not conform may be counseled to alter their bodies or encouraged to perfect a new gender presentation so that they may "pass" as the "other sex" (Raymond 1994). Those who start out challenging the dominant gender system by enacting gender in ways that are comfortable for themselves but disturbing to others often end up by redefining their identities in ways that conform to hegemonic belief systems and institutional demands.

We have both substantive and theoretical goals in writing this article. Substantively, we aim to enhance social scientific understandings of the coming-out experiences of a nonrandom sample of individuals whose gender expressions, gender identity, or both fall outside the gender binary. Theoretically, our goal is to demonstrate the ways in which interactional or identity-based challenges to gender are limited in the extent they can reform, radically alter, or eliminate the gender binary. Those whose gender identity and gender presentations fall outside the binary are stigmatized, ostracized, and socially delegitimized to the extent that they may fail to be socially recognized. With such social erasure, it becomes incumbent on the individual to adopt a social identity that falls within the confines of the dominant gender order. For many, "coming out" includes "crossing over," either permanently or temporarily, from one sex/gender category to the only acceptable alternative. While identities have been created for morphological men or women who wish to dress or live as "the other" gender, the binary gender system demands that individuals confess alternative identities and learn to present themselves in ways that convince others that they are, in fact, members of the sex category suggested by their gender.

In this article, we examine the coming-out experiences of a nonrandom sample of individuals who were members of the transgender community at the time we solicited volunteers for our project. Transgenderism refers to "the lives and experiences of diverse groups of people who live outside normative sex/gender relations" (Namaste 1994:228). Persons who enact alternative gender presentations or who have internalized alternative gender identities are referred to as "transgenderists" (Tewksbury and Gagné 1996).

Although barriers to self-awareness and acceptance are declining, transgenderists continue to grapple with many of the issues that confronted sexual minorities in the United States prior to the 1970s. Most masculine-to-feminine transgenderists conform to traditional beliefs about sex and gender, whereas a minority attempt to step outside the gender binary by defining themselves in nongendered or multiply gendered ways (Raymond 1994). For example, within the transgender community, the declassification of transsexualism as a psychiatric diagnosis has been hotly debated, with those seeking to challenge medical definitions arguing that it should be removed from the *Diagnostic and Statistical Manual of Mental Disorders* (DSM-IV) and those still seeking access to hormones and sex reassignment surgery (SRS) arguing that being diagnosed transsexual is the only way they may become the women they truly are. In other words, they must "confess" their transsexualism in ways that adhere to medical models in order to proceed from one sex to the other. Similarly, most transsexuals adhere to beliefs that their desires to live as women were the result of biological "mistakes" that left them as feminine persons in male bodies (Pauly 1990; Stoller 1971). Rather than choosing to live as feminine males, they opt to cross over to full-time womanhood. Similarly, most cross-dressers look on their sartorial transitions as opportunities to express their feminine selves (Talamini 1981; Woodhouse 1989). They deem feminine behavior in masculine attire to be highly inappropriate. Among our sample, the exceptions to these trends tended to exist among individuals who, at one time, identified as transsexuals and/or cross-dressers and who, in the process of trying to understand who they were, began to question the legitimacy of gender as a defining characteristic of self. At the time we talked with them, these people were members of the transgender community who self-identified as either a radical transgenderist, ambigendered, or a third gender. They were looking for ways to defy categorization based on gender, rather than find a way to fit within the gender system.

METHOD

We completed 65 semistructured, in-depth, tape-recorded interviews with masculine-to-feminine individuals from several points along the transgender spectrum (see Tewksbury and Gagné 1996). *Transgenderism* is an umbrella term that encompasses a variety of identities—including transsexual, fetish, and nonfetishistic cross-dresser; drag queen; and other terms—as devised by individuals who live outside the dominant gender system. In this study, we have categorized individuals on the basis of the identity they proclaimed to us. All volunteers in our sample were members of the transgender communities through which we recruited volunteers for our study. The majority in our sample had refined their self-identifications in the process of coming out. Included in our sample are individuals who self-identify as pre- ($n = 27$), post- ($n = 10$), and nonoperative ($n = 4$) transsexual. Transsexuals are people who believe themselves to be female and who wish to, or do, live full-time as women. Preoperative transsexuals are those who desire to have, but have not yet had, SRS. Postoperative transsexuals are those who have had SRS. Nonoperative transsexuals are those who live full-time or nearly full-time as women but who do not wish to have SRS. Some have availed themselves of other medical and cosmetic procedures—including female hormones, breast implants, and electrolysis, whereas others alter their gender presentations without bodily alteration. During childhood (before age 10), about one-third ($n = 16$) felt a strong desire to become a girl or believed themselves to be female. The remainder began to recognize a desire to be female during adolescence ($n = 15$) or adulthood ($n = 10$). They self-identified as heterosexual, bisexual, lesbian, and asexual. Although our sample included many male individuals who had had sexual relationships or encounters with other male persons, no one in our sample self-identified as gay at the time of the interview or at any time during their lives. Also included in our sample are 2 fetishistic cross-dressers, one of whom began erotically motivated cross-dressing during adolescence and the other during adulthood. Such individuals—referred to in the psychiatric literature as transvestites—are male individuals who have a masculine gender identity, self-identity as heterosexual, and dress in women's clothing for erotic purposes. Our sample also includes 17 (nonfetishistic) cross-dressers.[1] Cross-dressers are men who usually self-identify as heterosexual, with a minority identifying as bisexual (Feinbloom 1977; Prince and Bentler 1972; Talamini 1982; Woodhouse 1989). Thirteen of the cross-dressers began cross-dressing in childhood, and 4 during adolescence. Cross-dressers are men who wear women's clothing to relax and permit the expression of their feminine selves. Seven of the cross-dressers in our sample began "dressing" in response to erotic motivations. By the time we interviewed them, the eroticism had dissipated. The remaining cross-dressers in our sample had always dressed for nonerotic reasons. All but 1 of the transsexuals in our study had, at one time, self-identified as a cross-dresser prior to developing a transsexual identity, with 15 reporting that their earliest experiences with cross-dressing were erotically motivated. Each continued cross-dressing even after the erotic component was gone and finally adopted a transsexual identity. In our sample, 4 cross-dressers were in the process of exploring the possibility they might be transsexual. We have categorized them according to the identities they presented to us at the time of the interview. Most cross-dressers in our sample held very traditional opinions about sex, gender, and sexuality. They were masculine, heterosexual men who, when they dressed as women, wished to be perceived as feminine, heterosexual female persons.

A small number of persons ($n = 5$) who cross-dressed and had no desire for SRS referred to

---

[1] In this article, unless otherwise stated, "cross-dresser" refers to a nonfetishistic cross-dresser.

themselves in more politically oriented terms. While there are subtle differences in politics, all five of these people have used transgenderism to challenge binary assumptions about sex, gender, and sexuality. Their intent is not to "pass" as women but to challenge the idea that gender is a "natural" expression of sex and sexuality. This group of five includes one "radical transgenderist"—an anatomical, heterosexual male person with a masculine gender identity, who uses cross-dressing as a means to express feminine aspects of self and to challenge traditional binary conceptualizations of sex, gender, and sexuality. It also includes one "ambigenderist," an individual who lives alternatively as a man and a woman, and who believes that categories of sexual orientation do not exist and that sexuality is a spectrum. Depending on how he or she feels, he or she frequently went out "in between"—as neither a man nor a woman (with long hair, makeup, high heels, tight pants, and a two-day growth of beard). In addition, this group includes three people who self-identified as a "third gender." These three individuals believed that all people have both masculine and feminine attributes. Their desire was to develop and be able to publicly present both aspects of self and to live as a combination of both genders. Like the ambigenderist, they resisted categorizing themselves according to sexual identity. In our discussions of the transgendered people in our sample, we have self-consciously adhered to the self-identifications used by our volunteers, with the exception of the final group of five. For purposes of clarity, we refer to this group as gender radicals. We have taken the liberty of doing this because all of them emphasized their desire to eliminate the existing system of gender, rather than just their own gender.

We solicited volunteers through 14 transgender support groups, transgender online services, and by responding to personal ads in a national transgender publication. People in every region of the contiguous 48 states volunteered for interviews, making our research national in scope. Participants resided in large urban areas, small towns, suburbs, and rural areas. Our sample includes 4 African Americans,

2 Asians, 1 Hispanic, and 58 Whites. Participants ranged in age from 24 to 68 years, with a mean age of 44. Occupationally, they were diverse with jobs ranging from doctors, airline pilots, computer systems analysts, engineers, college professors, school teachers, enlisted members of the military, police officers, welders, mechanics, food service and clerical workers, and janitors. Although our sample was occupationally diverse, the majority was well educated and had long employment histories in the skilled trades and professions. Most members of our sample were either employed or voluntarily unemployed (i.e., retired or student) at the time we talked with them. Nonetheless, one postoperative and eight preoperative transsexuals were unemployed, and the majority of those who lived full-time as the gender into which they were not assigned at birth were vastly underemployed.[2]

To provide the greatest reliability among interviews, all but one were conducted by the first author. Where distance precluded a face-to-face meeting, interviews were conducted over the telephone. They were organized such that, after background information on age, education, occupational history, and family was gathered, respondents were encouraged to tell their life stories as they pertained to their transgendered feelings and experiences. Respondents were guided through several areas of inquiry, including their earliest transgender experiences or feelings; being discovered cross-dressed; acquiring girls' or women's clothing, makeup, and wigs; learning about and refining a feminine appearance or persona; participating in transgender support groups or on-line communities; finding therapists and surgeons and experiences with the medical community; identifying and labeling emotions, feelings, behaviors, and identity; telling others; transformations or stability in sexual fantasy, behavior, and identity; and political and gender attitudes. Interviews ranged from 45 minutes to eight hours in length, averaging about three hours.

---

[2] We recognize that there is a transgender community within the impoverished class, but we were unable to solicit volunteers from that segment of the population through the routes we used.

Interviews were transcribed in full. An analytic-inductive process was used in organizing and interpreting the descriptions and stories of the volunteers in our sample (Miles and Huberman 1984). Data analysis included three flows of activity: data reduction, which included the process of identifying emergent themes in the data; data display, the process of organizing and clustering the information to be used for deriving conclusions; and conclusion drawing and verification, the process of deciding what experiences mean, noting patterns and explanations, and verifying our findings (Miles and Huberman 1984).

FINDINGS

Appearance is a central component in the establishment and maintenance of self and identity (Stone 1975). An alternative gender may be achieved only through interaction, in which the recognition of others has the potential to legitimate and reinforce the emergent alternative identity. Therefore, in order to "be" themselves, whether on a temporary or permanent basis, transgenderists have a compelling need to present alternative expressions of gender. Many transgenderists choose to alter their external physical characteristics to conform to beliefs about "appropriate" appearance for the desired gender. Individual expressions of gender, as well as surgical, cosmetic, and medical procedures used to alter primary and secondary sex characteristics, are signifiers of identity. Such alternations help individuals explore and clarify who they are and may help them gain entrée to a community of others like themselves. Identity transformation is a social psychological process that develops with time, experiences, the management of emotions (Mason-Schrock 1996), conscious efforts, and interaction with others.

To examine the ways in which alternatively gendered identities are recognized, explored, evaluated, and declared (both privately and publicly), it is necessary to look at several developmental steps in the lives of transgendered persons.

Early Transgendered Experiences

Examination of the earliest recollections that transgendered individuals have of feeling that either their sex or gender was "wrong" or did not "fit" for them are useful in providing insight into the earliest manifestations that become alternative identities. Many recollections of childhood may, in fact, be reconstructed biographies. Nonetheless, these are materials from which individuals mold current identities and, therefore, are valid and significant.[3] This is the process in which the collective creation of biographical stories brings phenomenologically real "true selves" into being (Mason-Schrock 1996).

Gender constancy—a sense that a person's gender is a permanent aspect of self—is acquired between the ages of three and five years (Kohlberg 1966; Kohlberg and Ulian 1974). In our sample, 16 transsexuals recalled wanting to be girls or knowing that they really were girls during early childhood. For all but one of the remainder, feelings of being or wanting to be a woman emerged during adolescence or adulthood. Among cross-dressers, all reported knowing they were boys in early childhood and throughout adolescence, but four said they remembered wishing they could be girls during early childhood, and two reported knowing they were male but wishing they could become female during adolesence. Fetishistic cross-dressers and gender radicals did not report feeling they were or wanting to become women. Feminine behaviors and feelings of being or wanting to be girls created confusion for young children and adolescents, particularly when they received messages that they could not be or act that way.

For transsexuals and cross-dressers, one way of making sense of the incongruity between sex and gender was to explore whether a feminine boy might actually be able to become a girl. For example, one cross-dresser explained that at about the

---

[3] This view, however, is disputed by others who believe that retrospective biography construction is actually a search for ways "to fashion this information into a story that leads inexorably to the identity" that is being constructed (Mason-Schrock 1996:176–77).

age of five, "I remember . . . asking my mother out in the backyard, 'Am I always going to be a boy? Could I change and be a girl someday?' " Such questions are undoubtedly common among young children. For most children, clothing and other expressions of gender are signifiers of maleness or femaleness. Cross-dressers explained that they were satisfied with explanations that they could not change their anatomy and become female but that they continued to want to temporarily "become" girls by wearing feminine clothing, makeup, and wigs. As adults, all but four cross-dressers (who were exploring the possibility they might be transsexual) reported knowing they were male and being happy with their sex and gender identity. Throughout their lives, they were able to conceal their transgenderism much more easily than were transsexuals, who felt compelled to act and be feminine at all times.

Among transsexuals, confusion over gender, desires to be female, or feelings of being female were commonly reported in childhood and over the life course. Many of the transsexuals in our sample thought they really were girls (in the dominant cultural sense) until they began to receive messages to the contrary. For example, one postoperative transsexual explained her earliest understanding of gender and the way in which it started to be corrected. She said,

> I was probably three or four years old. . . . I remember playing with paper dolls and Barbie dolls and stuff with my sisters and wearing their clothes. I didn't even know I wasn't a girl until [at school] I was told it was time to line up for a restroom break.

Differentiating themselves from girls did not come easily for these 16 transsexuals. Socializing messages might be gentle and subtle, as the ones above, or more laden with overt hostility and anger. For example, another preoperative transsexual explained,

> I can remember begging my mother to let me wear her clothes. . . . I kicked and screamed. . . . Another time she was ironing and I wanted my own ironing board and iron and be just like mommy. This time she

got really angry and I guess I was becoming aware of the fact that I wasn't ever going to be a little girl, that it was socially unacceptable . . . because she said, "You want to be a little girl? Well, we'll put you in a little dress and tie your hair up in ribbons." . . . She became aggressive about it and at that point I understood that it was socially unacceptable.

In early childhood, cross-dressing and cross-gender behavior appear to have been tolerated. However, as children advanced beyond the "toddler" stage, they were pressured by adults and other children to recognize and adhere to traditional conceptualizations of gender and conform to masculine stereotypes. Pressures to conform to the gender binary were often based on homophobic assumptions about gender "deviants." For example, a nonoperative transsexual said,

> Around the time I was 9 or 10 years old, there was one boy in the neighborhood . . . [who] was never allowed to spend the night at my house. . . . All he would tell me is, "My dad won't let me." One afternoon I approached his dad about it. . . . This man turned an incredible red-purple color and shaking and pointing a finger in my face [said], "Because you're a fucking queer!" I didn't know what those words meant, but it was real clear from his body language that whatever those words were tied to was not OK.

The pressure to adhere to the masculine stereotype was strong, and many in our sample tried to conform. Cross-dressers hid their dressing, segmenting it off from the rest of their lives. Among transsexuals, such segmentation of the feminine aspect of self was more difficult. The majority felt more comfortable playing with girls, participating in "girls' " activities, and expressing and presenting themselves in more feminine ways. For those whose transgender feelings and behaviors began in early childhood, pressures to "fit" into the masculine stereotype and "act" like boys created confusion about identity, an internalized sense of deviance, and frequently strong self-loathing. For example, a preoperative transsexual said, "I didn't know it was transsexual. I just didn't feel like a male. Everyone was telling me I was and I felt

I had to act that way . . . I felt it was something very, very wrong."

After an initial period of confusion about sex and gender, most children recognized that cross-dressing and feminine behavior were deviant and, therefore, they tried to repress it and keep it secret. This suggests that as children begin to understand the binary gender system, they become ashamed of feminine or transgendered feelings, learn to hide their behaviors, and become confused about who they are and how they fit into the world. Many in our sample talked about becoming addicted to alcohol or drugs later in life, in an effort to numb the emotional pain they experienced and to repress the "true self," which did not fit and, therefore, needed to be repressed. Throughout adolescence and adulthood, most went through periods of "purging," when they would stop engaging in transgendered behavior and throw out feminine clothing, makeup, and wigs. Despite the stigma attached to transgenderism, however, the need to "be themselves" was strong. Even as they tried to stop, and as their feminine attributes were criticized and sanctioned, they found it impossible to stop and learned to become more and more secretive. For example, a preoperative transsexual explained,

> I was being beat up, called sissy. . . . I didn't feel normal. I felt like, "Why are you doing this? This isn't right. You're a boy." But I couldn't stop. The curiosity kept drawing me to it and I kept doing it. I felt guilty and I always thought after I . . . took the clothes off, "I'm not going to do this anymore. This is silly." A few days later . . . I was back doing it again.

Among our entire sample, for some transgenderists cross-dressing began during puberty ($n = 20$) or even adulthood ($n = 16$). Only six of our sample (three cross-dressers, one fetishistic cross-dresser, and two transsexuals) reported that their initial experiences with cross-dressing were erotically motivated during puberty. For the majority, cross-dressing was an expression of gender that, during puberty, became entangled with sexuality. Most would put on women's clothing;

read, watch television, or lounge around the house; and then, almost as an afterthought, before removing the clothing, they would masturbate. For example, one preoperative transsexual explained that she began wearing her mother's panty hose and shoes at age eight or nine. She liked the silky feeling and the way they looked. As she got older, she began putting the entire ensemble together. She said,

> I used to borrow [wigs and clothes]. . . . I would put this stuff on when [my parents] were gone and I went running around the house, and it just felt that I was relieved. A great burden was lifted off me. I felt like I'm fine now.

When she was finished "running around the house," she would masturbate before removing the clothing.

While most children and adolescents could achieve a temporary sense of relief by cross-dressing, a small portion of the transsexuals in our sample associated gender with genital construction. While transsexual children and adolescents felt that they were (or wished they could be) girls, most believed genital construction was something that could not be changed and that gender could only be altered through clothing and other accoutrements. For a small portion of our sample ($n = 4$), however, this was not the case, and efforts to alter or remove genitals were reported. This was related by one preoperative transsexual who was trying to find the means to pay for SRS when we talked with her. She said, "I started that when I was seven or eight. . . . I used to do some castration-type things. No real painful ones. Just like rubber band things. I just did not want what I had there."

In recalling initial experiences defined as transgendered, most individuals discussed activities that allowed them to experiment with feminine gender presentations. Secrecy was important, as there was a sense of needing to keep activities and feelings from being detected by punishing others. As individuals grappled with guilt, anxiety, feelings of being different, and with social pressures to conform to a gender that did not feel comfortable, they struggled to "find" their true identity.

This internal struggle is the precursor to coming out to one's self.

Coming Out to One's Self

For many transgendered individuals, coming to terms with identity is driven by three factors: (1) events that inform them that to feel as they do is "wrong" (discussed above), (2) finding that there are names for their feelings, and (3) learning that there are others who have had similar experiences. The search for authenticity is a motivating factor in the desire to resolve identity (Gecas 1991). Because of the centrality of community in the formation and legitimation of identity (see Taylor and Whittier 1992), the efforts of transgenderists to find and express a "true self" are mitigated by their contacts with the transgendered world, just as they are affected by the dominant culture. To "confess" gender (or transgenderism), one must communicate in an established idiom or risk the desired authenticity. While new identities are emergent, they are created within the constraints of current understandings. Furthermore, because of dominant beliefs that incongruity between assumed sex and presented gender is indicative of homosexuality, and that such is deviant, as transgenderists mix or replace masculinity with femininity on either a temporary or permanent basis, they frequently wonder what this implies about their sexuality.

When individuals fail to adhere to the gender binary, they are often told they are wrong or bad, so they tend to initially think of themselves as sick or deviant. Until they find similar others who have rejected stigma, self-blame and the internalization of deviance are common. As the transgenderists in our sample became aware that there were others in the world like them, they experienced a sense of self-recognition and most quickly aligned themselves with new potential identities. The refinement and adoption of relatively stable identities occurred within the possibilities offered by the transgender subculture, which has been heavily influenced by medical models of transgenderism.

For most individuals, the first display of feelings that are later labeled as transgendered come in the form of cross-dressing. Among adult transgenderists cross-dressing is symbolically more important than "playing dress up." For fetishistic and nonfetishistic cross-dressers, it is an opportunity to express the feminine self; for gender radicals, it is a chance to blend the masculine and feminine aspects of self; and for transsexuals, it is a time to be one's self. Children learn at a very early age to attribute their own and others' sex and gender on the basis of clothing (Cahill 1989), and they find cross-dressing an accessible means of gender exploration. When others, especially valued and respected significant others, strongly oppose such actions, they effectively communicate a sense of deviance. All but two of our participants who engaged in transgender behaviors as children or adolescents told us that the message came through loud and clear: to cross-dress, or for that matter to do anything that was not "appropriately" masculine, was deviant and not to be discussed with others. Such messages worked to drive transgendered children into a secret world, where feelings about what was "natural" were held in private.

Most transsexuals and a minority of the cross-dressers in our sample reported being labeled "sissies" by parents, siblings, and school mates. The difference in experiences may be due to the fact that transsexuals reported an overwhelming urge to be feminine at all times, whereas cross-dressers could more easily segment the feminine self away from public scrutiny. Those labeled "sissy" or "girl-like" experienced extreme stigmatization, isolation, and at times abuse. Derogative comments from family members seemed to affect the self-esteem and self-concept more than insults from peers or other non-relatives. One nonoperative transsexual married to a woman recounted how her parents and friends pressured her to be more masculine. She said,

> The kids in the neighborhood that I wanted to be friends with . . . were the girls. . . . I wanted my own doll and remember the boys in the neighborhood seemed to have a real problem with that. . . . In that same time period, my dad came into my bedroom one night and he took all the dolls out of my bed. He said I could keep the animals but the dolls had to go because, "You're a little boy and little boys don't sleep with dolls."

Even with such social sanctions, the feelings persisted. Among transsexuals and a minority of cross-dressers, to be doing what girls were doing felt comfortable and natural. For many, playing with boys was stressful, anxiety provoking, and often induced feelings of failure and low self-esteem. Consequently, many transgenderists found ways to separate themselves from those who reinforced the feeling of difference and deviance, staying to themselves as much as possible.

Just as children tried to conceal transgenderism or conform to the expectations of family and other socializing agents, adults were likely to engage in similar coping strategies until they began to accept themselves as transgenderists. Transsexuals tended to react to negative messages by being hypermasculine. As adults, many in our sample went into physically strenuous or high-risk occupations where they could prove their masculinity. Some joined the military and others married, hoping to "cure" themselves of transgendered longings and behavior. For example, one preoperative transsexual, who got married at a time in her life when she identified as a cross-dresser, explained, "[Now] I'm okay. I'm one of the guys. I've scored. I'm a guy. I fit in with all the other guys. This will cure everything. Well, it didn't." She was cross-dressing within months of the wedding. Or, as an attempt to not be perceived as different during her life as a man, one preoperative transsexual explained, "[Working for a] moving company and the fact that I played windmill softball were both indicative of the many people in my situation where we overcompensate." Another said, "I would avoid doing anything that someone might see as being a remotely feminine kind of thing. I wouldn't even help my ex-[wife] plant a flower garden." Out of our entire sample, 18 had served in the military. Most said they hoped the experience would make men out of them. Although an extreme example of this sentiment, another preoperative transsexual explained,

I knew there was something wrong with me and I wanted to do whatever I could to make a real man out of myself. So I joined the army. Voluntarily went to Vietnam. Voluntarily carried a machine gun in the jungle. I was a paratrooper. I was a Green Beret. I did everything I could do in a that three-year period to make a man out of myself. Cross-dressers were less likely to react in hypermasculine ways, primarily because they kept their feminine side hidden.

Most transgenderists who recalled childhood, adolescence, and early adulthood as periods of confusion and turmoil found cross-dressing to be relaxing and comfortable and functioning as a woman to be natural. Their struggles with identity and relationships arose from society's sanctions.

Throughout childhood, adolescence, and early to mid adulthood most transgenderists in our study experienced shame and confusion for not being "right." They lived in a social region for which there was no idiom. Because they were sanctioned for feminine attributes and behavior, they learned that there was no place for feminine boys or men in society. Feeling more comfortable with girls, they began to understand gender and sex within the social options presented to them. The socially constructed aspects of reality were so strong that believing they were born with the wrong genitals seemed more plausible than violating the gender binary. Even in adulthood, transsexuals frequently made efforts to conceal their genitals, even from themselves, by tucking them between the legs or taping them up. While relatively uncommon in our sample (during adulthood, $n = 2$), when transsexuals were unaware of available medical options or were unable to afford SRS, they attempted self-castration. These efforts indicate the degree to which gender is signified by genitalia.

It was common in our sample for transgenderists to experience sexual attractions to other men, to have sexual fantasies about men, or both. At the same time, they experienced social sanctions and pressures to conform to dominant conceptualizations of gender. While they worried they might be gay, they began to experience and explore sexuality within the binary system and its ancillary compulsory heterosexuality (Rich 1989). As a 36-year-old bisexual cross-dresser explained, "You're getting all kinds of messages that men are men and women are women. Sissy boys and fags. The adolescent years are really, really hard on homosexuals and anything not mainstream sexually." Within our sample, adolescent male persons and adult men in the early stages of identity formation were frequently confused about the implications feminine behavior had on their sexuality. As men, they knew sex with male individuals was unacceptable; but as women, it was a source of validation. Most reacted by repressing attractions to men, at least until they began to go out in public as women, when sexual interactions with men were indicative of passage into social womanhood. Nonetheless, sexual interaction between social men was perceived by everyone in our sample as problematic. As a postoperative transsexual explained,

> There's been a few boys that I would have probably liked to have gotten it on with. The so-called labels back then of being homosexual, or gay, or something like that, kept me from doing it. . . . The fifties was when I grew up and you just didn't talk about things like that.

None of the people in our sample adopted a gay identity, even temporarily, although sexual experimentation with male persons was a common aspect of the coming-out experience. Because of an understanding that transgenderism, homosexuality, and femininity were wrong, all but two transgenderists made efforts to conceal, to purge, to deny, and to cure themselves in order to avoid acceptance of their transgenderism.

Most commonly, the triggering event for acceptance of an identity came when, either accidentally or intentionally, the individual encountered others who served as symbols for available identities. However, role models who challenged binary conceptualizations of gender were largely unavailable. Because "there is no place for a person who is neither a woman or a man" (Lorber 1994:96), finding role models and formulating an identity outside the gender binary is virtually impossible. Thus, alternative identities were restricted to those available within the gender binary, usually found among those who had crossed *from* one gender *to* the only other one known to be legitimately available.

Symbolic others came from a variety of sources, including television, magazine articles, pornography, psychological or medical case reports, female impersonators and most recently, on-line computer services. However, most of these sources were not equally available to children and adolescents. Television appearances by pioneer transgenderists served to introduce many adolescents of the 1960s to Christine Jorgensen and Jan Morris, and to Renee Richards in the 1970s. Learning of the availability of transsexualism and seeing such women on television and reading about them in newspapers and magazines provided opportunities to know that there were alternative identities available. One newly postoperative transsexual looked back on her late teens as generally unhappy and confusing but says that she made a major discovery about both herself and society when

> I was in high school and I started to hear about Renee Richards. I graduated high school in '72, so she was just coming out when I was just starting high school. At that time, I still thought that I was alone in the world. . . . When I started to hear about Renee Richards, then I said, Maybe there is somebody else, but this is the only other person that knows where I'm coming from.

Finding others who felt as they did helped to alleviate, but not remove, the sense of isolation experienced by transgendered individuals. Nonetheless, through such initial exposures, many individuals learned that there were alternatives to living in confusion and shame, if one was willing to transform (either temporarily or permanently) to the other gender. Simply learning that SRS was possible led some to reconfigure their identities and reassess their place in the world. One transsexual, who more than 20 years later is still awaiting SRS, recalled that when she was entering her teen years,

> I still didn't have those feelings of wanting to be a woman probably until about the age of 10 when the Christine Jorgensen thing broke. At that time, I knew it was possible for men to have sex changes. That's when I got my first feeling that I wanted to be a girl.

From this point onward, the way she perceived herself was different. Whereas she says that during childhood "I didn't feel like a girl, and I didn't feel like a boy. I just wanted to be myself," after learning about the possibility of SRS, she lived in a state of identity limbo. Finally, she says, "When [my feminine self] took her first injection [of hormones], she became a reality to me. She became a real person." While available role models and medical procedures may not dictate identity changes, they do provide alternatives that contribute to identity clarification. Feminine gender is culturally signified and, in Western society, dictated by anatomy (Laqueur 1990). Because such beliefs are internalized, many transgendered individuals feel compelled to physically alter their bodies.

Finding a symbol of sex and gender possibilities did not always occur in such a positive way. Although one might, for the first time, learn that alternatives to the gender binary exist, some transgenderists simultaneously learned that such people were "freaks" to be objectified. For instance, a Mormon preoperative transsexual, recounted how at about age 18, "[We would] pass around the pornography and look at it. It really didn't do anything for me until I actually saw a transgendered person in the magazine. . . . I really identified with that."

In a more positive fashion, a few years later in life, while searching out more information and identity reinforcement, this same person discovered a copy of a transgender organizational magazine, and recalled, "I felt like there were people like me. That was my niche and I more or less identified with that. I got more education through that magazine than anything else."

Finally, in today's information age, on-line computer services appear to be emerging as a primary location for finding both virtual and real mentors. It was common for transgenderists who deciphered and accepted their identities in the 1990s to have done so with the assistance of on-line bulletin boards and personal conversations with already-identifying transgenderists. Here, in the privacy of one's home or work area, contacts could be made that allowed both experimentation with identities and informational inquiries that did not jeopardize existing identities or social, occupational, and familial relationships. In addition, on-line services allowed individuals to access information beyond that concerning the strictly erotic aspects of cross-dressing. For some transgenderists, this was a critical factor, as tabloid media and sensationalist reports have created a common misperception of cross-dressing as primarily an erotic activity. A self-identified radical transgenderist credits his subscription to one on-line service with helping him understand that cross-dressing need not be sexually charged. He said, "It wasn't until I got a hold of [on-line service] that I got exposed to aspects other than the erotic aspects, which are all over the place."

Similarly, a preoperative transsexual who says she didn't understand most of her feelings found virtual role models in cyberspace when

> I was on [a service]. I was browsing through an adult area. There was a single topic on [it] called "Cross Dressing," and I bumped in the cross-dressing place there and read a biography. When I read that, I was shocked because I could have written that myself word for word. And then I read more biographies and each one of them was the same story I had. So what I had done was I found people that had similar histories as children that I did, and that validated me.

Not all persons who found virtual models defined them as helpful. For some, the occassion of encountering both real and reported transgenderists served only to raise more issues to be resolved. For example, one cross-dresser recalled finding fetishistic cross-dressers and transsexuals in cyberspace. He related, "Although there were similarities, there were also some grave differences, primarily in the fact that I felt more romantic interest. I didn't feel I was a heterosexual female trapped in a male body. I liked my male body." Still, finding others even tangentially similar provided a forum in which to discover options and explore alternative identities. Thus, while we "do" gender in interaction with others, it appears that the emergence of transgender identity and alternatives to the gender binary are dependent on others who will recognize one as an authentic social actor (West and Zimmerman 1987).

Coming Out to Others

Simply discovering (quasi-)similar others is not all that is needed for the transgendered individual to complete the coming-out process. Rather, finding a symbolic role model provides initial validation of a newly emergent identity and potential avenues to find further sources of external validation. The sources of validation that are most important for the stabilization of identity are the significant others in one's life and the community of similar others.

Accepting an identity for one's self was one thing; proclaiming and working to get others to accept it was quite different. Going public with a transgendered identity could be an intimidating experience, to say the least. Among our sample, cross-dressers, fetishistic cross-dressers, and gender radicals had greater control over the coming-out process than did transsexuals, primarily because the former, as a group, were more limited in their need and desire to publicly enact the feminine self. The two fetishistic cross-dressers in our sample had revealed their transgenderism to their sexual partners and to members of the support groups to which they belonged. In those groups, they were encouraged to come to meetings "dressed," despite the fact that neither had a desire to cross-dress except for sexual purposes. Most nonfetishistic cross-dressers in our sample had come out to their spouses before joining a support group. For a minority, finding a community of similar others gave individual cross-dressers the support they needed to explore their identity as transgendered individuals and to later inform spouses or other significant others. One cross-dresser said that his wife was relieved when he came out to her. He had been attending support group meetings and transgender conferences in another state, and she thought he was having an affair. Like cross-dressers, gender radicals could selectively come out or not reveal their transgendered identity to others. For them, support groups provided access to a community in which they could explore their gender identities.

Despite the differences among these categories, the years of mainstream socialization and messages about "proper" gender performance were influential on everyone in our sample. The degree to which transgenderists were intimidated about revealing their transgenderism may be heard in the words of a 10-month, postoperative transsexual, who said,

> For somebody who's been a freak, a hippie, and a marijuana dealer, . . . and a flamboyant dresser, and somebody who refuses to get a conventional job and all this, somebody who's not been afraid of public

opinion, it's, I think, notable that the gender area of my life and the social expectations were the one area I was afraid of public opinion.

Intimidation was not limited to those desiring to go out publicly. One cross-dresser explained that his fear of coming out to his wife was so extreme that he thought the couple would have to separate so he could pursue his transgenderism. He said,

> I sat her down and we had a talk, and that's when I told her I couldn't live this way anymore and I was going to leave. [I told her] that I loved her and the kids, but I couldn't tell her why. . . . [After a few days] we talked this all out and I finally went ahead and told her. . . . She said, "You go in there and dress. I want to see what you look like." So then I dressed up for her the first time. I was nervous and scared to death. I was shaking from inside out. . . . We sat down and discussed the basic rules on how this was going to work. . . . That's been five years ago, and we're still together.

Intimidation came from two fronts: (1) fears about how one would be treated by others and (2) anxieties about how others would cope with what was certainly seen by many as "nontraditional" behavior. Fear of the responses one will receive is to be expected. With the close cultural association drawn between transgenderism and homosexuality (Altman 1982; Bullough and Bullough 1993; Talamini 1982), fears of violent and isolating homophobic reactions seem warranted.[4] In addition, as people involved in significant relationships with others, many expressed concerns about how the news that they were transgendered would affect those close to them. These concerns typically centered on one's family, both nuclear and extended.

According to the accounts of those who have proclaimed their transgender identities to significant others, the fears about negative reactions were largely

---

[4] A substantial minority of our sample talked about experiencing intimidation, harassment, and violence in public places. It was not uncommon for those learning to "pass" to be called "faggot" or other homophobic epithets. One very tall, muscular cross-dresser told us about having her wig pulled off and being physically assaulted, and one preoperative transsexual had to move after receiving death threats from her neighbors.

exaggerated, but not altogether unwarranted. Less than one-fourth of all persons interviewed for this project reported that their first experience of coming out to someone else lead to a negative reaction. This was related to several factors. First, transgenderists had exaggerated fears about the reactions of most significant others. Second, most individuals were actually successful at controlling knowledge of their transgenderism. They consciously selected individuals to come out to who were, in fact, sympathetic to the alternative identity. Who would be accepting was ascertained through discussions of various potentially volatile issues. In that way, transgenderists learned if there was a need for caution or preparatory education of the recipient. Those who received negative reactions to their proclamations were least likely to have gathered information or to have laid the necessary groundwork. Instead, they simply announced the new identity. For example, a preoperative transsexual decided to tell an 18-year-old daughter, who did not even know that her father had been cross-dressing, when the daughter moved back home. She said,

> After a week or two there, it seemed inappropriate not to tell my daughter. The girl lives in the house. For crying out loud, she's 18 years old. So I told her and I didn't really build up to it or anything. . . . She was always in the bathroom, doing hair and makeup and stuff. I stopped in to chat. I suppose it was like a bomb or something like that. "By the way. . . . I'm going to have a sex change." She turned into an ice cube.

Although the experience of telling one's first "other" was not necessarily a negative experience, fears remained, and careful, often painful, decisions were made regarding with whom to share an emergent identity. Interestingly, two factors stand out about these early disclosures. First, they were usually done only out of a sense of responsibility, when someone was perceived as "needing to know." Second, the individuals with whom this information was shared were almost always female, most often a significant other. This was true among all groups of transgenderists in our sample.

While some elected to share with their mothers, there was a characteristic tendency for most to report that it was extremely difficult to share their new identity with their parents. For some, this was more easily accomplished when the interaction with one's parents was not face-to-face or when the situation could be escaped quickly. Despite the urge to deliver the news and run, those who came out to others face-to-face, who had provided (or offered to provide) information about transgenderism, and gave others time and space to cope with the information were most likely to receive tolerant, accepting, or supportive reactions. Still, much of the reaction to being told was dependent on the values of the recipient of the news, as well as the relationship itself. For example, a two-year postoperative transsexual who had been living with her male partner prior to having surgery recalled telling her mother about her decision to have SRS. She said, "I told her, 'Mom, I'm transsexual and I'm going to have SRS.' My mom's response was, 'Oh, thank God! I can deal with this.' She thought I was going to tell her [my partner] and I were HIV positive." While cross-dressers commonly came out only to spouses and other transgenderists, transsexuals typically enlisted the supportive family members they had told to help them inform other relatives. Because their transitions are permanent and public, coming out cannot be restricted. One transsexual explained, "From my mom, I told my two sisters. . . . [Then] I think it was my grandmother, then my father. And I just couldn't bring myself to tell my kids, and so my mom told them." Coming out to those one expected to be supportive, based on an established past, provided both difficulties and benefits. While it might be hard to risk the support, there was often a belief that (at least after an initial period of shock) the established foundation of the relationship would win out and the informed other would be supportive.

The arena where transgenderists (usually transsexuals) were least likely to receive positive reactions was at work. Although there were a few people who were permitted to transition on the job, it was more common for transsexuals to be fired, demoted, pressured to quit, and harassed by other workers. Some found employment in unskilled, low-wage jobs, such as janitors or in fast-food restaurants; others worked for temporary agencies. A few in our sample went back to college, transitioning as students. The loss of identity and the structure of one's daily routine that comes with a career was more difficult for transsexuals to cope with than the actual loss of income. After accepting a severance package in exchange for her silence about her job termination, one postoperative transsexual wrote to the first author, "I have spent my entire life becoming the best [job title] I could be. Today I sold myself for 50 pieces of silver." Frequently, the loss of professional identity and income came at the same time that relationships with old friends and family members were being risked and sometimes lost.

Early excursions into the public domain were commonly as frightening as coming out to significant others or on the job. While going out and passing in public may be thought to be different from coming out, it is important to recognize that for the majority of transgenderists, the goal is to be perceived and accepted as woman, not a transgenderist. Telling others about their transgenderism is done primarily to lay the groundwork for greater expression, acceptance, and legitimation of a feminine identity, and this is accomplished in public and in private interactions. Although there was variation between going out in public or telling a significant other first, every person in our sample felt a need to expand their sphere of interaction with others. While control over access to information about the transgendered identity remained important, this became less salient as the need to interact with others publicly increased. Because of the fear of the danger inherent in negative public reactions, most transgenderists carefully planned and carried out their initial public excursions in limited-access locations.

When transgenderists began to go out in public, they did so because of a need to receive reactions from others to legitimate identity. While some have undoubtedly been driven back into the closet by their initial forays into public places, in our sample, such excursions served to increase commitment to the emergent identity. Selection of safe places for public ventures meant that transgenderists looked for locations where they could make quick and easy entrances and exits and where they are unlikely to

encounter disapproving others. Transgenderists most commonly reported that their first ventures were to gay community events or locations, simply driving in their cars, or going to known meeting places for transgenderists. The most common site for first ventures was gay bars. Here, among other marginalized community members, individuals could try out their new identities. Despite a strong desire to avoid being perceived as homosexual, gay bars were defined as safe havens (Levine, Shaiova, and Mihailovic 1975). For example, a preoperative transsexual, who had been living as a woman full-time for seven months, related that "while I was working on coming out full-time, I needed a safe place to go while I practiced. The bar was it. I know the drag queens might not like that. It was still a safe place for me though." For others, the thought of venturing into such a public setting and actually interacting with others, even if they might be expected to be understanding, was simply too intimidating. Instead, some felt a need to slowly transition into public outings. For these individuals, the easiest way to be out, but not relinquish too much control, was to drive through populated areas often including the vicinity of gay community settings. In this way, especially since most did so after dark, they could be seen, but not so well as to seriously threaten their ability to pass. A radical transgenderist, who has an understanding and supportive female partner reported that "I think the first time out was just to drive around with my girlfriend. We were going to a local gay bar, but it wasn't open at the time. We just drove and got fast food."

Typically, successful ventures while driving provided the impetus and courage for transgenderists to move forward and present themselves face-to-face with others; however, these steps were taken slowly and carefully. Movement from the car was usually into either a gay bar or a gathering of other transgenderists. For example, a preoperative transsexual who is fully out only to one family member and acquaintances in the transgender community, explained her first time out in public as follows:

> About 10 years ago. . . . I was out very late one night, got in my car, drove downtown to the north side of the city which is known for its gays, lesbians, and an

occasional transvestite. Walked to what I thought was a bar where transvestites hung out and sat down, had a couple of drinks, couple cigarettes. . . . I did things like get dressed and drove around. I'd go for a short walk around the block or something. I didn't think I was good enough yet to go out in daylight and try to pull it off as a woman.

In gay bars and neighborhoods, transgenderists were most likely to be interpreted as marginal members of the queer subculture. Such settings provide a place where one who is "neither woman nor man" (Lorber 1994:96) is most likely to find a social place that does not disturb the social order.

While transgenderists are likely to be interpreted as marginal members of the gay or queer subculture, they can experiment with sex, gender, and sexual identity in such locales. Frequently, while out as women who are (relatively) obviously male, transgenderists will have their first experiences being treated "like ladies." Woodhouse (1989:31) has described a category of male individuals who do not want to have sex with a man or with a woman but who still want sex; so, they have sex with men dressed as women. These so-called "punters" provide opportunities for transgenderists to perfect their feminine persona and, for those who wish to learn more about themselves, to explore their sexuality. The overwhelming motivation for flirting in the bar and having sexual relations with men was to be treated "like a lady" and to explore the gendered aspects of sexuality.[5] It is through such interactions that many transsexuals and some cross-dressers encounter the final rite of passage as authentic heterosexual women, whether or not they have undergone SRS.

For others, the impetus to appear in public for the first time surfaced when opportunities arose to meet other transgenderists in the context of a support group. Support groups were one location where the most important identity tests occurred, when the individual encountered other transgenderists. As they entered such groups, transgenderists commonly reported a feeling of total acceptance and freedom to be themselves, often for the first time in their lives. If these supposedly similar others were willing to accept the individual, and the individual felt safe in the group, this communicated that she or he truly was transgendered. The value of support groups, on-line services, organizations, and publications becomes most clear in this context.

Support groups can be very important in facilitating identity exploration and the arrival at a "final" identity, but they could also induce anxiety, confusion, and fright in individual transgenderists. While they may have already confronted their "difference" in their own minds and with others in their lives, to come face-to-face with "the real thing" could be intimidating. For those who were courageous enough to take such steps, support groups almost always functioned as they were intended. They provided support for a stigmatized identity. Nonetheless, such acceptance was provided within a narrow range of social options that were based on acceptance of a binary system of sex and gender. Transsexualism was commonly explained by biological theories, and those who had completed the transition process gave advice on how to gain access to medical procedures to those in earlier stages. Among cross-dressers, "dressing" was encouraged as an acceptable way for men to express the feminine self. All transgenderists were encouraged to perfect their ability to pass during informal interactions and copious seminars on style, makeup, feminine body language, and the feminine voice and diction.

In addition to the facilitating function of support groups, many transgenderists reported that their public proclamations were in large part propelled by encouragement (or instructions) from a therapist. The overwhelming majority of our samples were or had been active in counseling/therapy. Many therapists, especially those who seemed to be well liked by their clients, encouraged coming out, appearing to others, and learning to pass as women. If one were to view transgenderism as "normal," it should be treated as such, particularly

---

[5] Those who wished to determine whether they were gay reported having sex with men while not dressed as women. It appears that sexual interaction was a form of gender play and exploration of gender-based heterosexual identity.

by the transgenderist; however, "normality" was defined as the desire to be and pass as a woman. Among our sample, only a small minority was willing to be publicly known as transgendered.

Resolution of Identity

After a lifetime of being stigmatized and feeling as if they did not fit, the transgenderists in our sample engaged in a long process of identity exploration. The majority in our sample explained that they had arrived at a "true" identity, with which they felt they could "be themselves." Only a minority of men who cross-dressed but were exploring transsexualism had not yet resolved their identities. In their efforts to resolve and establish an identity that was comfortable for themselves, the individuals in our sample shared diverse goals and visions for themselves and the community. Transsexuals sought to "completely" transform and live convincingly as their true (female) selves. Cross-dressers sought only to have opportunities to temporarily vary their public identity presentations, express their femininity, and be recognized and treated as women. Only the gender radicals in our sample wished to live and be recognized as transgendered. Significant differences appeared among specific transgender identities. Among most transsexuals and cross-dressers, there was an overwhelming desire to pass as women, for it was through such interactions that femininity and treatment as a woman were achieved. For a minority, as experience and confidence were gained, passing was a desirable, but no longer essential, aspect of going out in public. These people tended to recognize that physical stature, including height and musculature, made it difficult, if not impossible, for them to pass. Among gender radicals, concerns with presenting a convincing appearance as a woman were secondary, if at all important. For them, the goal was to challenge dominant conceptualizations of gender and create new possibilities.

Among transsexuals, because of the internalized identity as women, it was most common to find an aspiration to be seen and identified by others as real women. When discussing this feeling, transsexuals expressed a need to "pass" in their daily interactions. This desire was paramount for such individuals and taken as a symbolic testament of final arrival at their desired self and socially constructed identity. One divorced, preoperative transsexual summarized this sentiment well when she commented, "[Passing] to me is the most important aspect of the whole thing. If you can't do that, I don't see the point of living this way." Enduring the internal and social struggles encountered in the process of recognizing and accepting a new identity and introducing oneself to the outside world was valued only if there could be a nonstigmatizing, "normal" resolution to the process. Transsexuals did not wish to challenge the gender binary, although most perceived their transitions as very radical actions. Rather, their goal was to "become" the women they "truly are" and to pass from being their masculine selves into full womanhood. Often, after learning to pass and completing the transformation process, transsexuals dropped out of the transgender community and assumed their place as women in society.

Within the transgender community, a desire to pass and blend into society sometimes introduced tensions and additional levels of hierarchy and structure. Those who sought to pass, and believed they had the ability to do so, sometimes believed that varying statuses of achievement (passing ability) were important. Some passable transgenderists, therefore, viewed those who could not pass as liabilities. Being seen with a detectable transgenderist was believed to bring suspicion and possible detection to those who would otherwise pass. Once again, the above transsexual showed her aptitude for clear expression when she explained her withdrawal from a local support group because, "I didn't feel the group gave me anything. I was too far ahead of them. . . . We're still friends, but I won't walk down the street with them."

Although most transgenderists were concerned with passing as well as possible, there is an emergent group within the community that seeks a free expression of gender, outside of the binary system. For example, the ambigenderist in our sample explained that she had moved beyond such concerns, focusing on her own welfare and identity, not the perceptions of others.

> At one time, [passing] was important. I don't care anymore. A lot of times I'll go out in a dress . . . no makeup on. I'm not trying to pass and I know I'm not going to pass. I am who I am. . . . It is political, everything's political. A social statement about who I am and I'm going to express myself.

Similarly, a former self-identified transsexual, turned gender radical, had kept a masculine name and avoided feminine pronouns while living as a woman. This person expressed the belief that passing is something that many transgenderists experience and then move through, saying, "I think passing is more a fear that has to be overcome and when I overcame that fear to being nonchalant about it, I didn't care that I passed or not."

For both those who were and were not seeking to pass when in public, the most common, overwhelming desire was to simply be accepted. This was difficult unless they could find ways to fit within the binary and symbolically communicate identity within the idiomatic system of gender expression. To "blend in" to society as a woman was something most transgenderists, especially transsexuals, saw as an ultimate goal. The ultimate resolution was an identity that was not wrapped in the language of transgenderism. To be known as simply just another person was desirable.

Despite one's own aspirations for individual identity and ability to blend socially, there was a sense of community among the vast majority of transgenderists that facilitated a desire to work with others and to contribute to the developmental processes of other community members. Regardless of the variety of community members, the plurality of individuals expressed a keen ambition to contribute to the psychological, social, and physical development of other transgendered community members. Helping others transform appears to be an important final "step" in the transformation process. Nonetheless, there are variations within the community. For transsexuals, the desire to participate in, and contribute to, the transgendered community appears to be relatively temporary. Once a stable identity as "woman" has been established, many leave the community. For cross-dressers, the community provides an opportunity to go out in public. For those who wish to challenge cultural conceptualizations of gender, support groups serve as potential social movement organizations.

This attempt to contribute to the development of others in the community came in both implicit and explicit forms. For some, this could be accomplished simply by being visible to other community members. More often, such forms of encouragement and assistance were much more direct and overt. For example, a gender radical, who is an active member of a local support group, editor of a local transgender community newsletter, and who conducts research on the structure of the transgender community, merged the implicit and explicit. This person explained,

> I feel the best thing I can do to create change is just to thrive, to be myself, to present myself in a way that I am comfortable with. The hell with everything else. . . . We need to be more open. We need to be more proud of who we are as opposed to being more ashamed. I think our movement could be much stronger. . . . I want people to start questioning things even though they may look at me oddly. People always say that I am sick or insane. Maybe one person may start to look at things differently. If other people start seeing that, we can act normally in the open with people knowing about you and that they don't have to be frightened.

To help other individual transgenderists, it was necessary to work at social change. Without changing the cultural context, the social infrastructure, and the idiom in which transgenderists are perceived and alternative genders are achieved, it is highly unlikely that the experiences and identities of individual transgenderists can be "normalized," without placing them back within a binary system.

CONCLUSION

Gender is so pervasive that it is taken for granted and often completely overlooked, until the norms of gender presentation, interaction, or organization are inadvertently violated or deliberately challenged (Lorber 1994). Gender receives constant surveillance and is continually policed through social interactions that socialize new and existing members of society and sanction those who violate the rules (see Gagné and Tewksbury 1996). At the organizational level, individuals are categorized and assigned meaning and roles on the basis of gender. For example, one of the first questions asked on organizational applications is one's sex. This is based on the erroneous assumption that gender will be congruent with sex. In organizational settings, sleeping arrangements are often based on sex/gender (as in dormitory arrangements) and bathrooms and locker rooms are segregated by sex/gender (see Rothblatt 1995). Where individuals' gender does not "match" their sex, there is little organizational space in which they can exist.

Individuals who attempt to challenge the binary conceptualization of sex and gender, by living androgynously between genders, are likely to be ridiculed and stigmatized (see Gagné and Tewksbury 1996). Those who attempt to live outside of the sex/gender binary, for example, by publicly confessing that they are male persons with (or who would like to have) breasts or vaginas, are also likely to be ostracized. Those who are willingly or unwittingly unconvincing in their gender presentations and interactions are subject to greater levels of emotional and physical abuse than are those who are able to pass. It is those who are publicly perceived as "not women/not men" who pose the greatest challenge to the binary system. Nonetheless, the goal of most is to be perceived as a woman and treated like a lady. Those who pass are perceived as women, and any challenge they might have posed to the gender system goes unnoticed.

To challenge the binary, individuals must overcome a number of interactional, organizational, and structural barriers. They must learn to live and find ways to cope with the discomfort and hostility that others express at not being able to categorize them within existing gender categories. They need to find ways to support themselves and interact with others in organizations that have social spaces for women and men only. And, they must find ways to

establish themselves as legal and social actors within institutions that recognize only two sexes and two congruent genders. Given these pressures, it is understandable why most transgendered individuals come out quickly and cross over to the "other" gender category.

REFERENCES

Cass, Vivien C. 1979. "Homosexual identity formation: A theoretical model." *Journal of Homosexuality* 4:219–35.

———. 1984. "Homosexual identity formation: Testing a theoretical model." *Journal of Sex Research* 20:143–67.

Cahill, Spencer. 1989. "Fashioning males and females: Appearance management and the social reproduction of gender." *Symbolic Interaction* 2:281–98.

Coleman, Eli. 1981–82. "Developmental stages of the coming out process." *Journal of Homosexuality* 7:31–43.

Feinbloom, Deborah H. 1977. *Transvestites and transsexuals.* New York: Delta Books.

Foucault, Michel. [1978] 1990. *The history of sexuality: An introduction.* Vol. 1, translated by Robert Hurley. Reprint, New York: Vintage.

Gagné, Patricia, and Richard Tewksbury. 1996. "No 'man's' land: Transgenderism and the stigma of the feminine man." In *Advances in Gender Research.* Vol. 1, edited by Marcia Texler Segal and Vasilikie Demos. Greenwich, CT: JAI.

Gecas, Viktor. 1991. "The self-consent as a basis for a theory of motivation." In *The Self-Society Dynamic,* edited by J. A. Howard and P. L. Callero. Cambridge, England: Cambridge University Press.

Huber, Joan. 1989. "A theory of gender stratification." In *Feminist Frontiers II: Rethinking Sex, Gender, and Society,* edited by Laurel Richardson and Verta Taylor. New York: Random House.

Huber, Joan, and Glenna Spitze. 1983. *Sex Stratification: Children, Housework, and Jobs.* New York: Academic Press.

Isay, Richard A. 1990. "Psychoanalytic theory and the therapy of gay men." In *Homosexuality/Heterosexuality: Concepts of Sexual Orientation,* edited by D. P. McWhirter, S. A. Sanders, and J. M. Reinisch. New York: Oxford University Press.

Kohlberg, Lawrence. 1966. "A cognitive-developmental analysis of children's sex-role concepts and attitudes." In *The Development of Sex Differences,* edited by Eleanor E. Maccoby. Stanford, CA: Stanford University Press.

Kohlberg, Lawrence, and D. Z. Ulian. 1974. "Stages in the development of psychosexual concepts and attitudes." In *Sex Differences in Behavior,* edited by R. C. Friedman, R. M. Richard, and R. L. Vande Wiele. New York: Wiley.

Laqueur, Thomas. 1990. *Making Sex: Body and Gender from the Greeks to Freud.* Cambridge, MA: Harvard University Press.

Mason-Schrock, Doug. 1996. "Transsexuals' narrative construction of the 'true self.'" *Social Psychology Quarterly* 59:176–92.

Miles, Matthew B., and A. Michael Huberman. 1984. *Qualitative Data Analysis: A Sourcebook of New Methods.* Beverly Hills, CA: Sage.

Namaste, Ki. 1994. "The politics of inside/out: Queer theory, poststructuralism, and a sociological approach to sexuality." *Sociological Theory* 12:220–31.

Pauly, Ira B. 1990. "Gender identity disorders: Evaluation and treatment." *Journal of Sex Education & Therapy* 16:2–24.

Prince, Virginia, and P. M. Bentler. 1972. "Survey of 504 cases of transvestism." *Psychological Reports* 31:903–17.

Raymond, Janice G. 1994. *The Transsexual Empire: The Making of the She-Male.* New York: Teachers College Press.

Rich, Adrienne. 1989. "Compulsory heterosexuality and lesbian existence." In *Feminist Frontiers II: Rethinking Sex, Gender, and Society,* edited by Laurel Richardson and Verta Taylor. New York: Random House.

Stoller, Robert J. 1971. "The term 'transvestism.'" *Archives of General Psychiatry* 24:230–37.

Stone, Gregory P. 1975. "Appearance and the self." In *Life as Theatre: A Dramaturgical Sourcebook,* edited by Dennis Brissett and Charles Edgley. Chicago: Aldine.

Talamini, John T. 1981. "Transvestism: Expression of a second self." *Free Inquiry in Creative Sociology* 9:72–74.

———. 1982. *Boys Will Be Girls: The Hidden World of the Heterosexual Male Transvestite.* Lanham, MD: University Press of America.

Taylor, Verta, and Nancy Whittier. 1992. "Collective identity and social movement communities: Lesbian feminist mobilization." In *Frontiers in Social Movement Theory,* edited by Aldon D. Morris and Carol McClurg Mueller. New Haven, CT: Yale University Press.

Tewksbury, Richard, and Patricia Gagné. 1996. "Transgenderists: Products of non-normative intersections of sex, gender, and sexuality." *Journal of Men's Studies* 5:105–29.

Troiden, Richard, and Erich Goode. 1980. "Variables related to the acquisition of a gay identity." *Journal of Homosexuality* 5:383–92.

Weinberg, Thomas S. 1978. "On 'doing' and 'being' gay: Sexual behavior and homosexual male self-identity." *Journal of Homosexuality* 4:563–78.

Woodhouse, Annie. 1989. *Fantastic Women: Sex, Gender and Transvestism.* New Brunswick, NJ: Rutgers University Press.

STUDY QUESTIONS

1. What are the stages of "becoming homosexual," as identified by Richard Troiden?
2. What research methods were used in Troiden's study?
3. What research methods were used in Murphy, Waldorf, and Reinarman's study of drug dealers?
4. Describe the different pathways into drug dealing described by Murphy, Waldorf, and Reinarman.
5. What impact does drug dealing have on the sellers' identities?
6. What research methods were used in the study of transgender persons by Gagné, Tewksbury, and McGaughey?
7. What are the main developmental stages in the process of becoming a transgendered person?
8. What unique challenges confront transgenders in their efforts to "come out" and gain acceptance from others?

MANAGING DEVIANCE: PASSING, DISCLOSURE, AND NEUTRALIZATION

Introduction

How do deviants cope with stigma and condemnation by others? Many feel compelled to "pass for normal" in their encounters with certain people, if not everyone. For those who wish to keep their deviance secret as well as those who "come out" only selectively, to a few people, some "passing" is necessary. As Erving Goffman (1963: 74) points out, "Because of the great rewards in being considered normal, almost all persons who are in a position to pass will do so on some occasion by intent." Passing offers major benefits, though it also requires sustained effort and is fraught with anxiety about being discovered. Deviants who attempt to pass as normal thus develop various techniques for managing the information available to others and structuring their contacts with others in order to minimize the chances for discovery and labeling. A good example is a person with AIDS, who may take pains to conceal his or her stigmatized affliction. Passing may be necessary to avoid losing one's job or to prevent being abandoned by one's family and friends. In her study, "Living with the Stigma of AIDS," Rose Weitz found that some persons-with-AIDS tried to conceal their illness from others, some selectively disclosed their condition, while others took the more active role of trying to combat stigmatization by educating others about the disease. Her article illustrates how stigmatization can radically affect the individuals' everyday lives as well as the coping mechanisms employed to manage or reduce stigma.

Many people who engage in behavior that they know to be wrong and punishable attempt to justify it to themselves and, if caught, to others. They may engage in what Sykes and Matza (1957) call "techniques of neutralization" to suspend or negate the norms that they violate and defuse any guilt over their deviant activities. Neutralization allows an actor to reconcile his or her deviance with conventional norms: the person can engage in deviant acts and still maintain a positive self-image. Types of neutralization include: denying that anyone was victimized, condemning the labelers, and appealing to "higher loyalties" to justify a deviant act. These and other neutralization techniques are featured in articles in this section of the book. Donald McCabe examines cheating among college students, and the students' reliance on "situational ethics" to defend their cheating. Situational ethics are invoked when people see their behavior as acceptable under the circumstances. Despite acknowledging that cheating is wrong in principle, students were found to excuse their own cheating using one or more neutralization techniques.

Even though powerful and affluent people have more resources at their disposal than other people, which increases their capacity to conceal deviant acts or avoid sanctions if discovered, they are occasionally branded deviant by others. The study reprinted here on white-collar criminals (Michael Benson's "Denying the Guilty Mind") shows that they, like other deviants, attempt to justify and excuse their criminal acts, albeit somewhat differently than the student cheaters studied by McCabe. Benson's affluent deviants attempt to deny criminal intent by claiming that their acts were nothing more than legitimate business practices or by attaching blame to someone else.

Diana Scully and Joseph Marolla's unique study of neutralization is based on in-depth interviews with 118 men convicted of rape, who were incarcerated in state prisons in Virginia. Interviews were designed to probe the ways in which rapists explained their attacks on women. More than half of the sample denied that they had committed a rape and offered justifications for their behavior, while the remainder admitted that they had raped and that it was wrong, but they nevertheless offered excuses for it. In rationalizing and defending their conduct, both groups drew on wider cultural views of women and myths about rape. This suggests that it is not only acceptance of unconventional beliefs that may lead to deviant behavior, but also that identification with prevailing, dominant values can be conducive to deviance.

Neutralization is engaged in not only by deviant actors—who have an obvious interest in avoiding censure and in normalizing their behavior—but also by some observers and even certain victims. When strangers act strangely, observers tend to view them with a "presumption of deviance," readily attaching a deviant label to the actor. A very different dynamic is found in primary groups—among significant others and friends. There is a strong likelihood that family members will, at least for a period of time, *normalize* the questionable behavior of a loved one. Studies of families where one member has begun to show signs of being an alcoholic, being mentally disturbed, exhibiting violence against another family member, or engaging in criminal conduct outside the home have found that other family members resist labeling the person deviant, accord him or her the benefit of the doubt, and stretch the range of "normality" in order to include the individual's questionable behavior (Fishman 1986; Jackson 1954; Sampson, Messinger, and Towne 1962; Yarrow et al. 1955). There is, in other words, a high tolerance for deviance in many families—until it becomes unmanageable. Such normalization in primary groups is explained by significant others' closeness to the actor, which allows them to see traits other than the deviant one—"normal" traits that tend to cancel out the deviant acts, at least at the beginning. The fact that the person is a close friend or family member produces what scholars call a "halo effect" that blinds loved ones and prevents them from seeing the actor's behavior as deviant—again, at least for some period of time. Kathleen Ferraro and John Johnson ("How Women Experience Battering") examine this phenomenon of accommodation in families where husbands beat their wives. Interviews with 120 battered women showed that most of them initially rationalized their husbands' violence. Ferraro and Johnson identify several factors that eventually led the wives to acknowledge that they were being victimized and to ultimately label their husbands deviant.

REFERENCES

Fishman, Laura T. 1986. "Prisoners' Wives' Interpretations of Male Criminality and Subsequent Arrest." *Deviant Behavior* 7:137–158.

Goffman, Erving. 1963. *Stigma*. Englewood Cliffs, NJ: Prentice Hall.

Jackson, Joan. 1954. "The Adjustment of the Family to the Crisis of Alcoholism." *Quarterly Journal of Studies on Alcohol* 5:564–586.

Sampson, Harold, Sheldon L. Messinger, and Robert D. Towne. 1962. "Family Processes and Becoming a Mental Patient." *American Journal of Sociology* 68:88–96.

Sykes, Gresham, and David Matza. 1957. "Techniques of Neutralization: A Theory of Delinquency." *American Sociological Review* 22:667–670.

Yarrow, Marian, Charlotte Schwartz, Harriet Murphy, and Leila Deasy. 1955. "The Psychological Meaning of Mental Illness in the Family." *Journal of Social Issues* 11:12–24.

Living with the Stigma of AIDS

Rose Weitz

Despite the mass media's extensive coverage of AIDS, few sociologists have yet written about the experience of having AIDS and none have focused on how stigma affects PWAs [persons with AIDS]. However, researchers have investigated how people with other illnesses are affected by and manage stigma. Studies suggest that ill people try to avoid stigma either by revealing their illnesses, so that others will not be shocked or confused by their unusual behaviors, or by concealing their illnesses, so that their differences will not lead others to reject them (Schneider and Conrad 1983; Hilbert 1984; Boutte 1987; Brooks and Matson 1987). Ill persons also can try to reduce stigma by teaching others the biology of their illnesses and arguing against punitive theological explanations for illness (Gussow and Tracy 1968).

This article describes how stigma affects PWAs' relationships with families, friends, lovers, colleagues, and health care workers. It explores how PWAs avoid or reduce stigma by concealing their illnesses, learning when and to whom they should reveal their illnesses, changing their social networks, educating others about AIDS, developing nonstigmatizing theories of illness causation, and using bravado to convince others that they are still functioning social beings.

METHODS AND SAMPLE

This article draws on interviews I conducted between July, 1986 and March, 1987 with 23 Arizona residents who either had AIDS or AIDS-Related Complex (ARC).

From *Qualitative Sociology* 13, No. 1, 1990, Reprinted by permission of Kluwer Academic Publishers and the author.

All respondents discussed in this article were men who described themselves as gay or bisexual (although none mentioned any recent relationships with women). Three of the men had used drugs as well. I also interviewed two heterosexual women who had used intravenous drugs and one man who was seropositive for HIV antibodies but had not yet been diagnosed as having AIDS or ARC. Because I interviewed only two women and one seropositive but asymptomatic individual, I have only limited understanding of how such individuals' experiences might differ from that of gay or bisexual PWAs. Consequently, I present in this article only data from the interviews with gay and bisexual men.

When my study began, the Arizona Department of Health Services believed that approximately 40 of the 110 known AIDS cases in the state were still living. To contact these and other PWAs, I posted signs in gay bars; announced the study in gay and mainstream newspapers and AIDS political action groups; asked physicians, AIDS support group leaders, and other respondents to inform PWAs of the study; and had non-profit groups which offer emotional or financial support to PWAs send letters describing the study to their clients. Eighteen of the 23 subjects learned of the study through the non-profit groups, two from friends, two from a political action group, and one from a notice in a gay newspaper.

The sample is comparable to the Arizona population in terms of religion and to the state's reported AIDS cases at the time of the study in terms of sex, geographical location (overwhelmingly urban), and mode of transmission (Arizona Dept. of Health Services, February 2, 1987). Because participating in the interviews required mental competence and some physical stamina, the sample undoubtedly underrepresents the most seriously ill PWAs. It also underrepresents persons with Kaposi's sarcoma (1 percent of the sample, but 21 percent of reported cases), even though they tend to be less ill than other PWAs, perhaps because these individuals do not want a stranger to see the disfiguring lesions which Kaposi's sarcoma can cause. In addition, the sample underrepresents nonwhites (0 percent of the sample but 13 percent of reported cases), who typically are less integrated into the AIDS support networks and therefore were less likely to have heard of the study. Finally, the sample overrepresents persons in their thirties (60 percent of the sample, but 42 percent of reported cases) and underrepresents older persons.

The data for this paper were obtained through semistructured interviews. I began with a set list of questions, but during each interview also probed into any unexpected topics that seemed potentially significant. These new topics were then incorporated into subsequent interviews. Thus, all the interviews covered the same basic questions, but the later interviews also included additional ones which emerged as significant in the earlier interviews. Interviews ranged from two to five hours in length, averaging about three hours, and were audiotaped and transcribed. Interviews took place at respondents' homes unless they preferred another location (usually my home).

I analyzed the data using themes which emerged from the respondents' statements. With each interview, I began to develop themes which I followed up in subsequent interviews. After completing the interviews, I reread them all to identify additional critical concepts. I then sorted the interview materials according to these concepts to see what patterns emerged. These patterns were used to develop the structure of my analysis in this article.

The Impact of Stigma

Given the extensive media coverage of AIDS, PWAs cannot avoid knowing that many people condemn them and consider AIDS a divine punishment for sin. Several of my subjects described PWAs as the modern world's equivalent of lepers. A few mentioned their fears that they would be quarantined or even killed if the public learned they had AIDS. One expressed the fear that if the "rednecks living across the street . . . found out a gay person was over here with AIDS, they may decide to get drunk one night and come over and kill the faggot." The sense of stigma was so strong that another said he would rather die than be cured for if he were cured he would have to live the rest of his life with the stigma of having once had AIDS.

The following sections describe how this sense of stigma develops, and how stigma pervades PWAs' relationships with family, friends, lovers, health care workers, and fellow workers. The final section discusses how PWAs cope with this stigma.

Family   All PWAs run a risk that their families will reject them, either because of their illness *per se* or because their illness exposes or emphasizes that they are gay or use drugs. One of the men I spoke with was a 27 year old computer operator whose parents lived in a small town in another state. He felt he had a good relationship with his parents, but had never told them of his sexual orientation. When asked how he thought his family would react to news of his diagnosis, he said:

> You just can't predict. They might find it so disgusting that you'll basically lose them. They'll be gone. Or they'll go through the adjustment period and not mind. You really don't know.

Virtually every respondent reported that at least one family member had ceased contact with him after learning of his illness. One source of this rejection is that diagnosis with AIDS can reinforce families' belief that homosexuality is immoral. Families who had always questioned the morality of homosexuality may interpret an individual's illness as divine punishment, regarding it as proof that homosexual behavior should not be tolerated. For example, a 26 year old tailor from a fundamentalist Christian family, whose relatives had not known he was gay, described how AIDS forced him to reveal his sexual orientation and thus "put a wedge" between him and his family. His family considered homosexuality sinful and questioned whether they should help him with his health problems if he would not change his behaviors. He was still in contact with his parents, even though his mother had told him that his homosexuality was an "embarrassment" to her. But he had stopped talking to his sister because he could not abide her constant admonitions "to repent" and "to confess sin."

Even PWAs whose families have in the past appeared to accept their lifestyles may find that their families reject them once their diagnosis becomes known. When questioned about this, the PWAs suggested that somehow AIDS had made their homosexuality more real and salient to their families. Just as pregnancy forces parents to recognize that their daughters are not just living with men but having sex, diagnosis with AIDS apparently forces families to recognize that their sons or brothers are not simply gay in some abstract way, but actually engage or engaged in homosexual activities. As a result, families who have tolerated their relatives' homosexuality despite deep reservations about its morality find that they can no longer do so. A 38 year old business manager reported that when he first told his parents he was gay "their reaction while it wasn't initially effusive at least it was grudgingly accepting." Now, however, he felt that his parents had "used this whole AIDS thing against me" by telling him that AIDS was "just desserts for the homosexual community." Similarly, a 29 year old blue collar worker recounted how his mother, who previously had seemed to tolerate his lifestyle, responded to news of his diagnosis by telling him "I think your lifestyle is vulgar. I have never understood it, I've never accepted it. . . . Your lifestyle repulses me." She subsequently refused to let him in her house or help him obtain medical insurance.

Even when families do not overtly reject ill relatives, their behavior may still create a sense of stigma. This can happen when families either hide news of their relatives' illnesses from others altogether or tell others that their relatives have some less stigmatized disease. A 39 year old floral designer, whose Catholic family had all known he was gay before he became ill, reported that his mother refused to tell his brothers and sisters that he had AIDS, and ordered him not to tell them as well.

When his siblings finally were told, they in turn would not tell their spouses. Such behavior forces PWAs to recognize that, as one fundamentalist Christian said, "it was an embarrassment to [the family] . . . that I was gay and . . . that I have AIDS." This imposed secrecy places heavy burdens on individuals who subsequently must "live a lie."

Families may reinforce a sense of stigma by adopting extreme and medically unwarranted anti-contagion measures. One family brought their own sheets when visiting their ill son's home. Others refused to allow PWAs to touch any food, share their bathrooms, or come closer than an arm's length away. A 29 year old Mormon salesperson, whose family believed he deserved AIDS as punishment for his sins, reported that initially his family "wouldn't come in the room unless they had gloves and a mask and they wouldn't touch me . . . [And] for a time I couldn't go over to somebody's house for dinner. And they still use paper plates [when I eat there]." Even PWAs who feel such precautions are necessary still miss the experience of physical warmth and intimacy. They report feeling stigmatized, isolated, and contaminated.

Although PWAs fear that their families will reject them once their illness becomes known, they also hope that news of their illness will bring their families closer together. A 38 year old store manager who had never had a particularly close relationship with his family described his fantasy "that something like this—an experience where you come this close to death or the reality of death—is when you realize what's really important and not who's right and who's wrong."

For the lucky ones, this fantasy materializes. The oldest man I interviewed, a 57 year old lawyer, had always considered his father a cold and selfish man, and had never been on good terms with him. This situation changed, at least partially, when he became ill. As he described it:

> We've gotten closer . . . There's the verbal "I love you," there's the letters. One of the nicest things that's ever happened to me . . . is my father sent me a personal card. In the inside he wrote "God bless you. I love you son" . . . . It meant the world to me.

Another man described how, despite their disapproval of his lifestyle, his fundamentalist Christian family had provided him with housing, money, and emotional support once they learned of his illness. As he described it, in his family, when "little brother needed help . . . that took priority over all the other bullshit. They were right there."

Diagnosis can also bring families together by ending previous sources of conflict. Whether to preserve their own health, protect others from infection, or because they simply lose interest in sex once diagnosed with a deadly, sexually transmitted disease, PWAs may cease all sexual activity. For health reasons, PWAs may also stop smoking and drinking. As a result, families that previously had disapproved of PWAs' lifestyles may stop considering them "sick" or "sinful," even if the PWAs continue to consider themselves gay. Consequently, some PWAs achieve a new acceptance from relatives who attach less stigma to AIDS than to their former behaviors.

Friends and Lovers At the time of diagnosis, only 7 of the 23 men had lovers (as opposed to sexual partners with whom they had no ongoing relationship). These seven naturally turned to their lovers as well as their families for emotional support. The two whose lovers were also HIV infected did, indeed, receive support from their lovers, as did one man whose lover was HIV negative and two whose lovers do not know their HIV status. The remaining two men, however, were almost immediately abandoned by their lovers.

The PWAs' friends have proven considerably less sympathetic. Typically, PWAs reported that some friends "are very supportive, come around, enjoy coming over here, whatever. But most of them have backed off." A young blue collar worker described how, when his best friend learned of his diagnosis:

> He couldn't get me out of his apartment fast enough. . . . It was to the point [my friends] didn't even want to be in the same room with me. . . . It was just like "don't call us, we'll call you . . ." They stopped returning calls. When I would see them out [at bars], they would see me coming and they would head out in the other direction.

Because housemates, like other friends, may also reject PWAs once they learn about their illness, PWAs may have to make new housing arrangements shortly after receiving their diagnoses. Some housemates left or asked the PWA to leave as soon as they learned that he had AIDS. In other cases, housemates asked the PWAs to leave once the housemates learned that they too were being shunned by others as possible sources of infection. Because of limited financial resources and social stigma, PWAs who need new housing may be forced to move in with their families or with other PWAs. Those who move in with their families risk retreating into a childlike dependency, while those who live with other PWAs must cope with their housemates' illnesses as well as their own.

Although rejection by friends and lovers is common, it is not universal. In fact, some men received acceptance and caring from friends and lovers beyond anything they had expected. The 57 year old lawyer quoted above had received many offers of support from friends. He told me, "I never knew I was [so] loved." Similar experiences led the 38 year old business manager described above to conclude "that family are those people who you can really love and trust and care for" and not necessarily one's blood relations.

Health Care Workers That persons who lack medical training should fear or abhor the victims of a new and deadly disease may not seem surprising. Yet even many health care professionals shun PWAs (Katz et al. 1987; Kelly et al. 1987). In Arizona, as in many other places, no nursing home or after-care facility, only a handful of dentists and ambulance services, and relatively few physicians will care for PWAs. Some respondents had experienced discrimination from professionals directly, while more knew of the problem from talking to others.

Through trial and error, most PWAs eventually find primary practitioners who, they believe, provide good and nonjudgmental care. They still face potential stigma, however, whenever they need specialist or hospital care. It may take several phone calls to find a willing specialist. If hospitalization is needed, the problem is less access to care than quality of care. Hospital staff usually cannot refuse to provide care, but they can make their ignorance and prejudice painfully obvious. One man described how hospital nurses made his friends and family "protect themselves" by donning isolation garb, even though his infection could not be transmitted through casual contact. He reported:

> A lot of the nurses were very nervous. It was obvious. Some of them double gloved and some wouldn't come in at all. I mean, they would if you forced them to, but they weren't going to just drop in and see how you were doing and stuff.

Other PWAs mentioned social workers who refused to enter their hospital rooms and hospital staff who disappeared suddenly once their diagnoses became known. One man first realized that he had AIDS when he suddenly found himself under the care of a new hospital staff team, all of whom appeared gay.

Work   By the time individuals receive diagnoses of AIDS, many are physically incapable of working. Others, faced with catastrophic medical bills, must quit their jobs to qualify for state-financed medical assistance.

PWAs who continue working risk additional stigma and discrimination if others learn of their illnesses. Although most courts have ruled that PWAs are disabled and thus qualify for protection under anti-discrimination laws (Leonard 1987), in practice employers can fire PWAs with impunity because few PWAs have the time, money, or stamina to sue successfully (personal communication, Jane Aiken, Arizona Governor's Task Force on AIDS).

Only one man, a mechanic for a large public institution with an established AIDS policy, described his working situation as satisfactory. Every other PWA who revealed his illness was either fired immediately or forced to quit when colleagues or employers made his situation intolerable. An outgoing and amiable young man who had worked as a tailor said that his fellow workers initially responded well, taking only reasonable precautions, such as not sharing drinking glasses.

Then little things happened . . . . If a pin came from [my department] they would immediately throw it away because [they thought] if they poked themselves, they could get AIDS . . . [Then they developed] a list of things for me to do at the end of the day like wipe down the scissors and the table and everything that I touched with a weak solution of ten-to-one [bleach] . . . . With all that happening, I kind of lost the desire to work.

He quit his job soon thereafter. Although he appeared to have a strong legal case, he (like all the others in similar situations) decided he did not have the energy, funds, or time to sue.

Managing the Stigma of AIDS

Avoiding Stigma   To maintain as much of their pre-diagnosis lives as possible, PWAs must find ways to avoid or reduce stigma. One basic strategem used by PWAs as well as by people with other stigmatized illnesses (Boutte 1987; Hilbert 1984; Schneider and Conrad 1983) is to hide the nature of their illness.

Hiding can begin at the time of diagnosis. Since AIDS was first identified, federal law has required physicians to report all cases to the government. A new Arizona law (enacted during the study period) requires physicians to report persons who have ARC or who test positive for HIV, the virus that causes AIDS. Although laws supposedly protect the confidentiality of these reports, physicians and patients fear that the information will leak out. As a result, to protect clients from possible legal, social, and financial repercussions, physicians may circumvent the reporting law. One man, for example, described how his physician diagnosed his illness as ARC rather than AIDS to avoid the stigma which the physician believed would result from a diagnosis of AIDS and the necessity to report him to the state. The physician told him:

> "If you diagnosed a person with AIDS, people really do back off from that one. I don't care how knowledgeable people are . . . . We don't want to diagnose people with AIDS if we don't have to diagnose." He [the physician] said, "the first time you go to the hospital with pneumonia or the cancer lesions and stuff

like that," he said, "then we got no choice and it has to be reported to the state. But as ARC we don't really have to report ARC cases."

Other physicians avoid reporting by using highly restrictive definitions of AIDS. One physician decided that only his client's pharynx and not his esophagus was infected with candidiasis. This slim distinction allowed the physician to conclude that the client had ARC rather than AIDS and hence did not have to be reported. Physicians can also diagnose each opportunistic infection a client contracts rather than diagnosing AIDS as the underlying cause of those infections.

Fearing that disclosure might result in loss of employment or insurance, PWAs and their physicians also used these tactics to hide diagnoses from insurance companies (and indirectly from employers). A computer operator who was well-read on the biology of AIDS and active in an AIDS political action group described how he and his physician avoided telling his insurance company he had ARC or AIDS:

> [We have] been very careful, even so far, never to put the three big letters [ARC] or four big letters [AIDS] on the [insurance] papers. It's always been just candidiasis or anemia or something ridiculous . . . . Anything but. And I prefer to keep it that way, and I think probably even [the physician's] notes reflect that.

For the same reason, and as long as they can afford it, PWAs may only request insurance reimbursement for treatments that will not trigger questions about whether they have AIDS.

In addition to hiding their illness from unknown bureaucrats, PWAs may also hide it from families, friends, and sexual partners as well. Shame about his sexuality had led one 41 year old Catholic man to sever all contact with his ex-wife and young children when he started having gay relationships years ago. After he received his diagnosis, and despite his realization that he was dying, he continued this silence:

> I haven't seen my kids for almost 12 years and when AIDS came down, I didn't know how to handle it. How do you tell your kids 2,000 miles away that you're not only homosexual, but you're dying from a

killer disease, the "gay plague" as I call it? How do you do that? How do you explain a lifetime in a thirty minute telephone conversation? So I chose not to.

Others chose not to tell their families because they assumed their families would reject them or because the PWAs could not cope with the anguish their news would bring.

Deciding whether to inform sexual partners with whom they were not in continuing relationships was more complex, for it raised the question not only of how to protect oneself from stigma but also how to protect others from infection. This was not an issue for the five men who were in continuing relationships with lovers who knew of their illness. Nor was it an issue for the 14 men who either had sex or had sex only on rare occasions when they were too drunk to make any conscious decisions. Of the remaining four men, two always told their lovers because they felt obliged to inform anyone whom they might infect that they were at risk. The other two disagreed, arguing that they need not disclose their diagnosis as long as they limited themselves to activities unlikely to transmit the virus. Besides, they argued, most gay or bisexual men already had been exposed to the virus. The well-informed computer operator described above stated that he felt no ethical obligation to reveal his diagnosis to sexual partners because "the level of infection in that group is so high that if, in fact, *you* are careful not to exchange body fluids to *them,* then their level of risk out of this encounter is much lower than what they probably did the week before. And they found *that* acceptable." (emphasis in original.)

PWAs use a variety of methods to hide their illnesses from people around them. One man routinely transferred his pills of zidovudine (formerly called azidothymidine or AZT) to an unmarked bottle because he feared others would recognize the drug as one used to treat AIDS. Some selected clothing or used make-up to hide their emaciation or skin problems. Men whose tongues showed the tell-tale whitish spots of candidiasis (an infection that frequently accompanies AIDS) closed their mouths partially while smiling or talking.

Most importantly, PWAs learned to gauge how sick they looked. Whenever possible, they tried to look healthy when out in public. A 23 year old salesperson who had always enjoyed going to bars and never enjoyed solitude described how "Every time I go out [to a bar] I try to hide it. I try to act energetic and normal and I always have them put a squeeze of lime in my drinks so it's like a mixed drink." When their health made it impossible to appear normal, PWAs stayed home. As another man explained, "There are days that I really feel shitty and I look bad and I won't let anybody see me. I won't go around anybody. And then there are days I really force myself to put myself together so I will look decent and I'm not afraid to go out then."

This strategy is no help, however, when PWAs must go out despite visible physical problems. To protect their secret in these circumstances, PWAs may devise plausible alternative explanations for their symptoms. One man explained his weight loss by telling co-workers that he had begun marathon training. Others attributed their physical problems to less stigmatized illnesses, such as leukemia or cancer.

Although hiding one's illness gives PWAs some protection against rejection, it carries a high price. PWAs who hide their illness from employers may lose their jobs when they cannot explain their increased absences and decreased productivity. Those who choose not to tell friends or relatives must endure their illness alone and in silence, without support they might otherwise receive. They must also endure the emotional strain caused by the secretiveness itself. As one man said, "I want to tell. I'm not used to hiding everything from everybody . . . . I'm a basically honest person and I don't like to lie." Finally, PWAs who keep their illnesses secret risk hearing painfully disparaging comments about how AIDS "serves those queers right." On such occasions, PWAs may feel that they cannot respond without risking exposure. A 33 year old salesperson involved with an AIDS political action group said:

> I was at my desk and three secretaries telling AIDS jokes were standing right behind me. It cut and it hurt. I grit my teeth and said nothing . . . . [Occasionally] I try and slide in a little bit of education . . . but I don't

push it to the point where they go, "how come he knows so much?"

To avoid questions about why they don't find AIDS jokes humorous, some PWAs even feel obliged to join in the laughter.

Because both concealing and revealing one's illness can create problems, it is difficult for a PWA to decide what to do. To deal with this dilemma, PWAs learn to predict how various others may react to news of their illness. For example, a PWA can tell a relative that he volunteers for an AIDS education group or that a friend of his has AIDS. The relative's reaction can help the PWA decide whether to tell of his own illness.

PWAs also learn not only whom to tell but when to tell of their illness. A 24 year old blue collar worker who had been abandoned by several close friends said, "I used to tell people up front about my diagnosis, but I don't anymore. I let them get to know me, because I really want them to get to know me before they pass judgment on me." A few PWAs whose families lived out of state had decided not to disclose their illness until they could see their families in person. Others, who expected their diagnosis to precipitate family crises, decided not to tell until death appeared imminent.

In the aftermath of disclosure, PWAs can avoid further stigma by reducing contact with friends and relatives who prove unsupportive. As a result, however, their social lives shrink significantly. The man who put lime in his water at bars said:

> [Before getting AIDS] I was out all the time, I loved to be around people. I hated to be by myself. But now, I find that I don't like to be around people that much except if it's people I know that are not going to reject me because I don't want the rejection. I don't want to be hurt; I'm tired of being hurt.

To replace their former social networks, PWAs can join support groups organized for persons who have this illness. These groups afford them a social life without risk of rejection or social awkwardness. One man who had experienced painful rejections explained that he socialized mostly with other PWAs "mainly because I guess I'm still afraid of people's reactions" but also "because I think they [other PWAs] can understand more what your feelings are, what is going through your head. It's a lot easier to sit around and have a conversation with someone who is also ill with this disease and you don't have to worry about avoiding certain topics." Similarly, the 39 year old floral designer described above, whose mother had refused to tell his siblings of his illness, experienced further trauma when most of his friends abandoned him. He told me of the pleasure he obtained from a recent potluck social for PWAs:

> I was not alone . . . I met a lot of really beautiful people, a lot of really nice friends. They took your phone number, they call you, socialize with you, you go to the show with them. You do things with them. If you need any help or whatever, they're there . . . . I went through hiding myself in my house and every time the facial sores started I would be afraid to go out and let people see me. These people don't care. You're not the only one that's had the facial sores and they don't care. You're welcome there . . . . Nobody [at the potluck] was afraid because a person with ARC or AIDS made a dish. We all rather enjoyed the food. It was like all the barriers went down when you were with these other people.

Although socializing with PWAs solves some problems, it creates others. First, PWAs may find that they have nothing but their illness in common. As a result, the relationships they develop are likely to be superficial and unrewarding. Second, as one man explained, these social circles do not permit the PWA "to get away from AIDS and be myself at the same time." Only with other PWAs can they act truly naturally. Yet when they are with other PWAs, they cannot avoid at least thinking about their illness. Third, PWAs who develop new friendships in these circles must then cope with their friends' illnesses and dying as well as their own. Thus seeking friendship from other PWAs in the end can increase their own sorrow.

Reducing Stigma Although hiding one's illness and restricting one's social circle help PWAs to avoid stigma, they will not reduce that stigma. Some PWAs therefore consider these strategies inadequate

and choose, at least in some situations, to attack the roots of the stigma.

To reduce the stigma of AIDS, PWAs may "come out of the closet" about their illness—working for community organizations that provide services to PWAs, becoming "resources" for acquaintances who have unanswered questions about AIDS, or even speaking for the media about having AIDS. PWAs who take this course believe it is the only way truly to improve their situation. For example, the man whose mother refused to help him obtain health insurance subsequently became an active speaker about AIDS. He explained, "the only way that I could see getting rid of that stigma is to stick up for myself and become publicly known, to say it's okay to be my friend, it's okay to hug me, it's okay to sit down on a couch with me and watch TV." Other PWAs continue to conceal their diagnosis but nonetheless try to teach people around them that PWAs should not be shunned. One man described a confrontation with a neighbor who accused him of having AIDS and asked him not to use the pool in their apartment complex. The PWA denied that he had AIDS, but told the neighbor that "ignorance is no excuse. You ought to read up on AIDS, you can't get it that way."

To reduce stigma, PWAs must go beyond educating others about the biology of the disease to challenging the idea that AIDS is a deserved punishment for sin. They do so in two ways. First, PWAs can argue that God is the source of love and not of punishment and that God would not have created gay people only to reject them as sinners. Second, they can argue that all illnesses are biological phenomena, not signs of divine judgment, and that it was simply bad luck that the first Americans affected by AIDS were gay. Several of the men stressed their belief that AIDS had originated among heterosexuals in Africa and thus could not be punishment for homosexuality. As one 28 year old construction worker said, "It didn't start out as a homosexual disease and it's not going to finish that way."

These alternative explanations for AIDS allow PWAs to reject their rejectors as prejudiced or ignorant. The construction worker just quoted went on to describe his reaction to Jerry Fallwell's statements that AIDS is God's punishment for sin:

> Somebody like that really ought to be put away. He's doing so much damage, it's pathetic and he doesn't know what he's talking about and that's real sad. And we don't need that—we need understanding.

Other PWAs, however, themselves believe that they deserve AIDS (Weitz 1989). In these circumstances, they can reduce stigma only by accepting responsibility for their actions, forswearing their former activities, and asking forgiveness from their families, churches, and God.

Finally, PWAs can reduce stigma through bravado—putting on what amounts to a show in order to convince others of the reality that they are functioning and worthwhile human beings. The man who chastised his neighbor for being ignorant about AIDS told how he and other PWAs occasionally go to a bar to "show these people that we can live with AIDS. That we can have a good time. That we can dance, that we can socialize, that we're not people with plagues." Describing a recent visit to his neighborhood bar, he said:

> I just walked in, put my arms around somebody, said "Hi, how're you doing? Everything going ok with you?" and he said, "Well, how are you doing?" and I said, "Well, ARC hasn't gotten me down yet, I don't think it will." I said, "I'm going to beat this thing." And I just acted like nothing was wrong.

CONCLUSIONS

Almost by definition, "to define something as a disease or illness is to deem it undesirable" (Conrad and Schneider 1980:36). By the same token, to say that someone has a disease or (more strongly) is diseased implies that the person is less whole, functioning, or worthy than "normal" people. Consequently, all chronically ill persons must struggle against stigma.

At present, however, no other physical illness in American society carries stigma as severe as AIDS.

For example, while some people believe that herpes or leprosy are divine punishments for sin, far more people believe that AIDS is a divine punishment. Similarly, some health care workers provide only grudging, low quality care to patients whom they consider demanding hypochondriacs, such as people who suffer chronic pain with no clear cause. Few if any health care workers, however, refuse to provide care to such persons. Yet many refuse to provide care to PWAs. The stigma of AIDS reflects the fact that it is contagious, deforming, fatal, imperfectly understood, and associated with already stigmatized groups.

Despite the differences between AIDS and other illnesses, however, PWAs manage stigma in much the same way as other chronically ill people. To avoid stigma, PWAs do not disclose their illness if it is invisible, mask the signs of illness if they are visible, lie about those signs if they cannot be masked, and minimize contact with people who reject them when their illness becomes known. Alternatively, PWAs can reveal their illness and either challenge their detractors' theological and biological assumptions or ask forgiveness for their former deviant conduct. In these ways, PWAs, like people with other illnesses, can limit the impact of illness on their social lives.

REFERENCES

Boutte, Marie I. 1987. "'The stumbling disease': A case study of stigma among Azorean-Portuguese." *Social Science and Medicine* 24(3):209–217.

Brooks, Nancy A., and Ronald R. Matson. 1987. "Managing multiple sclerosis." *Research in the Sociology of Health Care* 6:73–106.

Conrad, Peter, and Joseph Schneider. 1980. *Deviance and Medicalization: From Badness to Sickness*. St. Louis: C.V. Mosby.

Gussow, Zachary, and George S. Tracy. 1968. "Status, ideology, and adaptation to stigmatized illness: A study of leprosy." *Human Organization,* 27:316–325.

Hilbert, Richard A. 1984. "The acultural dimensions of chronic pain: Flawed reality construction and the problem of meaning." *Social Problems* 31:365–78.

Katz, Irwin, R. Glen Hass, Nina Parisi, Janetta Astone, and Denise McEvaddy. 1987. "Lay people's and health care personnel's perceptions of cancer, AIDS, cardiac, and diabetic patients." *Psychological Reports* 60:615–629.

Kelly, Jeffrey A., Janet S. St. Lawrence, Steve Smith, Harold V. Hood, and Donna J. Cook. 1987. "Stigmatization of AIDS patients by physicians." *American Journal of Public Health* 77:789–791.

Leonard, Arthur S. 1987. "AIDS in the workplace." Pp. 109–125 in Harlon L. Dalton, Scott Burris, and the Yale AIDS Law Project (eds.), *AIDS and the Law: A Guide for the Public.* New Haven: Yale University Press.

Schneider, Joseph, and Peter Conrad. 1983. *Having Epilepsy.* Philadelphia: Temple University Press.

Weitz, Rose. 1989. "Uncertainty and the lives of persons with AIDS." *Journal of Health and Social Behavior* 30:270–281.

READING 5-5

Situational Ethics and Cheating Among College Students

Donald L. McCabe

The concept of situational ethics may be particularly helpful in understanding student rationalizations for cheating. Extending the arguments of Norris and Dodder (1979), LaBeff et al. conclude

> that students hold qualified guidelines for behavior which are situationally determined. As such, the concept of situational ethics might well describe . . . college cheating [as having] rules for behavior [that] may not be considered rigid but depend on the circumstances involved (1990:191).

LaBeff et al. believe a utilitarian calculus of "the end justifies the means" underlies this reasoning process and "what is wrong in most situations might be considered right or acceptable if the end is defined as appropriate" (1990:191).

Sykes and Matza (1957) hypothesize that such rationalizations, that is, "justifications for deviance that are seen as valid by the delinquent but not by the legal system or society at large" (p. 666), are

From "The Influence of Situational Ethics on Cheating Among College Students." *Sociological Inquiry* 62, no. 3 (Summer 1992). Reprinted by permission of the University of Texas Press and the author.

common. However, they challenge conventional wisdom that such rationalizations typically follow deviant behavior as a means of protecting "the individual from self-blame and the blame of others after the act" (p. 666). They develop convincing arguments that these rationalizations may logically precede the deviant behavior and "[d]isapproval from internalized norms and conforming others in the social environment is neutralized, turned back, or deflated in advance. Social controls that serve to check or inhibit deviant motivational patterns are rendered inoperative, and the individual is freed to engage in delinquency without serious damage to his self-image" (pp. 666–667).

METHODOLOGY

The data discussed here were gathered as part of a study of college cheating conducted during the 1990–1991 academic year. A seventy-two-item questionnaire concerning cheating behavior was administered to students at thirty-one highly selective colleges across the country. Surveys were mailed to a minimum of five hundred students at each school and a total of 6,096 completed surveys were returned (38.3 percent response rate). Eighty-eight percent of the respondents were seniors, nine percent were juniors, and the remaining three percent could not be classified. Survey administration emphasized voluntary participation and assurances of anonymity to help combat issues of non-response bias and the need to accept responses without the chance to question or contest them.

The final sample included 61.2 percent females (which reflects the inclusion of five all-female schools in the sample and a slightly higher return rate among female students) and 95.4 percent U.S. citizens. The sample paralleled the ethnic diversity of the participating schools (85.5 percent Anglo, 7.2 percent Asian, 2.6 percent African American, 2.2 percent Hispanic and 2.5 percent other); their religious diversity (including a large percentage of students who claimed no religious preference, 27.1 percent); and their mix of undergraduate majors (36.0 percent humanities, 28.8 percent social sciences, 26.8 percent natural sciences and engineering, 4.5 percent business, and 3.9 percent other).

RESULTS

Of the 6,096 students participating in this research, over two-thirds (67.4 percent) indicated that they had cheated on a test or major assignment at least once while an undergraduate. This cheating took a variety of different forms, but among the most popular (listed in decreasing order of mention) were: (1) a failure to footnote sources in written work, (2) collaboration on assignments when the instructor specifically asked for individual work, (3) copying from other students on tests and examinations, (4) fabrication of bibliographies, (5) helping someone else cheat on a test, and (6) using unfair methods to learn the content of a test ahead of time. Almost one in five students (19.1 percent) could be classified as active cheaters (five or more self-reported incidents of cheating).

Students admitting to any cheating activity were asked to rate the importance of several specific factors that might have influenced their decisions to cheat. These data establish the importance of denial of responsibility and condemnation of condemners as neutralization techniques. For example, 52.4 percent of the respondents who admitted to cheating rated the pressure to get good grades as an important influence in their decision to cheat, with parental pressures and competition to gain admission into professional schools singled out as the primary grade pressures. Forty-six percent of those who had engaged in cheating cited excessive workloads and an inability to keep up with assignments as important factors in their decisions to cheat.

In addition to rating the importance of such preselected factors, 426 respondents (11.0 percent of the admitted cheaters) offered their own justifications for cheating in response to an open-ended question on motivations for cheating.

As shown in the table, denial of responsibility was the technique most frequently cited (216 responses, 61.0 percent of the total) in the 354 responses classified into one of Sykes and Matza's five categories of neutralization. The most common

NEUTRALIZATION STRATEGIES: SELF-ADMITTED CHEATERS

Strategy	Number	Percent
Denial of responsibility	216	61.0
Mind block	90	25.4
No understanding of material	31	8.8
Other	95	26.8
Condemnation of condemners	99	28.0
Pointless assignment	35	9.9
No respect for professor	28	7.9
Other	36	10.2
Appeal to higher loyalties	24	6.8
Help a friend	10	2.8
Peer pressure	9	2.5
Other	5	1.5
Denial of injury	15	4.2
Cheating is harmless	9	2.5
Does not matter	6	1.7

responses in this category were mind block, no understanding of the material, a fear of failing, and unclear explanations of assignments. (Although it is possible that some instances of mind block and a fear of failing included in this summary would be more accurately classified as rationalization, the wording of all responses included here suggests that rationalization preceded the cheating incident. Responses that seem to involve post hoc rationalizations were excluded from this summary.) Condemnation of condemners was the second most popular neutralization technique observed (99 responses, 28.0 percent) and included such explanations as pointless assignments, lack of respect for individual professors, unfair tests, parents' expectations, and unfair professors. Twenty-four respondents (6.8 percent) appealed to higher loyalties to explain their behavior. In particular, helping a friend and responding to peer pressures were influences some students could not ignore. Finally fifteen students (4.2 percent) provided responses that clearly fit into the category of denial of injury. These students dismissed their cheating as harmless since it did not hurt anyone or they felt cheating did not matter in some cases (for example, where an assignment counted for a small percentage of the total course grade).

Detailed examination of selected student responses provides additional insight into the neutralization strategies they employ.

Denial of Responsibility

Denial of responsibility invokes the claim that the act was "due to forces outside of the individual and beyond his control such as unloving parents" (Sykes and Matza 1957:667). For example, many students cite an unreasonable workload and the difficulty of keeping up as ample justification for cheating:

> Here at . . . , you must cheat to stay alive. There's so much work and the quality of materials from which to learn, books, professors, is so bad that there's no other choice.

> It's the only way to keep up.

> I couldn't do the work myself.

The following descriptions of student cheating confirm fear of failure is also an important form of denial of responsibility:

> . . . a take-home exam in a class I was failing.

> . . . was near failing.

Some justified their cheating by citing the behavior of peers:

> Everyone has test files in fraternities, etc. If you don't, you're at a great disadvantage.

> When most of the class is cheating on a difficult exam and they will ruin the curve, it influences you to cheat so your grade won't be affected.

All of these responses contain the essence of denial of responsibility: the cheater has deflected blame to others or to a specific situational context.

Denial of Injury

As noted in the table, denial of injury was identified as a neutralization technique employed by some respondents. A key element in denial of injury is whether one feels "anyone has clearly been hurt by [the] deviance." In invoking this defense, a cheater would argue "that his behavior does not really cause any great harm despite the fact that it runs counter to the law" (Sykes and Matza 1957:667–668). For example, a number of students argued that the assignment or test on which they cheated was so trivial that no one was really hurt by their cheating.

> These grades aren't worth much therefore my copying doesn't mean very much. I am ashamed, but I'd probably do it the same way again.

> If I extend the time on a take-home it is because I feel everyone does and the teacher kind of expects it. No one gets hurt.

As suggested earlier, these responses suggest the conclusion of LaBeff et al. that "[i]t is unlikely that students will . . . deny injury" (1990:196) must be re-evaluated.

The Denial of the Victim

LaBeff et al. failed to find any evidence of denial of the victim in their student accounts. Although the student motivations for cheating summarized in the table support this conclusion, at least four students (0.1% of the self-admitted cheaters in this study) provided comments elsewhere on the survey instrument which involved denial of the victim. The common element in these responses was a victim deserving of the consequences of the cheating behavior and cheating was viewed as "a form of rightful retaliation or punishment" (Sykes and Matza 1957:668).

This feeling was extreme in one case, as suggested by the following student who felt her cheating was justified by the

> realization that this school is a manifestation of the bureaucratic capitalist system that systematically keeps the lower classes down, and that adhering to their rules was simply perpetuating the institution.

This "we" versus "they" mentality was raised by many students, but typically in comments about the policing of academic honesty rather than as justification for one's own cheating behavior. When used to justify cheating, the target was almost always an individual teacher rather than the institution and could be more accurately classified as a strategy of condemnation of condemners rather than denial of the victim.

The Condemnation of Condemners

Sykes and Matza describe the condemnation of condemners as an attempt to shift "the focus of attention from [one's] own deviant acts to the motives and behavior of those who disapprove of [the] violations. [B]y attacking others, the wrongfulness of [one's] own behavior is more easily repressed or lost to view" (1957:668). The logic of this strategy for student cheaters focused on issues of favoritism and fairness. Students invoking this rationale describe "uncaring, unprofessional instructors with negative attitudes who were negligent in their behavior" (LaBeff et al. 1990:195). For example:

> In one instance, nothing was done by a professor because the student was a hockey player.
>
> The TAs who graded essays were unduly harsh.
>
> It is known by students that certain professors are more lenient to certain types, e.g., blondes or hockey players.

I would guess that 90% of the students here have seen athletes and/or fraternity members cheating on an exam or papers. If you turn in one of these culprits, and I have, the penalty is a five-minute lecture from a coach and/or administrator. All these add up to a "who cares, they'll never do anything to you anyway" attitude here about cheating.

Concerns about the larger society were an important issue for some students:

> When community frowns upon dishonesty, then people will change.
>
> If our leaders can commit heinous acts and then lie before Senate committees about their total ignorance and innocence, *then why can't I cheat a little?*
>
> In today's world you do anything to be above the competition.

In general, students found ready targets on which to blame their behavior and condemnation of the condemners was a popular neutralization strategy.

The Appeal to Higher Loyalties

The appeal to higher loyalties involves neutralizing "internal and external controls . . . by sacrificing the demands of the larger society for the demands of the smaller social groups to which the [offender] belongs. [D]eviation from certain norms may occur not because the norms are rejected but because other norms, held to be more pressing or involving a higher loyalty, are accorded precedence" (Sykes and Matza 1957:669). For example, a difficult conflict for some students is balancing the desire to help a friend against the institution's rules on cheating. The student may not challenge the rules, but rather views the need to help a friend, fellow fraternity/sorority member, or roommate to be a greater obligation which justifies the cheating behavior.

Fraternities and sororities were singled out as a network where such behavior occurs with some frequency. For example, a female student at a small university in New England observed:

> There's a lot of cheating within the Greek system. Of all the cheating I've seen, it's often been men and women in fraternities and sororities who exchange information or cheat.

The appeal to higher loyalties was particularly evident in student reactions concerning the reporting of cheating violations. Although fourteen of the thirty-one schools participating in this research had explicit honor codes that generally require students to report cheating violations they observe, less than one-third (32.3 percent) indicated that they were likely to do so. When asked if they would report a friend, only 4 percent said they would and most students felt that they should not be expected to do so. Typical student comments included:

> Students should not be sitting in judgment of their own peers.
>
> The university is not a police state.

For some this decision was very practical:

> A lot of students, 50 percent, wouldn't because they know they will probably cheat at some time themselves.

For others, the decision would depend on the severity of the violation they observed and many would not report what they consider to be minor violations, even those explicitly covered by the school's honor code or policies on academic honesty. Explicit examination or test cheating was one of the few violations where students exhibited any consensus concerning the need to report violations. Yet even in this case many students felt other factors must be considered. For example, a senior at a woman's college in the Northeast commented:

> It would depend on the circumstances. If someone was hurt, *very likely*. If there was no single victim in the case, if the victim was [the] institution . . . , then *very unlikely*.

Additional evidence of the strength of the appeal to higher loyalties as a neutralization technique is found in the fact that almost one in five respondents (17.8 percent) reported that they had helped someone cheat on an examination or major test. The percentage who have helped others cheat on papers and other assignments is likely much higher. Twenty-six percent of those students who helped someone else cheat on a test reported that they had never cheated on a test themselves, adding support to the argument that peer pressure to help friends is quite strong.

CONCLUSIONS

From this research it is clear that college students use a variety of neutralization techniques to rationalize their cheating behavior, deflecting blame to others and/or the situational context, and the framework of Sykes and Matza (1957) seems well-supported when student explanations of cheating behavior are analyzed. Unlike prior research (LaBeff et al. 1990), however, the present findings suggest that students employ all of the techniques described by Sykes and Matza, including denial of injury and denial of victim. Although there was very limited evidence of the use of denial of victim, denial of injury was not uncommon. Many students felt that some forms of cheating were victimless crimes, particularly on assignments that accounted for a small percentage of the total course grade. The present research does affirm LaBeff et al.'s finding that denial of responsibility and condemnation of condemners are the neutralization techniques most frequently utilized by college students. Appeal to higher loyalties is particularly evident in neutralizing institutional expectations that students report cheating violations they observe.

REFERENCES

LaBeff, Emily E., Robert E. Clark, Valerie J. Haines, and George M. Diekhoff. 1990. "Situational Ethics and College Student Cheating." *Sociological Inquiry* 60:190–198.

Norris, Terry D., and Richard A. Dodder. 1979. "A Behavioral Continuum Synthesizing Neutralization Theory, Situational Ethics and Juvenile Delinquency." *Adolescence* 55:545–555.

Sykes, Gresham M., and David Matza. 1957. "Techniques of Neutralization: A Theory of Delinquency." *American Sociological Review* 22:664–670.

READING 5-6

Denying the Guilty Mind

Michael L. Benson

The present study treats the accounts given by a sample of convicted white-collar offenders, focusing specifically on the techniques they use to deny their own criminality. The emphasis is on general patterns and regularities in the data. The central research question is: How do convicted white-collar offenders account for their adjudication as criminals? While researchers have frequently expressed outrage at the denial of criminality that is thought to be typical of white-collar criminals, few attempts have been made to understand how this process occurs or to relate it to general deviance theory. Rather, researchers have all too often concentrated on morally condemning offenders (Clinard and Yeager 1978).

Over 30 years ago, Sutherland (1949:222, 225) wrote,

> Businessmen develop rationalizations which conceal the fact of crime . . . . Even when they violate the law, they do not conceive of themselves as criminals . . . . Businessmen fight whenever words that tend to break down this rationalization are used.

This view of white-collar offenders has continued to the present day (Geis 1982; Meier and Geis 1982). Indeed, failure to confront and penetrate the rationalizations used by white-collar offenders and to get beyond a sympathetic view of the individual offender is considered by some to be one of the reasons for the continued widespread prevalence of white-collar crimes (Geis 1982:55–57; Meier and Geis 1982:98). In addition, others have argued that the leniency with which white-collar criminals

are treated by the justice system derives in part from their ability to evoke sympathy from judges (Conklin 1977).

THE STUDY

This study is based primarily on interviews conducted with a sample of 30 convicted white-collar offenders. The interviews were supplemented by an examination of the files maintained on 80 white-collar offenders and by further interviews with federal probation officers, federal judges, Assistant U.S. Attorneys, and defense attorneys specializing in white-collar cases.

The sample of interviewed offenders was essentially self-selected. A letter which introduced the researcher and described the nature of the study was sent to most of the 80 offenders in the sample.[1] The letter indicated that the researcher was interested in the subject's impressions of the way in which his case was handled and in the effect that conviction had on his self-image and life prospects.[2] Offenders were assured that their remarks would not be attributable to them as individuals. The proposed interviews would be open-ended and unstructured.

In light of the small and nonrandom nature of the sample, the results reported here must be viewed as provisional. There are no systematic differences between the offenders who agreed to be

---

[1] Some offenders whose files were examined were not available to be interviewed, because they were incarcerated at the time of the study.
[2] All of the offenders who consented to being interviewed were men.

interviewed and those who did not in terms of their social and offense characteristics, but there is some likelihood that the interviewees differed psychologically or experientially from those who refused to participate.

The letter inviting participation in the study was sent from the Probation Office, and it is possible that some offenders viewed their participation as a way of ingratiating themselves with their respective probation officers. They also may have felt under some coercion to participate in the study. While these potential sources of bias cannot be completely ruled out, it is the researcher's impression that most of the interviewees agreed to participate because they welcomed an opportunity to express their views on the criminal justice system in a confidential and nonjudgmental forum.

In the interviews no attempt was made to challenge the explanations or rationalizations given by offenders regarding their offenses. Rather, offenders were encouraged to talk of themselves and their feelings regarding the case and they were allowed to focus on the aspects they considered to be most important. This approach was followed for two reasons: first, the sensitive nature of the subject matter under discussion did not permit the use of an interrogatory or inquisitorial style. The emotional trauma wrought by conviction was, indeed, evident in many of the interviews and, considering the voluntary nature of the interviews, to challenge the subjects seemed insensitive and unnecessary. Second, the goal of the study was not to determine how strong the rationalizations were, nor was it to bring about a "rehabilitative" awareness in the offender of the criminality of past acts. Rather, it was to determine how offenders account for their actions to themselves and to significant others, who it is assumed are unlikely to challenge or refute their explanations.

The Offenders

For the purposes of this study, white-collar offenders were those convicted of economic offenses committed through the use of indirection, fraud, or collusion (Shapiro 1980). The offenses represented in the sample are those that are usually thought of as presumptively white-collar offenses, such as securities and exchange fraud, antitrust violations, embezzlement, false claims and statements, and tax violations. In terms of socioeconomic status, the sample ranges from a formerly successful practitioner of international law to a man currently self-employed as a seller of jewelry trinkets. For some offenders, particularly licensed professionals and those employed in the public sector, conviction was accompanied by loss of occupation and other major changes in life-style. For others, such as businessmen and those employed in the private sector, conviction was not accompanied by collateral disabilities other than the expense and trauma of criminal justice processing (Benson 1984).

DENYING THE GUILTY MIND

In court, defense lawyers are fond of presenting white-collar offenders as having suffered enough by virtue of the humiliation of public adjudication as criminals. On the other hand, prosecutors present them as cavalier individuals who arrogantly ignore the law and brush off its weak efforts to stigmatize them as criminals. Neither of these stereotypes is entirely accurate. The subjective effects of conviction on white-collar offenders are varied and complex. One suspects that this is true of all offenders, not only white-collar offenders.

The emotional responses of offenders to conviction have not been the subject of extensive research. However, insofar as an individual's emotional response to adjudication may influence the deterrent or crime-reinforcing impact of punishment on him or her, further study might reveal why some offenders stop their criminal behavior while others go on to careers in crime (Casper 1978:80).

Although the offenders displayed a variety of different emotions with respect to their experiences, they were nearly unanimous in denying basic criminality. To see how white-collar offenders justify and excuse their crimes, we turn to their accounts. The small number of cases rules out the use of any elaborate classification techniques. Nonetheless, it is useful to group offenders by offense when presenting their interpretations.

Antitrust Violators

Four of the offenders had been convicted of antitrust violations, all in the same case involving the building and contracting industry. Four major themes characterized their accounts. First, antitrust offenders focused on the everyday character and historical continuity of their offenses.

> It was a way of doing business before we even got into the business. So it was like why do you brush your teeth in the morning or something . . . . It was part of the everyday . . . . It was a method of survival.

The offenders argued that they were merely following established and necessary industry practices. These practices were presented as being necessary for the well-being of the industry as a whole, not to mention their own companies. Further, they argued that cooperation among competitors was either allowed or actively promoted by the government in other industries and professions.

The second theme emphasized by the offenders was the characterization of their actions as blameless. They admitted talking to competitors and admitted submitting intentionally noncompetitive bids. However, they presented these practices as being done not for the purpose of rigging prices nor to make exorbitant profits. Rather, the everyday practices of the industry required them to occasionally submit bids on projects they really did not want to have. To avoid the effort and expense of preparing full-fledged bids, they would call a competitor to get a price to use. Such a situation might arise, for example, when a company already had enough work for the time being, but was asked by a valued customer to submit a bid anyway.

> All you want to do is show a bid, so that in some cases it was for as small a reason as getting your deposit back on the plans and specs. So you just simply have no interest in getting the job and just call to see if you can find someone to give you a price to use, so that you didn't have to go through the expense of an entire bid preparation. Now that is looked on very

unfavorably, and it is a technical violation, but it was strictly an opportunity to keep your name in front of a desired customer. Or you may find yourself in a situation where somebody is doing work for a customer, has done work for many, many years and is totally acceptable, totally fair. There is no problem. But suddenly they (the customer) get an idea that they ought to have a few tentative figures, and you're called in, and you are in a moral dilemma. There's really no reason for you to attempt to compete in that circumstance. And so there was a way to back out.

Managed in this way, an action that appears on the surface to be a straightforward and conscious violation of antitrust regulations becomes merely a harmless business practice that happens to be a "technical violation." The offender can then refer to his personal history to verify his claim that, despite technical violations, he is in reality a law-abiding person. In the words of one offender, "Having been in the business for 33 years, you don't just automatically become a criminal overnight."

Third, offenders were very critical of the motives and tactics of prosecutors. Prosecutors were accused of being motivated solely by the opportunity for personal advancement presented by winning a big case. Further, they were accused of employing prosecution selectively and using tactics that allowed the most culpable offenders to go free. The Department of Justice was painted as using antitrust prosecutions for political purposes.

The fourth theme emphasized by the antitrust offenders involved a comparison between their crimes and the crimes of street criminals. Antitrust offenses differ in their mechanics from street crimes in that they are not committed in one place and at one time. Rather, they are spatially and temporally diffuse and are intermingled with legitimate behavior. In addition, the victims of antitrust offenses tend not to be identifiable individuals, as is the case with most street crimes. These characteristics are used by antitrust violators to contrast their own behavior with that of common stereotypes of criminality. Real crimes are pictured as discrete events that have beginnings and ends and involve individuals who directly and purposely victimize someone else in a particular place and at particular time.

> It certainly wasn't a premediated type of thing in our cases as far as I can see . . . . To me it's different than _____ and I sitting down and we plan, well, we're going to rob this bank tomorrow and premeditatedly go in there . . . . That wasn't the case at all . . . . It wasn't like sitting down and planning I'm going to rob this bank type of thing . . . . It was just a common everyday way of doing business and surviving.

A consistent thread running through all of the interviews was the necessity for antitrust-like practices, given the realities of the business world. Offenders seemed to define the situation in such a manner that two sets of rules could be seen to apply. On the one hand, there are the legislatively determined rules—laws—which govern how one is to conduct one's business affairs. On the other hand, there is a higher set of rules based on the concepts of profit and survival, which are taken to define what it means to be in business in a capitalistic society. These rules do not just regulate behavior; rather, they constitute or create the behavior in question. If one is not trying to make a profit or trying to keep one's business going, then one is not really "in business." Following Searle (1969:33–41), the former type of rule can be called a regulative rule and the latter type a constitutive rule. In certain situations, one may have to violate a regulative rule in order to conform to the more basic constitutive rule of the activity in which one is engaged.

This point can best be illustrated through the use of an analogy involving competitive games. Trying to win is a constitutive rule of competitive games in the sense that if one is not trying to win, one is not really playing the game. In competitive games, situations may arise where a player deliberately breaks the rules even though he knows or expects he will be caught. In the game of basketball, for example, a player may deliberately foul an opponent to prevent him from making a sure basket. In this instance, one would understand that the fouler was trying to win by gambling that the opponent would not make the free throws. The player violates

the rule against fouling in order to follow the higher rule of trying to win.

Trying to make a profit or survive in business can be thought of as a constitutive rule of capitalist economies. The laws that govern *how* one is allowed to make a profit are regulative rules, which can understandably be subordinated to the rules of trying to survive and profit. From the offender's point of view, he is doing what businessmen in our society are supposed to do—that is, stay in business and make a profit. Thus, an individual who violates society's laws or regulations in certain situations may actually conceive of himself as thereby acting more in accord with the central ethos of his society than if he had been a strict observer of its law. One might suggest, following Denzin (1977), that for businessmen in the building and contracting industry, an informal structure exists below the articulated legal structure, one which frequently supersedes the legal structure. The informal structure may define as moral and "legal" certain actions that the formal legal structure defines as immoral and "illegal."

Tax Violators

Six of the offenders interviewed were convicted of income tax violations. Like antitrust violators, tax violators can rely upon the complexity of the tax laws and an historical tradition in which cheating on taxes is not really criminal. Tax offenders would claim that everybody cheats somehow on their taxes and present themselves as victims of an unlucky break, because they got caught.

> Everybody cheats on their income tax, 95% of the people. Even if it's for ten dollars it's the same principle. I didn't cheat. I just didn't know how to report it.

The widespread belief that cheating on taxes is endemic helps to lend credence to the offender's claim to have been singled out and to be no more guilty than most people.

Tax offenders were more likely to have acted as individuals rather than as part of a group and, as a result, were more prone to account for their offenses by referring to them as either mistakes or the product of special circumstances. Violations were presented as simple errors which resulted from ignorance and poor recordkeeping. Deliberate intention to steal from the government for personal benefit was denied.

> I didn't take the money. I have no bank account to show for all this money, where all this money is at that I was supposed to have. They never found the money, ever. There is no Swiss bank account, believe me.
>
> My records were strictly one big mess. That's all it was. If only I had an accountant, this wouldn't even of happened. No way in God's creation would this ever have happened.

Other offenders would justify their actions by admitting that they were wrong while painting their motives as altruistic rather than criminal. Criminality was denied because they did not set out to deliberately cheat the government for their own personal gain. Like the antitrust offenders discussed above, one tax violator distinguished between his own crime and the crimes of real criminals.

> I'm not a criminal. That is, I'm not a criminal from the standpoint of taking a gun and doing this and that. I'm a criminal from the standpoint of making a mistake, a serious mistake. . . . The thing that really got me involved in it is my feeling for the employees here, certain employees that are my right hand. In order to save them a certain amount of taxes and things like that, I'd extend money to them in cash, and the money came from these sources that I took it from. You know, cash sales and things of that nature, but practically all of it was turned over to the employees, because of my feeling for them.

All of the tax violators pointed out that they had no intention of deliberately victimizing the government. None of them denied the legitimacy of the tax laws, nor did they claim that they cheated because the government is not representative of the people (Conklin 1977:99). Rather, as a result of ignorance or for altruistic reasons, they made decisions which turned out to be criminal when viewed from the perspective of the law. While they acknowledged the technical criminality of their actions, they tried to show that what they did was not criminally motivated.

Violations of Financial Trust

Four offenders were involved in violations of financial trust. Three were bank officers who embezzled or misapplied funds, and the fourth was a union official who embezzled from a union pension fund. Perhaps because embezzlement is one crime in this sample that can be considered *mala in se,* these offenders were much more forthright about their crimes. Like the other offenders, the embezzlers would not go so far as to say "I am a criminal," but they did say "What I did was wrong, was criminal, and I knew it was." Thus, the embezzlers were unusual in that they explicitly admitted responsibility for their crimes. Two of the offenders clearly fit Cressey's scheme as persons with financial problems who used their positions to convert other people's money to their own use.

Unlike tax evasion, which can be excused by reference to the complex nature of tax regulations or antitrust violations, which can be justified as for the good of the organization as a whole, embezzlement requires deliberate action on the part of the offender and is almost inevitably committed for personal reasons. The crime of embezzlement, therefore, cannot be accounted for by using the same techniques that tax violators or antitrust violators do. The act itself can only be explained by showing that one was under extraordinary circumstances which explain one's uncharacteristic behavior. Three of the offenders referred explicitly to extraordinary circumstances and presented the offense as an aberration in their life history. For example, one offender described his situation in this manner:

> As a kid, I never even—you know kids will sometimes shoplift from the dime store—I never even did that. I had never stolen a thing in my life and that was what was so unbelieveable about the whole thing, but there were some psychological and personal questions that I wasn't dealing with very well. I wasn't terribly happily married. I was married to a very strong-willed woman and it just wasn't working out.

The offender in this instance goes on to explain how, in an effort to impress his wife, he lived beyond his means and fell into debt.

A structural characteristic of embezzlement also helps the offender demonstrate his essential lack of criminality. Embezzlement is integrated into ordinary occupational routines. The illegal action does not stand out clearly against the surrounding set of legal actions. Rather, there is a high degree of surface correspondence between legal and illegal behavior. To maintain this correspondence, the offender must exercise some restraint when committing his crime. The embezzler must be discrete in his stealing; he cannot take all of the money available to him without at the same time revealing the crime. Once exposed, the offender can point to this restraint on his part as evidence that he is not really a criminal. That is, he can compare what happened with what could have happened in order to show how much more serious the offense could have been if he was really a criminal at heart.

> What I could have done if I had truly had a devious criminal mind and perhaps if I had been a little smarter—and I am not saying that with any degree of pride or any degree of modesty whatever, [as] it's being smarter in a bad, an evil way—I could have pulled this off on a grander scale and I might still be doing it.

Even though the offender is forthright about admitting his guilt, he makes a distinction between himself and someone with a truly "devious criminal mind."

Contrary to Cressey's (1953:57–66) findings, none of the embezzlers claimed that their offenses were justified because they were underpaid or badly treated by their employers. Rather, attention was focused on the unusual circumstances surrounding the offense and its atypical character when compared to the rest of the offender's life. This strategy is for the most part determined by the mechanics and organizational format of the offense itself. Embezzlement occurs within the organization but not for the organization. It cannot be committed accidentally or out of ignorance. It can be accounted for only by showing that the actor "was not himself" at the time of the offense or was under such extraordinary circumstances that embezzlement was an understandable response to an unfortunate situation. This may explain the finding that embezzlers tend to produce accounts that are viewed as more sufficient by the justice system than those produced by other offenders (Rothman and Gandossy 1982). The only plausible option open to a convicted embezzler trying to explain his offense is to admit responsibility while justifying the action, an approach that apparently strikes a responsive chord with judges.

Fraud and False Statements

Ten offenders were convicted of some form of fraud or false statements charge. Unlike embezzlers, tax violators, or antitrust violators, these offenders were much more likely to deny committing any crime at all. Seven of the ten claimed that they, personally, were innocent of any crime, although each admitted that fraud had occurred. Typically, they claimed to have been set up by associates and to have been wrongfully convicted by the U.S. Attorney handling the case. One might call this the scapegoat strategy. Rather than admitting technical wrongdoing and then justifying or excusing it, the offender attempts to paint himself as a victim by shifting the blame entirely to another party. Prosecutors were presented as being either ignorant or politically motivated.

The outright denial of any crime whatsoever is unusual compared to the other types of offenders studied here. It may result from the nature of the crime of fraud. By definition, fraud involves a conscious attempt on the part of one or more persons to mislead others. While it is theoretically possible to accidentally violate the antitrust and tax laws, or to violate them for altruistic reasons, it is difficult to imagine how one could accidentally mislead someone else for his or her own good. Furthermore, in many instances, fraud is an aggressively acquisitive crime. The offender develops a scheme to bilk other people out of money or property, and does this not because of some personal problem but because the scheme is an easy way to get rich. Stock swindles, fraudulent loan scams, and so on are often so large and complicated that they cannot possibly be excused as foolish and desperate solutions to personal problems. Thus, those involved in large-scale frauds do not have the option open to most embezzlers of presenting themselves as persons responding defensively to difficult personal circumstances.

Furthermore, because fraud involves a deliberate attempt to mislead another, the offender who fails to remove himself from the scheme runs the risk of being shown to have a guilty mind. That is, he is shown to possess the most essential element of modern conceptions of criminality: an intent to harm another. His inner self would in this case be exposed as something other than what it has been presented as, and all of his previous actions would be subject to reinterpretation in light of this new perspective. For this reason, defrauders are most prone to denying any crime at all. The cooperative and conspiratorial nature of many fraudulent schemes makes it possible to put the blame on someone else and to present oneself as a scapegoat. Typically, this is done by claiming to have been duped by others. Two illustrations of this strategy are presented below.

> I figured I wasn't guilty, so it wouldn't be that hard to disprove it, until, as I say, I went to court and all of a sudden they start bringing in these guys out of the woodwork implicating me that I never saw. Lot of it could be proved that I never saw.

> Inwardly, I personally felt that the only crime that I committed was not telling on these guys. Not that I deliberately, intentionally committed a crime against the system. My only crime was that I should have had the guts to tell on these guys, what they were doing, rather than putting up with it and then trying to gradually get out of the system without hurting them or without them thinking I was going to snitch on them.

Of the three offenders who admitted committing crimes, two acted alone and the third acted with only one other person. Their accounts were similar to the others presented earlier and tended to focus on either the harmless nature of their violations or on the unusual circumstances that drove them to commit their crimes. One claimed that his violations were only technical and that no one besides himself had been harmed.

> First of all, no money was stolen or anything of that nature. The bank didn't lose any money. . . . What I did was a technical violation. I made a mistake. There's no question about that, but the bank lost no money.

Another offender who directly admitted his guilt was involved in a check-kiting scheme. In a manner similar to embezzlers, he argued that his actions were motivated by exceptional circumstances.

> I was faced with the choice of all of a sudden, and I mean now, closing the doors or doing something else to keep that business open. . . . I'm not going to tell you that this wouldn't have happened if I'd had time to think it over, because I think it probably would have. You're sitting there with a dying patient. You are going to try to keep him alive.

In the other fraud cases more individuals were involved, and it was possible and perhaps necessary for each offender to claim that he was not really the culprit.

The investigation, prosecution, and conviction of a white-collar offender involves him in a very undesirable status passage (Glaser and Strauss 1971). The entire process can be viewed as a long and drawn-out degradation ceremony with the prosecutor as the chief denouncer and the offender's family and friends as the chief witnesses. The offender is moved from the status of law-abiding citizen to that of convicted felon. Accounts are developed to defeat the process of identity transformation that is the object of a degradation ceremony. They represent the offender's attempt to diminish the effect of his legal transformation and to prevent its becoming a publicly validated label.

SUMMARY AND IMPLICATIONS

In effect, offenders attempt to adjust the normative lens through which their offenses are viewed by society.[3] Societal reaction to crimes and criminals

---

[3] The idea of a "normative lens" and much of the following discussion is indebted to a paper presented at an annual meeting of the American Society of Criminology by Wheeler (1984).

varies according to many factors. Although there is no clear-cut consensus on the number and relative importance of factors, it can be assumed that two elements of significance are (1) the seriousness of the offense, and (2) the blameworthiness of the offender. Any offender interested in avoiding being labeled a criminal must be able to minimize the blameworthiness and seriousness of his actions to a degree such that the label "criminal" will be regarded as inappropriate.

Seriousness

The partial legitimacy of the outcomes of some white-collar crimes seems to play an important role in the offender's minimization of seriousness. Some antitrust offenses, tax violations, and false statements made to lending institutions have as their outcomes more than just illegal gain for the perpetrators. They may also shore up a failing business or provide stability in employment. While defrauding the Medicaid system, a doctor or dentist may also be providing at least some much-needed services for the poor. The harm experienced by the victim or victims is balanced against the benefits derived by other uninvolved parties, such as employees and family. The congruence of legitimacy and illegitimacy that characterizes the commission of white-collar and corporate crimes (Clinard and Quinney 1973) may be reproduced in the final products of those crimes and in the justifications presented by offenders.

A belief in widespread illegality was frequently expressed in the interviews. It seemed to be assumed that everybody is unscrupulous in one way or another. This fosters a callousness of attitude with regard to criminal behavior (Denzin 1977). Criminal behavior is seen as acceptable and necessary for survival in the business world. This belief leads to the view that certain types of law violations, since they are normal, are not really serious crimes, which provides a blanket excuse for illegal behavior.

The belief in widespread illegality extends beyond the legitimate business world to society at large, which offenders seem to assume is at the mercy of rampant and unpunished street criminality. The lack of identifiable individual victims has been suggested as one of the reasons for the lack of societal concern with white-collar criminality. This characteristic of white-collar offenses may also be used by offenders before they commit their crimes. That is, the lack of individual victims may help the offender in using the familiar neutralization techniques of denying the victim and the harm.

Blameworthiness

The complexity of the laws and regulations governing the business world seems to facilitate relieving the offender's sense of blameworthiness. Crimes committed out of ignorance or inattention to detail are less offensive to the social conscience than those deliberately committed. Unlike the common street crimes, it is possible to accidentally violate laws that govern the conduct of businesses, professions, and industries. This means that the motives underlying conduct cannot automatically be inferred from the conduct itself. An offense that would be considered blameworthy if committed knowingly may be excusable, or at least understandable, if committed out of ignorance. Complexity gives rise to an ambiguity in the connection between the act and its motive. This may allow offenders to persuade themselves and others that the motive was not really criminal, so therefore the act was not really a crime.

Such a process may even work in advance of the crime when offenders maintain a concerted ignorance of the law or of the activities of subordinates. Katz (1979) has argued that individuals involved in organizational crimes are frequently aware that there is a chance that the crime will eventually come to light. Yet, even though discovery is a possibility, offenders may nonetheless choose to participate provided that they can construct anticipatory defenses that will allow them to eventually deny blameworthiness. Many features of corporate organization facilitate the building of these "metaphysical escapes" (Katz 1979). In other words, offenders may purposely attempt to structure crimes so that the connection between act and motive remains ambiguous and deniable.

Individuals who commit crimes outside an organizational context or who act against organizations (embezzlers) may attempt to reduce their blameworthiness by setting the crime within the context of an otherwise impeccable life. If a crime can be shown to be an aberration, then its importance as an indicator of the offender's true character is dramatically reduced. His or her personality can be shown to have both good and bad points with the good outnumbering the bad. The obvious inconsistency of the offender's conviction vis-a-vis the rest of his life may be handled by family, friends, and perhaps society at large by denying the implications of the offender's actions in order to maintain a consistent and favorable attitude toward him (Geis 1982:97).

As with the use of concerted ignorance, the process of setting the crime within a context of impeccability may be used by offenders prior to the illegal act as a neutralization technique. A lifetime of socially acceptable and desirable behavior in one arena is used to excuse an occasional indiscretion in another.

What needs to be determined is how effective these strategies are in helping the offender avoid stigmatization as a criminal—that is, avoid being thought of and treated like a criminal by others. If certain classes of offenders can commit crimes, be convicted, and yet still, through the use of appropriate accounting strategies, avoid being labeled as criminals, then one of the primary functions of the criminal law and the criminal justice system— the symbolic separation of the offender from the community—is negated. A moral environment is thereby perpetuated in which the symbolic consequences of criminal behavior for some offenders can largely be ignored.

REFERENCES

Casper, Jonathan D. 1978. *Criminal Courts: The Defendant's Perspective.* Washington, D.C.: U.S. Department of Justice.

Clinard, Marshall B., and Richard Quinney. 1973. *Criminal Behavior Systems: A Typology.* New York: Holt, Rinehart, and Winston.

Clinard, Marshall B. and Peter C. Yeager. 1978. "Corporate crime: Issues in research." *Criminology* 16: 255–272.

Conklin, John E. 1977. *Illegal but Not Criminal: Business Crime in America.* Englewood Cliffs, NJ: Prentice Hall.

Cressey, Donald. 1953. *Other People's Money.* New York: Free Press.

Denzin, Norman K. 1977. "Notes on the criminogenic hypothesis: A case study of the American liquor industry." *American Sociological Review* 42:905–920.

Geis, Gilbert. 1982. *On White-Collar Crime.* Lexington, MA: Lexington.

Katz, Jack. 1979. "Concerted ignorance: The social construction of cover-up." *Urban Life* 8:295–316.

Meier, Robert, and Glbert Geis. 1982. "The psychology of the white-collar offender." In Gilbert Geis (ed.), *On White-Collar Crime*. Lexington, MA: Lexington.

Rothman, Martin, and Robert F. Gandossy. 1982. "Sad tales: The accounts of white-collar defendants and the decision to sanction." *Pacific Sociological Review* 4:449–473.

Shapiro, Susan P. 1980. *Thinking About White-Collar Crime: Matters of Conceptualization and Research.* Washington. D.C. U.S. Government Printing Office.

Searle, John R. 1969. *Speech Acts.* Cambridge: Cambridge University Press.

Sutherland, Edwin H. 1949. *White Collar Crime.* New York: Dryden.

Rapists' Vocabulary of Motive

Diana Scully and Joseph Marolla

We view rape as behavior learned socially through interaction with others; convicted rapists have learned the attitudes and actions consistent with sexual aggression against women. Learning also includes the acquisition of culturally derived vocabularies of motive, which can be used to diminish responsibility and to negotiate a non-deviant identity.

Sociologists have long noted that people can, and do, commit acts they define as wrong and, having done so, engage various techniques to disavow deviance and present themselves as normal. Through the concept of "vocabulary of motive," Mills (1940:904) was among the first to shed light on this seemingly perplexing contradiction. Wrong-doers attempt to reinterpret their actions through the use of a linguistic device by which norm-breaking conduct is socially interpreted. That is, anticipating the negative consequences of their behavior, wrong-doers attempt to present the act in terms that are both culturally appropriate and acceptable.

Scott and Lyman (1968) describe excuses and justifications, linguistic "accounts" that explain and remove culpability for an untoward act after it has been committed. *Excuses* admit the act was bad or inappropriate but deny full responsibility, often through appeals to accident, or biological drive, or through scapegoating. In contrast, *justifications* accept responsibility for the act but deny that it was wrong—that is, they show in this situation the act was appropriate. *Accounts* are socially approved vocabularies that neutralize an act or its consequences and are always a manifestation of an underlying negotiation of identity.

From *Social Problems* 31, No. 5, June 1984, 530–44. Reprinted by permission of the University of California Press and the authors. © 1984 by the Society for the Study of Social Problems.

This paper presents an analysis of interviews we conducted with a sample of 114 convicted, incarcerated rapists. We use the concept of accounts (Scott and Lyman 1968) as a tool to organize and analyze the vocabularies of motive which this group of rapists used to explain themselves and their actions. An analysis of their accounts demonstrates how it was possible for 83 percent (n = 114)[1] of these convicted rapists to view themselves as non-rapists.

When rapists' accounts are examined, a typology emerges that consists of admitters and deniers. Admitters (n = 47) acknowledged that they had forced sexual acts on their victims and defined the behavior as rape. In contrast, deniers[2] either eschewed sexual contact or all association with the victim (n = 35),[3] or admitted to sexual acts but did not define their behavior as rape (n = 32).

METHODS AND VALIDITY

From September, 1980, through September, 1981, we interviewed 114 male convicted rapists who were incarcerated in seven maximum or medium

---

[1] These numbers include pretest interviews. When the analysis involves either questions that were not asked in the pretest or that were changed, they are excluded and thus the number changes.

[2] There is, of course, the possibility that some of these men really were innocent of rape. However, while the U.S. criminal justice system is not without flaw, we assume that it is highly unlikely that this many men could have been unjustly convicted of rape, especially since rape is a crime with traditionally low conviction rates. Instead, for purposes of this research, we assume that these men were guilty as charged and that their attempt to maintain an image of non-rapist springs from some psychological or sociologically interpretable mechanism.

[3] Because of their outright denial, interviews with this group of rapists did not contain the data being analyzed here and, consequently, they are not included in this paper.

security prisons in the Commonwealth of Virginia. All of the rapists had been convicted of the rape or attempted rape (n = 8) of an adult woman, although a few had teenage victims as well. Men convicted of incest, statutory rape, or sodomy of a male were omitted from the sample.

Twelve percent of the rapists had been convicted of more than one rape or attempted rape, 39 percent also had convictions for burglary or robbery, 29 percent for abduction, 25 percent for sodomy, and 11 percent for first or second degree murder. Eighty-two percent had a previous criminal history but only 23 percent had records for previous sex offenses. Their sentences for rape and accompanying crimes ranged from 10 years to an accumulation by one man of seven life sentences plus 380 years; 43 percent of the rapists were serving from 10 to 30 years and 22 percent were serving at least one life term. Forty-six percent of the rapists were white and 54 percent were black. Their ages ranged from 18 to 60 years; 88 percent were between 18 and 35 years. Forty-two percent were either married or cohabiting at the time of their offense. Only 20 percent had a high school education or better, and 85 percent came from working-class backgrounds. Despite the popular belief that rape is due to a personality disorder, only 26 percent of these rapists had any history of emotional problems. When the rapists in this study were compared to a statistical profile of felons in all Virginia prisons, prepared by the Virginia Department of Corrections, rapists who volunteered for this research were disproportionately white, somewhat better educated, and younger than the average inmate.

All participants in this study were volunteers. We sent a letter to every inmate (n = 3500) at each of the seven prisons. The letters introduced us as professors at a local university, described our research as a study of men's attitudes toward sexual behavior and women, outlined our procedures for ensuring confidentiality, and solicited volunteers from all criminal categories. Using one follow-up letter, approximately 25 percent of all inmates, including rapists, indicated their willingness to be interviewed by mailing an information sheet to us at the university. From this pool of volunteers, we constructed a sample of rapists based on age, education, race, severity of current offenses, and previous criminal records. Obviously, the sample was not random and thus may not be representative of all rapists.

Each of the authors—one woman and one man—interviewed half of the rapists. Both authors were able to establish rapport and obtain information. However, the rapists volunteered more about their feelings and emotions to the female author and her interviews lasted longer.

All rapists were given an 89-page interview, which included a general background, psychological, criminal, and sexual history, attitude scales, and 30 pages of open-ended questions intended to explore their perceptions of their crimes, their victims, and theirselves. Because a voice print is an absolute source of identification, we did not use tape recorders. All interviews were hand recorded. With some practice, we found it was possible to record much of the interview verbatim. While hand recording inevitably resulted in some lost data, it did have the advantage of eliciting more confidence and candor in the men.

Interviews with the rapists lasted from three hours to seven hours; the average was about four-and-one-half hours. Most of the rapists were reluctant to end the interview. Once rapport had been established, the men wanted to talk, even though it sometimes meant, for example, missing a meal.

Because of the reputation prison inmates have for 'conning,' validity was a special concern in our research. Although the purpose of the research was to obtain the men's own perceptions of their acts, it was also necessary to establish the extent to which these perceptions deviated from other descriptions of their crimes. To establish validity, we used the same technique others have used in prison research: comparing factual information, including details of the crime, obtained in the interview with pre-sentence reports on file at the prisons (Athens 1977; Luckenbill 1977; Queen's Bench Foundation 1976). Pre-sentence reports, written by a court worker at the time of conviction, usually include general background information, a psychological evaluation, the offender's version of the details of the crime, and the victim's or police's version of the details of the crime. Using these records allowed us to clarify two important issues: first, the amount of change that had occurred in rapists' accounts from pre-sentencing to the time when we interviewed them; and, second, the amount of discrepancy between rapists' accounts, as told to us, and the victims' and/or police versions of the crime, contained in the pre-sentence reports.

The time between pre-sentence reports and our interviews (in effect, the amount of time rapists had spent in prison before we interviewed them) ranged from less than one year to 20 years; the average was three years. Yet despite this time lapse, there were no significant changes in the way rapists explained their crimes, with the exception of 18 men who had denied their crimes at their trials but admitted them to us. There were no cases of men who admitted their crime at their trial but denied them when talking to us.

However, there were major differences between the accounts we heard of the crimes from rapists and the police's and victim's versions. Admitters (including deniers turned admitters) told us essentially the same story as the police and victim versions. However, the admitters subtly understated the force they had used and, though they used words such as *violent* to describe their acts, they also omitted reference to the more brutal aspects of their crime.

In contrast, deniers' interview accounts differed significantly from victim and police versions. According to the pre-sentence reports, 11 of the 32 deniers had been acquainted with their victim. But an additional four deniers told us they had been acquainted with their victims. In the pre-sentence reports, police or victim versions of the crime described seven rapes in which the victim had been hitchhiking or was picked up in a bar; but deniers told us this was true of 20 victims. Weapons were present in 21 of the 32 rapes according to the pre-sentence reports, yet only

TABLE 7-1

COMPARISON OF ADMITTERS' AND DENIERS' CRIMES, POLICE/VICTIM VERSIONS IN PRE-SENTENCE REPORTS

Characteristics	Percent Admitters n = 47	Percent Deniers n = 32
White Assailant	57	41
Black Assailant	43	59
Group Rape	23	13
Multiple Rapes	43	34
Assailant a Stranger	72	66
Controversial Situation	06	22
Weapon and/or Injury Present (includes victim murdered)	74	69

nine men acknowledged the presence of a weapon and only two of the nine admitted they had used it to threaten or intimidate their victim. Finally, in at least seven of the rapes, the victim had been seriously injured,[4] but only three men admitted injury. In two of the three cases, the victim had been murdered; in these cases the men denied the rape but not the murder. Indeed, deniers constructed accounts for us which, by implicating the victim, made their own conduct appear to have been more appropriate. They never used words such as *violent,* choosing instead to emphasize the sexual component of their behavior.

It should be noted that we investigated the possibility that deniers claimed their behavior was not criminal because, in contrast to admitters, their crimes resembled what research has found the public define as a controversial rape, that is, victim an acquaintance, no injury or weapon, victim picked up hitchhiking or in a bar (Burt 1980; Burt and Albin 1981; Williams 1979). However, as Table 7-1 indicates, the crimes committed by

---

[4] It was sometimes difficult to determine the full extent of victim injury from the pre-sentence reports. Consequently, it is doubtful that this number accurately reflects the degree of injuries sustained by victims.

deniers were only slightly more likely to involve these elements.

This contrast between pre-sentence reports and interviews suggests several significant factors related to interview content validity. First, when asked to explain their behavior, our sample of convicted rapists (except deniers turned admitters) responded with accounts that had changed surprisingly little since their trials. Second, admitters' interview accounts were basically the same as others' versions of their crimes, while deniers systematically put more blame on the victims.

JUSTIFYING RAPE

Deniers attempted to justify their behavior by presenting the victim in a light that made her appear culpable, regardless of their own actions. Five themes run through attempts to justify their rapes: (1) women as seductresses; (2) women mean "yes" when they say "no"; (3) most women eventually relax and enjoy it; (4) nice girls don't get raped; and (5) guilty of a minor wrongdoing.

1) Women as Seductresses

Men who rape need not search far for cultural language which supports the premise that women provoke or are responsible for rape. In addition to common cultural stereotypes, the fields of psychiatry and criminology (particularly the subfield of victimology) have traditionally provided justifications for rape, often by portraying raped women as the victims of their own seduction (Albin 1977; Marolla and Scully 1979). For example, Hollander (1924:130) argues:

> Considering the amount of illicit intercourse, rape of women is very rare indeed. Flirtation and provocative conduct, i.e. tacit (if not actual) consent is generally the prelude to intercourse.

Since women are supposed to be coy about their sexual availability, refusal to comply with a man's sexual demands lacks meaning and rape appears normal. The fact that violence and, often, a weapon are used to accomplish the rape is not considered. As an example, Abrahamsen (1960:61) writes:

> The conscious or unconscious biological or psychological attraction between man and woman does not exist only on the part of the offender toward the woman but, also, on her part toward him, which in many instances may, to some extent, be the impetus for his sexual attack. Often a women [sic] unconsciously wishes to be taken by force—consider the theft of the bride in Peer Gynt.

Like Peer Gynt, the deniers we interviewed tried to demonstrate that their victims were willing and, in some cases, enthusiastic participants. In these accounts, the rape became more dependent upon the victim's behavior than upon their own actions.

Thirty-one percent (n = 10) of the deniers presented an extreme view of the victim. Not only willing, she was the aggressor, a seductress who lured them, unsuspecting, into sexual action. Typical was a denier convicted of his first rape and accompanying crimes of burglary, sodomy, and abduction. According to the pre-sentence reports, he had broken into the victim's house and raped her at knife point. While he admitted to the breaking and entry, which he claimed was for altruistic purposes ("to pay for the prenatal care of a friend's girlfriend"), he also argued that when the victim discovered him, he had tried to leave but she had asked him to stay. Telling him that she cheated on her husband, she had voluntarily removed her clothes and seduced him. She was, according to him, an exemplary sex partner who "enjoyed it very much and asked for oral sex.[5] Can I have it now?" he reported her as saying. He claimed they had spent hours in bed, after which the victim had told him he was good looking and asked to see him again. "Who would

---

[5] It is worth noting that a number of deniers specifically mentioned the victim's alleged interest in oral sex. Since our interview questions about sexual history indicated that the rapists themselves found oral sex marginally acceptable, the frequent mention is probably another attempt to discredit the victim. However, since a tape recorder could not be used for the interviews and the importance of these claims didn't emerge until the data was being coded and analyzed, it is possible that it was mentioned even more frequently but not recorded.

believe I'd meet a fellow like this?" he reported her as saying.

In addition to this extreme group, 25 percent (n = 8) of the deniers said the victim was willing and had made some sexual advances. An additional 9 percent (n = 3) said the victim was willing to have sex for money or drugs. In two of these three cases, the victim had been either an acquaintance or picked up, which the rapists said led them to expect sex.

2) Women Mean "Yes" When They Say "No"

Thirty-four percent (n = 11) of the deniers described their victim as unwilling, at least initially, indicating either that she had resisted or that she had said no. Despite this, and even though (according to pre-sentence reports) a weapon had been present in 64 percent (n = 7) of these 11 cases, the rapists justified their behavior by arguing that either the victim had not resisted enough or that her "no" had really meant "yes." For example, one denier who was serving time for a previous rape was subsequently convicted of attempting to rape a prison hospital nurse. He insisted he had actually completed the second rape, and said of his victim: "She semi-struggled but deep down inside I think she felt it was a fantasy come true." The nurse, according to him, had asked a question about his conviction for rape, which he interpreted as teasing. "It was like she was saying, 'rape me'." Further, he stated that she had helped him along with oral sex and "from her actions, she was enjoying it." In another case, a 34-year-old man convicted of abducting and raping a 15-year old teenager at knife point as she walked on the beach, claimed it was a pickup. This rapist said women like to be overpowered before sex, but to dominate after it begins.

> A man's body is like a coke bottle, shake it up, put your thumb over the opening and feel the tension. When you take a woman out, woo her, then she says "no, I'm a nice girl," you have to use force. All men do this. She said "no" but it was a societal no, she wanted to be coaxed. All women say "no" when they mean "yes" but its a societal no, so they won't have to feel responsible later.

Claims that the victim didn't resist or, if she did, didn't resist enough, were also used by 24 percent (n = 11) of admitters to explain why, during the incident, they believed the victim was willing and that they were not raping. These rapists didn't redefine their acts until some time after the crime. For example, an admitter who used a bayonet to threaten his victim, an employee of the store he had been robbing, stated:

> At the time I didn't think it was rape. I just asked her nicely and she didn't resist. I never considered prison. I just felt like I had met a friend. It took about five years of reading and going to school to change my mind about whether it was rape. I became familar with the subtlety of violence. But at the time, I believed that as long as I didn't hurt anyone it wasn't wrong. At the time, I didn't think I would go to prison, I thought I would beat it.

Another typical case involved a gang rape in which the victim was abducted at knife point as she walked home about midnight. According to two of the rapists, both of whom were interviewed, at the time they had thought the victim had willingly accepted a ride from the third rapist (who was not interviewed). They claimed the victim didn't resist and one reported her as saying she would do anything if they would take her home. In this rapist's view, "She acted like she enjoyed it, but maybe she was just acting. She wasn't crying, she was engaging in it." He reported that she had been friendly to the rapist who abducted her and, claiming not to have a home phone, she gave him her office number—a tactic eventually used to catch the three. In retrospect, this young man had decided, "She was scared and just relaxed and enjoyed it to avoid getting hurt." Note, however, that while he had redefined the act as rape, he continued to believe she enjoyed it.

Men who claimed to have been unaware that they were raping viewed sexual aggression as a man's prerogative at the time of the rape. Thus they regarded their act as little more than a minor wrongdoing even though most possessed or used a weapon. As long as the victim survived without major physical injury, from their perspective, a rape had not taken place. Indeed, even U.S. courts have often taken the position that physical injury is a necessary ingredient for a rape conviction.

3) Most Women Eventually Relax and Enjoy It

Many of the rapists expected us to accept the image, drawn from cultural stereotype, that once the rape began, the victim relaxed and enjoyed it.[6] Indeed, 69 percent (n = 22) of deniers justified their behavior by claiming not only that the victim was willing, but also that she enjoyed herself, in some cases to an immense degree. Several men suggested that they had fulfilled their victims' dreams. Additionally, while most admitters used adjectives such as "dirty," "humiliated," and "disgusted," to describe how they thought rape made women feel, 20 percent (n = 9) believed that their victim enjoyed herself. For example, one denier had posed as a salesman to gain entry to his victim's house. But he claimed he had had a previous sexual relationship with the victim, that she agreed to have sex for drugs, and that the opportunity to have sex with him produced "a glow, because she was really into oral stuff and fascinated by the idea of sex with a black man. She felt satisfied, fulfilled, wanted me to stay, but I didn't want her." In another case, a denier who had broken into his victim's house but who insisted the victim was his lover and let him in voluntarily, declared "She felt good, kept kissing me and wanted me to stay the night. She felt proud after sex with me." And another denier, who had hid in his victim's closet and later attacked her while she slept, argued that while she was scared at first, "once we

got into it, she was ok." He continued to believe he hadn't committed rape because "she enjoyed it and it was like she consented."

4) Nice Girls Don't Get Raped

The belief that "nice girls don't get raped" affects perception of fault. The victim's reputation, as well as characteristics or behavior which violate normative sex role expectations, are perceived as contributing to the commission of the crime. For example, Nelson and Amir (1975) defined hitchhike rape as a victim-precipitated offense.

In our study, 69 percent (n = 22) of deniers and 22 percent (n = 10) of admitters referred to their victims' sexual reputation, thereby evoking the stereotype that "nice girls don't get raped." They claimed that the victim was known to have been a prostitute, or a "loose" woman, or to have had a lot of affairs, or to have given birth to a child out of wedlock. For example, a denier who claimed he had picked up his victim while she was hitchhiking stated, "To be honest, we [his family] knew she was a damn whore and whether she screwed one or 50 guys didn't matter." According to presentence reports this victim didn't know her attacker and he abducted her at knife point from the street. In another case, a denier who claimed to have known his victim by reputation stated:

> If you wanted drugs or a quick piece of ass, she would do it. In court she said she was a virgin, but I could tell during sex [rape] that she was very experienced.

When other types of discrediting biographical information were added to these sexual slurs, a total of 78 percent (n = 25) of the deniers used the victim's reputation to substantiate their accounts. Most frequently, they referred to the victim's emotional state or drug use. For example, one denier claimed his victim had been known to be loose and, additionally, had turned state's evidence against her husband to put him in prison and save herself from a burglary conviction. Further, he asserted that she had met her current boyfriend, who was himself in and out of prison, in a drug rehabilitation center where they were both clients.

---

[6] Research shows clearly that women do not enjoy rape. Holmstrom and Burgess (1978) asked 93 adult rape victims, "How did it feel sexually?" Not one said they enjoyed it. Further, the trauma of rape is so great that it disrupts sexual functioning (both frequency and satisfaction) for the overwhelming majority of victims, at least during the period immediately following the rape and, in fewer cases, for an extended period of time (Burgess and Holmstrom 1979; Feldman-Summers et al. 1979). In addition, a number of studies have shown that rape victims experience adverse consequences prompting some to move, change jobs, or drop out of school (Burgess and Holmstrom 1974; Kilpatrick et al. 1979; Ruch et al. 1980; Shore 1979).

Evoking the stereotype that women provoke rape by the way they dress, a description of the victim as seductively attired appeared in the accounts of 22 percent (n = 7) of deniers and 17 percent (n = 8) of admitters. Typically, these descriptions were used to substantiate their claims about the victim's reputation. Some men went to extremes to paint a tarnished picture of the victim, describing her as dressed in tight black clothes and without a bra; in one case, the victim was portrayed as sexually provocative in dress and carriage. Not only did she wear short skirts, but she was observed to "spread her legs while getting out of cars." Not all of the men attempted to assassinate their victim's reputation with equal vengeance. Numerous times they made subtle and offhand remarks like, "She was a waitress and you know how they are."

The intent of these discrediting statements is clear. Deniers argued that the woman was a "legitimate" victim who got what she deserved. For example, one denier stated that all of his victims had been prostitutes; pre-sentence reports indicated they were not. Several times during his interview, he referred to them as "dirty sluts," and argued "anything I did to them was justified." Deniers also claimed their victim had wrongly accused them and was the type of woman who would perjure herself in court.

5) Only a Minor Wrongdoing

The majority of deniers did not claim to be completely innocent and they also accepted some accountability for their actions. Only 16 percent (n = 5) of deniers argued that they were totally free of blame. Instead, the majority of deniers pleaded guilty to a lesser charge. That is, they obfuscated the rape by pleading guilty to a less serious, more acceptable charge. They accepted being over-sexed, accused of poor judgement or trickery, even some violence, or guilty of adultery or contributing to the delinquency of a minor, charges that are hardly the equivalent of rape.

Typical of this reasoning is a denier who met his victim in a bar when the bartender asked him if he would try to repair her stalled car. After attempting unsuccessfully, he claimed the victim drank with him and later accepted a ride. Out riding, he pulled into a deserted area "to see how my luck would go." When the victim resisted his advances, he beat her and he stated:

> I did something stupid. I pulled a knife on her and I hit her as hard as I would hit a man. But I shouldn't be in prison for what I did. I shouldn't have all this time [sentence] for going to bed with a broad.

This rapist continued to believe that while the knife was wrong, his sexual behavior was justified.

In another case, the denier claimed he picked up his under-age victim at a party and that she voluntarily went with him to a motel. According to pre-sentence reports, the victim had been abducted at knife point from a party. He explained:

> After I paid for a motel, she would have to have sex but I wouldn't use a weapon. I would have explained. I spent money and, if she still said no, I would have forced her. If it had happened that way, it would have been rape to some people but not to my way of thinking. I've done that kind of thing before. I'm guilty of sex and contributing to the delinquency of a minor, but not rape.

In sum, deniers argued that, while their behavior may not have been completely proper, it should not have been considered rape. To accomplish this, they attempted to discredit and blame the victim while presenting their own actions as justified in the context. Not surprisingly, none of the deniers thought of himself as a rapist. A minority of the admitters attempted to lessen the impact of their crime by claiming the victim enjoyed being raped. But despite this similarity, the nature and tone of admitters' and deniers' accounts were essentially different.

EXCUSING RAPE

In stark contrast to deniers, admitters regarded their behavior as morally wrong and beyond justification. They blamed themselves rather than the victim, although some continued to cling to the belief that the victim had contributed to the crime somewhat, for example, by not resisting enough.

Several of the admitters expressed the view that rape was an act of such moral outrage that it was unforgivable. Several admitters broke into tears at intervals during their interviews. A typical sentiment was,

> I equate rape with someone throwing you up against a wall and tearing your liver and guts out of you. . . . Rape is worse than murder . . . and I'm disgusting.

Another young admitter frequently referred to himself as repulsive and confined:

> I'm in here for rape and in my own mind, its the most disgusting crime, sickening. When people see me and know, I get sick.

Admitters tried to explain their crime in a way that allowed them to retain a semblance of moral integrity. Thus, in contrast to deniers' justifications, admitters used excuses to explain how they were compelled to rape. These excuses appealed to the existence of forces outside of the rapists' control. Through the use of excuses, they attempted to demonstrate that either intent was absent or responsibility was diminished. This allowed them to admit rape while reducing the threat to their identity as a moral person. Excuses also permitted them to view their behavior as idiosyncratic rather than typical and, thus, to believe they were not "really" rapists. Three themes run through these accounts: (1) the use of alcohol and drugs; (2) emotional problems; and (3) nice guy image.

1) The Use of Alcohol and Drugs

A number of studies have noted a high incidence of alcohol and drug consumption by convicted rapists prior to their crime (Groth 1979; Queen's Bench Foundation 1976). However, more recent research has tentatively concluded that the connection between substance use and crime is not as direct as previously thought (Ladouceur 1983). Another facet of alcohol and drug use mentioned in the literature is its utility in disavowing deviance. McCaghy (1968) found that child molesters used alcohol as a technique for neutralizing their deviant identity. Marolla and Scully (1979), in a review of psychiatric literature, demonstrated how alcohol consumption is applied

differently as a vocabulary of motive. Rapists can use alcohol both as an excuse for their behavior and to discredit the victim and make her more responsible. We found the former common among admitters and the latter common among deniers.

Alcohol and/or drugs were mentioned in the accounts of 77 percent (n = 30) of admitters and 84 percent (n = 21) of deniers and both groups were equally likely to have acknowledged consuming a substance—admitters, 77 percent (n = 30); deniers, 72 percent (n = 18). However, admitters said they had been affected by the substance; if not the cause of their behavior, it was at least a contributing factor. For example, an admitter who estimated his consumption to have been eight beers and four "hits of acid" reported:

> Straight, I don't have the guts to rape. I could fight a man but not that. To say, "I'm going to do it to a woman," knowing it will scare and hurt her, takes guts or you have to be sick.

TABLE 7-2

RAPISTS' ACCOUNTS OF OWN AND VICTIMS' ALCOHOL AND/OR DRUG (A/D) USE AND EFFECT

	Admitters n = 39 %	Deniers n = 25 %
Neither Self nor Victim Used A/D	23	16
Self Used A/D	77	72
Of Self Used, no Victim Use	51	12
Self Affected by A/D	69	40
Of Self Affected, no Victim Use or Affect	54	24
Self A/D Users who were Affected	90	56
Victim Used A/D	26	72
Of Victim Used, no Self Use	0	0
Victim Affected by A/D	15	56
Of Victim Affected, no Self Use or Affect	0	40
Victim A/D Users who were Affected	60	78
Both Self and Victim Used and Affected by A/D	15	16

Another admitter believed that his alcohol and drug use,

> . . . brought out what was already there but in such intensity it was uncontrollable. Feelings of being dominant, powerful, using someone for my own gratification, all rose to the surface.

In contrast, deniers' justifications required that they not be substantially impaired. To say that they had been drunk or high would cast doubt on their ability to control themself or to remember events as they actually happened. Consistent with this, when we asked if the alcohol and/or drugs had had an effect on their behavior, 69 percent (n = 27) of admitters, but only 40 percent (n = 10) of deniers, said they had been affected.

Even more interesting were references to the victim's alcohol and/or drug use. Since admitters had already relieved themselves of responsibility through claims of being drunk or high, they had nothing to gain from the assertion that the victim had used or been affected by alcohol and/or drugs. On the other hand, it was very much in the interest of deniers to declare that their victim had been intoxicated or high: that fact lessened her credibility and made her more responsible for the act. Reflecting these observations, 72 percent (n = 18) of deniers and 26 percent (n = 10) of admitters maintained that alcohol or drugs had been consumed by the victim. Further, while 56 percent (n = 14) of deniers declared she had been affected by this use, only 15 percent (n = 6) of admitters made a similar claim. Typically, deniers argued that the alcohol and drugs had sexually aroused their victim or rendered her out of control. For example, one denier insisted that his victim had become hysterical from drugs, not from being raped, and it was because of the drugs that she had reported him to the police. In addition, 40 percent (n = 10) of deniers argued that while the victim had been drunk or high, they themselves either hadn't ingested or weren't affected by alcohol and/or drugs. None of the admitters made this claim. In fact, in all of the 15 percent (n = 6) of cases where an admitter said the victim was drunk or high, he also admitted to being similarly affected.

These data strongly suggest that whatever role alcohol and drugs play in sexual and other types of violent crime, rapists have learned the advantage to be gained from using alcohol and drugs as an account. Our sample were aware that their victim would be discredited and their own behavior excused or justified by referring to alcohol and/or drugs.

2) Emotional Problems

Admitters frequently attributed their acts to emotional problems. Forty percent (n = 19) of admitters said they believed an emotional problem had been at the root of their rape behavior, and 33 percent (n = 15) specifically related the problem to an unhappy, unstable childhood or a marital-domestic situation. Still others claimed to have been in a general state of unease. For example, one admitter said that at the time of the rape he had been depressed, feeling he couldn't do anything right, and that something had been missing from his life. But he also added, "being a rapist is not part of my personality." Even admitters who could locate no source for an emotional problem evoked the popular image of rapists as the product of disordered personalities to argue they also must have problems:

> The fact that I'm a rapist makes me different. Rapists aren't all there. They have problems. It was wrong so there must be a reason why I did it. I must have a problem.

Our data do indicate that a precipitating event, involving an upsetting problem of everyday living, appeared in the accounts of 80 percent (n = 38) of admitters and 25 percent (n = 8) of deniers. Of those experiencing a precipitating event, including deniers, 76 percent (n = 35) involved a wife or girlfriend. Over and over, these men described themselves as having been in a rage because of an incident involving a woman with whom they believed they were in love.

Frequently, the upsetting event was related to a rigid and unrealistic double standard for sexual conduct and virtue which they applied to "their" woman but which they didn't expect from men, didn't apply to themselves, and, obviously, didn't honor in other women. To discover that the "pedestal" didn't apply to their wife or girlfriend sent them into a fury. One especially articulate and typical admitter described his feeling as follows. After serving a short prison term for auto theft, he married his "childhood sweetheart" and secured a well-paying job. Between his job and the volunteer work he was doing with an ex-offender group, he was spending long hours away from home, a situation that had bothered his wife. In response to her request, he gave up his volunteer work, though it was clearly meaningful to him. Then, one day, he discovered his wife with her former boyfriend "and my life fell apart." During the next several days, he said his anger had made him withdraw into himself and, after three days of drinking in a motel room, he abducted and raped a stranger. He stated:

> My parents have been married for many years and I had high expectations about marriage. I put my wife on a pedestal. When I walked in on her, I felt like my life had been destroyed, it was such a shock. I was bitter and angry about the fact that I hadn't done anything to my wife for cheating. I didn't want to hurt her [victim], only to scare and degrade her.

It is clear that many admitters, and a minority of deniers, were under stress at the time of their rapes. However, their problems were ordinary—the types of upsetting events that everyone experiences at some point in life. The overwhelming majority of the men were not clinically defined as mentally ill in court-ordered psychiatric examinations prior to their trials. Indeed, our sample is consistent with Abel et al. (1980) who found fewer than 5 percent of rapists were psychotic at the time of their offense.

As with alcohol and drug intoxication, a claim of emotional problems works differently depending upon whether the behavior in question is being justified or excused. It would have been counterproductive for deniers to have claimed to have had emotional problems at the time of the rape. Admitters used psychological explanations to portray themselves as having been temporarily "sick" at the time of the rape. Sick people are usually blamed for neither the cause of their illness nor for acts committed while in that state of diminished capacity. Thus, adopting the sick role removed responsibility by excusing the behavior as having been beyond the ability of the individual to control. Since the rapists were not "themselves," the rape was idiosyncratic rather than typical behavior. Admitters asserted a non-deviant identity despite their self-proclaimed disgust with what they had done. Although admitters were willing to assume the sick role, they did not view their problem as a chronic condition, nor did they believe themselves to be insane or permanently impaired. Said one admitter, who believed that he needed psychological counseling: "I have a mental disorder, but I'm not crazy." Instead, admitters viewed their "problem" as mild, transient, and curable. Indeed, part of the appeal of this excuse was that not only did it relieve responsibility, but, as with alcohol and drug addiction, it allowed the rapist to "recover." Thus, at the time of their interviews, only 31 percent (n = 14) of admitters indicated that "being a rapist" was part of their self-concept. Twenty-eight percent (n = 13) of admitters stated they had never thought of themselves as rapists, 8 percent (n = 4) said they were unsure, and 33 percent (n = 16) asserted they had been a rapist at one time but now were recovered. A multiple "exrapist," who believed his "problem" was due to "something buried in my subconscious" that was triggered when his girlfriend broke up with him, expressed a typical opinion:

> I was a rapist, but not now. I've grown up, had to live with it. I've hit the bottom of the well and it can't get worse. I feel born again to deal with my problems.

3) Nice Guy Image

Admitters attempted to further neutralize their crime and negotiate a non-rapist identity by painting an image of themselves as a "nice guy." Admitters projected the image of someone who had made a serious mistake but, in every other respect, was a decent person. Fifty-seven percent (n = 27) expressed regret and sorrow for their victim indicating that they wished there were a way to apologize for or amend their behavior. For example, a participant in a rape-murder, who insisted his partner did the murder, confided, "I wish there was something I could do besides saying 'I'm sorry, I'm sorry.' I live with it 24 hours a day and, sometimes, I wake up crying in the middle of the night because of it."

Schlenker and Darby (1981) explain the significance of apologies beyond the obvious expression of regret. An apology allows a person to admit guilt while at the same time seeking a pardon by signalling that the event should not be considered a fair representation of what the person is really like. An apology separates the bad self from the good self, and promises more acceptable behavior in the future. When apologizing, an individual is attempting to say: "I have repented and should be forgiven," thus making it appear that no further rehabilitation is required.

The "nice guy" statements of the admitters reflected an attempt to communicate a message consistent with Schlenker's and Darby's analysis of apologies. It was an attempt to convey that rape was not a representation of their "true" self. For example,

> It's different from anything else I've ever done. I feel more guilt about this. It's not consistent with me. When I talk about it, it's like being assaulted myself. I don't know why I did it, but once I started, I got into it. Armed robbery was a way of life for me, but not rape. I feel like I wasn't being myself.

Admitters also used "nice guy" statements to register their moral opposition to violence and harming women, even though, in some cases, they had seriously injured their victims. Such was the case of an admitter convicted of a gang rape:

> I'm against hurting women. She should have resisted. None of us were the type of person that would use force on a woman. I never positioned myself on a woman unless she showed an interest in me. They would play to me, not me to them. My weakness is to follow. I never would have stopped, let along pick her up without the others. I never would have let anyone beat her. I never bothered women who didn't want

sex; never had a problem with sex or getting it. I loved her—like all women.

Finally, a number of admitters attempted to improve their self-image by demonstrating that, while they had raped, it could have been worse if they had not been a "nice guy." For example, one admitter professed to being especially gentle with his victim after she told him she had just had a baby. Others claimed to have given the victim money to get home or make a phone call, or to have made sure the victim's children were not in the room. A multiple rapist, whose pattern was to break in and attack sleeping victims in their homes, stated:

> I never beat any of my victims and I told them I wouldn't hurt them if they cooperated. I'm a professional thief. But I never robbed the women I raped because I felt so bad about what I had already done to them.

Even a young man, who raped his five victims at gun point and then stabbed them to death, attempted to improve his image by stating:

> Physically they enjoyed the sex [rape]. Once they got involved, it would be difficult to resist. I was always gentle and kind until I started to kill them. And the killing was always sudden, so they wouldn't know it was coming.

SUMMARY AND CONCLUSIONS

Convicted rapists' accounts of their crimes include both excuses and justifications. Those who deny what they did was rape justify their actions; those who admit it was rape attempt to excuse it or themselves. This study does not address why some men admit while others deny, but future research might address this question. This paper does provide insight on how men who are sexually aggressive or violent construct reality, describing the different strategies of admitters and deniers.

Admitters expressed the belief that rape was morally reprehensible. But they explained themselves and their acts by appealing to forces beyond their control, forces which reduced their capacity to act rationally and thus compelled them to rape. Two types of excuses predominated: alcohol/drug intoxication and emotional problems. Admitters used these excuses to negotiate a moral identity for themselves by viewing rape as idiosyncratic rather than typical behavior. This allowed them to reconceptualize themselves as recovered or "exrapists," someone who had made a serious mixtake which did not represent their "true" self.

In contrast, deniers' accounts indicate that these men raped because their value system provided no compelling reason not to do so. When sex is viewed as a male entitlement, rape is no longer seen as criminal. However, the deniers had been convicted of rape, and like the admitters, they attempted to negotiate an identity. Through justifications, they constructed a "controversial" rape and attempted to demonstrate how their behavior, even if not quite right, was appropriate in the situation. Their denials, drawn from common cultural rape stereotypes, took two forms, both of which ultimately denied the existence of a victim.

The first form of denial was buttressed by the cultural view of men as sexually masterful and women as coy but seductive. Injury was denied by portraying the victim as willing, even enthusiastic, or as politely resistent at first but eventually yielding to "relax and enjoy it." In these accounts, force appeared merely as a seductive technique. Rape was disclaimed: rather than harm the woman, the rapist had fulfilled her dreams. In the second form of denial, the victim was portrayed as the type of woman who "got what she deserved." Through attacks on the victim's sexual reputation and, to a lesser degree, her emotional state, deniers attempted to demonstrate that since the victim wasn't a "nice girl," they were not rapists. Consistent with both forms of denial was the self-interested use of alcohol and drugs as a justification. Thus, in contrast to admitters, who accentuated their own use as an excuse, deniers emphasized the victim's consumption in an effort to both discredit her and make her appear more responsible for the rape. It is important to remember that deniers did not invent these justifications.

Rather, they reflect a belief system which has historically victimized women by promulgating the myth that women both enjoy and are responsible for their own rape.

While admitters and deniers present an essentially contrasting view of men who rape, there were some shared characteristics. Justifications particularly, but also excuses, are buttressed by the cultural view of women as sexual commodities, dehumanized and devoid of autonomy and dignity. In this sense, the sexual objectification of women must be understood as an important factor contributing to an environment that trivializes, neutralizes, and, perhaps, facilitates rape.

Finally, we must comment on the consequences of allowing one perspective to dominate thought on a social problem. Rape, like any complex continuum of behavior, has multiple causes and is influenced by a number of social factors. Yet, dominated by psychiatry and the medical model, the underlying assumption that rapists are "sick" has pervaded research. Although methodologically unsound, conclusions have been based almost exclusively on small clinical populations of rapists—that extreme group of rapists who seek counseling in prison and are the most likely to exhibit psychopathology. From this small, atypical group of men, psychiatric findings have been generalized to all men who rape. Our research, however, based on volunteers from the entire prison population, indicates that some rapists, like deniers, viewed and understood their behavior from a popular cultural perspective. This strongly suggests that cultural perspectives, and not an idiosyncratic illness, motivated their behavior. Indeed, we can argue that the psychiatric perspective has contributed to the vocabulary of motive that rapists use to excuse and justify their behavior (Scully and Marolla 1984).

Efforts to arrive at a general explanation for rape have been retarded by the narrow focus of the medical model and the preoccupation with clinical populations. The continued reduction of such complex behavior to a singular cause hinders, rather than enhances, our understanding of rape.

REFERENCES

Albin, Rochelle. 1977. "Psychological studies of rape." *Signs* 3(2):423–435.

Athens, Lonnie. 1977. "Violent crimes: A symbolic interactionist study." *Symbolic Interaction* 1(1):56–71.

Burgess, Ann Wolbert, and Lynda Lytle Holmstrom. 1974. *Rape: Victims of Crisis.* Bowie: Robert J. Brady.

———. 1979. "Rape: Sexual disruption and recovery." *American Journal of Orthopsychiatry* 49(4):648–657.

Groth, Nicholas A. 1979. *Men Who Rape.* New York: Plenum Press.

Hollander, Bernard. 1924. *The Psychology of Misconduct, Vice, and Crime.* New York: Macmillan.

Holmstrom, Lynda Lytle, and Ann Wolbert Burgess. 1978. "Sexual behavior of assailant and victim during rape." Paper presented at the annual meetings of the American Sociological Association, San Francisco, September 2–8.

Kilpatrick, Dean G., Lois Veronen, and Patricia A. Resnick. 1979. "The aftermath of rape: Recent empirical findings." *American Journal of Orthopsychiatry* 49(4):658–669.

Ladouceur, Patricia. 1983. "The relative impact of drugs and alcohol on serious felons." Paper presented at the annual meetings of the American Society of Criminology, Denver, November 9–12.

Luckenbill, David. 1977. "Criminal homicide as a situated transaction." *Social Problems* 25(2):176–187.

McCaghy, Charles. 1968. "Drinking and deviance disavowal: The case of child molesters." *Social Problems* 16(1):43–49.

Marolla, Joseph, and Diana Scully. 1979. "Rape and psychiatric vocabularies of motive." Pp. 301–318 in Edith S. Gomberg and Violet Franks (eds.), *Gender and Disordered Behavior: Sex Differences in Psychopathology.* New York: Brunner/Mazel.

Mills, C. Wright. 1940. "Situated actions and vocabularies of motive." *American Sociological Review* 5(6): 904–913.

Queen's Bench Foundation. 1976. *Rape: Prevention and Resistence.* San Francisco: Queen's Bench Foundation.

Ruch, Libby O., Susan Meyers Chandler, and Richard A. Harter. 1980. "Life change and rape impact." *Journal of Health and Social Behavior* 21(3): 248–260.

Scott, Marvin, and Stanford Lyman. 1968. "Accounts." *American Sociological Review* 33(1):46–62.

Schlenker, Barry R., and Bruce W. Darby. 1981. "The use of apologies in social predicaments." *Social Psychology Quarterly* 44(3):271–278.

Shore, Barbara K. 1979. *An Examination of Critical Process and Outcome Factors in Rape.* Rockville, MD: National Institute of Mental Health.

Sykes, Gresham M., and David Matza. 1957. "Techniques of neutralization." *American Sociological Review* 22(6): 664–670.

READING 5-8

How Women Experience Battering

Kathleen J. Ferraro and John M. Johnson

Why do battered women stay in abusive relationships? Some observers answer facilely that they must like it. The masochism thesis was the predominant

From *Social Problems* 30, No. 3, February 1983, 325–39. Reprinted by permission of the University of California Press and the authors. © 1983 by the Society for the Study of Social Problems.

response of psychiatrists writing about battering in the 1960s (Saul 1972; Snell et al. 1964). More sympathetic studies of the problem have revealed the difficulties of disentangling oneself from a violent relationship (Hilberman 1980; Martin 1976; Walker 1979). These studies point to the social and cultural expectations of women and their status within the nuclear family as reasons for the reluctance of battered women to flee the relationship. The socialization of women emphasizes the primary value of being a good wife and mother, at the expense of personal achievement in other spheres of life. The patriarchal ordering of society assigns a secondary status to women, and provides men with ultimate authority, both within and outside the family unit. Economic conditions contribute to the dependency of women on men; in 1978 U.S. women earned, on the average, 58 percent of what men earned (U.S. Department of Labor 1980). In sum, the position of women in U.S. society makes it extremely difficult for them to reject the authority of men and develop independent lives free of marital violence (Dobash and Dobash 1979; Pagelow 1981).

Material and cultural conditions are the background in which personal interpretations of events are developed. Women who depend on their husbands for practical support also depend on them as sources of self-esteem, emotional support, and continuity. This paper looks at how women make sense of their victimization within the context of these dependencies. Without dismissing the importance of the macro forces of gender politics, we focus on inter- and intrapersonal responses to violence. We first describe six techniques of rationalization used by women who are in relationships where battering has occurred. We then turn to catalysts which may serve as forces to reevaluate rationalizations and to initiate serious attempts at escape. Various physical and emotional responses to battering are described, and finally, we outline the consequences of leaving or attempting to leave a violent relationship.

THE DATA

The data for this study were drawn from diverse sources. From July, 1978 to September, 1979 we were participant observers at a shelter for battered women located in the southwestern United States.

The shelter was located in a suburban city of a major urban center. The shelter served five cities as well as the downtown population, resulting in a service population of 170,000. It was funded primarily by the state through an umbrella agency concerned with drug, mental health, and alcoholism problems. It was initially staffed by paraprofessionals and volunteers, but since this research it has become professionalized and is run by several professional social workers.

During the time of the research, 120 women passed through the shelters; they brought with them 165 children. The women ranged in age from 17 to 68, generally had family incomes below $15,000, and did not work outside the home. The characteristics of shelter residents are summarized in Table 8-1.

We established personal relationships with each of these women, and kept records of their experiences and verbal accounts. We also tape-recorded informal conversations, staff meetings, and crisis phone conversations with battered women. This daily interaction with shelter residents and staff permitted first-hand observation of feelings and thoughts about the battering experience. Finally, we taped interviews with 10 residents and five battered women who had left their abusers without entering the shelter. All quotes in this paper are taken from our notes and tapes.

In addition to this participant study, both authors have been involved with the problem of domestic violence for more than 10 years. In 1976–77, Ferraro worked as a volunteer at Rainbow Retreat, the oldest shelter still functioning in the United States. In 1977–78, we both helped to found a shelter for battered women in our community. This involvement has led to direct contact with hundreds of women who have experienced battering, and many informal talks with people involved in the shelter movement in the United States and Europe.

The term battered woman is used in this paper to describe women who are battered repeatedly by men with whom they live as lovers. Marriage is not

TABLE 8-1

DEMOGRAPHIC CHARACTERISTICS OF SHELTER RESIDENTS DURING FIRST YEAR OF OPERATION (N = 120)

Age		Education	
−17	2%	Elementary School	2%
18−24	33%	Junior High	8%
25−34	43%	Some High School	28%
35−44	14%	High School Graduate	43%
45−54	6%	Some college	14%
55+	1%	College graduate	2%
		Graduate School	1%

Ethnicity		Number of Children	
White	78%	0	19%
Black	3%	1	42%
Mexican-American	10%	2	21%
American Indian	8%	3	15%
Other	1%	4	2%
		5+	1%
		Pregnant	7%

Family Income		Employment Status	
−$5,000	27%	Full time	23%
$ 6,000−10,000	36%	Part time	8%
$11,000−15,000	10%	Housewife	54%
$16,000 +	10%	Student	5%
No Response+	17%	Not employed	8%
		Receiving welfare	2%

Note:
*Many women had no knowledge of their husband's income.

a prerequisite for being a battered woman. Many of the women who entered the shelter we studied were living with, but were not legally married to, the men who abused them.

RATIONALIZING VIOLENCE

Marriages and their unofficial counterparts develop through the efforts of each partner to maintain feelings of love and intimacy. In modern, Western cultures, the value placed on marriage is high; individuals invest a great amount of emotion in their spouses, and expect a return on that investment. The majority of women who marry still adopt the roles of wives and mothers as primary identities, even when they work outside the home, and thus have a strong motivation to succeed in their domestic roles. Married women remain economically dependent on their husbands. In 1978, married men in the United States earned an average of $293 a week, while married women earned $167 a week (U.S. Department of Labor 1980). Given these high expectations and dependencies, the costs of recognizing failures and dissolving marriages are significant. Divorce is an increasingly common phenomenon in the United States, but it is still labeled a social problem and is seldom undertaken without serious deliberations and emotional upheavals (Bohannan 1971). Levels of commitment vary widely, but some degree of commitment is implicit in the marriage contract.

When marital conflicts emerge there is usually some effort to negotiate an agreement or bargain, to ensure the continuity of the relationship (Scanzoni 1972). Couples employ a variety of strategies, depending on the nature and extent of resources available to them, to resolve conflicts without dissolving relationships. It is thus possible for marriages to continue for years, surviving the inevitable conflicts that occur (Sprey 1971).

In describing conflict-management, Spiegel (1968) distinguishes between "role induction" and "role modification." Role induction refers to conflict in which "one or the other parties to the conflict agrees, submits, goes along with, becomes convinced, or is persuaded in some way" (1968: 402). Role modification, on the other hand, involves adaptations by both partners. Role induction seems particularly applicable to battered women who accommodate their husbands' abuse. Rather than seeking help or escaping, as people typically do when attacked by strangers, battered women often rationalize violence from their husbands, at least initially. Although remaining with a violent man does not indicate that a woman views violence as an acceptable aspect of the relationship, the length of time that a woman stays in the marriage after abuse begins is a rough index of her efforts to accommodate the situation. In a U.S. study of 350 battered women, Pagelow (1981) found the median length of stay after violence began was four years; some left in less than one year, others stayed as long as 42 years.

Battered women have good reasons to rationalize violence. There are few institutional, legal, or cultural supports for women fleeing violent marriages. In Roy's (1977:32) survey of 150 battered women, 90 percent said they "thought of leaving and would have done so had the resources been available to them." Eighty percent of Pagelow's (1981) sample indicated previous, failed attempts to leave their husbands. Despite the development of the international shelter movement, changes in police practices, and legislation to protect battered women since 1975, it remains extraordinarily difficult for a battered women [sic] to escape a violent husband determined to maintain his control. At least one woman, Mary Parziale, has been murdered by an abusive husband while residing in a shelter (Beverly 1978); others have been murdered after leaving shelters to establish new, independent homes (Garcia 1978). When these practical and social constraints are combined with love for and commitment to an abuser, it is obvious that there is a strong incentive—often a practical necessity—to rationalize violence.

Previous research on the rationalizations of deviant offenders has revealed a typology of "techniques of neutralization," which allow offenders to view their actions as normal, acceptable, or at least justifiable (Sykes and Matza 1957). A similar typology can be constructed for victims. Extending the concepts developed by Sykes and Matza, we assigned the responses of battered women we interviewed to one of six categories of rationalization: (1) the appeal to the salvation ethic; (2) the denial of the victimizer; (3) the denial of injury; (4) the denial of victimization; (5) the denial of options; and (6) the appeal to higher loyalties. The women usually employed at least one of these techniques to make sense of their situations; often they employed two or more, simultaneously or over time.

1) The appeal to the salvation ethic: This rationalization is grounded in a woman's desire to be of service to others. Abusing husbands are viewed as deeply troubled, perhaps "sick," individuals, dependent on their wives nurturance for survival. Battered women place their own safety and happiness below their commitment to "saving my man" from whatever malady they perceive as the source of their husbands' problems (Ferraro 1979a). The appeal to the salvation ethic is a common response to an alcoholic or drug-dependent abuser. The battered partners of substance-abusers frequently describe the charming, charismatic personality of their sober mates, viewing this appealing personality as the "real man" being destroyed by disease. They then assume responsibility for helping their partners to overcome their problems, viewing the batterings they receive as an index of their partners' pathology. Abuse must be endured while helping the man return to his "normal" self. One woman said:

> I thought I was going to be Florence Nightingale. He had so much potential; I could see how good he really was, and I was going to 'save' him. I thought I was the only thing keeping him going, and that if I left he'd lose his job and wind up in jail. I'd make excuses to everybody for him. I'd call work and lie when he was drunk, saying he was sick. I never criticized him, because he needed my approval.

2) The denial of the victimizer: This technique is similar to the salvation ethic, except that victims do not assume responsibility for solving their abusers' problems. Women perceive battering as an event beyond the control of both spouses, and blame it on some external force. The violence is judged situational and temporary, because it is linked to unusual circumstances or a sickness which can be cured. Pressures at work, the loss of a job, or legal problems are all situations which battered women assume as the causes of their partners' violence. Mental illness, alcoholism, and drug addiction are also viewed as external, uncontrollable afflictions by many battered women who accept the medical perspective on such problems. By focusing on factors beyond the control of their abuser, women deny their husbands' intent to do them harm, and thus rationalize violent episodes.

> He's sick. He didn't used to be this way, but he can't handle alcohol. It's really like a disease, being an alcoholic. . . . I think too that this is what he saw at home, his father is a very violent man, and alcohlic [sic] too, so it's really not his fault, because this is all he has ever known.

3) The denial of injury: For some women, the experience of being battered by a spouse is so discordant with their expectations that they simply refuse to acknowledge it. When hospitalization is not required—and it seldom is for most cases of battering—routines quickly return to normal. Meals are served, jobs and schools are attended, and daily chores completed. Even with lingering pain, bruises, and cuts, the normality of everyday life overrides the strange, confusing memory of the attack. When husbands refuse to discuss or acknowledge the event, in some cases even accusing their wives of insanity, women sometimes come to believe the violence never occurred. The denial of injury does not mean that women feel no pain. They know they are hurt, but define the hurt as tolerable or normal. Just as individuals tolerate a wide range of physical discomfort before seeking medical help, battered women tolerate a wide range of physical abuse before defining it as an injurious assault. One woman explained her disbelief at her first battering:

> I laid in bed and cried all night. I could not believe it had happened, and I didn't want to believe it. We had only been married a year, and I was pregnant and excited about starting a family. Then all of a sudden, this! The next morning he told me he was sorry and it wouldn't happen again, and I gladly kissed and made up. I wanted to forget the whole thing, and wouldn't let myself worry about what it meant for us.

4) The denial of victimization: Victims often blame themselves for the violence, thereby neutralizing the responsibility of the spouse. Pagelow (1981) found that 99.4 percent of battered women felt they did not deserve to be beaten, and 51 percent said they had done nothing to provoke an attack. The battered women in our sample did not believe violence against them was justified, but some felt it could have been avoided if they had been more passive and conciliatory. Both Pagelow's and our samples are biased in this area, because they were made up almost entirely of women who had already left their abusers, and thus would have been unlikely to feel major responsibility for the abuse they received. Retrospective accounts of victimization in our sample, however, did reveal evidence that some women believed their right to leave violent men was restricted by their participation in the conflicts. One subject said:

> Well, I couldn't really do anything about it, because I did ask for it. I knew how to get at him, and I'd keep after it and keep after it until he got fed up and knocked me right out. I can't say I like it, but I shouldn't have nagged him like I did.

As Pagelow (1981) noted, there is a difference between provocation and justification. A battered woman's belief that her actions angered her spouse to the point of violence is not synonymous with the belief that violence was therefore *justified*. But belief in provocation may diminish a woman's capacity for retaliation or self-defense, because it blurs her concept of responsibility. A woman's acceptance of responsibility for the violent incident is encouraged by an abuser who continually denigrates her and makes unrealistic demands. Depending on the social supports available, and the personality of the battered woman, the man's accusations of inadequacy may assume the status of truth. Such beliefs of inferiority inhibit the development of a notion of victimization.

5) The denial of options: This technique is composed of two elements: practical options and emotional options. Practical options, including alternative housing, source of income, and protection from an abuser, are clearly limited by the patriarchal structure of Western society. However, there are differences in the ways battered women respond to these obstacles, ranging from determined struggle to acquiescence. For a variety of reasons, some battered women do not take full advantage of the practical opportunities which are available to escape, and some return to abusers voluntarily even after establishing an independent lifestyle. Others ignore the most severe contraints

in their efforts to escape their relationships. For example, one resident of the shelter we observed walked 30 miles in her bedroom slippers to get to the shelter, and required medical attention for blisters and cuts to her feet. On the other hand, a woman who had a full-time job, had rented an apartment, and had been given by the shelter all the clothes, furniture, and basics necessary to set up housekeeping, returned to her husband two weeks after leaving the shelter. Other women refused to go to job interviews, keep appointments with social workers, or move out of the state for their own protection (Ferraro 1981b). Such actions are frightening for women who have led relatively isolated or protected lives, but failure to take action leaves few alternatives to a violent marriage. The belief of battered women that they will not be able to make it on their own—a belief often fueled by years of abuse and oppression—is a major impediment to acknowledge that one is a victim and taking action.

The denial of *emotional* options imposes still further restrictions. Battered women may feel that no one else can provide intimacy and companionship. While physical beating is painful and dangerous, the prospect of a lonely, celibate existence is often too frightening to risk. It is not uncommon for battered women to express the belief that their abuser is the only man they could love, thus severely limiting their opportunities to discover new, more supportive relationships. One woman said:

> He's all I've got. My dad's gone, and my mother disowned me when I married him. And he's really special. He understands me, and I understand him. Nobody could take his place.

6) The appeal to higher loyalties: This appeal involves enduring battering for the sake of some higher commitment, either religious or traditional. The Christian belief that women should serve their husbands as men serve God is invoked as a rationalization to endure a husband's violence for later rewards in the afterlife. Clergy may support this view by advising women to pray and try harder to please their husbands (Davidson 1978; McClinchey 1981). Other women have a strong commitment to the nuclear family, and find divorce repugnant. They may believe that for their children's sake, any marriage is better than no marriage. One woman we interviewed divorced her husband of 35 years after her last child left home. More commonly women who have survived violent relationships for that long do not have the desire or strength to divorce and begin a new life. When the appeal to higher loyalties is employed as a strategy to cope with battering, commitment to and involvement with an ideal overshadows the mundane reality of violence.

CATALYSTS FOR CHANGE

Rationalization is a way of coping with a situation in which, for either practical or emotional reasons, or both, a battered woman is stuck. For some women, the situation and the beliefs that rationalize it, may continue for a lifetime. For others, changes may occur within the relationship, within individuals, or in available resources which serve as catalysts for redefining the violence. When battered women reject prior rationalizations and begin to view themselves as true victims of abuse, the victimization process begins.

There are a variety of catalysts for redefining abuse; we discuss six: (1) a change in the level of violence; (2) a change in resources; (3) a change in the relationship; (4) despair; (5) a change in the visibility of violence; and (6) external definitions of the relationship.

1) A change in the level of violence: Although Gelles (1976) reports that the severity of abuse is an important factor in women's decisions to leave violent situations, Pagelow (1981) found no significant correlation between the number of years spent cohabiting with an abuser and the severity of abuse. On the contrary: the longer women lived with an abuser, the more severe the violence they

endured, since violence increased in severity over time. What does seem to serve as a catalyst is a sudden change in the relative level of violence. Women who suddenly realize that battering may be fatal may reject rationalizations in order to save their lives. One woman who had been severely beaten by an alcoholic husband for many years explained her decision to leave on the basis of a direct threat to her life:

> It was like a pendulum. He'd swing to the extremes both ways. He'd get drunk and beat me up, then he'd get sober and treat me like a queen. One day he put a gun to my head and pulled the trigger. It wasn't loaded. But that's when I decided I'd had it. I sued for separation of property. I knew what was coming again, so I got out. I didn't want to. I still loved the guy, but I knew I had to for my own sanity.

There are, of course, many cases of homicide in which women did not escape soon enough. In 1979, 7.6 percent of all murders in the United States where the relationship between the victim and the offender was known were murders of wives by husbands (Flanagan et al. 1982). Increases in severity do not guarantee a reinterpretation of the situation, but may play a part in the process.

2) A change in resources: Although some women rationalize cohabiting with an abuser by claiming they have no options, others begin reinterpreting violence when the resources necessary for escape become available. The emergence of safe homes or shelters since 1970 has produced a new resource for battered women. While not completely adequate or satisfactory, the mere existence of a place to go alters the situation in which battering is experienced (Johnson 1981). Public support of shelters is a statement to battered women that abuse need not be tolerated. Conversely, political trends which limit resources available to women, such as cutbacks in government funding to social programs, increase fears that life outside a violent marriage is economically impossible. One 55-year-old woman discussed this catalyst:

> I stayed with him because I didn't want my kids to have the same life I did. My parents were divorced, and I was always so ashamed of that. . . . Yes, they're all on their own now, so there's no reason left to stay.

3) A change in the relationship: Walker (1979), in discussing the stages of a battering relationship, notes that violent incidents are usually followed by periods of remorse and solicitude. Such phases deepen the emotional bonds, and make rejection of an abuser more difficult. But as battering progresses, periods of remorse may shorten, or disappear, eliminating the basis for maintaining a positive outlook on the marriage. After a number of episodes of violence, a man may realize that this victim will not retaliate or escape, and thus feel no need to express remorse. Extended periods devoid of kindness or love may alter a woman's feelings toward her partner so much so that she eventually begins to define herself as a victim of abuse. One woman recalled:

> At first, you know, we used to have so much fun together. He has kind've, you know, a magnetic personality; he can be really charming. But it isn't fun anymore. Since the baby came, it's changed completely. He just wants me to stay at home, while he goes out with his friends. He doesn't even talk to me, most of the time. . . . No, I don't really love him anymore, not like I did.

4) Despair: Changes in the relationship may result in a loss of hope that "things will get better." When hope is destroyed and replaced by despair, rationalizations of violence may give way to the recognition of victimization. Feelings of hopelessness or despair are the basis for some efforts to assist battered women, such as Al-Anon. The director of an Al-Anon organized shelter explained the concept of "hitting bottom":

> Before the Al-Anon program can really be of benefit, a woman has to hit bottom. When you hit bottom, you realize that all of your own efforts to control the situation have failed; you feel helpless and lost and worthless and completely disenchanted with the world. Women can't really be helped unless they're ready for it and want it. Some women come here when things get bad, but they aren't really ready to be committed to Al-Anon. Things haven't gotten bad enough for them, and they go right back. We see this all the time.

5) A change in the visibility of violence: Creating a web of rationalizations to overlook violence is accomplished more easily if no intruders are present to question their validity. Since most violence between couples occurs in private, there are seldom conflicting interpretations of the event from outsiders. Only 7 percent of the respondents in Gelles' (1979) study who discussed spatial location of violence indicated events which took place outside the home, but all reported incidents within the home. Others report similar findings (Pittman and Handy 1964; Pokorny 1965; Wolfgang 1958). If violence does occur in the presence of others, it may trigger a reinterpretation process. Battering in private is degrading, but battering in public is humiliating, for it is a statement of subordination and powerlessness. Having others witness abuse may create intolerable feelings of shame which undermine prior rationalizations.

> He never hit me in public before—it was always at home. But the Saturday I got back [returned to husband from shelter], we went Christmas shopping and he slapped me in the store because of some stupid joke I made. People saw it, I know, I felt so stupid, like, they must all think what a jerk I am, what a sick couple, and I thought, 'God, I must be crazy to let him do this.'

6) External definitions of the relationship: A change in visibility is usually accomplished by the interjection of external definitions of abuse. External definitions vary depending on their source and the situation; they either reinforce or undermine rationalizations. Battered women who request help frequently find others—and especially officials—don't believe their story or are unsympathetic (Pagelow 1981; Pizzey 1974). Experimental research by Shotland and Straw (1976) supports these reports. Observers usually fail to respond when a woman is attacked by a man, and justify nonintervention on the grounds that they assumed the victim and offender were married. One young woman discussed how lack of support from her family left her without hope:

> It wouldn't be so bad if my own family gave a damn about me. . . . Yeah, they know I'm here, and they don't care. They didn't care about me when I was a kid, so why should they care now? I got raped and beat as a kid, and now I get beat as an adult. Life is a big joke.

Clearly, such responses from family members contribute to the belief among battered women that there are no alternatives and that they must tolerate the abuse. However, when outsiders respond with unqualified support of the victim and condemnation of violent men, their definitions can be a potent catalyst toward victimization. Friends and relatives who show genuine concern for a woman's well-being may initiate an awareness of danger which contradicts previous rationalizations.

> My mother-in-law knew what was going on, but she wouldn't admit it. . . . I said, 'Mom, what do you think these bruises are?' and she said 'Well, some people just bruise easy. I do it all the time, bumping into things.' . . . And he just denied it, pretended like nothing happened, and if I'd said I wanted to talk about it, he'd say, 'life goes on, you can't just dwell on things.' . . . But this time, my neighbor *knew* what happened, she saw it, and when he denied it, she said, 'I can't believe it! You know that's not true!' . . . and I was so happy that finally, somebody else saw what was goin' on, and I just told him then that this time I wasn't gonna' come home!

Shelters for battered women serve not only as material resources, but as sources of external definitions which contribute to the victimization process. They offer refuge from a violent situation in which a woman may contemplate her circumstances and what she wants to do about them. Within a shelter, women meet counselors and other battered women who are familiar with rationalizations of violence and the reluctance to give up commitment to a spouse. In counseling sessions, and informal conversations with other residents, women hear horror stories from others who have already defined themselves as victims. They are supported for expressing anger and rejecting responsibility for their abuse (Ferraro 1981a). The goal of many shelters is to overcome feelings of guilt and inadequacy so that women can make choices in their best interests. In this atmosphere, violent incidents are reexamined and redefined as assaults in which the woman was victimized.

How others respond to a battered woman's situation is critical. The closer the relationship of others, the more significant their response is to a woman's perception of the situation. Thus, children can either help or hinder the victim. Pizzey (1974) found adolescent boys at a shelter in Chiswick, England, often assumed the role of the abusing father and themselves abused their mothers, both verbally and physically. On the other hand, children at the shelter we observed often became extremely protective and nurturing toward their mothers. This phenomenon has been thoroughly described elsewhere (Ferraro 1981a). Children who have been abused by fathers who also beat their mothers experience high levels of anxiety, and rarely want to be reunited with their fathers. A 13-year-old, abused daughter of a shelter resident wrote the following message to her stepfather:

> I am going to be honest and not lie. No, I don't want you to come back. It's not that I am jealous because mom loves you. It is [I] am afraid I won't live to see 18. I did care about you a long time ago, but now I can't care, for the simple reason you[']re always calling us names, even my friends. And another reason is, I am tired of seeing mom hurt. She has been hurt enough in her life, and I don't want her to be hurt any more.

No systematic research has been conducted on the influence children exert on their battered mothers, but it seems obvious that the willingness of children to leave a violent father would be an important factor in a woman's own decision to leave.

The relevance of these catalysts to a woman's interpretation of violence vary [sic] with her own situation and personality. The process of rejecting rationalizations and becoming a victim is ambiguous, confusing, and emotional. We now turn to the feelings involved in victimization.

THE EMOTIONAL CAREER OF VICTIMIZATION

As rationalizations give way to perceptions of victimization, a woman's feelings about herself, her spouse, and her situation change. These feelings are imbedded in a cultural, political, and interactional structure. Initially, abuse is contrary to a woman's cultural expectations of behavior between intimates, and therefore engenders feelings of betrayal. The husband has violated his wife's expectations of love and protection, and thus betrayed her confidence in him. The feeling of betrayal, however, is balanced by the husband's efforts to explain his behavior, and by the woman's reluctance to abandon faith. Additionally, the political dominance of men within and outside the family mediate [sic] women's ability to question the validity of their husband's actions.

At the interpersonal level, psychological abuse accompanying violence often invokes feelings of guilt and shame in the battered victim. Men define violence as a response to their wives' inadequacies or provocations, which leads battered women to feel that they have failed. Such character assaults are devastating, and create long-lasting feelings of inferiority (Ferraro 1979b):

> I've been verbally abused as well. It takes you a long time to . . . you may say you feel good and you

may . . . but inside, you know what's been said to you and it hurts for a long time. You need to build up your self-image and make yourself feel like you're a useful person, that you're valuable, and that you're a good parent. You might think these things, and you may say them. . . . I'm gonna prove it to myself.

Psychologists working with battered women consistently report that self-confidence wanes over years of ridicule and criticism (Hilberman and Munson 1978; Walter 1979).

Feelings of guilt and shame are also mixed with a hope that things will get better, at least in the early stages of battering. Even the most violent man is nonviolent much of the time, so there is always a basis for believing that violence is exceptional and the "real man" is not a threat. The vascillation between violence and fear on the one hand, and nonviolence and affection on the other was described by a shelter resident:

> First of all, the first beatings—you can't believe it yourself. I'd go to bed, and I'd cry, and I just couldn't believe this was happening. And I'd wake up the next morning thinking that couldn't of happened, or maybe it was my fault. It's so unbelievable that this person that you're married to and you love would do that to you, but yet you can't leave either because, ya'know, for the other 29 days of the month that person loves you and is with you.

Hope wanes as periods of love and remorse dwindle. Feelings of love and intimacy are gradually replaced with loneliness and pessimism. Battered women who no longer feel love for their husbands but remain in their marriages enter a period of emotional dormancy. They survive each day, performing necessary tasks, with a dull depression and lack of enthusiasm. While some battered women live out their lives in this emotional desert, others are spurred by catalysts to feel either the total despair or mortal fear which leads them to seek help.

Battered women who perceive their husbands' actions as life-threatening experience a penetrating fear that consumes all their thoughts and energies. The awareness of murderous intent by a presumed ally who is a central figure in all aspects of her life destroys all bases for safety. There is a feeling that death is imminent, and that there is nowhere to hide. Prior rationalizations and beliefs about a "good marriage" are exploded, leaving the woman in a crisis of ambiguity (Ridington 1978).

Feelings of fear are experienced physiologically as well as emotionally. Battered women experience aches and fatigue, stomach pains, diarrhea or constipation, tension headaches, shakes, chills, loss of appetite, and insomnia. Sometimes, fear is expressed as a numbed shock, similar to rape trauma syndrome (Burgess and Holmstrom 1974), in which little is felt or communicated.

If attempts to seek help succeed, overwhelming feelings of fear subside, and a rush of new emotions are felt: the original sense of betrayal re-emerges, creating strong feelings of anger. For women socialized to reject angry feelings as unfeminine, coping with anger is difficult. Unless the expression of anger is encouraged in a supportive environment, such women may suppress anger and feel only depression (Ball and Wyman 1978). When anger is expressed, it often leads to feelings of strength and exhilaration. Freedom from threats of violence, the possibility of a new life, and the unburdening of anger create feelings of joy. The simple pleasures of going shopping, taking children to the park, or talking with other women without fear of criticism or punishment from a husband, constitute amazing freedoms. One middle-aged woman expressed her joy over her newly acquired freedom this way:

> Boy, tomorrow I'm goin' downtown, and I've got my whole day planned out, and I'm gonna' do what *I* wanna' do, and if somebody doesn't like it, to *hell* with them! You know, I'm having so much fun, I should've done this years ago!

Probably the most typical feeling expressed by women in shelters is confusion. They feel both sad and happy, excited and apprehensive, independent, yet in need of love. Most continue to feel attachment to their husbands, and feel ambivalent about divorce. There is grief over the loss of an intimate, which must be acknowledged and mourned. Although shelters usually discourage women from contacting their abusers while staying at the shelter, most women do communicate with their husbands—and most receive desperate pleas for forgiveness and reconciliation. If there is not strong emotional support and potential material support, such encouragement by husbands often rekindles hope for the relationship. Some marriages can be revitalized through counseling, but most experts agree that long-term batterers are unlikely to change (Pagelow 1981; Walker 1979). Whether they seek refuge in shelters or with friends, battered women must decide relatively quickly what actions to take. Usually, a tentative commitment is made, either to independence or working on the relationship, but such commitments are usually ambivalent. As one woman wrote to her counselor:

> My feelings are so mixed up sometimes. Right now I feel my husband is really trying to change. But I know that takes time. I still feel for him some. I don't know how much. My mind still doesn't know what it wants. I would really like when I leave here to see him once in a while, get my apartment, and sort of like start over with our relationship for me and my baby and him, to try and make it work. It might. It kind of scares me. I guess I am afraid it won't. . . . I can only hope this works out. There's no telling what could happen. No one knows.

The emotional career of battered women consists of movement from guilt, shame, and depression to fear and despair, to anger, exhilaration, and confusion. Women who escape violent relationships must deal with strong, sometimes conflicting, feelings in attempting to build new lives for themselves free of violence. The kind of response women receive when they seek help largely determines the effects these feelings have on subsequent decisions.

CONCLUSION

The process of victimization is not synonymous with experiencing violent attacks from a spouse. Rationalizing the violence inhibits a sense of outrage and efforts to escape abuse. Only after rationalizations are rejected, through the impact of one or more catalysts, does the victimization process begin. When previously rationalized violence is reinterpreted as dangerous, unjustified assault, battered women actively seek alternatives. The success of their efforts to seek help depends on available resources, external supports, reactions of husbands and children, and their own adaptation to the situation. Victimization includes not only cognitive interpretations, but feelings and physiological responses. Creating a satisfying, peaceful environment after being battered involves emotional confusion and ambiguity, as well as enormous practical and economic obstacles. It may take years of struggle and aborted attempts before a battered woman is able to establish a safe and stable lifestyle; for some, this goal is never achieved.

REFERENCES

Ball, Patricia G., and Elizabeth Wyman. 1978. "Battered wives and powerlessness: What can counselors do?" *Victimology* 2(3–4):545–552.

Beverly. 1978. "Shelter resident murdered by husband." *Aegis,* September/October:13.

Bohannan, Paul (ed.). 1971. *Divorce and After.* Garden City, NY: Anchor.

Burgess, Ann W., and Lynda Lytle Holmstrom. 1974. *Rape: Victims of Crisis.* Bowie, MD: Brady.

Dobash, R. Emerson, and Russell P. Dobash. 1979. *Violence Against Wives.* New York: Free Press.

Ferraro, Kathleen J. 1979a. "Hard love: Letting go of an abusive husband." *Frontiers* 4(2):16–18.

———. 1979b. "Physical and emotional battering: Aspects of managing hurt." *California Sociologist* 2(2):134–149.

———. 1981a. "Battered women and the shelter movement." Unpublished Ph.D. dissertation, Arizona State University.

———. 1981b. "Processing battered women." *Journal of Family Issues* 2(4):415–438.

Flanagan, Timothy J., David J. van Alstyne, and Michael R. Gottfredson (eds.). 1982. *Sourcebook of Criminal Justice Statistics:1981.* U.S. Department of Justice, Bureau of Justice Statistics. Washington, D.C.: U.S. Government Printing Office.

Garcia, Dick. 1978. "Slain women 'lived in fear.'" *The Times* (Erie, Pa.), June 14:B1.

Hilberman, Elaine. 1980. "Overview: The 'wife-beater's wife' reconsidered." *American Journal of Psychiatry* 137(11):1336–1347.

Hilberman, Elaine, and Kit Munson. 1978. "Sixty battered women." *Victimology* 2(3–4):460–470.

Martin, Del. 1976. *Battered Wives.* San Francisco: Glide.

Pagelow, Mildred Daley. 1981. *Woman-Battering.* Beverly Hills: Sage.

Pittman, D. J., and W. Handy. 1964. "Patterns in criminal aggravated assault." *Journal of Criminal Law, Criminology, and Police Science* 55(4):462–470.

Pizzey, Erin. 1974. *Scream Quietly or the Neighbors Will Hear.* Baltimore: Penguin.

Pokorny, Alex. D. 1965. "Human violence: A comparison of homicide, aggravated assault, suicide, and attempted suicide." *Journal of Criminal Law, Criminology, and Police Science* 56(December): 488–497.

Ridington, Jillian. 1978. "The transition process: A feminist environment as reconstitutive milieu." *Victimology* 2(3–4):563–576.

Shotland, R. Lance, and Margret K. Straw. 1976. "Bystander response to an assault: When a man attacks a woman." *Journal of Personality and Social Psychology* 34(5):990–999.

Snell, John E., Richard Rosenwald, and Ames Robey. 1964. "The wifebeater's wife: A study of family interaction." *Archives of General Physhiatry* 11(August): 107–112.

Spiegel, John P. 1968. "The resolution of role conflict within the family." Pp. 391–411 in N. W. Bell and E. F. Vogel (eds.), *A Modern Introduction to the Family.* New York: Free Press.

Sprey, Jetse. 1971. "On the management of conflict in families." *Journal of Marriage and the Family* 33(4): 699–706.

Sykes, Gresham M., and David Matza. 1957. "Techniques of neutralization: A theory of delinquency." *American Sociological Review* 22(6):667–670.

Wolfgang, Marvin E. 1958. *Patterns in Criminal Homicide.* New York: John Wiley.

STUDY QUESTIONS

1. In what ways do persons with AIDS attempt to pass for normal, according to Rose Weitz's study?
2. What special challenges are faced by persons who attempt to cope with the stigma of AIDS?
3. What research methods were used in Donald McCabe's study of college student cheating?
4. Give one example of each of the neutralization techniques students used to justify their cheating.
5. Critically evaluate the justifications made by corporate criminals in Michael Benson's study.
6. Describe the research methods used in Diana Scully and Joseph Marolla's study of rapists.
7. How did the claims made by the "deniers" differ from those made by the "admitters"?
8. Which theory of deviance best explains the claims of deniers who proffer justifications for their acts?
9. What research methods were used in Kathleen Ferraro and John Johnson's study of battered wives?
10. The wives employed what kinds of techniques to explain their husbands' violent behavior?
11. What kinds of changes led some of the wives eventually to label their husbands deviant?

FIGHTING BACK: ORGANIZED RESISTANCE BY DEVIANTS

Introduction

Most theories of deviance portray deviant actors as powerless in the face of overwhelming stigmatization and discrimination by conforming individuals. (Conflict theory is the exception, insofar as it examines deviance by powerful people and institutions.) Labeling theory, in particular, has depicted deviants as "underdogs" who seek to conceal their deviance from others or who passively accept degrading treatment by other people. This is indeed the case for many deviant individuals, who are powerless to defend themselves. However, some "fight back"—individually or collectively—to challenge the labelers, make a scene in public, reject rules and stereotypes, trumpet positive self-images, and demand their rights. Some deviants have gone so far as to organize in what Edwin Schur (1980) calls "deviance liberation movements," or what opponents might castigate as "immoral crusades." Such resistance became particularly pronounced in the 1970s, in contrast to the more submissive response of deviants in earlier decades (Kitsuse 1980). It is important to carefully examine the ways in which deviants attempt to fight for their interests and change the status quo. This section of the book features studies of several deviance liberation campaigns: organized movements by gays and lesbians, prostitutes, mental patients, the physically disabled, and pedophiles.

Such campaigns struggle to change not only public opinion and official policies but also the *identities* of their constituents. They attempt to destigmatize and validate their behaviors and enhance self-esteem and pride—an "identity politics" directed as much to bolstering their own self-image as to proclaiming their dignity to audiences in the outside world.

Some of these crusades (gays, the disabled) have managed to win significant victories—in building alliances with third parties, generating favorable media coverage, gaining some tolerance among the public, and changing some laws and the policies of some employers and institutions. But this is obviously an uphill battle, fraught with many disappointments and failures along the way. Since deviance is a discredited behavior or condition, any attempt to defend it is likely to be denounced as well. Ronald Weitzer's study ("The Prostitutes' Rights Campaign") identifies a number of variables that shape whether or not a deviance liberation movement will be successful, and the importance of these factors is also evident in the chapters by Mary deYoung, Renee Anspach, and Steven Epstein.

REFERENCES

Kitsuse, John I. 1980. "Coming Out all Over: Deviants and the Politics of Social Problems." *Social Problems* 28:1–13.

Schur, Edwin. 1980. *The Politics of Deviance.* Englewood Cliffs: Prentice Hall.

READING 5-9

The Prostitutes' Rights Campaign

Ronald Weitzer

In the 1970s, groups of deviants began to mobilize to challenge popular stereotypes and discriminatory treatment (Adam 1987; Anderson 1981; Anspach 1979; D'Emilio 1983; deYoung 1988; Johnson 1983). One analyst observed that deviants were "coming out all over," embracing positive self-images and demanding equal rights (Kitsuse 1980:9). Theories of deviance were ill-equipped to explain this new activism. Labeling theory, in particular, tended to portray deviants as "underdogs" who passively accepted humiliating treatment and rarely fought back.

Schur (1980; cf. Mauss 1975) was one of the first to examine collective resistance to labeling in the form of "deviance liberation" movements. Such campaigns confront the standard problems of more conventional movements: mobilizing resources, building effective organizations, locating charismatic leaders, winning third party support, attracting mass media attention, and obtaining favorable responses from the authorities. But they also must overcome a host of problems less salient, albeit not absent, in conventional movements, including stigmatization of the group's life-style, occupation, or condition; low self-esteem among potential movement participants; and major obstacles to organization and mobilization due to fear of harassment from citizens or control agents (Schur 1980: 195–196). Movements of homosexuals, mental patients, drug users, and pedophiles operate under an extremely heavy yoke of disrepute. Not only must they struggle for legal and institutional changes but also for normalization of the deviant status of members/constituents.

The social science literature contains few studies of unsuccessful social movements and of the contemporary politics of prostitution (exceptions include Dominelli 1986; Haft 1974; Hobson 1987; McLeod 1981, 1982; Roby 1969). This article partially fills that gap by analyzing the structure, objectives, and distinctive problems faced by the prostitutes' rights movement in the U.S.[1] Data sources include movement documents, interviews

From *The Sociological Quarterly* 32, No. 1, pp. 23–41, Spring 1991. © 1991 by JAI Press. Reprinted by permission of the University of California Press.

---

[1] Although the literature variously defines "social movement," this campaign can be considered one in that it is an organized effort to promote social change, using both institutionalized and noninstitutionalized means.

with the two most prominent movement leaders, press coverage in the *New York Times* and *San Francisco Chronicle,* 1973–1988, and secondary, survey data. The data show that this movement largely has failed to attract popular support, build alliances with third parties, alter conventional attitudes, and convince authorities of the need for decriminalization.

After outlining campaign claims and goals, I examine its relative failure in comparison with the record of the gay rights movement. Consistent with resource mobilization theory (Jenkins 1983; McCarthy and Zald 1977; Oberschall 1973), I suggest that a critical mass of constituents or alliances with third parties may provide sufficient resources (money, facilities, labor) to compensate for a deviance liberation movement's lack of moral assets, and thus enhance its prospects for success. The prostitutes' rights movement has been crippled by a poverty of moral, material, and human capital.

CLAIMS AND GOALS

The struggle to decriminalize and normalize prostitution in the U.S. emerged in the relatively tolerant climate of the early 1970s:

> The rise of the women's movement, expanding notions of the laws of privacy and equal protection, the encouragement of a number of civil rights lawyers, and a new concern about victimless crimes, all have contributed. Most importantly, an increasingly frank, public discussion of sexual mores has helped lift the shroud of secrecy and ignorance enveloping prostitution and has made the time propitious. (Haft 1974:10)

While the time may have been propitious for the rise of a prostitutes' movement, its success was considerably more problematic.

This study focuses on the most prominent organization in the prostitutes' rights campaign, COYOTE (Call Off Your Old Tired Ethics). COYOTE was formed in San Francisco under the leadership of Margo St. James (a flamboyant former prostitute) in 1973, when no comparable organizations existed elsewhere in the U.S. During

the 1970s a number of COYOTE affiliates appeared, some transitory and others persisting (in Georgia, New York, Massachusetts, Minnesota, and Colorado). Since 1979 COYOTE has also been known as the National Task Force on Prostitution (NTFP). These organizations are affiliated with the International Committee for Prostitutes' Rights, formed in 1985 in Amsterdam, which has sponsored several international conventions on prostitution (Pheterson 1989).

COYOTE insists that prostitutes have basic *rights* to occupational choice and sexual self-determination: prostitution is legitimate work and women have the right to control their own bodies, including sale of sexual favors. Denial of these twin rights constitutes the central grievance of COYOTE, whose chief goals are (1) public education regarding the costs of existing prostitution controls, (2) decriminalization of all aspects of voluntary adult prostitution, and (3) normalization of the occupation and the individuals involved in prostitution (NTFP 1987a, 1984–1986).

Public Education

COYOTE seeks to enlighten the public about the adverse consequences of existing prostitution controls to kindle sentiment for decriminalization. These consequences include (1) cost-ineffective law enforcement, (2) harms caused by criminalization, and (3) unconstitutional laws and enforcement practices.

Enforcement of prostitution laws is seen as both fruitless and a significant drain on limited criminal justice resources. According to the San Francisco Committee on Crime (1971:20), spending on prostitution control "buys essentially nothing of a positive nature, and a great deal that is negative." Atlanta's Task Force on Prostitution (Atlanta 1986) concluded that this spending is a "waste" and the revolving-door arrest and prosecution of prostitutes results in "hardening the individuals, burdening the court system, . . . and adversely affecting police morale." Pearl (1987) found that each of the 16 largest American cities spent an average $7.5 million and a total of $120 million in 1985 enforcing prostitution laws; half of the cities spent more on prostitution control than on education or public welfare, and 5 spent more than on health services and hospitals. The costs were not offset by revenues from convictions. Fines averaged $100, at an average cost per arrest of $2,000. The study suggests expenditures might be more cost-effective if redirected to the control of violent and property crimes.

A second claim is that many of the harms associated with prostitution are attributable to criminalization and that decriminalization would help ameliorate these problems.[2] The illegality of prostitution rather than anything intrinsic to it may increase prostitutes' vulnerability to exploitation by pimps, managers, and other third parties; present opportunities for their drift into criminal street networks; and perpetuate their victimization by customers, strangers, and vice cops (Silbert and Pines 1982).

The movement views many prostitution laws as unconstitutional, either as drafted or enforced (COYOTE 1974c; cf. Decker 1979; Rosenbleet and Pariente 1973). These laws allegedly infringe upon the rights to privacy, due process, free speech, and equal protection; contain vague and overly broad language; criminalize a status instead of behavior; and are enforced primarily against one category of offender (female streetwalkers).

COYOTE claims that the material costs, ancillary problems, and dubious constitutionality of existing controls constitute an impeccable case for decriminalization. Other important considerations, however, receive little attention from movement leaders. Unaddressed is the concern that legalization or decriminalization could give prostitution the state's blessing and perhaps lead to its proliferation; illegality affirms the state's disapproval and may help contain prostitution, which the public seems to value. In short, however costly, ineffec-

tive, or conducive to other social problems, criminalization may serve valued practical and symbolic functions (Boles and Tatro 1978; Gusfield 1963) that, in the public arena, overshadow the instrumental case for reform.

Decriminalization

COYOTE favors full decriminalization, that is, the elimination of all legal restrictions on prostitution.[3] It flatly opposes legalization, whether in the form of registration and licensing, special taxes, compulsory health examinations, "red light" districts, or brothels.[4] Regulations are rejected as likely to perpetuate the stigma attached to prostitution; as inherently "oppressive" (Alexander 1987:211)—maintaining male control of, or being applied only to, women; and as allowing the government to "regulate what a woman does with her own body" (COYOTE 1974a). St. James states, "We want to legitimize prostitution rather than ghettoize it or license it. Any kind of regulation is bad, because it gives the pimps a stranglehold" (Hamilton 1979:2).

Movement leaders point to Nevada as proof positive that legalization should be avoided. Eleven of Nevada's 17 counties permit brothel prostitution; in 1987, 37 legal brothels employed a total of 275–375 women (Stein 1987). According to COYOTE, these women are shackled by local restrictions that seriously limit their freedom and are stigmatized as "known prostitutes." While the controls are indeed extensive and some brothels resemble total institutions, evidence does not show widespread stigmatization. Interviews conducted in Nevada in the mid-1970s (Symanski 1974:357; Stingley 1976b) found popular support for brothel prostitution, and a 1988 statewide poll revealed

---

[2] Other harms commonly associated with prostitution are denied by the movement: that prostitution contributes significantly to the spread of VD, that it is controlled by organized crime, and that prostitutes are AIDS carriers. The first two beliefs have been refuted by most studies, but the last remains controversial.

---

[3] National decriminalization throughout the U.S. is necessary because reform in only some states "will result in marked shifts in the prostitute population to the areas where it is legal" (COYOTE 1978a).

[4] COYOTE proposes that existing business codes be used to confine prostitution businesses to commercial or mixed residential-commercial areas (Alexander 1979).

that 71.3% disagreed (22.4% agreed) that legal prostitution "hurts the state's tourism economy."[5] Residents of rural counties, where prostitution is a significant source of tax revenues, subscribed to this opinion least (only 14.1% agreed). Against this backdrop of tolerance, a minority of elites in the legislature, media, gaming industry, and churches have attempted—unsuccessfully—to repeal legalized prostitution (Taylor 1988).

Some observers argue that full decriminalization would give prostitutes advantages not enjoyed by purveyors of other commercial services. Skolnick and Dombrink (1978:201) note that prostitution "provides a commercial as well as a sexual service. Why should sexual services be exempted from regulation when other consenting commercial activities are regulated?" (cf. James and Owens 1977; Decker 1979; Kaplan 1977; Milman 1980; Parnas 1981). Policy-makers and criminal justice officials tend to reject decriminalization (see below), at best finding attractive only those proposals that include some viable controls, such as health examinations, taxation, and zoning. Similarly, the public is more inclined to support some form of regulation than full decriminalization (see below).

Normalization

COYOTE seeks to alter public stereotypes about and enhance the self-esteem of prostitutes. Its public portrayal of prostitutes challenges common stereotypes: they are ordinary, psychologically well-adjusted people, having normal needs and aspirations.[6] Movement literature insists that these women have "integrity" and "dignity" and that prostitution is valid "work." Yet, highly-charged derogatory labels, such as "hooker," "harlot," and "whore," are also used approvingly by movement activists in an effort to reclaim and strip them of their negative associations.[7] While such terms may indeed have shock-value and garner public attention, they arguably undermine the normalization process and have an alienating effect on the audience.

In the 1970s, COYOTE staged counter-degradation ceremonies—Hookers' Balls, Prostitutes' Conventions, and Hookers' Film Festivals—which celebrated prostitution. These events were designed not only for public consumption but also to transform the consciousness and self-image of prostitutes. Other consciousness-raising activities include COYOTE's "rap sessions," support groups, legal assistance, and other services for prostitutes.

Deviance liberation movements typically face tremendous problems in confronting moral questions. Although it exhorts Americans to "call off your old tired ethics," COYOTE claims that the notion that prostitution threatens the moral order "is difficult to change because it is based on emotion, rather than reason" (COYOTE 1974b). Perhaps because of this difficulty, COYOTE focuses on the instrumental logic for decriminalization discussed above: costly and ineffective law enforcement, harms due to criminalization, and dubious constitutionality. It asserts that once the rational basis for legal reform is accepted, moral concerns will subside.

Although moral objections are rarely addressed by them (Richards 1979), movement leaders occasionally counter with "techniques of neutralization" (Sykes and Matza 1957): (1) reversal of blame and denial of victims: for example, "the real undermining of morality results from making illegal

---

[5] Responses were grouped as strongly disagree (53.7%), disagree (17.6%), agree (9.5%), and strongly agree (12.9%). The poll (N = 1213) was conducted in November 1988 by the Center for Survey Research at the University of Nevada, Las Vegas.

[6] Variation among types of prostitutes in levels of psychological adjustment is found in a study by Exner and colleagues (1977). Evaluations of 95 prostitutes found that housewife prostitutes and streetwalker/addict prostitutes exhibited various signs of psychopathology. Non-addict streetwalkers, however, were not pathological, merely "immature and dependent"; house prostitutes and call girls were well-adjusted, "capable of handling themselves well, manifesting good emotional controls, being well aware of conventionality, and doing well in the occupation of their choice."

[7] COYOTE's logo proclaims it a "loose women's organization." The brochure announcing the Fourth National Whore's Congress in San Francisco in 1987 states, "The word whore is used to stigmatize women and the word prostitute is used to criminalize women. We reclaim and identify with both words and we demand our rights as whores, as prostitutes, and as working women."

conduct engaged in between consenting adults and in which no one is victimized" (COYOTE, quoted in Stingley 1976a); (2) condemning the condemners: for example, those most concerned about immorality are a vocal minority with a "vice-cop mentality" (*San Francisco Chronicle* 1977); (3) denial of responsibility: for example, "to suggest that society's moral fiber is undermined by 'sex-for-pay' but not by promiscuous sexual behavior without pay . . . is logically inconsistent and clearly unsupportable . . ." (COYOTE, quoted in Stingley 1976a). In any case, decriminalization would not imply that prostitution is moral, but only that the state should not legislate morality (COYOTE 1974b; NOW 1973; cf. Richards 1979).

Data presented below suggest that these definitional struggles have done little to normalize prostitution. Nevertheless, the movement hopes to eventually convince elites and the public to reconsider their views, thus producing a more favorable climate for decriminalization—which, could, in turn, lessen the stigma of prostitution. As COYOTE's director suggests, "Once they don't go to jail, they can come out of the closet and become normalized."[8]

IMPACT OF THE MOVEMENT

A deviance liberation movement's success can be measured in part by its impact on popular attitudes, legislation, and the practices of control agents.

Public Opinion

While public attitudes toward the prostitutes' rights movement *per se* have not been surveyed, attitudinal data relevant to its goals are available. These data suggest that a sizeable proportion of the public holds views the movement and much of the scholarly literature consider grossly misinformed (Haft 1974; James 1977; Milman 1980; Wandling 1976),

and that there is public dissensus regarding legalization and decriminalization.[9]

National U.S. data on beliefs about the effects of prostitution are not available, but the findings of a representative Canadian study may approximate American patterns. It reveals that 59% disagreed (16% agreed) that violence rarely accompanies prostitution; 69% agreed (20% disagreed) that prostitution is a major cause of venereal disease (VD); and 60% agreed (11% disagreed) that prostitution degrades prostitutes (Peat, Marwick, and Partners 1984). A study of business, neighborhood, and police groups in Boston shows that 85% of this sample thought prostitution breeds crime where it is concentrated; 70% thought it contributes significantly to the spread of VD; and 77% believed it is often accompanied by muggings and violent crimes (Milman 1980). The movement does not appear to have demystified what it considers popular myths accepted by Americans.

Public attitudes on prostitution's social effects seem to shape policy preferences. COYOTE leaders assert that "a majority of the population supports a change in the law," and that 60–70% believe that prostitutes should have the right to pursue the oldest profession (Alexander 1987:198; St. James 1987:85). Yet virtually every survey fails to substantiate this. Moreover, longitudinal data (Table 9-1) suggest that *the movement has had no positive impact on public opinion* regarding the legal status of prostitution; in fact, attitudes have *hardened* since the movement's emergence.

Evidence in Table 9-1 does not indicate that the public's "predominant attitude" is one of "resigned acceptance, if not actual tolerance" for "what is perceived as a benign form of human eccentricity . . ." (McClosky and Brill 1983:211). The vast majority

---

[8] Interview with Priscilla Alexander, San Francisco, March 16, 1987.

[9] Apparent inconsistencies among some of the findings may be due to the wording of questions and the response options offered. Similar inconsistencies appear in survey data on other kinds of deviance (McClosky and Brill 1983). In the prostitution polls it is rarely clear how "prostitution" is interpreted by respondents, that is, whether it is identified with street prostitution or includes less visible kinds.

TABLE 9-1

ATTITUDES ON PROSTITUTION

"Is it a good idea or bad idea to legalize prostitution to provide more tax revenues and help control the disease and crime that now result from uncontrolled prostitution?"

1971		1983	
Good idea	50%	Good idea	41%
Bad idea	42	Bad idea	54
No opinion	8	No opinion	5

Source: Field polls, May 1971 and March 1983, Field Research Institute.
N = 750, random sample. California sample, 1983 poll.

"It should be legal for a woman to receive pay for sex."

Strongly agree	Agree	Disagree	Strongly disagree
5%	35%	37%	23%

"It should be legal for a man to visit a prostitute."

Strongly agree	Agree	Disagree	Strongly disagree
7%	40%	36%	17%

Source: Illinois Survey Research Laboratory, March–April 1984, University of Illinois, Urbana.
N = 480, random sample, Chicago SMSA sample.

"Tell me how important to society you feel it is that laws prohibiting prostitution be strictly enforced."

	March 1979	March 1983
Very important	42%	47%
Fairly important	23	22
Not very important	18	18
Not at all important	14	10
Don't know/No answer	4	3

Source: Roper Poll, Roper Reports 83-04, March 1983, University of Connecticut, Storrs.
N = 2,000, national sample.

"Do you favor or oppose the legalization of prostitution?"

Favor	23%
Oppose	72
Not sure	6

*Source: Time/*Yankelovich, Skelly, and White, September 1985.
N = 1,014, national sample of registered voters.

"In dealing with prostitution, the government should . . . "

License and regulate it	47%
Arrest or fine the people who have anything to do with it	30
Neither/Undecided	23

Source: Civil Liberties Survey, 1978–1979 (cited in McClosky and Brill 1983).
N = 1,993.

want prostitution laws "strictly enforced." Taken together, these data suggest that a bedrock of support for continued criminalization remains, but a sizeable minority favor some liberalization. The movement has failed to capitalize on this latent support.

Response of the Authorities

Constitutional challenges to prostitution laws occasionally have succeeded. Some courts have ruled prostitution statutes unconstitutional due to gender-biased wording, the right to privacy, lack of demonstrable harm to public safety and health, or discriminatory enforcement against one category of offender, female streetwalkers. But these few victories have not substantially altered prostitutes' treatment by most courts (Hobson 1987; Milman 1980; Murray 1979). Consequently, COYOTE favors statutory decriminalization over piecemeal court challenges.

The legal community is divided on questions of legalization and decriminalization. A 1971 poll of 124 California judges finds a majority (54%) favored legalization (Jennings 1976:1258). Some state bar associations have passed resolutions endorsing decriminalization, and the American Bar Association nearly did so in 1976 (Strobel 1976). Other groups have taken a conservative position. The Federation of New York State Judges, for example, opposed a proposal by the State Bar Association advocating red-light prostitution districts, in part because it considered prostitution a "grave moral evil" (*New York Times* 1986).

Police departments have rarely altered policies in response to movement pressures. One exception was COYOTE's success in 1975 in convincing the San Francisco Police Department to lift its three-day VD quarantine on arrested prostitutes on grounds that customers were not arrested and examined for VD and prostitutes were not a significant source of VD.

Generally, police respond to street prostitution with geographical containment and order-maintenance, rather than vigorous law enforcement (Cohen 1980, ch. 5). But they also tend to reject proposals for liberalization, anticipating that it would increase street crimes (James 1977; cf. Pearl 1987). A small national survey of 41 police chiefs in large cities shows support for intensified enforcement and very little support for alternatives to criminalization (Milman 1980). Only 17% favored total decriminalization, 11% decriminalization of everything but public solicitation, 14% legalization in designated zones, 24% legalized houses of prostitution, and 41% licensing for public health purposes. Similarly, a survey of 88 officers in a small midwestern city finds little support for de facto decriminalization (Wilson et al. 1985). Only 4.5% supported non-enforcement for pimps, 5.7% for street prostitutes, 19.3% for call girls, and 31.8% for clients.

In the legislative arena the most significant reform since the movement's rise is the rationalizing of prostitution statutes (incorporating gender-neutral language and revising some overly vague laws). Changes in the letter of the law have had little affect [sic] on law enforcement practices, however (Hobson 1987:213). Several state criminal justice commissions have recommended decriminalization on fiscal grounds, but mustered little legislative support. No state legislature has seriously entertained formal decriminalization. Legalization of brothel prostitution in Nevada in 1971 was shaped by historical and economic factors unique to Nevada and somewhat removed from the discourse of the prostitutes' rights campaign (Symanski 1974), which it preceded. At the national level, COYOTE lobbied Congress in 1976 for a resolution on decriminalization, to no avail.

Legislators liberally inclined on the issue realize reform efforts would likely be fruitless and might backfire by arousing opposition among constituents. The few attempts made validate this view—for example, California State Assemblyman Leroy Greene's vain efforts throughout the 1970s to win support for legalization. My review of listings under "prostitution" in the indexes to the *New York Times* and the *San Francisco Chronicle* 1973–1988 finds virtually all reported state and municipal activity on prostitution issues has centered on passage of increasingly punitive measures (cf. Parnas 1981).[10] (This activity was often in response to the clamor of constituents.) Frustrated with the legislative record, COYOTE complains that "for most legislators [prostitution] remains a joke except when they think they can gain prominence by attacking prostitutes" (NTFP 1987a:2). As late as 1987 COYOTE was "just beginning to educate legislators," but its leader noted that it is "hard to evaluate whether we're having an effect."[11]

If the authorities have granted few tangible concessions, have they demonstrated acceptance of movement leaders as representing a legitimate set of interests? Gamson (1975) proposes four indicators of official "acceptance" of a movement: consultation, sustained negotiation, formal recognition, and inclusion. In the mid-1970s COYOTE seemed to gain some acceptance among elites in San Francisco in terms of consultation. Informal support was also evident: the police chief, district attorney, and sheriff (among other elites) endorsed some of COYOTE's goals and attended some of its functions. This honeymoon was short-lived. Elsewhere in the country activists are occasionally consulted (e.g., appointment to a task force studying prostitution), but the movement has not been able to sustain acceptance from the authorities. In general, it continues to be regarded as either a rather eccentric "immoral crusade" or a cause offering no political advantages for elites who might spearhead reform on such a politically risky issue. Even in the single state permitting legalized brothel prostitution, legislators and state officials are reluctant to discuss the topic; the governor's executive assistant recently stated that the governor "doesn't have a position on this issue" (Taylor 1988:3). Elsewhere, policymakers' abiding indifference or active opposition

constitutes an almost insurmountable obstacle in the movement's path.

A POVERTY OF RESOURCES

Despite widespread public sentiment that homosexuality is immoral, declining approval of homosexual relations, and extremely low support for the gay rights movement, homosexuals have achieved important gains: judicial victories, passage of gay rights ordinances, repeal of sodomy statutes in many states, tolerance by some church denominations, growing access to political elites, and sympathetic media coverage (see Adam 1987; Barron 1989; D'Emilio 1983). They have affected, *inter alia,* the outcomes of some political campaigns and have influenced AIDS-related policies. These victories should not be exaggerated, in light of political and legal setbacks, but are undeniably significant.

The movement is fortunate to have a broad support base with disposable income, which can be relied on for financial support and mobilized for protest events (e.g., over 200,000 marched in support of gay rights in Washington, D.C., in October 1987). The organizational development of the movement is also striking. More than 3,000 gay organizations exist today, including political action committees, lobbying groups, support networks, and nonprofit foundations. These [were] built in the 1960s on the foundations of preexisting groups—mainly gay bars—which nurtured a collective identity and the growth of a gay subculture (D'Emilio 1983; Adam 1987). Vibrant gay communities emerged in several American cities, providing the movement with unique organizational advantages.

The prostitutes' rights movement lacks both subcultural foundations and material assets. Moreover, its resources have become increasingly scarce over time, partly due to the growth of political and sexual conservatism in the 1980s. In San Francisco, the 1978 assassination of liberal mayor George Moscone brought to power a less tolerant successor, Diane Feinstein. St. James (1989:xix) says the "climate changed" as a result of Feinstein's incumbency and

---

[10] The movement in America has been less successful legislatively than that in England, where it has generated some parliamentary support for decriminalization, culminating in the introduction of bills to eliminate incarceration for soliciting and loitering (McLeod 1982).

[11] Interview with Alexander, March 16, 1987.

suggests this adversely affected COYOTE's resources and ties to liberal elites in the city. Nationally, the 1980s witnessed a decided shift toward political conservatism, a growing intolerance of sexual deviance, and the appearance of AIDS. This changed environment made movement goal-attainment more difficult, but its explanatory power should not be exaggerated. As I show below, relations between COYOTE and key environmental actors (potential recruits, mass media, third party sponsors) have remained relatively constant since 1973. In addition, important intraorganizational problems have hindered movement success from the very beginning.

Income and Leadership

COYOTE's income in the 1980s diminished considerably, largely because the primary revenue source of the 1970s (from among donations, memberships, fundraising events, and speakers' fees)—the annual Hookers' Ball—was discontinued after 1979.[12] In 1980, "lack of money" was cited to explain "lack of success."[13] When asked in 1987 about available funds, the director responded, "We have almost none."[14]

The movement also suffered from lack of human capital—staff and skilled organizers. Unlike gay rights organizations, COYOTE has never attracted more than a handful of committed activists, and many affiliates have been run by lone organizers. St. James, principal leader for more than a decade, admitted, "I hate organizing" (St. James 1976:129). She was successful in the 1970s in building ties to certain groups and staging spectacular events, but less active in more mundane duties: responsibilities were insufficiently delegated and decision-making faltered (*San Francisco Chronicle* 1986;

Thomas 1978). She left COYOTE in 1985 and became co-director of the International Committee for Prostitutes' Rights; COYOTE is now run on a part-time basis by Priscilla Alexander and Gloria Lockett.

Support Base

Popular support facilitates a movement's acceptance and legitimacy, if not tangible gains (Gamson 1975:51). Movement support can be measured by the number of its (1) constituents, who provide resources, and (2) adherents, who support goals (McCarthy and Zald 1977). Available figures on constituents—members paying annual dues—may be unreliable. COYOTE claimed 8,500 members in 1974; 8,000 in 1977; and 10,000–15,000 in 1980.[15] Whatever the real numbers, almost all were "paper" constituents: on the mailing list and paying nominal dues but quite inactive.

Public opinion data presented in Table 9-1 indicate significant support for some form of legalization and much less for decriminalization. While the pool of adherents (supporters of decriminalization) is not insignificant, they, like COYOTE's constituents, remain unmobilized. In this movement, leaders typically speak on behalf of, rather than involve, prostitutes and non-prostitute adherents: mobilization events (picketing, demonstrations, conventions) have been few and far between. This is a professional or entrepreneurial campaign, not a mass-based movement (McCarthy and Zald 1977).

The beneficiaries of decriminalization and thus potential constituents might be expected to include customers and prostitutes (particularly streetwalkers, most vulnerable under criminalization).[16] Some customers may favor legalization—for health and

---

[12] Six Hookers' Balls were held from 1974 to 1979, each drawing large crowds and income. The Ball netted $10,000 in 1975, $30,000 in 1977, and $60,000 in 1978 (COYOTE 1976, 1978b; St. James 1989). The event was dropped due to a legal dispute between COYOTE and a professional organizer over ownership rights to the Ball.

[13] Interview with Margo St. James and Priscilla Alexander, San Francisco, September 12, 1980.

[14] Interview with Alexander, March 16, 1987.

[15] COYOTE 1974a: St. James 1977; Interview with St. James and Alexander, September 12, 1980.

[16] Hilton (n.d., p. 15) identifies the types of persons with interests likely threatened by decriminalization: "high-income prostitutes; pimps; members of the vice squad; bellhops; cab drivers and all others who earn fees from disseminating information in the illegal market; criminals and others who can extort money from prostitutes; and, finally, people who derive satisfaction from feeling that something they consider nasty is illegal" (cf. Heyl 1979; Sheehy 1973, ch. 5).

safety reasons—but few have "come out" in support, apparently lacking strong incentives and/or anticipating fallout among friends, spouses, and associates. COYOTE's attitude toward customers may also play a part: as one leader remarked, "COYOTE is contemptuous of johns."[17]

Mobilization of prostitutes has been equally elusive, despite the estimated reservoir of one million adult prostitutes nationally. It was premature for one observer to argue in 1974 that "prostitutes at last are willing to act in concert to assert their rights" (Haft 1974:10). St. James (1989:xix) estimates that only 3% of COYOTE's members are prostitutes. This quiescence among beneficiaries can be explained by factors internal and external to the movement. Internally, COYOTE has not prioritized recruitment: "We don't go looking for constituents," St. James told me, "they come to COYOTE."[18] Given the lack of recruitment efforts, many prostitutes may be unaware of the movement's very existence.

Among those aware of the movement, several factors discourage open participation. They may, as COYOTE claims, simply be "too busy" trying to survive.[19] But other constraints seem more salient: fear of police surveillance and harassment, discouragement from pimps and other managers, and anticipated repercussions among family and friends. Structural difficulties compound these interpersonal deterrents. Unlike gays, prostitutes lack the preexisting networks and the kind of subculture or sense of community suited to political activism. Solidarities among prostitutes (where they exist) are largely survival-oriented, and those prostitutes most involved in criminal subcultures (involving mainly drug dealing and theft) are particularly likely to eschew movement involvement.

Alliances

Strong alliances with other groups inside or outside the movement may offset an organization's lack of internal resources and constituent support

(Zald and McCarthy 1980). COYOTE has maintained very loose and intermittent relations with affiliates, both nationally and internationally. Leaders of these organizations occasionally meet at conferences, but do not coordinate local activities.

Various influential third parties have formally supported decriminalization but their contribution to the movement has been limited. Some organizations have done little more than issue a call for decriminalization. Others have mounted legal challenges to the constitutionality of prostitution laws. In addition to the ACLU's formal support for decriminalization (since 1975), it occasionally has filed taxpayers' and class action suits, informally lobbied legislators, and defended individuals prosecuted under prostitution laws. In general, however, the ACLU accords prostitution low priority. A COYOTE leader remarked that the ACLU "doesn't want to get involved" in litigation on behalf of prostitutes and is "interested in more popular things."[20]

A number of writers (Schur 1980:207; McLeod 1981, 1982; Musheno and Seeley 1986) maintain that prostitutes' rights organizations benefitted from association with the women's movement. In 1973, the National Organization for Women (NOW) issued a formal resolution supporting decriminalization. NOW is in a position to contribute to COYOTE's finances, legitimacy, and support base (through bloc recruitment of some of its 270,000 members [Matthews 1990]), but has offered little material support and its formal endorsement of decriminalization has not appreciably enhanced the standing of prostitutes' rights organizations.[21] As COYOTE's director recently complained, "Some NOW chapters are doing more, but I'm still not getting the cooperation I want."[22] Similarly, the International Committee for Prostitutes' Rights (1986:1) has accused the

---

[17] Interview with Alexander, September 12, 1980.
[18] Interview with St. James, September 12, 1980.
[19] Interview with St. James, San Francisco, November 14, 1980.

[20] Interview with Alexander, March 16, 1987.
[21] Political organizations, such as the League of Women Voters and the National Women's Political Caucus, have never taken a position on prostitution (personal communication). COYOTE has called on both organizations to make prostitution a priority (Alexander 1979).
[22] Interview with Alexander, March 16, 1987.

women's movement in other countries of giving lip service to the issue of prostitution and displaying "hesitation or refusal to accept prostitution as legitimate work and to accept prostitutes as working women. . . ."

Two factors explain the half-hearted support from the women's movement. First, prostitution is an unpopular cause, unlikely to yield gains for and more likely to discredit the women's movement if embraced in a prominent and sustained fashion. The "contamination" resulting from an individual's association with deviants (Goffman 1963) also may apply to organizations that champion deviant causes.

Second, feminists disagree fundamentally on prostitution, not unlike the heated debates on pornography. A libertarian faction sees it as a valid occupational alternative, which decriminalization would make safer; abolitionists consider it inherently sexist and degrading. The dominant view among feminists consists of opposition to criminalization and state regulation, which expose prostitutes to exploitation and victimization, coupled with moral indignation over the institution of prostitution, as an extreme form of gender oppression (Hobson 1987; MacMillan 1977; Musheno and Seeley 1986; Women Endorsing Decriminalization 1973). The favored solution is immediate decriminalization and ultimate abolition of the oldest profession.

Tensions within the women's movement over prostitution are reflected in fundamental ideological divisions among those organizations campaigning for changes in prostitution. The dominant, abolitionist view among feminists is not shared by COYOTE and comes closer to that of two lesser known organizations: the U.S. Prostitutes Collective and WHISPER (Women Hurt in Systems of Prostitution Engaged in Revolt). Both endorse decriminalization as an interim measure. The U.S. Prostitutes Collective seeks "economic independence for women, so that none of us will be forced into prostitution for economic reasons" (West 1987:280). Spearheading a "revolt" against prostitution, WHISPER (founded in 1985) denies that

women freely choose prostitution, that prostitution is a valid career, and that it can ever be organized humanely. Prostitution is based on male domination, women's commodification, and "enforced sexual access and sexual abuse" (WHISPER 1985/86:1; cf. Barry 1979; Pivar 1973). Hardly victimless, it is "a crime committed against women by men" since it violates women's human dignity (Wynter 1987:270). Buying sexual favors is by definition "violence against women" (WHISPER n.d.). As an abolitionist organization, WHISPER does not fit within the prostitutes' rights movement: it advocates not the rights of prostitutes as prostitutes but the right to escape from prostitution; seeks not normalization but intensification of the stigma attached to women of ill repute; and champions the universal eradication of prostitution.

COYOTE denies that victimization is intrinsic to prostitution, that most prostitution is forced, and that abolition is required. It views prostitution as neither innately degrading nor the ultimate in sexist objectification and considers it naive to view decriminalization as a precursor to prostitution's eventual elimination (see Alexander 1987; Bell 1987; NTFP 1987b; Richards 1979; Withers 1977). Calling on feminists to respect "the integrity of prostitute women," the International Committee for Prostitutes' Rights (1986:1) claims that prostitutes "reject support that requires them to leave prostitution" and "object to being treated as symbols of oppression and demand recognition as workers."

The Media

The mass media are crucial contributors to the success or failure of modern social movements, shaping access to the public and vital resources. They can distort, selectively depict, or accurately portray movement activities and goals. COYOTE regards the media as its most important resource, since they allow direct and cost-free public access.[23]

Movement leaders have appeared on national and local talk shows and newscasts, albeit infrequently.

---

[23] Interview with St. James, September 12, 1980.

The media have approached COYOTE for information on prostitution, interviewed its spokespersons, and covered events such as the Hookers' Balls and Conventions, usually in a more amused than serious manner. But my examination of the indexes of the *New York Times* and the *San Francisco Chronicle* shows at no point since the movement's rise sustained press coverage of the grievances, goals, and activities of prostitutes' rights organizations—unlike the more frequent reporting on the gay rights movement. Limited media attention to COYOTE's concerns has negatively affected acquisition of material resources and opportunities to influence public attitudes.

CONCLUSION

COYOTE has not failed in every area. It appears to have enhanced the self-images of affiliated prostitutes (Delacoste and Alexander 1987; Pheterson 1989). It has aided individual prostitutes, attracted some media attention, extracted concessions from some city governments and police forces, and won legal battles in some courtrooms. Quite possibly, "If COYOTE didn't exist, it would be worse" than currently for prostitutes.[24] COYOTE's survival for 17 years is also noteworthy. Perhaps "simply continuing to fight over a period of years, one gains a measure of credibility" (St. James 1980:199), but this longevity effect is difficult to discern in this movement.

St. James (1980:199) claims that "publicity has educated the public [and] gained us some respectability among community groups." However, her colleague, Priscilla Alexander, considers it "unclear" whether public education has occurred.[25] St. James also argues that the "basic injustice" of prostitution law and enforcement patterns "makes the movement succeed."[26] Generally, however, arguments regarding "basic injustices" have fallen on deaf ears among elites and the wider public. COYOTE has not altered public opinion nor won major concessions or lasting acceptance from authorities.

Our findings support the resource mobilization theory of social movements, which considers ideological and moral factors secondary to material and organizational variables in shaping movement outcomes. Deviance liberation movements are not sentenced to fail because of high levels of perceived immorality. "Immoral crusades" may prevail on authorities (if not the wider public) if they aggregate and mobilize the material and human resources of (1) a mass base of constituents and/or (2) well-endowed, influential third parties (groups, movements, elites). The gay rights and abortion rights campaigns have succeeded in mobilizing both of the above. The prostitutes' rights movement has failed in both domains and thus remains in a weak position to overcome its lack of moral capital and to attain its goals.

REFERENCES

Adam, Barry. 1987. *The Rise of a Gay and Lesbian Movement.* Boston: Twayne.

Alexander, Priscilla. 1977. "An Ideal." *COYOTE Howls* 4.

———. 1979. "National Decriminalization a Must as Hypocritical, Sexist Vigilante Groups Spring into Action across the U.S." *NTFP News* 1 (Sept./Oct.).

———. 1987. "Prostitution: A Difficult Issue for Feminists." Pp. 184–214 in *Sex Work: Writings by Women in the Sex Industry,* edited by Frederique Delacoste and Priscilla Alexander. Pittsburgh: Cleis.

Anderson, Patrick. 1981. *High in America: The True Story Behind NORML and the Politics of Marijuana.* New York: Viking.

Anspach, Renee R. 1979. "From Stigma to Identity Politics: Political Activism among the Physically Disabled and Former Mental Patients." *Social Science and Medicine* 13A:765–773.

Atlanta. 1986. *The Mayor's Task Force on Prostitution: Findings and Recommendations.* Bureau of Planning.

Barron, James. 1989. "Homosexuals See 2 Decades of Gains, but Fear Setbacks." *New York Times,* June 25: 1, 25.

---

[24] Interview with Alexander, March 16, 1987.
[25] Interview with Alexander, March 16, 1987.
[26] Interview with St. James, September 12, 1980.

Barry, Kathleen. 1979. *Female Sexual Slavery.* Englewood Cliffs: Prentice Hall.

Bell, Laurie, ed. 1987. *Good Girls/Bad Girls: Feminists and Sex Trade Workers Face to Face.* Seattle: Seal Press.

Boles, Jacqueline, and Charlotte Tatro. 1978. "Legal and Extra-Legal Methods of Controlling Female Prostitution." *International Journal of Comparative and Applied Criminal Justice* 2:71–85.

Cohen, Bernard. 1980. *Deviant Street Networks: Prostitution in New York City.* Lexington, MA: Lexington.

COYOTE. 1974a. "COYOTE Background." *COYOTE Howls* 1(2).

———. 1974b. "Fiction versus Fact." *COYOTE Howls* 1(2).

———. 1974c. "Prostitution and the Constitution." Press release.

———. 1976. *COYOTE Howls* 3:6.

———. 1978a. "Universal Decriminalization." *COYOTE Howls* 5(1):11.

———. 1978b. "Where Does the Money Go?" *COYOTE Howls* 5(2):9.

Decker, John. 1979. *Prostitution: Regulation and Control.* Littleton. CO: Rothman.

Delacoste, Frederique, and Priscilla Alexander, eds. 1987. *Sex Work: Writings by Women in the Sex Industry.* Pittsburgh: Cleis.

D'Emilio, John. 1983. *Sexual Politics, Sexual Communities: The Making of a Homosexual Minority in the United States.* Chicago: University of Chicago Press.

deYoung, Mary. 1988. "The Indignant Page: Techniques of Neutralization in the Publications of Pedophile Organizations." *Child Abuse and Neglect* 12:583–591.

Dominelli, Lena. 1986. "The Power of the Powerless: Prostitution and the Reinforcement of Submissive Femininity." *Sociological Review* 34:65–92.

Exner, John E., Joyce Wylie, Antonia Leura, and Tracey Parrill. 1977. "Some Psychological Characteristics of Prostitutes." *Journal of Personality Assessment* 41:474–485.

Gamson, William. 1975. *The Strategy of Social Protest.* Homewood, IL: Dorsey.

Goffman, Erving. 1963. *Stigma.* Englewood Cliffs: Prentice Hall.

Gusfield, Joseph. 1963. *Symbolic Crusade.* Urbana: University of Illinois Press.

Haft, Marilyn G. 1974. "Hustling for Rights." *Civil Liberties Review* 1:8–26.

Hamilton, Mildred. 1979. "Margo." *San Francisco Sunday Examiner and Chronicle,* April 29:1–2.

Heyl, Barbara. 1979. "Prostitution: An Extreme Case of Sex Stratification." Pp. 196–210 in *The Criminology of Deviant Women,* edited by Freda Adler and Rita James Simon. Boston: Houghton Mifflin.

Hilton, George. n.d. "The Prohibition of Prostitution: An Economic Analysis." Unpublished paper, Department of Economics, UCLA.

Hobson, Barbara. 1987. *Uneasy Virtue: The Politics of Prostitution and the American Reform Tradition.* New York: Basic Books.

International Committee for Prostitutes' Rights. 1986. *Draft Statement on Prostitution and Feminism.* Second World Whore's Congress, Brussels, Oct. 1–4.

James, Jennifer. 1977. "Answers to the Twenty Questions Most Frequently Asked about Prostitution." Pp. 37–67 in *The Politics of Prostitution,* edited by Jennifer James. Seattle: Social Research Associates.

James, Jennifer, and Mary Owen. 1977. "The Development of Model Prostitution Laws." Pp. 95–114 in *The Politics of Prostitution,* edited by Jennifer James. Seattle: Social Research Associates.

Jenkins, J. Craig. 1983. "Resource Mobilization Theory and the Study of Social Movements." *Annual Review of Sociology* 9:527–553.

Jennings, M. Anne. 1976. "The Victim as Criminal: A Consideration of California's Prostitution Law." *California Law Review* 64:1235–1284.

Johnson, Roberta Ann. 1983. "Mobilizing the Disabled." Pp. 82–100 in *Social Movements of the Sixties and Seventies,* edited by Jo Freeman. New York: Longman.

Kaplan, John. 1977. "Non-victim Crime and the Regulation of Prostitution." *West Virginia Law Review* 79:593–606.

Kitsuse, John. 1980. "Coming Out All Over: Deviants and the Politics of Social Problems." *Social Problems* 28:1–13.

Mathews, Jay. 1990. "NOW Leaders Threaten Boycott over Abortion Pill." *Washington Post,* July 1.

McCarthy, John, and Mayer Zald. 1977. "Resource Mobilization and Social Movements." *American Journal of Sociology* 82:1212–1241.

McClosky, Herbert, and Alida Brill. 1983. *Dimensions of Tolerance: What Americans Believe about Civil Liberties.* New York: Russell Sage.

McLeod, Eileen. 1981. "Man-made Laws for Men? The Street Prostitutes' Campaign against Control."

Pp. 61–78 in *Controlling Women: The Normal and the Deviant,* edited by Bridget Hutter and G. Williams. London: Croom Helm.

———. 1982. *Working Women: Prostitution Now.* London: Croom Helm.

MacMillan, Jackie. 1977. "Prostitution as Sexual Politics." *Quest* 4:41–50.

Mauss, Armand. 1975. *Social Problems as Social Movements.* Philadelphia: Lippincott.

Milman, Barbara. 1980. "New Rules for the Oldest Profession: Should We Change our Prostitution Laws?" *Harvard Women's Law Journal* 3:1–82.

Murray, Ellen F. 1979. "Anti-prostitution Laws: New Conflicts in the Fight against the World's Oldest Profession." *Albany Law Review* 43:360–387.

Musheno, Michael, and Kathryn Seeley. 1986. "Prostitution Policy and the Women's Movement: Historical Analysis of Feminist Thought and Organization." *Contemporary Crises* 10:237–255.

National Organization for Women. 1973. *Text of the Resolution Calling for the Decriminalization of Prostitution.* Resolution no. 141.

National Task Force on Prostitution [NTFP]. 1984–1986. *NTFP Policies.* San Francisco.

———. 1987a. *About the NTFP.* San Francisco.

———. 1987b. *On Prostitution.* San Francisco.

New York Times. 1986. "Judges" Group Opposes State Red-light Areas." May 12:D11.

Oberschall, Anthony. 1973. *Social Conflict and Social Movements.* Englewood Cliffs: Prentice Hall.

Parnas, Raymond. 1981. "Legislative Reform of Prostitution Laws." *Santa Clara Law Review* 21: 669–696.

Pearl, Julie. 1987. "The Highest Paying Customer: America's Cities and the Costs of Prostitution Control." *Hastings Law Journal* 38:769–800.

Peat, Marwick, and Partners. 1984. *A National Population Study of Prostitution and Pornography.* Report no. 6. Ottawa, Canada: Department of Justice.

Pheterson, Gail, ed. 1989. *A Vindication of the Rights of Whores.* Seattle: Seal Press.

Pivar, David J. 1973. *Purity Crusade: Sexual Morality and Social Control, 1868–1900.* Westport: Greenwood.

Richards, David. 1979. "Commercial Sex and the Rights of the Person: A Moral Argument for the Decriminalization of Prostitution." *University of Pennsylvania Law Review* 127:1195–1287.

Roby, Pamela A. 1969. "Politics and the Criminal Law: Revision of the New York State Penal Law on Prostitution." *Social Problems* 17:83–109.

Rosenbleet, Charles, and Barbara Pariente. 1973. "The Prostitution of the Criminal Law." *American Criminal Law Review* 11:373–427.

St. James, Margo. 1976. "Penthouse Interview." *Penthouse,* Sept.

———. 1977. "COYOTE Is Closing: What Is COYOTE?" *COYOTE Howls* 4:8.

———. 1980. "What's a Nice Girl Like You . . . ?" Pp. 191–201 in *Prostitutes: Our Life,* edited by Claude Jaget. Bristol. Falling Wall Press.

———. 1987. "The Reclamation of Whores." Pp. 81–87 in *Good Girls/Bad Girls: Feminists and Sex Trade Workers Face to Face,* edited by Laurie Bell. Seattle: Seal Press.

———. 1989. "Preface." Pp. xvii–xx in *A Vindication of the Rights of Whores,* edited by Gail Pheterson. Seattle: Seal Press.

San Francisco Chronicle. 1977. "A Move to Halt Opening of Hookers Film Festival." March 28:4.

———. 1986. "COYOTE's New Leadership." February 25:21.

San Francisco Committee on Crime. 1971. *A Report on Non-Victim Crime in San Francisco, Part 2: Sexual Conduct, Gambling, Pornography.* Submitted to the Mayor's Office.

Schur, Edwin. 1980. *The Politics of Deviance.* Englewood Cliffs: Prentice Hall.

Sheehy, Gail. 1973. *Hustling: Prostitution in Our Wide-Open Society.* New York: Delacoste.

Skolnick, Jerome, and John Dombrink. 1978. "The Legalization of Deviance." *Criminology* 16: 193–208.

Stein, Mark. 1987. "Bordellos of Nevada Try to Lure Patrons, Banish AIDS." *Los Angeles Times,* June 8.

Stingley, Jim. 1976a. "Issues Raised by Decriminalization." *Los Angeles Times,* February 9.

———. 1976b. "Their Houses in Order." *Los Angeles Times,* February 8.

Strobel, Lee. 1976. "Is Hooking Actually Crooking? Lawyers Unit Almost Votes 'No'." *Chicago Tribune,* February 17:5.

Sykes, Gresham, and David Matza. 1957. "Techniques of Neutralization: A Theory of Delinquency." *American Sociological Review* 22:666–670.

Symanski, Richard. 1974. "Prostitution in Nevada." *Annals of the Association of American Geographers* 64:357–377.

Taylor, Ronald. 1988. "Business Leaders in Nevada Ask: Can State Afford Prostitution?" *Los Angeles Times*, August 8:3, 16.

Thomas, Stephanie. 1978. "COYOTE Energy = Social Change." *COYOTE Howls* 5.

Wandling, Therese. 1976. "Decriminalization of Prostitution: The Limits of the Criminal Law." *Oregon Law Review* 55:553–566.

West, Rachel. 1987. "U.S. Prostitutes Collective." Pp. 279–289 in *Sex Work: Writings by Women in the Sex Industry*, edited by Frederique Delacoste and Priscilla Alexander. Pittsburgh: Cleis.

WHISPER. n.d. "WHISPER Resolution against Trafficking in Women." Pamphlet.

———. 1985/86. *Newsletter* 1.

Will, George F. 1974. "The Conservative Case for Legal Prostitution." *San Francisco Sunday Examiner and Chronicle*, Sept. 1.

Wilson, George P., Francis T. Cullen, Edward J. Latessa, and John Steven Wills. 1985. "State Intervention and Victimless Crimes: A Study of Police Attitudes." *Journal of Police Science and Administration* 13:22–29.

Withers, Jean. 1977. "Evaluating Prostitution: The Feminist Dilemma." Pp. 1–8 in *The Politics of Prostitution*, edited by Jennifer James. Seattle: Social Research Associates.

Women Endorsing Decriminalization. 1973. "Prostitution: A Non-victim Crime?" *Issues in Criminology* 8: 137–162.

Wynter, Sarah. 1987. "Whisper." Pp. 266–270 in *Sex Work: Writings by Women in the Sex Industry*, edited by Frederique Delacoste and Priscilla Alexander. Pittsburgh: Cleis.

Zald, Mayer, and John McCarthy. 1980. "Social Movement Industries: Competition and Conflict among Movement Organizations." Pp. 1–20 in *Research in Social Movements, Conflicts, and Change*, vol. 3, edited by Louis Kriesberg. Greenwich, CT: JAI Press.

READING 5-10

Pedophile Organizations

Mary deYoung

The René Guyon Society, the Childhood Sensuality Circle, and the North American Man/Boy Love Association (NAMBLA) are pedophile organizations that are striving to gain respectability and support in society. Because they have a philosophy that supports and encourages adult sexual behavior with children, these organizations are condemned by the larger society. In order to make their unpopular philosophy more palatable and their members more acceptable,

From *Human Organization* 43, No. 1, Spring 1984, 72–74. Reprinted by permission of the Society for Applied Anthropology.

these organizations have created a code of ethics that places parameters on their philosophy and restrictions on the behavior of their members. This paper examines the philosophy, goals, and strategies of these three organizations.

The René Guyon Society, created in 1962 by a small group of parents after attending a conference on sexuality, took its name from a French jurist and Freudian psychologist who had been an outspoken advocate of adult-child sex. It also adopted his motto as its slogan: "Sex by year eight or else it's too late." The society champions the abolition of statutory rape laws so parents can give their consent for their children to engage in sexual activities with adults, and provides counseling and support services for those parents attracted to, yet skeptical of, its philosophy and practices. Believing that affection often overlooks age differences, the Childhood Sensuality Circle was established in 1971 for the purpose of promoting sexual self-determination for adults and children. It advocates the abolition of age of consent laws and encourages children to use their own standards in the selection of adult sexual partners. The North American Man/Boy Love Association (NAMBLA) was formed in 1978 in reaction to the arrests of 24 Revere, Massachusetts, men for sexual activity with adolescent boys. Promoting an end to what it refers to as the state's repression of sexuality, NAMBLA also champions the abolition of all age of consent laws and works for the release of all men incarcerated or hospitalized for noncoercive sex with minors.

Shielded by a small but vocal movement that views the taboo against adult sexual behavior with children as unenlightened and anachronistic (De Mott 1980), these pedophile organizations have emerged from the "lunatic fringe" into public attention; their arrival has been greeted by a smattering of support and an abundance of criticism. Viewing themselves as beleaguered minority groups whose time has not yet come, these pedophile organizations have a vested interest in making their unpopular philosophy palatable, a difficult task indeed, in view of the deeply ingrained taboo against adult-child sex. A second goal of the pedophile organizations is to disavow the deviance of their members. In order to achieve these two goals— making their unpopular philosophy palatable and their members acceptable—the pedophile organizations have created a code of ethics, of sorts, that places parameters on their philosophy and limitations on the behavior of their members.

Through an examination of the publications, bulletins, and newsletters of the René Guyon Society, the Childhood Sensuality Circle, and the North American Man/Boy Love Association, several features of the code of ethics of these pedophile organizations become evident: (1) a "pro-child" ideology, (2) emphasis on consensual sexual activity, and (3) the placing of limitations on members' behavior. Each of these aspects will be discussed in turn.

PRO-CHILD IDEOLOGY

In order to reduce society's condemnation, the first priority of pedophile organizations in creating a code of ethics has been to make broad "pro-child" proclamations, couched in the rhetoric of children's rights. NAMBLA, for example, states that it believes that "children need more than sexual freedom; they need the right to control all aspects of their lives and bodies, without the interference of adults, whether the family, the state or the church. They should be treated like full human beings, not as the private property of their parents and the state" (1980:2). A similar declaration is made by the Childhood Sensuality Circle: "To live a full life is every individual's birthright. We advocate the total liberation of children, not to confer on them the same legal status as adults, but to accord them the opportunity to be all that they can be as children" (1981:1).

Apparently recognizing that skeptics and detractors may not be convinced of the sincerity of such pro-child statements when they are issued by organizations that advocate pedophilia and incest, these pedophile organizations have also allied themselves with pro-child movements that exist in the larger society. The Childhood Sensuality Circle advocates and actively promotes sex education of children (CSC 1981:1), an end to corporal punishment in schools (1981:2), child abuse prevention and treatment (1981:3), and other such esoterically pro-child ideologies as home births (1982b:15), anti-circumcision (1982a:10), and the abolition of the peace-time military draft (1982c:11). In a statement of philosophy by one of its spokespersons, NAMBLA also opposes the military draft, the circumcision of male infants, and the "sexual mutilation" of female infants, and advocates birth control, sex education, abortion on demand, and even the World Health Organization's baby formula code (1983:2).

In testimony before a senate subcommittee investigating the sexual exploitation of children, René Guyon Society spokesperson Tim O'Hara offered what comes closest to a pro-child pronouncement from that pedophile organization: "[We] feel that sexual abuse is not a crime. The real crime is making a child ashamed of their body" (Subcommittee on Select Education 1977:168). Less articulate than the other pedophile organizations in making sweeping statements about children's rights and freedoms, the society nonetheless has actively spoken out against a variety of social ills that have left victimized children in its wake: prostitution, drug abuse, and murder, to name but a few (René Guyon Society 1982:1).

All of these pro-child proclamations, of course, are made for a very specific purpose: to convince the larger society that the philosophy of these organizations is built upon a foundation of respect, care, and love for children in general, and that the members of the organizations, in practice, are lovers, not abusers, of children. And to further demonstrate that their love of children extends into their sexual activities, they develop a second feature of the code of ethics: an emphasis on consensual sexual activity with children.

CONSENSUAL SEXUAL ACTIVITY

The issue of consent is a thorny one. Each pedophile organization believes that a child can give full and knowledgeable consent for sexual activity with an adult, yet none is so ignorant as to disregard the inherent difference in power between a child and an adult that may render that consent invalid. In an effort to resolve that dilemma, the pedophile organizations redefine the issue of consent in terms of the age of the child.

The most evasive and apparently the most troubled of these groups on this issue, NAMBLA publicly focuses on its members' sexual activities with adolescents rather than children. There is an implied morality in that emphasis: adolescents,

presumably, are less likely to be intimidated or coerced by an adult and are therefore more likely to be able to give free consent.

Yet many NAMBLA members are sexually attracted to children, not adolescents, so the question that organization must answer is whether children can give consent to sexual activities with adults. "The lower the age," a NAMBLA founder conceded in a recent interview, "the more complicated it becomes" (NAMBLA 1982:7), and although that does not answer the question, one of the stated goals of the organization does: NAMBLA advocates and lobbies for the abolition of any age of consent laws. If successful in that mission, neither age nor consent will remain a "complicated issue."

The Childhood Sensuality Circle also has difficulties with the age at which children can give consent for sexual activities with adults. In a recent publication, the Circle states that a child is not able to fully cope with his or her physical environment until age six (1981:5). That statement would seem to imply that a child cannot give consent for sexual behavior with an adult until that age, but the Circle never states that explicitly, nor does it cite any evidence in support of its assumption that a six year old can fully cope with his or her physical environment. Like NAMBLA, the Childhood Sensuality Circle circumvents this delicate issue by advocating the abolition of all age of consent laws.

The René Guyon Society is the most explicit in regard to the issue of age, standing firm as it does on its motto: "Sex by year eight or else it's too late." This pedophile organization simply assumes that the child's physiological ability to tolerate the adult's sexual behavior is sufficient to constitute consent. Even infants can tolerate masturbation, fondling, and oral contact, but the Society does not believe that a female child can physiologically tolerate sexual intercourse until she is "eleven or twelve" years old. The Society, however, cites enigmatic scientific studies that "prove" that a four-year-old child's anus is large enough to accommodate an adult male's penis without discomfort (1982:1).

LIMITATIONS ON MEMBERS' BEHAVIOR

A third component of the ethical code of pedophile organizations is the setting of limits on the behavior of the individual members. The René Guyon Society grudgingly urges all members to "obey all bad sex laws until they are changed. . . . No scofflaws welcome" (1982:1). Its primary limitation, however, and the one most persistently demanded, is that condoms be used by adults in their sexual activities with children. This, then, becomes "moral" sexual activity, and the Society openly advocates adult sexual intercourse and anal intercourse with children, incest, children's sexual activity with other children, and child pornography (1982:1).

The Childhood Sensuality Circle is the least explicit in placing limitations on members' behavior, and limits itself to brief statements such as "we are resolutely against the [sexual] traffic in children" (1982b:2). Vague admonitions are frequently found in the Circle's *Nusletter,* such as this response to a father worried about how to approach his young daughters for sexual activities:

> Because of the power imbalance between children and adults, I think child-adult sex is better conducted in a context where the child can stay or walk away, take it or leave it. . . . I would urge you to find a teen or adult to take care of your orgasm needs, and involve the children only in an occasional romp in bed with mommy and daddy (1982a:11).

NAMBLA has placed the most limitations on its members' behavior. In a recent interview, a NAMBLA spokesperson stated, "We have strict rules against members being involved in such crimes as prostitution, the production of commercial pornography, or sex by force. If I ever knew of a member of NAMBLA who [had done this], I would report him to the police" (NAMBLA 1982:7). Asserting that the primary purpose of the organization is to provide "backup support for men and boys involved with each other in consensual ways," NAMBLA spokespersons disabuse anyone of the idea that the organization exists to "provide sexual outlets for people" (1983:1).

Again, the function of these organizational limitations on members' behavior is to keep that behavior within moral bounds as defined by that organization. It also serves to convey to the larger society that the most exploitative and abusive behavior of people sexually attracted to children is condemned by the organizations just as it is by the larger society.

Pedophile organizations have a philosophy that is generally considered repugnant by the larger society and a membership that is judged as perverted. In order to make their unpopular philosophy palatable and their members acceptable, these pedophile organizations have created an ethical code. This code makes pro-child statements and allies itself with pro-child movements in the larger society. It also emphasizes consensual sexual activity with minors in order to present its members as lovers rather than abusers of children. Finally, it places limitations on the behavior of its members in an effort to demonstrate to the larger society that the organization, too, takes a stand against the abuse and exploitation of innocent children.

REFERENCES

Childhood Sensuality Circle. 1981. CSC Pamphlet. V. Davila, ed. San Diego, Calif.
———. 1982a. *Nusletter* 8(2).
———. 1982b. *Nusletter* 8(3).
———. 1982c. *Nusletter* 8(5).
DeMott, B. 1980. "The Pro-Incest Lobby." *Psychology Today* 13(10):11–13.
North American Man/Boy Love Association (NAMBLA)
———. 1980. *What Is NAMBLA?* New York.
———. 1982. *Bulletin* 3(10).
———. 1983. *Bulletin* 4(1).
René Guyon Society. 1982. *Bulletin.* T. O'Hara, ed. May. Los Angeles, Calif.
Subcommittee on Select Education. 1977. *Sexual Exploitation of Children*. Washington, D.C.: House of Representatives, 95th Congress, 1st Session.

Political Activism Among the Disabled and Mental Patients

Renee R. Anspach

INTRODUCTION

Among other legacies of the 1960s was what might be termed the "politicization of life." As political organizers extended their efforts to the most disenfranchised groups—welfare recipients, poor tenants, and prisoners—power, once seen as elusive, was now considered attainable. And as "deviant" groups such as hippies, Hell's Angels, and Gay Liberationists began to articulate their demands in quasi-political terms, the once hard-and-fast distinction between social deviance and political marginality became blurred (Horowitz and Liebowitz 1968). Most significantly, the sixties witnessed a widening definition of politics to embrace all aspects of the person. An ever-increasing array of personal habits, from long hair to the discarding of brassieres to vegetarianism, came to be equated with conscious rebellion against the confines of the normative order. The language of political protest and persuasion, no longer a specialized vocabulary, became the available idiom for the expression of discontent. Sociologically, these developments pointed to the existence of a political as well as a social construction of reality.

This politically-charged climate set the stage for the subject of this paper: a nascent political activism among former mental patients and the physically disabled. On April 6, 1977, the politicization of the handicapped was dramatically and vividly displayed to the American public. About 300 blind, deaf, and physically disabled activists assembled in front of Washington's Department of Health, Education, and Welfare, carrying placards, shouting slogans, and chanting songs from the civil rights movement. The issue was H.E.W. Secretary Califano's failure to sign Section 504 of the Rehabilitation Act, which forbids architectural and economic discrimination on the basis of disability. The 30-hr sit-in coincided with demonstrations in other major cities. In San Francisco, the sit-in lasted almost a month, until final victory was achieved with the signing of the bill.[1, 2] Former mental patients, too, have recently joined the ranks of the politically active. In 1975, for example, 250 persons from several states and Canada and representing about twenty organizations attended a conference on "Human Rights and Psychiatric Oppression." The names of the most militant organizations—Mental Patients' Liberation Front, Network Against Psychiatric Assault, and Committee Against Psychiatric Oppression—give testimony to their concern with such issues as the quality of mental hospitals, aftercare, civil rights, and forced medication and shock treatments (Conference on Human Rights and Psychiatric Oppression 1975). How many of the nation's disabled and former mental patients have been swept up by this tide of politicization, and how many others are "fellow travellers," passive onlookers, apathetic, or opposed? No one knows. While the scope of the new activism is elusive, it is clear from these events and from the spate of publications such as *Mainstream* and *Madness Network News* that a social movement has been born.

From *Social Science and Medicine* 13A (1979):765 – 773. Reprinted by permission of Elsevier Science.

[1] *Washington Post.* April 7, 1977.
[2] *Los Angeles Times.* April 6, 1977.

While it is difficult to delineate the contours of a social movement which is only now taking shape, it is clear that this growing politicization differs qualitatively from two traditional organizational modalities of the disabled, the voluntary organization and the self-help group. Since various forms of disability have historically captured the sympathetic imagination of the American public, charitable voluntary associations, such as the Muscular Dystrophy Association and the National Foundation for Infantile Paralysis, have proliferated. The Mental Hygiene Movement, founded at the turn of the century by Clifford Beers, established the tradition of advocacy and social brokerage characteristic of contemporary Mental Health Associations (Deutsch 1937). However, unlike these voluntary associations and lobbies, the new activist groups are composed of the disabled themselves, seeking social change through their own efforts, rather than through others acting as surrogates. The new activist groups also differ from self-help groups, such as colostomy clubs and Recovery, Incorporated. While the emerging activist groups borrow from the self-help movements the emphasis on indigenous organization and self-reliance, they are political, rather than therapeutic, in orientation. They seek not to modify their own behavior in conformance to a pre-existing normative mold, but rather to influence the behaviour of groups, organizations, and institutions. For, unlike its predecessors, the new activism, with its spate of organizations and its outpouring of publications, is self-consciously polemical in tone, characterized by its open agitation for legislative change and architectural reform, its militant opposition to job discrimination, and its frequent reliance on demonstrations and the tactics of social protest.

Political activism among the handicapped and former mental patients, exemplifies a type of politics which we will term *identity politics.* Among its goals are forging an image or conception of self and propagating this self to attentive publics.

Not only is the fashioning of collective identity an explicitly articulated *goal* of the politicized disabled, but the very act of political participation in itself induces others to impute certain characteristics to the activist. For once (s)he has entered the realm of polity, the political actor assumes a certain persona. We attribute certain qualities to political action which sharply contrast to personal deviation, which is assumed to be individualistic and non-rational, seemingly without purpose. Political action, on the other hand, is viewed as prima facie evidence of rational, goal-directed, voluntaristic, and change-oriented behavior. The agitation of the disabled and former mental patients demonstrates, in word and deed, that they are capable of purposive political action.

POLITICAL ACTIVISM OF THE DISABLED: AN ANOMALY

Political Activism and Commonsense Notions of Disability

These attributes of the political actor are a direct affront to deeply-rooted notions of what the handicapped should be like. For while the physically handicapped often conjure images of pathos and pity, militant political action evokes responses of anger and outrage. Hence "normal" viewers were apt to experience a mixture of conflicting emotions and to perceive a certain incongruity in the demonstrations of April 6, 1977, when disabled activists converged on Washington. National television played the event to the hilt, presumably mindful of the newsworthiness of contradictory imagery: the march on Washington (how could *they* have the stamina?); the sight of wheelchairs and seeing-eye dogs (must they be so . . . well . . . obtrusive?); and the angry chants and epithets hurled at Califano (the poster children suddenly turned belligerent). While the demonstrators received extensive coverage on national television networks, they failed to make the front page in most newspapers, since this was, after all, a *visual* event. But the incongruities did not escape reporters, who were careful to paint a vivid portrait for readers, as seen in this account in the *Los Angeles Times:*

> About 300 persons—*some led by seeing eye dogs and speaking with their hands* (italics added)—staged a sit-in at H.E.W. to demand the civil rights bill be signed and enforced.[3]

The point is that political activism among the disabled is an assault upon our taken-for-granted conceptions of disability. It is therefore important to examine the incongruities of the demonstration, for they reveal our basic assumption that the handicapped are consummately passive and powerless.

Political action on the part of those labelled as "mentally ill" presents a similar anomaly. The traditional medical model creates a conception of the helplessness of the "mentally ill." Mental patients are viewed as not entirely responsible for their actions. Professionals, too, endorse this notion of powerlessness as the very essence of "mental disorder." When I asked a psychiatric social worker why mental patients do not unite in political action, he replied:

> If they could get into a group they wouldn't be mentally ill. There's a joke about a man who visited a mental institution. He asked the psychiatrist, "What if all these lunatics ganged up on you?" The psychiatrist answered, "If they could get together they wouldn't be crazy." Mental patients are so preoccupied with the distortions they see, they don't think in political terms.

In short, mental patients are often conceived deterministically, as fundamentally powerless and irrational beings, who are at the mercy of their "distortions." Such notions about "mental illness" are intrinsically incompatible with political action, which is by definition conscious, rational, and goal-directed.

A Theoretical Anomaly

Not only is political action on the part of the disabled and former mental patients phenomenologically troublesome from the standpoint of the commonsense actor, but such action also presents an anomaly in terms of sociological theory, particularly the various sociologies of deviance. Generally sociologists have conceptualized problems of handicap, "mental disorder," and stigma as some sort of personal deviation. But most of the prevailing thinking on deviance conceives of its phenomenon in a way that does not provide *sufficiently* for the possibility of politicized deviants, collectively engaged in attempts to reweave the fabric of identity. According to Horowitz and Liebowitz, theories which conceptualize deviance as a social, rather than as a political, problem tend to obscure its political dimensions. They fault prevailing theories for their reliance on a "social welfare model," which tends to evaluate deviance in largely therapeutic terms. Presumably, Horowitz and Liebowitz are referring to those structural-functional and subcultural perspectives which utilize notions of "improper socialization" or socially-induced individual pathology. Such theories, argue the authors, fail to recognize that deviance is a "conflict between superordinates who make the rules and subordinates whose behavior violates them" (Horowitz and Liebowitz 1968).

But although labelling theorists may be credited with introducing a political dimension into the study of deviance, their notion of power ultimately proves to be limited and one-sided. Most studies of deviance generated by the labelling perspective portray the deviant as powerless, passive, and relatively uninvolved in the labelling process (Davis 1975; Mankoff 1971; Akers 1976). Part of this bias stems from the decision of many labelling theorists to focus on "total institutions" (Goffman 1961), where those labelled are perforce compelled to accept identities enforced by institutional dictates and where there is little latitude for negotiation with officials. But this portrait of the determined deviant goes much deeper, and is rooted in a *one-way* model of the role-taking process, in which identities are simply *imposed* upon the deviant rather than negotiated. This problem is most apparent in the work of Scheff, who portrays the mental patient as a

---

[3] Ibid.

tabula rasa, who in one fell swoop, casts off the trappings of an old self and steps into the strait jacket of an imposed, deviant role (Scheff 1968). But the assumption of deviant passivity creeps into the work of almost all labelling theorists, reliant as they are on the notion of "victimization" and an ideological commitment to the "underdog." Labelling theory, then, is conceptually ill-equipped to deal with the identity politics of the "mentally ill" and the physically disabled. Demonstrations and social protest provide these politicized deviants with a forum where identity is negotiated on a grand scale with the American public.

STRATAGEMS FOR IDENTITY MANAGEMENT

So far I have spoken as though identity politics were the only, or the prevailing, response to handicap or stigma. Political activism is, however, only one of an array of possible stratagems for the management of a somewhat problematic identity. It is theoretically worthwhile to contrast political activism with these other responses in order to delineate its essential features.

These stratagems can, I believe, be contrasted with respect to two central dimensions: the individual's conception of self and his/her relationship to prevailing societal values. To begin with, the handicapped and those labelled as "mentally ill" must develop some posture *vis-à-vis* certain salient cultural values which portray them in a less than favorable light. As Davis points out in his study of polio children and their families, the handicapped person must contend with that fact that

> he is at a disadvantage with respect to several important values emphasized in our society; e.g., physical attractiveness; wholeness and symmetry of body parts; and various physiognomic attributes felt to be prerequisite for a pleasant and engaging personality (Davis 1972a).

The former mental patient, while usually free from the obtrusiveness of an immediately visible stigma, is also said to violate some of the sacred principles of our society: the canons of rationality, self-determination, and full responsibility for the consequences of one's actions. No matter what the particulars of the stigma, the individual must ultimately, consciously or unwittingly, accept or reject the societal values which his/her very ontology contradicts. Moreover, the stigmatized person invariably adopts a stratagem which carries profound implications for his/her identity or conception of self. By combining these two dimensions—stance toward societal values and self-concept—it is possible to develop a typology of four* modal responses to stigma, represented schematically below:

Stratagems for Stigma Management
Societal values

		Accepts	Rejects
Self-concept	**Positive**	Normalization	Political Activism
	Negative	Disassociation	Retreatism

The terms "normalization" and "disassociation" were drawn from Davis' study of polio children and their families. In the first stratagem, *normalization,* the individual is firmly committed to cultural conceptions of normalcy and endorses commonly-held assumptions about the "ideal" person. But while accepting these societal values and cognizant that (s)he fails to measure up to them, the individual makes a concerted effort to minimize, rationalize, explain away, and downplay the stigma attached to his/her differentness. The typical existential stance of the normalizer is that (s)he is "superficially different but basically the same as everyone else," or that ultimately "differences don't really matter." Generally, the normalizer attempts, insofar as possible, to participate in the

---

* Davis and Goffman discuss a fifth stratagem, passing, in which the individual accepts the normal standard yet attempts to conceal his/her condition. This response, while available to the former mental patient, is, of course, impossible for the person with a visible handicap.

round of activities available to "normals" and to aspire to "normal" attainments. As Davis indicates, the societal "idealization of the normal, healthy, and physically attractive," and the "democratic fiction" that differences wither away in the face of a fundamental equality of human beings, make normalization the favored response (Davis 1972a). There is another societal factor which often impels the disabled toward normalization: the ever present American myth of success. Our culture abounds with symbolic inducements to overcome even the weightiest of obstacles. F.D.R. and Helen Keller may be said to be the Horatio Algers of the handicapped, reminders that, given hard work, diligence, and individual effort, the courageous disabled can reach the loftiest pinnacles of achievement.

Normalization carries a certain undeniable advantage: the individual is able to maintain a relatively sanguine and confident attitude toward the self. Yet the normalizer purchases this positive self-conception at a certain price. First, interactions with "normals" are necessarily strained, for an obvious disability inevitably tends to obtrude upon the social situation. In their gambits to "disavow their deviance," normalizers must continually manage and contend with the inescapable tension of an interaction which is fragile, problematic, and easily subject to "slips" and disruptions (Davis 1972b).

Secondly, normalization is premised on a number of contradictory beliefs, and hence the normalizer is fated to experience a certain degree of "cognitive dissonance." Most obvious of these contradictions is the gap between the "democratic fiction"—the "You-can't-tell-a-book-by-its-cover" ideology—and the actual obsession with ascriptive attributes which plagues our culture. Then there is the discrepancy between the canons of civility— the norms of polite society which proffer a superficial acceptance to the handicapped—and the actual emotional displays conveyed non-verbally by "normals" in social intercourse. This gap between what Goffman (1959) terms the "expressions given" and the "expressions given off" renders the

existential state of the normalizer one of profound *distrust* and suspicion of a rejection that may lurk beneath the façade of civility. Finally, there is the economic gap between the myth of success and individual achievement propagated by rehabilitative ideology and the harsh realities of economic discrimination against the handicapped and former mental patients. The list of gaps between myth and reality could be multiplied indefinitely, but the point is that the normalizer's valiant attempts to preserve a positive self image are undoubtedly punctuated by moments of anguish, despair, and internal turmoil.

The next two responses—disassociation and retreatism—require little explanation and entail for the disabled person a less than felicitous conception of self. In *disassociation,* the individual remains attached to the values of the wider society and aware that (s)he is disqualified according to them. Unable to accept the harsh fact of their disqualification and unwilling to aspire to acceptance by "normals," those who disassociate live with an identity that is tainted and tarnished. This negative self-conception leads them to avoid contacts with "normals," perhaps in an effort to spare themselves the pain of impending rejection. Self-exclusion, resentment, and anger toward "normals"—these are the emotional concomitants of the disassociative response (Davis 1972a).

In the third response, *retreatism* (a term borrowed from Merton), the self-image of the individual is profoundly negative, and (s)he neither accepts societal values nor aspires to "normal" attainments. The profound despair of retreatists lead them to withdraw from the world of "normals" to a world of private hopes and fears. These are the people who have "given up"—found in mental hospitals, flophouses, welfare hotels, and other margins of "civilization."

Political activism has recently come to represent a viable collective alternative to the previous individualistic responses. Like the normalizer, the activist seeks to attain a favorable conception of self, often asserting a claim to superiority over "normals." But unlike the normalizer, the activist relinquishes any claim to an acceptance which (s)he views as artificial and consciously repudiates prevailing societal values. The new activist demands institutional equality rather than friendship. Because of this separatist stance on the part of the activist, (s)he may be apt to experience less internal turmoil than the normalizer. Although some emotional conflicts undoubtedly ensue whenever the allure of "acceptance" and the strain of militancy beckon the activist to return to a normalizing response, political activism is a response which is less conflictual and less frought with dissonance than is normalization. Paul Hunt, a disabled writer, provides perhaps the most eloquent statement of the activist's repudiation of societal values and exaltation of self:

> What I *am* rejecting is society's tendency to set up rigid standards of what is right and proper and to force the individual into a mould. . . .
>
> For the disabled person with a fair intelligence or other gifts, perhaps the greatest temptation is to use them just to escape from his disabledness, to buy a place in the sun, a share in the illusory normal world where all is light and pleasure and happiness. Naturally we want to get away from and forget the sickness, depression, pain, loneliness, and poverty of which we probably see more than our share. But if we deny our special relation to the dark in this way, we shall have ceased to recognize the most important asset of disabled people in our society—the uncomfortable subversive position from which we act as a living reproach to any scale of values that puts attributes or possessions before the person (Hunt 1966).

FACTORS IN THE ADOPTION OF STRATAGEMS

These typical responses to disability—normalization, disassociation, retreatism, and political activism—provide the individual with an array of possible "solutions" to the dilemmas of problematic identity. There are a myriad of factors which may lead the individual to adopt a particular stratagem. While not exhaustive, the list of such factors includes physical, interactional, social, structural, and societal variables. Naturally the choice of stratagem is subject to the impress of historical events, for definitions of disability and responses to them are historical, as well as interactional, emergents.

First, the nature of the disability, its "severity and restrictiveness," and its relationship to prevailing societal conceptions of disability, undoubtedly has some influence on the adoption of a stratagem. For example, a severely restrictive impairment may limit associations with others, inhibit participation in "normal" activities, and, hence, curtail opportunities for normalization. Some visible stigmata, such as facial deformities, may produce a profound dissonance when followed by an exclusionary response. In MacGregor's study of the impact of facial deformities, impaired individuals simply could not come to terms with the fact that although they were ostensibly fully qualified for employment, they nonetheless faced job discrimination. Her research implies profound disassociative tendencies among those whose appearance is a symbolic affront to societal standards of physical beauty (MacGregor 1958). The type of disability, then, may influence, but does not in itself determine the choice of stratagem.

Equally important are the interactional factors, the nature of the relationships in which individuals are embedded. Handicapped persons who are well-integrated into the social networks of "normals" and who can draw upon community resources and supports are probably more apt to normalize. On the other hand, those in close association with other handicapped persons may find themselves caught up in the tide of political activism. The reactions of significant others to the individual—the responses of teachers, friends, family members, and business associates, as gleaned from both overt and non-verbal cues, leave an imprint upon the self-concept of the individual. It is likely that exclusionary responses, over a period of time, impel the individual toward some sort of repudiation of self or societal values, while "accepting" responses on the part of significant others would invite normalization.

The individual's relationship to social control agents and professionals presumably has a powerful effect upon the choice of stratagem. Mental hospitals and other "total institutions" necessarily produce responses of passivity and withdrawal which severely inhibit the capacity to unite. Mental patients, especially, are subjected to the transformatory socialization process so eloquently described by Goffman (1961). The institutional context induces the survival strategies of retreatism, or, in "successful" cases, normalization, but scarcely inspires inmates to engage in concerted political action. (Although "bitter memories" can provide the emotional foundation for a later activist stance.)

The importance of the network of professionals in which most disabled persons are embedded cannot be overestimated. The ideology of rehabilitation, a fusion of welfare liberalism and the medical model, has been a powerful historical force favoring normalization. Infused with optimism and a belief in human perfectability, imbued with a belief in the efficacy of individual effort, rehabilitation agents promulgate a rhetoric of "coping" with disability and "adjustment" to the prevailing normative structure. Rehabilitation provides the disabled with a set of formulae and recipes, accommodative strategies which exhort them to "live with" their disability, while trying insofar as possible, to transcend its limitations. Bitterness, resentment, and anger, typical of the disassociative response, are viewed as symptoms of "maladjustment," to be avoided at all costs. The disabled must struggle against these feelings and maintain a cheerful and sanguine attitude toward their disability. Without belaboring the point, we can see that rehabilitation, with its commitment to individual adjustment and "acceptance" of disability, not only encourages normalization, but diffuses dissent and *depoliticizes* deviance.

Given the pervasiveness of the Protestant Ethic, the power of the rehabilitation model, and the efficacy of social control, it is small wonder that former mental patients and the physically disabled were late to politicize. During the sixties, however, there were some ideological changes among segments of the American public which made political action on the part of the disabled a possibility. While a detailed analysis of broad societal change

is well beyond the scope of this paper, it is possible to sketch the outlines of these historical transformations. An important development was the return of newly politicized disabled veterans of the Vietnam War, who actively sought significant institutional reforms. Moreover, during the late 1960's, liberalism and the welfare state, and their progeny, social welfare, rehabilitation, and the "helping ideology," were assaulted from all sides of the political spectrum. The writings of Goffman, Laing, and Szasz revealed a disillusionment with the medical model and a profound dissatisfaction with professionals. But the writings of Szasz (1961) and Goffman implied that there was little that mental patients could do to better their own conditions. Change must come from the "oppressors." While such theories may have inspired professionals to seek institutional reform, they provided little incentive for patients to unite in concerted political action. These writers speak of oppression but they do not speak to the oppressed. Only the writings of R. D. Laing (1960, 1964) (and we are not addressing their "correctness," but only their sociological implications) with their celebration of insanity and their vision of the mad as the symbol of sanity in an "insane society," provided those labelled as "mentally ill" with an exalted sense of self which at the same time repudiates the values of the wider society. Among critics of psychiatry, Laing's writings were alone in creating the cognitive and ideational foundations for an incipient political activism.

In addition to the revolt against the medical model, other forces were at work which ultimately served to inspire political action on the part of the disabled. The previously mentioned "politicization of life" obliterated the distinction between deviance and political marginality, as deviants adopted militant strategies and political radicals assumed "deviant" life styles (Horowitz and Liebowitz 1968). The growing Gay Liberation movement perhaps reflects a general "de-closetization" of deviance in American society. Finally, the Black Power movement, with its militancy, its rejection of assimilation, and its celebration of differentness, reflected an ideology which tied stigma to other forms of political oppression.

Until the 1960s there were simply no alternatives to the ideology of rehabilitation. And without an ideology or a set of constituent ideas, a social movement is impossible. The social movements of the sixties provided the disabled and the "mentally ill" with just that ideology. From the radical psychiatry movement, former mental patients learned to extoll the validity of their experience. From the Gay Liberationists, the disabled learned that stigma was not a thing to be hidden, but could be openly displayed. And from the Black Power movement, the disabled and former mental patients learned that their stigma was not stigma at all, but perhaps a superior differentness, to be celebrated but never to be submerged in the abyss of assimilation. Together, these social movements and historical trends broke the spell of the ideology of rehabilitation, exposed the false allure of fictional acceptance, and, above all, provided a language or metaphor for political action.

THE STRATAGEMS OF IDENTITY POLITICS

Political activism, as contrasted with other responses to disability, seeks, in repudiating societal values, to elevate the self-concept of its participants. In this section I will explore in greater detail just how these two aspects of identity social movements— repudiation and self-elevation—are accomplished. In so doing, I am relying largely on the published statements of articulate disabled activists, especially those generated by the 1975 Conference on Human Rights and Psychiatric Oppression. While such pronouncements cannot be construed as "representative" of the breadth and scope of identity politics, and while they are biased toward the "official," such official ideologies do reveal basic themes of identity politics. And ideology, after all, is one medium through which selves are created.

Most activists endeavor to dispel stigma by viewing their deviation in non-medical terms. The politicized mental patient groups adhere to some notion of *societal etiology*. The cause of mental disorder is to be sought not in individual pathology, but rather in perceived political, economic, or social repression. The Mental Patients' Liberation Front, a Boston-based activist group, provides perhaps the most militant illustration of this tenet, when it states its goal to be "to transform the classist, racist, and sexist society, with its oppressive power relations, that caused our pain and incarceration." Project Release, an organization based in New York City, is concerned with the problem of recidivism, or the "revolving door," in which patients are released, only to return quickly to the confines of the mental hospital. But Project Release explains an otherwise conventional problem for the psychiatric profession by reference to a socio-economic model: its leaders state that their "ideology is that recidivism is primarily caused by *socio-economic conditions* and not by 'mental illness'."[4]

Another group attending the conference runs a halfway house based on Laingian principles, which emphasizes the creative aspects of madness and expressly condemns the use of psychotropic drugs. Its leaders expressed another variant of this theme:

> The "system" is set up to keep many people struggling for a living, for a place in society, for a feeling of self worth. People in emotional crises are experiencing their pain for legitimate reasons. The pressures of living in the world today are many and can severely tax anyone's emotional stability. It is a myth that "emotional breakdown" is due to an individual's weakness or inadequacies, a myth perpetrated by existing "mental health" facilities and other social and economic power structures.[5]

In this framework, those who suffer "crises" (and this term is substituted for "mental illness") are neither weak not emotionally unstable. Rather, their crises are viewed as legitimate and reasonable responses to the travails of an oppressive civilization. In providing a rationale for suffering, the Laingian ideology legitimates mental patients' experience

---

[4] Conference on Human Rights and Psychiatric Oppression, *Newsletter* 1974.
[5] Ibid.

and, in so doing, allows them to sustain viable conceptions of self. This same group adds an additional nuance, echoed by other activist groups:

> In traditional psychiatric settings, people's expressions of emotional distress are usually labelled as "mental illness," and are invalidated rather than listened to with respect. The patients are cut off from their feelings by mind-numbing psychotropic drugs, and by their environment . . . . We will help people to find their own solutions to problems, rather than having solutions imposed by psychiatric authorities.[6]

This blame of and disdain for "psychiatric authorities" and professionals is a salient theme found in the ideological pronouncements of most patient activist groups. Psychoactive drugs and shock treatments in particular, and enforced medical interventions in general, are viewed as infringements upon patients' integrity and dignity. The Network Against Psychiatric Assault, an organization in San Francisco claiming more than 100 members, has successfully halted enforced shock treatments at Langley-Porter Neuropsychiatric Institute, and has agitated, with some degree of success, for broader legislative restrictions on enforced treatments. Similar lawsuits and demonstrations are being carried out in other states. This struggle against institutions and professionals on the part of activist groups indicates that the rehabilitative model has been supplanted by an ideology of overt conflict.

Physically disabled activists, unlike mental patients, cannot fault "society" for their disability. Yet even here we find a variant on the theme of societal culpability: disabled activists blame society for the stigmatization of a mere difference. Paul Hunt, a muscular dystrophy victim, faults contemporary society for its mindless obsession with achievement, its fetishism of commodities and conformity, and its use of ascriptive attributes and material possessions as the salient yardstick of personal worth (Hunt 1966). In creating such a portrait of the world around him, Hunt safeguards his own sense of integrity and the validity of the experience of disability.

Hunt's writings, with their religious overtones, begin to define the parameters of a "pedagogy of the oppressed" (Freire 1970). He not only legitimates the experience of disability but equates disability with revolution against the constraints of rigid normative standards. The handicapped, by their very *being,* reproach materialism and petty conformity, standing as a reminder to all of their own tragedy and finitude. The disabled, then, play a symbolic missionary role. Former patients who adhere to Laingian ideology also celebrate their own condition and equate madness with revolutionary experience:

> Our basic philosophy is that "breakdown" or extreme emotional crisis, with suitable conditions of emotional and physical support, can be a constructive and growth-producing experience; "breakdown" is potentially "break through."[7]

In identifying handicap with subversion and madness with revolution, the activists conceive themselves as playing an *active* role in transforming the social order. Hence the tendency of the disabled and former patients to "elevate" their status by identifying themselves with more politicized and active minority groups and revolutionaries:

> Our constant experience of this pressure towards unthinking conformity in some way relates us to other obvious deviants and outcasts like the Jew in a gentile world, the Negro in a white world, homosexuals, the mentally handicapped; and also the more voluntary rebels in every sphere—artists, philosophers, prophets, who are essentially subversive elements in society. This is an area where disabled people can play an important role (Hunt 1966).

One can only marvel at the power of these stratagems of self-affirmation. Madness emerges not as affliction, but as creative rebellion, and the disabled emerge not as passive victims, but as prophets, visionaries, and revolutionaries.

Language, too, is of paramount importance. The older self-help groups and many professionals sought to replace the usual names for disabilities with

---

[6] Ibid.

[7] Ibid.

more delicate labels, such as "hard of hearing."[8] Some disabled activists have attempted, usually unsuccessfully, to find substitute terms which remove the pejorative connotations of the words "handicapped" and "disabled." (And this is a testimony to the power of language in structuring experience.) But the most militant proudly and self-consciously flaunt the most degrading terms: "cripple," "inmate," "madness," and "proud paranoids" are found in their published statements. This stratagem—*de-euphemization*—demonstrates a subtle mastery of the language game of "normals." Like Richard Wright before them, who created a linguistic revolution when he coined the term "black power," these activists use the very terms which directly assault the "liberal toleration" of "normal" outsiders. Their words, then, are at once an affront to "normals," a signal of conflict and battle, a repudiation of the illusory acceptance implicit in the euphemism, and a testimony to the intrinsic viability of their own experience.

Societal etiology, identification of deviation with revolution, and de-euphemization—these are the stratagems by which the politicized disabled seek to reformulate their condition and to redefine their situation. Identity politics, then, is a sort of phenomenological warfare, a struggle over the social meanings attached to attributes rather than an attempt to assimilate these attributes to the dominant meaning structure.

CONCLUDING REMARKS

Throughout, I have used the concept of identity politics to describe the incipient political activism of the disabled and former mental patients. The new political activists attempt to create an identity for themselves and to propagate this newly-created sense of self to "normals." This is accomplished in two ways. First, the *actions* of the disabled, their militancy and their reliance on social protest, demonstrate that they are independent, rational beings, capable of self-determination and political action. These actions *symbolically* assault the prevailing commonsense (and sociological) imagery of passivity and victimization. Secondly, unlike other responses to stigma and disability, political activism creates an *ideology* which repudiates societal values and normative standards and, in so doing, creates a viable self-conception for participants.

The political activism of the handicapped and former mental patients has far-reaching significance for the professionals who work with them and the sociologists who study them. Many rehabilitative tenets, appropriate to an era when normalization was the favored and modal response to disability, no longer seem applicable to those whose aspirations transcend an often illusory social acceptance by "normals." The identity politics of the disabled and "mentally ill" also challenges the sociologies of deviance, stigma, and disability to create new conceptions of the deviant actor, which embrace concerted political action which resists, rather than subscribes to, societal imputations.

REFERENCES

Akers, R. 1976. "Problems in the sociology of deviance: Social definitions and behavior." *Soc. Forces*, 455–465.

Davis, F. 1972a. "The family of the polio child: Some problems of identity." In *Illness. Interaction and the Self*, edited by F. Davis. Belmont: Wadsworth.

———. 1972b. "Deviance disavowal: The management of strained interaction by the visibly handicapped." In *Illness, Interaction, and the Self*, edited by F. Davis. Belmont: Wadsworth.

———. 1975. *Sociological Constructions of Deviance: Perspectives and Issues in the Field*. New York: Brown.

Deutsch, A. 1937. *The Mentally Ill in America*. New York: Doubleday.

Freire, P. 1970. *The Pedagogy of the Oppressed*. New York: Herder & Herder.

Goffman, E. 1959. *The Presentation of Self in Everyday Life,* Garden City: Doubleday.

———. 1961. *Asylums: Essays on the Social Situation of Patients and Other Inmates*. Garden City: Doubleday.

Horowitz, I., and M. Liebowitz. 1968. "Social deviance and political marginality." *Soc. Probl.* 281–296.

Hunt, P. 1966. "A critical condition." In *Stigma: The Experience of Disability,* edited by P. Hunt. London: Chapman.

---

[8] Ibid.

Laing, R. D. 1960. *The Divided Self*. London: Tavistock.

Laing, R. D., and A. Esterson. 1964. *Sanity, Madness, and the Family*. London: Tavistock.

Mankoff, M. 1971. "Societal reaction and career deviance: A critical analysis." *Sociol. Q.* 12:205–217.

MacGregor, F. 1958. "Some psycho-social problems associated with facial deformities." In *Patients,* *Physicians, and Illness,* edited by E. G. Jaco. New York: Free Press.

Scheff, T. 1968. *Being Mentally Ill: A Sociological Theory*. Chicago: Aldine.

Szasz, T. 1961. *The Myth of Mental Illness: Foundations of a Theory of Personal Conduct*. New York: Hoeber-Harper.

READING 5-12

Gay and Lesbian Movements

Steven Epstein

OUT OF THE CLOSETS AND INTO THE STREETS

By the end of the 1960s, as social attitudes about sexual expressiveness became more liberal, the idea of a radical challenge to the oppression of gay men and lesbians began to be more conceivable. At the same time, the tactics even of the more militant homophile activists, modeled after the nonviolent tradition of the Negro civil rights movement, seemed increasingly timid in contrast to the disruptive protests ever more visible on the streets of U.S. cities and on the evening news broadcasts—the confrontational tactics of the anti–Vietnam war protesters, the Black Power movement, and others dedicated to radical change or revolutionary upheaval in the United States (D'Emilio 1983: 223). Increasingly, conditions seemed right for a new politics of sexuality, but what was lacking was a transformation of consciousness, or "cognitive liberation" (McAdam 1982): gay men and lesbians needed not only to perceive the existing sexual and social order as unjust but to acquire "a new sense

From Barry D. Adam, Jan Willem Duyvendak, and Andre Krouwel (eds.), *The Global Emergence of Gay and Lesbian Politics* (Philadelphia: Temple Univ. Press), 1999. Reprinted by permission of Temple University Press, © 1999 by Temple University.

of efficacy," whereby those "who ordinarily consider themselves helpless come to believe that they have some capacity to alter their lot" (Piven and Cloward 1979).

Though the development of such efficacy is inevitably a gradual process, in historical retrospect it may appear as a shift of startling abruptness. Such is the story of the patrons of a gay bar called the Stonewall Inn, located in the Greenwich Village neighborhood of New York City, shortly after 1:00 A.M. on 28 July 1969. When police raided the bar, as they were in the habit of doing periodically, and began hauling the customers into paddy wagons for transport to jail, some of the bar's patrons, including black and Puerto Rican drag queens and lesbians, decided they had had enough. A melee erupted as the crowd began throwing coins, bottles, cans, and bricks, yelling, "Gay power," and shouting epithets at the police (Duberman 1993:196–201). Disturbances continued in the streets outside the Stonewall for several nights running. To be sure, the Stonewall rebellion was not as unique or consequential an event at the time as it came to be portrayed later (Murray 1996:59–65). "But if the Stonewall riots did not *begin* the gay revolution," acknowledges Martin Duberman, the historian who has chronicled the events in greatest detail, "it remains true that those riots became a symbolic event of international importance," one that "occupies a central place in the iconography of lesbian and gay awareness" (Duberman 1993:224, xv).

Members of the New York Mattachine Society, who viewed these turbulent developments with alarm, put a sign outside the Stonewall Inn: "We homosexuals plead with our people to please help maintain peaceful and quiet conduct on the streets of the Village" (Duberman 1993:207). But within weeks, young gay men and women had formed a new group, the Gay Liberation Front (GLF), which would become the prototypical organization of the gay liberation movement (Marotta 1981). In a telling example of how the frames and tactics of one social movement will very often spill over to influence other, contemporary or subsequent, movements (Meyer and Whittier 1994), gay liberation activists borrowed heavily from the movements that they, as individuals, were already active in: the antiwar movement lent a suspicion of the government; the New Left lent an "apocalyptic rhetoric and sense of impending revolution" (D'Emilio 1983:233–34); the women's liberation movement lent a critique of sexism and the idea that "the personal"—even "the sexual"—is "political"; Third World liberation movements lent the prideful affirmation of a stigmatized identity and the notion of resistance to an imperial state; and the hippie movement and counterculture lent an injunction to "do your own thing," a distrust of authority and dismissal of the older generation (here including older, "closeted" gay men and lesbians), and a belief that protest tactics could be playful and celebratory while still being subversive (Altman 1971:234; D'Emilio 1983:224; Adam 1987:76; Cruikshank 1992:61, 76; Duberman 1993:220).

Gay liberation–style activism quickly spread around the country—in particular, the "action technology" (Oliver and Marwell 1992:251–72) known as the "zap," which called for the graphic and confrontational disruption of the day-to-day routines of opponents. In October 1969 a "suicide squadron" of GLF members in New York interrupted a meeting of mayoral candidates after waiting two hours for candidates to reply to questions submitted to them. That same month gay students at Berkeley staged guerrilla theater and gay power demonstrations during orientation week. The following May, members of GLF, chanting "Suck cock; beat the draft" and "Bring our boys home," participated in a Washington, D.C., antiwar protest and held a "nude-in" in the Lincoln Memorial reflecting pool (Thompson 1994:22–35). On the first anniversary of the Stonewall riot, two thousand men and women held a commemorative march through the streets of New York, while hundreds of others marched in other U.S. cities. By the following year the Stonewall anniversary celebration had spread to Paris and London and become an official, international gay event (Duberman 1993:279).

Liberationists challenged corporations over their hiring practices, continued the fight against police entrapment, and organized large dances in cities around the country where, in the past, men and women had been arrested for dancing with partners of the same sex. One noteworthy struggle—which was over the very definition and character of gayness, as well as the personal safety of lesbians and gay men seeking to live their lives free of fear of confinement and stigmatization—was the campaign waged against the "war criminals" of the American Psychiatric Association to remove homosexuality from the list of mental illnesses and halt the attempts to "cure" homosexuals. This battle was won in 1973, after many disruptive "zaps" both outside and inside the association's conventions (Bayer 1981; Marcus 1992).

Earlier, homophile activists had begun to consolidate a "minority group" identity that emphasized the stability of sexual identity and called for homosexuals to take their place in U.S. society. Radical gay liberationists repudiated this agenda and put forward claims about sexuality, identity and difference, and the public and private that differed in nearly every particular from those of homophile activists. Where homophiles had had little to say about sexuality as such, liberationists saw sexuality as a subversive and revolutionary force. Adopting philospher Herbert Marcuse's (1966) hybrid "Freudo-Marxism," they called for the liberation of the "polymorphous-perverse" forms of sexuality believed to lie latent within every individual. Lesbians and gay men, in this conception, were the vanguard in a vast struggle to redefine the family, gender roles, and our erotic and relational capacities as human beings. As writer and activist Dennis Altman noted, "Liberation . . . would involve a breakdown of the barriers between male and female homosexuals, and between gays and straights. Masculinity and femininity would cease to be sharply differentiated categories" (1971: 106). The appeal to a universal bisexual potential was widespread in early movement rhetoric. By implication, the collective subject of the new movement was necessarily transitory: paradoxically, the victory of the movement would result in the withering away of both "the homosexual" and "the heterosexual," with each replaced by "a new human for whom such distinctions no longer are necessary for the establishment of identity" (Altman 1971:237).

Where homophile activists had endorsed a strong separation between public and private realms, liberationists, arguing that "the personal is political," placed at the center of their politics the act of coming out—the public and defiant affirmation of identity. As D'Emilio notes, in the years before gay liberation, "coming out" meant revealing one's homosexuality to other homosexuals; after gay liberation the public avowal of one's sexual desires and identity became a strategy for movement building and heightening the commitment of recruits. Liberationists connected the collective action frame of visible confrontation—epitomized by the slogan, "Out of the closets and into the streets!"—to the "Gay is good" frame by arguing that a healthy, liberated gay person simply had nothing to hide (D'Emilio 1983:235–36). Liberationists "engaged in public displays of affection, violated gender conventions, and gloried in the discomfort they deliberately provoked in others" (D'Emilio 1992:243).

These distinctive ways of framing sexuality, identity, and the relation between public and private resonated with young gay men and lesbians around the country and pulled them into activism. These frames also implied particular strategies and tactics for the gay liberation movement. Because homosexuality was too transgressive ever to be integrated into the existing society, and because radical gays and lesbians were committed to the broader social struggle against capitalism, imperialism, racism, and sexism, it followed that gay liberation was a revolutionary movement with the goal of social and cultural transformation. Perhaps more so in rhetoric than in reality, gay liberation emphasized the importance of forming coalitions with other oppressed groups. Thus at the 1970 NACHO meeting in San Francisco, radicals fought against oldline homophiles to pass resolutions supporting women's liberation and the Black Panthers and calling for the removal of U.S. forces from Vietnam (Adam 1987:79).

Yet, for all its flash and dazzle, gay liberation, as an organized movement, was short-lived, and the utopian notion of challenging fixed categories of identity proved particularly difficult to sustain or institutionalize. Almost immediately, tensions arose concerning the comprehensive political vision of radical gay liberation. In November 1969 several New York activists who found GLF too anarchic, impractical, and preoccupied with rhetoric split off to found a new, more focused organization called the Gay Activists Alliance (GAA) (Adam 1987:80). Though it engaged in actions similar to those of GLF and used many of the same tactics, GAA conceived of itself as "exclusively devoted to issues involving gay rights" (Evans 1973) and was less committed to overthrowing the categories of gender and sexuality.

Gay liberation impelled a rapid proliferation of gay organizations: at the time of Stonewall, there were only about fifty lesbian or gay groups in the entire United States; by the end of 1973, there were more than a thousand, ranging from gay newspapers to crisis hotlines to social clubs (D'Emilio 1992:244). But the groups with a radical and comprehensive political agenda soon faded from the scene. By 1971, New York's GLF had splintered into factions, and within a few years GLF and GAA chapters had disbanded around the country. As the political climate became conservative, "the belief that a revolution was imminent and that gays should get on board, was losing whatever momentary plausibility it had" (D'Emilio 1992:245).

LESBIAN AND GAY RIGHTS IN THE 1970s

The irony of radical gay liberation is that its most profound effect was to promote the development of forms of identity, community, and politics that were antithetical to the liberationist vision. Radical activists who foresaw the "end of the homosexual" and the transcendence of constraining categories of gender and sexuality discovered instead that they were helping to build communities organized around the notion that gays and lesbians were a distinct class of people with unique political interests. Liberationists who had connected the freedom of gay men and lesbians to a socialist agenda found, to their chagrin, that the new gay male culture was organized substantially around profit-making businesses, such as bars and bathhouses, and that homosexuality, far from posing a revolutionary challenge to U.S. society through its radical incompatibility with it, in fact seemed to do fine—perhaps even to thrive—under capitalism. Those who had promoted an androgynous style of personal dress and expression in the hopes of challenging gender roles greeted with some ambivalence the rise, among gay men, of the pervasive, so-called "Castro clone" style of exaggerated masculinity: short hair, mustaches, denim, plaid shirts, leather, and boots (Altman 1982:20, 85, 104; Fitzgerald 1986:54, 58; Adam 1987:100).

The developing gay neighborhoods, such as San Francisco's Castro District, became "a kind of laboratory for experimentation with alternate ways to live. [They were] also a carnival where social conventions were turned upside down just for the pleasure of seeing what they looked like the wrong way up" (Fitzgerald 1986:12). As Frances Fitzgerald has noted, the pioneering of these new communities reflected the "extraordinary" and "quintessentially American" notion that people could "start all over again from scratch"—that they could make "new lives, new families, even new societies" by, in effect, reinventing themselves (Fitzgerald 1986:23). Indeed, the 1970s was the era of the consolidation of a new, quasi-ethnic form of gay identity, community, and politics (Murray 1979, 1996; Altman 1982; Epstein 1987). Within more-or-less defined territorial enclaves (Castells 1983; Davis 1995:284–303), gay men and, to a lesser degree, lesbians established gay restaurants, gay choruses, gay newspapers, gay churches and synagogues, and (by the 1980s) gay savings and loan associations. The distinctive rainbow flag, designed in San Francisco in 1978 (Thompson 1994:23) and soon flying outside residences and businesses in the gay ghettoes, would come to mark the territory and welcome the "immigrants" who poured in from smaller, less hospitable towns and rural areas around the country. Hundreds of thousands of people would turn out each year for the Lesbian and Gay Freedom Day parades held in commemoration of Stonewall in cities around the United States—simultaneously an official holiday and a political and cultural event for the lesbian and gay population. Although the parade crowds were extraordinarily diverse, the gay enclaves themselves were narrower in their social composition—largely white and, with the increasing gentrification of property within them, largely middle class.

As Dennis Altman has noted, the widespread acceptance, by both straights and gays, of the notion that gay men and lesbians constituted a sort of ethnic group, roughly analogous to Jewish Americans or Italian Americans, represented not only an extraordinary change from twenty years earlier (when homosexuality was widely understood as a form of deviance or pathology, like alcoholism) but also a very American response: the ethnic model made sense in a country where people tend to identify themselves by ethnicity rather

[than] by class and where interest-group politics typically reflects the jockeying among ethnic groups for their "piece of the pie" (Altman 1982:viii–ix, 224). The combined reliance on a quasi-ethnic, essentialist identity and the political model of the civil rights movement would distinguish this new, more mainstream "lesbian and gay rights movement" from gay political formations elsewhere around the world—and from alternatives within the United States.

The communal and middle-class character of the new gay enclaves made it easier for the lesbian and gay rights movement to mobilize resources. People who are well integrated into community institutions and organizations are more readily drawn into social movements (McAdam 1982; Lo 1992: 224–47), and many within the gay, quasi-ethnic communities were prepared to make substantial commitments of time and money. In this sense the formation of quasi-ethnic communities proved central to the rise of the lesbian and gay rights movement. Increasingly, the mainstream lesbian and gay rights movement, despite its white, middle-class base and its particular conception of the political agenda, would seek to present itself in hegemonic fashion as "the movement"—as what all gay politics boiled down to in the end.

Questions of sexuality, identity and difference, and the relation between public and private were framed by the lesbian and gay rights movement in ways that fostered the goal of defining and defending the interests of a gay quasi-ethnicity. Consistent with the quasi-ethnic model, the lesbian and gay rights movement expressed the view that being gay was a fixed or immutable condition, and gay men and lesbians (sometimes together, more often separately) were portrayed as belonging to communities that had distinctive cultural forms. Internal differences within the culture, such as racial or class differences, were overlooked in the dominant rhetoric. Often the lineage of this culture was traced in ways that paid little attention to the particularities of the organization of desire in other societies, as in the attempt to lay claim to Plato, Sappho, or Michelangelo as "famous homosexuals

in history." For similar reasons, activists tended to trumpet scientific arguments suggesting that homosexuality was biologically based, since such claims seemed to undercut the position that homosexuality was a chosen, sinful lifestyle and seemed to support the view that lesbians and gay men deserved protection as a legitimate minority. Indeed, the political corollary of this essentialist conception was that the state should be pressured to ensure the formal legal equality of lesbians and gay men as a people, much as had been done for African Americans and for women.

This movement did not present a coherent or sustained analysis of the place of sexuality in modern society. It did, however, disseminate a widely influential conception of "homophobia," which reframed the "social problem" of homosexuality by arguing that the real problem was the irrational fear of homosexuality on the part of many ill-informed straight people. This conception was distinctly Freudian—ironically so, since Freud and his followers were themselves often denounced as homophobes by members of the movement. It assumed that homophobic attitudes and behaviors often were defense mechanisms for warding off recognition of one's own repressed homoerotic impulses (what Freud would call a "reaction-formation" [Weinberg 1972:12])—hence the folk wisdom that the most violent homophobes and gay bashers were themselves "closet cases."

Finally, in terms of the public/private distinction, the lesbian and gay rights movement retained the liberationist rhetoric of gay pride while also endorsing the notion of a right to privacy in the expression of sexuality. The right to privacy was seen as a cornerstone of the struggle to "get government out of the bedroom" by abolishing laws against sodomy. These conceptions of sexuality, identity, and privacy came together in the form of a single-issue politics, modeled loosely on the civil rights movement and put forward by organizations that had much more formal bureaucratic and leadership structures than those of the gay liberation era (D'Emilio 1992:246). Indeed, where liberationist, nonidentitarian politics seemed by their nature to be evanescent and resistant to institutionalization, gay ethnicity lent itself easily to the construction of organizations (Armstrong 1998).

The lesbian and gay rights movement sought to bring about social change through a variety of approaches. First, over the course of the 1970s, the movement built national organizations, such as the National Gay Task Force (later renamed the National Gay and Lesbian Task Force, or NGLTF), an advocacy group founded in 1973, which by the end of the decade claimed ten thousand mostly white, male, and middle-class members (Altman 1982:123). Three years later the Gay Rights National Lobby (GRNL) was founded as a lobbying group to bring pressure to bear on the U.S. Congress, and in 1980 the Human Rights Campaign Fund (later shortened to Human Rights Campaign, or HRC) was created as a fund-raising tool to support candidates perceived to be "gay friendly." Compared with the size of the emergent gay and lesbian communities, these organizations were small, and compared with the diversity of lesbians and gay men in terms of race and class, their social composition was fairly monolithic. The first national organization formed by gay men and lesbians of color, the National Coalition of Black Lesbians and Gays, opened its doors in 1978 and held its first national convention in 1982 (Ridinger 1996:188–89).

Second, in line with a familiar American tendency to turn to the courts to ensure legal protection for minorities, activists created legal support organizations, such as the Lambda Legal Defense and Education Fund (LLDEF) founded in New York in 1972, and the Gay and Lesbian Advocates and Defenders (GLAD) founded in Boston in 1978. These organizations took on the legal cases of lesbians and gay men fighting discrimination and also filed many "friend of the court" briefs in the hope of influencing judicial decisions.

Third, activists sought to overturn sodomy laws and pass antidiscrimination laws. In California an activist lobbying effort proved successful in overturning the state's sodomy law, and in many other states—twenty-one of them by the end of 1978— sodomy statutes were removed as part of a general process of penal code reform (Bernstein 1997a:44). The first federal civil rights bill for gay men and lesbians was introduced into Congress in 1974 by Bella Abzug and Ed Koch, both Democrats from New York. But the fierce opposition to legislation at the federal level meant that lesbians and gay men, in the interim, faced the time-consuming challenge of proceeding state by state or city by city in pursuit of antidiscrimination statutes within the decentralized governance structure of the United States.

Fourth, the movement sought to make inroads into the Democratic Party, which—given the absence of powerful leftist parties in the American two-party system—was perceived by many activists as the only game in town. At the local level, lesbians and gay men formed groups such as San Francisco's Alice B. Toklas Lesbian and Gay Democratic Club, expressing support for liberal candidates who were willing to call for equal rights for gays and lesbians (Faderman 1991:199). At the national level, activists sought to convince the party to adopt a gay rights plank in its platform; this effort failed in 1976 after Democratic presidential nominee Jimmy Carter retracted his support (Thompson 1994:132).

Fifth, the lesbian and gay rights movement sought to elect openly gay men and women to local office. In 1974, activist and former college teacher Elaine Nobel was elected by a six-hundred-vote margin to the Massachusetts House of Representatives, becoming the first openly gay legislator in the United States (Ridinger 1996:212). In 1977, after several unsuccessful tries, Harvey Milk, owner of a camera shop in San Francisco's Castro District, was elected to the city's Board of Supervisors. When Milk, along with San Francisco Mayor George Moscone, was shot dead by a conservative member of the Board of Supervisors in 1978, the new mayor quickly named another gay leader, Harry Britt, to take Milk's place on the board. The power of the gay community within the city was further demonstrated in the White Night riots, which broke out when Dan White, Milk's killer, was convicted of manslaughter rather than murder:

thousands of protesters marched on City Hall and set fire to police cars to protest the verdict.

In addition to legislative, judicial, and electoral activism, the lesbian and gay rights movement of the 1970s pursued change on many other fronts. It pressured businesses to adopt nondiscrimination policies, achieving victories with companies such as AT&T, with more than one million employees nationwide. Activists sought acceptance within church congregations and also formed their own gay congregations. The Metropolitan Community Church, for example, founded in 1968 by a Los Angeles activist, the Reverend Troy Perry, soon spread around the country. Activists created new organizations to document and respond to antigay violence (Jenness and Broad 1994; Jenness 1995). They also used the arts to educate the public about the goals of the movement; one noteworthy example is the 1978 documentary *Word Is Out: Stories of Some of Our Lives,* by filmmakers Nancy Adair and Casey Adair, which was based on lengthy interviews with twenty-six gay men and lesbians.

Beginning in the mid-1970s, the terrain of political contention for the lesbian and gay rights movement was radically altered by the rise of an organized opponent, the New Right, a social movement concerned in large part with the defense of "traditional" family, gender, and sexual forms. This is a clear case in which the particularities of the United States affected the trajectory of lesbian and gay movements: because the centrality of religion in general and fundamentalism in particular made such an opponent possible in the United States, gay men and lesbians here faced a set of challenges that their counterparts in most other countries escaped.

In June 1977, voters in Dade County, Florida, galvanized by former beauty pageant winner Anita Bryant and her Save Our Children organization, repealed a recently passed ordinance that would have protected gays and lesbians against discrimination. The news, which hit gay and lesbian communities like a bombshell, proved to be only the first in a series of repeal efforts that spread across the country. The emergent threat provided leaders of gay

and lesbian movements with a new agenda and a clear rhetorical target; increasingly, activists pointed to the dangers posed by the New Right as the reason that gays and lesbians needed to get involved in political work. In this way, movement organizers painted a picture of the antagonist (see Hunt, Benford, and Snow 1994:185–208) as means of recruitment and mobilization.

The response was a considerable upswing in attendance at lesbian and gay demonstrations and Gay Pride Day events, including a turnout of 250,000 for a highly politicized Gay Pride Day in San Francisco in 1978 (Adam 1987:105). In California more than thirty organizations sprang up, as activists fought a successful grassroots organizing campaign against an antigay referendum sponsored by state senator John Briggs, which called for the dismissal of all gay and lesbian teachers from California public schools. Following the repeal of a lesbian and gay rights ordinance in St. Paul, Minnesota, in 1978, support began building for a national show of strength against the rising tide of conservatism. The first national March on Washington for Gay and Lesbian Rights, held in Washington, D.C., on 14 October 1979, drew a sizable crowd; estimates ranged from 25,000, according to the U.S. Park Police, to 125,000, according to conference organizers.

A conference of Third World lesbians and gays was held just before the march, in part in an effort to increase participation by lesbians and gay men of color in the event and in gay and lesbian politics more generally (Ridinger 1996:192–97). But in the aftermath of the march, it was hard to discern many long-term consequences of the mobilization. If the energy did not dissipate entirely, it was redirected to local organizing that emphasized building durable community institutions and organizations but lacked a comprehensive or radical agenda for social change.

ACTING UP

Around 1987, with the growing fear that most or perhaps all of those infected with HIV—estimated to be about half the gay men in the most densely concentrated gay neighborhoods—would eventually progress to symptomatic illness, disquiet about the pace and politics of biomedical research swelled into mass unrest. As in the early 1980s, this upswing of grassroots AIDS activism originated in gay and lesbian communities and spread from there. In New York, activist and playwright Larry Kramer, cofounder of GMHC, helped create a radical activist organization, the AIDS Coalition to Unleash Power—better known by its acronym, ACT UP. Soon there were ACT UP chapters in San Francisco, Boston, Chicago, Houston, Los Angeles, New Orleans, Seattle, and other cities as ACT UP became, briefly, the most visible social movement organization in the United States.

A magnet for radical young gay men and lesbians, ACT UP practiced an in-your-face politics of "no business as usual." Adopting styles of political and cultural practice derived from the gay liberation movement of the early 1970s, the peace movement, and the punk subculture, ACT UP became famous for its imaginative street theater, its skill at attracting the news cameras, and its well-communicated sense of urgency. ACT UP chapters typically had no formal leaders; in many cities, meetings operated by the consensus process. As Joshua Gamson describes in a participant/observer study of the San Francisco chapter, ACT UP shared the basic characteristics of "new social movements"—"a (broadly) middle-class membership and a mix of instrumental, expressive, and identity-oriented activities" (1989:354; Elbaz 1992).

On the national scene, the New York City chapter dominated—with upward of 150 members at regular weekly meetings and a $300,000 budget by the end of 1988—though chapters in San Francisco, Los Angeles, and Boston were also prominent in the movement. Ostensibly, since AIDS was not a "gay disease," ACT UP was not a "gay organization," but members in fact tended to be gay or lesbian, and many of the group's activities—and the pink-triangle background of its distinctive "Silence = Death" logo—suggested the centrality of gayness to its organizational identity

(Gamson 1989). The history of gay challenges to medical authorities, as in the early-1970s campaign against the psychiatric profession, informed ACT UP's undeferential approach to scientists and medical experts.

During the late 1980s, ACT UP activists engaged in manifold projects directed at a variety of social institutions, including the state, the church, the mass media, and the health care sector (Crimp and Rolston 1990)—though at times, like the queer activist groups that sprang up in their wake, they seemed less concerned with achieving institutional change than with posing general challenges to cultural norms (Gamson 1989). Although some within gay communities were openly disgruntled with ACT UP's confrontational tactics and its tone of abrasive self-righteousness, others noted the creative ways in which the activists marshalled their moral outrage, retained an emphasis on sexual freedom as part of a political agenda, and challenged the conventional division between public and private. The deaths of prominent activists were often marked by loud and angry "political funerals" winding through city streets; in this way, traditionally private moments of death were transformed into public displays of defiance against an indifferent or hostile society and government.

ACT UP and other groups based in gay and lesbian communities were also central to the project of remaking biomedicine in the United States. Activists challenged the authority of experts and, by immersing themselves in technical details of virology and immunology, constituted themselves as grassroots experts who could debate scientists on research directions and priorities. They waged a successful campaign against the U.S. Food and Drug Administration for faster approval of experimental AIDS therapies. Subsequently, activists turned their attention to the National Institutes of Health, successfully demanding changes in the methods of testing AIDS drugs in order to speed up the process, get more patients into clinical trials, and ensure that trials were ethically conducted (Epstein 1995, 1996, 1997).

Once again in the trajectory of gay and lesbian activism, the radical grassroots challenge proved short-lived, but it provided the spark for more enduring, if more mainstream, organizational forms. By the early 1990s, activism focused on AIDS treatments had become more professionalized, and the more confrontational and controversial street activism of ACT UP had subsided.

LESBIAN AND GAY RIGHTS IN THE 1980s

Although it often seemed that gay and lesbian politics in the 1980s were preoccupied with AIDS, the mainstream lesbian and gay rights movement maintained a diverse political agenda throughout the decade. The quasi-ethnic/territorial model of organizing remained central, concretely symbolized by a 1984 vote for the incorporation of West Hollywood, which promptly elected a majority of openly gay or lesbian city council members. In San Francisco the institutionalization of the lesbian and gay rights movement was mirrored in an explosion of local civic and political organizations: only 93 lesbian and gay organizations existed between 1975 and 1979, but that number jumped to 255 between 1980 and 1983 and the numbers stayed roughly at that level through the mid-1990s (Armstrong 1998: chap. 1).

The emphasis on civil rights legislation and protection from discrimination also continued, though the 1980s saw a proliferation of new, nationwide organizations with different emphases—including Parents and Friends of Lesbians and Gays (PFLAG), which brought relatives of gay men and lesbians into the movement, and the Gay and Lesbian Alliance Against Defamation (GLAAD), which focused public attention on representations of gay men and lesbians in the mass media and the entertainment industry. The decade was also marked by new cultural and political movements, such as the lesbian "baby boom," the grassroots development of lesbian and gay history projects, the rise of gay and lesbian studies in universities (Escoffier 1990), and the birth of many lesbian

and gay professional groups (Taylor and Raeburn 1995). Two members of Congress, Gerry Studds and Barney Frank, both from Massachusetts, came out of the closet; and gays and lesbians both expressed support for and sought to pressure the Democratic Party in a large demonstration outside the Democratic National Convention in San Francisco in 1984. In Oregon, however, voters repealed a ban on job discrimination in 1988, as skirmishes continued between lesbian and gay activists and the New Right.

In 1982, when Georgia police officers entered the home of a man named Michael Hardwick to serve a warrant for traffic violations, they found him having sex with another man. Hardwick was arrested and convicted under Georgia's sodomy law, and the verdict in *Bowers v. Hardwick* was appealed all the way to the United States Supreme Court. Rejecting the argument that gay sex was protected by a "right to privacy," the Court upheld the constitutionality of Georgia's sodomy law in a split (five-four) vote in 1986, sparking angry demonstrations outside federal buildings across the United States. The NGLTF formed a Privacy Project, directed by Sue Hyde, designed to assist activists around the country in contesting state sodomy laws; but only one sodomy statute, in Washington, D.C., was overturned partly as a result of these efforts (Bernstein 1997a:69).

Frustration with the court's ruling, along with mounting concern about AIDS, was a primary force behind a mass mobilization the following year: the second National March on Washington for Gay and Lesbian Rights, held on 15 October 1987. More than two hundred thousand people from around the United States poured into Washington for the five-hour demonstration, which called for legal recognition of gay relationships, passage of the federal gay rights bill, and a ban on discrimination based on HIV status, among other issues. Two days before the march, more than six hundred demonstrators were arrested in a large act of civil disobedience at the U.S. Supreme Court building in protest of the Hardwick decision. The week's events also included a display of 1,920 panels of the Names

Project's AIDS Quilt and a public "commitment ceremony" attended by two thousand lesbian and gay male couples (Ridinger 1996:198–201). Roughly coinciding with the advent of ACT UP, this national mobilization reflected a rare moment in which the mainstream lesbian and gay rights movement seemed to move in sync with more radical, grassroots activism. But it was indeed a moment, not an enduring political formation.

SOCIAL MOVEMENT ORGANIZATIONS AND THEIR ANTAGONISTS IN THE 1990s

Unlike gay and lesbian movements in other countries, U.S. activists in the 1990s found themselves in the extraordinary and unenviable position of fighting not only the repeal of gay rights ordinances at the local level (Adam 1995:133) but also the passage of citywide and statewide referenda that sought to make it legally impossible for gay rights laws ever to be established (Bernstein 1997a: 74). Activists in Oregon fought bitter but successful battles against such initiatives in 1992 and 1993, also dividing among themselves over whether to put forward a least-common-denominator antidiscrimination agenda or a more radical defense of queer sexualities (Bull and Gallagher 1996; Bernstein 1997b:555). In Colorado 53 percent of voters supported a 1992 referendum that scrapped existing gay rights laws in the more liberal cities of Denver, Boulder, and Aspen and prohibited the establishment of any such laws in the future (Adam 1995:133). National outrage on the part of lesbians and gay men prompted an organized boycott of travel to the state of Colorado, as well as a court challenge that eventually made its way to the United States Supreme Court. In 1996, in an important six-three decision for gays and lesbians from the Supreme Court, which was not known to favor them, the Court ruled that the state had no compelling interest in preemptively banning gays and lesbians from attempting to pass legislation securing their rights.

The creation of unity amid diversity was also the significant but transient result of two visible national mobilizations in the early 1990s: the third National March on Washington for Lesbian, Gay, and Bi Equal Rights and Liberation and New York City's Stonewall 25 which commemorated the twenty-fifth anniversary of the Stonewall riot. The National March drew as few as three hundred thousand and as many as one million participants, depending on who did the counting. Planners insisted on racial diversity and gender balance in all local delegations to the national steering committee that helped prepare for the march. And, as the name reflects, the march signaled a more complete inclusion of bisexuals in the political agenda, as well as a stated desire to accommodate both those who sought equal rights and those who insisted on a more radical politics of liberation. The following year, Stonewall Twenty-five put more than one million marchers, including many international contingents, on the streets of Manhattan, with participants marching past the United Nations building, demanding respect for the human rights of lesbians, gays, and bisexuals around the world. Unlike earlier national marches, these events attracted significant attention in the mass media, but like earlier marches, these national shows of strength seemed to have little lasting impact on movement mobilization either nationally or locally.

The failure to build on these national demonstrations in any significant way was accompanied by another conspicuous lack: there were no widely recognized, charismatic leaders. As commentators had been noting for some time (Jernigan 1988), gay and lesbian movements in the United States seemed to produce remarkably few such leaders. There was no shortage of popular heroes, such as the gay men and lesbians who became public figures through their legal battles against dismissal from the military. And celebrities, such as Chastity Bono (the lesbian daughter of Sonny Bono and Cher) and Candace Gingrich (the sister of right-wing politician Newt Gingrich), had become a familiar presence at marches and parades. But—perhaps because of the proliferation and diversity of movements and organizations—gay and lesbian movements seemed to have difficulty generating or sustaining leaders with the imagination and personal qualities needed to mobilize or redirect collective sentiments in powerful ways, to generate solidarity across the divisions within the movements, or to construct coalitions with movements of other kinds.

As activists waged trench warfare against the New Right in local initiatives around the United States, many held out the hope that larger successes might be won at the national level. Particularly in contrast to the overt, antigay hate mongering that marked the 1992 Republican National Convention, the stated positions of Democratic presidential candidate Bill Clinton seemed to hold open the prospect of a new political opportunity structure for gay and lesbian movements. Clinton explicitly mentioned gay people in his nomination acceptance speech at the Democratic National Convention and included openly gay people in his campaign team and, later, in his administration. However, when his attempt to make good on a campaign promise to end the persecution of gay men and lesbians in the U.S. military met with energetic political opposition, Clinton quickly backed down and proposed a regressive "compromise" that, in practice, continued to lead to the dismissal of gay men and lesbians from the military. This and subsequent actions by Clinton—on issues such as gay marriage—demonstrated that there was no political party of consequence in the U.S. political system with which lesbian and gay activists could unproblematically ally and that the U.S. two-party system provided restricted opportunities for the advancement of a gay rights agenda.

These two issues—gays in the military and gay marriage—merit additional attention for the extraordinary amount of controversy that they provoked. Given that no other country that has openly considered the issue of military service by lesbians and gay men has greeted the prospect with any great degree of panic or preoccupation, the popular hysteria surrounding the issue in the United States testified to unique aspects of the U.S. political and cultural environment. As Barry Adam notes, an explanation that points to the power of the New Right alone seems insufficient to account

for the psychological charge of the debate (Adam 1994:103–18), which raised the specter of "vulnerable" heterosexual soldiers being eyed by predatory homosexuals in shower rooms and pointed, in rather Freudian terms, to the threat that overt homosexual desire posed to sublimated male bonding and esprit de corps. Much like the targeting of homosexuals during the McCarthy era, the debate about gays in the military seemed wrapped up in concerns about the "feminization" of the state, in a country whose whole national identity in the period since the Second World War has centered on its global military might (Adam 1994:113).

The debate over gay marriage was equally freighted with symbolic power for all concerned. In the 1980s and early 1990s, lesbians and gay men won substantial victories in obtaining domestic partner benefits such as health insurance for the lovers of gay men and lesbians employed by many businesses, city governments, and universities around the United States—no small matter in a country without national health care. A number of cities, such as San Francisco, had formal provisions for couples to register at City Hall as domestic partners. No one seemed quite prepared, however, when the Hawaii Supreme Court ruled in 1993, that a lower court had improperly dismissed a lawsuit challenging the state's policy of denying marriage licenses to gay or lesbian couples. The court suggested that it would most likely rule in favor of the lawsuit, and a lower court eventually did so in 1997. Meanwhile, conservatives around the country were shocked to realize that if Hawaii permitted gay marriages, then the U.S. Constitution might require every other state to recognize those marriages. Even as gay men and lesbians throughout the United States began imagining wedding-and-honeymoon trips to Hawaii, conservatives in many state legislatures began introducing measures to define marriage strictly as the union of a man and a woman. Such measures had become law in twenty-five states by mid-1997. At the same time, members of the U.S. Congress proposed a national Defense of Marriage Act, which Clinton announced in

September 1996 that he would sign, effectively ensuring its passage.

The marriage debate was revealing for what it suggested about the limits of popular endorsement of the equality of gay men and lesbians. While substantial percentages of those surveyed in opinion polls disapproved of discrimination against gays and lesbians in the workplace, far fewer were able to conceive of gay marriage as anything other than an oxymoron.

In 1960 no cities or states in the United States guaranteed equal rights to gay men and lesbians. Every state outlawed sodomy, and there were no openly gay elected officials anywhere in the United States. By 1997 thirty states and the District of Columbia had abolished their sodomy laws. Eleven states and dozens of cities and counties had passed laws protecting lesbians and gay men (and sometimes bisexuals and transgendered people) from various forms of discrimination based on sexual orientation, and elsewhere gubernatorial executive orders and mayoral proclamations officially banned discrimination. As a result, by the mid-1990s more than one-fifth of Americans lived in cities or counties providing legal protection (Wald, Button, and Rienzo 1996:1153). In addition, five states, including New York, now offer domestic partner benefits to gay and lesbian state employees. With the exception of Wisconsin and Minnesota, however, every state that has banned discrimination (including Hawaii) is on the Atlantic or Pacific Coast, leaving the inhabitants of the vast interior without protection (Sherrill 1996:469). Sodomy laws remain on the books in most of the South, several western states, Michigan, and even liberal Massachusetts. And, although in 1997 the U.S. Senate came surprisingly close to passing a bill banning employment discrimination, relief is not very likely to come soon at the federal level.

At this writing, three members of the U.S. House of Representatives are openly gay—though all were closeted when first elected to that office—as are eleven other men and women in state-level governments. In late 1997, Virginia Apuzzo, a former executive director of the NGLTF, became the highest-ranking openly gay or lesbian person in government in U.S. history when she was appointed assistant to the president for management and administration. Increasingly, large segments of the society appear ready to countenance the presence of lesbian and gay men in roles that were previously unthinkable—gay and lesbian ministers, gay and lesbian athletes, gay and lesbian characters in popular television shows and films. Newspapers that in the recent past covered homosexuality as a crime story or a titillating social problem now routinely present commentary and analysis on lesbian and gay politics, community, and identity. Television talk shows provide a forum, however constrained, for those with the most marginalized sexualities to tell their stories to a national audience (Gamson 1998). Even in the domain of organized religion, there have been significant changes. In 1997, for example, the Interfaith Alliance, a nationwide organization of more than fifty denominations, announced its support for a federal antidiscrimination law protecting lesbians and gay men in the workplace.

These indicators of social change are significant, and they speak, at least in part, to the power of political activism and the diffuse effects of the visibility of lesbian/gay/bisexual/transgender communities. At the same time, other measures suggest that the gains of U.S. gay and lesbian movements of recent decades coexist with strong antipathy toward gay men and lesbians that has varied little over time. For example, the General Social Survey, the most complete statistical survey of public attitudes on a range of social issues over the years, revealed no meaningful change in beliefs about the acceptability of gay sexuality between 1973 and 1991 (Smith 1994:63–97). In 1973, 73 percent of those surveyed said that sex between members of the same sex was "always wrong"; in the 1991 survey, that figure was 77 percent. Another survey, the American National Election Study, asks respondents to rank different social groups using a "feeling thermometer." Responses over time reveal that feelings toward gays and lesbians are "colder" than feelings for many other oppressed groups, including blacks and people on welfare, and "warmer" only than feelings for illegal aliens (Sherrill 1996:470). Findings such as these are consistent with Urvashi Vaid's contention that lesbians, gay men, bisexuals, and transgendered people in the United States have been granted "virtual equality"—"a state of conditional equality based more on the appearance of acceptance by straight America than on genuine civic parity" (Vaid 1995:xvi).

Such attitudes reflect not only the power of religious fundamentalism in the United States but also the deep undercurrents of anxiety about sexuality and the legacy of the "sexual revolution." Numerous episodes—from the public furor in 1989 and 1990 over the exhibition of sexually explicit and sadomasochistic work by acclaimed gay photographer Robert Mapplethorpe (Cruikshank 1992: 51) to recent laws in California and other states mandating the "chemical castration" of sex offenders—demonstrate that sexuality remains a fertile domain for staging moral panic. The most comprehensive recent survey of sexual behaviors and attitudes in the United States found that respondents could be clustered into seven distinct subsets based on their responses to questions about the acceptability of homosexuality, premarital sex, extramarital sex, abortion, and pornography. In five of the seven clusters, accounting for three-quarters of the entire population surveyed, "same-gender sex" was rated as "always wrong" by heavy majorities (between 65 percent and 98 percent). In the remaining two clusters, less than 10 percent of respondents agreed that same-gender sex was always wrong (Laumann et al. 1994:509–40, esp. 514). The results suggest not only that discomfort with lesbian and gay sexuality in U.S. society extends far beyond the New Right but also that there is little middle ground between the attitudinal clusters that are heavily opposed and those that are quite supportive.

These findings also underscore the point that the ways in which gay and lesbian movements frame sexuality and identity matter. A substantial sector of the population is more inclined at present to accept the argument that gays, as a people, deserve protection from discrimination than to feel really comfortable with the idea of sex between men or sex between women (see Yang 1997). So, on one hand, social movements that play down questions of sexuality and emphasize issues of fairness would seem to have a short-term, tactical advantage. But, on the other hand, this approach may well jettison the possibility of long-term, fundamental improvement either in the social standing of gay men, lesbians, bisexuals, and transgendered people or in the overall political climate surrounding sexuality.

REFERENCES

Adam, Barry D. 1987. *The Rise of a Gay and Lesbian Movement*. Boston: Twayne.

———. 1994. "Anatomy of a Panic: State Voyeurism, Gender Politics, and the Cult of Americanism." In *Gays and Lesbians in the Military: Issues, Concerns, and Contrasts*. Ed. Wilbur J. Scott and Sandra Carson Stanley. Hawthorne, N.Y.: Aldine de Gruyter.

———. 1995. *The Rise of a Gay and Lesbian Movement*. Rev. ed. New York: Twayne.

Altman, Dennis. 1971. *Homosexual: Oppression and Liberation*. New York: Avon.

———. 1982. *The Homosexualization of America*. Boston: Beacon.

Armstrong, Elizabeth. 1998. "Multiplying Identities: Identity Elaboration in San Francisco's Lesbian/Gay Organizations." Ph.D. diss., Department of Sociology, University of California, Berkeley.

Bayer, Ronald. 1981. *Homosexuality and American Psychiatry: The Politics of Diagnosis*. New York: Basic.

———. 1997b. "Celebration and Suppression: The Strategic Uses of Identity by the Lesbian and Gay Movement." *American Journal of Sociology* 103, no. 3 (November):531–65.

Bernstein, Mary. 1997a. "*Sexual Orientation Policy, Protest, and the State*." Ph.D. diss., Department of Sociology, New York University.

Bull, Chris, and John Gallagher. 1996. *Perfect Enemies: The Religious Right, the Gay Movement, and the Politics of the 1990s*. New York: Crown.

Castells, Manuel. 1983. *The City and the Grassroots*. Berkeley and Los Angeles: University of California Press.

Crimp, Douglas, and Adam Rolston. 1990. *AIDS Demographics*. Seattle: Bay.

Cruikshank, Margaret. 1992. *The Gay and Lesbian Liberation Movement*. New York: Routledge.

Davis, Tim. 1995. "The Diversity of Queer Politics and the Redefinition of Sexual Identity and Community in Urban Space." In *Mapping Desire*. Ed. David Bell and Gill Valentine. London: Routledge.

D'Emilio, John. 1983. *Sexual Politics, Sexual Communities: The Making of a Homosexual Minority in the United States, 1940–1970*. Chicago: University of Chicago Press.

———. 1992. *Making Trouble: Essays on Gay History, Politics, and the University*. New York: Routledge.

Duberman, Martin. 1993. *Stonewall*. New York: Dutton.

Elbaz, Gilbert. 1992. "The Sociology of AIDS Activism: The Case of ACT UP/New York, 1987–1992." Ph.D. diss., City University of New York.

Epstein, Steven. 1987. "Gay Politics, Ethnic Identity: The Limits of Social Constructionism." *Socialist Review* 17, no. 3–4 (May–August): 9–54.

———. 1995. "The Construction of Lay Expertise: AIDS Activism and the Forging of Credibility in the Reform of Clinical Trials." *Science, Technology and Human Values* 20, no. 4 (Fall):408–37.

———. 1996. *Impure Science: AIDS, Activism, and the Politics of Knowledge*. Berkeley and Los Angeles: University of California Press.

———. 1997. "AIDS Activism and the Retreat from the Genocide Frame." *Social Identities* 3, no. 3 (October): 415–38.

Evans, Arthur. 1973. "How to zap straights." In *The Gay Liberation Book*. Ed. Len Richmond and Gary Noguera. San Francisco: Ramparts Press.

Fitzgerald, Frances. 1986. *Cities on a Hill: A Journey through Contemporary American Cultures*. New York: Simon and Schuster.

Gamson, Joshua. 1989. "Silence, Death, and the Invisible Enemy: AIDS Activism and Social Movement 'Newness.' " *Social Problems* 36, no. 4 (October): 351–65.

———. 1998. *Freaks Talk Back: Television Talk and Sexual Nonconformity*. Chicago: University of Chicago Press.

Hunt, Scott A., Robert D. Benford, and David A. Snow. 1994. "Identity Fields: Framing Processes and the Social Construction of Movement Identities." In *New Social Movements: From Ideology to Identity*. Ed. Enrique Laraña, Hank Johnston, and Joseph R. Gusfield. Philadelphia: Temple University Press.

Jenness, Valerie. 1995. "Social Movement Growth, Domain Expansion, and Framing Processes: The Case of Violence against Gays and Lesbians as a Social Problem." *Social Problems* 42, no. 1 (February): 145–70.

Jenness, Valerie, and Kendal Broad. 1994. "Antiviolence Activism and the (In)visibility of Gender in the Gay/Lesbian and Women's Movements." *Gender and Society* 8, no. 3 (September):402–23.

Jernigan, David. 1988. "Why Gay Leaders Don't Last: The First Ten Years After Stonewall." *Out/Look,* no. 2 (Summer 1988):33–49.

Laumann, Edward O., John H. Gagnon, Robert T. Michael, and Stuart Michaels. 1994. *The Social Organization of Sexuality: Sexual Practices in the United States*. Chicago: University of Chicago Press.

Lo, Clarence Y. H. 1992. "Communities of Challengers in Social Movement Theory." In *Frontiers in Social Movement Theory*. Ed. Aldon D. Morris and Carol McClurg Mueller. New Haven: Yale University Press.

Marcus, Eric. 1992. *Making History: The Struggle for Gay and Lesbian Equal Rights, 1945–1990: An Oral History*. New York: HarperCollins.

Marcuse, Herbert. 1966. *Eros and Civilization*. Boston: Beacon.

Marotta, Toby. 1981. *The Politics of Homosexuality*. Boston: Houghton-Mifflin.

McAdam, Doug. 1982. *Political Process and the Development of Black Insurgency, 1930–1970*. Chicago: University of Chicago Press.

Meyer, David S., and Nancy Whittier. 1994. "Social Movement Spillover." *Social Problems* 41 (May): 277–98.

Murray, Stephen O. 1979. "Institutional Elaboration of a Quasi-Ethnic Community." *International Review of Modern Sociology* 9:165–78.

Oliver, Pamela, and Gerald Marwell. 1992. "Mobilizing Technologies for Collective Action." In *Frontiers in Social Movement Theory*. Ed. Aldon D. Morris and Carol McClurg Mueller. New Haven: Yale University Press.

Ridinger, Robert B. Marks. 1996. *The Gay and Lesbian Movement: References and Resources*. New York: Hall.

Sherrill, Kenneth. 1996. "The Political Power of Lesbians, Gays, and Bisexuals." *PS: Political Science and Politics* 29, no. 3 (September): 469–73.

Smith, Tom W. 1994. "Attitudes toward Sexual Permissiveness: Trends, Correlates, and Behavioral

Connections." In *Sexuality across the Life Course*. Ed. Alice S. Rossi, Chicago and London: University of Chicago Press.

Thompson, Mark, ed. 1994. *Long Road to Freedom: The Advocate History of the Gay and Lesbian Movement*. New York: St. Martin's.

Vaid, Urvashi. 1995. *Virtual Equality: The Mainstreaming of Gay and Lesbian Liberation*. New York: Anchor.

Wald, Kenneth D., James W. Button, and Barbara A. Rienzo. 1996. "The Politics of Gay Rights in American Communities: Explaining Antidiscrimination Ordinances and Policies." *American Journal of Political Science* 40:1152–78.

Weinberg, George. 1972. *Society and the Healthy Homosexual*. New York: St. Martin's.

STUDY QUESTIONS

1. What variables determine whether a deviance liberation movement will succeed, according to Ronald Weitzer?
2. In what ways do the unpopular pedophile organizations discussed by Mary de Young attempt to justify their goal of relaxing controls on adult sexual contact with children?
3. What are the main goals of the organizations fighting for prostitutes, pedophiles, mental patients, the disabled, and gays as described in the chapters by Ronald Weitzer, Mary deYoung, Renee Anspach, and Steven Epstein?
4. To what degree have each of these groups been successful in achieving their goals?

Recommended Readings

Becker, Howard, *Outsiders: Studies in the Sociology of Deviance*

Ben-Yehuda, Nachman, *Deviance and Moral Boundaries*

Braithwaite, John, *Crime, Shame, and Reintegration*

Cloward, Richard, and Lloyd Ohlin, *Delinquency and Opportunity: A Theory of Juvenile Gangs*

Cohen, Albert, *Delinquent Boys: The Subculture of the Gang*

Erikson, Kai, *Wayward Puritans: A Study in the Sociology of Deviance*

Goffman, Erving, *Asylums*

Goffman, Erving, *Stigma: Notes on the Management of Spoiled Identity*

Goode, Erich, *Deviant Behavior*

Gusfield, Joseph, *Symbolic Crusade: Symbolic Politics and American Temperance*

Humphreys, Laud, *Tearoom Trade: Impersonal Sex in Public Places*

Katz, Jack, *Seductions of Crime: Moral and Sensual Attractions in Doing Evil*

Laumann, Edward, *The Social Organization of Sexuality: Sexual Practices in the U.S.*

Lemert, Edwin, *Social Pathology*

Lofland, John, *Deviance and Identity*

Matza, David, *Delinquency and Drift*

Matza, David, *Becoming Deviant*

Scheff, Thomas, *Being Mentally Ill*

Schur, Edwin, *Crimes Without Victims*

Schur, Edwin, *Politics of Deviance*

Sutherland, Edwin, *White-Collar Crime*

Weitzer, Ronald, *Sex for Sale*

Wolfgang, Marvin, and Franco Ferracuti, *The Subculture of Violence*